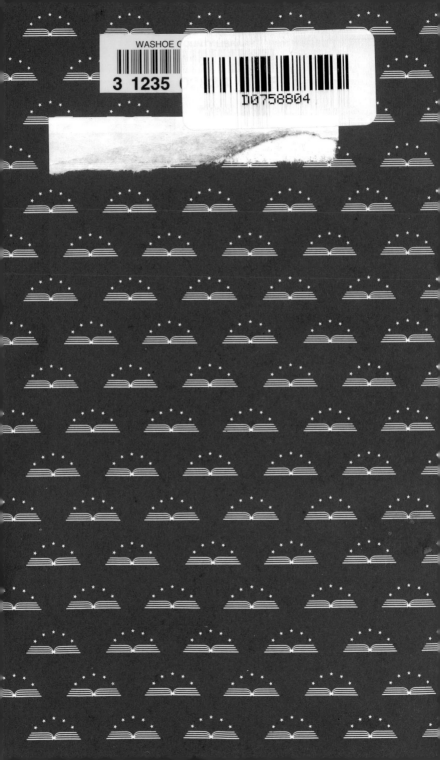

EZRA POUND

Ezra Pound

POEMS AND TRANSLATIONS

THE LIBRARY OF AMERICA

Special thanks are due to Mary de Rachewiltz and Omar Pound, the heirs of Ezra Pound, for their support of this project.

Volume compilation, notes, and chronology copyright © 2003 by Literary Classics of the United States, Inc., New York, N.Y. All rights reserved.
No part of this book may be reproduced commercially by offset-lithographic or equivalent copying devices without the permission of the publisher.

Some of the material in this volume is reprinted by permission of the holders of the copyright and publication rights. Acknowledgments are on pages 1253–54 of the Note on the Texts.

The paper used in this publication meets the minimum requirements of the American National Standard for Information Sciences—Permanence of Paper for Printed Library Materials, ANSI Z39.48–1984.

Distributed to the trade in the United States by Penguin Putnam Inc. and in Canada by Penguin Books Canada Ltd.

Library of Congress Catalog Number: 2003040142
For cataloging information, see end of Index.
ISBN 1–931082–41–3

First Printing
The Library of America–144

Manufactured in the United States of America

RICHARD SIEBURTH
SELECTED THE CONTENTS AND WROTE
THE CHRONOLOGY AND NOTES FOR THIS VOLUME

Contents

HILDA'S BOOK

Child of the grass
The years pass Above us
Shadows of air All these shall Love us
Winds for our fellows
The browns and the yellows
            Of autumn our colors
Now at our life's morn. Be we well sworn
Ne'er to grow older
Our spirits be bolder At meeting
Than e'er before All the old lore
Of the forests & woodways
Shall aid us: Keep we the bond & seal
Ne'er shall we feel
            Aught of sorrow

            Let light flow about thee
            As   a cloak of air

            ———————

I strove a little book to make for her,
Quaint bound, as 'twere in parchment very old,
That all my dearest words of her should hold,
Wherein I speak of mystic wings that whirr
Above me when within my soul do stir
Strange holy longings
That may not be told
Wherein all autumn's crimson and fine gold
And wold smells subtle as far-wandered myrrh
Should be as burden to my heart's own song.
I pray thee love these wildered words of mine:
Tho I be weak, is beauty alway strong,
So be they cup-kiss to the mingled wine
That life shall pour for us life's ways among.
Ecco il libro: for the book is thine.

Being alone where the way was full of dust, I said
> "*Era mea*
> *In qua terra*
> *Dulce myrrtii floribus*
> *Rosa amoris*
> *Via erroris*
> *Ad te coram veniam*"

And afterwards being come to a woodland place where the sun was warm amid the autumn, my lips, striving to speak for my heart, formed those words which here follow.

La Donzella Beata

Soul
Caught in the rose hued mesh
Of o'er fair earthly flesh
Stooped you again to bear
This thing for me
And be rare light
For me, gold white
In the shadowy path I tread?
Surely a bolder maid art thou
Than one in tearful fearful longing
That would wait Lily-cinctured
Star-diademed at the gate
Of high heaven crying that I should come
To thee.

The Wings

A wondrous holiness hath touched me
And I have felt the whirring of its wings
Above me, Lifting me above all terrene things
As her fingers fluttered into mine
Its wings whirring above me as it passed

I know no thing therelike, lest it be
A lapping wind among the pines
Half shadowed of a hidden moon
A wind that presseth close
            and kisseth not
But whirreth, soft as light
Of twilit streams in hidden ways
This is base thereto and unhallowed . . .
Her fingers layed on mine in fluttering benediction
And above the whirring of all-holy wings.

Ver Novum

Thou that art sweeter than all orchards' breath
And clearer than the sun gleam after rain
Thou that savest my soul's self from death
As scorpion's is, of self-inflicted pain
Thou that dost ever make demand for the best I have to give
Gentle to utmost courteousy bidding only my pure-purged
     spirits live:
Thou that spellest ever gold from out my dross
Mage powerful and subtly sweet
Gathering fragments that there be no loss
Behold the brighter gains lie at thy feet.

If any flower mortescent lay in sun-withering dust
If any old forgotten sweetness of a former drink
Naught but stilt fragrance of autumnal flowers
Mnemonic of spring's bloom and parody of powers
That make the spring the mistress of our earth—
If such a perfume of a dulled rebirth
Lingered, obliviate with o'er mistrust,
Marcescent, fading on the dolorous brink
That border is to that marasmic sea
Where all desire's harmony

Tendeth and endeth in sea monotone
Blendeth wave and wind and rocks most drear

Into dull sub-harmonies of light; out grown
From man's compass of intelligence,
Where love and fear meet
Having ceased to be:

All this, and such disconsolate finery
As doth remain in this gaunt castle of my heart
Thou gatherest of thy clemency
Sifting the fair and foul apart,
Thou weavest for thy self a sun-gold bower
By subtily incanted raed
Every unfavorable and ill-happed hour
Turneth blind and potently is stayed
Before the threshold of thy dwelling place

Holy, as beneath all-holy wings
Some sacred covenant had passed thereby
Wondrous as wind murmurings
That night thy fingers laid on mine their benediction
When thru the interfoliate strings
Joy sang among God's earthly trees
Yea in this house of thine that I have found at last
Meseemeth a high heaven's antepast
And thou thyself art unto me
Both as the glory head and sun
Casting thine own anthelion
Thru this dull mist
My soul was wont to be.

To One That Journeyeth with Me

"Naethless, whither thou goest I will go"
    Let, Dear, this sweet thing be, if be it may
    But hear this truth for truth,
    Let hence and alway whither soe'er I wander there I know
    Thy presence, if the waning wind move slow
    Thru woodlands where the sun's last vassals stray
    Or if the dawn with shimmering array

Doth spy the land where eastward peaks bend low.
Yea all day long as one not wholly seen
Nor ever wholly lost unto my sight
Thou mak'st me company for love's sweet sake
Wherefor this praising from my heart I make
To one that brav'st the way with me for night
Or day, and drinks with me the soft wind and the keen.

Domina

My Lady is tall and fair to see
She swayeth as a poplar tree
    When the wind bloweth merrily
Her eyes are grey as the grey of the sea
Not clouded much to trouble me
    When the wind bloweth merrily
My Lady's glance is fair and straight
My Lady's smile is changed of late
    Tho the wind bloweth merrily
Some new soul in her eyes I see
Not as year-syne she greeteth me
    When the wind bloweth merrily
Some strange new thing she can not tell
Some mystic danaan spell
    When the wind bloweth merrily
Maketh her long hands tremble some
Her lips part, tho no words come
    When the wind bloweth merrily
Her hair is brown as the leaves that fall
She hath no villeiny at all
    When the wind bloweth merrily
When the wind bloweth my Lady's hair
I bow with a murmured prayer
    For the wind that bloweth merrily
With my lady far, the days be long
For her homing I'd clasp the song
    That the wind bloweth merrily

Wind song: this is my Lady's praise
What be lipped words of all men's lays
      When the wind bloweth merrily
To my Lady needs I send the best
Only the wind's song serves that behest.
      For the wind bloweth merrily.

The Lees

There is a mellow twilight 'neath the trees
Soft and hallowed as is a thought of thee,
Low soundeth a murmurous minstrelsy
A mingled evensong beneath the breeze
Each creeping, leaping chorister hath ease
To sing, to whirr his heart out, joyously;
Wherefor take thou my laboured litany
Halting, slow pulsed it is, being the lees
Of song wine that the master bards of old
Have left for me to drink thy glory in.
Yet so these crimson cloudy lees shall hold
Some faint fragrance of that former wine
O Love, my White-flower-o-the-Jasamin
Grant that the kiss upon the cup be thine.

Per Saecula

Where have I met thee? Oh Love tell me where
In the aisles of the past were thy lips known
To me, as where your breath as roses blown
Across my cheek? Where through your tangled hair
Have I seen the eyes of my desire bear
Hearts crimson unto my heart's heart? As mown
Grain of the gold brown harvest from seed sown
Bountifully amid spring's emeralds fair
So is our reaping now: But speak that spring
Whisper in the murmurous twilight where
I met thee mid the roses of the past

Where you gave your first kiss in the last,
Whisper the name thine eyes were wont to bear
The mystic name whereof my heart shall sing.

Shadow

Darkness hath descended upon the earth
And there are no stars
The sun from zenith to nadir is fallen
And the thick air stifleth me.
Sodden go the hours
Yea the minutes are molten lead, stinging and heavy
I saw her yesterday.
And lo, there is no time
Each second being eternity.
Peace! trouble me no more.
Yes, I know your eyes clear pools
Holding the summer sky within their depth
But trouble me not
I saw HER yesterday.
Peace! your hair is spun gold fine wrought and wondrous
But trouble me not
I saw her yester e'en.
Darkness hath filled the earth at her going
And the wind is listless and heavy
When will the day come: when will the sun
Be royal in bounty
From nadir to zenith up-leaping?
For lo! his steeds are weary, not having beheld her
Since sun set.
Oh that the sun steeds were wise
Arising to seek her!
The sun sleepeth in Orcus.
From zenith to nadir is fallen his glory
Is fallen, is fallen his wonder
I saw her yesterday
Since when there is no sun.

ONE WHOSE SOUL WAS
SO FULL OF ROSE
LEAVES STEEPED IN
GOLDEN WINE THAT THERE
WAS NO ROOM THEREIN
FOR ANY VILLEINY—

The Banners

My wandring brother wind wild bloweth now
October whirleth leaves in dusty air
September's yellow gold that mingled fair
With green and rose tint on each maple bough
Sulks into deeper browns and doth endow
The wood-way with a tapis broidered rare—And where
King oak tree his brave panoply did wear
Of quaint device and colored
The dawn doth show him but a shorn stave now.
If where the wood stood in its pageantry
A castle holyday'd to greet its queen
Now but the barren banner poles be seen
Yea that the ruined walls stand ruefully
I make no grief, nor do I feel this teen
Sith thou mak'st autumn as spring's noon to me.

"To draw back into the soul of things." PAX

Meseemeth that 'tis sweet this wise to lie
Somewhile quite parted from the stream of things
Watching alone the clouds' high wanderings
As free as they are in some wind-free sky
While naught but thoughts of thee as clouds glide by
Or come as faint blown wind across the strings
Of this odd lute of mine imaginings
And make it whisper me quaint things and high
Such peace as this would make death's self most sweet
Could I but know, Thou maiden of the sun,

That thus thy presence would go forth with me
Unto that shadow land where ages' feet
Have wandered, and where life's dreaming done
Love may dream on unto eternity.

Green Harping

Thou that wearest the doeskins' hue
"Hallew!" "Hallew!"
Tho the elfin horn shall call to you
'true   be true
By the violets in thy leaf brown hair
'ware   be ware
Tho the elfin knights shall find thee fair
'ware   too fair
Tho hosts of night shall hail thee queen
         In the Eringreen
The elf old queen hath sorrow seen
and teen   much teen
Tho the shadow lords shall marshall their might
         afore thy sight
Hold thou thy heart of my heart's right
         in their despite
Tho night shall dwell in thy child eyes
'wise   be wise
That thy child heart to mine emprise
'plies   replies
For night shall flee from the fore-sun's flame
'shame   in shame
Tho my heart to thee embeggared came
'same   'tis the same
That lordship o'er the light doth hold
'bold   quite bold
And thee to my kingdom I enfold
By spell of old.

From another sonnet.

THY FINGERS MOVE AGAIN ACROSS MY FACE
AS LITTLE WINDS THAT DREAM
BUT DARE IN NO WISE TELL THEIR DREAM ALOUD—

Li Bel Chasteus

That castle stands the highest in the Land
Far seen and mighty
—Of the great hewn stones
What shall I say?
And deep foss-way
That far beneath us bore of old
A swelling turbid sea
Hill-born and torrent-wise
Unto the fields below, where
Staunch villein and wandered
Burgher held the land and tilled
Long labouring for gold of wheat grain
And to see the beards come forth
For barley's even-tide.

But circle arched above the hum of life
We dwelt, amid the
Ancient boulders
Gods had hewn
And druids runed
Unto the birth most wondrous
That had grown
A mighty fortress while the world had slept
And we awaited in the shadows there
While mighty hands had laboured sightlessly
And shaped this wonder 'bove the ways of men.

Meseems we could not see the great green waves
Nor rocky shore by Tintagoel
From this our hold

But came faint murmuring as undersong
E'en as the burgher's hum arose
And died as faint wind melody
Beneath our gates.

The Arches

That wind-swept castle hight with thee alone
Above the dust and rumble of the earth:
It seemeth to mine heart another birth
To date the mystic time, whence I have grown
Unto new mastery of dreams and thrown
Old shadows from me as of lesser worth.
For 'neath the arches where the winds make mirth
We two may drink a lordship all our own.
Yea alway had I longed to hold real dreams
Not laboured things we make beneath the sun
But such as come unsummoned in our sleep,
And this above thine other gifts, meseems
Thou'st given me. So when the day is done
Thou meet me 'bove the world in this our keep.

Era Venuta

Some times I feel thy cheek against my face
Close pressing, soft as is the South's first breath
That all the soft small earth things summoneth
To spring in woodland and in meadow space
Yea sometimes in a dusty man-filled place
Meseemeth somewise thy hair wandereth
Across my eyes as mist that halloweth
My sight and shutteth out the world's disgrace
That is apostasy of them that fail
Denying that God doth God's self disclose
In every beauty that they will not see.
Naethless when this sweetness comes to me
I know thy thought doth pass as elfin "Hail"
That beareth thee, as doth the wind a rose.

The Tree

I stood still and was a tree amid the wood
Knowing the truth of things unseen before
Of Daphne and the laurel bow
And that god-feasting couple old
That grew elm-oak amid the wold
'Twas not until the gods had been
Kindly entreated and been brought within
Unto the hearth of their hearts' home
That they might do this wonder thing.
Naethless I have been a tree amid the wood
And many new things understood
That were rank folly to my head before.

Being before the vision of Li Bel Chasteus

"E'en as lang syne from shadowy castle towers
"Thy striving eyes did wander to discern
"Which compass point my homeward way should be."
For you meseem some strange strong soul of wine . . .

Hair some hesitating wind shall blow Backward as some
    brown haze
That drifteth from thy face as fog that shifteth from fore some
Hidden light and slow discloseth that the light is fair—

Thu Ides Til

O thou of Maydes all most wonder sweet
That art my comfort eke and my solace
Whan thee I find in any wolde or place
I doon thee reverence as is most meet.
To cry thy prayse I nill nat be discreet
Thou hast swich debonairite and grace
Swich gentyl smile thy alderfayrest face
To run thy prayse I ne hold not my feet.
My Lady, tho I ne me hold thee fro
Nor streyve with thee by any game to play
But offer only thee myn own herte reede
I prey by love that thou wilt kindness do
And that thou keep my song by night and day
As shadow blood from myn own herte y-blede.

L'Envoi

Full oft in musty, quaint lined book of old
Have I found rhyming for some maiden quaint
In fashioned chançonnette and teen's compleynt
The sweet-scent loves of chivalry be told
With fair conceit and flower manifold
Right subtle tongued in complex verse restraint
Against their lyric might my skill's but faint.
My flower's outworn, the later rhyme runs cold
Naethless, I loving cease me not to sing
Love song was blossom to the searching breeze
E'er Paris' rhyming had availed to bring
Helen and Greece for towered Troy's disease
Wherefor, these petals to the winds I fling
'Vail they or fail they as the winds shall please.

The Wind

"I would go forth into the night" she saith.
The night is very cold beneath the moon
'Twere meet, my Love that thou went forth at noon
For now the sky is cold as very death.
And then she drew a little sobbing breath
"Without a little lonely wind doth crune
And calleth me with wandered elfin rune
That all true wind-born children summoneth
Dear, hold me closer! so, till it is past
Nay I am gone the while. Await!"
And I await her here for I have understood.
Yet held I not this very wind—bound fast
Within the castle of my soul I would
For very faintness at her parting, die.

Sancta Patrona
Domina Caelae

Out of thy purity
Saint Hilda pray for me.
Lay on my forehead
The hands of thy blessing.
Saint Hilda pray for me
Lay on my forehead
Cool hands of thy blessing
Out of thy purity
Lay on my forehead
White hands of thy blessing.
Virgo caelicola
Ora pro nobis.

Rendez-vous

She hath some tree-born spirit of the wood
About her, and the wind is in her hair
Meseems he whisp'reth and awaiteth there
As if somewise he also understood.
The moss-grown kindly trees, meseems, she could
As kindred claim, for tho to some they wear
A harsh dumb semblance, unto us that care
They guard a marvelous sweet brotherhood
And thus she dreams unto the soul of things
Forgetting me, and that she hath it not
Of dull man-wrought philosophies I wot,
She dreameth thus, so when the woodland sings
I challenge her to meet my dream at Astalot
And give him greeting for the song he brings.

FROM

A LUME SPENTO

This Book was

LA FRAISNE

(THE ASH TREE)

dedicated

to such as love this same
beauty that I love, somewhat
after mine own fashion.

But sith one of them has gone out very quickly from amongst us it given

A LUME SPENTO

(WITH TAPERS QUENCHED)

in memorian eius mihi caritate primus

William Brooke Smith

Painter, Dreamer of dreams.

Grace Before Song

Lord God of heaven that with mercy dight
Th' alternate prayer wheel of the night and light
Eternal hath to thee, and in whose sight
Our days as rain drops in the sea surge fall,

As bright white drops upon a leaden sea
Grant so my songs to this grey folk may be:

As drops that dream and gleam and falling catch the sun,
Evan'scent mirrors every opal one
Of such his splendor as their compass is,
So, bold My Songs, seek ye such death as this.

Note Precedent to "La Fraisne"

"When the soul is exhausted of fire, then doth the spirit re-
turn unto its primal nature and there is upon it a peace great
and of the woodland
        "*magna pax et silvestris.*"
Then becometh it kin to the faun and the dryad, a wood-
land-dweller amid the rocks and streams
        "*consociis faunis dryadisque inter saxa sylvarum*"
                                        Janus of Basel.*
Also has Mr. Yeats in his "Celtic Twilight" treated of such,
and I because in such a mood, feeling myself divided between
myself corporal and a self aetherial "a dweller by streams and
in woodland," eternal because simple in elements
        "*Aeternus quia simplex naturae*"
Being freed of the weight of a soul "capable of salvation
or damnation," a grievous striving thing that after much

---

*Referendum for contrast. "Daemonalitas" of the Rev. Father Sinistrari of
Ameno (1600 circ). "A treatise wherein is shown that there are in existence
on earth rational creatures besides man, endowed like him with a body and
soul, that are born and die like him, redeemed by our Lord Jesus-Christ, and
capable of receiving salvation or damnation." Latin and English text. pub.
Liseux. Paris, 1879.

straining was mercifully taken from me; as had one passed say-
ing as one in the Book of the Dead,

"I, lo I, am the assembler of souls," and had taken it with
him, leaving me thus *simplex naturae*, even so at peace and
trans-sentient as a wood pool I made it.

The Legend thus: "Miraut de Garzelas, after the pains he
bore a-loving Riels of Calidorn and that to none avail, ran
mad in the forest.

"Yea even as Peire Vidal ran as a wolf for her of Penautier
tho some say that twas folly or as Garulf Bisclavret so ran
truly, till the King brought him respite (See "Lais" Marie de
France), so was he ever by the Ash Tree."

Hear ye his speaking: (low, slowly he speaketh it, as one
drawn apart, reflecting) (égaré).

La Fraisne

(Scene: The Ash Wood of Malvern)

For I was a gaunt, grave councilor
Being in all things wise, and very old,
But I have put aside this folly and the cold
That old age weareth for a cloak.

I was quite strong—at least they said so—
The young men at the sword-play;
But I have put aside this folly, being gay
In another fashion that more suiteth me.

I have curled mid the boles of the ash wood,
I have hidden my face where the oak
Spread his leaves over me, and the yoke
Of the old ways of men have I cast aside.

By the still pool of Mar-nan-otha
Have I found me a bride
That was a dog-wood tree some syne.
She hath called me from mine old ways

She hath hushed my rancour of council,
Bidding me praise

Naught but the wind that flutters in the leaves.

She hath drawn me from mine old ways,
Till men say that I am mad;
But I have seen the sorrow of men, and am glad,
For I know that the wailing and bitterness are a folly.

And I? I have put aside all folly and all grief.
I wrapped my tears in an ellum leaf
And left them under a stone
And now men call me mad because I have thrown
All folly from me, putting it aside
To leave the old barren ways of men,
Because my bride
Is a pool of the wood and
Tho all men say that I am mad
It is only that I am glad,
Very glad, for my bride hath toward me a great love
That is sweeter than the love of women
That plague and burn and drive one away.

Aie-e! 'Tis true that I am gay
        Quite gay, for I have her alone here
        And no man troubleth us.

Once when I was among the young men . . . .
And they said I was quite strong, among the young men.
Once there was a woman . . . .
. . . . but I forget . . . . she was . . . .
. . . . I hope she will not come again.

. . . . I do not remember . . . .
I think she hurt me once but . . . .
That was very long ago.

I do not like to remember things any more.

I like one little band of winds that blow
In the ash trees here:
For we are quite alone
Here mid the ash trees.

Cino

(Italian Campagna 1309, the open road)

Bah! I have sung women in three cities,
But it is all the same;
And I will sing of the sun.

Lips, words, and you snare them,
Dreams, words, and they are as jewels,
Strange spells of old deity,
Ravens, nights, allurement:
And they are not;
Having become the souls of song.

Eyes, dreams, lips, and the night goes.
Being upon the road once more,
They are not.
Forgetful in their towers of our tuneing
Once for Wind-runeing
They dream us-toward and
Sighing, say "Would Cino,
"Passionate Cino, of the wrinkling eyes,
"Gay Cino, of quick laughter,
"Cino, of the dare, the jibe,
"Frail Cino, strongest of his tribe
"That tramp old ways beneath the sun-light,
"Would Cino of the Luth were here!"

Once, twice, a year—
Vaguely thus word they:
        "Cino?" "Oh, eh, Cino Polnesi
        "The singer is't you mean?"

"Ah yes, passed once our way,
"A saucy fellow, but . . . .
"(Oh they are all one these vagabonds),
"Peste! 'tis his own songs?
"Or some other's that he sings?
"But *you*, My Lord, how with your city?"

But you "My Lord," God's pity!
And all I knew were out, My Lord, you
Were Lack-land Cino, e'en as I am
O Sinistro.

I have sung women in three cities.
But it is all one.
I will sing of the sun.
. . . . eh? . . . . they mostly had grey eyes,
But it is all one, I will sing of the sun.

> "'Pollo Phoibee, old tin pan you
> Glory to Zeus' aegis-day
> Shield o'steel-blue, th' heaven o'er us
> Hath for boss thy lustre gay!

> 'Pollo Phoibee, to our way-fare
> Make thy laugh our wander-lied;
> Bid thy 'fulgence bear away care.
> Cloud and rain-tears pass they fleet!

> Seeking e'er the new-laid rast-way
> To the gardens of the sun . . . .

I have sung women in three cities
But it is all one.

I will sing of the white birds
In the blue waters of heaven,
The clouds that are spray to its sea.

In Epitaphium Eius

Servant and singer, Troubadour
That for his loving, loved each fair face more
Than craven sluggard can his life's one love,

Dowered with love, "whereby the sun doth move
And all the stars."
They called him fickle that the lambent flame
Caught "Bicé" dreaming in each new-blown name,

And loved all fairness tho its hidden guise
Lurked various in half an hundred eyes;

That loved the essence tho each casement bore
A different semblance than the one before.

Na Audiart

(*Que be-m vols mal*)

Note: Any one who has read anything of the troubadours knows
well the tale of Bertran of Born and My Lady Maent of Mon-
taignac, and knows also the song he made when she would none
of him, the song wherein he, seeking to find or make her equal,
begs of each preëminent lady of Langue d'Oc some trait or some
fair semblance: thus of Cembelins her "esgart amoros" to wit, her
love-lit glance, of Aelis her speech free-running, of the Vicomptess
of Chales her throat and her two hands, at Roacoart of Anhes her
hair golden as Iseult's; and even in this fashion of Lady Audiart
"altho she would that ill come unto him" he sought and praised
the lineaments of the torse. And all this to make "Una dompna
soiseubuda" a borrowed lady or as the Italians translated it "Una
donna ideale."

Tho thou well dost wish me ill
                              Audiart, Audiart,
Where thy bodice laces start
As ivy fingers clutching thru
Its crevices,
                    Audiart, Audiart,

Stately, tall and lovely tender
Who shall render
Audiart, Audiart
Praises meet unto thy fashion?
Here a word kiss!
Pass I on
Unto Lady "Miels-de-Ben,"
Having praised thy girdle's scope,
How the stays ply back from it;
I breathe no hope
That thou shouldst . . . .
Nay no whit
Bespeak thyself for anything.
Just a word in thy praise, girl,
Just for the swirl
Thy satins make upon the stair,
'Cause never a flaw was there
Where thy torse and limbs are met:
Tho thou hate me, read it set
In rose and gold,*
Or when the minstrel, tale half told
Shall burst to lilting at the phrase
"Audiart, Audiart". . . .

Bertrans, master of his lays,
Bertrans of Aultaforte thy praise
Sets forth, and tho thou hate me well,
Yea tho thou wish me ill
Audiart, Audiart
Thy loveliness is here writ till,
Audiart,
Oh, till thou come again.†
And being bent and wrinkled, in a form
That hath no perfect limning, when the warm
Youth dew is cold
Upon thy hands, and thy old soul
Scorning a new, wry'd casement

*i. e. in illumed manuscript.
†reincarnate.

Churlish at seemed misplacement
Finds the earth as bitter
As now seems it sweet,
Being so young and fair
As then only in dreams,
Being then young and wry'd,
Broken of ancient pride
Thou shalt then soften
Knowing I know not how
Thou wert once she
                                Audiart, Audiart
For whose fairness one forgave
                                Audiart, Audiart
Que be-m vols mal.

Villonaud for This Yule

Towards the Noel that morte saison
(*Christ make the shepherds' homage dear!*)
Then when the grey wolves everychone
Drink of the winds their chill small-beer
And lap o' the snows food's gueredon
Then makyth my heart his yule-tide cheer
(Skoal! with the dregs if the clear be gone!)
Wineing the ghosts of yester-year.

Ask ye what ghosts I dream upon?
(*What of the magians' scented gear?*)
The ghosts of dead loves éveryone
That make the stark winds reek with fear
Lest love return with the foison sun
And slay the memories that me cheer
(Such as I drink to mine fashion)
Wineing the ghosts of yester-year.

Where are the joys my heart had won?
(*Saturn and Mars to Zeus drawn near!*)*

*signum Nativitatis.

Where are the lips mine lay upon,
Aye! where are the glances feat and clear
That bade my heart his valor don?
I skoal to the eyes as grey-blown mere
(Who knows whose was that paragon?)
Wineing the ghosts of yester-year.

Prince: ask me not what I have done
Nor what God hath that can me cheer
But ye ask first where the winds are gone
Wineing the ghosts of yester-year.

A Villonaud. Ballad of the Gibbet

Or the Song of the Sixth Companion

(Scene: *"En cest bourdel où tenons nostre estat"*)
It being remembered that there were six of us with Master
Villon, when that expecting presently to be hanged he writ
a ballad whereof ye know:
"Frères humains qui après nous vivez."

Drink ye a skoal for the gallows tree!
François and Margot and thee and me,
Drink we the comrades merrily
That said us, "Till then" for the gallows tree!

Fat Pierre with the hook gauche-main,
Thomas Larron "Ear-the-less,"
Tybalde and that armouress
Who gave this poignard its premier stain
Pinning the Guise that had been fain
To make him a mate of the "Hault Noblesse"
And bade her be out with ill address
As a fool that mocketh his drue's disdeign.

Drink we a skoal for the gallows tree!
François and Margot and thee and me,
Drink we to Marienne Ydole,
That hell brenn not her o'er cruelly.

Drink we the lusty robbers twain,
Black is the pitch o' their wedding dress,*
Lips shrunk back for the wind's caress
As lips shrink back when we feel the strain
Of love that loveth in hell's disdeign
And sense the teeth thru the lips that press
'Gainst our lips for the soul's distress
That striveth to ours across the pain.

Drink we skoal to the gallows tree!
François and Margot and thee and me,
For Jehan and Raoul de Vallerie
Whose frames have the night and its winds in fee.

Maturin, Guillaume, Jacques d'Allmain,
Culdou lacking a coat to bless
One lean moiety of his nakedness
That plundered St. Hubert back o' the fane:
Aie! the lean bare tree is widowed again
For Michault le Borgne that would confess
In "faith and troth" to a traitoress
"Which of his brothers had he slain?"

But drink we skoal to the gallows tree!
François and Margot and thee and me:

These that we loved shall God love less
And smite alway at their faibleness?

Skoal!! to the Gallows! and then pray we:
God damn his hell out speedily
And bring their souls to his "Haulte Citee."

---

*Certain gibbeted corpses used to be coated with tar as a preservative;
thus one scare crow served as warning for considerable time. See Hugo
"L'Homme qui Rit."

Mesmerism

"And a cat's in the water-butt"
Robt. Browning, *Mesmerism*

Aye you're a man that! ye old mesmerizer
Tyin' your meanin' in seventy swadelin's,
One must of needs be a hang'd early riser
To catch you at worm turning. Holy Odd's bodykins!

"Cat's i' the water butt!" Thought's in your verse-barrel,
Tell us this thing rather, then we'll believe you,
You, Master Bob-Browning, spite your apparel
Jump to your sense and give praise as we'd lief do.

You wheeze as a head-cold long-tonsilled Calliope,
But God! what a sight you ha' got o' our innards,
Mad as a hatter but surely no Myope,
Broad as all ocean and leanin' man-kin'ards.

Heart that was big as the bowels of Vesuvius,
Words that were wing'd as her sparks in eruption,
Eagled and thundered as Jupiter Pluvius,
Sound in your wind past all signs o' corruption.

Here's to you, Old Hippety-hop o'the accents,
True to the Truth's sake and crafty dissector,
You grabbed at the gold sure; had no need to pack cents
Into your versicles.
                    Clear sight's elector!

Fifine Answers

"Why is it that, disgraced, they seem to relish life the more?"
Fifine at the Fair, VII, 5.

Sharing his exile that hath borne the flame,
Joining his freedom that hath drunk the shame
And known the torture of the Skull-place hours

Free and so bound, that mingled with the powers
Of air and sea and light his soul's far reach
Yet strictured did the body-lips beseech
"To drink": "I thirst." And then the sponge of gall.

Wherefor we wastrels that the grey road's call
Doth master and make slaves and yet make free,
Drink all of life and quaffing lustily
Take bitter with the sweet without complain
And sharers in his drink defy the pain
That makes you fearful to unfurl your souls.

We claim no glory. If the tempest rolls
About us we have fear, and then
Having so small a stake grow bold again.
We know not definitely even this
But 'cause some vague half knowing half doth miss
Our consciousness and leaves us feeling
That somehow all is well, that sober, reeling
From the last carouse, or in what measure
Of so called right or so damned wrong our leisure
Runs out uncounted sand beneath the sun,
That, spite your carping, still the thing is done
With some deep sanction, that, we know not how,
Without our thought gives feeling; You allow
That 'tis not need we *know* our every thought
Or see the work shop where each mask is wrought
Wherefrom we view the world of box and pit,
Careless of wear, just so the mask shall fit
And serve our jape's turn for a night or two.

Call! eh bye! the little door at twelve!

I meet you there myself.

Anima Sola

"Then neither is the bright orb of the sun greeted nor yet either the shaggy might of earth or sea, thus then, in the firm vessel of harmony is fixed God, a sphere, round, rejoicing in complete solitude."

Empedokles

Exquisite loneliness
Bound of mine own caprice
I fly on the wings of an unknown chord
    That ye hear not,
    Can not discern.
My music is weird and untamed
Barbarous, wild, extreme,
I fly on the note that ye hear not
On the chord that ye can not dream.
And lo, your out-worn harmonies are behind me
    As ashes and mouldy bread,
I die in the tears of the morning
    I kiss the wail of the dead.
My joy is the wind of heaven,
    My drink is the gall of night,
My love is the light of meteors;
    The autumn leaves in flight.

I pendant sit in the vale of fate
  I twine the Maenad strands
And lo, the three Eumenides
    Take justice at my hands.
For I fly in the gale of an unknown chord.
The blood of light is God's delight
And I am the life blood's ward.

O Loneliness, O Loneliness,
Thou boon of the fires blown
From heaven to hell and back again
Thou cup of the God-man's own!

For I am a weird untamed
That eat of no man's meat
My house is the rain ye wail against
    My drink is the wine of sleet.

My music is your disharmony
    Intangible, most mad,
For the clang of a thousand cymbals
Where the sphinx smiles o'er the sand,
    And viol strings that out-sing kings
Are the least of my command.
Exquisite, alone, untrammeled
I kiss the nameless sign
And the laws of my inmost being
    Chant to the nameless shrine.
I flee on the wing of a note ye know not,
My music disowns your law,
Ye can not tread the road I wed

And lo! I refuse your bidding.
I will not bow to the expectation that ye have.
Lo! I am gone as a red flame into the mist,
My chord is unresolved by your counter-harmonies.

In Tempore Senectutis

    For we are old
And the earth passion dyeth;
We have watched him die a thousand times,
When he wanes an old wind cryeth,
    For we are old
And passion hath died for us a thousand times
    But we grew never weary.

Memory faileth, as the lotus-loved chimes
    Sink into fluttering of wind,
    But we grow never weary
    For we are old.

The strange night-wonder of your eyes
Dies not, tho passion flyeth
        Along the star fields of Arcturus
And is no more unto our hands;
        My lips are cold
And yet we twain are never weary,
And the strange night-wonder is upon us,
The leaves hold our wonder in their flutterings,
The wind fills our mouths with strange words
        For our wonder that grows not old.

The moth hour of our day is upon us
        Holding the dawn;
There is strange Night-wonder in our eyes
Because the Moth-Hour leadeth the dawn
As a maiden, holding her fingers,
The rosy, slender fingers of the dawn.

He: "Red spears bore the warrior dawn
                        "Of old.
        "Strange! Love, hast thou forgotten
                "The red spears of the dawn,
                "The pennants of the morning?"

She: "Nay, I remember, but now
        "Cometh the Dawn, and the Moth-Hour
        "Together with him; softly
        "For we are old."

Famam Librosque Cano

Your songs?
                Oh! The little mothers
Will sing them in the twilight,
And when the night
Shrinketh the kiss of the dawn
That loves and kills,
What time the swallow fills
Her note, then the little rabbit folk

That some call children,
Such as are up and wide
Will laugh your verses to each other,
Pulling on their shoes for the day's business,
Serious child business that the world
Laughs at, and grows stale;
Such is the tale
—Part of it—of thy song-life.

Mine?

      A book is known by them that read
      That same. Thy public in my screed
      Is listed. Well! Some score years hence
      Behold mine audience,
      As we had seen him yesterday.

      Scrawny, be-spectacled, out at heels,
Such an one as the world feels
A sort of curse against its guzzling
And its age-lasting wallow for red greed
And yet; full speed
Tho it should run for its own getting,
Will turn aside to sneer at
'Cause he hath
No coin, no will to snatch the aftermath
Of Mammon.
Such an one as women draw away from
For the tobacco ashes scattered on his coat
And sith his throat
Shows razor's unfamiliarity
And three days' beard;

Such an one picking a ragged
Backless copy from the stall,
Too cheap for cataloguing,
Loquitur,

"Ah-eh! the strange rare name. . . .
"Ah-eh! He must be rare if even *I* have not. . . ."
And lost mid-page
Such age
As his pardons the habit,
He analyzes form and thought to see
How I 'scaped immortality.

The Cry of the Eyes

Rest Master, for we be aweary, weary
And would feel the fingers of the wind
Upon these lids that lie over us
Sodden and lead-heavy.

Rest brother, for lo! the dawn is without!
The yellow flame paleth
And the wax runs low.

Free us, for without be goodly colors,
Green of the wood-moss and flower colors,
And coolness beneath the trees.

Free us, for we perish
In this ever-flowing monotony
Of ugly print marks, black
Upon white parchment.

Free us, for there is one
Whose smile more availeth
Than all the age-old knowledge of thy books:
And we would look thereon.

Scriptor Ignotus

To K. R. H.
Ferrara 1715

When I see thee as some poor song-bird
Battering its wings, against this cage we call Today,
Then would I speak comfort unto thee,
From out the heights I dwell in, when
That great sense of power is upon me
And I see my greater soul-self bending
Sibylwise with that great forty-year epic
That you know of, yet unwrit
But as some child's toy 'tween my fingers,
And see the sculptors of new ages carve me thus,
And model with the music of my couplets in their hearts:
Surely if in the end the epic
And the small kind deed are one;
If to God, the child's toy and the epic are the same.
E'en so, did one make a child's toy,
He might wright it well
And cunningly, that the child might
Keep it for his children's children
And all have joy thereof.

Dear, an this dream come true,
Then shall all men say of thee
"She 'twas that played him power at life's morn,
And at the twilight Evensong,
And God's peace dwelt in the mingled chords
She drew from out the shadows of the past,
And old world melodies that else
He had known only in his dreams
Of Iseult and of Beatrice."

Dear, an this dream come true,
I, who being poet only,
Can give thee poor words only,
Add this one poor other tribute,
This thing men call immortality.

A gift I give thee even as Ronsard gave it.
Seeing before time, one sweet face grown old,
And seeing the old eyes grow bright
From out the border of Her fire-lit wrinkles,
As she should make boast unto her maids
"Ronsard hath sung the beauty, *my* beauty,
                    Of the days that I was fair."

So hath the boon been given, by the poets of old time
(Dante to Beatrice—an I profane not—)
Yet with my lesser power shall I not strive
                    To give it thee?

All ends of things are with Him
From whom are all things in their essence.
If my power be lesser
Shall my striving be less keen?
But rather more! if I would reach the goal,
                    Take then the striving!
"And if," for so the Florentine hath writ
When having put all his heart
Into his "Youth's Dear Book"
He yet strove to do more honor
To that lady dwelling in his inmost soul,
He would wax yet greater
To make her earthly glory more.
Though sight of hell and heaven were
                    price thereof,
If so it be His will, with whom
Are all things and through whom
Are all things good,
Will I make for thee and for the beauty of thy music
A new thing
As hath not heretofore been writ.
                    Take then my promise!

Note. Bertold Lomax, English Dante scholar and mystic, died in Ferrara
1723, with his "great epic," still a mere shadow, a nebula crossed with some
few gleams of wonder light. The lady of the poem an organist of Ferrara,
whose memory has come down to us only in Lomax' notes.

Vana

In vain have I striven
　　　to teach my heart to bow;
In vain have I said to him
"There be many singers　　greater than thou."

But his answer cometh,　　as winds and as lutany,
As a vague crying upon the night
That leaveth me no rest,　　saying ever,
　　　　　"Song,　　a song."
Their echoes play upon each other in the twilight
Seeking ever a song.
Lo, I am worn with travail
And the wandering of many roads hath made my eyes
As dark red circles filled with dust.
Yet there is a trembling upon me in the twilight,
　　　And little red elf words　　crying "A song,"
　　　Little grey elf words　　crying for a song,
　　　Little brown leaf words　　crying "A song,"
　　　Little green leaf words　　crying for a song.
The words are as leaves, old brown leaves in the spring time
Blowing they know not whither, seeking a song.

That Pass Between the False Dawn and the True

Blown of the winds whose goal is "No-man-knows"
As feathered seeds upon the wind are borne,
To kiss as winds kiss and to melt as snows
And in our passing taste of all men's scorn,
Wraiths of a dream that fragrant ever blows
From out the night we know not to the morn,
Borne upon winds whose goal is "No-man-knows."
An hour to each! We greet. The hour flows
And joins its hue to mighty hues out-worn
Weaving the Perfect Picture, while we torn
Give cry in harmony, and weep the Rose
Blown of the winds whose goal is "No-man-knows."

In Morte De

Oh wine-sweet ghost how are we borne apart
Of winds that restless blow we know not where
As little shadows smoke-wraith-sudden start
If music break the freighted dream of air;
So, fragile curledst thou in my dream-wracked heart,
So, sudden summoned dost thou leave it bare.
O wine-sweet ghost how are we borne apart!
As little flames amid the dead coal dart
And lost themselves upon some hidden stair,
So futile elfin be we well aware
Old cries I cry to thee as I depart,
"O wine-sweet ghost how are we borne apart."

Threnos

No more for us the little sighing
No more the winds at twilight trouble us.

Lo the fair dead!

No more do I burn.
No more for us the fluttering of wings
That whirred the air above us.

Lo the fair dead!

No more desire flayeth me,
No more for us the trembling
At the meeting of hands.

Lo the fair dead!

No more for us the wine of the lips
No more for us the knowledge.

Lo the fair dead!

No more the torrent
No more for us the meeting-place
(Lo the fair dead!)
Tintagoel.

Ballad Rosalind

Our Lord is set in his great oak throne
For our old Lord liveth all alone
    These ten years and gone.

A book on his knees and bent his head
For our old Lord's love is long since dead.
    These ten years and gone.

For our young Lord Hugh went to the East,
And fought for the cross and is crows' feast
    These ten years and gone.

"But where is our Lady Rosalind,
Fair as day and fleet as wind
    These ten years and gone?"

For our old Lord broodeth all alone
Silent and grey in his black oak throne
    These ten years and gone.

Our old Lord broodeth silent there
For to question him none will dare
    These ten years and more.

Where is our Lady Rosalind
Fair as dawn and fleet as wind.
    These ten years and gone?

Our old Lord sits with never a word
And only the flame and the wind are heard
    These ten years and more.

.   .   .   .   .   .

"Father! I come," and she knelt at the throne,
"Father! know me, I am thine own.
    "These ten years and more

"Have they kept me for ransom at Chastel d' Or
"And never a word have I heard from thee
    "These ten years and more."

But our Lord answered never a word
And only sobbing and wind were heard.
    (These ten years and gone.)

We took our Lord and his great oak throne
And set them deep in a vault of stone
    These ten years and gone,

A book on his knees and bow'd his head
For the Lord of our old Lord's love is dead
    These ten years and gone,

And Lady Rosalind rules in his stead
(Thank we God for our daily bread)
    These ten years and more.

Malrin

Malrin, because of his jesting stood without, till all the guests were entered in unto the Lord's house. Then there came an angel unto him saying, "Malrin, why hast thou tarried?"

To whom, Malrin, "There is no feeding till the last sheep be gone into the fold. Wherefor I stayed chaffing the laggards and mayhap when it was easy helping the weak."

Saith the angel, "The Lord will be wroth with thee, Malrin, that thou art last."

"Nay sirrah!" quipped Malrin, "I knew my Lord when thou and thy wings were yet in the egg."

Saith the angel, "Peace! hasten lest there be no bread for thee, rattle-tongue."

"Ho," quoth Malrin, "is it thus that thou knowest my Lord? Aye! I am his fool and have felt his lash but meseems that thou hast set thy ignorance to my folly, saying 'Hasten lest there be an end to his bread.'"

Whereat the angel went in in wrath. And Malrin, turning slowly, beheld the last blue of twilight and the sinking of the silver of the stars. And the suns sank down like cooling gold in their crucibles, and there was a murmuring amid the azure curtains and far clarions from the keep of heaven, as a Muezzin crying, "Allah akbar, Allah il Allah! *it is finished*."

And Malrin beheld the broidery of the stars become as wind-worn tapestries of ancient wars. And the memory of all old songs swept by him as an host blue-robèd trailing in dream, Odysseus, and Tristram, and the pale great gods of storm, the mailed Campeador and Roland and Villon's women and they of Valhalla; as a cascade of dull sapphires so poured they out of the mist and were gone. And above him the stronger clarion as a Muezzin crying "Allah akbar, Allah il Allah, *it is finished*."

And again Malrin, drunk as with the dew of old world druidings, was bowed in dream. And the third dream of Malrin was the dream of the seven and no man knoweth it.

And a third time came the clarion and after it the Lord called softly unto Malrin, "Son, why hast thou tarried? Is it not fulfilled, thy dream and mine?"

And Malrin, "O Lord, I am thy fool and thy love hath been my scourge and my wonder, my wine and mine extasy. But one left me awroth and went in unto thy table. I tarried till his anger was blown out."

"Oh Lord for the ending of our dream I kiss thee. For his anger is with the names of Deirdre and Ysolt. And our dream is ended, PADRE."

Masks

These tales of old disguisings, are they not
Strange myths of souls that found themselves among
Unwonted folk that spake an hostile tongue,
Some soul from all the rest who'd not forgot
The star-span acres of a former lot
Where boundless mid the clouds his course he swung,
Or carnate with his elder brothers sung
Ere ballad-makers lisped of Camelot?

Old singers half-forgetful of their tunes,
Old painters color-blind come back once more,
Old poets skill-less in the wind-heart runes,
Old wizards lacking in their wonder-lore:

All they that with strange sadness in their eyes
Ponder in silence o'er earth's queynt devyse?

On His Own Face in a Glass

O strange face there in the glass!

O ribald company, O saintly host!
O sorrow-swept my fool,

What answer?
                O ye myriad
That strive and play and pass,
Jest, challenge, counterlie,

I   ?   I   ?   I   ?
                                And ye?

Invern

Earth's winter cometh
And I being part of all
And sith the spirit of all moveth in me
I must needs bear earth's winter
Drawn cold and grey with hours
And joying in a momentary sun,
Lo I am withered with waiting till my spring cometh!
Or crouch covetous of warmth
O'er scant-logged ingle blaze,
Must take cramped joy in tomed Longinus
That, read I him first time
The woods agleam with summer
Or mid desirous winds of spring,
Had set me singing spheres
Or made heart to wander forth among warm roses
Or curl in grass nest neath a kindly moon.

Plotinus

As one that would draw thru the node of things,
    Back sweeping to the vortex of the cone,
    Cloistered about with memories, alone
In chaos, while the waiting silence sings:

Obliviate of cycles' wanderings
    I was an atom on creation's throne
    And knew all nothing my unconquered own.
God! Should I be the hand upon the strings?!

But I was lonely as a lonely child.
I cried amid the void and heard no cry,
And then for utter loneliness, made I
New thoughts as crescent images of *me*.
And with them was my essence reconciled
While fear went forth from mine eternity.

Prometheus

For we be the beaten wands
And the bearers of the flame.
    Our selves have died lang syne, and we
Go ever upward as the sparks of light
Enkindling all
'Gainst whom our shadows fall.

Weary to sink, yet ever upward borne,
Flame, flame that riseth ever
To the flame within the sun,
Tearing our casement ever
For the way is one
That beareth upward
To the flame within the sun.

Aegupton

I—even I—am he who knoweth the roads
Thru the sky and the wind thereof is my body.

I have beheld the Lady of Life.
I, even I, that fly with the swallows.

Green and grey is her raiment
Trailing along the wind.

I—even I—am he who knoweth the roads
Thru the sky and the wind thereof is my body.

Manus animam pinxit—
My pen is in my hand

To write the acceptable word,
My mouth to chaunt the pure singing:

Who hath the mouth to receive it?
The Song of the Lotus of Kumi?

I—even I—am he who knoweth the roads
Thru the sky and the wind thereof is my body.

I am flame that riseth in the sun,
I, even I, that fly with the swallows

For the moon is upon my forehead,
The winds are under my kiss.

The moon is a great pearl in the waters of sapphire;
Cool to my fingers the flowing waters.

I—even I—am he who knoweth the roads
Of the sky and the wind thereof is my body.

I will return unto the halls of the flowing
Of the truth of the children of Ashu.

I—even I—am he who knoweth the roads
Of the sky and the wind thereof is my body.

Ballad for Gloom

For God, our God, is a gallant foe
That playeth behind the veil.

I have loved my God as a child at heart
That seeketh deep bosoms for rest,
I have loved my God as maid to man
But lo this thing is best:

To love your God as a gallant foe
                    that plays behind the veil,
To meet your God as the night winds meet
                    beyond Arcturus' pale.

I have played with God for a woman,
I have staked with my God for truth,

I have lost to my God as a man, clear eyed,
    His dice be not of ruth,

For I am made as a naked blade
    But hear ye this thing in sooth:

Who loseth to God as man to man
    Shall win at the turn of the game.
I have drawn my blade where the lightnings meet
    But the ending is the same:
Who loseth to God as the sword blades lose
    Shall win at the end of the game.

For God, our God, is a gallant foe
           that playeth behind the veil
Whom God deigns not to overthrow
           Hath need of triple mail.

For E. McC.

That was my counter-blade under
Leonardo Terrone, Master of Fence.

Gone while your tastes were keen to you,
Gone where the grey winds call to you,
By that high fencer, even Death,
Struck of the blade that no man parrieth,
Such is your fence, one saith,
    one that hath known you.
Drew you your sword most gallantly
Made you your pass most valiantly
    'Gainst that grey fencer, even Death.

Gone as a gust of breath.
Faith! no man tarrieth,
"*Se il cor ti manca,*" but it failed thee not!
"*Non ti fidar,*" it is the sword that speaks

"In me." *

Thou trusted'st in thyself and met the blade
'Thout mask or gauntlet, and art laid
As memorable broken blades that be
Kept as bold trophies of old pageantry,
As old Toledos past their days of war
Are kept mnemonic of the strokes they bore,
So art thou with us, being good to keep
In our heart's sword-rack, tho thy sword-arm sleep.

ENVOI

Struck of the blade that no man parrieth
Pierced of the point that toucheth lastly all,
'Gainst that grey fencer, even Death,
Behold the shield! He shall not take thee all.

*Sword-rune! "If thy heart fail thee trust not in me."

Salve O Pontifex!

To Swinburne; an hemichaunt

One after one do they leave thee,
          High Priest of Iacchus,
Toning thy melodies even as winds tone
The whisper of tree leaves, on sun-lit days.
Even as the sands are many
And the seas beyond the sands are one
In ultimate; so we here being many
Are unity. Nathless thy compeers
          Knowing thy melody,
Lulled with the wine of thy music
Go seaward silently, leaving thee sentinel
O'er all the mysteries,
          High Priest of Iacchus,
For the lines of life lie under thy fingers,
And above the vari-colored strands
Thine eyes look out unto the infinitude

Of the blue waves of heaven,
And even as Triplex Sisterhood
Thou fingerest the threads knowing neither
Cause nor the ending.
                    High Priest of Iacchus
Draw'st forth a multiplicity
Of strands, and beholding
The color thereof, raisest thy voice
Toward the sunset,
                    O High Priest of Iacchus!
And out of the secrets of the inmost mysteries
Thou chantest strange far-sourced canticles;
                    O High Priest of Iacchus!
Life and the ways of Death her
Twin born sister, being Life's counterpart
(And evil being inversion of blessing
That blessing herself might have being)
And night and the winds of night;
Silent voices ministering to the souls
Of hamadryads that hold council concealed
In streams and tree-shadowing
Forests on hill slopes,
                    O High Priest of Iacchus
All the manifold mystery
Thou makest wine of song of,
And maddest thy following
Even with visions of great deeds
And their futility, and the worship of love,
                    O High Priest of Iacchus.
Wherefor tho thy co-novices bent to the scythe
Of the magian wind that is voice of Prosephone,
Leaving thee solitary, master of initiating
Maenads that come thru the
Vine-entangled ways of the forest
Seeking, out of all the world
                    Madness of Iacchus,
That being skilled in the secrets of the double cup
They might turn the dead of the world
Into beauteous paeans,
                    O High Priest of Iacchus

Wreathed with the glory of years of creating
Entangled music that men may not
Over readily understand:
                    Breathe!
Now that evening cometh upon thee,
Breathe upon us that low-bowed and exultant
Drink wine of Iacchus
                That since the conquering*
Hath been chiefly contained in the numbers
Of them that even as thou, have woven
Wicker baskets for grape clusters
Wherein is concealèd the source of the vintage,
                O High Priest of Iacchus
Breathe thou upon us
                Thy magic in parting!
Even as they thy co-novices
Being mingled with the sea
While yet thou mad'st canticles
Serving upright before the altar
That is bound about with shadows
Of dead years wherein thy Iacchus
Looked not upon the hills, that being
Uncared for, praised not him in entirety,
                O High Priest of Iacchus
Being now near to the border of the sands
Where the sapphire girdle of the sea
                Encinctureth the maiden
Prosephone, released for the spring.
Look! Breathe upon us
The wonder of the thrice encinctured mystery
Whereby thou being full of years art young,
Loving even this lithe Prosephone
That is free for the seasons of plenty;

Whereby thou being young art old
And shalt stand before this Prosephone
                Whom thou lovest,
In darkness, even at that time

*Vicisti, Nazarenus!

That she being returned to her husband
Shall be queen and a maiden no longer,

Wherein thou being neither old nor young,
Standing on the verge of the sea
Shalt pass from being sand,
        O High Priest of Iacchus,
And becoming wave
            Shalt encircle all sands,
Being transmuted thru all
The girdling of the sea.
        O High Priest of Iacchus,
Breathe thou upon us!

To the Dawn: Defiance

Ye blood-red spears-men of the dawn's array
That drive my dusk-clad knights of dream away,
Hold! For I will not yield.

My moated soul-shall dream in your despite
A refuge for the vanquished hosts of night
That *can* not yield.

The Decadence

Tarnished we! Tarnished! Wastrels all!
And yet the art goes on, goes on.
Broken our strength, yea as crushed reeds we fall,
And yet the art, the *art* goes on.

Bearers of beauty flame and wane,
The sunset shadow and the rose's bloom.
The sapphire seas grow dull to shine again
As new day glistens in the old day's room.

Broken our manhood for the wrack and strain;
Drink of our hearts the sunset and the cry
"Io Triumphe!" Tho our lips be slain
We see Art vivant, and exult to die.

Redivivus

Hail Michael Agnolo! my soul lay slain
Or else in torpor such, death seems more fair,
I looked upon the light, if light were there
I knew it not. There seemed not any pain,
Nor joy, nor thought nor glorious deed nor strain
Of any song that half remembered were
For sign of quickness in that soul; but bare
Gaunt walls alone me seemed it to remain.

Thou praisest Dante well, My Lord: "No tongue
"Can tell of him what told of him should be
"For on blind eyes his splendor shines too strong."
If so his soul goes on unceasingly
Shall mine own flame count flesh one life too long
To hold its light and bear ye company?

Fistulae

"To make her madrigal
"Who shall the rose sprays bring;
"To make her madrigal
"And bid my heart to sing?"

Song

Love thou thy dream
All base love scorning,
Love thou the wind
And here take warning
That dreams alone can truly be,
For 'tis in dream I come to thee.

Motif

I have heard a wee wind searching
Thru still forests for me,
I have seen a wee wind searching
O'er still sea.

Thru woodlands dim
Have I taken my way,
And o'er silent waters, night and day
Have I sought the wee wind.

La Regina Avrillouse

Lady of rich allure,
Queen of the spring's embrace,
Your arms are long like boughs of ash,
Mid laugh broken streams, spirit of rain unsure,
Breath of the poppy flower,
All the wood thy bower
And the hills thy dwelling place.

This will I no more dream,
Warm is thine arm's allure
Warm is the gust of breath
That ere thy lips meet mine
Kisseth my cheek and saith:
"This is the joy of earth,
Here is the wine of mirth
Drain ye one goblet sure,

Take ye the honey cup
The honied song raise up,
Drink of the spring's allure
April and dew and rain,
Brown of the earth sing sure,
Cheeks and lips and hair
And soft breath that kisseth where
Thy lips have come not yet to drink."

Moss and the mold of earth
These be thy couch of mirth,
Long arms thy boughs of shade
April-alluring, as the blade
Of grass doth catch the dew
And make it crown to hold the sun,
Banner be you
      Above my head
Glory to all wold display'd
      April-alluring, glory-bold.

A Rouse

Save ye, Merry gentlemen! Vagabonds and Rovers,
    Hell take the hin'most,
      We're for the clovers!
"Soul" sings the preacher.
    Our joy's the light.
"Goal" bawls ambition.
    Grass our delight!

Save ye, merry gentlemen!
    Whirr and dew of earth,
    Beauty 'thout raiment,
Reed pipes and mellow mirth
Scot free, no payment!

Gods be for heaven,
Clay the poet's birth!
    Save ye merry gentlemen!
Wind and dew and spray o' sea
    Hell take the hin'most,
Foot or sail for Arcady
Voice o' lark and breath of bee
    Hell take the hin'most!
Our drink shall be the orange wine,
House o' boughs and roof o' vine
    Hell take the hin'most!

Laugh and lips and gleam o' hair
Fore-kiss breath, and shoulders bare,
    Save you queen o April!

(*La Regina Avrillouse loquitur*).

    Follow! follow!

    Breath of mirth,
My bed, my bower green of earth,
    Naught else hath any worth.
Save ye "jolif bachillier"!
    Hell take the hin'most!

Nicotine
A Hymn to the Dope

Goddess of the murmuring courts,
        Nicotine, my Nicotine,
Houri of the mystic sports,
        trailing-robed in gabardine,
Gliding where the breath hath glided,
Hidden sylph of filmy veils,
Truth behind the dream is veiléd
E'en as thou art, smiling ever, ever gliding,
Wraith of wraiths, dim lights dividing
Purple, grey, and shadow green
        Goddess, Dream-grace, Nicotine.

Goddess of the shadow's lights,
        Nicotine, my Nicotine,
Some would set old Earth to rights,
        Thou and I none such I ween.
Veils of shade our dream dividing,
Houris dancing, intergliding,
Wraith of wraiths and dream of faces,

Silent guardian of the old unhallowed places,
Utter symbol of all old sweet druidings,
Mem'ry of witched wold and green,
            Nicotine, my Nicotine:

Neath the shadows of thy weaving
Dreams that need no undeceiving,
Loves that longer hold me not,
Dreams I dream not any more,
Fragrance of old sweet forgotten places,
Smiles of dream-lit, flit-by faces
All as perfume Arab-sweet
Deck the high road to thy feet

As were Godiva's coming fated
And all the April's blush belated
Were lain before her, carpeting
The stones of Coventry with spring,
So thou my mist-enwreathéd queen,
Nicotine, white Nicotine,
            Riding engloried in thy hair
Mak'st by-road of our dreams
            Thy thorough-fare.

In Tempore Senectutis
(*An Anti-stave for Dowson*)

When I am old
I will not have you look apart
From me, into the cold,
Friend of my heart,
Nor be sad in your remembrance
Of the careless, mad-heart semblance
That the wind hath blown away
When I am old.

When I am old
And the white hot wonder-fire
Unto the world seem cold,

My soul's desire
Know you then that all life's shower,
The rain of the years, that hour
Shall make blow for us one flower,
Including all, when we are old.

When I am old
If you remember
Any love save what is then
Hearth light unto life's December
Be your joy of past sweet chalices
To know then naught but this
"How many wonders are less sweet
Than love I bear to thee
When I am old."

Oltre La Torre: Rolando

There dwelt a lady in a tower high,
Foul beasts surrounded it,
I scattered them and left her free.

O-la! Oll-aa! The green-wood tree
Hath many a smooth sward under it!

My lady hath a long red cloak,
Her robe was of the sun,
This blade hath broke a baron's yoke,
That hath such guerdon won.

Yea I have broke my Lord Gloom's yoke
New yoke will I have none,
Save the yoke that shines in the golden bow
Betwixt the rain and the sun.

Ol-la! Ol-la! the good green-wood!
The good green wood is free!
Say who will lie in the bracken high
And laugh, and laugh for the winds with me?

Make-strong old dreams lest this our world lose heart.

For man is a skinfull of wine
But his soul is a hole full of God
And the song of all time blows thru him
As winds thru a knot-holed board.

Tho man be a skin full of wine
Yet his heart is a little child
That croucheth low beneath the wind
When the God-storm battereth wild.

THE SAN TROVASO NOTEBOOK

San Vio. June

Old powers rise and do return to me
Grace to thy bounty, O Venetian sun.
Weary I came to thee, my romery
A cloth of day-strands raveled and ill-spun,
My soul a swimmer weary of the sea,
The shore a desert place with flowers none.

Old powers rise and do return to me.
The strife of waves, their lusty harmony
A thundered thorough bass the rocks upon,
Makes strong forgotten chanteys, and anon
My heart's loud-shouted burden proves to thee
Old powers risen have returned to me.

June 22

Roundel for Arms

All blood and body for the sun's delight,
Such be forms, that in my song bid spring,
Should lead my lyric where the ways be dight
With flowers fit for any garlanding
And bid the lustre of arms be bright
Who do our chaunting 'gainst the "Lord Gloom" fling.

All blood and body for the sun's delight,
I bid ye stand, my words, and in the fight
Bear ye as men and let your glaive-strokes ring
Basnet on falchion 'till the chorusing
Proclaim your triumph and ye stand aright,
All blood and body for the sun's delight.

Cino. June.

Roundel
After Joachim du Bellay

I come unto thee thru the hidden ways,
Soul of my soul, whose beauty quivereth
Within her eyes to whom my former days
As wined libation poured I, while my breath
Strove to her homage in unskillful lays
And bade my heart make his high vaunt 'gainst death.

I come unto thee thru the hidden ways
Who art the soul of beauty, and whose praise
Or color, or light, or song championeth,
And of whom Time as but an herald saith,
"Trust tho thou sense not, spite of my delays,
Her whom I bring thee thru the hidden ways."

Cino. June

To Ysolt. For Pardon.

My songs remade that I send greet the world
Thou knowest as at first they came to me,
Freighted with fragrance of thyself and furled
In stumbling words that yet us seemed to be
True music, sith thy heart and mine empurled
Their outer sense with inner subtlety.

My songs remade that I send greet the world
Me seem as red leaves of the Autumn whirled
Out thru the dust-grey ways, that dearer we,
As green bough-banners, held more lovingly
With simpler color than these turn-coats hurled,
As songs remade sent forth to greet the world.

?San Trovaso

Piazza San Marco.

June.

I

Master Will, so cussed human,
Careless-clouted god o' speech,
Is there twist o' man or woman
Too well-hidden for thy reach?

Diadems and broken roses,
Wind and Tritons loud at horn,
Sack-stains half thy screed discloses,
Th' other half doth hold the morn.

II

Some comfort 'tis to catch Will Shaxpeer stealing.
All bards are thieves save Villon, master thief,
Who pilfered naught but wine and then, wide reeling,
Lilted his heart out, Ballad-Lord in chief.
(True to his song's good, spit the fate hands dealing,
With lips the bolder for a soul-hid grief.)

III—AFTER SHAKESPEARE'S SONNET XCVIII

When proud-pied April leadeth in his train
And yellow crocus quick'neth to the breath
Of Zephyr fleeting from the sun-shot rain,
Then seek I her whom mine heart honoureth.
She is a woodland sprite and suzerain
Of every power that flouteth wintry death.

When proud-pied April leadeth in his train
And freeth all the earth from cold's mort-main,
Then with her fairness mine heart journeyeth
Thru bourgeon wood-ways wherein tourneyeth
Earth's might of laughter 'gainst all laughter slain
Ere proud-pied April led in feat his train.

For a Play
(Maeterlinck)

Personality—amour
    brings me to death,

My lady Willow-wisp
    that brings me to light
(a wandered forest gleam that fades)
leaving me to see the rocks turn
as if sans her connection
    and then the sun,
The sea sapphire, the grass emerald
and the white-blue above.

                S. Vio. June

Alma Sol Veneziae
(Baritone)

Thou that hast given me back
    Strength for the journey,
Thou that hast given me back
    Heart for the Tourney,

O Sun venezian,
    Thou that thru all my veins
Hast bid the life-blood run,
Thou that hast called my soul
    From out the far crevices,
Yea, the far dark crevices
    And caves of ill-fearing,

        Alma tu sole!
Cold, ah a-cold
    Was my soul in the caves
    Of ill-fearing.

                S. Vio.

Ballad of Wine Skins

As winds thru a round smooth knot-hole
Make tune to the time of the storm,
The cry of the bard in the half-light
Is chaos bruised into form.

The skin of my wine is broken,
Is sunken and shrunken and old.
My might is the might of thistle down,
My name as a jest out-told.

Yet there cometh one in the half-light
That shieldeth a man with her hair,
And what man crouch from in his soul
The child of his heart shall bear.

———

Thoughts moving
            in her eyes
as sunset color
            shadows
                    on Giudecca.

The haze
            that
            doth the sun prolong.

———

I have felt the lithe wind
            blowing
                    under one's fingers
            sinuous.

A QUINZAINE FOR THIS YULE

Being selected from a
Venetian sketch-book
—"San Trovaso"—

TO

THE AUBE OF THE WEST DAWN

Beauty should never be presented explained. It is Marvel and Wonder, and in art we should find first these doors—Marvel and Wonder—and, coming through them, a slow understanding (slow even though it be a succession of lightning understandings and perceptions) as of a figure in mist, that still and ever gives to each one his own right of believing, each after his own creed and fashion.

Always the desire to know and to understand more deeply must precede any reception of beauty. Without holy curiosity and awe none find her, and woe to that artist whose work wears its "heart on its sleeve."

WESTON ST. LLEWMYS

Prelude: Over the Ognisanti

High-dwelling 'bove the people here,
Being alone with beauty most the while,
Lonely?
            How can I be,
Having mine own great thoughts for paladins
Against all gloom and woe and every bitterness?

Also have I the swallows and the sunset
And I see much life below me,
            In the garden, on the waters,
And hither float the shades of songs they sing
To sound of wrinkled mandolin, and plash of waters,
Which shades of song re-echoed
Within that somewhile barren hall, my heart,
Are found as I transcribe them following.

Night Litany

O Dieu, purifiez nos coeurs!
            purifiez nos coeurs!

Yea the lines hast thou laid unto me
            in pleasant places,
And the beauty of this thy Venice
            hast thou shewn unto me
Until is its loveliness become unto me
            a thing of tears.

O God, what great kindness
            have we done in times past
            and forgotten it,
That thou givest this wonder unto us,
            O God of waters?

O God of the night
              What great sorrow
Cometh unto us,
              That thou thus repayest us
Before the time of its coming?

O God of silence,
              Purifiez nos coeurs
              Purifiez nos coeurs
For we have seen
The glory of the shadow of the
      likeness of thine handmaid,
Yea, the glory of the shadow
      of thy Beauty hath walked
Upon the shadow of the waters
      In this thy Venice.
              And before the holiness
Of the shadow of thy handmaid
      Have I hidden mine eyes,
              O God of waters.

O God of silence,
              Purifiez nos coeurs,
              Purifiez nos coeurs,
O God of waters,
              make clean our hearts within us
And our lips to show forth thy praise,
              For I have seen the
shadow of this thy Venice
floating upon the waters,
              And thy stars
have seen this thing out of their far courses
have they seen this thing,
              O God of waters.
Even as are thy stars
Silent unto us in their far-coursing,
Even so is mine heart
              become silent within me.

(*Fainter*)
>   Purifiez nos coeurs
O God of the silence,
>   Purifiez nos coeurs
O God of waters.

Purveyors General

Praise to the lonely ones!
Give praise out of your ease
To them whom the farther seas
Bore out from amongst you.

We, that through all the world
Have wandered seeking new things
And quaint tales, that your ease
May gather such dreams as please
>   you, the Home-stayers.

We, that through chaos have hurled
Our souls riven and burning,
Torn, mad, even as windy seas
Have we been, that your ease
Should keep bright amongst you:

That new tales and strange peoples
Such as the further seas
Wash on the shores of,
That new mysteries and increase
Of sunlight should be amongst you,
>   you, the home-stayers.

Even for these things, driven from you,
Have we, drinking the utmost lees
Of all the world's wine and sorrowing
Gone forth from out your ease,
>   And borrowing
Out of all lands and realms
>   of the infinite,
New tales, new mysteries,

New songs from out the breeze
That maketh soft the far evenings,
Have brought back these things
        Unto your ease,
Yours unto whom peace is given.

Aube of the West Dawn.
Venetian June

From the Tale "How Malrin chose for his Lady the
reflection of the Dawn and was thereafter true to her."

When svelte the dawn reflected in the west,
As did the sky slip off her robes of night,
I see to stand mine armouress confessed,
Then doth my spirit know himself aright,
And tremulous against her faint-flushed breast
Doth cast him quivering, her bondsman quite.

When I the dawn reflected in the west,
Fragile and maiden to my soul have pressed,
Pray I, her mating hallowed in God's sight,
That none asunder me with bale of might
From her whose lips have bade mine own be blest,
My bride, "The dawn reflected in the west."

I think from such perceptions as this arose the ancient myths of the demi-
gods; as from such as that in "The Tree" (*A Lume Spento*), the myths of
metamorphosis.

To La Contessa Bianzafior (Cent. XIV)
(*Defense at Parting*)

I

And all who read these lines shall love her then
Whose laud is all their burthen, and whose praise
Is in my heart forever, tho' my lays

But stumble and grow startled dim again
When I would bid them, mid the courts of men,
Stand and take judgment. Whoso in new days
Shall read this script, or wander in the ways
My heart hath gone, shall praise her then.
Knowing this thing, "White Flower," I bid thy thought
Turn toward what thing a singer's love should be;
Stood I within thy gates and went not on,
One poor fool's love were all thy gueredon.
I go—my song upon the winds set free—
And lo!
  A thousand souls to thine are brought.

II

"This fellow mak'th his might seem over strong!"

Hath there a singer trod our dusty ways
And left not twice this hoard to weep her praise,
Whose name was made the glory of his song?

Hear ye, my peers! Judge ye, if I be wrong.
Hath Lesbia more love than all Catullus' days
Should've counted her of love? Tell me where strays
Her poet now, what ivory gates among?

Think ye? Ye think it not; my vaunt o'er bold?
Hath Deirdre, or Helen, or Beatrys,
More love than to maid unsung there is?

Be not these other hearts, when his is cold,
That seek thy soul with ardor manifold,
A better thing than were the husk of his?

III

Whose is the gift of love? Tell me, whose is
The right to give or take? The thing is mine?
Think ye, O fools! It is not mine nor thine
Though I should strive, and I might strive y-wis,
Though I should strive what would we make o' this

Love for her soul, a love toward the divine,
A might within what heart that seeks such wine
As is the love betwixt her lips and his?

Were I to stand alone and guard this drink
To shut it off from such as come to pray,
What were the gueredon I bid ye think
To one that strove to hold the sun in goal?
Know ye first love, then come to me and say,
"Thou art inconstant and hast shamed thy soul."

IV

Night and the wax wanes. Night, and the text grows dim.
Who hath more love? Who brings more love?
    Speak strait.
Sung? Or unsung? Wedded? Or maid to wait
A thousand hearts who at the rune of him
That saw thy soul amid the Seraphim
Shall bear their incense to the horny gate
Whereby true dreams arise and hold their state?

Ye mock the lines. Pardon a poor fool's whim.

I, that have seen amid the dreams so much,
Speak dimly, stumble and draw forth your scorn.
Whether availeth more one prisoned man
Giving such labor as a bonds-man can,
Or a host of vagrants crying the morn
With "Hail" and "Day's grace" from the hearts o' such.

"queren lo jorn"

Partenza di Venezia

Ne'er felt I parting from a woman loved
As feel I now my going forth from thee,
Yea, all thy waters cry out "Stay with me!"
And laugh reflected flames up luringly.

O elf-tale land that I three months have known,
Venice of dreams, if where the storm-wrack drave
As some uncertain ghost upon the wave,
For cloud thou hidest and then fitfully
For light and half-light feign'st reality,
If first we fear the dim dread of the unknown
Then reassured for the calm clear tone
"I am no spirit. Fear not me!"

As once the twelve storm-tossed on Galilee
Put off their fear yet came not nigh
Unto the holier mystery.
So we bewildered, yet have trust in thee,
And thus thou, Venice,
                    show'st thy mastery.

Lucifer Caditurus

By service clomb I heaven
And the law that smites the spheres,
Turning their courses even,
Served me as I serve God.

And shall all fears
Of chaos or this hell the Mover dreams—
Because *he knows* what is to me yet dim—
Bid me to plod
An huckster of the sapphire beams
From star to star
Giving to each his small embraced desire,
Shall I not bear this light
Unto what far
Unheavened bourne shall meet my fire
With some toward sympathy
That wills not rule?

By service clomb I heaven
And the Law served me, even
As I serve God; but shall this empery

Bid me restrict my course, or plod
A furrow worker in a space-set sod
Or turn the emeralds of the empyrean
Because I dread some pale remorse
Should gnaw the sinews of m' effulgent soul
Deigned I to break His bonds
        That hold the law?

Sandalphon

And these about me die,
Because the pain of the infinite singing
Slayeth them.
Ye that have sung of the pain of the earth-horde's
        age-long crusading,
Ye know somewhat the strain,
        the sad-sweet wonder-pain of such singing.
And therefore ye know after what fashion
This singing hath power destroying.

Yea, these about me, bearing such song in homage
Unto the Mover of Circles,
Die for the might of their praising,
And the autumn of their marcescent wings
Maketh ever new loam for my forest;
And these grey ash trees hold within them
All the secrets of whatso things
They dreamed before their praises,
And in this grove my flowers,
Fruit of prayerful powers,
Have first their thought of life
        And then their being.

Ye marvel that I die not! *forsitan!*
Thinking me kin with such as may not weep,
Thinking me part of them that die for praising
—yea, tho' it be praising,
past the power of man's mortality to

dream or name its phases,
—yea, tho' it chaunt and paean
past the might of earth-dwelt
soul to think on,
—yea, tho' it be praising
as these the winged ones die of.

Ye think me one insensate
              else die I also
Sith these about me die,
and if I, watching
ever the multiplex jewel, of beryl and jasper
      and sapphire
Make of these prayers of earth ever new flowers;
Marvel and wonder!
Marvel and wonder even as I,
Giving to prayer new language
and causing the works to speak
of the earth-horde's age-lasting longing,
Even as I marvel and wonder, and know not,
Yet keep my watch in the ash wood.

Note on Sandalphon. The angel of prayer according to the Talmud stands
unmoved among the angels of wind and fire, who die as their one song is
finished; also as he gathers the prayers they turn to flowers in his hands.
   Longfellow also treats of this, but as a legend rather than a reality.

Fortunatus

Resistless, unresisting, as some swift spear upon the flood
Follow'th the river's course and tarries not
But hath the stream's might for its on-sped own,
So towards my triumph, and so reads the will,
'Gainst which I will not, or mine eyes grow dim,
And dim they seem not, nor are willed to be.
For beauty greet'th them through your London rain,
That were of Adriatic beauty loved and won,
And though I seek all exile, yet my heart
Doth find new friends and all strange lands
Love me and grow my kin, and bid me speed.

Caught sometimes in the current of strange happiness, borne upon such winds as Dante beheld whirling the passion-pale shapes in the nether-gloom,* so here in the inner sunlight, or above cool, dew-green pasture lands, and again in caves of the azure magic.

WESTON ST. LLEWMYS

*"*E paion sì al vento esser leggieri.*"
"*Ombre portate dalla detta briga.*"

Beddoesque

——and going heavenward leaves
An opal spray to wake, a track that gleams
With new-old runes and magic of past time
Caught from the sea deep of the whole man-soul,
The "mantra" of our craft, that to the sun,
New brought and broken by the fearless keel,
That were but part of all the sun-smit sea,
Have for a space their individual being,
And do seem as things apart from all Time's hoard,
The great whole liquid jewel of God's truth.

Greek Epigram

Day and night are never weary,
Nor yet is God of creating
For day and night their torch-bearers
The aube and the crepuscule.

So, when I weary of praising the dawn and the sunset,
Let me be no more counted among the immortals;
But number me amid the wearying ones,
Let me be a man as the herd,
And as the slave that is given in barter.

Christophori Columbi Tumulus

(From the Latin of Hippolytus Capilupus, Early Cent. MDC)

Genoan, glory of Italy, Columbus thou sure light,
Alas the urn takes even thee so soon out-blown,
Its little space

Doth hold thee, whom Oceanus had not the might
Within his folds to hold, altho' his broad embrace
Doth hold all lands.

Bark-borne beyond his boundries unto Hind thou wast
Where scarce Fame's volant self the way had cast.

To T. H.   The Amphora.

Bring me this day some poet of the past,
Some unknown shape amid the wonder lords!
Yea of such wine as all time's store affords
From rich amphorae that nor years can blast
With might of theirs and blows down-rainèd fast,
Falernian and Massic of the Roman hoards,
I've drunk the best that any land accords,
Yet dread the time that I shall drink the last.

Bring me this day from out the smoky room
Some curved clay guardian of untasted wine,
That holds the sun at heart. Search i' the gloom
Boy, well, and mark you that the draught be good.
Then as an answer to this jest of mine,
Luck brought th' amphora, and the clasp was "Hood."

Histrion

No man hath dared to write this thing as yet,
And yet I know, how that the souls of all men great
At times pass through us,
And we are melted into them, and are not
Save reflexions of their souls.
Thus am I Dante for a space and am
One François Villon, ballad-lord and thief
Or am such holy ones I may not write,
Lest blasphemy be writ against my name;
This for an instant and the flame is gone.

'Tis as in midmost us there glows a sphere
Translucent, molten gold, that is the "I"
And into this some form projects itself:
Christus, or John, or eke the Florentine;
And as the clear space is not if a form's
Imposed thereon,
So cease we from all being for the time,
And these, the Masters of the Soul, live on.

Nel Biancheggiar

Blue-grey, and white, and white-of-rose,
The flowers of the West's fore-dawn unclose.
I feel the dusky softness whirr
of color, as upon a dulcimer
"Her" dreaming fingers lay between the tunes,
As when the living music swoons
But dies not quite, because for love of us
—knowing our state
How that 'tis troublous—
It wills not die to leave us desolate.

With thanks to Marco Londonio for his delightful Italian paraphrase of these lines appearing in "La Bauta" for Aug. 9th.

"Make-strong old dreams lest this our world lose heart."

THIS BOOK IS FOR
MARY MOORE
OF TRENTON, IF SHE
WANTS IT

Praise of Ysolt

In vain have I striven
      to teach my heart to bow;
In vain have I said to him
"There be many singers greater than thou."

But his answer cometh, as winds and as lutany,
As a vague crying upon the night
That leaveth me no rest, saying ever,
          "Song, a song."

Their echoes play upon each other in the twilight
Seeking ever a song.
Lo, I am worn with travail
And the wandering of many roads hath made my eyes
As dark red circles filled with dust.
Yet there is a trembling upon me in the twilight,
    And little red elf words   crying "A song,"
    Little grey elf words   crying for a song,
    Little brown leaf words   crying "A song,"
    Little green leaf words   crying for a song.
The words are as leaves, old brown leaves in the
    spring time
Blowing they know not whither, seeking a song.

White words as snow flakes but they are cold
Moss words, lip words, words of slow streams.

In vain have I striven
      to teach my soul to bow,
In vain have I pled with him,
    "There be greater souls than thou."

For in the morn of my years there came a woman
As moon light calling
As the moon calleth the tides,
          "Song, a song."
Wherefore I made her a song and she went from me
As the moon doth from the sea,

But still came the leaf words, little brown elf words
Saying "The soul sendeth us."
                    "A song, a song!"
And in vain I cried unto them "I have no song
For she I sang of hath gone from me."

But my soul sent a woman, a woman of the wonderfolk,
A woman as fire upon the pine woods
        crying "Song, a song."
As the flame crieth unto the sap.
My song was ablaze with her and she went from me
As flame leaveth the embers so went she unto new
        forests
And the words were with me
        crying ever "Song, a song."

And I "I have no song,"
Till my soul sent a woman as the sun:
Yea as the sun calleth to the seed,
As the spring upon the bough
So is she that cometh the song-drawer
She that holdeth the wonder words within her eyes
The words little elf words
        that call ever unto me
            "Song, a song."

ENVOI

In vain have I striven with my soul
        to teach my soul to bow.
What soul boweth
        while in his heart art thou?

Tally-O

What ho! the wind is up and eloquent.
Through all the Winter's halls he crieth Spring.
Now will I get me up unto mine own forests
And behold their bourgeoning.

At the Heart o' Me

A.D. 751

With ever one fear at the heart o' me
Long by still sea-coasts
    coursed my Grey-Falcon,
And the twin delights
    of shore and sea were mine,
Sapphire and emerald with
    fine pearls between.

Through the pale courses of
    the land-caressing in-streams
Glided my barge and
    the kindly strange peoples
Gave to me laugh for laugh,
    and wine for my tales of wandering.
And the cities gave me welcome
    and the fields free passage,
With ever one fear
    at the heart o' me.

An thou should'st grow weary
    ere my returning,
An "*they*" should call to thee
    from out the borderland,
What should avail me
    booty of whale-ways?
What should avail me
    gold rings or the chain-mail?
What should avail me
    the many-twined bracelets?
What should avail me,
    O my beloved,
Here in this "Middan-gard"*
    what should avail me
Out of the booty and
    gain of my goings?

*Anglo-Saxon, "Earth."

Xenia

And
Unto thine eyes my heart
Sendeth old dreams of the spring-time,
Yea of wood-ways my rime
Found thee and flowers in and of all streams
That sang low burthen, and of roses,
That lost their dew-bowed petals for the dreams
We scattered o'er them passing by.

Occidit

Autumnal breaks the flame upon the sun-set herds.
The sheep on Gilead as tawn hair gleam
Neath Mithra's dower and his slow departing,
While in the sky a thousand fleece of gold
Bear, each his tribute, to the waning god.

Hung on the rafters of the effulgent west,
Their tufted splendour shields his decadence,
As in our southern lands brave tapestries
Are hung king-greeting from the ponticells
And drag the pageant from the earth to air,
Wherein the storied figures live again,
Wind-molden back unto their life's erst guise,
All tremulous beneath the many-fingered breath
That Aufidus* doth take to house his soul.

*The West Wind.

An Idyl for Glaucus

Nel suo aspetto tal dentro mi fei
Qual si fe' Glauco nel gustar dell' erba
Che il fe' consorto in mar degli altri dei.
                    Paradiso, 1, 67–9.

"As Glaucus tasting the grass that made
him sea-fellow with the other gods."

I

Whither he went I may not follow him. His eyes
Were strange to-day. They always were,
After their fashion, kindred of the sea.

To-day I found him. It is very long
That I had sought among the nets, and when I asked
The fishermen, they laughed at me.
I sought long days amid the cliffs thinking to find
The body-house of him, and then
There at the blue cave-mouth my joy
Grew pain for suddenness, to see him 'live.
Whither he went I may not come, it seems
He is become estranged from all the rest,
And all the sea is now his wonder-house.
And he may sink unto strange depths, he tells me of,
That have no light as we it deem.
E'en now he speaks strange words. I did not know
One half the substance of his speech with me.

And then when I saw naught he sudden leaped
And shot, a gleam of silver, down, away.
And I have spent three days upon this rock
And yet he comes no more.
He did not even seem to know
I watched him gliding through the vitreous deep.

II

They chide me that the skein I used to spin
Holds not my interest now,
They mock me at the route, well, I have come again.
Last night I saw three white forms move
Out past the utmost wave that bears the white foam crest.
I somehow knew that he was one of them.

Oimè, Oimè! I think each time they come
Up from the sea heart to the realm of air
They are more far-removèd from the shore.

When first I found him here, he slept
E'en as he might after a long night's taking on the deep.
And when he woke some whit the old kind smile
Dwelt round his lips and held him near to me.
But then strange gleams shot through the grey-deep eyes
As though he saw beyond and saw not me.
And when he moved to speak it troubled him.
And then he plucked at grass and bade me eat.
And then forgot me for the sea its charm
And leapt him in the wave and so was gone.

III

I wonder why he mocked me with the grass.
I know not any more how long it is
Since I have dwelt not in my mother's house.
I know they think me mad, for all night long
I haunt the sea-marge, thinking I may find
Some day the herb he offered unto me.
Perhaps he did not jest; they say some simples have
More wide-spanned power than old wives draw from them.
Perhaps, found I this grass, he'd come again.
Perhaps 'tis some strange charm to draw him here,
'Thout which he may not leave his new-found crew
That ride the two-foot coursers of the deep,
And laugh in storms and break the fishers' nets.
Oimè, Oimè!

SONG
Voices in the Wind.

We have worn the blue and vair,
And all the sea-caves
Know us of old, and know our new-found mate.
There's many a secret stair
The sea-folk climb . . .

Out of the Wind.
Oimè, Oimè!

I wonder why the wind, even the wind doth seem
To mock me now, all night, all night, and
Have I strayed among the cliffs here.
They say, some day I'll fall
Down through the sea-bit fissures, and no more
Know the warm cloak of sun, or bathe
The dew across my tired eyes to comfort them.
They try to keep me hid within four walls.
I will not stay!
                    Oimè!
And the wind saith; Oimè!

I am quite tired now. I know the grass
Must grow somewhere along this Thracian coast,
If only he would come some little while and find it me.

ENDETH THE LAMENT FOR GLAUCUS

In Durance

I am homesick after mine own kind,
Oh I know that there are folk about me, friendly faces,
But I am homesick after mine own kind.

"These sell our pictures"! Oh well,
They reach me not, touch me some edge or that,
But reach me not and all my life's become
One flame, that reacheth not beyond
Mine heart's own hearth,
Or hides among the ashes there for thee.
"Thee"? Oh "thee" is who cometh first
Out of mine own soul-kin,
For I am homesick after mine own kind
And ordinary people touch me not.
                              Yea, I am homesick
After mine own kind that know, and feel
And have some breath for beauty and the arts.

Aye, I am wistful for my kin of the spirit
And have none about me save in the shadows
When come *they*, surging of power, "DAEMON,"
"Quasi KALOUN." S.T. says, Beauty is most that, a
    "calling to the soul."
Well then, so call they, the swirlers out of the mist
    of my soul,
They that come mewards bearing old magic.

But for all that, I am homesick after mine own kind
And would meet kindred e'en as I am,
Flesh-shrouded bearing the secret.
"All they that with strange sadness"
Have the earth in mock'ry, and are kind to all,
My fellows, aye I know the glory
Of th' unbounded ones, but ye, that hide
As I hide most the while
And burst forth to the windows only whiles or whiles
For love, or hope, or beauty or for power,
Then smoulder, with the lids half closed
And are untouched by echoes of the world.

Oh ye, my fellows: with the seas between us some be,
Purple and sapphire for the silver shafts
Of sun and spray all shattered at the bows
Of such a "Veltro" of the vasty deep
As bore my tortoise house scant years agone:
And some the hills hold off,
The little hills to east us, though here we
Have damp and plain to be our shutting in.

And yet my soul sings "Up!" and we are one.
Yea thou, and Thou, and THOU, and all my kin
To whom my breast and arms are ever warm,
For that I love ye as the wind the trees
That holds their blossoms and their leaves in cure
And calls the utmost singing from the boughs
That 'thout him, save the aspen, were as dumb
Still shade, and bade no whisper speak the birds of how
"Beyond, beyond, beyond, there lies . . ."

Guillaume de Lorris Belated
A Vision of Italy

Wisdom set apart from all desire,
A hoary Nestor with youth's own glad eyes,
Him met I at the style, and all benign
He greeted me an equal and I knew,
By this his lack of pomp, he was himself.

Slow-Smiling is companion unto him,
And Mellow-Laughter serves, his trencherman.
And I a thousand beauties there beheld.
And he and they made merry endlessly.
And love was rayed between them as a mist,
And yet so fine and delicate a haze
It did impede the eyes no whit,
Unless it were to make the halo round each one
Appear more myriad-jewelled marvellous,
Than any pearled and ruby diadem the courts o' earth
      ha' known.

Slender as mist-wrought maids and hamadryads
Did meseem these shapes that ministered,
These formed harmonies with lake-deep eyes,
And first the cities of north Italy
I did behold,
Each as a woman wonder-fair,
And svelte Verona first I met at eve;
And in the dark we kissed and then the way
Bore us somewhile apart.
And yet my heart keeps tryst with her,
So every year our thoughts are interwove
As fingers were, such times as eyes see much, and tell.
And she that loved the master years agone,
That bears his signet in her "Signor Square,"
"Che lo glorifico."
                    She spread her arms,
And in that deep embrace
All thoughts of woe were perished
And of pain and weariness and all the wrack

Of light-contending thoughts and battled-gleams,
(That our intelligence doth gain by strife against itself)
Of things we have not yet the earnèd right to clearly see.
And all, yea all that dust doth symbolize
Was there forgot, and my enfranchised soul
Grew as the liquid elements, and was infused
With joy that is not light, nor might nor harmony,
And yet hath part and quality of all these three,
Whereto is added calm past earthly peace.

Thus with Verona's spirit, and all time
Swept on beyond my ken, and as the sea
Hath in no wise a form within itself,
Cioè, as liquid hath no form save where it bounden is
By some enshrouding chalice of hard things—
As wine its graven goblet, and the sea
Its wave-hewn basalt for a bordering,
So had my thought and now my thought's remembrance
No "*in*formation" of whatso there passed
For this long space the dream-king's horny gate.

And when that age was done and the transfusion
Of all my self through her and she through me,
I did perceive that she enthroned two things:
Verona, and a maid I knew on earth;
And dulled some while from dream, and then become
That lower thing, deductive intellect, I saw
How all things are but symbols of all things,
And each of many, do we know
But the equation governing.
And in my rapture at this vision's scope
I saw no end or bourn to what things mean,
So praised Pythagoras and once more raised
By this said rapture to the house of Dream,
Beheld Fenicè as a lotus flower
Drift through the purple of the wedded sea
And grow a wraith and then a dark-eyed she,
And knew her name was "All-forgetfulness,"
And hailed her: "Princess of the Opiates,"
And guessed her evil and her good thereby.

And then a maid of nine "Pavia" hight,
Passed with a laugh that was all mystery,
And when I turned to her
She reached me one clear chalice of white wine,
Pressed from the recent grapes that yet were hung
Adown her shoulders, and were bound
Right cunningly about her elfish brows;
So hale a draught, the life of every grape
Lurked without ferment in the amber cloud.
And memory, this wine was, of all good.

And more I might have seen: Firenza, Goito,
Or that proudest gate, Ligurian Genoa,
Cornelia of Colombo of far sight,
That, man and seer in one, had well been twain,
And each a glory to his hills and sea;
And past her a great band
Bright garlanded or rich with purple skeins,
And crimson mantles and queynt fineries
That tarnished held but so the more
Of dim allurement in their half-shown folds:
So swept my vision o'er their filmy ranks,
Then rose some opaque cloud,
Whose name I have not yet discerned,
And music as I heard it one clear night
Within our earthly night's own mirroring,
Cioè, San?——San Pietro by Adige,
Where altar candles blazed out as dim stars,
And all the gloom was soft, and shadowy forms
Made and sang God, within the far-off choir.
And in a clear space high behind
Them and the tabernacle of that place,
Two tapers shew the master of the keys
As some white power pouring forth itself.

And all the church rang low and murmured
Thus in my dream of forms the music swayed.
And I was lost in it and only woke
When something like a mass bell rang, and then
That white-foot wind, pale Dawn's annunciatrice,

Me bore to earth again, but some strange peace
I had not known so well before this swevyn
Clung round my head and made me hate earth less.

In the Old Age of the Soul

I do not choose to dream; there cometh on me
Some strange old lust for deeds.
As to the nerveless hand of some old warrior
The sword-hilt or the war-worn wonted helmet
Brings momentary life and long-fled cunning,
So to my soul grown old—
Grown old with many a jousting, many a foray,
Grown old with many a hither-coming and hence-going—
Till now they send him dreams and no more deed;
So doth he flame again with might for action,
Forgetful of the council of the elders,
Forgetful that who rules doth no more battle,
Forgetful that such might no more cleaves to him
So doth he flame again toward valiant doing.

Alba Belingalis

Phoebus shineth ere his splendour flieth
Aurora drives faint light athwart the land
And the drowsy watcher crieth,
                    "Arise."

REF.
O'er cliff and ocean the white dawn appeareth
It passeth vigil and the shadows cleareth.

They be careless of the gates, delaying,
Whom the ambush glides to hinder,
Whom I warn and cry to, praying,
                    "Arise."

REF.

O'er cliff and ocean the white dawn appeareth
It passeth vigil and the shadows cleareth.

Forth from out Arcturus, North Wind bloweth
The stars of heaven sheathe their glory
And sun-driven forth-goeth
                              Settentrion.

REF.

O'er sea mist, and mountain is the dawn display'd
It passeth watch and maketh night afraid.

From a tenth-century ms.

From Syria

The song of Peire Bremon "Lo Tort" that he made for
his Lady in Provença: he being in Syria a crusader.

In April when I see all through
Mead and garden new flowers blow,
And streams with ice-bands broken flow,
Eke hear the birds their singing do;
When spring's grass-perfume floateth by
Then 'tis sweet song and birdlet's cry
Do make mine old joy come anew.

Such time was wont my thought of old
To wander in the ways of love.
Burnishing arms and clang thereof,
And honour-services manifold
Be now my need. Whoso combine
Such works, love is his bread and wine,
Wherefore should his fight the more be bold.

Song bear I, who tears should bring
Sith ire of love mak'th me annoy,
With song think I to make me joy.
Yet ne'er have I heard said this thing:

"He sings who sorrow's guise should wear."
Natheless I will not despair
That sometime I'll have cause to sing.

I should not to despair give way
That somewhile I'll my lady see.
I trust well He that lowered me
Hath power again to make me gay.
But if e'er I come to my Love's land
And turn again to Syrian strand,
God keep me there for a fool, alway!

God for a miracle well should
Hold my coming from her away,
And hold me in His grace alway
That I left her, for holy-rood.
An I lose her, no joy for me,
Pardi, hath the wide world in fee.
Nor could He mend it, if He would.

Well did she know sweet wiles to take
My heart, when thence I took my way.
'Thout sighing, pass I ne'er a day
For that sweet semblance she did make
To me, saying all in sorrow:
"Sweet friend, and what of me to-morrow?"
"Love mine, why wilt me so forsake?"

ENVOI

Beyond sea be thou sped, my song,
And, by God, to my Lady say
That in desirous, grief-filled way
My nights and my days are full long.
And command thou William the Long-Seer
To tell thee to my Lady dear,
That comfort be her thoughts among.

The only bit of Peire Bremon's work that has come down to us, and
through its being printed with the songs of Giraut of Bornelh he is like to
lose credit for even this.—E.P.

From the Saddle
D'Aubigné to Diane

Wearied by wind and wave death goes
With gin and snare right near alway
Unto my sight. Behind me bay
As hounds the tempests of my foes.
Ever on ward against such woes,
Pistols my pillow's service pay,
Yet Love makes me the poet play.
Thou know'st the rime demands repose,
So if my line disclose distress,
The soldier and my restlessness
And teen, Pardon, dear Lady mine,
For since mid war I bear love's pain
'Tis meet my verse, as I, show sign
Of powder, gun-match and sulphur stain.

Marvoil

A poor clerk I, "Arnaut the less" they call me,
And because I have small mind to sit
Day long, long day cooped on a stool
A-jumbling o' figures for Maitre Jacques Polin,
I ha' taken to rambling the South here.

The Vicomte of Beziers's not such a bad lot.
I made rimes to his lady this three year:
Vers and canzone, till that damn'd son of Aragon,
Alfonso the half-bald, took to hanging
His helmet at Beziers.
Then came what might come, to wit: three men and
     one woman,
Beziers off at Mont-Ausier, I and his lady
Singing the stars in the turrets of Beziers,
And one lean Aragonese cursing the seneschal
To the end that you see, friends:

Aragon cursing in Aragon, Beziers busy at Beziers—
Bored to an inch of extinction,
Tibors all tongue and temper at Mont-Ausier,
Me! in this damn'd inn of Avignon,
Stringing long verse for the Burlatz;
All for one half-bald, knock-knee'd king of the
          Aragonese,
Alfonso, Quatro, poke-nose.

And if when I am dead
They take the trouble to tear out this wall here,
They'll know more of Arnaut of Marvoil
Than half his canzoni say of him.
As for will and testament I leave none,
Save this: "Vers and canzone to the Countess of
          Beziers
In return for the first kiss she gave me."
May her eyes and her cheek be fair
To all men except the King of Aragon,
And may I come speedily to Beziers
Whither my desire and my dream have preceded me.

O hole in the wall here! be thou my jongleur
As ne'er had I other, and when the wind blows,
Sing thou the grace of the Lady of Beziers,
For even as thou art hollow before I fill thee with
          this parchment,
So is my heart hollow when she filleth not mine eyes,
And so were my mind hollow, did she not fill utterly
          my thought.

Wherefore, O hole in the wall here,
When the wind blows sigh thou for my sorrow
That I have not the Countess of Beziers
Close in my arms here.
Even as thou shalt soon have this parchment.

O hole in the wall here, be thou my jongleur,
And though thou sighest my sorrow in the wind,
Keep yet my secret in thy breast here;
Even as I keep her image in my heart here.

Mihi pergamena deest.

Revolt

Against the Crepuscular Spirit in Modern Poetry

I would shake off the lethargy of this our time,
    and give
For shadows—shapes of power
For dreams—men.

"It is better to dream than do"?
         Aye! and, No!

Aye! if we dream great deeds, strong men,
Hearts hot, thoughts mighty.

No! if we dream pale flowers,
Slow-moving pageantry of hours that languidly
Drop as o'er-ripened fruit from sallow trees.
If so we live and die not life but dreams,
Great God, grant life in dreams,
Not dalliance, but life!

Let us be men that dream,
Not cowards, dabblers, waiters
For dead Time to reawaken and grant balm
For ills unnamed.

Great God, if we be damn'd to be not men but only dreams,
Then let us be such dreams the world shall tremble at
And know we be its rulers though but dreams!
Then let us be such shadows as the world shall tremble at
And know we be its masters though but shadow!

Great God, if men are grown but pale sick phantoms
That must live only in these mists and tempered lights
And tremble for dim hours that knock o'er loud
Or tread too violent in passing them;

Great God, if these thy sons are grown such thin ephemera,
I bid thee grapple chaos and beget
Some new titanic spawn to pile the hills and stir
This earth again.

And Thus in Nineveh

"Aye! I am a poet and upon my tomb
Shall maidens scatter rose leaves
And men myrtles, ere the night
Slays day with her dark sword.

"Lo! this thing is not mine
Nor thine to hinder,
For the custom is full old,
And here in Nineveh have I beheld
Many a singer pass and take his place
In those dim halls where no man throubleth
His sleep or song.
And many a one hath sung his songs
More craftily, more subtle-souled than I;
And many a one now doth surpass
My wave-worn beauty with his wind of flowers,
Yet am I poet, and upon my tomb
Shall all men scatter rose leaves
Ere the night slay light
With her blue sword.

"It is not, Raama, that my song rings highest
Or more sweet in tone than any, but that I
Am here a Poet, that doth drink of life
As lesser men drink wine."

The White Stag

I ha' seen them 'mid the clouds on the heather.
Lo! they pause not for love nor for sorrow,
Yet their eyes are as the eyes of a maid to her lover,
When the white hart breaks his cover
And the white wind breaks the morn.

> *"'Tis the white stag, Fame, we're a hunting,*
> *Bid the world's hounds come to horn!"*

Piccadilly

Beautiful, tragical faces,
Ye that were whole, and are so sunken;
And, O ye vile, ye that might have been loved,
That are so sodden and drunken,
Who hath forgotten you?

O wistful, fragile faces, few out of many!

The gross, the coarse, the brazen,
God knows I cannot pity them, perhaps, as I should do,
But, oh, ye delicate, wistful faces,
Who hath forgotten you?

EXULTATIONS

I am an eternal spirit and the things I make are but ephemera, yet I endure:

Yea, and the little earth crumbles beneath our feet and we endure.

Guido Invites You Thus*

"Lappo I leave behind and Dante too,
Lo, I would sail the seas with thee alone!
Talk me no love talk, no bought-cheap fiddl'ry,
Mine is the ship and thine the merchandise,
All the blind earth knows not th' emprise
Whereto thou calledst and whereto I call.

Lo, I have seen thee bound about with dreams,
Lo, I have known thy heart and its desire;
Life, all of it, my sea, and all men's streams
Are fused in it as flames of an altar fire!

Lo, thou hast voyaged not! The ship is mine."

*The reference is to Dante's sonnet "Guido vorrei . . ."

Sestina: Altaforte

LOQUITUR: *En* Bertrans de Born.
      Dante Alighieri put this man in hell for that he was a
      stirrer-up of strife.
      Eccovi!
      Judge ye!
      Have I dug him up again?
The scene is at his castle, Altaforte. "Papiols" is his jongleur.
"The Leopard," the *device* of Richard (Cœur de Lion).

I

Damn it all! all this our South stinks peace.
You whoreson dog, Papiols, come! Let's to music!
I have no life save when the swords clash.
But ah! when I see the standards gold, vair, purple, opposing
And the broad fields beneath them turn crimson,
Then howl I my heart nigh mad with rejoicing.

II

In hot summer have I great rejoicing
When the tempests kill the earth's foul peace,
And the light'nings from black heav'n flash crimson,
And the fierce thunders roar me their music
And the winds shriek through the clouds mad, opposing,
And through all the riven skies God's swords clash.

III

Hell grant soon we hear again the swords clash!
And the shrill neighs of destriers in battle rejoicing,
Spiked breast to spiked breast opposing!
Better one hour's stour than a year's peace
With fat boards, bawds, wine and frail music!
Bah! there's no wine like the blood's crimson!

IV

And I love to see the sun rise blood-crimson.
And I watch his spears through the dark clash
And it fills all my heart with rejoicing
And pries wide my mouth with fast music
When I see him so scorn and defy peace,
His lone might 'gainst all darkness opposing.

V

The man who fears war and squats opposing
My words for stour, hath no blood of crimson
But is fit only to rot in womanish peace
Far from where worth's won and the swords clash
For the death of such sluts I go rejoicing;
Yea, I fill all the air with my music.

VI

Papiols, Papiols, to the music!
There's no sound like to swords swords opposing,

No cry like the battle's rejoicing
When our elbows and swords drip the crimson
And our charges 'gainst "The Leopard's" rush clash.
May God damn for ever all who cry "Peace!"

VII

And let the music of the swords make them crimson!
Hell grant soon we hear again the swords clash!
Hell blot black for alway the thought "Peace"!

Piere Vidal Old

> It is of Piere Vidal, the fool par excellence of all Provence, of
> whom the tale tells how he ran mad, as a wolf, because of his
> love for Loba of Penautier, and how men hunted him with
> dogs through the mountains of Cabaret and brought him for
> dead to the dwelling of this Loba (she-wolf) of Penautier,
> and how she and her Lord had him healed and made wel-
> come, and he stayed some time at that court. He speaks:

When I but think upon the great dead days
And turn my mind upon that splendid madness,
Lo! I do curse my strength
And blame the sun his gladness;
For that the one is dead
And the red sun mocks my sadness.

Behold me, Vidal, that was fool of fools!
Swift as the king wolf was I and as strong
When tall stags fled me through the alder brakes,
And every jongleur knew me in his song,
And the hounds fled and the deer fled
And none fled over long.

Even the grey pack knew me and knew fear.
God! how the swiftest hind's blood spurted hot
Over the sharpened teeth and purpling lips!

Hot was that hind's blood yet it scorched me not
As did first scorn, then lips of the Penautier!
Aye ye are fools, if ye think time can blot

From Piere Vidal's remembrance that blue night.
God! but the purple of the sky was deep!
Clear, deep, translucent, so the stars me seemed
Set deep in crystal; and because my sleep
—Rare visitor—came not,—the Saints I guerdon
For that restlessness—Piere set to keep

One more fool's vigil with the hollyhocks.
Swift came the Loba, as a branch that's caught,
Torn, green and silent in the swollen Rhone,
Green was her mantle, close, and wrought
Of some thin silk stuff that's scarce stuff at all,
But like a mist wherethrough her white form fought,

And conquered! Ah God! conquered!
Silent my mate came as the night was still.
Speech? Words? Faugh! Who talks of words and love?!
Hot is such love and silent,
Silent as fate is, and as strong until
It faints in taking and in giving all.

Stark, keen, triumphant, till it plays at death.
God! she was white then, splendid as some tomb
High wrought of marble, and the panting breath
Ceased utterly. Well, then I waited, drew,
Half-sheathed, then naked from its saffron sheath
Drew full this dagger that doth tremble here.

Just then she woke and mocked the less keen blade.
Ah God, the Loba! and my only mate!
Was there such flesh made ever and unmade!
God curse the years that turn such women grey!
Behold here Vidal, that was hunted, flayed,
Shamed and yet bowed not and that won at last.

And yet I curse the sun for his red gladness,
I that have known strath, garth, brake, dale,
And every run-way of the wood through that great madness,
Behold me shrivelled as an old oak's trunk
And made men's mock'ry in my rotten sadness!

No man hath heard the glory of my days:
No man hath dared and won his dare as I:
One night, one body and one welding flame!
What do ye own, ye niggards! that can buy
Such glory of the earth? Or who will win
Such battle-guerdon with his "prowesse high"?

O Age gone lax! O stunted followers,
That mask at passions and desire desires,
Behold me shrivelled, and your mock of mocks;
And yet I mock you by the mighty fires
That burnt me to this ash.

.   .   .   .

Ah! Cabaret! Ah Cabaret, thy hills again!

.   .   .   .

Take your hands off me! . . .   [*Sniffing the air.*
                              Ha! this scent is hot!

Ballad of the Goodly Fere *

Simon Zelotes speaketh it somewhile after the Crucifixion.

Ha' we lost the goodliest fere o' all
For the priests and the gallows tree?
Aye lover he was of brawny men,
O' ships and the open sea.

When they came wi' a host to take Our Man
His smile was good to see,
"First let these go!" quo' our Goodly Fere,
"Or I'll see ye damned," says he.

*Fere = Mate, Companion.

Aye he sent us out through the crossed high spears
And the scorn of his laugh rang free,
"Why took ye not me when I walked about
Alone in the town?" says he.

Oh we drank his "Hale" in the good red wine
When we last made company,
No capon priest was the Goodly Fere
But a man o' men was he.

I ha' seen him drive a hundred men
Wi' a bundle o' cords swung free,
That they took the high and holy house
For their pawn and treasury.

They'll no' get him a' in a book I think
Though they write it cunningly;
No mouse of the scrolls was the Goodly Fere
But aye loved the open sea.

If they think they ha' snared our Goodly Fere
They are fools to the last degree.
"I'll go to the feast," quo' our Goodly Fere,
"Though I go to the gallows tree."

"Ye ha' seen me heal the lame and blind,
And wake the dead," says he,
"Ye shall see one thing to master all:
'Tis how a brave man dies on the tree."

A son of God was the Goodly Fere
That bade us his brothers be.
I ha' seen him cow a thousand men.
I have seen him upon the tree.

He cried no cry when they drave the nails
And the blood gushed hot and free,
The hounds of the crimson sky gave tongue
But never a cry cried he.

I ha' seen him cow a thousand men
On the hills o' Galilee,
They whined as he walked out calm between,
Wi' his eyes like the grey o' the sea.

Like the sea that brooks no voyaging
With the winds unleashed and free,
Like the sea that he cowed at Genseret
Wi' twey words spoke' suddently.

A master of men was the Goodly Fere,
A mate of the wind and sea,
If they think they ha' slain our Goodly Fere
They are fools eternally.

I ha' seen him eat o' the honey-comb
Sin' they nailed him to the tree.

Hymn III

From the Latin of Marc Antony Flaminius, sixteenth century

As a fragile and lovely flower unfolds its gleaming foliage
   on the breast of the fostering earth, if the dew and
   the rain draw it forth;
So doth my tender mind flourish, if it be fed with the sweet
   dew of the fostering spirit,
Lacking this, it beginneth straightway to languish, even as a
   floweret born upon dry earth, if the dew and the rain
   tend it not.

Sestina for Ysolt

There comes upon me will to speak in praise
Of things most fragile in their loveliness;
Because the sky hath wept all this long day
And wrapped men's hearts within its cloak of greyness,
Because they look not down I sing the stars,
Because 'tis still mid-March I praise May's flowers.

Also I praise long hands that lie as flowers
Which though they labour not are worthy praise,
And praise deep eyes like pools wherein the stars
Gleam out reflected in their loveliness,
For whoso look on such there is no greyness
May hang about his heart on any day.

The other things that I would praise to-day?
Besides white hands and all the fragile flowers,
And by their praise dispel the evening's greyness?
I praise dim hair that worthiest is of praise
And dream upon its unbound loveliness,
And how therethrough mine eyes have seen the stars.

Yea, through that cloud mine eyes have seen the stars
That drift out slowly when night steals the day,
Through such a cloud meseems their loveliness
Surpasses that of all the other flowers.
For that one night I give all nights my praise
And love therefrom the twilight's coming greyness.

There is a stillness in this twilight greyness
Although the rain hath veiled the flow'ry stars,
They seem to listen as I weave this praise
Of what I have not seen all this grey day,
And they will tell my praise unto the flowers
When May shall bid them in in loveliness.

O ye I love, who hold this loveliness
Near to your hearts, may never any greyness
Enshroud your hearts when ye would gather flowers,
Or bind your eyes when ye would see the stars;
But alway do I give ye flowers by day,
And when day's plucked I give ye stars for praise.

But most, thou Flower, whose eyes are like the stars,
With whom my dreams bide all the live-long day,
Within thy hands would I rest all my praise.

Portrait

From "La Mère Inconnue"

Now would I weave her portrait out of all dim splendour.
Of Provence and far halls of memory,
Lo, there come echoes, faint diversity
Of blended bells at even's end, or
As the distant seas should send her
The tribute of their trembling, ceaselessly
Resonant. Out of all dreams that be,
Say, shall I bid the deepest dreams attend her?

Nay! For I have seen the purplest shadows stand
Always with reverent chere that looked on her,
Silence himself is grown her worshipper
And ever doth attend her in that land
Wherein she reigneth, wherefore let there stir
Naught but the softest voices, praising her.

"Fair Helena" by Rackham

"What I love best in all the world?"

When the purple twilight is unbound,
　　　To watch her slow, tall grace
　　　　　　and its wistful loveliness,
And to know her face
　　　　　　is in the shadow there,
Just by two stars beneath that cloud—
The soft, dim cloud of her hair,
And to think my voice
　　　　　　can reach to her
As but the rumour of some tree-bound stream,
Heard just beyond the forest's edge,
Until she all forgets I am,
And knows of me
Naught but my dream's felicity.

Laudantes Decem Pulchritudinis Johannae Templi

I

When your beauty is grown old in all men's songs,
And my poor words are lost amid that throng,
Then you will know the truth of my poor words,
And mayhap dreaming of the wistful throng
That hopeless sigh your praises in their songs,
You will think kindly then of these mad words.

II

I am torn, torn with thy beauty,
O Rose of the sharpest thorn!
O Rose of the crimson beauty,
Why hast thou awakened the sleeper?
Why hast thou awakened the heart within me,
O Rose of the crimson thorn?

III

The unappeasable loveliness
              is calling to me out of the wind,
And because your name
              is written upon the ivory doors,
The wave in my heart is as a green wave, unconfined,
Tossing the white foam toward you;
And the lotus that pours
Her fragrance into the purple cup,
Is more to be gained with the foam
Than are you with these words of mine.

IV

He speaks to the moonlight concerning the Beloved.

Pale hair that the moon has shaken
Down over the dark breast of the sea,
O magic her beauty has shaken
About the heart of me;

Out of you have I woven a dream
That shall walk in the lonely vale
Betwixt the high hill and the low hill,
Until the pale stream
Of the souls of men quench and grow still.

V

Voices speaking to the sun.

Red leaf that art blown upward and out and over
The green sheaf of the world,
And through the dim forest and under
The shadowed arches and the aisles,
We, who are older than thou art,
Met and remembered when his eyes beheld her
In the garden of the peach-trees,
In the day of the blossoming.

VI

I stood on the hill of Yrma
          when the winds were a-hurrying,
With the grasses a-bending
          I followed them,
Through the brown grasses of Ahva
          unto the green of Asedon.
I have rested with the voices
          in the gardens of Ahthor,
I have lain beneath the peach-trees
          in the hour of the purple:

Because I had awaited in
          the garden of the peach-trees,
Because I had feared not
          in the forest of my mind,
Mine eyes beheld the vision of the blossom
There in the peach-gardens past Asedon.

O winds of Yrma, let her again come unto me,
Whose hair ye held unbound in the gardens of Ahthor!

VII

Because of the beautiful white shoulders and the
    rounded breasts
I can in no wise forget my beloved of the peach-trees,
And the little winds that speak when the dawn is unfurled
And the rose-colour in the grey oak-leaf's fold

When it first comes, and the glamour that rests
On the little streams in the evening; all of these
Call me to her, and all the loveliness in the world
Binds me to my beloved with strong chains of gold.

VIII

If the rose-petals which have fallen upon my eyes
And if the perfect faces which I see at times
When my eyes are closed—
Faces fragile, pale, yet flushed a little, like petals of roses:
If these things have confused my memories of her
So that I could not draw her face
Even if I had skill and the colours,
Yet because her face is so like these things
They but draw me nearer unto her in my thought
And thoughts of her come upon my mind gently,
As dew upon the petals of roses.

IX

He speaks to the rain.

O pearls that hang on your little silver chains,
The innumerable voices that are whispering
Among you as you are drawn aside by the wind,
Have brought to my mind the soft and eager speech
Of one who hath great loveliness,

Which is subtle as the beauty of the rains
That hang low in the moonshine and bring
The May softly among us, and unbind
The streams and the crimson and white flowers and reach
Deep down into the secret places.

X

The glamour of the soul hath come upon me,
And as the twilight comes upon the roses,
Walking silently among them,
So have the thoughts of my heart
Gone out slowly in the twilight
Toward my beloved,
Toward the crimson rose, the fairest.

Aux Belles de Londres

I am aweary with the utter and beautiful weariness
And with the ultimate wisdom and with things terrene,
I am aweary with your smiles and your laughter,
And the sun and the winds again
Reclaim their booty and the heart o' me.

Francesca

You came in out of the night
And there were flowers in your hands,
Now you will come out of a confusion of people,
Out of a turmoil of speech about you.

I who have seen you amid the primal things
Was angry when they spoke your name
In ordinary places.
I would that the cool waves might flow over my mind,
And that the world should dry as a dead leaf,
Or as a dandelion seed-pod and be swept away,
So that I might find you again,
Alone.

Nils Lykke

Beautiful, infinite memories
That are a-plucking at my heart,
Why will you be ever calling and a-calling,
And a-murmuring in the dark there?
And a-reaching out your long hands
Between me and my beloved?

And why will you be ever a-casting
The black shadow of your beauty
On the white face of my beloved
And a-glinting in the pools of her eyes?

A Song of the Virgin Mother

In the play "Los Pastores de Belen"
From the Spanish of Lope de Vega

As ye go through these palm-trees
O holy angels;
Sith sleepeth my child here
Still ye the branches.

O Bethlehem palm-trees
That move to the anger
Of winds in their fury,
Tempestuous voices,
Make ye no clamour,
Run ye less swiftly,
Sith sleepeth the child here
Still ye your branches.

He the divine child
Is here a-wearied
Of weeping the earth-pain,
Here for his rest would he
Cease from his mourning,

Only a little while,
Sith sleepeth this child here
Stay ye the branches.

Cold be the fierce winds,
Treacherous round him.
Ye see that I have not
Wherewith to guard him,
O angels, divine ones
That pass us a-flying,
Sith sleepeth my child here
Stay ye the branches.

Planh for the Young English King

That is, Prince Henry Plantagenet, elder brother to Richard "Cœur de Lion."

From the Provençal of Bertrans de Born "Si tuit li dol elh plor elh marrimen."

If all the grief and woe and bitterness,
All dolour, ill and every evil chance
That ever came upon this grieving world
Were set together they would seem but light
Against the death of the young English King.
Worth lieth riven and Youth dolorous,
The world o'ershadowed, soiled and overcast,
Void of all joy and full of ire and sadness.

Grieving and sad and full of bitterness
Are left in teen the liegemen courteous,
The joglars supple and the troubadours.
O'er much hath ta'en Sir Death that deadly warrior
In taking from them the young English King,
Who made the freest hand seem covetous.
'Las! Never was nor will be in this world
The balance for this loss in ire and sadness!

O skilful Death and full of bitterness,
Well mayst thou boast that thou the best chevalier
That any folk e'er had, hast from us taken;
Sith nothing is that unto worth pertaineth
But had its life in the young English King,
And better were it, should God grant his pleasure
That he should live than many a living dastard
That doth but wound the good with ire and sadness.

From this faint world, how full of bitterness
Love takes his way and holds his joy deceitful,
Sith no thing is but turneth unto anguish
And each to-day 'vails less than yestere'en,
Let each man visage this young English King
That was most valiant mid all worthiest men!
Gone is his body fine and amorous,
Whence have we grief, discord and deepest sadness.

Him, whom it pleased for our great bitterness
To come to earth to draw us from misventure,
Who drank of death for our salvacioun,
Him do we pray as to a Lord most righteous
And humble eke, that the young English King
He please to pardon, as true pardon is,
And bid go in with honouréd companions
There where there is no grief, nor shall be sadness.

Alba Innominata

From the Provençal

In a garden where the whitethorn spreads her leaves
My lady hath her love lain close beside her,
Till the warder cries the dawn—Ah dawn that grieves!
Ah God! Ah God! That dawn should come so soon!

"Please God that night, dear night should never cease,
Nor that my love should parted be from me,
Nor watch cry 'Dawn'—Ah dawn that slayeth peace!
Ah God! Ah God! That dawn should come so soon!

"Fair friend and sweet, thy lips! Our lips again!
Lo, in the meadow there the birds give song!
Ours be the love and Jealousy's the pain!
Ah God! Ah God! That dawn should come so soon!

"Sweet friend and fair take we our joy again
Down in the garden, where the birds are loud,
Till the warder's reed astrain
Cry God! Ah God! That dawn should come so soon!

"Of that sweet wind that comes from Far-Away
Have I drunk deep of my Belovèd's breath,
Yea! of my Love's that is so dear and gay.
Ah God! Ah God! That dawn should come so soon!"

ENVOI

Fair is this damsel and right courteous,
And many watch her beauty's gracious way.
Her heart toward love is no wise traitorous.
Ah God! Ah God! That dawn should come so soon!

Planh

It is of the white thoughts that he saw in the Forest.

White Poppy, heavy with dreams,
O White Poppy, who art wiser than love,
Though I am hungry for their lips
        When I see them a-hiding
And a-passing out and in through the shadows
—There in the pine wood it is,
And they are white, White Poppy,
They are white like the clouds in the forest of the sky
Ere the stars arise to their hunting.

O White Poppy, who art wiser than love,
I am come for peace, yea from the hunting

Am I come to thee for peace.
Out of a new sorrow it is,
That my hunting hath brought me.

White Poppy, heavy with dreams,
Though I am hungry for their lips
        When I see them a-hiding
And a-passing out and in through the shadows
—And it is white they are—
But if one should look at me with the old hunger in her eyes,
How will I be answering her eyes?
For I have followed the white folk of the forest.

Aye! It's a long hunting
And it's a deep hunger I have when I see them a-gliding
And a-flickering there, where the trees stand apart.

But oh, it is sorrow and sorrow
When love dies-down in the heart.

THE SPIRIT OF ROMANCE

Inscriptio Fontis
From the Latin of Andrea Navagero
(16th Century)

Lo! the fountain is cool and
      none more hale of waters.
Green is the land about it,
      soft with the grasses.
And twigged boughs of elm
      stave off* the sun.

There is no place more charmed
      with light-blown airs,
Though Titan in utmost flame
      holdeth the middle sky,
And the parched fields burn with
      the oppressing star.

Stay here thy way, O voyager,
      for terrible is now the heat;
Thy tired feet can go no further now.
Balm here for weariness is
      sweet reclining,
Balm 'gainst the heat, the winds,
      and greeny shade!
And for thy thirst the lucid fount's assuaging.

* Arceo.

A War Song
From the Provençal of Bertrand de Born
(c. 1140–1214)

Well pleaseth me the sweet time of Easter
That maketh the leaf and the flower come out.
And it pleaseth me when I hear the clamor
Of the birds, their song through the wood;
And it pleaseth me when I see through the meadows
The tents and pavilions set up, and great joy have I
When I see o'er the campagna knights armed and horses
     arrayed.

And it pleaseth me when the scouts set in flight the folk
     with their goods;
And it pleaseth me when I see coming together after them
     an host of armed men.
And it pleaseth me to the heart when I see strong castles
     besieged,
And barriers broken and riven, and I see the host on the
     shore all about shut in with ditches,
And closed in with lisses of strong piles.

The Lark
From Bernart de Ventadorn

When I see the lark a-moving
For joy his wings against the sunlight,
Who forgets himself and lets himself fall
For the sweetness which goes into his heart;
Ai! what great envy comes unto me for him whom I see so
     rejoicing!

I marvel that my heart melts not for desiring.
Alas! I thought I knew so much
Of Love, and I know so little of it, for I cannot
Hold myself from loving

Her from whom I shall never have anything toward.
She hath all my heart from me, and she hath from me all
    my wit
And myself and all that is mine.
And when she took it from me she left me naught
Save desiring and a yearning heart.

"*Vedut' Ho la Lucente Stella Diana*"

From the Italian of Guido Guinicelli

(died 1274)

I have seen the shining star of the dawn
Appearing ere the day yieldeth its whiteness.
It has taken upon itself the form of a human face,
Above all else meseems it gives splendor.
A face of snow, color of the ivy-berry,
The eyes are brilliant, gay, and full of love,
And I do not believe that there is a Christian maid in the
    world
So full of fairness or so valorous.
Yea, I am so assailed of her worth,
With such cruel battling of sighs,
That I am not hardy to return before her;
Thus may she have cognizance of my desires:
That without speaking, I would be her servitor
For naught save the pity that she might have of my anguish.

Sequaire

Godeschalk

(805–869)

The Pharisee murmurs when the woman weeps, conscious of guilt.

Sinner, he despises a fellow-in-sin. Thou, unacquainted with sin, hast regard for the penitent, cleansest the soiled one, loved her to make her most fair.

She embraces the feet of the master, washes them with tears, dries them with her hair; washing and drying them she anointed them with unguent, covered them with kisses.

These are the feasts which please thee, O Wisdom of the Father!

Born of the Virgin, who disdained not the touch of a sinner.

Chaste virgins, they immaculately offer unto the Lord the sacrifice of their pure bodies, choosing Christ for their deathless bridegroom.

O happy bridals, whereto there are no stains, no heavy dolors of childbirth, no rival mistress to be feared, no nurse molestful!

Their couches, kept for Christ alone, are walled about by angels of the guard, who, with drawn swords, ward off the unclean lest any paramour defile them.

Therein Christ sleepeth with them: happy is this sleep, sweet the rest there, wherein true maid is fondled in the embraces of her heavenly spouse.

Adorned are they with fine linen, and with a robe of purple; their left hands hold lilies, their right hands roses.

On these the lamb feedeth, and with these is he refreshed; these flowers are his chosen food.

He leapeth, and boundeth and gamboleth among them.

With them doth he rest through the noon-heat.

It is upon their bosoms that he sleepeth at mid-day, placing his head between their virgin breasts.

Virgin Himself, born of a virgin mother, virginal retreats above all he seeketh and loveth.

Quiet is his sleep upon their bosoms, that no spot by any chance should soil His snowy fleece.

Give ear unto this canticle, most noble company of virgin devotees, that by it our devotion may with greater zeal prepare a temple for the Lord.

Cantico del Sole
From the Italian of St. Francis of Assisi
(1182–1226)

Most high Lord,
Yours are the praises,
The glory and the honors,
And to you alone must be accorded
All graciousness; and no man there is
Who is worthy to name you.
Be praisèd, O God, and be exalted,
My Lord, of all creatures,
And in especial of the most high Sun
Which is your creature, O Lord, that makes clear
The day and illumines it,
Whence by its fairness and its splendor
It is become thy face;
And of the white moon (be praisèd, O Lord)
And of the wandering stars,
Created by you in the heaven
So brilliant and so fair.
Praisèd be my Lord, by the flame
Whereby night groweth illumined
In the midst of its darkness,
For it is resplendent,
Is joyous, fair, eager; is mighty.
Praisèd be my Lord, of the air,
Of the winds, of the clear sky,
And of the cloudy, praisèd
Of all seasons whereby
Live all these creatures
Of lower order.
Praisèd be my Lord
By our sister the water,
Element meetest for man,
Humble and chaste in its clearness.
Praisèd be the Lord by our mother
The Earth that sustaineth,
That feeds, that produceth

Multitudinous grasses
And flowers and fruitage.
Praisèd be my Lord, by those
Who grant pardons through his love,
Enduring their travail in patience
And their infirmity with joy of the spirit.
Praisèd be my Lord by death corporal
Whence escapes no one living.
Woe to those that die in mutual transgression
And blessed are they w ho shall
Find in death's hour thy grace that comes
From obedience to thy holy will,
Wherethrough they shall never see
The pain of the death eternal.
Praise and give grace to my Lord,
Be grateful and serve him
In humbleness e'en as ye owe.
Praise him all creatures!

CANZONI

"Quos ego Persephonae maxima dona feram."
PROPERTIUS

TO
OLIVIA AND DOROTHY SHAKESPEAR

Canzon: The Yearly Slain

(Written in reply to Manning's "Korè")

"Et huiusmodi stantiae usus est fere in omnibus cantionibus suis Arnaldus Danielis et nos eum secuti sumus."
Dante, *De Vulgari Eloquio*, II. 10.

I

Ah! red-leafed time hath driven out the rose
And crimson dew is fallen on the leaf
Ere ever yet the cold white wheat be sown
That hideth all earth's green and sere and red;
The Moon-flower's fallen and the branch is bare,
Holding no honey for the starry bees;
The Maiden turns to her dark lord's demesne.

II

Fairer than Enna's field when Ceres sows
The stars of hyacinth and puts off grief,
Fairer than petals on May morning blown
Through apple-orchards where the sun hath shed
His brighter petals down to make them fair;
Fairer than these the Poppy-crowned One flees,
And Joy goes weeping in her scarlet train.

III

The faint damp wind that, ere the even, blows
Piling the west with many a tawny sheaf,
Then when the last glad wavering hours are mown
Sigheth and dies because the day is sped;
This wind is like her and the listless air
Wherewith she goeth by beneath the trees,
The trees that mock her with their scarlet stain.

IV

Love that is born of Time and comes and goes!
Love that doth hold all noble hearts in fief!
As red leaves follow where the wind hath flown,
So all men follow Love when Love is dead.
O Fate of Wind! O Wind that cannot spare,
But drivest out the Maid, and pourest lees
Of all thy crimson on the wold again,

V

Korè my heart is, let it stand sans gloze!
Love's pain is long, and lo, love's joy is brief!
My heart erst alway sweet is bitter grown;
As crimson ruleth in the good green's stead,
So grief hath taken all mine old joy's share
And driven forth my solace and all ease
Where pleasure bows to all-usurping pain.

VI

Crimson the hearth where one last ember glows!
My heart's new winter hath no such relief,
Nor thought of Spring whose blossom he hath known
Hath turned him back where Spring is banishèd.
Barren the heart and dead the fires there,
Blow! O ye ashes, where the winds shall please,
But cry, "Love also is the Yearly Slain."

VII

Be sped, my Canzon, through the bitter air!
To him who speaketh words as fair as these,
Say that I also know the "Yearly Slain."

Canzon: The Spear

I

'Tis the clear light of love I praise
That steadfast gloweth o'er deep waters,
A clarity that gleams always.
Though man's soul pass through troubled waters,
Strange ways to him are openèd.
To shore the beaten ship is sped
If only love of light give aid.

II

That fair far spear of light now lays
Its long gold shaft upon the waters.
Ah! might I pass upon its rays
To where it gleams beyond the waters,
Or might my troubled heart be fed
Upon the frail clear light there shed,
Then were my pain at last allay'd.

III

Although the clouded storm dismays
Many a heart upon these waters,
The thought of that far golden blaze
Giveth me heart upon the waters,
Thinking thereof my bark is led
To port wherein no storm I dread;
No tempest maketh me afraid.

IV

Yet when within my heart I gaze
Upon my fair beyond the waters,
Meseems my soul within me prays
To pass straightway beyond the waters.
Though I be alway banishèd
From ways and woods that she doth tread,
One thing there is that doth not fade,

V

Deep in my heart that spear-print stays,
That wound I gat beyond the waters,
Deeper with passage of the days
That pass as swift and bitter waters,
While a dull fire within my head
Moveth itself if word be said
Which hath concern with that far maid.

VI

My love is lovelier than the sprays
Of eglantine above clear waters,
Or whitest lilies that upraise
Their heads in midst of moated waters.
No poppy in the May-glad mead
Would match her quivering lips' red
If 'gainst her lips it should be laid.

VII

The light within her eyes, which slays
Base thoughts and stilleth troubled waters,
Is like the gold where sunlight plays
Upon the still o'ershadowed waters.
When anger is there minglèd
There comes a keener gleam instead,
Like flame that burns beneath thin jade.

VIII

Know by the words here minglèd
What love hath made my heart his stead,
Glowing like flame beneath thin jade.

Canzon

To be sung beneath a window

I

Heart mine, art mine, whose embraces
Clasp but wind that past thee bloweth?
E'en this air so subtly gloweth,
Guerdoned by thy sun-gold traces,
That my heart is half afraid
For the fragrance on him laid;
Even so love's might amazes!

II

Man's love follows many faces,
My love only one face knoweth;
Towards thee only my love floweth,
And outstrips the swift stream's paces.
Were this love well here displayed,
As flame flameth 'neath thin jade
Love should glow through these my phrases.

III

Though I've roamed through many places,
None there is that my heart troweth
Fair as that wherein fair groweth
One whose laud here interlaces
Tuneful words, that I've essayed.
Let this tune be gently played
Which my voice herward upraises.

IV

If my praise her grace effaces,
Then 'tis not my heart that showeth,
But the skilless tongue that soweth
Words unworthy of her graces.
Tongue, that hath me so betrayed,
Were my heart but here displayed,
Then were sung her fitting praises.

Canzon: Of Incense

I

Thy gracious ways,
        O Lady of my heart, have
O'er all my thought their golden glamour cast;
As amber torch-flames, where strange men-at-arms
Tread softly 'neath the damask shield of night,
Rise from the flowing steel in part reflected,
So on my mailed thought that with thee goeth,
Though dark the way, a golden glamour falleth.

II

The censer sways
        And glowing coals some art have
To free what frankincense before held fast
Till all the summer of the eastern farms
Doth dim the sense, and dream up through the light,
As memory, by new-born love corrected—
With savour such as only new love knoweth—
Through swift dim ways the hidden pasts recalleth.

III

On barren days,
        At hours when I, apart, have
Bent low in thought of the great charm thou hast,
Behold with music's many-stringed charms
The silence groweth thou. O rare delight!
The melody upon clear strings inflected
Were dull when o'er taut sense thy presence floweth,
With quivering notes' accord that never palleth.

IV

The glowing rays
      That from the low sun dart, have
Turned gold each tower and every towering mast;
The saffron flame, that flaming nothing harms
Hides Khadeeth's pearl and all the sapphire might
Of burnished waves, before her gates collected:
The cloak of graciousness, that round thee gloweth,
Doth hide the thing thou art, as here befalleth.

V

All things worth praise
      That unto Khadeeth's mart have
From far been brought through perils over-passed,
All santal, myrrh, and spikenard that disarms
The pard's swift anger; these would weigh but light
'Gainst thy delights, my Khadeeth! Whence protected
By naught save her great grace that in him showeth,
My song goes forth and on her mercy calleth.

VI

O censer of the thought that golden gloweth,
Be bright before her when the evening falleth.

VII

Fragrant be thou as a new field one moweth,
O song of mine that "Hers" her mercy calleth.

Canzone: Of Angels

I

He that is Lord of all the realms of light
Hath unto me from His magnificence
Granted such vision as hath wrought my joy.
Moving my spirit past the last defence
That shieldeth mortal things from mightier sight,
Where freedom of the soul knows no alloy,
I saw what forms the lordly powers employ;
Three splendours, saw I, of high holiness,
From clarity to clarity ascending
Through all the roofless, tacit courts extending
In æther which such subtle light doth bless
As ne'er the candles of the stars hath wooed;
Know ye herefrom of their similitude.

II

Withdrawn within the cavern of his wings,
Grave with the joy of thoughts beneficent,
And finely wrought and durable and clear,
If so his eyes showed forth the mind's content,
So sate the first to whom remembrance clings,
Tissued like bat's wings did his wings appear,
Not of that shadowy colouring and drear,
But as thin shells, pale saffron, luminous;
Alone, unlonely, whose calm glances shed
Friend's love to strangers though no word were said,
Pensive his godly state he keepeth thus.
Not with his surfaces his power endeth,
But is as flame that from the gem extendeth.

III

My second marvel stood not in such ease,
But he, the cloudy pinioned, winged him on
Then from my sight as now from memory,
The courier aquiline, so swiftly gone!

The third most glorious of these majesties
Give aid, O sapphires of th' eternal see,
And by your light illume pure verity.
That azure feldspar hight the microcline,
Or, on its wing, the Menelaus weareth
Such subtlety of shimmering as beareth
This marvel onward through the crystalline,
A splendid calyx that about her gloweth,
Smiting the sunlight on whose ray she goeth.

IV

The diver at Sorrento from beneath
The vitreous indigo, who swiftly riseth,
By will and not by action as it seemeth,
Moves not more smoothly, and no thought surmiseth
How she takes motion from the lustrous sheath
Which, as the trace behind the swimmer, gleameth
Yet presseth back the æther where it streameth.
To her whom it adorns this sheath imparteth
The living motion from the light surrounding;
And thus my nobler parts, to grief's confounding,
Impart into my heart a peace which starteth
From one round whom a graciousness is cast
Which clingeth in the air where she hath past.

V—TORNATA

Canzon, to her whose spirit seems in sooth
Akin unto the feldspar, since it is
So clear and subtle and azure, I send thee, saying:
That since I looked upon such potencies
And glories as are here inscribed in truth,
New boldness hath o'erthrown my long delaying,
And that thy words my new-born powers obeying—
Voices at last to voice my heart's long mood—
Are come to greet her in their amplitude.

To Our Lady of Vicarious Atonement

(*Ballata*)

I

Who are you that the whole world's song
Is shaken out beneath your feet
Leaving you comfortless,
Who, that, as wheat
Is garnered, gather in
The blades of man's sin
And bear that sheaf?
Lady of wrong and grief,
Blameless!

II

All souls beneath the gloom
That pass with little flames,
All these till time be run
Pass one by one
As Christs to save, and die;
What wrong one sowed,
Behold, another reaps!
Where lips awake our joy
The sad heart sleeps
Within.

No man doth bear his sin,
But many sins
Are gathered as a cloud about man's way.

To Guido Cavalcanti

Dante and I are come to learn of thee,
Ser Guido of Florence, master of us all,
Love, who hath set his hand upon us three,
Bidding us twain upon thy glory call.
Harsh light hath rent from us the golden pall

Of that frail sleep, *His* first light seigniory,
And we are come through all the modes that fall
Unto their lot who meet him constantly.
Wherefore, by right, in this Lord's name we greet thee,
Seeing we labour at his labour daily.
Thou, who dost know what way swift words are crossed
O thou, who hast sung till none at song defeat thee,
Grant! by thy might and hers of San Michele,
Thy risen voice send flames this pentecost.

Sonnet in Tenzone

LA MENTE

"O Thou mocked heart that cowerest by the door
And durst not honour hope with welcoming,
How shall one bid thee for her honour sing,
When song would but show forth thy sorrow's store?
What things are gold and ivory unto thee?
Go forth, thou pauper fool! Are these for naught?
Is heaven in lotus leaves? What hast thou wrought,
Or brought, or sought, wherewith to pay the fee?"

IL CUORE

"If naught I give, naught do I take return.
'Ronsard me celebroit!' behold I give
The age-old, age-old fare to fairer fair
And I fare forth into more bitter air;
Though mocked I go, yet shall her beauty live
Till rimes unrime and Truth shall truth unlearn."

Sonnet: Chi È Questa?

Who is she coming, that the roses bend
Their shameless heads to do her passing honour?
Who is she coming with a light upon her
Not born of suns that with the day's end end?
Say is it Love who hath chosen the nobler part?

Say is it Love, that was divinity,
Who hath left his godhead that his home might be
The shameless rose of her unclouded heart?
If this be Love, where hath he won such grace?
If this be Love, how is the evil wrought,
That all men write against his darkened name?
If this be Love, if this . . .
     O mind give place!
What holy mystery e'er was noosed in thought?
Own that thou scan'st her not, nor count it shame!

Ballata, Fragment

II

Full well thou knowest, song, what grace I mean,
E'en as thou know'st the sunlight I have lost.
Thou knowest the way of it and know'st the sheen
About her brows where the rays are bound and crossed,
E'en as thou knowest joy and know'st joy's bitter cost.
Thou know'st her grace in moving,
Thou dost her skill in loving,
Thou know'st what truth she proveth,
Thou knowest the heart she moveth,
O song where grief assoneth!

Canzon: The Vision

I

When first I saw thee 'neath the silver mist,
Ruling thy bark of painted sandal-wood,
Did any know thee? By the golden sails
That clasped the ribbands of that azure sea,
Did any know thee save my heart alone?
O ivory woman with thy bands of gold,
Answer the song my luth and I have brought thee!

II

Dream over golden dream that secret cist,
Thy heart, O heart of me, doth hold, and mood
On mood of silver, when the day's light fails,
Say who hath touched the secret heart of thee,
Or who hath known what my heart hath not known!
O slender pilot whom the mists enfold,
Answer the song my luth and I have wrought thee!

III

When new love plucks the falcon from his wrist,
And cuts the gyve and casts the scarlet hood,
Where is the heron heart whom flight avails?
O quick to prize me Love, how suddenly
From out the tumult truth has ta'en his own,
And in this vision is our past unrolled.
Lo! With a hawk of light thy love hath caught me.

IV

And I shall get no peace from eucharist,
Nor doling out strange prayers before the rood,
To match the peace that thine hands' touch entails;
Nor doth God's light match light shed over me
When thy caught sunlight is about me thrown,
Oh, for the very ruth thine eyes have told,
Answer the rune this love of thee hath taught me.

V

After an age of longing had we missed
Our meeting and the dream, what were the good
Of weaving cloth of words? Were jewelled tales
An opiate meet to quell the malady
Of life unlived? In untried monotone
Were not the earth as vain, and dry, and old,
For thee, O Perfect Light, had I not sought thee?

VI

Calais, in song where word and tone keep tryst
Behold my heart, and hear mine hardihood!
Calais, the wind is come and heaven pales
And trembles for the love of day to be.
Calais, the words break and the dawn is shown.
Ah, but the stars set when thou wast first bold,
Turn! lest they say a lesser light distraught thee.

VII

O ivory thou, the golden scythe hath mown
Night's stubble and my joy. Thou royal souled,
Favour the quest! Lo, Truth and I have sought thee!

Octave

Fine songs, fair songs, these golden usuries
Her beauty earns as but just increment,
And they do speak with a most ill intent
Who say they give when they pay debtor's fees.

I call him bankrupt in the courts of song
Who hath her gold to eye and pays her not,
Defaulter do I call the knave who hath got
Her silver in his heart, and doth her wrong.

Sonnet

If on the tally-board of wasted days
They daily write me for proud idleness,
Let high Hell summons me, and I confess,
No overt act the preferred charge allays.

To-day I thought—what boots it what I thought?
Poppies and gold! Why should I blurt it out?
Or hawk the magic of her name about
Deaf doors and dungeons where no truth is bought?

Who calls me idle? I have thought of her.
Who calls me idle? By God's truth I've seen
The arrowy sunlight in her golden snares.

Let him among you all stand summonser
Who hath done better things! Let whoso hath been
With worthier works concerned, display his wares!

Ballatetta

The light became her grace and dwelt among
Blind eyes and shadows that are formed as men;
Lo, how the light doth melt us into song:

The broken sunlight for a healm she beareth
Who hath my heart in jurisdiction.
In wild-wood never fawn nor fallow fareth
So silent light; no gossamer is spun
So delicate as she is, when the sun
Drives the clear emeralds from the bended grasses
Lest they should parch too swiftly, where she passes.

Madrigale

Clear is my love but shadowed
By the spun gold above her,
Ah, what a petal those bent sheaths discover!

The olive wood hath hidden her completely,
She was gowned that discreetly
The leaves and shadows concealed her completely.

Fair is my love but followed
In all her goings surely
By gracious thoughts, she goeth so demurely.

Era Mea

Era mea
In qua terra
Dulce myrti floribus,
Rosa amoris
Via erroris
Ad te coram
Veniam?

ANGLICÈ REDDITA
Mistress mine, in what far land,
Where the myrtle bloweth sweet
Shall I weary with my way-fare,
Win to thee that art as day fair,
Lay my roses at thy feet?

Paracelsus in Excelsis

"Being no longer human why should I
Pretend humanity or don the frail attire?
Men have I known, and men, but never one
Was grown so free an essence, or become
So simply element as what I am.
The mist goes from the mirror and I see!
Behold! the world of forms is swept beneath—
Turmoil grown visible beneath our peace,
And we, that are grown formless, rise above—
Fluids intangible that have been men,
We seem as statues round whose high-risen base
Some overflowing river is run mad,
In us alone the element of calm!"

Prayer for His Lady's Life

From Propertius, *Elegiae*, Lib. III, 26

Here let thy clemency, Persephone, hold firm,
Do thou, Pluto, bring here no greater harshness.
So many thousand beauties are gone down to Avernus
Ye might let one remain above with us.

With you is Iope, with you the white-gleaming Tyro,
With you is Europa and the shameless Pasiphae,
And all the fair from Troy and all from Achaia,
From the sundered realms, of Thebes and of aged Priamus;
And all the maidens of Rome, as many as they were,
They died and the greed of your flame consumes them.

> *Here let thy clemency, Persephone, hold firm,*
> *Do thou, Pluto, bring here no greater harshness.*
> *So many thousand fair are gone down to Avernus,*
> *Ye might let one remain above with us.*

Speech for Psyche
in the Golden Book of Apuleius

All night, and as the wind lieth among
The cypress trees, he lay,
Nor held me save as air that brusheth by one
Close, and as the petals of flowers in falling
Waver and seem not drawn to earth, so he
Seemed over me to hover light as leaves
And closer me than air,
And music flowing through me seemed to open
Mine eyes upon new colours.
O winds, what wind can match the weight of him!

"*Blandula, Tenulla, Vagula*"

What hast thou, O my soul, with paradise?
Will we not rather, when our freedom's won,
Get us to some clear place wherein the sun
Lets drift in on us through the olive leaves
A liquid glory? If at Sirmio
My soul, I meet thee, when this life's outrun,
Will we not find some headland consecrated
By aery apostles of terrene delight,
Will not our cult be founded on the waves,
Clear sapphire, cobalt, cyanine,
On triune azures, the impalpable
Mirrors unstill of the eternal change?

Soul, if She meet us there, will any rumour
Of havens more high and courts desirable
Lure us beyond the cloudy peak of Riva?

Erat Hora

"Thank you, whatever comes." And then she turned
And, as the ray of sun on hanging flowers
Fades when the wind hath lifted them aside,
Went swiftly from me. Nay, whatever comes
One hour was sunlit and the most high gods
May not make boast of any better thing
Than to have watched that hour as it passed.

Epigrams

I

O ivory, delicate hands!
O face that hovers
Between "To-come" and "Was,"
Ivory thou wast,
A rose thou wilt be.

II
(THE SEA OF GLASS)

I looked and saw a sea
                    roofed over with rainbows,
In the midst of each
                    two lovers met and departed;
Then the sky was full of faces
                    with gold glories behind them.

La Nuvoletta

Dante to an unknown lady, beseeching her not to
interrupt his cult of the dead Beatrice.
From "Il Canzoniere," Ballata II.

Ah little cloud that in Love's shadow lief
Upon mine eyes so suddenly alightest,
Take some faint pity on the heart thou smitest
That hopes in thee, desires, dies, in brief.

Ah little cloud of more than human fashion
Thou settest a flame within my mind's mid space
With thy deathly speech that grieveth;

Then as a fiery spirit in thy ways
Creates hope, in part a rightful passion,
Yet where thy sweet smile giveth
His grace, look not! For in Her my faith liveth.

Think on my high desire whose flame's so great
That nigh a thousand who were come too late,
Have felt the torment of another's grief.

Rosa Sempiterna

A rose I set within my "Paradise"
Lo how his red is turned to yellowness,
Not withered but grown old in subtler wise
Between the empaged rime's high holiness
Where Dante sings of that rose's device

Which yellow is, with souls in blissfulness.
Rose whom I set within my paradise,
Donor of roses and of parching sighs,
Of golden lights and dark unhappiness,
Of hidden chains and silvery joyousness,
Hear how thy rose within my Dante lies,
O rose I set within my paradise.

The Golden Sestina

From the Italian of Pico della Mirandola

In the bright season when He, most high Jove,
From welkin reaching down his glorying hand,
Decks the Great Mother and her changing face,
Clothing her not with scarlet skeins and gold
But with th' empurpling flowers and gay grass,
When the young year renewed, renews the sun,

When, then, I see a lady like the sun,
One fashioned by th' high hand of utmost Jove,
So fair beneath the myrtles on gay grass
Who holdeth Love and Truth, one by each hand,
It seems, if I look straight, two bands of gold
Do make more fair her delicate fair face.

Though eyes are dazzled, looking on her face
As all sight faileth that looks toward the sun,
New metamorphoses, to rained gold,
Or bulls or whitest swans, might fall on Jove
Through her, or Phoebus, his bag-pipes in hand,
Might, mid the droves, come barefoot o'er our grass.

Alas, that there was hidden in the grass
A cruel shaft, the which, to wound my face,
My Lady took in her own proper hand.
If I could not defend me 'gainst that sun
I take no shame, for even utmost Jove
Is in high heaven pierced with darts of gold.

Behold the green shall find itself turned gold
And spring shall be without her flowers and grass,
And hell's deep be the dwelling place of Jove
Ere I shall have uncarved her holy face
From my heart's midst, where 'tis both Sun and sun;
And yet she beareth me such hostile hand!

O sweet and holy and O most light hand,
O intermingled ivory and gold,
O mortal goddess and terrestrial sun
Who comest not to foster meadow grass,
But to show heaven by a likened face
Wert sent amongst us by th' exalted Jove,

I still pray Jove that he permit no grass
To cover o'er thy hands, thy face, thy gold
For heaven's sufficèd with a single sun.

Rome

From the French of Joachim du Bellay

"Troica Roma resurges."
PROPERTIUS

O thou new comer who seek'st Rome in Rome
And find'st in Rome no thing thou canst call Roman;
Arches worn old and palaces made common,
Rome's name alone within these walls keeps home.

Behold how pride and ruin can befall
One who hath set the whole world 'neath her laws,
All-conquering, now conquerèd, because
She is Time's prey and Time consumeth all.

Rome that art Rome's one sole last monument,
Rome that alone hast conquered Rome the town,
Tiber alone, transient and seaward bent,
Remains of Rome. O world, thou unconstant mime!
That which stands firm in thee Time batters down,
And that which fleeteth doth outrun swift time.

Her Monument, the Image Cut Thereon

From the Italian of Leopardi (Written 1831–3 circa)

Such wast thou,
Who art now
But buried dust and rusted skeleton.
Above the bones and mire,
Motionless, placed in vain,
Mute mirror of the flight of speeding years,
Sole guard of grief
Sole guard of memory
Standeth this image of the beauty sped.

O glance, when thou wast still as thou art now,
How hast thou set the fire
A-tremble in men's veins; O lip curved high
To mind me of some urn of full delight,
O throat girt round of old with swift desire,
O palms of Love, that in your wonted ways
Not once but many a day
Felt hands turn ice a-sudden, touching ye,
That ye were once! of all the grace ye had
That which remaineth now
Shameful, most sad
Finds 'neath this rock fit mould, fit resting place!

And still when fate recalleth,
Even that semblance that appears amongst us
Is like to heaven's most 'live imagining.
All, all our life's eternal mystery!
To-day, on high
Mounts, from our mighty thoughts and from the fount
Of sense untellable, Beauty
That seems to be some quivering splendour cast
By the immortal nature on this quicksand,
And by surhuman fates
Given to mortal state
To be a sign and an hope made secure
Of blissful kingdoms and the aureate spheres;
And on the morrow, by some lightsome twist,

Shameful in sight, abject, abominable
All this angelic aspect can return
And be but what it was
With all the admirable concepts that moved from it
Swept from the mind with it in its departure.

Infinite things desired, lofty visions
'Got on desirous thought by natural virtue,
And the wise concord, whence through delicious seas
The arcane spirit of the whole Mankind
Turns hardy pilot . . . and if one wrong note
Strike the tympanum,
Instantly
That paradise is hurled to nothingness.

O mortal nature,
If thou art
Frail and so vile in all,
How canst thou reach so high with thy poor sense;
Yet if thou art
Noble in any part
How is the noblest of thy speech and thought
So lightly wrought
Or to such base occasion lit and quenched?

Victorian Eclogues

I
EXCUSES

Ah would you turn me back now from the flowers,
You who are different as the air from sea is,
Ah for the pollen from our wreath of hours,
You who are magical, not mine as she is,
Say will you call us from our time of flowers?

You whom I loved and love, not understanding,
Yea we were ever torn with constant striving,

Seeing our gods are different, and commanding
One good from them, and in my heart reviving
Old discords and bent thought, not understanding.

We who have wept, we who have lain together
Upon the green and sere and white of every season,
We who have loved the sun but for the weather
Of our own hearts have found no constant reason,
What is your part, now *we* have come together?

What is your pain, Dear, what is your heart now
A little sad, a little . . . . . Nay, I know not
Seeing I never had and have no part now
In your own secret councils wherein blow not
My roses. My vineyard being another heart now?

You who were ever dear and dearer being strange,
How shall I "go" who never came anear you?
How could I stay, who never came in range
Of anything that halved; could never hear you
Rightly in your silence; nay, your very speech was strange.

You, who have loved not what I was or will be,
You who but loved me for a thing I could be,
You who love not a song whate'er its skill be
But only love the cause or what cause should be,
How could I give you what I am or will be?

Nay, though your eyes are sad, you will not hinder,
You, who would have had me only near not nearer,
Nay though my heart had burned to a bright cinder
Love would have said to me: "Still fear her,
Pain is thy lot and naught she hath can hinder."

So I, for this sad gladness that is mine now,
Who never spoke aright in speaking to you,
Uncomprehending anything that's thine now,
E'en in my spoken words more wrong may do you
In looking back from this new grace that's mine now.

Sic semper finis deest.

II
SATIEMUS

What if I know thy speeches word by word?
And if thou knew'st I knew them wouldst thou speak?
What if I know thy speeches word by word,
And all the time thou sayest them o'er I said,
"Lo, one there was who bent her fair bright head,
Sighing as thou dost through the golden speech."
Or, as our laughters mingle each with each,
As crushed lips take their respite fitfully,
What if my thoughts were turned in their mid reach
Whispering among them, "The fair dead
Must know such moments, thinking on the grass;
Oh how white dogwoods murmured overhead
In the bright glad days!"
How if the low dear sound within thy throat
Hath as faint lute-strings in its dim accord
Dim tales that blind me, running one by one
With times told over as we tell by rote;
What if I know thy laughter word by word
Nor find aught novel in thy merriment?

III
ABELARD
"Pere Esbaillart a Sanct Denis." Villon

"Because my soul cried out, and only the long ways
Grown weary, gave me answer and
Because she answered when the very ways were dumb
With all their hoarse, dry speech grown faint and chill.
Because her answer was a call to me,
Though I have sinned, my God, and though thy angels
Bear no more now my thought to whom I love;
Now though I crouch afraid in all thy dark
Will I once cry to thee:
                    Once more! Once more my strength!
Yea though I sin to call him forth once more,
Thy messengers for mine,
Their wings my power!

And let once more my wings fold down above her,
Let their cool length be spread
Over her feet and head
And let thy calm come down
To dwell within her, and thy gown of peace
Clothe all her body in its samite.
O Father of all the blind and all the strong,
Though I have left thy courts, though all the throng
Of thy gold-shimmering choir know me not,
Though I have dared the body and have donned
Its frail strong-seeming, and although
Its lightening joy is made my swifter song,
Though I have known thy stars, yea all, and chosen one.
Yea though I make no barter, and repent no jot,
Yet for the sunlight of that former time
Grant me the boon, O God,
Once more, once more, or I or some white thought
Shall rise beside her and, enveloping
All her strange glory in its wings of light,
Bring down thy peace upon her way-worn soul.
Oh sheathe that sword of her in some strong case,
The doe-skin scabbard of thy clear Rafael!
Yea let thy angels walk, as I have seen
Them passing, or have seen their wings
Spread their pavilions o'er our twin delight.
Yea I have seen them when the purple light
Hid all her garden from my drowsy eyes.

A Prologue

SCENE — IN THE AIR

The Lords of the Air:
>   What light hath passed us in the silent ways?

The Spirits of Fire:
>   We are sustainèd, strengthened suddenly.

The Spirits of Water:
>   Lo, how the utmost deeps are clarified!

The Spirits Terrene:
　　What might is this more potent than the spring?
　　Lo, how the night
　　Which wrapped us round with its most heavy cloths
　　Opens and breathes with some strange-fashioned
　　　　brightness!

IN HEAVEN

*Christ, the eternal Spirit in Heaven speaketh thus, over the child
　　of Mary:*
　　O star, move forth and write upon the skies,
　　"This child is born in ways miraculous."

　　　　　.　　.　　.　　.

　　O windy spirits, that are born in Heaven,
　　Go down and bid the powers of Earth and Air
　　Protect his ways until the Time shall come.

　　　　　.　　.　　.　　.

　　O Mother, if the dark of things to be
　　Wrap round thy heart with cloudy apprehensions,
　　Eat of thy present corn, the aftermath
　　Hath its appointed end in whirling light.
　　Eat of thy present corn, thou so hast share
　　In mightier portents than Augustus hath.

　　　　　.　　.　　.

　　In every moment all to be is born,
　　Thou art the moment and need'st fear no scorn.

Echo of the Angels singing "Exultasti:"
　　Silence is born of many peaceful things,
　　Thus is the starlight woven into strings
　　Whereon the Powers of peace make sweet accord.
　　Rejoice, O Earth, thy Lord
　　Hath chosen Him his holy resting-place.

　　Lo, how the wingèd sign
　　Flutters above that hallowed chrysalis.

IN THE AIR

The invisible Spirit of the Star answers them:
Bend in your singing, gracious potencies,
Bend low above your ivory bows and gold!
That which ye know but dimly hath been wrought
High in the luminous courts and azure ways:
Bend in your praise;
For though your subtle thought
Sees but in part the source of mysteries,
Yet are ye bidden in your songs, sing this:
     "Gloria! gloria in excelsis
     Pax in terra nunc natast."

Angels continuing in song:
Shepherds and kings, with lambs and frankincense
Go and atone for mankind's ignorance:
Make ye soft savour from your ruddy myrrh.
Lo, how God's son is turned God's almoner.
Give ye this little
Ere he give ye all.

ON EARTH

One of the Magi:
How the deep-voicèd night turns councillor!
And how, for end, our starry meditations
Admit us to his board!

A Shepherd:
Sir, we be humble and perceive ye are
Men of great power and authority,
And yet we too have heard.

DIANA IN EPHESUS

(Lucina dolentibus:)
     "Behold the deed! Behold the act supreme!
With mine own hands have I prepared my doom,
Truth shall grow great eclipsing other truth,
And men forget me in the aging years.
             Explicit.

Maestro di Tocar

(W.R.)

You, who are touched not by our mortal ways
Nor girded with the stricture of our bands,
Have but to loose the magic from your hands
And all men's hearts that glimmer for a day,
And all our loves that are so swift to flame
Rise in that space of sound and melt away.

Aria

My love is a deep flame
                    that hides beneath the waters.

—My love is gay and kind,
My love is hard to find
        as the flame beneath the waters.

The fingers of the wind
                            meet hers
With a frail
            swift greeting.
My love is gay
                and kind
                        and hard
                                of meeting,
As the flame beneath the waters
                    hard of meeting.

L'Art

When brightest colours seem but dull in hue
And noblest arts are shown mechanical,
When study serves but to heap clue on clue
That no great line hath been or ever shall,
But hath a savour like some second stew

Of many pot-lots with a smack of all.
'Twas one man's field, another's hops the brew,
'Twas vagrant accident not fate's fore-call.

Horace, that thing of thine is overhauled,
And "Wood notes wild" weaves a concocted sonnet.
Here aery Shelley on the text hath called,·
And here, Great Scott, the Murex, Keats comes on it.
And all the lot howl, "Sweet Simplicity!"
'Tis Art to hide our theft exquisitely.

Song in the Manner of Housman

O woe, woe,
People are born and die,
We also shall be dead pretty soon
Therefore let us act as if we were
                                dead already.

The bird sits on the hawthorn tree
But he dies also, presently.
Some lads get hung, and some get shot.
Woeful is this human lot.
                    Woe! woe, etcetera. . . .

London is a woeful place,
Shropshire is much pleasanter.
Then let us smile a little space
Upon fond nature's morbid grace.
                    Oh, Woe, woe, woe, etcetera. . . .

Translations from Heine
Von "Die Heimkehr"

I

Is your hate, then, of such measure?
Do you, truly, so detest me?
Through all the world will I complain
Of *how* you have addressed me.

O ye lips that are ungrateful,
Hath it never once distressed you,
That you can say such *awful* things
Of *any* one who ever kissed you?

II

So thou hast forgotten fully
That I so long held thy heart wholly,
Thy little heart, so sweet and false and small
That there's no thing more sweet or false at all.

Love and lay thou hast forgotten fully,
And my heart worked at them unduly.
I know not if the love or if the lay were better stuff,
But I know now, they both were good enough.

III

Tell me where thy lovely love is,
Whom thou once did sing so sweetly,
When the fairy flames enshrouded
Thee, and held thy heart completely.

All the flames are dead and sped now
And my heart is cold and sere;
Behold this book, the urn of ashes,
'Tis my true love's sepulchre.

IV

I dreamt that I was God Himself
Whom heavenly joy immerses,
And all the angels sat about
And praised my verses.

V

The mutilated choir boys
When I begin to sing
Complain about the awful noise
And call my voice too thick a thing.

When light their voices lift them up,
Bright notes against the ear,
Through trills and runs like crystal,
Ring delicate and clear.

They sing of Love that's grown desirous,
Of Love, and joy that is Love's inmost part,
And all the ladies swim through tears
Toward such a work of art.

VI

This delightful young man
Should not lack for honourers,
He propitiates me with oysters,
With Rhine wine and liqueurs.

How his coat and pants adorn him!
Yet his ties are more adorning,
In these he daily comes to ask me:
Are you feeling well this morning?

He speaks of my extended fame,
My wit, charm, definitions,
And is diligent to serve me,
Is detailed in his provisions.

In evening company he sets his face
In most spiritu*el* positions,
And declaims before the ladies
My *god-like* compositions.

O what comfort is it for me
To find him such, when the days bring
No comfort, at my time of life when
All good things go vanishing.

Translator to Translated

O Harry Heine, curses be,
I live too late to sup with thee!
Who can demolish at such polished ease
Philistia's pomp and Art's pomposities!

VII
SONG FROM "DIE HARZREISE"

I am the Princess Ilza
In Ilsenstein I fare,
Come with me to that castle
And we'll be happy there.

Thy head will I cover over
With my waves' clarity
Till thou forget thy sorrow,
O wounded sorrowfully.

Thou wilt in my white arms there,
Nay, on my breast thou must
Forget and rest and dream there
For thine old legend-lust.

My lips and my heart are thine there
As they were his and mine.
His? Why the good King Harry's,
And he is dead lang syne.

Dead men stay alway dead men,
Life is the live man's part,
And I am fair and golden
With joy breathless at heart.

If my heart stay below there,
My crystal halls ring clear
To the dance of lords and ladies
In all their splendid gear.

The silken trains go rustling,
The spur-clinks sound between,
The dark dwarfs blow and bow there
Small horn and violin.

Yet shall my white arms hold thee,
That bound King Harry about.
Ah, I covered his ears with them
When the trumpet rang out.

Und Drang

Nay, dwells he in cloudy rumour alone?
                                        Binyon

I

I am worn faint,
The winds of good and evil
Blind me with dust
And burn me with the cold,
There is no comfort being over-man;
Yet are we come more near
The great oblivions and the labouring night,
Inchoate truth and the sepulchral forces.

II

Confusion, clamour, 'mid the many voices
Is there a meaning, a significance?

That life apart from all life gives and takes,
This life, apart from all life's bitter and life's sweet,
Is good.
        Ye see me and ye say: exceeding sweet
Life's gifts, his youth, his art,
And his too soon acclaim.

I also knew exceeding bitterness,
Saw good things altered and old friends fare forth,
And what I loved in me hath died too soon,
Yea I have seen the "gray above the green";
Gay have I lived in life;
        Though life hath lain
Strange hands upon me and hath torn my sides,
Yet I believe.

    .   .   .   .   .   .

Life is most cruel where she is most wise.

III

The will to live goes from me.
        I have lain
Dull and out-worn
        with some strange, subtle sickness.
Who shall say
That love is not the very root of this,
O thou afar?

Yet she was near me,
        that eternal deep.
O it is passing strange that love
Can blow two ways across one soul.

    .   .   .   .   .

And I was Aengus for a thousand years,
And she, the ever-living, moved with me
And strove amid the waves, and
        would not go.

IV

ELEGIA

"Far buon tempo e trionfare"

"I have put my days and dreams out of mind"
For all their hurry and their weary fret
Availed me little. But another kind
Of leaf that's fast in some more sombre wind,
Is man on life, and all our tenuous courses
Wind and unwind as vainly.

     . . . . .

I have lived long, and died,
Yea I have been dead, right often,
And have seen one thing:
The sun, while he is high, doth light our wrong
And none can break the darkness with a song.

To-day's the cup. To-morrow is not ours:
Nay, by our strongest bands we bind her not,
Nor all our fears and our anxieties
Turn her one leaf or hold her scimitar.

The deed blots out the thought
And many thoughts, the vision;
And right's a compass with as many poles
As there are points in her circumference,
'Tis vain to seek to steer all courses even,
And all things save sheer right are vain enough.
The blade were vain to grow save toward the sun,
And vain th' attempt to hold her green forever.

All things in season and no thing o'er long!
Love and desire and gain and good forgetting,
Thou canst not stay the wheel, hold none too long!

V

How our modernity,
Nerve-wracked and broken, turns
Against time's way and all the way of things,
Crying with weak and egoistic cries!

. . . . .

All things are given over,
Only the restless will
Surges amid the stars
Seeking new moods of life,
New permutations.

. . . . .

See, and the very sense of what we know
Dodges and hides as in a sombre curtain
Bright threads leap forth, and hide, and leave no pattern.

VI

I thought I had put Love by for a time
And I was glad, for to me his fair face
Is like Pain's face.
                    A little light,
The lowered curtain and the theatre!
And o'er the frail talk of the inter-act
Something that broke the jest! A little light,
The gold, and half the profile!
                              The whole face
Was nothing like you, yet that image cut
Sheer through the moment.

VI*b*

I have gone seeking for you in the twilight,
Here in the flurry of Fifth Avenue,
Here where they pass between their teas and teas.
Is it such madness? though you could not be
Ever in all that crowd, no gown
Of all their subtle sorts could be your gown.

Yet I am fed with faces, is there one
That even in the half-light mindeth me.

VII
THE HOUSE OF SPLENDOUR

'Tis Evanoe's,
A house not made with hands,
But out somewhere beyond the worldly ways
Her gold is spread, above, around, inwoven,
Strange ways and walls are fashioned out of it.

And I have seen my Lady in the sun,
Her hair was spread about, a sheaf of wings,
And red the sunlight was, behind it all.

And I have seen her there within her house,
With six great sapphires hung along the wall,
Low, panel-shaped, a-level with her knees,
And all her robe was woven of pale gold.

There are there many rooms and all of gold,
Of woven walls deep patterned, of email,
Of beaten work; and through the claret stone,
Set to some weaving, comes the aureate light.

Here am I come perforce my love of her,
Behold mine adoration
Maketh me clear, and there are powers in this
Which, played on by the virtues of her soul,
Break down the four-square walls of standing time.

VIII
THE FLAME

'Tis not a game that plays at mates and mating,
Provençe knew;
'Tis not a game of barter, lands and houses,
Provençe knew.
We who are wise beyond your dream of wisdom,
Drink our immortal moments; we "pass through."

We have gone forth beyond your bonds and borders,
Provençe knew;
And all the tales they ever writ of Oisin
Say but this:
That man doth pass the net of days and hours.
Where time is shrivelled down to time's seed corn
We of the Ever-living, in that light
Meet through our veils and whisper, and of love.

O smoke and shadow of a darkling world,
Barters of passion, and that tenderness
That's but a sort of cunning! O my Love,
These, and the rest, and all the rest we knew.

'Tis not a game that plays at mates and mating,
'Tis not a game of barter, lands and houses,
'Tis not "of days and nights" and troubling years,
Of cheeks grown sunken and glad hair gone gray;
There *is* the subtler music, the clear light
Where time burns back about th' eternal embers.
We are not shut from all the thousand heavens:
Lo, there are many gods whom we have seen,
Folk of unearthly fashion, places splendid,
Bulwarks of beryl and of chrysoprase.

Sapphire Benacus, in thy mists and thee
Nature herself's turned metaphysical,
Who can look on that blue and not believe?

Thou hooded opal, thou eternal pearl,
O thou dark secret with a shimmering floor,
Through all thy various mood I know thee mine;

If I have merged my soul, or utterly
Am solved and bound in, through aught here on earth,
There canst thou find me, O thou anxious thou,
Who call'st about my gates for some lost me;
I say my soul flowed back, became translucent.
Search not my lips, O Love, let go my hands,

This thing that moves as man is no more mortal.
If thou hast seen my shade sans character,
If thou hast seen that mirror of all moments,
That glass to all things that o'ershadow it,
Call not that mirror me, for I have slipped
Your grasp, I have eluded.

IX

(HORAE BEATAE INSCRIPTIO)

How will this beauty, when I am far hence,
Sweep back upon me and engulf my mind!

How will these hours, when we twain are gray,
Turned in their sapphire tide, come flooding o'er us!

X

(THE ALTAR)

Let us build here an exquisite friendship,
The flame, the autumn, and the green rose of love
Fought out their strife here, 'tis a place of wonder;
Where these have been, meet 'tis, the ground is holy.

XI

(AU SALON)

Her grave, sweet haughtiness
Pleaseth me, and in like wise
Her quiet ironies.
Others are beautiful, none more, some less.

I suppose, when poetry comes down to facts,
When our souls are returned to the gods
                    and the spheres they belong in,
Here in the every-day where our acts
Rise up and judge us;

I suppose there are a few dozen verities
That no shift of mood can shake from us:

One place where we'd rather have tea
(Thus far hath modernity brought us)
"Tea" (Damn you)
                    Have tea, damn the Caesars,
Talk of the latest success, give wing to some scandal,
Garble a name we detest, and for prejudice?
Set loose the whole consummate pack
                    to bay like Sir Roger de Coverley's.

This our reward for our works,
                    sic crescit gloria mundi:
Some circle of not more than three
                    that we prefer to play up to,

Some few whom we'd rather please
        than hear the whole aegrum vulgus
Splitting its beery jowl
        a-meaowling our praises.

Some certain peculiar things,
        cari laresque, penates,
Some certain accustomed forms,
        the absolute unimportant.

XII
(AU JARDIN)

O you away high there,
                    you that lean
From amber lattices upon the cobalt night,
I am below amid the pine trees,
Amid the little pine trees, hear me!

"The jester walked in the garden."
                    Did he so?
Well, there's no use your loving me
That way, Lady;
For I've nothing but songs to give you.

I am set wide upon the world's ways
To say that life is, some way, a gay thing,
But you never string two days upon one wire
But there'll come sorrow of it.
                              And I loved a love once,
Over beyond the moon there,
                              I loved a love once,
And, may be, more times,

But she danced like a pink moth in the shrubbery.

Oh, I know you women from the "other folk,"
And it'll all come right,
O' Sundays.

"The jester walked in the garden."
                              Did he so?

POEMS WITHDRAWN
FROM CANZONI

Leviora

I
AGAINST FORM

Whether my Lady will to hear of me
The unrimed speech wherein the heart is heard,
Or whether she prefer to the perfumed word
And powdered cheek of masking irony?
Decorous dance steps ape simplicity,
The well-groomed sonnet is to truth preferred;
Let us be all things so we're not absurd,
Dabble with forms and damn the verity.
Bardlets and bardkins, I do bite my thumb.
Corset the muse and "directoire" her grace,
Marcel the elf-looks of *sa chevelure*,
Enamel Melpomene's too sun-kissed face
And then to have your fame forged doubly sure
Let taste rule all and bid the heart be dumb.

II
HIC JACET

When we be buried in anthologies,
Subjective egoists, objective makers
Tied cheek by jowl, the true and false partakers
Of semi-fame, and drear eternities
Warmed by no fire save scholastic comment,
Will those among us who have pleased ourselves
Not sit more snugly than the crabbed elves
Who made the work a trade, as if 'twere so meant?
And when the eyes we sing to are grown dim,
Think you we fellows who have loved our loving
Think you that we, who for their sake we've sung to,

Have jammed our words within the sonnet's rim
And for love's sake set all our lines a-moving,
Think you we'll care what shelf the tomes are flung to?

IV

TO MY VERY DEAR FRIEND — REMONSTRATING
FOR HIS ESSAY UPON "MIGHTY MOUTHS"

Deaf . . . dericus, deaf . . . ingides,
Thou passest Midas, if the truth be told,
I mean in hearing and in manifold
Bombastic statement of unverities.
Leave, Friend, ah leave such wordy fields as these,
Thou deck'st poor plaster with thin leaves of gold,
And then thou chokest e'en as Midas old,
Whose fated touch begat such bright disease.

Disturb not high Olympus with the claims
Of this bemotlied mimic of the great,
Priapus hides him 'neath Jehova's coat.
Some musty corner in the tomb of fame
Where thou and ——— ——— shall hold future state
Would better fit this "Mouth" whom thou dost note.

To Hulme (T. E.) and Fitzgerald (A Certain)

Is there for feckless poverty
That grins at ye for a' that!
A hired slave to none am I,
But underfed for a' that;
For a' that and a' that;
The tails I shun and a' that,
My name but mocks the guinea stamp,
And Pound's dead broke for a' that.

Although my linen still is clean,
My socks fine silk and a' that,
Although I dine and drink good wine—

Say, twice a week, and a' that;
For a' that and a' that,
My tinsel show and a' that,
These breeks 'll no last many weeks
'Gainst wear and tear and a' that.

Ye see this birkie ca'ed a bard,
Wi' cryptic eyes and a' that,
Aesthetic phrases by the yard;
It's but E. P. for a' that,
For a' that and a' that,
My verses, books and a' that,
The man of independent means
He looks and laughs at a' that.

One man will make a novelette
And sell the same and a' that.
For verse nae man can siller get,
Nae editor maun fa' that
For a' that and a' that,
Their royalties and a' that,
Wi' time to loaf and will to write
I'll stick to rhyme for a' that.

And ye may praise or gang your ways
Wi' pity, sneers and a' that,
I know my trade and God has made
Some men to rhyme and a' that,
I maun gang on for a' that
Wi' verse to verse until the hearse
Carts off me wame and a' that.

Redondillas, or Something of That Sort

I sing the gaudy to-day and cosmopolite civilization
Of my hatred of crudities, of my weariness of banalities,
I sing of the ways that I love, of Beauty and delicate savours.

No man may pass beyond
     the nets of good and evil
For joy's in deepest hell
     and in high heaven,
About the very ports
     are subtle devils.

I would sing of exquisite sights,
     of the murmur of Garda:
I would sing of the amber lights,
     or of how Desenzano
Lies like a topaz chain
     upon the throat of the waters.

I sing of natural forces
     I sing of refinements
I would write of the various moods
     of nuances, of subtleties.
I would sing of the hatred of dullness,
     of the search for sensation.

I would sing the American people,
     God send them some civilization;
I would sing of the nations of Europe,
     God grant them some method of cleansing
The fetid extent of their evils.
     I would sing of my love "To-morrow,"
But Yeats has written an essay,
     Why should I stop to repeat it?
I don't like this hobbledy metre
     but find it easy to write in,
I would sing to the tune of "*Mi Platz*"
     were it not for the trouble of riming,
Besides, not six men believe me
     when I sing in a beautiful measure.

I demonstrate the breadth of my vision.
     I am bored of this talk of the tariff,
I too have heard of T. Roosevelt.
     I have met with the "Common Man,"

I admit that he usually bores me,
        He is usually stupid or smug.
I praise God for a few royal fellows
        like Plarr and Fred Vance and Whiteside,
I grant them fullest indulgence
        each one for his own special queerness.

I believe in some lasting sap
        at work in the trunk of things;
I believe in a love of deeds,
        in a healthy desire for action;
I believe in double-edged thought
        in careless destruction.

I believe in some parts of Nietzsche,
        I prefer to read him in sections;
In my heart of hearts I suspect him
        of being the one modern christian;
Take notice I never have read him
        except in English selections.
I am sick of the toothless decay
        of God's word as they usually preach it;
I am sick of bad blasphemous verse
        that they sell with their carols and hymn tunes.

I would sing of the soft air
        and delight that I have in fine buildings,
Pray that God better my voice
        before you are forced to attend me.
I would turn from superficial things
        for a time, into the quiet
I would draw your minds to learn
        of sorrow in quiet,
To watch for signs and strange portents.

          .   .   .   .   .

Delicate beauty on some sad, dull face
Not very evil, but just damned, through weakness,
Drawn down against hell's lips by some soft sense;
When you shall find such a face
        how far will your thought's lead fathom?

Oh, it's easy enough to say
       'tis this, that and the other,
But when some truth is worn smooth
       how many men really do think it?
We speak to a surfeited age,
       Grant us keen weapons for speaking.

Certain things really do matter:
       Love, and the comfort of friendship.
After we are burnt clear,
       or even deadened with knowledge;
After we have gone the whole gamut,
       exhausted our human emotions,
Still is there something greater,
       some power, some recognition,
Some bond beyond the ordinary bonds
       of passion and sentiment
And the analyzed method of novels,
       some saner and truer course
That pays us for foregoing blindness.

Whenever we dare, the angels crowd about us.
There is no end to the follies
       sprung from the full fount of weakness;
There is great virtue in strength
       even in passive resistance.
God grant us an open mind
       and the poise and balance to use it.
They tell me to "Mirror my age,"
       God pity the age if I do do it,
Perhaps I myself would prefer
       to sing of the dead and the buried:
At times I am wrapped in my dream
       of my mistress "To-morrow"
We ever live in the now
       it is better to live in than sing of.

Yet I sing of the diverse moods
       of effete modern civilization.

I sing of delicate hues
        and variations of pattern;
I sing of risorgimenti,
        of old things found that were hidden,
I sing of the senses developed,
        I reach towards perceptions scarce heeded.
If you ask me to write world prescriptions
        I write so that any can read it:
A little less Paul Verlaine,
        A good sound stave of Spinoza,
A little less of our nerves
        A little more will toward vision.

I sing of the fish and the sauce,
        I sing of the *rôti de dindon*;
I sing of delectable things that
        I scarcely ever can pay for.
I love the subtle accord
        of rimes wound over and over;
I sing of the special case,
        The truth is the individual.

Tamlin is the truest of ballads,
        There is more in heaven and earth
Than the priest and the scientists think of.
        The core in the heart of man
Is tougher than any "system."
        I sing devils, thrones and dominions
At work in the air round about us,
        Of powers ready to enter
And thrust our own being from us.
        I sing of the swift delight
Of the clear thrust and riposte in fencing,
        I sing of the fine overcoming,
I sing of the wide comprehension.
        I toast myself against the glow of life
I had a trace of mind, perhaps some heart
        Nature I loved, in her selected moods,
And art,
        perhaps a little more than need be.

I have no objection to wealth,
        the trouble is the acquisition,
It would be rather a horrible sell
        to work like a dog and not get it.
Arma, virumque cano, qui primus, etcetera, ab oris,
Even this hobbledy-hoy
        is not my own private invention.
We are the heirs of the past,
        it is asinine not to admit it.
O Virgil, from your green elysium
        see how that dactyl stubs his weary toes.

I too have been to the play-house,
        often bored with vapid inventions;
I too have taken delight
        in the maze of the Russian dancers.
I am that terrible thing,
        the product of American culture,
Or rather that product improved
        by considerable care and attention.
I am really quite modern, you know,
        despite my affecting the ancients.
I sing of the pleasure of teas
        when one finds someone brilliant to talk to.
I know this age and its works
        with some sort of moderate intelligence,
It does nothing so novel or strange
        except in the realm of mechanics.
Why should I cough my head off
        with that old gag of "Nascitur ordo"?
(The above is not strictly the truth
        I've just heard of a German named Ehrlich.
Medical science is jolted,
        we'll have to call back Fracastori
To pen a new end for "De Morbo.")
        But setting science aside
To return to me and my status;
        I'm not specifically local,
I'm more or less Europe itself,
        More or less Strauss and De Bussy.

I even admire and am
     Klimt and that horrible Zwintscher.
Shall I write it: *Admiror, sum ergo?*
     Deeds are not always first proof,
Write it thus: By their Gods ye shall know them.
The chief god in hell is convention,
     'got by that sturdy sire Stupidity
Upon pale Fear, in some most proper way.
     Where people worship a sham
There is hardly room for a devil.
     You'll find some such thing in Hen. Ibsen.
I'm sorry Dame Fashion has left him
     and prefers to imbibe him diluted
In . . . Why name our whole tribe of playwrights?
     Mistrust the good of an age
That swallows a whole code of ethics.
     Schopenhauer's a gloomy decadent
Somewhat chewed by the worms of his wisdom.
     Our mud was excreted of mind,
That mudless the mind should be clearer.
     Behold how I chivvy Lucretius,
Behold how I dabble in cosmos.
     Behold how I copy my age,
Dismissing great men with a quibble.
     I know not much save myself,
I know myself pretty completely.
     I prefer most white wine to red,
Bar only some lordly Burgundy.
     We all of us make mistakes,
Give us reasonable time to retrieve them.
     The future will probably meet
With people who know more than we do.
     There's no particular end
To this sort of a statement of being,
     no formal envoi or tornata
But perhaps a sort of a bow.
     The musician returns to the dominant.
Behold then the the the that I am;
     Behold me sententious, *dégagé*,
Behold me my saeculum in parvo,

Bergson's objective fact,
London's last foible in poets.
I love all delicate sounds,
The purple fragrance of incense;
I love the flaked fire of sunlight
Where it glints like red rain on the water;
I love the quaint patterns inwoven
In Mozart, Steibelt, Scarlatti,
I love their quavers and closes,
The passionate moods of singing.

THE SONNETS AND BALLATE
OF
GUIDO CAVALCANTI

AS MUCH OF THIS BOOK AS IS MINE
I SEND TO MY FRIENDS
VIOLET AND FORD MADDOX HUEFFER

I have owned service to the deathless dead
Grudge not the gold I bear in livery.

OH dissi lui, non se' tu Oderisi,
   L' onor d' Agobbio, e l' onor di quell' arte
   Ch' alluminare è chiamala in Parisi?

FRATE, diss' egli, piu ridon le carte,
   Che pennelleggia Franco Bolognese:
   L' onore è tullo or suo, e mio in parte.

BEN non sare' io stato sì cortese
   Mentre ch' io vissi, per lo gran disio
   Dell' eccellenza, ove mio core intese.

DI tal superbia qui si paga 'l fio:
   Ed ancor non sarei qui, se non fosse,
   Che, possendo peccar, mi volsi a Dio.

O VANAGLORIA dell' umane posse,
   Com' poco verde su la cima dura,
   Se non è giunta dall' elati grosse!

CREDETTE Cimabue nella pintura
   Tener lo campo, ed ora ha Giotto il grido,
   Sì che la fama di colui oscura.

COSÌ ha tolto l' uno all' altro Guido
   La gloria della lingua: e forse e nato
   Chi l' uno e l' altro caccerà di nido.

NON è il mondan romore altro ch' un fiato
   Di vento, ch' or vien quinci ed or vien quindi,
   E muta nome, perchè muta lato.

Dante in "Purgatorio," XI.

INTRODUCTION

"Cimabue thought that in portraiture
  He held the field; now Giotto hath the cry
  And all the former fame is turned obscure;
  Thus hath one Guido from the other reft
  The glory of our tongue, and there's perchance
  One born who shall un-nest both him and him."

Even the qualification in the last line of this speech which
Oderesi, honour of Agobbio, illuminator of fair pages, makes
to Dante in the terrace for the purgation of Pride, must be
balanced by Dante's reply to Guido's father among the burn-
ing tombs (Inf. X), sic.

Cavalcante di Cavalcanti:
    "If by the height of genius thou dost go
    Through this blind prison house; where is my son?
    Why is he not with thee?"
Dante:
    "I come not of myself,
    But he, who awaiteth there (i.e. Virgil), doth lead
        me through."

After these passages from "The Commedia" there should be
small need of my writing introductions to the poems of Guido
Cavalcanti, for if he is not among the major prophets, he has
at least his place in the canon, in the second book of The Arts,
with Sappho and Theocritus; with all those who have sung, not
all the modes of life, but some of them, unsurpassedly; those
who in their chosen or fated field have bowed to no one.

It is conceivable that poetry of a far-off time or place re-
quires a translation not only of word and of spirit, but of "ac-
companiment," that is, that the modern audience must in
some measure be made aware of the mental content of the
older audience, and of what these others drew from certain
fashions of thought and speech. Six centuries of derivative
convention and loose usage have obscured the exact signifi-

cances of such phrases as: "The death of the heart," and "The departure of the soul."

Than Guido Cavalcanti no psychologist of the emotions is more keen in his understanding, more precise in his expression; we have in him no rhetoric, but always a true description, whether it be of pain itself, or of the apathy that comes when the emotions and possibilities of emotion are exhausted, or of that stranger state when the feeling by its intensity surpasses our powers of bearing and we seem to stand aside and watch it surging across some thing or being with whom we are no longer identified.

The relation of certain words in the original to the practice of my translation may require gloze. *L'anima* and *la Morte* are feminine, but it is not always expeditious to retain this gender in English. *Gentile* is 'noble'; 'gentleness' in our current sense would be *soavitate*. *Mente* is 'mind,' 'consciousness,' 'apperception.' The *spiriti* are the 'senses,' or the 'intelligences of the senses,' perhaps even 'the moods,' when they are considered as 'spirits of the mind.' *Valore* is 'power.' *Virtute*, 'virtue,' 'potency,' requires a separate treatise. Pater has explained its meaning in the preface to his "The Renaissance," but in reading a line like

> *"Vedrai la sua virtù nel ciel salita"*

one must have in mind the connotations alchemical, astrological, metaphysical, which Swedenborg would have called the correspondences.

The equations of alchemy were apt to be written as women's names and the women so named endowed with the magical powers of the compounds. *La virtù* is the potency, the efficient property of a substance or person. Thus modern science shows us radium with a noble virtue of energy. Each thing or person was held to send forth magnetisms of certain effect; in Sonnet XXXV, the image of his lady has these powers.

It is a spiritual chemistry, and modern science and modern mysticism are both set to confirm it.

> *"Vedrai la sua virtù nel ciel salita."*

The heavens were, according to the Ptolemaic system, clear concentric spheres with the earth as their pivot; they moved

more swiftly as they were far-removed from it, each one en-
dowed with its *virtue*, its property for affecting man and des-
tiny; in each its star, the sign visible to the wise and guiding
them. A logical astrology, the star a sort of label of the spiri-
tual force, an indicator of the position and movement of that
spiritual current. Thus "her" presence, his Lady's, corre-
sponds with the ascendency of the star of that heaven which
corresponds to her particular emanation or potency. Likewise,

> *"Vedrai la sua virtù nel ciel salita."*

Thou shalt see the rays of this emanation going up to heaven
as a slender pillar of light, or, more strictly in accordance with
the stanza preceding: thou shalt see depart from her lips her
subtler body, and from that a still subtler form ascends and
from that a star, the body of pure flame surrounding the
source of the *virtù*, which will declare its nature.

I would go so far as to say that "Il Paradiso" and the form
of "The Commedia" might date from this line; very much as
I think I find in Guido's "Place where I found people whereof
each one grieved overly of Love," some impulse that has ulti-
mate fruition in Inferno V.

These are lines in the sonnets; is it any wonder that "F. Z."
is able to write:

"His (Guido's) canzone solely on the nature of Love was
so celebrated that the rarest intellects, among them 'il beato
Egidio Colonna,' set themselves to illustrating it with com-
mentaries, of which the most cited is that of Mazzuchelli."

Another line, of which Rossetti completely loses the signif-
icance is

> *"E la beltate per sua Dea la mostra."*   (Sonnet VII, 11.)

"Beauty displays her for her goddess." That is to say, as the
spirit of God became incarnate in the Christ, so is the spirit of
the eternal beauty made flesh dwelling amongst us in her.
And in the line preceding,

> *"Ch' a lei s'inchina ogni gentil virtute"*

means, that "she" acts as a magnet for every "gentil virtute,"
that is, the noble spiritual powers, the invigorating forces of
life and beauty bend toward her; not

"To whom are subject all things virtuous."

The *inchina* implies not the homage of an object but the direction of a force.

In the matter of these translations and of my knowledge of Tuscan poetry, Rossetti is my father and my mother, but no one man can see everything at once.

The twelfth ballata, being psychological and not metaphysical, needs hardly be explained. Exhausted by a love born of fate and of the emotions, Guido turns to an intellectual sympathy,

"Love that is born of loving like delight,"

and in this new force he is remade,

"formando di disio nova persona"

yet with some inexplicable lack. His sophistication prevents the complete enthusiasm. This "new person" which is formed about his soul

"amar gia non osa"

knowing "The end of every man's desire."

The facts of Guido's life, as we know them from other evidence than that of his own and his friends' poems, are about as follows: Born 1250 (circa), his mother probably of the Conti Guidi. In 1266 or 1267 "Cavalcante di Cavalcanti gave for wife to his son Guido one of the Uberti," i. e., the daughter of Farinata. Thus Villani. Some speak of it as a "betrothal." In 1280 he acted as one of the sureties of the peace arranged by Cardinal Latino. We may set 1283 as the date of his reply to Dante's first sonnet. In 1284 he was a member of the grand council with Dino Compagni and Brunetto Latino. In party feuds of Florence Guelf, then a "White" with the Cherci, and most violent against Corso Donati. 1292–96 is the latitude given us for the pilgrimage to the holy house of Galicia. Corso, it is said, tried to assassinate him on this pilgrimage. It is more plausible to accept 1292 as the date of the feud between the Cavalcanti and the Bundelmonti, dating so the sonnet to Neronne. For upon his return from the pilgrimage which had extended only to Toulouse, Guido attacks Corso in the streets of Florence, and for the general turmoil ensuing, the leaders of both factions were exiled. Guido was sent with the "Whites" to Sarzana, where he caught his death fever. Dante at this time (1300) being a prior of Florence, was party to decree of exile, and perhaps aided in procuring Cavalcanti's speedy recall. "Il nostro Guido" was buried on August 29, whence writes Villani, "and his death is a great loss, for as he was philosopher, so was he man of parts in more things, although somewhat punctilious and fiery." Boccaccio considers him "probably" the "other just man," in Dante's statement that there were two in Florence.

Benevenuto says so positively, "*alter oculus Florentiae.*" In the Decameron we hear that, "He was of the best logicians in the world, a very fine natural philosopher. Thus was he *leggiadrisimo,*" and there is much in this word with which to confute those who find no irony in his sonnets; "and habile and a great talker." On the "sixth day" (novel nine) the queen herself tells how he leapt over an exceeding great tomb to escape from that bore Betto Brunelleschi. Other lines we have of him as: "noble and pertinent and better than another at whatever he set his hand to"; among the critics, Crescimbene notes, "*robustezza e splendore*"; Cristofore Landiano, "*sobrio e dotto,* and surpassed by a greater light he became not as the moon to the sun. Of Dante and Petrarcha, I speak elsewhere."

Filippo Villani, with his translator Mazzuchelli, set him above Petrarch, speaking of him as "Guido of the noble line of the Cavalcanti, most skilled in the liberal arts, Dante's contemporary and very intimate friend, a man surely diligent and given to speculation, 'physicus' (? natural philosopher) of authority . . . worthy of laud and honor for his joy in the study of 'rhetoric,'* he brought over the fineness of this art into the rhyming compositions of the common tongue (*eleganter traduxit*). For canzoni in vulgar tongue and in the advancement of this art he held second place to Dante, nor hath Petrarch taken it from him."

---

*"Rhetoric" must not here be understood in the current sense of our own day. "Exact and adequate speech" might be a closer rendering.

Dino Compagni, who knew him, has perhaps left us the most apt description, saying that Guido was "*cortes e ardito, ma sdegnoso e solitario,*" at least I would so think of him, "courteous, bold, haughty and given to being alone." It is so we find him in the poems themselves.

Dante delays in answering the elder Cavalcante's question (Inf. X) "What said you? 'He (Guido) *had?*' Lives he not still, with the sweet light beating upon his eyes?" This delay is, I think, a device for reminding the reader of the events of the year 1300. One who had signed a decree of exile against his friend, however much civic virtue was thereby displayed, might well delay his answer.

And if that matchless and poignant ballad,

"*Perch' io non spero di tornar già mai*"

had not reached Florence before Dante saw the vision, it was at least written years before he wrote the tenth canto of the Inferno.

Guido left two children, Andrea and Tancia. Mandetta of Toulouse is an incident. As to the identity of "our own Lady," that Giovanna "presumably" of whom Dante writes in the Vita Nuova, sonnet fourteen, and the prose preceding, weaving his fancy about Primavera, the first coming Spring, St. John the Forerunner, with Beatrice following Monna Vanna, as the incarnate love: Again in the sonnet of the enchanted ship, "*Guido vorrei . . .*" we find her mentioned in the chosen company. One modern writer would have us follow out the parallels between the Commedia and "Book of His Youth," and identify her with the "Matilda" of the Earthly Paradise. By virtue of her position and certain similarities of phrasing in Purgatory XXVIII and one of the lives of the saint, we know that Matilda in some way corresponds to or balances John the Baptist. Dante is undoubtedly reminded of his similar equation in the Vita Nuova and shows it in his

"*Tu mi fai remembrar, dove e qual era*
Proserpina, nel tempo che perdette
La madre lei, ed ella primavera."

Dante's commentators in their endless search for exact correspondences, seem never to suspect him of poetical innuendo, of calling into the spectrum of the reader's mind associated things which form no exact allegory. So far as the personal Matilda is concerned, the great Countess of Tuscany has some claims, and we have nothing to show that Giovanna was dead at the time of the vision.

As to the actual identity of Guido's lady—granting her to have been one and not several—no one has been rash enough to suggest that *il nostro Guido* was in love with his own wife, to whom he had been wedded or betrothed at sixteen. True it would have been contrary to the laws of chivalric love, but Guido was not one to be bound by a convention if the whim had taken him otherwise. The discussion of such details and theories is futile except in so far as it may serve to bring us more intimately in touch with the commune of Florence and the year of grace one thousand three hundred.

As for the verse itself: I believe in an ultimate and absolute rhythm as I believe in an absolute symbol or metaphor. The perception of the intellect is given in the word, that of the emotions in the cadence. It is only, then, in perfect rhythm joined to the perfect word that the two-fold vision can be recorded. I would liken Guido's cadence to nothing less powerful than line in Blake's drawing.

In painting, the color is always finite. It may match the color of the infinite spheres, but it is in a way confined within the frame and its appearance is modified by the colors about it. The line is unbounded, it marks the passage of a force, it continues beyond the frame.

Rodin's belief that energy is beauty holds thus far, namely, that all our ideas of beauty of line are in some way connected with our ideas of swiftness or easy power of motion, and we consider ugly those lines which connote unwieldy slowness in moving.

Rhythm is perhaps the most primal of all things known to us. It is basic in poetry and music mutually, their melodies depending on a variation of tone quality and of pitch respectively, as is commonly said, but if we look more closely we will see that music is, by further analysis, pure rhythm; rhythm and nothing else, for the variation of pitch is the variation in rhythms of the individual notes, and harmony the blending of these varied rhythms. When we know more of overtones we will see that the tempo of every masterpiece is absolute, and is exactly set by some further law of rhythmic accord. Whence it should be possible to show that any given rhythm implies about it a complete musical form—fugue, sonata, I cannot say what form, but a form, perfect, complete. Ergo, the rhythm set in a line of poetry connotes its symphony, which, had we a little more skill, we could score for orchestra. *Sequitur*, or rather *inest*: the rhythm of any poetic line corresponds to emotion.

It is the poet's business that this correspondence be exact, i. e., that it be the emotion which surrounds the thought expressed. For which cause I have set here Guido's own words, that those few of you who care, may read in them the signs of his genius. By the same token, I consider Carducci and Arnone blasphemous in accepting the reading

E fa di claritate tremar l'are

instead of following those *mss.* which read

E fa di clarità l'aer tremare.

I have in my translations tried to bring over the qualities of Guido's rhythm, not line for line, but to embody in the whole of my English some trace of that power which implies the man. The science of the music of words and the knowledge of their magical powers has fallen away since men invoked Mithra by a sequence of pure vowel sounds. That there might be less interposed between the reader and Guido, it was my first intention to print only his poems and an unrhymed gloze. This has not been practicable. I can not trust the reader to read the Italian for the music after he has read the English for the sense.

These are no sonnets for an idle hour. It is only when the emotions illumine the perceptive powers that we see the reality. It is in the light born of this double current that we look upon the face of the mystery unveiled. I have lived with these sonnets and ballate daily month in and month out, and have been daily drawn deeper into them and daily into contemplation of things that are not of an hour. And I deem, for this, that *voi altri pochi* who understand, will love me better for my labor in proportion as you read more carefully.

For the rest, I can but quote an envoi, that of Guido's Canzone "*Donna mi prega*":

> Thou mayest go assurèd, my Canzone,
> Whither thou wilt, for I have so adorned thee
> That praise shall rise to greet thy reasoning
> Mid all such folk as have intelligence;
> To stand with any else, thou 'st no desire.

EZRA POUND.

November 15, 1910.

Sonnet I

You, who do breach mine eyes and touch the heart,
And start the mind from her brief reveries,
Might pluck my life and agony apart,
Saw you how love assaileth her with sighs,
And lays about him with so brute a might
That all my wounded senses turn to flight.
There's a new face upon the seigniory,
And new is the voice that maketh loud my grief.

Love, who hath drawn me down through devious ways,
Hath from your noble eyes so swiftly come!
'Tis he hath hurled the dart, wherefrom my pain,
First shot's resultant! and in flanked amaze
See how my affrighted soul recoileth from
That sinister side wherein the heart lies slain.

Sonnet II

I saw the eyes, where Amor took his place
When love's might bound me with the fear thereof,
Look out at me as they were weary of love.
I say: The heart rent him as he looked on this,
And were't not that my Lady lit her grace,
Smiling upon me with her eyes grown glad,
Then were my speech so dolorously clad
That Love should mourn amid his victories.

The instant that she deigned to bend her eyes
Toward me, a spirit from high heaven rode
And chose my thought the place of his abode
With such deep parlance of love's verities
That all Love's powers did my sight accost
As though I'd won unto his heart's mid-most.

Sonnet III

O Lady mine, doth not thy sight allege
Him who hath set his hand upon my heart,
When parched responses from my faint throat start
And shudder for the terror of his edge?
He was Amor, who since he found you, dwells
Ever with me, and he was come from far;
An archer is he as the Scythians are
Whose only joy is killing someone else.

My sobbing eyes are drawn upon his wrack,
And such harsh sighs upon my heart he casteth
That I depart from that sad me he wasteth,
With Death drawn close upon my wavering track,
Leading such tortures in his sombre train
As, by all custom, wear out other men.

Sonnet IV

If I should pray this lady pitiless
That Mercy to her heart be no more foeman,
You'd call me clownish, vile, and say that no man
Was so past hope and filled with vanities.

Where find you now these novel cruelties?
For still you seem humility's true leaven,
Wise and adorned, alert and subtle even,
And fashioned out in ways of gentleness.

My soul weeps through her sighs for grievous fear
And all those sighs, which in the heart were found,
Deep drenched with tears do sobbing thence depart,
Then seems that on my mind there rains a clear
Image of a lady, thoughtful, bound
Hither to keep death-watch upon that heart.

Sonnet V

Lady, my most rash eyes, the first who used
To look upon thy face, the power-fraught,
Were, Lady, those by whom I was accused
In that harsh place where Amor holdeth court.
And there before him was their proof adduced,
And judgment wrote me down: "Bondslave" to thee,
Though still I stay Grief's prisoner, unloosed,
And Fear hath lien upon the heart of me.
For the which charges, and without respite,
They dragged me to a place where a sad horde
Of such as love and whom Love tortureth
Cried out, all pitying as I met their sight,
"Now art thou servant unto such a Lord
Thou'lt have none other one save only Death."

Sonnet VI

Thou fill'st my mind with griefs so populous
That my soul irks him to be on the road.
Mine eyes cry out, "We cannot bear the load
Of sighs the grievous heart sends upon us."
Love, sensitive to thy nobility,
Saith, "Sorrow is mine that thou must take thy death
From this fair lady who will hear no breath
In argument for aught save pitying thee."
And I, as one beyond life's compass thrown,
Seem but a thing that's fashioned to design,
Melted of bronze or carven in tree or stone.
A wound I bear within this heart of mine
Which by its mastering quality is grown
To be of that heart's death an open sign.

Sonnet VII

Who is she coming, drawing all men's gaze,
Who makes the air one trembling clarity
Till none can speak but each sighs piteously
Where she leads Love adown her trodden ways?

Ah God! The thing she's like when her glance strays,
Let Amor tell. 'Tis no fit speech for me.
Mistress she seems of such great modesty
That every other woman were called "Wrath."

No one could ever tell the charm she hath
For all the noble powers bend toward her,
She being beauty's godhead manifest.

Our daring ne'er before held such high quest;
But ye! There is not in you so much grace
That we can understand her rightfully.

Sonnet VIII

Ah why! why were mine eyes not quenched for me,
Or stricken so that from their vision none
Had ever come within my mind to say:
"Listen, dost thou not hear me in thine heart?"
Fear of new torments was then so displayed
To me, so cruel and so sharp of edge
That my soul cried, "Ah mistress, bring us aid,
Lest th'eyes and I remain in grief always."

But thou hast left them so that Amor cometh
And weepeth over them so piteously
That there's a deep voice heard whose sound in part
Turned unto words, is this: "Whoever knoweth
Pain's depth, let him look on this man whose heart
Death beareth in his hand cut cruciform."

Sonnet IX

At last I am reduced to self compassion,
For the sore anguish that I see me in;
At my great weakness; that my soul hath been
Concealed beneath her wounds in such a fashion:

Such mine oppression that I know, in brief,
That to my life ill's worst starred ills befall;
And this strange lady on whose grace I call
Maintains continuous my stour of grief,
For when I look in her direction,
She turns upon me her disdeigning eyen
So harshly that my waiting heart is rent
And all my powers and properties are spent,
Till that heart lieth for a sign ill-seen,
Where Amor's cruelty hath hurled him down.

Sonnet X

Alas, my spirits, that ye come to find me
So painful, poor, waylaid in wretchedness,
Yet send no words adorned with deep distress
Forth from my mind to say what sorrows bind me.
Alas, ye see how sore my heart is wounded
By glance, by fair delight and by her meekness;
'Las! Must I pray ye that ye aid his weakness,
Seeing him power-stripped, naked, confounded.

And now a spirit that is noble and haut
Appeareth to that heart with so great might
That all th' heart's virtues turn in sudden flight.

Woe! And I pray you greet my soul as friend,
Who tells through all her grief what things were wrought
On her by Love, and will be to the end.

Sonnet XI

If Mercy were the friend of my desires,
Or Mercy's source of movement were the heart,
Then, by this fair, would Mercy show such art
And power of healing as my pain requires.
From torturing delights my sighs commence,

Born of the mind where Love is situate,
Go errant forth and naught save grief relate
And find no one to give them audience.

They would return to the eyes in galliard mode,
With all harsh tears and their deep bitterness
Transmuted into revelry and joy;
Were't not unto the sad heart such annoy,
And to the mournful soul such rathe distress
That none doth deign salute them on the road.

Sonnet XII

The grace of youth in Toulouse ventureth;
She's noble and fair, with quaint sincerities,
Direct she is and is about her eyes
Most like to our Lady of sweet memories.
So that within my heart desirous
She hath clad the soul in fashions peregrine.*
Pilgrim to her he hath too great chagrin
To say what Lady is lord over us.
This soul looks deep into that look of hers,
Wherein he rouseth Love to festival,
For deep therein his rightful lady resteth.
Then with sad sighing in the heart he stirs,
Feeling his death-wound as that dart doth fall
Which this Tolosan by departure casteth.

* *Vita Nuova* XLI, l.46: "*In guisa che da lui si svia e vanne a lei*," and Sonnet XXIV and Sonnet V, l.4.

Sonnet XIII

Concerning the source, the affects and the progeny of the little spirit of pure love: Born of the perception of beauty, he arouseth that power of the mind whence is born that quality of love which ennobleth every sense and every desire; misunderstood of base minds who comprehend not his

power, he is the cause of that love in woman which teach-
eth modesty. Thus from him is born that love in woman
whence is born Mercy, and from Mercy "as a gentle rain
from heaven" descend those spirits which are the keys of
every spirit; perforce of the one spirit which seeth.

Subtle the spirit striking through the eyes
Which rouseth up a spirit in the mind
Whence moves a spirit unto love inclined
Which breeds, in other sprites, nobilities.
No turbid spirit hath the sense which sees
How greatly empowered a spirit he appeareth;
He is the little breath which that breath feareth,
Which breedeth virginal humilities.
Yet from this spirit doth another move
Wherein such tempered sweetness rightly dwells
That Mercy's spirit followeth his ways,
And Mercy's spirit as it moves above
Rains down those spirits that ope all things else,
Perforce of One who seeth all of these.

Sonnet XIV

Surely thine intellect gives no embrace
To him who hath bred this day's dishonesty;
How art thou shown for beggared suddenly
By that red spirit showing in thy face!
Perhaps it is some love within thee breedeth
For her who's folly's circumscription,
Perhaps some baser light doth call thee on
To make thee glad where mine own grief exceedeth.

Thou art my grief, my grief to such extent
That I trust not myself to meet Milady,
Starving myself of what Love sweetest lent me
So that before my face that key's forbent
Which her disdeign turned in my heart and made me
Suitor to wrath and sadness and lamenting.

Sonnet XV

Thou hast in thee the flower and the green
And that which gleameth and is fair of sight,
Thy form is more resplendent than sun's sheen;
Who sees thee not, can ne'er know worth aright.
Nay, in this world there is no creature seen
So fashioned fair and full of all delight;
Who fears Amor, and fearing meets thy mien,
Thereby assured, he solveth him his fright.

The ladies of whom thy cortège consisteth
Please me in this, that they've thy favour won;
I bid them now, as courtesy existeth,
Holding most dear thy lordship of their state,
To honour thee with powers commensurate,
Sith thou art thou, that art sans paragon.

Sonnet XVI

To Guido Orlando

This most lief lady, where doth Love display him
So full of valour and so vestured bright,
Bids thy heart "Out!" He goes and none gainsay him;
And he takes life with her in long delight.
Her cloister's guard is such that should you journey
To Ind you'd see each unicorn obey it;
Its armèd might against thee in sweet tourney
Cruel riposteth, thou canst not withstay it.
And she is surely in her valliancies
Such that she lacks not now worth's anything,
And yet He made her for a mortal creature.
Then showed her forth, and here His foresight is,
And His providence, Ah, how fair a thing
If by her likeness thou mayst learn its nature!

For the final lines Rossetti gives:
  Yet she's created for a mortal creature;
  In her is shown what God's providence is;
  Sufficeth she unto thy mind to bring
  Knowledge of it, seeing it shares her nature.

Sonnet XVII

Concerning Pinella, he replies to a sonnet
by Bernardo da Bologna and explains why they have
sweet waters in Galicia (Liscian)

Now every cool small spring that springeth sweetly
Takes clarity and virtue in Liscian climes,
Bernard my friend, from one sole source, discretely:
So she who answereth thy sharpened rimes.
For in that place where Love's reports are laid
Concerning all who to his sight are led,
He saith that this so gracious and fair maid
Hath in herself all graces gatherèd.

Whereas my grief in this is grown more grave
And sighs have turned me to one light and flame,
I send my burning heart, in her acclaim
Unto Pinella, upon a magic stream
Where fairies and their fair attendants gleam,
In this wrecked barque! where their show is so brave!

Sonnet XVIII

Beauty of woman, of the knowing heart,
And courtly knights in bright accoutrement
And loving speeches and the small birds' art,
Adorned swift ships which on high seas are sent,
And airs grown calm when white the dawn appeareth
And white snow falling where no wind is bent,
Brook-marge and mead where every flower flareth,
And gold and silver and azure and ornament:

Effective 'gainst all these think ye the fairness
And valour of my Lady's lordly daring?

Yea, she makes all seem base vain gathering,
And she were known above whome'er you'd bring
As much as heaven is past earth's comparing;
Good seeketh out its like with some address.

Sonnet XIX

He suggests to his kinsman Nerone that there
may be one among all the Buondelmonti of whom
they might in time make a man

News have I now for thee, so hear, Nerone,
How that the Buondelmonti shake with fear,
And all the Florentines cannot assure them,
Seeing thou hast in thee the lion-heart.
They fear thee more than they would fear a dragon,
Seeing that face of thine, how set it is
That neither bridge nor walls could hold against it
Lest they were strong as is King Pharaoh's tomb.
Oh how thou dost of smoky sins the greatest
In that thou wouldst drive forth such haughty blood
Till all be gone, gone forth without retention.
But sooth it is, thou might'st extend the pawn
Of one whose soul thou *mightest* give salvation
Wert thou more patient in thine huckstering.

Sonnet XX

So vilely is this soul of mine confounded
By strife grown audible within the heart,
That if toward her some frail Love but start
With unaccustomed speed, she swoons astounded.

She is as one in whom no power aboundeth;
Lo, she forsakes my heart through fearfulness,
And any seeing her, how prone she is,
Would deem her one whom death's sure cloak surroundeth.

Through th' eyes, as through the breach in wall, her foes
Came first to attack and shattered all defence,
Then spoiled the mind with their down-rained blows.

Whoe'er he be who holdeth joy most close
Would, should he see my spirit going hence,
Weep for the pity and make no pretence.

Cf. Sonnet I

Sonnet XXI

The Dred Spirit

Thou mayest see, who seest me face to face,
That most dred spirit whom Love summoneth
To meet with man when a man meets with Death;
One never seen in any other case.
So close upon me did this presence show
That I thought he would slay my heart his dolour,
And my sad soul clad her in the dead colour
That most accords the will and ways of woe.
Then he restrained him, seeing in true faith
The piteous lights forth-issue from your eyes
The which bore to my heart their foreign sweetness,
While the perceptive sense with subtle fleetness
Rescued those others* who had considered death
The one sure ending for their miseries.

*The senses or the spirits of the senses.

Sonnet XXII

To Dante, in answer to the first sonnet of the Vita Nuova.

Thou sawest, it seems to me, all things availing,
And every joy that ever good man feeleth.
Thou wast in proof of that lord valorous
Who through sheer honour lords it o'er the world.
Thou livest in a place where baseness dieth,
And holdest reason in the piteous mind:
So gently move the people in this sleep
That the heart bears it 'thout the feel of grief.

Love bore away thy heart, because in his sight
Was Death grown clamorous for one thou lovest,
Love fed her with thy heart in dread of this,
Then, when it seemed to thee he left in sadness,
A dear dream was it which was there completed
Seeing it contrary came conquering.

Note: Dante, V. n. III. "The true significance of the dream was not then seen by anyone."

Sonnet XXIII

To Dante, rebuking him for his way of life
after the death of Beatrice.

I daily come to thee uncounting times
And find thee ever thinking over vilely;
Much doth it grieve me that thy noble mind
And virtue's plenitude are stripped from thee;

Thou wast so careless in thy fine offending,
Who from the rabble alway held apart,
And spoke of me so straightly from the heart
That I gave welcome to thine every rime.

And now I care not, sith thy life is baseness
To give the sign that thy speech pleaseth me,
Nor come I to thee in guise visible,
Yet if thou 'lt read this sonnet many a time,
That malign spirit which so hunteth thee
Will sound forloyn* and spare thy affrighted soul.

*The recall of the hounds.

Sonnet XXIV

Dante, I pray thee, if thou Love discover
In any place where Lappo Gianni is,—
If 't irk thee not to move thy mind in this,
Write me these answered: "Doth he style him Lover?";
And, "Doth the lady seem as one approving?";
And, "Makes he show of service with fair skill?";
For many a time folk made as he is, will
To assume importance, make a show of loving.

Thou know'st that in that court where Love puts on
His royal robes, no vile man can be servant
To any lady who were lost therein;
If servant's suff'ring doth assistance win,
Our style could show unto the least observant,
It beareth mercy for a gonfalon.

Sonnet XXV

"Hoot Zah!!!"

Come, come Manetto, look upon this scarecrow
And set your mind upon its deformations,
Compute th' extent of its sad aberrations,
Say what it looks like where she scarcely dare go!

Nay, were she in a cloak most well concealèd
And snugly hooded and most tightly veiled
If, by her, daylight should once be assailed
Though by some noble woman partly healèd,

Still you could not be so sin-laden or quite
So bound by anguish or by love's abstractions
Nor so enwrapped in naked melancholy
But you were brought to deathly danger, solely
By laughter, till your sturdy sides grew fractions,
'Struth you were dead, or sought your life in flight.

Sonnet XXVI

Of Love in a Dead Vision

Nay, when I would have sent my verses to thee
To say how harshly my heart is oppressed,
Love in an ashen vision manifest
Appeared and spake: "Say not that I foredo thee,

For though thy friend be he I understand
He will not yet have his mind so enured
But that to hear of all thou hast endured,
Of that blare flame that hath thee 'neath its hand,

Would blear his mind out. Verily before!
Yea, he were dead, heart, life, ere he should hear
To the last meaning of the portent wrought.

And thou; thou knowest well I am Amor
Who leave with thee mine ashen likeness here
And bear away from thee thine every thought."

Sonnet XXVII

Were I that I that once was worthy of Love
(Of whom I find naught now save the remembrance)
And if the lady had another semblance,
Then would this sort of sign please me enough.

Do thou, who art from Love's clear realm returned,
Where Mercy giveth birth to hopefulness,
Judge as thou canst from my dim mood's distress
What bowman and what target are concerned.

Straining his arc, behold Amor the bowman
Draweth so gaily that to see his face
You'd say he held his rule for merriment,
Yet hear what's marvelous in all intent:
The smitten spirit pardoneth his foeman
Which pardon doth that foeman's power debase.

Anyone who can, from the text as it stands, discern what happens to
whom in the final lines of this sonnet, is at liberty to emend my translation.

Sonnet XXVIII

A love-lit glance, with living powers fraught,
Renewed within me love's extreme delight,
So love assails me with unwonted might,
And cordially he driveth me in thought
Towards my lady with whom 'vaileth not
Mercy nor pity nor the suffering wrought.
So oft and great, her torments on me fall
That my heart scarce can feel his life at all.

But when I feel that her so sweet regard
Passeth mine eyes and to the heart attaineth
Setting to rest therein spirits of joy,
Then do I give her thanks and without retard;
Love asked her to do this, and that explaineth
Why this first pity doth no annoy.

Sonnet XXIX

Dante, a sigh, that's the heart's messenger
Assailed me suddenly as I lay sleeping;
Aroused, I fell straightway into fear's keeping,
For Love came with that sigh as curator.

And I turned straight and saw the servitor
Of Monna Lagia, who came there a-crying,
"Ah pity! Aid me!" and at this his sighing
I took from Pity this much power and more:

That I found Love a-filing javelins
And asked him of both torment and solution,
And in this fashion came that Lord's replies:
"Say to the servant that his service wins.
He holds the Lady to his pleasure won.
If he'd believe it, let him watch her eyes."

Sonnet XXX

I fear me lest unfortune's counter thrust
Pierce through my throat and rip out my despair.
I feel my heart and that thought shaking there
Which shakes the aspen mind with his distrust,
Seeming to say, "Love doth not give thee ease
So that thou canst, as of a little thing,
Speak to thy Lady with full verities,
For fear Death set thee in his reckoning."

By the chagrin that here assails my soul
My heart's parturèd of a sigh so great
It cryeth to the spirits: "Get ye gone!"
And of all piteous folk I come on none
Who seeing me so in my grief's control
Will aid by saying e'en: "Nay, Spirits, wait!"

Sonnet XXXI

You, who within your eyes so often carry
That Love who holdeth in his hand three arrows,
Behold my spirit, by his far-brought sorrows,
Commends to you a soul whom hot griefs harry.

A mind thrice wounded she* already hath,
By this keen archer's Syrian shafts twice shot.
The third, less tautly drawn, hath reached me not,
Seeing your presence is my shield 'gainst wrath.

Yet this third shot had made more safe my soul,
Who almost dead beneath her members lies;
For these two arrows give three wounds in all:

The first: delight, which payeth pain his toll;
The second brings desire for the prize
Of that great joy which with the third doth fall.

*I.e. The Soul. I have kept the Italian gender in those few sonnets where there is no danger of confusing "her," the soul, with the subjects of other feminine pronouns.

Sonnet XXXII

To Cecco

If Santalena does not come unto you
Down in the plow-lands where the clods are hard,
But falls into the hands of some hot clod-pole
Who'll wear her out and hardly then return her;
Then tell me if the fruit which this land beareth
Is born of drought or heat or from the dampness,
And say what wind it is doth blight and wither
And which doth bring the tempest and the mist.

Say if it please you when at break of morning
You hear the farmer's workman bawling out
And all his family meddling in the noise?

Egad! I think that if your sweet Bettina
Beareth a mellow spirit in her heart
She'll rescue you once more from your last choice.

Sonnet XXXIII

With Death

Death who art haught, the wretched's remedy,
Grace! Grace! hands joined I do beseech it thee,
Come, see and conquer for worse things on me
Are launched by love. My senses that did live,
Consumèd are and quenched, and e'en in this place
Where I was galliard, now I see that I am
Fallen away, and where my steps I misplace,
Fall pain and grief; to open tears I nigh am.
And greater ills He'd send if greater may be.
Sweet Death, now is the time thou may'st avail me
And snatch me from His hand's hostility.
Ah woe! how oft I cry "Love tell me now:
Why dost thou ill only unto thine own,
Like him of hell who maketh the damned groan?"

Sonnet XXXIV

Amore and Mona Lagia and Guido and I
Can give true thanks unto Ser Such-a-one
Who hath now ridded us of Know-you-who?
I'll name no name for I'd have it forgotten.
And these three people have no wish for it
Though they were servants to him in such wise
That they, in sooth, could not have served him more
Had they mistaken him for God himself.

Let Love be thanked who was first made aware,
And then give thanks unto the prudent lady
Who at Love's instance hath called back her heart;

Then thanks to Guido* who's not here concerned
And to me too who drove him back to virtue,
If then he please me, think it not perchance.

*I.e. Guido Orlando

Sonnet XXXV

To Guido Orlando
He explains the miracles of the Madonna of Or San
Michele, by telling whose image it is

My Lady's face it is they worship there,
At San Michele in Orto, Guido mine,
Near her fair semblance that is clear and holy,
Sinners take refuge and get consolation.
Whoso before her kneeleth reverently
No longer wasteth but is comforted;
The sick are healed and devils driven forth,
And those with crooked eyes see straightway straight.
Great ills she cureth in an open place,
With reverence the folk all kneel unto her,
And two lamps shed the glow about her form.
Her voice is borne out through far-lying ways
'Till brothers minor cry: "Idolatry,"
For envy of her precious neighborhood.

Madrigal

O world gone blind and full of false deceits,
Deadly's the poison with thy joys connected,
O treacherous thou, and guileful and suspected:
Sure he is mad who for thy checks retreats
And for scant nothing loseth that green prize
Which over-gleams all other loveliness;

Wherefore the wise man scorns thee at all hours
When he would taste the fruit of pleasant flowers.

Ballata I

Sith need hath bound my heart in bands of grief,
Sith I turn flame in pleasure's saffron fire,
I sing how I lost a treasure by desire
And left all virtue and am low descended.

I tell, with senses dead, what scant relief
My heart from war hath in his life's small might.
Nay! were not death turned pleasure in my sight
Then Love would weep to see me so offended.

Yet, for I'm come upon a madder season,
The firm opinion which I held of late
Stands in a changèd state,
And I show not how much my soul is grieved
There where I am deceived
Since through my heart midway a mistress went
And in her passage all mine hopes were spent.

Note: This is not really a ballata but is the first stanza of a lost canzone, one mentioned by Dante in the D.V.E.

Ballata II

Ladies I saw a-passing where she passed;
Not that they seemed as ladies to my vision,
Who were like nothing save her shadow cast.

I praise her in no cause save verity's
None other dispraise, if ye comprehend me.
A spirit moveth speaking prophecies
Foretelling: Spirits mine, swift death shall end ye,
Cruel! if seeing me no tears forelend ye,
Sith but the being in thought sets wide mine eyes
For sobbing out my heart's full memories.

Ballata III

Tho' all thy piteous mercy fall away
Not for thy failing shall my faith so fall,
That Faith speaks on of services unpaid
To the unpitièd heart.

What that heart feeleth? Ye believe me not.
Who sees such things? Surely no one at all,
For Love me gives a spirit on his part
Who dieth if portrayed.

Thence when that pleasure so assaileth me,
And the sighing faileth me,
Within my heart a rain of love descendeth
So fragrantly, so purely
That I cry out, "Lady, thou hold'st me surely!"

Ballata IV

Weeping ye see me, in Grief's company,
One showing forth Love's jurisdiction.
Of pity-shrouded hearts I find not one
Who sigheth, seeing me disconsolate.

New is the grief that's come upon my heart,
And mournful is the press of my deep sighs,
And oft Death greeteth me, by tricksome art
Drawn close upon me with his agonies,
Yea close, drawn close till every dullard sees;
I hear their murmuring, "How grief hath bent
This man! And we from the apparent testament,
    Deem stranger torments in him sublimate."

Within my heart this grievous weight descended
Hath slain that band of spirits which was bent
Heartward, that th' heart might by them be defended.

When the sad heart had summoned them they'd left
Mine eyes of every other guard bereft
Till Rumour, courier through the mind, ran crying,
"A vileness in the heart, Oyez! lies dying
        On guard lest vileness strike at *your* estate!"

Ballata V

Light do I see within my Lady's eyes
And loving spirits in its plenisphere
Which bear in strange delight on my heart's care
Till Joy's awakened from that sepulchre.

    That which befalls me in my Lady's presence
Bars explanations intellectual,
I seem to see a lady wonderful
Forth issue from Her lips, one whom no sense
Can fully tell the mind of and one whence
Another fair, swift born, moves marvelous,
From whom a star goes forth and speaketh thus:
"Lo, thy salvation is gone forth from thee."

    There where this Lady's loveliness appeareth,
There's heard a voice which goes before her ways
And seems to sing her name with such sweet praise
That my mouth fears to speak what name she beareth,
And my heart trembles for the grace she weareth,
While far in my soul's deep the sighs astir
Speak thus: "Look well! For if thou look on her,
Then shalt thou see her virtue risen in heaven."

Vid. Introduction.

Ballata VI

The harshness of my strange and new misventure
Hath in my mind distraught
The wonted fragrance of love's every thought.

Already is my life in such part shaken
That she, my gracious lady of delight,
Hath left my soul most desolate forsaken
And e'en the place she was, is gone from sight;
And there rests not within me so much might
That my mind can reach forth
To comprehend the flower of her worth.

This noble thought is come well winged with death,
Namely, that I shall ne'er see her again,
And this harsh torment, with no pity fraught,
Increaseth bitterness and in its strain
I cry, and find none to attend my pain,
While for the flame I feel,
I thank that lord who turns grief's fortune wheel.

Full of all anguish and within Fear's gates
The spirit of my heart lies sorrowfully,
Thanks to that Fortune who my fortune hates,
Who'th spun death's lot where it most irketh me
And given hope that's ta'en in treachery,
Which ere it died aright
Had robbed me of mine hours of delight.

O words of mine foredone and full of terror,
Whither it please ye, go forth and proclaim
Grief. Throughout all your wayfare, in your error
Make ye soft clamour of my Lady's name,
While I downcast and fallen upon shame
Keep scant shields over me,
To whomso runs, death's colours cover me.

Ballata VII

Being in thought of love I came upon
Two damsels strange
Who sang, "The joyous rains
Of love descend within us."

So quiet in their modest courtesies
Their aspect coming softly on my vision
Made me reply, "Surely ye hold the keys
O' the virtues noble, high, without omission.
Ah, little maids, hold me not in derision,
For the wound I bear within me
And this heart o' mine ha' slain me.
I was in Toulouse lately."

And then toward me they so turned their eyes
That they could see my wounded heart's ill ease,
And how a little spirit born of sighs
Had issued forth from out the cicatrice.
Perceiving so the depth of my distress,
She who was smiling, said,
"Love's joy hath vanquished
This man. Behold how greatly!"

Then she who had first mocked me, in better part
Gave me all courtesy in her replies.
She said, "That Lady, who upon thine heart
Cut her full image, clear, by Love's device,
Hath looked so fixedly in through thine eyes
That she's made Love appear there;
If thou great pain or fear bear
Recommend thee unto him!"

Then the other piteous, full of misericorde,
Fashioned for pleasure in love's fashioning:
"His heart's apparent wound, I give my word,
Was gat from eyes whose power's an o'er great thing,
Which eyes have left in his a glittering

That mine can not endure.
Tell me, hast thou a sure
Memory of those eyes?"

To her dred question with such fears attended,
"Maid o' the wood," I said, "my memories render
Tolosa and the dusk and these things blended:
A lady in a corded bodice, slender
—Mandetta is the name Love's spirits lend her—
A lightning swift to fall,
And naught within recall
Save, Death! My wounds! Her eyes!"

(Envoi)
Speed Ballatet' unto Tolosa city
And go in softly neath the golden roof
And there cry out, "Will courtesy or pity
Of any most fair lady, put to proof,
Lead me to her with whom is my behoof?"
Then if thou get *her* choice
Say, with a lowered voice,
"It is *thy* grace I seek here."

Ballata VIII

The eyes of this gentle maid of the forest
Have set my mind in such bewilderment
That all my wistful thoughts on her are bent.

So doth she pierce me when mine eyes regard her
That I hear sighs a-trembling in mine heart
As from her eyes aye sources of mine ardour
The quaint small spirits of Amor forth-dart
From which small sprites such greater powers start
That when they reach me my faint soul is sent
Exhausted forth to swoon in banishment.

I feel how from my eyes the sighs forth-fare
When my mind reasoneth with me of her,
Till I see torments raining through the air.
Draggled by griefs, which I by these incur,
Mine every strength turns mine abandoner,
And I know not what place I am toward,
Save that Death hath me in his castle-yard.

And I am so outworn that now for mercy
I am not bold to cry out even in thought,
And I find Love, who speaking saith of her, "See,
She is not one whose image could be wrought.
Unto her presence no man could be brought
Who did not well to tremble for the daring."
And I? Would swoon if I should meet her faring.

(Envoi)
Go! Ballad mine, and when thy journey has won
Unto my Lady's presence wonderful,
Speak of my anguish in some fitting fashion,
Sorrowfully thus, "My sender is sorrowful,
Lo, how he saith, he hath no hope at all
Of drawing pity from such Courtesy
As keeps his Lady's gracious company."

Ballata IX

In wood-way found I once a shepherdess,
More fair than stars are was she to my seeming.

Her hair was wavy somewhat, like dull gold.
Eyes? Love-worn, and her face like some pale rose.
With a small twig she kept her lambs in hold,
And bare her feet were bar the dew-drop's gloze;
She sang as one whom mad love holdeth close,
And joy was on her for an ornament.

I greeted her in love without delaying:
"Hast thou companion in thy solitude?"
And she replied to me most sweetly, saying,
"Nay, I am quite alone in all this wood,
But when the birds 'gin singing in their coverts
My heart is fain that time to find a lover."

As she was speaking thus of her condition
I heard the bird-song 'neath the forest shade
And thought me how 't was but the time's provision
To gather joy of this small shepherd maid.
Favour I asked her, but for kisses only,
And then I felt her pleasant arms upon me.

She held to me with a dear willfulness
Saying her heart had gone into my bosom,
She drew me on to a cool leafy place
Where I gat sight of every coloured blossom,
And there I drank in so much summer sweetness
Meseemed Love's god connived at its completeness.

Ballata X

Now can I tell you tidings of mine eyes,
News which such pleasure to my heart supplyeth
That Love himself for glory of it sigheth.

This new delight which my heart drinketh in
Was drawn from nothing save a woman seen
Who hath such charm and a so courtly mien
And such fair fashion that the heart is fain
To greet her beauty, which nor base nor mean
Can know, because its hue and qualities demand
Intelligence in him who would understand.

I see Love grow resplendent in her eyes
With such great power and such noble thought
As hold therein all gracious ecstacies,

From them there moves a soul so subtly wrought
That all compared thereto are set at naught
And judgment of her speaks no truth save this:
"A splendour strange and unforeseen she is."

(Envoi)
Go Ballatetta, forth and find my Lady,
Ask if she have it this much of mercy ready,
This namely, that she turn her eyes toward thee?
Ask in his name whose whole faith rests in her,
And if she gracious, this much grace accord thee,
Offer glad-voiced incense of sweet savour
Proclaiming of whom thou receiv'st such favour.

Ballata XI

Because no hope is left me, Ballatetta,
Of return to Tuscany,
Light-foot go thou some fleet way
Unto my Lady straightway,
And out of her courtesy
Great honour will she do thee.

Tidings thou bearest with thee sorrow-fain
Full of all grieving, overcast with fear.
On guard! Lest any one see thee or hear,
Any who holds high nature in disdeign,
For sure if so, to my increase of pain,
Thou wert made prisoner
And held afar from her,
Hereby new harms were given
Me, and after death even
Dolour and griefs renewed.

Thou knowest, Ballatetta, that Death layeth
His hand upon me whom hath Life forsaken;
Thou knowest well how great a tumult swayeth
My heart at sound of her whom each sense cryeth

Till all my mournful body is so shaken
That I can not endure here,
Would'st thou make service sure here?
Lead forth my soul with thee
(I pray thee earnestly)
When it parts from my heart here.

Ah, Ballatetta, to thy friendliness,
I do give o'er this trembling soul's poor case.
Bring thou it there where her dear pity is,
And when thou hast found that Lady of all grace
Speak through thy sighs, my Ballad, with thy face
Low bowed, thy words in sum:
"Behold, thy servant is come,
This soul who would dwell with thee,
Assundered suddenly
From Him, Love's servitor."

O smothered voice and weak that tak'st the road
Out from the weeping heart and dolorous
Go crying out my most sad mind's alarm
Forth with my soul and this song piteous
Until thou find a lady of such charm,
So sweetly intelligent
That e'en thy sorrow is rent.
Take thy fast place before her.
And thou, Soul mine, adore her
Alway, with all thy might.

Ballata XII

If all my life be but some deathly moving,
Joy dragged from heaviness;
Seeing my deep distress
How doth Love's spirit call me unto loving?

How summon up my heart for dalliance?
When 't is so sorrowful
And manacled by sighs so mournfully
That e'en the will for grace dare not advance?
Weariness over all
Spoileth that heart of power, despoiling me.
And song, sweet laughter and benignity
Are grown three grievous sighs,
Till all men's careless eyes
May see Death risen to my countenance.

Love that is born of loving like delight,
Within my heart sojourneth
And fashions a new person from desire
Yet toppleth down to vileness all his might,
So all Love's daring spurneth
That man who knoweth service and its hire.
For Love, then why doth he of me inquire?
Only because he sees
Me cry on Death for ease,
While Death doth point me on toward all mischance.

And I can cry for Grief so heavily
As hath man never,
For Death drags to my heart a heart so bent
With wandering speech of her, who cruely
Outwearieth me ever. . . .
O Mistress spoiler of my good intent.
Accursed be the hour when Amor
Was born in such a wise
That my life in his eyes
Grew matter of pleasure and acceptable!

Ballata XIII

For naught save pity do I pray thy youth
That thou have care for Mercy's cast-away;
Lo, Death's upon me in his battle array!

And my soul finds him in his decadence
So over-wearied by that spirit wried
(For whom thou car'st not till his ways be tried,
Showing thyself thus wise in ignorance
To hold him hostile) that I pray that mover
And victor and slayer of every hard-wrought thing
That ere mine end he show him conquering.

Sith at his blows, who holds life in despite,
Thou seest clear how in my barbed distress
He wounds me there where dwells mine humbleness,
Till my soul living turneth in my sight
To speech, in words that grievous sighs o'ercover.
Till mine eyes see worth's self wavering
Grant me thy mercies for my covering!

Ballata XIV

I pray ye gentles, ye who speak of grief,
Out of new clemency, for my relief
That ye disdeign not to attend my pain.

I see my heart stand up before mine eyes
While my self-slaying mournful soul receiveth
Love's mortal stroke and in that moment dies,
Yea, in the very instant he perceiveth
Milady, and yet that smiling sprite who cleaveth
To her in joy, this very one is he
Who sets the seal of my mortality.

But should ye hear my sad heart's lamentation
Then would a trembling reach your heart's mid-most.
For Love holds with me such sweet conversation
That Pity, by your sighs, ye would accost.
To all less keen than ye the sense were lost,
Nor other hearts could think soft nor speak loudly
How dire the throng of sorrows that enshroud me.

Yea from my mind behold what tears arise
As soon as it hath news of Her, Milady,
Forth move they making passage through the eyes
Wherethrough there goes a spirit sorrowing,
Which entereth the air so weak a thing
That no man else its place discovereth
Or deems it such an almoner of Death.

RIPOSTES

Gird on thy star, We'll have this out with fate.

Silet

When I behold how black, immortal ink
Drips from my deathless pen—ah, well-away!
Why should we stop at all for what I think?
There is enough in what I chance to say.

It is enough that we once came together;
What is the use of setting it to rime?
When it is autumn do we get spring weather,
Or gather may of harsh northwindish time?

It is enough that we once came together;
What if the wind have turned against the rain?
It is enough that we once came together;
Time has seen this, and will not turn again;

And who are we, who know that last intent,
To plague to-morrow with a testament!

In Exitum Cuiusdam

On a certain one's departure

"Time's bitter flood"! Oh, that's all very well,
But where's the old friend hasn't fallen off,
Or slacked his hand-grip when you first gripped fame?

I know your circle and can fairly tell
What you have kept and what you've left behind:
I know my circle and know very well
How many faces I'd have out of mind.

Apparuit

Golden rose the house, in the portal I saw
thee, a marvel, carven in subtle stuff, a
portent. Life died down in the lamp and flickered,
caught at the wonder.

Crimson, frosty with dew, the roses bend where
thou afar moving in the glamorous sun
drinkst in life of earth, of the air, the tissue
            golden about thee.

Green the ways, the breath of the fields is thine there,
open lies the land, yet the steely going
darkly hast thou dared and the dreaded æther
            parted before thee.

Swift at courage thou in the shell of gold, cast-
ing a-loose the cloak of the body, camest
straight, then shone thine oriel and the stunned light
            faded about thee.

Half the graven shoulder, the throat aflash with
strands of light inwoven about it, loveli-
est of all things, frail alabaster, ah me!
            swift in departing,

Clothed in goldish weft, delicately perfect,
gone as wind! The cloth of the magical hands!
Thou a slight thing, thou in access of cunning
            dar'dst to assume this?

The Tomb at Akr Çaar

"I am thy soul, Nikoptis. I have watched
These five millennia, and thy dead eyes
Moved not, nor ever answer my desire,
And thy light limbs, wherethrough I leapt aflame,
Burn not with me nor any saffron thing.

See, the light grass sprang up to pillow thee,
And kissed thee with a myriad grassy tongues;
But not thou me.

I have read out the gold upon the wall,
And wearied out my thought upon the signs.
And there is no new thing in all this place.

I have been kind. See, I have left the jars sealed,
Lest thou shouldst wake and whimper for thy wine.
And all thy robes I have kept smooth on thee.

O thou unmindful! How should I forget!
—Even the river many days ago,
The river, thou wast over young.
And three souls came upon Thee—
And I came.
And I flowed in upon thee, beat them off;
I have been intimate with thee, known thy ways.
Have I not touched thy palms and finger-tips,
Flowed in, and through thee and about thy heels?
How 'came I in'? Was I not thee and Thee?

And no sun comes to rest me in this place,
And I am torn against the jagged dark,
And no light beats upon me, and you say
No word, day after day.

Oh! I could get me out, despite the marks
And all their crafty work upon the door,
Out through the glass-green fields. . . .
.   .   .   .
Yet it is quiet here:
I do not go."

Portrait d'une Femme

Your mind and you are our Sargasso Sea,
London has swept about you this score years
And bright ships left you this or that in fee:
Ideas, old gossip, oddments of all things,
Strange spars of knowledge and dimmed wares of price.
Great minds have sought you—lacking someone else.

You have been second always. Tragical?
No. You preferred it to the usual thing:
One dull man, dulling and uxorious,
One average mind—with one thought less, each year.
Oh, you are patient, I have seen you sit
Hours, where something might have floated up.
And now you pay one. Yes, you richly pay.
You are a person of some interest, one comes to you
And takes strange gain away:
Trophies fished up; some curious suggestion;
Fact that leads nowhere; and a tale for two,
Pregnant with mandrakes, or with something else
That might prove useful and yet never proves,
That never fits a corner or shows use,
Or finds its hour upon the loom of days:
The tarnished, gaudy, wonderful old work;
Idols and ambergris and rare inlays,
These are your riches, your great store; and yet
For all this sea-hoard of deciduous things,
Strange woods half sodden, and new brighter stuff:
In the slow float of differing light and deep,
No! there is nothing! In the whole and all,
Nothing that's quite your own.
                    Yet this is you.

N.Y.

My City, my beloved, my white! Ah, slender,
Listen! Listen to me, and I will breathe into thee a soul.
Delicately upon the reed, attend me!

Now do I know that I am mad,
For here are a million people surly with traffic;
This is no maid.
Neither could I play upon any reed if I had one.

My City, my beloved,
Thou art a maid with no breasts,
Thou art slender as a silver reed.
Listen to me, attend me!
And I will breathe into thee a soul,
And thou shalt live for ever.

A Girl

The tree has entered my hands,
The sap has ascended my arms,
The tree has grown in my breast—
Downward,
The branches grow out of me, like arms.

Tree you are,
Moss you are,
You are violets with wind above them.
A child—*so* high—you are,
And all this is folly to the world.

"Phasellus Ille"

This *papier-mâché*, which you see, my friends,
Saith 'twas the worthiest of editors.
Its mind was made up in "the seventies,"
Nor hath it ever since changed that concoction.
It works to represent that school of thought
Which brought the hair-cloth chair to such perfection,
Nor will the horrid threats of Bernard Shaw
Shake up the stagnant pool of its convictions;
Nay, should the deathless voice of all the world
Speak once again for its sole stimulation,
'Twould not move it one jot from left to right.

Come Beauty barefoot from the Cyclades,
She'd find a model for St. Anthony
In this thing's sure *decorum* and behaviour.

An Object

This thing, that hath a code and not a core,
Hath set acquaintance where might be affections,
And nothing now
Disturbeth his reflections.

Quies

This is another of our ancient loves.
Pass and be silent, Rullus, for the day
Hath lacked a something since this lady passed;
Hath lacked a something. 'Twas but marginal.

The Seafarer

(From the early Anglo-Saxon text)

May I for my own self song's truth reckon,
Journey's jargon, how I in harsh days
Hardship endured oft.
Bitter breast-cares have I abided,
Known on my keel many a care's hold,
And dire sea-surge, and there I oft spent
Narrow nightwatch nigh the ship's head
While she tossed close to cliffs. Coldly afflicted,
My feet were by frost benumbed.
Chill its chains are; chafing sighs
Hew my heart round and hunger begot
Mere-weary mood. Lest man know not
That he on dry land loveliest liveth,
List how I, care-wretched, on ice-cold sea,
Weathered the winter, wretched outcast
Deprived of my kinsmen;
Hung with hard ice-flakes, where hail-scur flew,
There I heard naught save the harsh sea
And ice-cold wave, at whiles the swan cries,
Did for my games the gannet's clamour,
Sea-fowls' loudness was for me laughter,
The mews' singing all my mead-drink.

Storms, on the stone-cliffs beaten, fell on the stern
In icy feathers; full oft the eagle screamed
With spray on his pinion.
      Not any protector
May make merry man faring needy.
This he little believes, who aye in winsome life
Abides 'mid burghers some heavy business,
Wealthy and wine-flushed, how I weary oft
Must bide above brine.
Neareth nightshade, snoweth from north,
Frost froze the land, hail fell on earth then
Corn of the coldest. Nathless there knocketh now
The heart's thought that I on high streams
The salt-wavy tumult traverse alone.
Moaneth alway my mind's lust
That I fare forth, that I afar hence
Seek out a foreign fastness.
For this there's no mood-lofty man over earth's midst,
Not though he be given his good, but will have in his
   youth greed;
Nor his deed to the daring, nor his king to the faithful
But shall have his sorrow for sea-fare
Whatever his lord will.
He hath not heart for harping, nor in ring-having
Nor winsomeness to wife, nor world's delight
Nor any whit else save the wave's slash,
Yet longing comes upon him to fare forth on the water.
Bosque taketh blossom, cometh beauty of berries,
Fields to fairness, land fares brisker,
All this admonisheth man eager of mood,
The heart turns to travel so that he then thinks
On flood-ways to be far departing.
Cuckoo calleth with gloomy crying,
He singeth summerward, bodeth sorrow,
The bitter heart's blood. Burgher knows not—
He the prosperous man—what some perform
Where wandering them widest draweth.
So that but now my heart burst from my breast-lock,
My mood 'mid the mere-flood,
Over the whale's acre, would wander wide.

On earth's shelter cometh often to me,
Eager and ready, the crying lone-flyer,
Whets for the whale-path the heart irresistibly,
O'er tracks of ocean; seeing that anyhow
My lord deems to me this dead life
On loan and on land, I believe not
That any earth-weal eternal standeth
Save there be somewhat calamitous
That, ere a man's tide go, turn it to twain.
Disease or oldness or sword-hate
Beats out the breath from doom-gripped body.
And for this, every earl whatever, for those speaking after—
Laud of the living, boasteth some last word,
That he will work ere he pass onward,
Frame on the fair earth 'gainst foes his malice,
Daring ado, . . .
So that all men shall honour him after
And his laud beyond them remain 'mid the English,
Aye, for ever, a lasting life's-blast,
Delight mid the doughty.
                                        Days little durable,
And all arrogance of earthen riches,
There come now no kings nor Cæsars
Nor gold-giving lords like those gone.
Howe'er in mirth most magnified,
Whoe'er lived in life most lordliest,
Drear all this excellence, delights undurable!
Waneth the watch, but the world holdeth.
Tomb hideth trouble. The blade is layed low.
Earthly glory ageth and seareth.
No man at all going the earth's gait,
But age fares against him, his face paleth,
Grey-haired he groaneth, knows gone companions,
Lordly men are to earth o'ergiven,
Nor may he then the flesh-cover, whose life ceaseth,
Nor eat the sweet nor feel the sorry,
Nor stir hand nor think in mid heart,
And though he strew the grave with gold,
His born brothers, their buried bodies
Be an unlikely treasure hoard.

Echoes

I

GUIDO ORLANDO, SINGING

Befits me praise thine empery, Lady of Valour,
Past all disproving;
Thou art the flower to me—
    Nay, by Love's pallor—
Of all good loving.

Worthy to reap men's praises
Is he who'd gaze upon
    Truth's mazes.
In like commend is he,
Who, loving fixedly,
Love so refineth,

Till thou alone art she
    In whom love's vested;
As branch hath fairest flower
    Where fruit's suggested.

II*

Thou keep'st thy rose-leaf
Till the rose-time will be over,
Think'st thou that Death will kiss thee?
Think'st thou that the Dark House
    Will find thee such a lover
As I? Will the new roses miss thee?

Prefer my cloak unto the cloak of dust
    'Neath which the last year lies,
For thou shouldst more mistrust
    Time than my eyes.

* Asclepiades, Julianus Ægyptus.

This great joy comes to me,
 To me observing
How swiftly thou hast power
 To pay my serving.

An Immorality

Sing we for love and idleness,
Naught else is worth the having.

Though I have been in many a land,
There is naught else in living.

And I would rather have my sweet,
Though rose-leaves die of grieving,

Than do high deeds in Hungary
To pass all men's believing.

Dieu! Qu'Il La Fait

From Charles D'Orleans
For music

God! that mad'st her well regard her,
How she is so fair and bonny;
For the great charms that are upon her
Ready are all folk to reward her.

Who could part him from her borders
When spells are alway renewed on her?
God! that mad'st her well regard her,
How she is so fair and bonny.

From here to there to the sea's border,
Dame nor damsel there's not any
Hath of perfect charms so many.
Thoughts of her are of dream's order:
God! that mad'st her well regard her.

Δώρια

Be in me as the eternal moods
          of the bleak wind, and not
     As transient things are—
          gaiety of flowers.
Have me in the strong loneliness
          of sunless cliffs
And of grey waters.
               Let the gods speak softly of us
In days hereafter,
               The shadowy flowers of Orcus
Remember Thee.

The Needle

Come, or the stellar tide will slip away.
Eastward avoid the hour of its decline,
Now! for the needle trembles in my soul!

Here have we had our vantage, the good hour.
Here we have had our day, your day and mine.
Come now, before this power
That bears us up, shall turn against the pole.

Mock not the flood of stars, the thing's to be.
O Love, come now, this land turns evil slowly.
The waves bore in, soon will they bear away.

The treasure is ours, make we fast land with it.
Move we and take the tide, with its next favour,
Abide
Under some neutral force
Until this course turneth aside.

Sub Mare

It is, and is not, I am sane enough,
Since you have come this place has hovered round me,
This fabrication built of autumn roses,
Then there's a goldish colour, different.

And one gropes in these things as delicate
Algæ reach up and out, beneath
Pale slow green surgings of the underwave,
'Mid these things older than the names they have,
These things that are familiars of the god.

Plunge

I would bathe myself in strangeness:
These comforts heaped upon me, smother me!
I burn, I scald so for the new,
New friends, new faces,
Places!
Oh to be out of this,
This that is all I wanted
            —save the new.
And you,
Love, you the much, the more desired!
Do I not loathe all walls, streets, stones,
All mire, mist, all fog,
All ways of traffic?
You, I would have flow over me like water,
Oh, but far out of this!
Grass, and low fields, and hills,
And sun,
Oh, sun enough!
Out and alone, among some
Alien people!

A Virginal

No, no! Go from me. I have left her lately.
I will not spoil my sheath with lesser brightness,
For my surrounding air has a new lightness;
Slight are her arms, yet they have bound me straitly
And left me cloaked as with a gauze of æther;
As with sweet leaves; as with a subtle clearness.
Oh, I have picked up magic in her nearness
To sheathe me half in half the things that sheathe her.

No, no! Go from me. I have still the flavour,
Soft as spring wind that's come from birchen bowers.
Green come the shoots, aye April in the branches,
As winter's wound with her sleight hand she staunches,
Hath of the trees a likeness of the savour:
As white their bark, so white this lady's hours.

Pan Is Dead

Pan is dead. Great Pan is dead.
Ah! bow your heads, ye maidens all,
And weave ye him his coronal.

There is no summer in the leaves,
And withered are the sedges;
How shall we weave a coronal,
Or gather floral pledges?

That I may not say, Ladies.
Death was ever a churl.
That I may not say, Ladies.
How should he show a reason,
That he has taken our Lord away
Upon such hollow season?

The Picture*

The eyes of this dead lady speak to me,
For here was love, was not to be drowned out,
And here desire, not to be kissed away.

The eyes of this dead lady speak to me.

* "Venus Reclining," by Jacopo del Sellaio (1442–93)

Of Jacopo del Sellaio

This man knew out the secret ways of love,
No man could paint such things who did not know.

And now she's gone, who was his Cyprian,
And you are here, who are "The Isles" to me.

And here's the thing that lasts the whole thing out:
The eyes of this dead lady speak to me.

The Return

See, they return; ah, see the tentative
    Movements, and the slow feet,
    The trouble in the pace and the uncertain
Wavering!

See, they return, one, and by one,
With fear, as half-awakened;
As if the snow should hesitate
And murmur in the wind,
            and half turn back;
These were the "Wing'd-with-Awe,"
            Inviolable.

Gods of the wingèd shoe!
With them the silver hounds,
            sniffing the trace of air!

Haie! Haie!
>These were the swift to harry;
>These the keen-scented;
>These were the souls of blood.

>Slow on the leash,
>>>>pallid the leash-men!

Effects of Music upon a Company of People

I

DEUX MOUVEMENTS
>1. *Temple qui fut.*
>2. *Poissons d'or.*

1

A soul curls back,
>Their souls like petals,
>Thin, long, spiral,
Like those of a chrysanthemum curl
Smoke-like up and back from the
Vavicel, the calyx,
Pale green, pale gold, transparent,
Green of plasma, rose-white,
Spirate like smoke,
Curled,
Vibrating,
Slowly, waving slowly.
O Flower animate!
O calyx!
O crowd of foolish people!

2

The petals!
On the tip of each the figure
Delicate.
See, they dance, step to step.
Flora to festival,

Twine, bend, bow,
Frolic involve ye.
Woven the step,
Woven the tread, the moving.
Ribands they move,
Wave, bow to the centre.
Pause, rise, deepen in colour,
And fold in drowsily.

II
FROM A THING BY SCHUMANN

Breast high, floating and welling
　　Their soul, moving beneath the satin,
　　Plied the gold threads,
Pushed at the gauze above it.
The notes beat upon this,
Beat and indented it;
Rain dropped and came and fell upon this,
Hail and snow,
My sight gone in the flurry!

And then across the white silken,
Bellied up, as a sail bellies to the wind,
Over the fluid tenuous, diaphanous,
Over this curled a wave, greenish,
Mounted and overwhelmed it.
This membrane floating above,
And bellied out by the up-pressing soul.

Then came a mer-host,
And after them legion of Romans.
The usual, dull, theatrical!

FROM

CATHAY

FOR THE MOST PART FROM THE CHINESE
OF RIHAKU, FROM THE NOTES OF THE
LATE ERNEST FENOLLOSA, AND
THE DECIPHERINGS OF THE
PROFESSORS MORI
AND ARIGA

RIHAKU flourished in the eighth century of our era. The Anglo-Saxon Seafarer is of about this period. The other poems from the Chinese are earlier.

Song of the Bowmen of Shu

Here we are, picking the first fern-shoots
And saying: When shall we get back to our country?
Here we are because we have the Ken-nin for our foemen,
We have no comfort because of these Mongols.
We grub the soft fern-shoots,
When anyone says "Return," the others are full of sorrow.
Sorrowful minds, sorrow is strong, we are hungry and thirsty.
Our defence is not yet made sure, no one can let his friend
    return.
We grub the old fern-stalks.
We say: Will we be let to go back in October?
There is no ease in royal affairs, we have no comfort.
Our sorrow is bitter, but we would not return to our country.
What flower has come into blossom?
Whose chariot? The General's.
Horses, his horses even, are tired. They were strong.
We have no rest, three battles a month.
By heaven, his horses are tired.
The generals are on them, the soldiers are by them
The horses are well trained, the generals have ivory arrows
    and quivers ornamented with fish-skin.
The enemy is swift, we must be careful.
When we set out, the willows were drooping with spring,
We come back in the snow,
We go slowly, we are hungry and thirsty,
Our mind is full of sorrow, who will know of our grief?

By Kutsugen.
4th Century B.C.

The Beautiful Toilet

Blue, blue is the grass about the river
And the willows have overfilled the close garden.
And within, the mistress, in the midmost of her youth,
White, white of face, hesitates, passing the door.
Slender, she puts forth a slender hand,

249

And she was a courtezan in the old days,
And she has married a sot,
Who now goes drunkenly out
And leaves her too much alone.

By Mei Sheng.
B.C. *140*.

The River Song

This boat is of shato-wood, and its gunwales are cut
    magnolia,
Musicians with jewelled flutes and with pipes of gold
Fill full the sides in rows, and our wine
Is rich for a thousand cups.
We carry singing girls, drift with the drifting water,
Yet Sennin needs
A yellow stork for a charger, and all our seamen
Would follow the white gulls or ride them.
Kutsu's prose song
Hangs with the sun and moon.

King So's terraced palace
                        is now but a barren hill,
But I draw pen on this barge
Causing the five peaks to tremble,
And I have joy in these words
                        like the joy of blue islands.
(If glory could last forever
Then the waters of Han would flow northward.)

And I have moped in the Emperor's garden, awaiting an
    order-to-write!
I looked at the dragon-pond, with its willow-coloured water
Just reflecting the sky's tinge,
And heard the five-score nightingales aimlessly singing.

The eastern wind brings the green colour into the island
    grasses at Yei-shu,
The purple house and the crimson are full of Spring softness.

South of the pond the willow-tips are half-blue and bluer,
Their cords tangle in mist, against the brocade-like palace.
Vine-strings a hundred feet long hang down from carved
    railings,
And high over the willows, the fine birds sing to each other,
    and listen,
Crying—"Kwan, Kuan," for the early wind, and the feel of it.
The wind bundles itself into a bluish cloud and wanders off.
Over a thousand gates, over a thousand doors are the sounds
    of spring singing,
And the Emperor is at Ko.
Five clouds hang aloft, bright on the purple sky,
The imperial guards come forth from the golden house with
    their armour a-gleaming.
The emperor in his jewelled car goes out to inspect his
    flowers,
He goes out to Hori, to look at the wing-flapping storks,
He returns by way of Sei rock, to hear the new nightingales,
For the gardens at Jo-run are full of new nightingales,
Their sound is mixed in this flute,
Their voice is in the twelve pipes here.

By Rihaku.
8th Century A.D.

The River-Merchant's Wife: A Letter

While my hair was still cut straight across my forehead
I played about the front gate, pulling flowers.
You came by on bamboo stilts, playing horse,
You walked about my seat, playing with blue plums.
And we went on living in the village of Chokan:
Two small people, without dislike or suspicion.

At fourteen I married My Lord you.
I never laughed, being bashful.
Lowering my head, I looked at the wall.
Called to, a thousand times, I never looked back.

At fifteen I stopped scowling,
I desired my dust to be mingled with yours
Forever and forever, and forever.
Why should I climb the look out?

At sixteen you departed,
You went into far Ku-to-Yen, by the river of swirling eddies,
And you have been gone five months.
The monkeys make sorrowful noise overhead.
You dragged your feet when you went out.
By the gate now, the moss is grown, the different mosses,
Too deep to clear them away!
The leaves fall early this autumn, in wind.
The paired butterflies are already yellow with August
Over the grass in the West garden,
They hurt me.
I grow older,
If you are coming down through the narrows of the river
      Kiang,
Please let me know beforehand,
And I will come out to meet you,
                              As far as Cho-fu-Sa.

                                            By Rihaku.

The Jewel Stairs' Grievance

The jewelled steps are already quite white with dew,
It is so late that the dew soaks my gauze stockings,
And I let down the crystal curtain
And watch the moon through the clear autumn.

                                            By Rihaku.

NOTE.—Jewel stairs, therefore a palace. Grievance, therefore there is something to complain of. Gauze stockings, therefore a court lady, not a servant who complains. Clear autumn, therefore he has no excuse on account of weather. Also she has come early, for the dew has not merely whitened the stairs, but has soaked her stockings. The poem is especially prized because she utters no direct reproach.

Poem by the Bridge at Ten-Shin

March has come to the bridge head,
Peach boughs and apricot boughs hang over a thousand
    gates,
At morning there are flowers to cut the heart,
And evening drives them on the eastward-flowing waters.
Petals are on the gone waters and on the going,
    And on the back-swirling eddies,
But to-day's men are not the men of the old days,
Though they hang in the same way over the bridge-rail.

The sea's colour moves at the dawn
And the princes still stand in rows, about the throne,
And the moon falls over the portals of Sei-go-yo,
And clings to the walls and the gate-top.
With head-gear glittering against the cloud and sun,
The lords go forth from the court, and into far borders.
They ride upon dragon-like horses,
Upon horses with head-trappings of yellow-metal,
And the streets make way for their passage.
        Haughty their passing,
Haughty their steps as they go into great banquets,
To high halls and curious food,
To the perfumed air and girls dancing,
To clear flutes and clear singing;
To the dance of the seventy couples;
To the mad chase through the gardens.
Night and day are given over to pleasure
And they think it will last a thousand autumns,
        Unwearying autumns.
For them the yellow dogs howl portents in vain,
And what are they compared to the lady Riokushu,
      That was cause of hate!
Who among them is a man like Han-rei
      Who departed alone with his mistress,
With her hair unbound, and he his own skiffs-man!

By Rihaku.

Lament of the Frontier Guard

By the North Gate, the wind blows full of sand,
Lonely from the beginning of time until now!
Trees fall, the grass goes yellow with autumn.
I climb the towers and towers
                    to watch out the barbarous land:
Desolate castle, the sky, the wide desert.
There is no wall left to this village.
Bones white with a thousand frosts,
High heaps, covered with trees and grass;
Who brought this to pass?
Who has brought the flaming imperial anger?
Who has brought the army with drums and with
        kettle-drums?
Barbarous kings.
A gracious spring, turned to blood-ravenous autumn,
A turmoil of wars-men, spread over the middle kingdom,
Three hundred and sixty thousand,
And sorrow, sorrow like rain.
Sorrow to go, and sorrow, sorrow returning,
Desolate, desolate fields,
And no children of warfare upon them,
            No longer the men for offence and defence.
Ah, how shall you know the dreary sorrow at the
            North Gate,
With Rihoku's name forgotten,
And we guardsmen fed to the tigers.

                                                              Rihaku.

Exile's Letter

To So-Kin of Rakuyo, ancient friend, Chancellor of Gen.
Now I remember that you built me a special tavern
By the south side of the bridge at Ten-Shin.
With yellow gold and white jewels, we paid for songs and
        laughter
And we were drunk for month on month, forgetting the
        kings and princes.

Intelligent men came drifting in from the sea and from the
    west border,
And with them, and with you especially
There was nothing at cross purpose,
And they made nothing of sea-crossing or of mountain
    crossing,
If only they could be of that fellowship,
And we all spoke out our hearts and minds, and without
    regret.

And then I was sent off to South Wei,
              smothered in laurel groves,
And you to the north of Raku-hoku,
Till we had nothing but thoughts and memories in common.

And then, when separation had come to its worst,
We met, and travelled into Sen-Go,
Through all the thirty-six folds of the turning and twisting
    waters,
Into a valley of the thousand bright flowers,
That was the first valley;
And into ten thousand valleys full of voices and pine-winds.
And with silver harness and reins of gold,
Out come the East of Kan foreman and his company.
And there came also the "True man" of Shi-yo to meet me,
Playing on a jewelled mouth-organ.
In the storied houses of San-Ko they gave us more Sennin
    music,
Many instruments, like the sound of young phoenix broods.
The foreman of Kan Chu, drunk, danced
            because his long sleeves wouldn't keep still
With that music-playing.
And I, wrapped in brocade, went to sleep with my head on
    his lap,
And my spirit so high it was all over the heavens,
And before the end of the day we were scattered like stars, or
    rain.
I had to be off to So, far away over the waters,
You back to your river-bridge.

And your father, who was brave as a leopard,
Was governor in Hei Shu, and put down the barbarian rabble.
And one May he had you send for me,
         despite the long distance.
And what with broken wheels and so on, I won't say it
    wasn't hard going,
Over roads twisted like sheeps' guts.
And I was still going, late in the year,
         in the cutting wind from the North,
And thinking how little you cared for the cost,
         and you caring enough to pay it.
And what a reception:
Red jade cups, food well set on a blue jewelled table,
And I was drunk, and had no thought of returning.
And you would walk out with me to the western corner of
    the castle,
To the dynastic temple, with water about it clear as blue jade,
With boats floating, and the sound of mouth-organs and
    drums,
With ripples like dragon-scales, going grass green on the
    water,
Pleasure lasting, with courtezans, going and coming without
    hindrance,
With the willow flakes falling like snow,
And the vermilioned girls getting drunk about sunset,
And the water a hundred feet deep reflecting green eyebrows
—Eyebrows painted green are a fine sight in young
    moonlight,
Gracefully painted—
And the girls singing back at each other,
Dancing in transparent brocade,
And the wind lifting the song, and interrupting it,
Tossing it up under the clouds.
         And all this comes to an end.
         And is not again to be met with.
I went up to the court for examination,
Tried Layu's luck, offered the Choyo song,
And got no promotion,
         and went back to the East Mountains white-
         headed.

And once again, later, we met at the South bridge-head.
And then the crowd broke up, you went north to San palace,
And if you ask how I regret that parting:
    It is like the flowers falling at Spring's end
            Confused, whirled in a tangle.
What is the use of talking, and there is no end of talking,
There is no end of things in the heart.

I call in the boy,
Have him sit on his knees here
            To seal this,
And send it a thousand miles, thinking.

By Rihaku.

From Rihaku

Four Poems of Departure

Light rain is on the light dust.
The willows of the inn-yard
Will be going greener and greener,
But you, Sir, had better take wine ere your departure,
For you will have no friends about you
When you come to the gates of Go.

SEPARATION ON THE RIVER KIANG

Ko-jin goes west from Ko-kaku-ro,
The smoke-flowers are blurred over the river.
His lone sail blots the far sky.
And now I see only the river,
            The long Kiang, reaching heaven.

TAKING LEAVE OF A FRIEND

Blue mountains to the north of the walls,
White river winding about them;
Here we must make separation
And go out through a thousand miles of dead grass.

Tenzone

Will people accept them?
    (i.e. these songs).
As a timorous wench from a centaur
    (or a centurion),
Already they flee, howling in terror.

Will they be touched with the verisimilitudes?
    Their virgin stupidity is untemptable.
I beg you, my friendly critics,
Do not set about to procure me an audience.

I mate with my free kind upon the crags;
    the hidden recesses
Have heard the echo of my heels,
    in the cool light,
    in the darkness.

The Condolence

A mis soledades voy,
De mis soledades vengo,
Porque por andar conmigo
Mi bastan mis pensamientos.
          Lope de Vega.

O my fellow sufferers, songs of my youth,
A lot of asses praise you because you are "virile,"
We, you, I! We are "Red Bloods"!
Imagine it, my fellow sufferers—
Our maleness lifts us out of the ruck,
    Who'd have foreseen it?

O my fellow sufferers, we went out under the trees,
We were in especial bored with male stupidity.
We went forth gathering delicate thoughts,
Our "*fantastikon*" delighted to serve us.
We were not exasperated with women,
    for the female is ductile.

263

And now you hear what is said to us:
We are compared to that sort of person
Who wanders about announcing his sex
As if he had just discovered it.
Let us leave this matter, my songs,
                and return to that which concerns us.

The Garret

Come, let us pity those who are better off than we are.
Come, my friend, and remember
            that the rich have butlers and no friends,
And we have friends and no butlers.
Come, let us pity the married and the unmarried.

Dawn enters with little feet
            like a gilded Pavlova,
And I am near my desire.
Nor has life in it aught better
Than this hour of clear coolness,
            the hour of waking together.

The Garden

En robe de parade.
                Samain

Like a skein of loose silk blown against a wall
She walks by the railing of a path in Kensington Gardens,
And she is dying piece-meal
            of a sort of emotional anæmia.

And round about there is a rabble
Of the filthy, sturdy, unkillable infants of the very poor.
They shall inherit the earth.

In her is the end of breeding.
Her boredom is exquisite and excessive.

She would like some one to speak to her,
And is almost afraid that I
      will commit that indiscretion.

Ortus

How have I laboured?
How have I not laboured
To bring her soul to birth,
To give these elements a name and a centre!

She is beautiful as the sunlight, and as fluid.
She has no name, and no place.
How have I laboured to bring her soul into separation;
To give her a name and her being!

Surely you are bound and entwined,
You are mingled with the elements unborn;
I have loved a stream and a shadow.

I beseech you enter your life.
I beseech you learn to say "I"
When I question you:
For you are no part, but a whole;
No portion, but a being.

Salutation

O generation of the thoroughly smug
      and thoroughly uncomfortable,
I have seen fishermen picnicking in the sun,
I have seen them with untidy families,
I have seen their smiles full of teeth
      and heard ungainly laughter.
And I am happier than you are,
And they were happier than I am;
And the fish swim in the lake
      and do not even own clothing.

Salutation the Second

You were praised, my books,
           because I had just come from the country;
I was twenty years behind the times
           so you found an audience ready.
I do not disown you,
           do not you disown your progeny.

Here they stand without quaint devices,
Here they are with nothing archaic about them.
Watch the reporters spit,
Watch the anger of the professors,
Watch how the pretty ladies revile them:

"Is this," they say, "the nonsense
           that we expect of poets?"
"Where is the Picturesque?"
           "Where is the vertigo of emotion?"
"No! his first work was the best."
           "Poor Dear! he has lost his illusions."

Go, little naked and impudent songs,
Go with a light foot!
(Or with two light feet, if it please you!)
Go and dance shamelessly!
Go with an impertinent frolic!

Greet the grave and the stodgy,
Salute them with your thumbs at your noses.

Here are your bells and confetti.
Go! rejuvenate things!
Rejuvenate even "The Spectator."
           Go! and make cat calls!
Dance and make people blush,
Dance the dance of the phallus
           and tell anecdotes of Cybele!
Speak of the indecorous conduct of the Gods!

(Tell it to Mr. Strachey)

Ruffle the skirts of prudes,
      speak of their knees and ankles.
But, above all, go to practical people—
      go! jangle their door-bells!
Say that you do no work
      and that you will live forever.

The Spring

Cydonian Spring with her attendant train,
Meliads and water-girls.
Stepping beneath a boisterous wind from Thrace,
Throughout this sylvan place
Spreads the bright tips,
And every vine-stock is
Clad in new brilliancies.
                And wild desire
Falls like black lightning.
O bewildered heart,
Though every branch have back what last year lost,
She, who moved here amid the cyclamen,
Moves only now a clinging tenuous ghost.

Albâtre

This lady in the white bath-robe which she calls a peignoir
Is, for the time being, the mistress of my friend,
And the delicate white feet of her little white dog
Are not more delicate than she is,
Nor would Gautier himself have despised their contrasts in
      whiteness
As she sits in the great chair
Between the two indolent candles.

Causa

I join these words for four people,
Some others may overhear them,
O world, I am sorry for you,
You do not know these four people.

Commission

Go, my songs, to the lonely and the unsatisfied,
Go also to the nerve-wracked, go to the enslaved-by-
    convention,
Bear to them my contempt for their oppressors.
Go as a great wave of cool water,
Bear my contempt of oppressors.

Speak against unconscious oppression,
Speak against the tyranny of the unimaginative,
Speak against bonds.
Go to the bourgeoise who is dying of her ennuis,
Go to the women in suburbs.
Go to the hideously wedded,
Go to them whose failure is concealed,
Go to the unluckily mated,
Go to the bought wife,
Go to the woman entailed.

Go to those who have delicate lust,
Go to those whose delicate desires are thwarted,
Go like a blight upon the dulness of the world;
Go with your edge against this,
Strengthen the subtle cords,
Bring confidence upon the algae and the tentacles of the soul.

Go in a friendly manner,
Go with an open speech.
Be eager to find new evils and new good,
Be against all forms of oppression.
Go to those who are thickened with middle age,
To those who have lost their interest.

Go to the adolescent who are smothered in family—
Oh how hideous it is
To see three generations of one house gathered together!
It is like an old tree with shoots,
And with some branches rotted and falling.

Go out and defy opinion,
Go against this vegetable bondage of the blood.
Be against all sorts of mortmain.

A Pact

I make a pact with you, Walt Whitman—
I have detested you long enough.
I come to you as a grown child
Who has had a pig-headed father;
I am old enough now to make friends.
It was you that broke the new wood,
Now is a time for carving.
We have one sap and one root—
Let there be commerce between us.

Surgit Fama

There is a truce among the gods,
Korè is seen in the North
Skirting the blue-gray sea
In gilded and russet mantle.

The corn has again its mother and she, Leuconoë,
That failed never women,
Fails not the earth now.

The tricksome Hermes is here;
He moves behind me
Eager to catch my words,
Eager to spread them with rumour;

To set upon them his change
Crafty and subtle;
To alter them to his purpose;
But do thou speak true, even to the letter:

"Once more in Delos, once more is the altar a-quiver.
Once more is the chant heard.
Once more are the never abandoned gardens
Full of gossip and old tales."

Preference

It is true that you say the gods are more use to you than
       fairies,
But for all that I have seen you
       on a high, white, noble horse,
Like some strange queen in a story.

It is odd that you should be covered with long robes and
       trailing tendrils and flowers;
It is odd that you should be changing your face
       and resembling some other woman to plague me;
It is odd that you should be hiding yourself
In the cloud of beautiful women who do not concern me.

And I, who follow every seed-leaf upon the wind?
You will say that I deserve this.

Dance Figure

For the Marriage in Cana of Galilee

Dark eyed,
O woman of my dreams,
Ivory sandaled,
There is none like thee among the dancers,
None with swift feet.

I have not found thee in the tents,
In the broken darkness.
I have not found thee at the well-head
Among the women with pitchers.

Thine arms are as a young sapling under the bark;
Thy face as a river with lights.

White as an almond are thy shoulders;
As new almonds stripped from the husk.

They guard thee not with eunuchs;
Not with bars of copper.

Gilt turquoise and silver are in the place of thy rest.
A brown robe, with threads of gold woven in patterns,
          hast thou gathered about thee,
O Nathat-Ikanaie, "Tree-at-the-river."

As a rillet among the sedge are thy hands upon me;
Thy fingers a frosted stream.

Thy maidens are white like pebbles;
Their music about thee!

There is none like thee among the dancers;
None with swift feet.

April

Nympharum membra disjecta

Three spirits came to me
And drew me apart
To where the olive boughs
Lay stripped upon the ground:
Pale carnage beneath bright mist.

Gentildonna

She passed and left no quiver in the veins, who now
Moving among the trees, and clinging

in the air she severed,
Fanning the grass she walked on then, endures:

Grey olive leaves beneath a rain-cold sky.

The Rest

O helpless few in my country,
O remnant enslaved!

Artists broken against her,
A-stray, lost in the villages,
Mistrusted, spoken-against,

Lovers of beauty, starved,
Thwarted with systems,
Helpless against the control;

You who can not wear yourselves out
By persisting to successes,
You who can only speak,
Who can not steel yourselves into reiteration;

You of the finer sense,
Broken against false knowledge,
You who can know at first hand,
Hated, shut in, mistrusted:

Take thought:
I have weathered the storm,
I have beaten out my exile.

Les Millwin

The little Millwins attend the Russian Ballet.
The mauve and greenish souls of the little Millwins
Were seen lying along the upper seats
Like so many unused boas.

The turbulent and undisciplined host of art students—
The rigorous deputation from "Slade"—
Was before them.
With arms exalted, with fore-arms
Crossed in great futuristic X's, the art students
Exulted, they beheld the splendours of *Cleopatra*.

And the little Millwins beheld these things;
With their large and anæmic eyes they looked out upon this
    configuration.

Let us therefore mention the fact,
For it seems to us worthy of record.

Further Instructions

Come, my songs, let us express our baser passions,
Let us express our envy of the man with a steady job and no
    worry about the future.
You are very idle, my songs.
I fear you will come to a bad end.
You stand about in the streets,
You loiter at the corners and bus-stops,
You do next to nothing at all.

You do not even express our inner nobilities,
You will come to a very bad end.

And I?
I have gone half cracked,
I have talked to you so much that
                    I almost see you about me,
Insolent little beasts, shameless, devoid of clothing!

But you, newest song of the lot,
You are not old enough to have done much mischief,
I will get you a green coat out of China
With dragons worked upon it,
I will get you the scarlet silk trousers
From the statue of the infant Christ at Santa Maria Novella,
Lest they say we are lacking in taste,
Or that there is no caste in this family.

A Song of the Degrees

I

Rest me with Chinese colours,
For I think the glass is evil.

II

The wind moves above the wheat—
With a silver crashing,
A thin war of metal.

I have known the golden disc,
I have seen it melting above me.
I have known the stone-bright place,
       The hall of clear colours.

III

O glass subtly evil, O confusion of colours!
O light bound and bent in, O soul of the captive,
Why am I warned? Why am I sent away?
Why is your glitter full of curious mistrust?
O glass subtle and cunning, O powdery gold!
O filaments of amber, two-faced iridescence!

Ité

Go, my songs, seek your praise from the young and from the
    intolerant,
Move among the lovers of perfection alone.
Seek ever to stand in the hard Sophoclean light
And take your wounds from it gladly.

Dum Capitolium Scandet

How many will come after me
        singing as well as I sing, none better;
Telling the heart of their truth
        as I have taught them to tell it;
Fruit of my seed,
        O my unnameable children.
Know then that I loved you from afore-time,
Clear speakers, naked in the sun, untrammelled.

Το Καλόν

Even in my dreams you have denied yourself to me
And sent me only your handmaids.

The Study in Aesthetics

The very small children in patched clothing,
Being smitten with an unusual wisdom,
Stopped in their play as she passed them
And cried up from their cobbles:
        Guarda! Ahi, guarda! ch' è be'a*!

But three years after this
I heard the young Dante, whose last name I do not know—

* Bella.

For there are, in Sirmione, twenty-eight young Dantes and
    thirty-four Catulli;
And there had been a great catch of sardines,
And his elders
Were packing them in the great wooden boxes
For the market in Brescia, and he
Leapt about, snatching at the bright fish
And getting in both of their ways;
And in vain they commanded him to *sta fermo!*
And when they would not let him arrange
The fish in the boxes
He stroked those which were already arranged,
Murmuring for his own satisfaction
This identical phrase:
      Ch' è be'a.
And at this I was mildly abashed.

The Bellaires

*Aus meinen grossen Schmerzen
Mach' ich die kleinen Lieder*

The good Bellaires
Do not understand the conduct of this world's affairs.
In fact they understood them so badly
That they have had to cross the Channel.
Nine lawyers, four counsels, five judges and three proctors of
    the King,
Together with the respective wives, husbands, sisters and
    heterogeneous connections of the good Bellaires,
Met to discuss their affairs;
But the good Bellaires have so little understood their affairs
That now there is no one at all
Who can understand any affair of theirs. Yet
Fourteen hunters still eat in the stables of
The good Squire Bellaire;
But these may not suffer attainder,
For they may not belong to the good Squire Bellaire
But to his wife.

On the contrary, if they do not belong to his wife,
He will plead
A "freedom from attainder"
For twelve horses and also for twelve boarhounds
From Charles the Fourth;
And a further freedom for the remainder
Of horses, from Henry the Fourth.
But the judges,
Being free of mediæval scholarship,
Will pay no attention to this,
And there will be only the more confusion,
Replevin, estoppel, espavin and what not.

Nine lawyers, four counsels, etc.,
Met to discuss their affairs,
But the sole result was bills
From lawyers to whom no one was indebted,
And even the lawyers
Were uncertain who was supposed to be indebted to them.

Wherefore the good Squire Bellaire
Resides now at Agde and Biaucaire.
To Carcassonne, Pui, and Alais
He fareth from day to day,
Or takes the sea air
Between Marseilles
And Beziers.

And for all this I have considerable regret,
For the good Bellaires
Are very charming people.

The New Cake of Soap

Lo, how it gleams and glistens in the sun
Like the cheek of a Chesterton.

Salvationists

I

Come, my songs, let us speak of perfection—
We shall get ourselves rather disliked.

II

Ah yes, my songs, let us resurrect
The very excellent term *Rusticus*.
Let us apply it in all its opprobrium
To those to whom it applies.
And you may decline to make them immortal,
For we shall consider them and their state
In delicate
Opulent silence.

III

Come, my songs,
Let us take arms against this sea of stupidities—
Beginning with Mumpodorus;
And against this sea of vulgarities—
Beginning with Nimmim;
And against this sea of imbeciles—
All the Bulmenian literati.

Epitaph

Leucis, who intended a Grand Passion,
Ends with a willingness-to-oblige.

Arides

The bashful Arides
Has married an ugly wife,
He was bored with his manner of life,
Indifferent and discouraged he thought he might as
Well do this as anything else.

Saying within his heart, "I am no use to myself,
"Let her, if she wants me, take me."
He went to his doom.

The Bath Tub

As a bathtub lined with white porcelain,
When the hot water gives out or goes tepid,
So is the slow cooling of our chivalrous passion,
O my much praised but-not-altogether-satisfactory lady.

Amitiés

Old friends the most.
W.B.Y.

I
To one, on returning certain years after.

You wore the same quite correct clothing,
You took no pleasure at all in my triumphs,
You had the same old air of condescension
Mingled with a curious fear
        That I, myself, might have enjoyed them.

Te voilà, mon Bourrienne, you also shall be immortal.

II
To another.

And we say good-bye to you also,
For you seem never to have discovered
That your relationship is wholly parasitic;

Yet to our feasts you bring neither
Wit, nor good spirits, nor the pleasing attitudes
  Of discipleship.

III

But you, *bos amic*, we keep on,
For to you we owe a real debt:
In spite of your obvious flaws,
You once discovered a moderate chop-house.

IV

Iste fuit vir incultus,
Deo laus, quod est sepultus,
Vermes habent eius vultum
      A-a-a-a—A-men.
Ego autem jovialis
Gaudero contubernalis
Cum jocunda femina.

Meditatio

When I carefully consider the curious habits of dogs
I am compelled to conclude
That man is the superior animal.

When I consider the curious habits of man
I confess, my friend, I am puzzled.

To Dives

Who am I to condemn you, O Dives,
I who am as much embittered
With poverty
As you are with useless riches?

Ladies

Agathas

Four and forty lovers had Agathas in the old days,
All of whom she refused;
And now she turns to me seeking love,
And her hair also is turning.

Young Lady

I have fed your lar with poppies,
I have adored you for three full years;
And now you grumble because your dress does not fit
And because I happen to say so.

Lesbia Illa

Memnon, Memnon, that lady
Who used to walk about amongst us
With such gracious uncertainty,
Is now wedded
To a British householder.
Lugete, Venere! Lugete, Cupidinesque!

Passing

Flawless as Aphrodite,
Thoroughly beautiful,
Brainless,
The faint odour of your patchouli,
Faint, almost, as the lines of cruelty about your chin,
Assails me, and concerns me almost as little.

Phyllidula

Phyllidula is scrawny but amorous,
Thus have the gods awarded her
That in pleasure she receives more than she can give;
If she does not count this blessed
Let her change her religion.

The Patterns

Erinna is a model parent,
Her children have never discovered her adulteries.
Lalage is also a model parent,
Her offspring are fat and happy.

Coda

O my songs,
Why do you look so eagerly and so curiously into people's
    faces,
Will you find your lost dead among them?

The Seeing Eye

The small dogs look at the big dogs;
They observe unwieldly dimensions
And curious imperfections of odor.

Here is a formal male group:
The young men look upon their seniors,
They consider the elderly mind
And observe its inexplicable correlations.

Said Tsin-Tsu:
It is only in small dogs and the young
That we find minute observation.

Ancora

Good God! They say you are *risqué*,
O canzonetti!
We who went out into the four A.M. of the world
Composing our albas,
We who shook off our dew with the rabbits,
We who have seen even Artemis a-binding her sandals,
Have we ever heard the like?
O mountains of Hellas!!

Gather about me, O Muses!
When we sat upon the granite brink in Helicon
Clothed in the tattered sunlight,
O Muses with delicate shins,
O Muses with delectable knee-joints,
When we splashed and were splashed with
The lucid Castilian spray,
Had we ever such an epithet cast upon us!!

"Dompna Pois de Me No'us Cal"

A Translation
from the Provençal of En Bertrans de Born

Lady, since you care nothing for me,
And since you have shut me away from you
Causelessly,
I know not where to go seeking,
For certainly
I will never again gather
Joy so rich, and if I find not ever
A lady with look so speaking
To my desire, worth yours whom I have lost,
I'll have no other love at any cost.

And since I could not find a peer to you,
Neither one so fair, nor of such heart,
So eager and alert,
Nor with such art
In attire, nor so gay
Nor with gift so bountiful and so true,
I will go out a-searching,
Culling from each a fair trait
To make me a borrowed lady
Till I again find you ready.

Bels Cembelins, I take of you your colour,
For it's your own, and your glance
Where love is,

A proud thing I do here,
For, as to colour and eyes
I shall have missed nothing at all,
Having yours.
I ask of Midons Aelis (of Montfort)
Her straight speech free-running,
That my phantom lack not in cunning.

At Chalais of the Viscountess, I would
That she give me outright
Her two hands and her throat,
So take I my road
To Rochechouart,
Swift-foot to my Lady Anhes,
Seeing that Tristan's lady Iseutz had never
Such grace of locks, I do ye to wit,
Though she'd the far fame for it.

Of Audiart at Malemort,
Though she with a full heart
Wish me ill,
I'd have her form that's laced
So cunningly,
Without blemish, for her love
Breaks not nor turns aside.
I of Miels-de-ben demand
Her straight fresh body,
She is so supple and young,
Her robes can but do her wrong.

Her white teeth, of the Lady Faidita
I ask, and the fine courtesy
She hath to welcome one,
And such replies she lavishes
Within her nest;
Of Bels Mirals, the rest,
Tall stature and gaiety,
To make these avail
She knoweth well, betide
No change nor turning aside.

Ah, Bels Senher, Maent, at last
I ask naught from you,
Save that I have such hunger for
This phantom
As I've for you, such flame-lap,
And yet I'd rather
Ask of you than hold another,
Mayhap, right close and kissed.
Ah, lady, why have you cast
Me out, knowing you hold me so fast!

The Coming of War: Actaeon

An image of Lethe,
  and the fields
Full of faint light
  but golden,
Gray cliffs,
  and beneath them
A sea
Harsher than granite,
  unstill, never ceasing;
High forms
  with the movement of gods,
Perilous aspect;
  And one said:
"This is Actaeon."
  Actaeon of golden greaves!
  Over fair meadows,
  Over the cool face of that field,
  Unstill, ever moving,
  Hosts of an ancient people,
  The silent cortège.

After Ch'u Yuan

I will get me to the wood
Where the gods walk garlanded in wistaria,
By the silver blue flood
    move others with ivory cars.
There come forth many maidens
    to gather grapes for the leopards, my friend,
For there are leopards drawing the cars.

I will walk in the glade,
I will come out of the new thicket
    and accost the procession of maidens.

Liu Ch'e

The rustling of the silk is discontinued,
Dust drifts over the court-yard,
There is no sound of foot-fall, and the leaves
Scurry into heaps and lie still,
And she the rejoicer of the heart is beneath them:

A wet leaf that clings to the threshold.

Fan-Piece, for Her Imperial Lord

A fan of white silk,
    clear as frost on the grass-blade,
You also are laid aside.

Ts'ai Chi'h

The petals fall in the fountain,
    the orange-coloured rose-leaves,
Their ochre clings to the stone.

In a Station of the Metro

The apparition of these faces in the crowd;
Petals on a wet, black bough.

Alba

As cool as the pale wet leaves
                              of lily-of-the-valley
She lay beside me in the dawn.

Heather

The black panther treads at my side,
And above my fingers
There float the petal-like flames.

The milk-white girls
Unbend from the holly-trees,
And their snow-white leopard
Watches to follow our trace.

The Faun

Ha! sir, I have seen you sniffing and snoozling about
                              among my flowers.
And what, pray, do you know about horticulture,
                              you capriped?
"Come, Auster, come, Apeliota,
And see the faun in our garden.
But if you move or speak
This thing will run at you
And scare itself to spasms."

Coitus

The gilded phaloi of the crocuses
         are thrusting at the spring air.
Here is there naught of dead gods
But a procession of festival,
A procession, O Giulio Romano,
Fit for your spirit to dwell in.
Dione, your nights are upon us.

The dew is upon the leaf.
The night about us is restless.

The Encounter

All the while they were talking the new morality
Her eyes explored me.
And when I arose to go
Her fingers were like the tissue
Of a Japanese paper napkin.

Tempora

Io! Io! Tamuz!
The Dryad stands in my court-yard
With plaintive, querulous crying.
(Tamuz. Io! Tamuz!)
Oh, no, she is not crying: "Tamuz."
She says, "May my poems be printed this week?
The god Pan is afraid to ask you,
May my poems be printed this week?"

Black Slippers: Bellotti

At the table beyond us
With her little suede slippers off,
With her white-stockin'd feet

Carefully kept from the floor by a napkin,
She converses:
           Connaissez-vous Ostende?
The gurgling Italian lady on the other side of the restaurant
Replies with a certain hauteur,
But I await with patience
To see how Celestine will re-enter her slippers.
She re-enters them with a groan.

Society

The family position was waning,
And on this account the little Aurelia,
Who had laughed on eighteen summers,
Now bears the palsied contact of Phidippus.

Image from d'Orleans

Young men riding in the street
In the bright new season
Spur without reason,
Causing their steeds to leap.

And at the pace they keep
Their horses' armoured feet
Strike sparks from the cobbled street
In the bright new season.

Papyrus

Spring . . .
Too long . . .
Gongula . . .

"Ione, Dead the Long Year"

Empty are the ways,
Empty are the ways of this land
And the flowers
                    Bend over with heavy heads.
They bend in vain.
Empty are the ways of this land
                    Where Ione
Walked once, and now does not walk
But seems like a person just gone.

ʹΙμέρρω

    Thy soul
Grown delicate with satieties,
Atthis.
                    O Atthis,
I long for thy lips.
I long for thy narrow breasts,
Thou restless, ungathered.

Shop Girl

For a moment she rested against me
Like a swallow half blown to the wall,
And they talk of Swinburne's women,
And the shepherdess meeting with Guido.
And the harlots of Baudelaire.

To Formianus' Young Lady Friend

After Valerius Catullus

All Hail! young lady with a nose
                    by no means too small,
With a foot unbeautiful,
                    and with eyes that are not black,

With fingers that are not long, and with a mouth undry,
And with a tongue by no means too elegant,
You are the friend of Formianus, the vendor of cosmetics,
And they call you beautiful in the province,
And you are even compared to Lesbia.

O most unfortunate age!

Tame Cat

"It rests me to be among beautiful women.
   Why should one always lie about such matters?

I repeat:
It rests me to converse with beautiful women
Even though we talk nothing but nonsense,

The purring of the invisible antennæ
Is both stimulating and delightful."

L'Art, 1910

Green arsenic smeared on an egg-white cloth,
Crushed strawberries! Come, let us feast our eyes.

Simulacra

Why does the horse-faced lady of just the unmentionable age
Walk down Longacre reciting Swinburne to herself, inaudibly?
Why does the small child in the soiled-white imitation fur
      coat
Crawl in the very black gutter beneath the grape stand?
Why does the really handsome young woman approach me in
   Sackville Street
Undeterred by the manifest age of my trappings?

Women Before a Shop

The gew-gaws of false amber and false turquoise attract them.
"Like to like nature": these agglutinous yellows!

Epilogue

O chansons foregoing
You were a seven days' wonder,
When you came out in the magazines
You created considerable stir in Chicago,
And now you are stale and worn out,
You're a very depleted fashion,
A hoop-skirt, a calash,
An homely, transient antiquity.

Only emotion remains.

Your emotions?
                    Are those of a maître-de-café.

The Social Order

I

This government official
Whose wife is several years his senior,
Has such a caressing air
When he shakes hands with young ladies.

II
(Pompes Funèbres)

This old lady,
Who was "so old that she was an atheist,"
Is now surrounded
By six candles and a crucifix,

While the second wife of a nephew
Makes hay with the things in her house.
Her two cats
Go before her into Avernus;
A sort of chloroformed suttee,
And it is to be hoped that their spirits will walk
With their tails up,
And with a plaintive, gentle mewing,
For it is certain that she has left on this earth
No sound
Save a squabble of female connections.

The Tea Shop

The girl in the tea shop
                is not so beautiful as she was,
The August has worn against her.
She does not get up the stairs so eagerly;
Yes, she also will turn middle-aged,
And the glow of youth that she spread about us
                as she brought us our muffins
Will be spread about us no longer.
                She also will turn middle-aged.

Ancient Music

Winter is icummen in,
Lhude sing Goddamm,
Raineth drop and staineth slop,
And how the wind doth ramm!
                Sing: Goddamm.
Skiddeth bus and sloppeth us,
An ague hath my ham.
Freezeth river, turneth liver,
              Damn you, sing: Goddamm.

Goddamm, Goddamm, 'tis why I am, Goddamm,
                    So 'gainst the winter's balm.
Sing goddamm, damm, sing Goddamm,
Sing goddamm, sing goddamm, DAMM.

NOTE.—This is not folk music, but Dr. Ker writes that the tune is to be found under the Latin words of a very ancient canon.

The Lake Isle

O God, O Venus, O Mercury, patron of thieves,
Give me in due time, I beseech you, a little tobacco-shop,
With the little bright boxes
            piled up neatly upon the shelves
And the loose fragrant cavendish
            and the shag,
And the bright Virginia
            loose under the bright glass cases,
And a pair of scales not too greasy,
And the whores dropping in for a word or two in passing,
For a flip word, and to tidy their hair a bit.

O God, O Venus, O Mercury, patron of thieves,
Lend me a little tobacco-shop,
            or install me in any profession
Save this damn'd profession of writing,
            where one needs one's brains all the time.

Epitaphs

Fu I

Fu I loved the high cloud and the hill,
Alas, he died of alcohol.

Li Po

And Li Po also died drunk.
He tried to embrace a moon
In the Yellow River.

Our Contemporaries

When the Taihaitian princess
Heard that he had decided,
She rushed out into the sunlight and swarmed up a cocoanut
    palm tree,

But he returned to this island
And wrote ninety Petrarchan sonnets.

NOTE.—Il s'agit d'un jeune poète qui a suivi le culte de Gauguin jusqu'à
Tahiti même (et qui vit encore). Étant fort bel homme, quand la princesse
bistre entendit qu'il voulait lui accorder ses faveurs elle montra son allegresse
de la façon dont nous venons de parler. Malheureusement ses poèmes ne sont
remplis que de ses propres subjectivités, style Victorien de la "Georgian An-
thology."

Ancient Wisdom, Rather Cosmic

So Shu dreamed,
And having dreamed that he was a bird, a bee, and a
    butterfly,
He was uncertain why he should try to feel like anything else,

Hence his contentment.

The Three Poets

Candidia has taken a new lover
And three poets are gone into mourning.
The first has written a long elegy to "Chloris,"
To "Chloris chaste and cold," his "only Chloris."
The second has written a sonnet
                upon the mutability of woman,
And the third writes an epigram to Candidia.

The Gypsy

"Est-ce que vous avez vu des autres—des camarades—
avec des singes ou des ours?"
                    A Stray Gipsy—A.D. 1912

That was the top of the walk, when he said:
"Have you seen any others, any of our lot,
"With apes or bears?"
                    —A brown upstanding fellow
Not like the half-castes,
                    up on the wet road near Clermont.
The wind came, and the rain,
And mist clotted about the trees in the valley,
And I'd the long ways behind me,
                    gray Arles and Biaucaire,
And he said, "Have you seen any of our lot?"
I'd seen a lot of his lot . . .
                    ever since Rhodez,
Coming down from the fair
                    of St. John,
With caravans, but never an ape or a bear.

The Game of Chess

Dogmatic Statement Concerning the Game of Chess:
Theme for a Series of Pictures

Red knights, brown bishops, bright queens,
Striking the board, falling in strong "L"s of colour,
Reaching and striking in angles,
                    holding lines in one colour.
This board is alive with light;
                    these pieces are living in form,
Their moves break and reform the pattern:
                    Luminous green from the rooks,
Clashing with "X"s of queens,
                    looped with the knight-leaps.

"Y" pawns, cleaving, embanking!
Whirl! Centripetal! Mate! King down in the vortex,
Clash, leaping of bands, straight strips of hard colour,
Blocked lights working in. Escapes. Renewal of contest.

Provincia Deserta

At Rochecoart,
Where the hills part
        in three ways,
And three valleys, full of winding roads,
Fork out to south and north,
There is a place of trees . . . gray with lichen.
I have walked there
        thinking of old days.
At Chalais
        is a pleached arbour;
Old pensioners and old protected women
Have the right there—
        it is charity.
I have crept over old rafters,
        peering down
Over the Dronne,
        over a stream full of lilies.
Eastward the road lies,
        Aubeterre is eastward,
With a garrulous old man at the inn.
I know the roads in that place:
Mareuil to the north-east,
        La Tour,
There are three keeps near Mareuil,
And an old woman,
        glad to hear Arnaut,
Glad to lend one dry clothing.

I have walked
        into Perigord,
I have seen the torch-flames, high-leaping,

Painting the front of that church;
Heard, under the dark, whirling laughter.
I have looked back over the stream
                    and seen the high building,
Seen the long minarets, the white shafts.
I have gone in Ribeyrac
                    and in Sarlat,
I have climbed rickety stairs, heard talk of Croy,
Walked over En Bertran's old layout,
Have seen Narbonne, and Cahors and Chalus,
Have seen Excideuil, carefully fashioned.

I have said:
                    "Here such a one walked.
"Here Cœur-de-Lion was slain.
                    "Here was good singing.
"Here one man hastened his step.
                    "Here one lay panting."
I have looked south from Hautefort,
                    thinking of Montaignac, southward.
I have lain in Rocafixada,
                    level with sunset,
Have seen the copper come down
                    tingeing the mountains,
I have seen the fields, pale, clear as an emerald,
Sharp peaks, high spurs, distant castles.
I have said: "The old roads have lain here.
"Men have gone by such and such valleys
"Where the great halls are closer together."
I have seen Foix on its rock, seen Toulouse, and Arles
    greatly altered,
I have seen the ruined "Dorata."
                    I have said:
"Riquier! Guido."
                    I have thought of the second Troy,
Some little prized place in Auvergnat:
Two men tossing a coin, one keeping a castle,
One set on the highway to sing.
                    He sang a woman.
Auvergne rose to the song;

The Dauphin backed him.
"The castle to Austors!"
                    "Pieire kept the singing—
"A fair man and a pleasant."
            He won the lady,
Stole her away for himself, kept her against armed force:
So ends that story.
That age is gone;
Pieire de Maensac is gone.
I have walked over these roads;
I have thought of them living.

Sennin Poem by Kakuhaku

The red and green kingfishers
            flash between the orchids and clover,
One bird casts its gleam on another.

Green vines hang through the high forest,
They weave a whole roof to the mountain,
The lone man sits with shut speech,
He purrs and pats the clear strings.
He throws his heart up through the sky,
He bites through the flower pistil
            and brings up a fine fountain.
The red-pine-tree god looks on him and wonders.
He rides through the purple smoke to visit the sennin,
He takes "Floating Hill"* by the sleeve,
He claps his hand on the back of the great water sennin.

But you, you dam'd crowd of gnats,
Can you even tell the age of a turtle?

* Name of a sennin.

A Ballad of the Mulberry Road

(Fenollosa MSS., very early)

The sun rises in south east corner of things
To look on the tall house of the Shin
For they have a daughter named Rafu,
      (pretty girl)
She made the name for herself: "Gauze Veil,"
For she feeds mulberries to silkworms,
      She gets them by the south wall of the town.
With green strings she makes the warp of her basket,
She makes the shoulder-straps of her basket
      from the boughs of Katsura,
And she piles her hair up on the left side of her head-piece.

Her earrings are made of pearl,
Her underskirt is of green pattern-silk,
Her overskirt is the same silk dyed in purple,
And when men going by look on Rafu
      They set down their burdens,
They stand and twirl their moustaches.

Old Idea of Choan by Rosoriu

I

The narrow streets cut into the wide highway at Choan,
Dark oxen, white horses,
      drag on the seven coaches with outriders.
The coaches are perfumed wood,
The jewelled chair is held up at the crossway,
Before the royal lodge
      a glitter of golden saddles, awaiting the princess,
They eddy before the gate of the barons.
The canopy embroidered with dragons
      drinks in and casts back the sun.

Evening comes.
      The trappings are bordered with mist.

The hundred cords of mist are spread through
        and double the trees,
Night birds, and night women,
        spread out their sounds through the gardens.

II

Birds with flowery wing, hovering butterflies
        crowd over the thousand gates,
Trees that glitter like jade,
        terraces tinged with silver,
The seed of a myriad hues,
A net-work of arbours and passages and covered ways,
Double towers, winged roofs,
        border the net-work of ways:
A place of felicitous meeting.
Riu's house stands out on the sky,
        with glitter of colour
As Butei of Kan had made the high golden lotus
        to gather his dews,
Before it another house which I do not know:
How shall we know all the friends
        whom we meet on strange roadways?

To-Em-Mei's "The Unmoving Cloud"

"Wet springtime," says To-Em-Mei. "Wet spring in
the garden."

I

The clouds have gathered, and gathered,
        and the rain falls and falls,
The eight ply of the heavens
        are all folded into one darkness,
And the wide, flat road stretches out.
I stop in my room toward the East, quiet, quiet,
I pat my new cask of wine.
My friends are estranged, or far distant,
I bow my head and stand still.

II

Rain, rain, and the clouds have gathered,
The eight ply of the heavens are darkness,
The flat land is turned into river.
            "Wine, wine, here is wine!"
I drink by my eastern window.
I think of talking and man,
And no boat, no carriage, approaches.

III

The trees in my east-looking garden
            are bursting out with new twigs,
They try to stir new affection,

And men say the sun and moon keep on moving
            because they can't find a soft seat.

The birds flutter to rest in my tree,
            and I think I have heard them saying,
"It is not that there are no other men
But we like this fellow the best,
But however we long to speak
He can not know of our sorrow."

                                        T'ao Yuan Ming
                                        A.D. 365–427

Near Perigord

*A Perigord, pres del muralh
Tan que i puosch' om gitar ab malh*

You'd have men's hearts up from the dust
And tell their secrets, Messire Cino,
Right enough? Then read between the lines of Uc St. Circ,
Solve me the riddle, for you know the tale.

Bertrans, En Bertrans, left a fine canzone:
"Maent, I love you, you have turned me out.

The voice at Montfort, Lady Agnes' hair,
Bel Miral's stature, the viscountess' throat,
Set all together, are not worthy of you. . . ."
And all the while you sing out that canzone,
Think you that Maent lived at Montaignac,
One at Chalais, another at Malemort
Hard over Brive—for every lady a castle,
Each place strong.

          Oh, *is* it easy enough?
Tairiran held hall in Montaignac,
His brother-in-law was all there was of power
In Perigord, and this good union
Gobbled all the land, and held it later for some hundred years.
And our En Bertrans was in Altafort,
Hub of the wheel, the stirrer-up of strife,
As caught by Dante in the last wallow of hell—
The headless trunk "that made its head a lamp."
For separation wrought out separation,
And he who set the strife between brother and brother
And had his way with the old English king,
Viced in such torture for the "counterpass."

   How would you live, with neighbours set about you—
Poictiers and Brive, untaken Rochecouart,
Spread like the finger-tips of one frail hand;
And you on that great mountain of a palm—
Not a neat ledge, not Foix between its streams,
But one huge back half-covered up with pine,
Worked for and snatched from the string-purse of Born—
The four round towers, four brothers—mostly fools:
What could he do but play the desperate chess,
And stir old grudges?
          "Pawn your castles, lords!
Let the Jews pay."
          And the great scene—
(That, maybe, never happened!)
          Beaten at last,
Before the hard old king:
          "Your son, ah, since he died

My wit and worth are cobwebs brushed aside
In the full flare of grief. Do what you will."

   Take the whole man, and ravel out the story.
He loved this lady in castle Montaignac?
The castle flanked him—he had need of it.
You read to-day, how long the overlords of Perigord,
The Talleyrands, have held the place, it was no transient fiction.
And Maent failed him? Or saw through the scheme?

   And all his net-like thought of new alliance?
Chalais is high, a-level with the poplars.
Its lowest stones just meet the valley tips
Where the low Dronne is filled with water-lilies.
And Rochecouart can match it, stronger yet,
The very spur's end, built on sheerest cliff,
And Malemort keeps its close hold on Brive,
While Born, his own close purse, his rabbit warren,
His subterranean chamber with a dozen doors,
A-bristle with antennæ to feel roads,
To sniff the traffic into Perigord.
And that hard phalanx, that unbroken line,
The ten good miles from thence to Maent's castle,
All of his flank—how could he do without her?
And all the road to Cahors, to Toulouse?
What would he do without her?

        "Papiol,
Go forthright singing—Anhes, Cembelins.
There is a throat; ah, there are two white hands;
There is a trellis full of early roses,
And all my heart is bound about with love.
Where am I come with compound flatteries—
What doors are open to fine compliment?"
And every one half jealous of Maent?
He wrote the catch to pit their jealousies
Against her, give her pride in them?

Take his own speech, make what you will of it—
And still the knot, the first knot, of Maent?

Is it a love poem? Did he sing of war?
Is it an intrigue to run subtly out,
Born of a jongleur's tongue, freely to pass
Up and about and in and out the land,
Mark him a craftsman and a strategist?
(St. Leider had done as much as Polhonac,
Singing a different stave, as closely hidden.)
Oh, there is precedent, legal tradition,
To sing one thing when your song means another,
"*Et albirar ab lor bordon—*"
Foix' count knew that. What is Sir Bertrans' singing?

Maent, Maent, and yet again Maent,
Or war and broken heaumes and politics?

II

End fact. Try fiction. Let us say we see
En Bertrans, a tower-room at Hautefort,
Sunset, the ribbon-like road lies, in red cross-light,
South toward Montaignac, and he bends at a table
Scribbling, swearing between his teeth; by his left hand
Lie little strips of parchment covered over,
Scratched and erased with *al* and *ochaisos*.
Testing his list of rhymes, a lean man? Bilious?
With a red straggling beard?
And the green cat's-eye lifts toward Montaignac.

Or take his "magnet" singer setting out,
Dodging his way past Aubeterre, singing at Chalais
    In the vaulted hall,
Or, by a lichened tree at Rochecouart
Aimlessly watching a hawk above the valleys,
Waiting his turn in the mid-summer evening,
Thinking of Aelis, whom he loved heart and soul . . .
To find her half alone, Montfort away,
And a brown, placid, hated woman visiting her,
Spoiling his visit, with a year before the next one.
Little enough?
Or carry him forward. "Go through all the courts,
My Magnet," Bertrans had said.

We came to Ventadour
In the mid love court, he sings out the canzon,
No one hears save Arrimon Luc D'Esparo—
No one hears aught save the gracious sound of compliments.
Sir Arrimon counts on his fingers, Montfort,
Rochecouart, Chalais, the rest, the tactic,
Malemort, guesses beneath, sends word to Cœur-de-Lion:
The compact, de Born smoked out, trees felled
About his castle, cattle driven out!
Or no one sees it, and En Bertrans prospered?

   And ten years after, or twenty, as you will,
Arnaut and Richard lodge beneath Chalus:
The dull round towers encroaching on the field,
The tents tight drawn, horses at tether
Further and out of reach, the purple night,
The crackling of small fires, the bannerets,
The lazy leopards on the largest banner,
Stray gleams on hanging mail, an armourer's torch-flare
Melting on steel.

     And in the quietest space
They probe old scandals, say de Born is dead;
And we've the gossip (skipped six hundred years).
Richard shall die to-morrow—leave him there
Talking of *trobar clus* with Daniel.
And the "best craftsman" sings out his friend's song,
Envies its vigour . . . and deplores the technique,
Dispraises his own skill?—That's as you will.
And they discuss the dead man,
Plantagenet puts the riddle: "Did he love her?"
And Arnaut parries: "Did he love your sister?
True, he has praised her, but in some opinion
He wrote that praise only to show he had
The favour of your party; had been well received."

"You knew the man."
     "*You* knew the man.
I am an artist, you have tried both métiers."
"You were born near him."

"Do we know our friends?"
"Say that he saw the castles, say that he loved Maent!"
"Say that he loved her, does it solve the riddle?"
    End the discussion, Richard goes out next day
And gets a quarrel-bolt shot through his vizard,
Pardons the bowman, dies,

            Ends our discussion. Arnaut ends
"In sacred odour"—(that's apocryphal!)
And we can leave the talk till Dante writes:
Surely I saw, and still before my eyes
Goes on that headless trunk, that bears for light
Its own head swinging, gripped by the dead hair,
And like a swinging lamp that says, "Ah me!
I severed men, my head and heart
Ye see here severed, my life's counterpart."

Or take En Bertrans?

                        III
            Ed eran due in uno, ed uno in due
                Inferno, XXVIII, 125

"Bewildering spring, and by the Auvezere
Poppies and day's-eyes in the green émail
Rose over us; and we knew all that stream,
And our two horses had traced out the valleys;
Knew the low flooded lands squared out with poplars,
In the young days when the deep sky befriended.
    And great wings beat above us in the twilight,
And the great wheels in heaven
Bore us together . . . surging . . . and apart . . .
Believing we should meet with lips and hands.

    High, high and sure . . . and then the counter-thrust:
'Why do you love me? Will you always love me?
But I am like the grass, I can not love you.'
Or, 'Love, and I love and love you,
And hate your mind, not *you*, your soul, your hands.'

So to this last estrangement, Tairiran!

There shut up in his castle, Tairiran's,
She who had nor ears nor tongue save in her hands,
Gone—ah, gone—untouched, unreachable!
She who could never live save through one person,
She who could never speak save to one person,
And all the rest of her a shifting change,
A broken bundle of mirrors . . .!"

Villanelle: The Psychological Hour

I had over-prepared the event,
        that much was ominous.
With middle-ageing care
        I had laid out just the right books.
I had almost turned down the pages.

      Beauty is so rare a thing.
      So few drink of my fountain.

So much barren regret,
So many hours wasted!
And now I watch, from the window,
        the rain, the wandering busses.

"Their little cosmos is shaken"—
        the air is alive with that fact.
In their parts of the city
        they are played on by diverse forces.
How do I know?
        Oh, I know well enough.
For them there is something afoot.
        As for me:
I had over-prepared the event—

      Beauty is so rare a thing.
      So few drink of my fountain.

Two friends: a breath of the forest . . .
Friends? Are people less friends
    because one has just, at last, found them?
Twice they promised to come.
    "Between the night and morning?"

Beauty would drink of my mind.
Youth would awhile forget
      my youth is gone from me.

II

("Speak up! You have danced so stiffly?
    Someone admired your works,
    And said so frankly.

    "Did you talk like a fool,
    The first night?
    The second evening?"

"*But* they promised again:
      'To-morrow at tea-time.'")

III

Now the third day is here—
      no word from either;
No word from her nor him,
Only another man's note:
      "Dear Pound, I am leaving England."

Dans un Omnibus de Londres

Les yeux d'une morte aimée
M'ont salué,
Enchassés dans un visage stupide
Dont tous les autres traits étaient banals,
Ils m'ont salué
Et alors je vis bien des choses
Au dedans de ma mémoire

Remuer,
S'éveiller.

Je vis des canards sur le bord d'un lac minuscule,
Auprès d'un petit enfant gai, bossu.

Je vis les colonnes anciennes en "toc"
Du Parc Monceau,
Et deux petites filles graciles,
Des patriciennes,
           aux toisons couleur de lin,
Et des pigeonnes
Grasses
         comme des poulardes.
Je vis le parc,
Et tous les gazons divers
Où nous avions loué des chaises
Pour quatre sous.

Je vis les cygnes noirs,
Japonais,
Leurs ailes
Teintées de couleur sang-de-dragon,
Et toutes les fleurs
D'Armenonville.

Les yeux d'une morte
M'ont salué.

Pagani's, November 8

Suddenly discovering in the eyes of the very beautiful
Normande cocotte
The eyes of the very learned British Museum assistant.

To a Friend Writing on Cabaret Dancers

"Breathe not the word to-morrow in her ears"
Vir Quidem, on Dancers

Good "Hedgethorn," for we'll anglicize your name
Until the last slut's hanged and the last pig disemboweled,
Seeing your wife is charming and your child
Sings in the open meadow—at least the kodak says so—

My good fellow, you, on a cabaret silence
And the dancers, you write a sonnet;
Say "Forget To-morrow," being of all men
The most prudent, orderly, and decorous!

"Pepita" has no to-morrow, so you write.

Pepita has such to-morrows: with the hands puffed out,
The pug-dog's features encrusted with tallow
Sunk in a frowsy collar—an unbrushed black.
She will not bathe too often, but her jewels
Will be a stuffy, opulent sort of fungus
Spread on both hands and on the up-pushed bosom—
It juts like a shelf between the jowl and corset.

Have you, or I, seen most of cabarets, good Hedgethorn?

Here's Pepita, tall and slim as an Egyptian mummy,
Marsh-cranberries, the ribbed and angular pods
Flare up with scarlet orange on stiff stalks
And so Pepita
            flares on the crowded stage before our tables
Or slithers about between the dishonest waiters—

        "CARMEN EST MAIGRE, UN TRAIT DE BISTRE
        CERNE SON ŒIL DE GITANA"

And "rend la flamme"
            you know the deathless verses.
I search the features, the avaricious features

Pulled by the kohl and rouge out of resemblance—
Six pence the object for a change of passion.

"Write me a poem."
                Come now, my dear Pepita,
"-ita, bonita, chiquita,"
                that's what you mean you advertising spade,
Or take the intaglio, my fat great-uncle's heirloom:
Cupid, astride a phallus with two wings,
Swinging a cat-o'-nine-tails.
                No. Pepita,
I have seen through the crust.
                I don't know what you look like
But your smile pulls one way
                and your painted grin another,
While that cropped fool,
                that tom-boy who can't earn her living,
Come, come to-morrow,
                To-morrow in ten years at the latest,
She will be drunk in the ditch, but you, Pepita,
Will be quite rich, quite plump, with pug-bitch features,
With a black tint staining your cuticle,
Prudent and svelte Pepita.
                "Poète, writ me a poème!"
Spanish and Paris, love of the arts part of your geisha-culture!

Euhenia, in short skirts, slaps her wide stomach,
Pulls up a roll of fat for the pianist,
"Pauvre femme maigre!" she says.
                He sucks his chop bone,
That some one else has paid for,
                grins up an amiable grin,
Explains the decorations.
                Good Hedgethorn, they all have futures,
All these people.
                Old Popkoff
Will dine next week with Mrs. Basil,
Will meet a duchess and an ex-diplomat's widow
From Weehawken—who has never known
Any but "Majesties" and Italian nobles.

Euhenia will have a *fonda* in Orbajosa.
The amorous nerves will give way to digestive;
"Delight thy soul in fatness," saith the preacher.
We can't preserve the elusive "*mica salis*,"
It may last well in these dark northern climates,
Nell Gwynn's still here, despite the reformation,
And Edward's mistresses still light the stage,
A glamour of classic youth in their deportment.
The prudent whore is not without her future,
Her bourgeois dulness is deferred.

       Her present dulness . . .
Oh well, her present dulness . . .

Now in Venice, 'Storante al Giardino, I went early,
Saw the performers come: him, her, the baby,
A quiet and respectable-tawdry trio;
An hour later: a show of calves and spangles,

"*Un e duo fanno tre*,"
       Night after night,
No change, no change of program, "*Che!*
La donna è mobile."

Homage to Quintus Septimius Florentis Christianus

(*Ex libris Graecæ*)

I

Theodorus will be pleased at my death,
And someone else will be pleased at the death of Theodorus,
And yet everyone speaks evil of death.

II

This place is the Cyprian's, for she has ever the fancy
To be looking out across the bright sea,

Therefore the sailors are cheered, and the waves
Keep small with reverence, beholding her image.

Anyte

III

A sad and great evil is the expectation of death—
And there are also the inane expenses of the funeral;
Let us therefore cease from pitying the dead
For after death there comes no other calamity.

Palladas

IV
Troy

Whither, O city, are your profits and your gilded shrines,
And your barbecues of great oxen,
And the tall women walking your streets, in gilt clothes,
With their perfumes in little alabaster boxes?
Where is the work of your home-born sculptors?

Time's tooth is into the lot, and war's and fate's too.
Envy has taken your all,
Save your douth and your story.

Agathas Scholasticus

V

Woman? Oh, woman is a consummate rage,
        but dead, or asleep, she pleases.
Take her. She has two excellent seasons.

Palladas

VI
Nicharcus upon Phidon his doctor

Phidon neither purged me, nor touched me,
But I remembered the name of his fever medicine and died.

Fish and the Shadow

The salmon-trout drifts in the stream,
The soul of the salmon-trout floats over the stream
                    Like a little wafer of light.

The salmon moves in the sun-shot, bright shallow sea. . . .

As light as the shadow of the fish
                    that falls through the water,
She came into the large room by the stair,
Yawning a little she came with the sleep still upon her.

"I am just from bed. The sleep is still in my eyes.
"Come. I have had a long dream."
And I: "That wood?
And two springs have passed us."
"Not so far, no, not so far now,
There is a place—but no one else knows it—
A field in a valley . . .
                    Qu'ieu sui avinen,
Ieu lo sai."

She must speak of the time
Of Arnaut de Mareuil, I thought, "*qu'ieu sui avinen.*"

Light as the shadow of the fish
That falls through the pale green water.

Impressions of François-Marie Arouet (de Voltaire)

I
Phyllidula and the Spoils of Gouvernet

Where, Lady, are the days
When you could go out in a hired hansom
Without footmen and equipments?
And dine in a soggy, cheap restaurant?

Phyllidula now, with your powdered Swiss footman
Clanking the door shut,
                and lying;
And carpets from Savonnier, and from Persia,
And your new service at dinner,
And plates from Germain,
And cabinets and chests from Martin (almost lacquer),
And your white vases from Japan,
And the lustre of diamonds,
Etcetera, etcetera, and etcetera?

II
To Madame du Châtelet

If you'd have me go on loving you
Give me back the time of the thing.

Will you give me dawn light at evening?
Time has driven me out of the fine plaisaunces,
The parks with the swards all over dew,
And grass going glassy with the light on it,
The green stretches where love is and the grapes
Hang in yellow-white and dark clusters ready for pressing.

And if now we can't fit with our time of life
There is not much but its evil left us.

Life gives us two minutes, two seasons—
                One to be dull in;
Two deaths—and to stop loving and being lovable,
That is the real death,
The other is little beside it.

Crying after the follies gone by me,
Quiet talking is all that is left us—
Gentle talking, not like the first talking, less lively;
And to follow after friendship, as they call it,
Weeping that we can follow naught else.

III
To Madame Lullin

You'll wonder that an old man of eighty
Can go on writing you verses. . . .

Grass showing under the snow,
Birds singing late in the year!

And Tibullus could say of his death, in his Latin:
"Delia, I would look on you, dying."

And Delia herself fading out,
Forgetting even her beauty.

The Temperaments

Nine adulteries, 12 liaisons, 64 fornications and something
      approaching a rape
Rest nightly upon the soul of our delicate friend Florialis,
And yet the man is so quiet and reserved in demeanour
That he is held to be both bloodless and sexless.

Bastidides, on the contrary, who both talks and writes of
      nothing but copulation,
Has become the father of twins,
But he accomplished this feat at some cost;
He had to be four times cuckold.

Three Cantos of a Poem of Some Length

I

Hang it all, there can be but the one "Sordello,"
But say I want to, say I take your whole bag of tricks,
Let in your quirks and tweeks, and say the thing's an
    art-form,
Your "Sordello," and that the "modern world"
Needs such a rag-bag to stuff all its thought in;
Say that I dump my catch, shiny and silvery
As fresh sardines flapping and slipping on the marginal cobbles?
I stand before the booth (the speech), but the truth
Is inside this discourse: this booth is full of the marrow of
    wisdom.
Give up the intaglio method?
                Tower by tower,
Red-brown the rounded bases, and the plan
Follows the builder's whim; Beaucaire's slim gray
Leaps from the stubby base of Altaforte—
Mohammed's windows, for the Alcazar
Has such a garden, split by a tame small stream—
The Moat is ten yards wide, the inner court-yard
Half a-swim with mire.
Trunk-hose?
        There are not. The rough men swarm out
In robes that are half Roman, half like the Knave of Hearts.
And I discern your story:
                Peire Cardinal
Was half fore-runner of Dante. Arnaut's the trick
Of the unfinished address,
And half your dates are out; you mix your eras;
For that great font, Sordello sat beside—
'Tis an immortal passage, but the font
Is some two centuries outside the picture—
And no matter.
        Ghosts move about me patched with histories.
You had your business: to set out so much thought,
So much emotion, and call the lot "Sordello."
Worth the evasion, the setting figures up

And breathing life upon them.
Has it a place in music? And your: "Appear Verona!"?
　　　　　I walk the airy street,
See the small cobbles flare with the poppy spoil.
'Tis your "Great Day," the Corpus Domini,
And all my chosen and peninsular village
Has spread this scarlet blaze upon its lane,
Oh, before I was up,—with poppy-flowers.
Mid-June, and up and out to the half ruined chapel,
Not the old place at the height of the rocks
But that splay barn-like church, the Renaissance
Had never quite got into trim again.
As well begin here, here began Catullus:
"Home to sweet rest, and to the waves deep laughter,"
The laugh they wake amid the border rushes.
This is our home, the trees are full of laughter,
And the storms laugh loud, breaking the riven waves
On square-shaled rocks, and here the sunlight
Glints on the shaken waters, and the rain
Comes forth with delicate tread, walking from Isola Garda,

　　　　　Lo Soleils plovil.

It is the sun rains, and a spatter of fire
Darts from the "Lydian" ripples, *lacus undae,*
And the place is full of spirits, not *lemures,*
Not dark and shadow-wet ghosts, but ancient living,
Wood-white, smooth as the inner-bark, and firm of aspect
And all a-gleam with colour?
　　　　　Not a-gleam
But coloured like the lake and olive leaves,
GLAUKOPOS, clothed like the poppies, wearing golden
　　　greaves,
Light on the air. Are they Etruscan gods?
The air is solid sunlight, *apricus.*
Sun-fed we dwell there (we in England now)
For Sirmio serves my whim, better than Asolo,
Yours and unseen. Your palace step?
My stone seat was the Dogana's vulgarest curb,
And there were not "those girls," there was one flare,

One face, 'twas all I ever saw, but it was real . . .
And I can no more say what shape it was . . .
But she was young, too young.
                              True, it was Venice,
And at Florian's under the North arcade
I have seen other faces, and had my rolls for breakfast,
Drifted at night and seen the lit, gilt cross-beams
Glare from the Morosini.
                              And for what it's worth
I have my background; and you had your background,
Watched "the soul," Sordello's soul, flare up
And lap up life, and leap "to th' Empyrean";
Worked out the form, meditative, semi-dramatic,
Semi-epic story; and what's left?
Pre-Daun-Chaucer, Pre-Boccacio? Not Arnaut,
Not Uc St Circ.
                              Gods float in the azure air,
Bright gods and Tuscan, back before dew was shed;
It is a world like Puvis'?
                              Never so pale, my friend,
'Tis the first light—not half-light—Panisks
And oak-girls and the Maelids have all the wood;
                              Our olive Sirmio
Lies in its burnished mirror, and the Mounts Balde and Riva
Are alive with song, and all the leaves are full of voices.
"*Non è fuggi.*"
                              "It is not gone." Metastasio
Is right, we have that world about us.
And the clouds bowe above the lake, and there are folk
      upon them
Going their windy ways, moving by Riva,
By the western shore, far as Lonato,
And the water is full of silvery almond-white swimmers,
The silvery water glazes the upturned nipple.

          "*When Atlas sat down with his astrolabe,
          He brother to Prometheus, physicist.*"

We let Ficino
Start us our progress, say it was Moses' birth year?

Exult with Shang in squatness? The sea-monster
Bulges the squarish bronzes.
Daub out, with blue of scarabs, Egypt,
Green veins in the turquoise?
                    Or gray gradual steps
Lead up beneath flat sprays of heavy cedars:
Temple of teak-wood, and the gilt-brown arches
Triple in tier, banners woven by wall,
Fine screens depicted: sea-waves curled high,
Small boats with gods upon them,
Bright flame above the river: Kuanon,
Footing a boat that's but one lotus petal,
With some proud four-square genius
Leading along, one hand upraised for gladness,
Saying, "'Tis she, his friend, the mighty Goddess.
Sing hymns, ye reeds, and all ye roots and herons and swans,
    be glad.
Ye gardens of the nymphs, put forth your flowers."
What have I of this life?
                    Or even of Guido?
A pleasant lie that I knew Or San Michaele,
Believe the tomb he leapt was Julia Laeta's,
Do not even know which sword he'd with him in the street-
    charge.
I have but smelt this life, a whiff of it,
The box of scented wood
Recalls cathedrals. Shall I claim;
Confuse my own phantastikon
Or say the filmy shell that circumscribes me
Contains the actual sun;
                        confuse the thing I see
With actual gods behind me?
                        Are they gods behind me?
Worlds we have, how many worlds we have.
                        If Botticelli
Brings her ashore on that great cockle-shell,
His Venus (Simonetta?), and Spring
And Aufidus fill all the air
With their clear-outlined blossoms?
World enough. Behold, I say, she comes

"Apparelled like the Spring, Graces her subjects"
                 ("Pericles"),
Such worlds enough we have, have brave decors
And from these like we guess a soul for man
And build him full of aery populations.
                       (Painting and Faustus),
Mantegna a sterner line, and the new world about us:
Barred lights, great flares, and write to paint, not music,
O Casella.

II

O "Virgilio mio,"
Send out your thought upon the Mantuan palace,
Drear waste, great halls; pigment flakes from the stone;
Forlorner quarter:
Silk tatters still in the frame, Gonzaga's splendour,
Where do we come upon the ancient people,
Or much or little,
Where do we come upon the ancient people?
"All that I know is that a certain star"—
All that I know of one, Joios, Tolosan,
Is that in middle May, going along
A scarce discerned path, turning aside
In "level poplar lands," he found a flower, and wept;
"Y a la primera flor," he wrote,
"Qu'ieu trobei, tornei em plor."
One stave of it, I've lost the copy I had of it in Paris,
Out of a blue and gilded manuscript:
Couci's rabbits, a slim fellow throwing dice,
Purported portraits serving in capitals.
Joios we have, by such a margent stream,
He strayed in the field, wept for a flare of colour
When Cœur de Lion was before Chalus;
Arnaut's a score of songs, a wry sestina;
The rose-leaf casts her dew on the ringing glass,
Dolmetsch will build our age in witching music,
Viols da Gamba, tabors, tympanons.

Yin-yo laps in the reeds, my guest departs,
The maple leaves blot up their shadows,
The sky is full of Autumn,
We drink our parting in saki.
Out of the night comes troubling lute music,
And we cry out, asking the singer's name,
And get this answer:
    "Many a one
Brought me rich presents, my hair was full of jade,
And my slashed skirts were drenched in the secret dyes,
Well dipped in crimson, and sprinkled with rare wines;
I was well taught my arts at Ga-ma-rio
And then one year I faded out and married."
The lute-bowl hid her face. We heard her weeping.

Society, her sparrows, Venus' sparrows.
Catullus hung on the phrase (played with it as Mallarmé
Played for a fan: "Rêveuse pour que je plonge.");
Wrote out his crib from Sappho:
God's peer, yea and the very gods are under him
Facing thee, near thee; and my tongue is heavy,
And along my veins the fire; and the night is
Thrust down upon me.
That was one way of love, *flamma demanat*,
And in a year: "I love her as a father,"
And scarce a year, "Your words are written in water,"
And in ten moons: "O Caelius, Lesbia illa,
Caelius, Lesbia, our Lesbia, that Lesbia
Whom Catullus once loved more
Than his own soul and all his friends,
Is now the drab of every lousy Roman";
So much for him who puts his trust in woman.

Dordoigne! When I was there
There came a centaur, spying the land
And there were nymphs behind him;
Or procession on procession by Salisbury,
Ancient in various days, long years between them;
Ply over ply of life still wraps the earth here.

Catch at Dordoigne!
                                    Vicount St. Antoni—
"D'amor tug miei cossir"—hight Raimon Jordans
Of land near Caortz. The Lady of Pena
"Gentle and highly prized."
And he was good at arms and *bos trobaire*,
"Thou art the pool of worth, flood-land of pleasure,
And all my heart is bound about with love,
As rose in trellis that is bound over and over";
Thus were they taken in love beyond all measure.
But the Viscount Pena
Went making war into an hostile country,
And was sore wounded. The news held him dead,
"And at this news she had great grief and teen,"
And gave the church such wax for his recovery
That he recovered,
"And at this news she had great grief and teen"
And fell a-moping, dismissed St. Antoni,
"Thus was there more than one in deep distress,"
So ends that novel. Here the blue Dordoigne
Placid between white cliffs, pale
As the background of a Leonardo. Elis of Montfort
Then sent him her invitations (wife of de Gordon).
It juts into the sky, Gordon that is,
Like a thin spire. Blue night pulled down about it
Like tent-flaps or sails close hauled. When I was there,
La Noche de San Juan, a score of players
Were walking about the streets in masquerade,
Pike-staves and paper helmets, and the booths
Were scattered align, the rag ends of the fair.
False arms, true arms:
A flood of people storming about Spain:
                                    My Cid rode up to Burgos,
Up to the studded gate between two towers,
Beat with his lance butt. A girl child of nine years
Comes to the shrine-like platform in the wall,
Lisps out the words a-whisper, the King's writ:
Let no man speak to Diaz (Ruy Diaz, Myo Cid)
Or give him help or food, on pain of death:
His heart upon a pike, his eyes torn out, his goods sequestered.

Cid from Bivar, from empty perches of dispersed hawks,
From empty presses,
Came riding with his company up the great hill
(*Afe Minaya!*) to Burgos in the Spring,
And thence to fighting, to down-throw of Moors
And to Valencia rode he. By the beard! *Muy velida!*
Of onrush of lances, of splintered staves
Riven and broken casques, dismantled castles;
Of painted shields split up, blazons hacked off,
Piled men and bloody rivers. Or
"Of sombre light upon reflected armour"
When De las Nieblas sails—
"Y dar nueva lumbre las armas y hierros"—
And portents in the wind, a pressing air;
Full many a fathomed sea-change in the eyes
That sought with him the salt sea victories,
Rumble of balladist.
                Another gate:
And Kumasaka's ghost comes back to explain
How well the young man fenced who ended him.
Another gate:
            The kernelled walls of Toro, *las almenas,*
Afield, a king come in an unjust cause,
Atween the chinks aloft flashes the armoured figure,
"Muy linda!", "Helen!", "a star,"
            Lights the king's features . . .
"No use, my liege. She is your highness' sister,"
Breaks in Ancures.
            "Mal fuego s'enciende!"
Such are the gestes of war.
            A tire-woman,
Court sinecure, the court of Portugal,
And the young prince loved her, Pedro,
Called later, Cruel. Jealousy, two stabbed her,
Courtiers, with king's connivance.
And he, the prince, kept quiet a space of years.
And came to reign, after uncommon quiet,
And had his will upon the dagger-players:
A wedding ceremonial: he and the dug-up corpse in cerements.
Who winked at murder kisses the dead hand,

Does loyal homage
        "Que despois de ser morta foy Rainha."
Dig up Camoens:
                "That once as Proserpine
Gatheredst thy soul's light fruit, and every blindness;
Thy Enna the flary mead-land of Mondego,
Long art thou sung by Maidens in Mondego."
What have we now of her, his "*linda Ignez*"?
Houtmans in jail for debt in Lisbon, how long after,
Contrives a company, the Dutch eat Portugal,
Follow her ships tracks. Roemer Vischer's daughters
Talking some Greek, dally with glass engraving:
Vondel, the Eglantine, Dutch Renaissance.
The old tale out of fashion, daggers gone,
And Gaby wears Braganza on her throat,
Another pearl, tied to a public gullet.

I knew a man, but where 'twas is no matter,
Born on a farm, he hankered after painting,
His father kept him at work, no luck,
Married and got four sons,
Three died, the fourth he sent to Paris. And this son:
Ten years of Julians' and the ateliers,
Ten years of life, his pictures in the salons,
Name coming in the press;
                        and when I knew him:
Back once again in middle Indiana,
Acting as usher in the theatre,
Painting the local drug-shop and soda bars,
The local doctor's fancy for a mantel-piece:
Sheep! jabbing the wool upon their flea-bit backs.
"Them sheep! Them goddamd sheep!!" Adoring Puvis,
Giving his family back what they had spent on him,
Talking Italian cities,
Local excellence at Perugia;
                        dreaming his renaissance,
Take my Sordello!

III

Another one, half-cracked: John Heydon,
Worker of miracles, dealer in levitation,
"Servant of God and secretary of nature,"
The half transparent forms, in trance at Bulverton:
"Decked all in green," with sleeves of yellow silk
Slit to the elbow, slashed with various purples,
(Thus in his vision)   Her eyes were green as glass,
Her foot was leaf-like, and she promised him,
Dangling a chain of emeralds, promised him
The way of holiest wisdom.
                                   "Omniformis
Omnis intellectus est": thus he begins
By spouting half of Psellus; no, not "Daemonibus,"
But Porphyry's "Chances," the 13th chapter,
That every intellect is omniform.
"A daemon is a substance in the locus of souls."
Munching Ficino's mumbling Platonists.

Valla, more earth and sounder rhetoric,
Prefacing praise to his Pope, Nicholas:
A man of parts skilled in the subtlest sciences;
A patron of the arts, of poetry; and of a fine discernment.
A catalogue, his jewels of conversation.
"Know then the Roman speech: a sacrament"
Spread for the nations, eucharist of wisdom,
Bread of the liberal arts.
                                   Ha! Sir Blancatz,
Sordello would have your heart up, give it to all the princes;
Valla, the heart of Rome,
                                   sustaining speech,
Set out before the people. "Nec bonus
Christianus" (in the Elegantiae) "ac bonus Tullianus."
Shook the church. Marius, Du Bellay, wept for the buildings;
Baldassar Castiglione saw Raphael
"Lead back the soul into its dead, waste dwelling,"
Laniato corpore. Lorenzo Valla
"Broken in middle life? Bent to submission?
Took a fat living from the Papacy"

(That's in Villari, but Burckhardt's statement's different).
"More than the Roman city the Roman speech"
Holds fast its part among the ever living.
"Not by the eagles only was Rome measured."
"Wherever the Roman speech was, there was Rome."
Wherever the speech crept, there was mastery,
Spoke with the law's voice, while your greek logicians. . . .

More greeks than one! Doughty's "Divine Homeros"
Came before sophistry. Justinopolitan, uncatalogued,
One Andreas Divus gave him in latin,
In Officina Wecheli, M.D. three "Xs." eight,
Caught up his cadence, word and syllable:
"Down to the ships we went, set mast and sail,
Black keel and beasts for bloody sacrifice,
Weeping we went."
I've strained my ear for -ensa, ombra, and -ensa,
And cracked my wit on delicate canzoni,
                    Here's but rough meaning:
"And then went down to the ship, set keel to breakers,
Forth on the godly sea,
We set up mast and sail on the swart ship,
Sheep bore we aboard her, and our bodies also,
Heavy with weeping; and winds from sternward
Bore us out onward with bellying canvas,
Circe's this craft, the trim-coifed goddess.
Then sat we amidships—wind jamming the tiller—
Thus with stretched sail
                    we went over sea till day's end.
Sun to his slumber, shadows o'er all the ocean,
Came we then to the bounds of deepest water,
To the Kimmerian lands and peopled cities
Covered with close-webbed mist, unpierced ever
With glitter of sun-rays,
Nor with stars stretched, nor looking back from heaven,
Swartest night stretched over wretched men there,
The ocean flowing backward, came we then to the place
Aforesaid by Circe.
Here did they rites, Perimedes and Eurylochus,
And drawing sword from my hip

I dug the ell-square pitkin,
Poured we libations unto each the dead,
First mead and then sweet wine, water mixed with white
    flour,
Then prayed I many a prayer to the sickly death's-heads,
As set in Ithaca, sterile bulls of the best
For sacrifice, heaping the pyre with goods.
Sheep, to Tiresias only; black and a bell sheep.
Dark blood flowed in the fosse,
Souls out of Erebus, cadaverous dead,
Of brides, of youths, and of much-bearing old;
Virgins tender, souls stained with recent tears,
Many men mauled with bronze lance-heads,
Battle spoil, bearing yet dreary arms,
These many crowded about me,
With shouting. Pallor upon me, cried to my men for more
    beasts.
Slaughtered the herds, sheep slain of bronze,
Poured ointment, cried to the gods,
To Pluto the strong, and praised Proserpine,
Unsheathed the narrow sword,
I sat to keep off the impetuous, impotent dead
Till I should hear Tiresias.
But first Elpenor came, our friend Elpenor,
Unburied, cast on the wide earth,
Limbs that we left in the house of Circe,
Unwept, unwrapped in sepulchre, since toils urged other.
Pitiful spirit, and I cried in hurried speech:
"Elpenor, how art thou come to this dark coast?
Cam'st thou a-foot, outstripping seamen?"
                 And he in heavy speech:
"Ill fate and abundant wine! I slept in Circe's ingle,
Going down the long ladder unguarded, I fell against the
    buttress,
Shattered the nape-nerve, the soul sought Avernus.
But thou, O King, I bid remember me, unwept, unburied,
Heap up mine arms, be tomb by sea-board, and inscribed:
'A man of no fortune and with a name to come.'
And set my oar up, that I swung mid fellows."

Came then another ghost, whom I beat off, Anticlea,
And then Tiresias, Theban,
Holding his golden wand, knew me and spoke first
"Man of ill hour, why come a second time,
Leaving the sunlight, facing the sunless dead, and this joyless
        region?
Stand from the fosse, move back, leave me my bloody bever,
And I will speak you true speeches."
                              And I stepped back,
Sheathing the yellow sword. Dark blood he drank then,
And spoke: "Lustrous Odysseus
Shalt return through spiteful Neptune, over dark seas,
Lose all companions." Foretold me the ways and the signs.
Came then Anticlea, to whom I answered:
"Fate drives me on through these deeps. I sought Tiresias,"
Told her the news of Troy. And thrice her shadow
                              Faded in my embrace.

Lie quiet Divus. Then had he news of many faded women,
Tyro, Alcmena, Chloris,
Heard out their tales by that dark fosse, and sailed
By sirens and thence outward and away,
And unto Circe. Buried Elpenor's corpse.
Lie quiet Divus, plucked from a Paris stall
With a certain Cretan's "Hymni Deorum";
The thin clear Tuscan stuff
                      Gives way before the florid mellow phrase,
Take we the goddess, Venerandam
Auream coronam habentem, pulchram. . . .
Cypri munimenta sortita est, maritime,
Light on the foam, breathed on by Zephyrs
And air-tending Hours, mirthful, orichalci, with golden
Girdles and breast bands, Thou with dark eyelids,
Bearing the golden bough of Argicida.

'NOH'

OR

ACCOMPLISHMENT

A Study of the Classical Stage of Japan

BY
ERNEST FENOLLOSA
AND
EZRA POUND

NOTE

The vision and the plan are Fenollosa's. In the prose I have had but the part of literary executor; in the plays my work has been that of translator who has found all the heavy work done for him and who has had but the pleasure of arranging beauty into the words.

I wish to express my very deep thanks to Mr. Arthur Waley, who has corrected a number of mistakes in the orthography of proper names from such Japanese texts as were available, and who has assisted me out of various impasses where my own ignorance would have left me.

EZRA POUND

CONTENTS

PART I

PART II

PART III

PART IV

Part I

INTRODUCTION

THE life of Ernest Fenollosa was the romance par excellence of modern scholarship. He went to Japan as a professor of economics. He ended as Imperial Commissioner of Arts. He had unearthed treasure that no Japanese had heard of. It may be an exaggeration to say that he had saved Japanese art for Japan, but it is certain that he had done as much as any one man could have to set the native art in its rightful pre-eminence and to stop the apeing of Europe. He had endeared himself to the government and laid the basis for a personal tradition. When he died suddenly in England the Japanese government sent a warship for his body, and the priests buried him within the sacred enclosure at Miidera. These facts speak for themselves.

His present reputation in Europe rests upon his "Epochs of Chinese and Japanese Art." In America he is known also for his service to divers museums. His work on Japanese and Chinese literature has come as a surprise to the scholars. It forms, I think, the basis for a new donation, for a new understanding of "the East." For instance, as I look over that section of his papers which deals with the Japanese Noh, having read what others have written in English about these plays, I am in a position to say definitely that Professor Fenollosa knew more of the subject than any one who has yet written in our tongue.

The Noh is unquestionably one of the great arts of the world, and it is quite possibly one of the most recondite.

In the eighth century of our era the dilettante of the Japanese court established the tea cult and the play of "listening to incense."*

In the fourteenth century the priests and the court and the players all together produced a drama scarcely less subtle.

* Vide Brinkley, Oriental Series, vol. iii.

For "listening to incense" the company was divided into two parties, and some arbiter burnt many kinds and many blended sorts of perfume, and the game was not merely to know which was which, but to give to each one of them a beautiful and allusive name, to recall by the title some strange event of history or some passage of romance or legend. It was a refinement in barbarous times, comparable to the art of polyphonic rhyme, developed in feudal Provence four centuries later, and now almost wholly forgotten.

The art of allusion, or this love of allusion in art, is at the root of the Noh. These plays, or eclogues, were made only for the few; for the nobles; for those trained to catch the allusion. In the Noh we find an art built upon the god-dance, or upon some local legend of spiritual apparition, or, later, on gestes of war and feats of history; an art of splendid posture, of dancing and chanting, and of acting that is not mimetic. It is, of course, impossible to give much idea of the whole of this art on paper. One can only trace out the words of the text and say that they are spoken, or half-sung and chanted, to a fitting and traditional accompaniment of movement and colour, and that they are themselves but half shadows. Yet, despite the difficulties of presentation, I find these words very wonderful, and they become intelligible if, as a friend says, "you read them all the time as though you were listening to music."

If one has the habit of reading plays and imagining their setting, it will not be difficult to imagine the Noh stage—different as it is from our own or even from Western mediaeval stages—and to feel how the incomplete speech is filled out by the music or movement. It is a symbolic stage, a drama of masks—at least they have masks for spirits and gods and young women. It is a theatre of which both Mr. Yeats and Mr. Craig may approve. It is not, like our theatre, a place where every fineness and subtlety must give way; where every fineness of word or of word-cadence is sacrificed to the "broad effect"; where the paint must be put on with a broom. It is a stage where every subsidiary art is bent precisely upon holding the faintest shade of a difference; where the poet may even be silent while the gestures consecrated by four centuries of usage show meaning.

"We work in pure spirit," said Umewaka Minoru, through whose efforts the Noh survived the revolution of 1868, and the fall of the Tokugawa.

Minoru was acting in the Shogun's garden when the news of Perry's arrival stopped the play. Without him the art would have perished. He restored it through poverty and struggle, "living in a poor house, in a poor street, in a kitchen, selling his clothes to buy masks and costumes from the sales of bankrupt companies, and using 'kaiyu' for rice."

The following prospectus from a programme of one of his later performances (March 1900) will perhaps serve to show the player's attitude toward the play.

Programme Announcement

Our ancestor was called Umegu Hiogu no Kami Tomotoki. He was the descendant in the ninth generation of Tachibana no Moroye Sadaijin, and lived in Umedzu Yamashiro, hence his family name. After that he lived in Oshima, in the province of Tamba, and died in the fourth year of Ninwa Moroye's descendant, the twenty-second after Tomotoki, was called Hiogu no Kami Tomosato. He was a samurai in Tamba, as his fathers before him. The twenty-eighth descendant was Hiogu no Kami Kagehisa. His mother dreamed that a Noh mask was given from heaven; she conceived, and Kagehisa was born. From his childhood Kagehisa liked music and dancing, and he was by nature very excellent in both of these arts. The Emperor Gotsuchi Mikado heard his name, and in January in the 13th year of Bunmei he called him to his palace and made him perform the play Ashikari. Kagehisa was then sixteen years old. The Emperor admired him greatly and gave him the decoration (Monsuki) and a curtain which was purple above and white below, and he gave him the honorific ideograph "waka" and thus made him change his name to Umewaka. By the Emperor's order, Ushoben Fugiwara no Shunmei sent the news of this and the gifts to Kagehisa. The letter of the Emperor, given at that time, is still in our house. The curtain was, unfortunately, burned in the great fire of Yedo on the 4th of March in the third year of Bunka. Kagehisa died in the second year of Kioroku and after him the family of Umewaka became professional actors of Noh. Hironaga, the thirtieth descendant of Umewaka Taiyu Rokuro, served Ota Nobunaga.* And he was given a territory of 700 koku in Tamba. And he died in Nobunaga's battle, Akechi.

---

* Nobunaga died in 1582.

His son, Taiyu Rokuro Ujimori, was called to the palace of Tokugawa Iyeyasu in the fourth year of Keicho, and given a territory of 100 koku near his home in Tamba. He died in the third year of Kambun. After that the family of Umewaka served the Tokugawa shoguns with Noh for generation after generation down to the revolution of Meiji (1868). These are the outlines of the genealogy of my house.

This is the 450th anniversary of Tomosato, and so to celebrate him and Kagehisa and Ujimori, we have these performances for three days. We hope that all will come to see them.

The head of the performance is the forty-fifth of his line, the Umewaka Rokoro, and is aided by Umewaka Manzaburo.

(Dated,) In the 33rd year of Meiji, 2nd month.

You see how far this is from the conditions of the Occidental stage. Pride of descent, pride in having served dynasties now extinct, fragments of ceremony and religious ritual, all serve at first to confuse the modern person, and to draw his mind from the sheer dramatic value of Noh.

Some scholars seem to have added another confusion. They have not understood the function of the individual plays in the performance, and have thought them fragmentary, or have complained of imperfect structure. The Noh plays are often quite complete in themselves; certain plays are detachable units, comprehensible as single performances, and without annotation or comment. Yet even these can be used as part of the Ban-gumi, the full Noh programme. Certain other plays are only "formed" and intelligible when considered as part of such a series of plays. Again, the texts or libretti of certain other plays, really complete in themselves, seem to us unfinished, because their final scene depends more upon the dance than on the words. The following section of Professor Fenollosa's notes throws a good deal of light on these questions. It is Notebook J, Section I., based on the authority of Mr. Taketi Owada, and runs as follows:

In the time of Tokugawa (A.D. 1602 to 1868), Noh became the music of the Shogun's court and it was called O-no, the programme O-no-gumi, the actor O-no-yakusha, and the stage O-no-butai, with honorific additions. The first ceremony of the year, Utai-zome, was considered very important at the court. In the palaces of the daimyos, also, they had their proper ceremonies. This ceremony of Utai-zome began with the Ashikaga shoguns (in the fourteenth century). At that time on the fourth day of the first month, Kanze (the head of one of the five chartered and hereditary companies of court actors) sang a play in Omaya, and the Shogun gave him jifuku ("clothes of the season"), and this became a custom. In the time of Toyotomi, the second day of the first month was set apart for the ceremony. But in the time of Tokugawa, the third day of the first month was fixed "eternally" as the day for Utai-zome. On that day, at the hour of "tori no jō" (about 5 A.M.), the Shogun presented himself in a large hall in Hon-Maru (where the imperial palace now is), taking with him the San-ke, or three relative daimyos, the ministers, and all the other daimyos and officials, all dressed in the robes called "noshime-kami-shimo." And the "Tayus" (or heads) of the Kanze and Komparu schools of acting come every year, and the Tayus of Hosho and Kita on alternate years, and the Waki actors, that is, the actors of second parts, and the actors of Kiogen or farces, and the hayashikata ("cats," or musicians) and the singers of the chorus, all bow down on the verandah of the third hall dressed in robes called "suo," and in hats called "yeboshi."

And while the cup of the Shogun is poured out three times, Kanze sings the "Shikai-nami" passage from the play of Takasago, still bowing. Then the plays Oi-matsu, Tōbuku, and Takasago are sung with music, and when they are over the Shogun gives certain robes, called the "White-aya," with crimson lining, to the three chief actors, and robes called "orikami" to the other actors. Then the three chief actors put on the new robes over their "suos" and begin at once to dance the Dance of the Match of Bows and Arrows. And the chant that accompanies it is as follows:

The chief actor sings—

"Shakuson, Shakuson!" (Buddha, Buddha!)

And the chorus sings this rather unintelligible passage—

"Taking the bow of Great Love and the arrow of Wisdom, he awakened Sandoku from sleep. Aisemmyō-o displayed these two as the symbols of IN and YO.* Monju (another deity) appeared in the form of Yo-yu and caught the serpent, Kishu-ja, and made it into a bow. From its eyes he made him his arrows.†

"The Empress Jingō of our country defeated the rebels with these arrows and brought the peace of Ciyo-shun to the people. O Hachiman Daibosatsu, Emperor Ojin, War-god Yumi-ya, enshrined in Iwashimidzu, where the clear water-spring flows out! O, O, O! This water is water flowing forever."

* [In and yo are divisions of metric, and there is a Pythagorean-like symbolism attached to them.]

† [The serpent is presumably the sky, and the stars the eyes made into arrows.]

This "yumi-ya" text cannot be used anywhere save in this ceremony at the Shogun's court, and in the "Takigi-No" of the Kasuga temple at Nara (where a few extra lines are interpolated).

When the above chant and dance are finished, the Shogun takes the robe "Kataginu" from his shoulders and throws it to the samurai in attendance. The samurai hands it to the minister, who walks with it to the verandah and presents it to the Taiyu of Kanze very solemnly. Then all the daimyos present take off their "kata-ginus" and give them to the chief actors, and thus ends the ceremony of Utai-zome. The next day the tayus, or chief actors, take the robes back to the daimyos and get money in exchange for them.

There are performances of Noh lasting five days at the initiations, marriages, and the like, of the Shoguns; and at the Buddhist memorial services for dead Shoguns for four days. There are performances for the reception of imperial messengers from Kyoto, at which the actors have to wear various formal costumes. On one day of the five-day performances the town people of the eight hundred and eight streets of Yedo are admitted, and they are marshalled by the officers of every street. The nanushi, or street officers, assemble the night before by the gates of Ote and Kikyo, and each officer carries aloft a paper lantern bearing the name of his street. They take sake and refreshments and wait for the dawn. It looks like a place on fire, or like a camp before battle.

The Kanze method of acting was made the official style of the Tokugawa Shoguns, and the tayus, or chief actors, of Kanze were placed at the head of all Noh actors. To the Kanze tayu alone was given the privilege of holding one subscription performance, or Kanjin-No, during his lifetime, for the space of ten days. And for this performance he had the right to certain dues and levies on the daimyos and on the streets of the people of Yedo. The daimyos were not allowed to attend the common theatre, but they could go to the Kanjin-No. (Note that the common theatre, the place of mimicry and direct imitation of life, has always been looked down upon in Japan. The Noh, the symbolic and ritual stage, is a place of honour to actor and audience alike.) The daimyos and even their wives and daughters could see Kanjin-No without staying behind the blinds. Programmes were sold in the streets, and a drum was beaten as a signal, as is still done to get an audience for the wrestling matches.

The privilege of holding one subscription performance was later granted to the Hosho company also.

BAN-GUMI

In the performance of Utai, or Noh, the arrangement of pieces for the day is called "Ban-gumi." "Gumi" means a setting in order, and "Ban" is derived from the old term "Ban-no-mai," which was formerly used when the two kinds of mai, or dancing, the Korean "u-ho" and the Chinese "sa-ho," were performed one after the other.

Now the Ka-den-sho, or secret book of Noh, decrees that the arrangement of plays shall be as follows:

A "Shugen" must come first. And Shugen, or congratulatory pieces, are limited to Noh of the Gods (that is, to pieces connected with some religious rite), because this country of the rising sun is the country of the gods. The gods have guarded the country from Kami-yo (the age of the gods) down to the time of the present reign. So in praise of them and in prayer we perform first this Kami-No.

The Shura, or battle-piece, comes second, for the gods and emperors pacified this country with bows and arrows; therefore, to defeat and put out the devils, we perform the Shura. (That is to say, it is sympathetic magic.)

Kazura, or Onna-mono, "wig-pieces," or pieces for females, come third. Many think that any Kazura will do, but it must be a "female Kazura," for after battle comes peace, or Yu-gen, mysterious calm, and in time of peace the cases of love come to pass. Moreover, the battle-pieces are limited to men; so we now have the female piece in contrast like in and yo (the different divisions of the metric, before mentioned).

The fourth piece is Oni-No, or the Noh of spirits. After battle comes peace and glory, but they soon depart in their turn. The glory and pleasures of man are not reliable at all. Life is like a dream and goes with the speed of lightning. It is like a dewdrop in the morning; it soon falls and is broken. To suggest these things and to lift up the heart for Buddha (to produce "Bodai-shin") we have this sort of play after the Onna-mono, that is, just after the middle of the programme, when some of the audience will be a little tired. Just to wake them out of their sleep we have these plays of spirits ("Oni"). Here are shown the struggles and the sins of mortals, and the audience, even while they sit for pleasure, will begin to think about Buddha and the coming world. It is for this reason that Noh is called Mu-jin-Kyo, the immeasurable scripture.*

Fifth comes a piece which has some bearing upon the moral duties of man, Jin, Gi, Rei, Chi, Shin; that is, Compassion, Righteousness, Politeness, Wisdom, and Faithfulness. This fifth piece teaches the duties of man here in this world as the fourth piece represents the results of carelessness to such duties.

Sixth comes another Shugen, or congratulatory piece, as conclusion to the whole performance, to congratulate and call down blessings on the lords present, the actors themselves, and the place. To show that though the spring may pass, still there is a time of its return, this Shugen is put in again just as at the beginning.

This is what is written in the Ka-den-sho. Then some one, I think Mr. Owada, comments as follows:

Though it is quite pedantic in wording, still the order of the performance is always like this. To speak in a more popular manner, first comes the Noh of the Divine Age (Kamiyo); then the battle-piece; then the play of women; fourth, the pieces which have a very quiet and deep interest, to touch the audience to their very hearts; fifth, the pieces which have stirring or lively scenes; and, sixth, pieces which praise the lords and the reign.

This is the usual order. When we have five pieces instead of six, we sing at the end of the performance the short passage from the play Takasago, beginning at "Senshuraku wa tami wo nade," "Make the people glad with the joy of a Thousand Autumns." (From the final chorus of Takasago.) This is called the "adding Shugen." But if in the fifth piece there are phrases like "Medeta kere" or "Hisashi kere"—"Oh, how happy!" or "O everlasting,"—then there is no necessity to sing the extra passage. In performances in memory of the dead, Tsuizen-No, they sing short passages from Toru and Naniwa.

Though five or six pieces are the usual number, there can be more or even fewer pieces, in which case one must use the general principles of the above schedule in designing and arranging the programme.

---

* These pieces are the most interesting because of their profound and subtle psychology and because of situations entirely foreign to our Western drama, if not to our folk-lore and legend.—E.P.

I think I have quoted enough to make clear one or two points.

First: There has been in Japan from the beginning a clear distinction between serious and popular drama. The merely mimetic stage has been despised.

Second: The Noh holds up a mirror to nature in a manner very different from the Western convention of plot. I mean the Noh performance of the five or six plays in order presents a complete service of life. We do not find, as we find in Hamlet, a certain situation or problem set out and analysed. The Noh service presents, or symbolizes, a complete diagram of life and recurrence.

The individual pieces treat for the most part known situations, in a manner analogous to that of the Greek plays, in which we find, for instance, a known Oedipus in a known predicament.

Third: As the tradition of Noh is unbroken, we find in the complete performance numerous elements which have disappeared from our Western stage; that is, morality plays, religious mysteries, and even dances—like those of the mass—which have lost what we might call their dramatic significance.

Certain texts of Noh will therefore be interesting only to students of folk-lore or of comparative religion. The battle-pieces will present little of interest, because Chansons de Geste are pretty much the same all the world over. The moralities are on a par with Western moralities, for ascetic Buddhism and ascetic Christianity have about the same set of preachments. These statements are general and admit of numerous exceptions, but the lover of the stage and the lover of drama and of poetry will find his chief interest in the psychological pieces, or the Plays of Spirits; the plays that are, I think, more Shinto than Buddhist. These plays are full of ghosts, and the ghost psychology is amazing. The parallels with Western spiritist doctrines are very curious. This is, however, an irrelevant or extraneous interest, and one might set it aside if it were not bound up with a dramatic and poetic interest of the very highest order.

I think I can now give a couple of texts, without much more preface than saying that the stage is visible from three sides. It is reached by a bridge which is divided into three sections by three real pine trees which are small and in pots. There is one scene painted on the background. It is a pine tree, the symbol of the unchanging. It is painted right on the back of the stage, and, as this cannot be shifted, it remains the same for all plays.

A play very often represents some one going on a journey. The character walks along the bridge or about the stage, announces where he is and where he is going, and often explains the meaning of his symbolic gestures, or tells what the dance means, or why one is dancing.

Thus, in Sotoba Komachi, a play by Kiyotsugu, two priests are going from Koyosan to Kioto, and in Settsu they meet with Ono no Komachi; that is to say, they meet with what appears to be an old woman sitting on a roadside shrine— though she is really the wraith of Ono, long dead.

SOTOBA KOMACHI

ONO

When I was young I had pride
And the flowers in my hair
Were like spring willows.
I spoke like the nightingales, and now am old,
Old by a hundred years, and wearied out.
I will sit down and rest.

THE WAKI
(one of the priests, is shocked at her impiety and says)

It is near evening; let us be getting along. Now will you
look at that beggar. She is sitting on a sotoba (*a carved
wooden devotional stick, or shrine*). Tell her to come off it and
sit on some proper thing.

ONO

Eh, for all your blather it has no letters on it, not a smudge
of old painting. I thought it was only a stick.

WAKI

Is it only a stick or a stump? May be it had once fine flow-
ers—in its time, in its time; and now it is a stick, to be sure,
with the blessed Buddha cut in it.

ONO

Oh, well then, I'm a stump, too, and well buried, with a
flower at my heart. Go on and talk of the shrine.

*The Tsure, in this case the second priest, tells the legend of the
shrine, and while he is doing it, the Waki notices some-
thing strange about the old hag, and cries out—*
Who are you?

ONO

I am the ruins of Ono,
The daughter of Ono no Yoshizane.

WAKI AND TSURE
(*together*)

How sad a ruin is this:
Komachi was in her day a bright flower;
She had the blue brows of Katsura;
She used no powder at all;
She walked in beautiful raiment in palaces.
Many attended her verse in our speech
And in the speech of the foreign court.   [*That is, China.*]
White of winter is over her head,
Over the husk of her shoulders;
Her eyes are no more like the colour on distant mountains.
She is like a dull moon that fades in the dawn's grip.
The wallet about her throat has in it a few dried beans,
A bundle is wrapped on her back, and on her shoulder is a
      basket of woven roots;
She cannot hide it at all.
She is begging along the road;
She wanders, a poor, daft shadow.

   [*I cannot quite make out whether the priest is still sceptical,
and thinks he has before him merely an old woman who thinks
she is Komachi. At any rate, she does not want commiseration,
and replies.*]

ONO

   Daft! Will you hear him? In my own young days I had a
hundred letters from men a sight better than he is. They came
like rain-drops in May. And I had a high head, may be, that
time. And I sent out no answer. You think because you see
me alone now that I was in want of a handsome man in the
old days, when Shosho came with the others—Shii no Shosho
of Fukakusa [Deep Grass] that came to me in the moonlight
and in the dark night and in the nights flooded with rain, and
in the black face of the wind and in the wild swish of the
snow. He came as often as the melting drops fall from the
eaves, ninety-nine times, and he died. And his ghost is about
me, driving me on with the madness.

———

Umewaka Minoru acted Ono in this play on March 8, 1899. It is quite usual for an old actor, wearing a mask, to take the part of a young woman. There is another play of Ono and Shosho called Kayoi Komachi, "Komachi Going"; it is by a Minoru, and Umewaka acted it on November 19, 1899; and it was followed by Suma Genji. I shall give both of these plays complete without further comment.

TECHNICAL TERMS IN NOH

Shite (pronounced "*Sch'tay*"): The hero or chief character.
Tsure: The follower of the hero.
Waki: Guest or guests, very often a wandering priest.
Waki no tsure, or *Wadzure*: Guest's attendant.
Tomo: An insignificant attendant.
Kogata: A very young boy.
Kiogenshi: Sailor or servant.
Hannya: An evil spirit.

The speaking part of Noh is called "Kataru," the singing parts "Utai."

KAYOI KOMACHI*

The Scene is in Yamashiro

CHARACTERS

SHITE, SHOSHO, the ghost of ONO NO KOMACHI's lover.
WAKI, or subsidiary character, a priest.
TSURE, Ono no Komachi.

WAKI

I am a priest in the village of Yase. And there's an odd little woman comes here every day with fruit and fuel. If she comes to-day I shall ask her who she is.

TSURE
(*announcing herself to the audience*)

I am a woman who lives out about Itchiharano. There are many rich houses in Yase, and I take fruit and wood to them, and there's where I'm going now.

WAKI

Then you are the woman. What sort of fruit have you there?

TSURE

I've nuts and kaki and chestnuts and plums and peaches, and big and little oranges, and a bunch of tachibana, which reminds me of days that are gone.

WAKI

Then that's all right—but who are you?

TSURE

(*To herself.*) I can't tell him that now. (*To him.*) I'm just a woman who lives out by Ichihara-no-be, in all that wild grass there.

> [*So saying she disappears.*

* [NOTE.—The crux of the play is that Shosho would not accept Buddhism, and thus his spirit and Ono's are kept apart. There is nothing like a ghost for holding to an idée fixe. In Nishikigi, the ghosts of the two lovers are kept apart because the woman had steadily refused the hero's offering of charm sticks. The two ghosts are brought together by the piety of a wandering priest. Mr. Yeats tells me that he has found a similar legend in Arran, where the ghosts come to a priest to be married.—E.P.]

WAKI

That's queer. I asked her her name. She won't tell me. She says she's just a woman from Ichihara, and then she's gone like a mist. If you go down by Ichihara you can hear the wind in the Susuki bushes as in the poem of Ono no Komachi's, where she says, "Ono, no I will not tell the wind my name is Ono, as long as Susuki has leaves." I dare say it is she or her spirit. I will go there the better to pray for her.

CHORUS
(announcing the action and change of scene)

So he went out of his little cottage in the temple enclosure. He went to Ichihara and prayed.

TSURE
(her voice heard from the furze bush, speaking to the priest)

There's a heap of good in your prayers; do you think you could bring me to Buddha?

SHITE
(the spirit of SHOSHO)

It's an ill time to do that. Go back. You move in ill hours.

TSURE

I say they were very fine prayers. I will not come back without a struggle.

SHITE

I've a sad heart to see you looking up to Buddha, you who left me alone, I diving in the black rivers of hell. Will soft prayers be a comfort to you in your quiet heaven, you who know that I'm alone in that wild, desolate place? To put you away from me! That's all he has come for, with his prayers. Will they do any good to my sort?

TSURE

O dear, you can speak for yourself, but my heart is clear as new moonlight.

CHORUS

See, she comes out of the bush.
        [*That is, the spirit has materialized.*]

SHITE

Will nothing make you turn back?

TSURE

Faith is like a wild deer on the mountain. It will not stop when you call it.

SHITE

Then I'll be the dog of your Buddha; I will not be beaten away from you.

TSURE

How terrible, how terrible his face is!*

CHORUS

See, he has caught at her sleeve.

WAKI

(*This apparently trivial speech of the* WAKI's *arrests them. It is most interesting in view of the "new" doctrine of the suggestibility or hypnotizability of ghosts. The* WAKI *says merely:*) Are you Ono no Komachi? And you, Shosho? Did you court her a hundred nights? Can you show this?

[*Then they begin the dance of this Noh, the image of the coming of* SHOSHO.

TSURE

I did not know you had such deep thirst for me.

SHITE

You deceived me by telling me to drive out a hundred nights. I thought you meant it. I took my carriage and came.

TSURE

I said, "Change your appearance, or people will see you and talk."

SHITE

I changed my carriage. Though I had fresh horses in Kohata, I even came barefoot.

* Shosho is not by any means bringing a humble and contrite heart to his conversion.

TSURE
You came in every sort of condition.

SHITE
It was not such a dark way by moonlight.

TSURE
You even came in the snow.

SHITE
I can, even now, seem to be shaking it off my sleeves.
[*This movement is developed into a dance.*

TSURE
In the evening rain.

SHITE
That devil in your rain was my invisible terror.

TSURE
On the night when there was no cloud——

SHITE
I had my own rain of tears; that was the dark night, surely.

TSURE
The twilight was always my terror.

SHITE
She will wait for the moon, I said, but she will never wait
for me.

CHORUS
The dawn! oh, the dawn is also a time of many thoughts.

SHITE
Yes, for me.

CHORUS
Though the fowls crow, though the bells ring, and though
the night shall never come up, it is less than nothing to her.

SHITE
With many struggles——

CHORUS

—I went for ninety-nine nights. And this is the hundredth
night. This night is the longing fulfilled. He hurries. What is
he wearing?

SHITE

His kasa is wretched; it is a very poor cloak, indeed.

CHORUS

His hat is in tatters.

SHITE

His under-coat is in rags.
[*All this refers both to* SHOSHO'S *having come dis-
guised, and being now in but the tatters of some
sort of astral body. Then presumably a light shows
in his spirit, as probably he had worn some rich
garment under his poor disguise.*

CHORUS

He comes in the dress with patterns;
He comes oversprinkled with flowers.
It is Shosho!

SHITE

In a garment with many folds.

CHORUS

The violet-coloured hakama. He thought she would wait
for his coming.

SHITE

I hurried to her as now.

CHORUS
(*speaking for* SHOSHO'S *thoughts*)
Though she only asks me to drink a cup of moonlight, I
will not take it. It is a trick to catch one for Buddha.

CHORUS
(*in a final statement*)
Both their sins vanished. They both became pupils of Bud-
dha, both Komachi and Shosho.

THE END

———

The final dance means that the lovers are spirits fluttering in the grass.

This eclogue is very incomplete. Ono seems rather like Echo, and without the last two lines of the chorus one could very well imagine her keeping up her tenzone with Shosho until the end of time.

In the performance of November 19, as stated before, this play was followed by Manzaburo's Suma Genji (Genji at Suma).

I must ask the reader to suspend his judgment of the dramatic values of such plays until he has read Nishikigi and some of the longer eclogues, at least some of those in which the utai or libretto set by itself conveys a fuller sense of the meaning.

SUMA GENJI

CHARACTERS

SHITE, an old wood-cutter, who is an apparition of the hero, GENJI, as a sort of place-spirit, the spirit of the seashore at Suma.

WAKI, FUJIWARA, a priest with a hobby for folk-lore, who is visiting sacred places.

SECOND SHITE, or the SHITE in his second manner or apparition, GENJI's spirit appearing in a sort of glory of waves and moonlight.

WAKI
(announcing himself)

I, Fujiwara no Okinori,
Am come over the sea from Hiuga;
I am a priest from the shinto temple at Miyazaki,
And, as I lived far afield,
I could not see the temple of the great god at Ise;
And now I am a-mind to go thither,
And am come to Suma, the sea-board.
Here Genji lived, and here I shall see the young cherry,
The tree that is so set in the tales——

SHITE

And I am a wood-cutter of Suma.
I fish in the twilight;
By day I pack wood and make salt.
Here is the mount of Suma.
There is the tree, the young cherry.*

And you may be quite right about Genji's having lived here. That blossom will flare in a moment.†

WAKI

I must find out what that old man knows. (*To* SHITE.) Sir, you seem very poor, and yet you neglect your road; you stop

---

* It must be remembered that the properties and scene are not represen-tational but symbolic, the hero-actor simply says in effect, "Pretend that that is the tree and that the mountain."

† There is here the double-entente. The blossom will really come out: it is a day of anniversary or something of that kind; also Genji will appear in his proper glory, as the audience knows, though the Waki does not.

on your way home, just to look at a flower. Is that the tree of the stories?

SHITE
I dare say I'm poor enough; but you don't know much if you're asking about that tree, "Is it the fine tree of Suma?"

WAKI
Well, *is* it the tree? I've come on purpose to see it.

SHITE
What! you really have come to see the cherry-blossom, and not to look at Mount Suma?

WAKI
Yes; this is where Genji lived, and you are so old that you ought to know a lot of stories about him.

CHORUS
(*telling out* GENJI'S *thoughts*)
If I tell over the days that are gone,
My sleeves will wither.*
The past was at Kiritsubo;
I went to the lovely cottage, my mother's,
But the emperor loved me.

I was made esquire at twelve, with the hat. The soothsayers unrolled my glories.† I was called Hikaru Genji. I was chujo in Hahakigi province. I was chujo in the land of the maple-feasting.‡ At twenty-five I came to Suma, knowing all sorrow of seafare, having none to attend my dreams, no one to hear the old stories.

Then I was recalled to the city. I passed from office to office. I was naidaijin in Miwotsukushi, I was dajodaijin in the lands of Otome, and daijotenno in Fuji no Uraba; for this I was called Hikam Kimi.

WAKI
But tell me exactly where he lived. Tell me all that you know about him.

---

* That is, this present manifestation in the shape of an old man will fade.
† The "soothsayer" is literally "the physiognomist from Corea."
‡ Chujo, naidaijin, etc. are names for different grades of office.

SHITE

One can't place the exact spot; he lived all along here by the waves. If you will wait for the moonlight you might see it all in a mist.

CHORUS

He was in Suma in the old days——

SHITE

(*stepping behind a screen or making some sign of departure, he completes the sentence of the chorus*)
—but now in the aery heaven.

CHORUS
(*to* WAKI)

Wait and the moon will show him.
That woodman is gone in the clouds.

WAKI

That "woodman" was Genji himself, who was here talking live words. I will wait for the night. I will stay here to see what happens. (*Announcing his act.**) Then Fujiwara no Okinori lay down and heard the waves filled with music.

SCENE II. *begins with the appearance of the* SECOND SHITE, *that is to say, a bright apparition of* GENJI *in supernatural form.*

GENJI

How beautiful this sea is! When I trod the grass here I was called "Genji the gleaming," and now from the vaulting heaven I reach down to set a magic on mortals. I sing of the moon in this shadow, here on this sea-marge of Suma. Here I will dance Sei-kai-ha, the blue dance of the sea waves.

[*And then he begins to dance.*

CHORUS
(*accompanying and describing the dance*)

The flower of waves-reflected
Is on his white garment;
That pattern covers the sleeve.
The air is alive with flute-sounds,

* The characters often give their own stage directions or explain the meaning of their acts, as in the last line here.

With the song of various pipes
The land is a-quiver,
And even the wild sea of Suma
Is filled with resonant quiet.

Moving in clouds and in rain,
The dream overlaps with the real;
There was a light out of heaven,
There was a young man at the dance here;
Surely it was Genji Hikaru,
It was Genji Hikaru in spirit.

GENJI

My name is known to the world;
Here by the white waves was my dwelling;
But I am come down out of sky
To put my glamour on mortals.

CHORUS

Gracious is the presence of Genji,
It is like the feel of things at Suma.

GENJI
(*referring also to a change in the dance*)
The wind is abated.

CHORUS

A thin cloud——

GENJI
—clings to the clear-blown sky.
It seems like the spring-time.

CHORUS

He came down like Brahma, Indra, and the Four Kings
    visiting the abode of Devas and Men.*
He, the soul of the place.†
He, who seemed but a woodman,
He flashed with the honoured colours,

---

* The Four Kings, i.e. of the four points of the compass. Devas (spirits)
and Men occupy the position immediately below the Gods.

† More precisely "He became the place." You can compare this with
Buckle, or Jules Romains' studies in unanimism.

He the true-gleaming.
Blue-grey is the garb they wear here,
Blue-grey he fluttered in Suma;
His sleeves were like the grey sea-waves;
They moved with curious rustling,
Like the noise of the restless waves,
Like the bell of a country town
'Neath the nightfall.

THE END

———

I dare say the play, Suma Genji, will seem undramatic to
some people the first time they read it. The suspense is the
suspense of waiting for a supernatural manifestation—which
comes. Some will be annoyed at a form of psychology which
is, in the West, relegated to spiritistic séances. There is, how-
ever, no doubt that such psychology exists. All through the
winter of 1914–15 I watched Mr. Yeats correlating folk-lore
(which Lady Gregory had collected in Irish cottages) and data
of the occult writers, with the habits of charlatans of Bond
Street. If the Japanese authors had not combined the psy-
chology of such matters with what is to me a very fine sort of
poetry, I would not bother about it.

The reader will miss the feel of suspense if he is unable to
put himself in sympathy with the priest eager to see "even in a
vision" the beauty lost in the years, "the shadow of the past in
bright form." I do not say that this sympathy is easily ac-
quired. It is too unusual a frame of mind for us to fall into it
without conscious effort. But if one can once get over the feel-
ing of hostility, if one can once let himself into the world of
the Noh, there is undoubtedly a new beauty before him. I
have found it well worth the trial, and can hope that others
will also.

The arrangement of five or six Noh into one performance
explains, in part, what may seem like a lack of construction in
some of the pieces; the plays have, however, a very severe
construction of their own, a sort of musical construction.

When a text seems to "go off into nothing" at the end, the reader must remember "that the vagueness or paleness of words is made good by the emotion of the final dance," for the Noh has its unity in emotion. It has also what we may call Unity of Image.* At least, the better plays are all built into the intensification of a single Image: the red maple leaves and the snow flurry in Nishikigi, the pines in Takasago, the blue-grey waves and wave pattern in Suma Genji, the mantle of feathers in the play of that name, Hagoromo.

When it comes to presenting Professor Fenollosa's records of his conversations with Umewaka Minoru, the restorer of Noh, I find myself much puzzled as to where to begin. I shall, however, plunge straight into the conversation of May 15, 1900, as that seems germane to other matters already set forth in this excerpt, preceding it only by the quaint record of an earlier meeting, December 20, 1898, as follows:

Called on old Mr. Umewaka with Mr. Hirata. Presented him with large box of eggs. He thanked me for presenting last Friday 18 yen to Takeyo for my six lessons, which began on November 18. I apologized to him for the mistake of years ago, thanked him for his frankness, his reticence to others, and his kindness in allowing me to begin again with him, asked him to receive 15 yen as a present in consideration of his recent help.

He was very affable, and talked with me for about 1½ hours. He asked me to sing, and I sang "Hansakaba." He praised me, said everything was exactly right and said that both he and Takeyo considered my progress wonderful; better than a Japanese could make. He said I was already advanced enough to sing in a Japanese company.†

Mosse and I are the only foreigners who have ever been taught Noh, and I am the only foreigner now practising it.

We spoke much of the art of it, I giving him a brief account of Greek drama. He already knew something about opera.

He said the excellence of Noh lay in emotion, not in action or externals. Therefore there were no accessories, as in the theatres.

* This intensification of the Image, this manner of construction, is very interesting to me personally, as an Imagiste, for we Imagistes knew nothing of these plays when we set out in our own manner. These plays are also an answer to a question that has several times been put to me: "Could one do a long Imagiste poem, or even a long poem in vers libre?"

† This is in Fenollosa's diary, not in a part of a lecture or in anything he had published, so there is no question of its being an immodest statement.

"Spirit" (tamashii) was the word he used. The pure spirit was what it (Noh) worked in, so it was higher than other arts. If a Noh actor acted his best, Umewaka could read his character. The actor could not conceal it. The spirit must out, the "whole man," he said. Therefore he always instructed his sons to be moral, pure and true in all their daily lives, otherwise they could not become the greatest actors.

He spoke much about the (popular) theatre, of its approximation of Noh when he was about thirteen years old. The present Danjuro's father and his troop disguised themselves and came to the performance of Kanjin Noh, from which they were normally excluded. This was the one opportunity for the public to see Noh, it is (as said elsewhere) the single benefit performance allowed to each master Noh actor. Other actors were excluded.

Then it was that Ichikawa, having seen these Noh plays, imitated them in the famous "Kanjiinjo," which the present Danjuro still plays as one of his 18 special pieces. Under the present regime, the popular actors have access to the Noh plays, and the popular plays have imitated them still further. Almost all forms of music and recitation have now (1898) taken more or less of their style from Noh.

Noh has been a purification of the Japanese soul for 400 years. Kobori Enshu classified the fifteen virtues of Noh, among which he counted mental and bodily health as one, calling it "Healing without medicine."

"Dancing is especially known, by its circulation of the blood, to keep off the disease of old age."

Now Minoru and his sons occasionally go to Danjuro's theatre. He spoke much about the Shogun's court. When a Noh actor was engaged by the Shogun he had to sign long articles to the effect that he would never divulge even to his wife or his relatives any of the doings or descriptions of things in the palace, also that he would not visit houses of pleasure or go to the theatre. If caught doing these things he was severely punished. Occasionally a Noh actor would go to the theatre in disguise.

With the exception of the Kanjin Noh, common people could not, at that time, see the Noh, but a very few were occasionally let in to the monthly rehearsals.

The notes for May 15, 1900, begin as follows:

He (Minoru) says that Mitsuni (a certain actor) has learning and great Nesshin, or technique, but that, after all the technique is learned, the great difficulty is to grasp the spirit of the piece.

He always tells the newspaper men to-day not to write criticisms of Noh. They can criticize the popular theatre, for there even the plots may change, and amateurs can judge it. But in Noh everything comes down by tradition from early Tokugawa days and cannot be judged by any living man, but can only be followed faithfully.*

Although there is no general score for actors and cats (i.e. the four musicians who have sat at the back of the Noh stage for so many centuries that no one quite knows what they mean or how they came there), there is in the hands of the Taiyu, or actor-manager, a roll such as he (Minoru) himself has, which gives general directions, not much detail. This contains only the ordinary text, with no special notations for singing, but for the dances there are minute diagrams showing where to stand, how far to go forward, the turns in a circle, the turns to right or left, how far to go with the right or left foot, how many steps, eyes right, eyes left, what mask and what clothes are to be worn, the very lines in which the clothes must hang, and the exact position of the arms. There are drawings of figures naked for old men, women, girls, boys, ghosts, and all kinds of characters sitting and standing; they show the proper relation of limbs and body. Then there are similar drawings of the same figures clothed.

But one cannot trust merely to such a set of instructions. There is a great deal that must be supplied by experience, feeling, and tradition, and which has always been so supplied. Minoru feels this so strongly that he has not yet shown the rolls to his sons, for fear it might make them mechanical.

"KUDEN" (TRADITION)

A book of this sort has been handed down by his ancestors from early Tokugawa days, but it is only a rough draft. He has written a long supplement on the finer points, but has shown it to no one. One should not trust to it, either. Such fine things as Matsukaze, the pose for looking at the moon, or at the dawn, or at the double reflection of the moon in two tubs, and all the detail of business cannot be written down, at such places he writes merely "kuden" (tradition), to show that this is something that can be learned only from a master. Sometimes his teacher used to beat him with a fan when he was learning.

Relying on record plus such tradition, we can say with fair certitude that there has been no appreciable change in Noh since the early days of Tokugawa (that is to say, since the beginning of the seventeenth century, or about the end of Shakespeare's lifetime).

Kuden, or this feeling for the traditional intensity, is not to be gained by mere teaching or mimicry, or by a hundred times trying;

---

* This is not so stupid as it seems; we might be fairly grateful if some private or chartered company had preserved the exact Elizabethan tradition for acting Shakespeare.

but it must be learned by a grasp of the inner spirit. In a place, for instance, where a father comes to his lost son, walks three steps forward, pats him twice on the head and balances his stick, it is very difficult to get all this into grace and harmony, and it certainly cannot be written down or talked into a man by word of mouth.

Imitation must not be wholly external. There is a tradition of a young actor who wished to learn Sekidera Komachi, the most secret and difficult of the three plays, which alone are so secret that they were told and taught only by father to eldest son. He followed a fine old woman, eighty years of age, in the street and watched her every step. After a while she was alarmed and asked him why he was following her. He said she was interesting. She replied that she was too old. Then he confessed that he was an ambitious Noh actor and wanted to play Komachi.

An ordinary woman would have praised him, but she did not. She said it was bad for Noh, though it might be good for the common theatre, to imitate facts. For Noh he must feel the thing as a whole, from the inside. He would not get it copying facts point by point. All this is true.

You must lay great stress upon this in explaining the meaning and aesthetics of the Noh.

There is a special medium for expressing emotion. It is the voice.

Each pupil has his own voice; it cannot be made to imitate the voice of an old woman or a spirit (oni). It must remain always the same, his own; yet with that one individual voice of his he must so express himself as to make it clear that it is the mentality of an old woman, or whatever it happens to be, who is speaking.

It is a Noh saying that "The heart is the form."

COSTUMES

There is a general tradition as to costumes. Coloured garments cannot be interchanged for white. The general colour is a matter of record, but not the minute patterns, which may be changed from time to time. It is not necessary that one dress should be reserved for one particular character in one particular piece. Even in Tokugawa days there was not always a costume for each special character. Some were used for several parts and some were unique; so also were the masks.

The general colour and colour-effect of the dress cannot be changed: say it were small circular patterns on a black ground, this must remain, but the exact flower or ornament inside the circles may vary. The length and cut of the sleeve could not be altered, but only the small details of the pattern. The size of the pattern might be changed just a little.

MASKS

The hannia, or daemonic masks, are different. The hannia in Awoi no Uye is lofty in feeling; that of Dojoji is base. They are very different. The masks of Shunkan, Semimaru, Kagekiyo, and Yoroboshi cannot be used for any other parts. Kontan's mask can be used for several parts, as, for example, the second shite in Takasago. Of course if one has only one hannia mask one must use it for all hannia, but it is better not to do so. The Adachigahara hannia is the lowest in feeling.

Fifty years ago they tried to copy the old masks exactly. The Shogun had Kanze's masks copied even to the old spots. Now it is difficult to get good sculptors.

Turning the head is very difficult, for the actor must be one piece with the mask.

An ordinary mask is worth 30 yen; a great one, 200. At first one cannot distinguish between them. But the longer you look at a good mask the more charged with life it becomes. A common actor cannot use a really good mask. He cannot make himself one with it. A great actor makes it live.

MUSIC

In the notes for a conversation of May 6, there are the following remarks about the singing or chanting [the Noh texts are part in prose and part in verse; some parts are sung and some spoken, or one might better say, intoned]:

The importance of the music is in its intervals [he seems to mean intervals between beats, i.e. rhythm intervals, not "intervals" of pitch]. It is just like the dropping of rain from the eaves.

The musical bar is a sort of double bar made up of five notes and seven notes, or of seven notes and then seven more notes, the fourteen notes being sung in the same time as the twelve first ones.

The division of seven syllables is called "yo," that of five is called "in"; the big drum is called "yo," and the small drum "in." The seven syllables are the part of the big drum, the five syllables are the part of the small drum—but if they come in succession it is too regular; so sometimes they reverse and the big drum takes the "in" part and the small drum the "yo."

The head of the chorus naturally controls the musicians. The chorus is called "kimi," or lord, and the "cats," or musicians, are called "subjects." When Minoru acts as head of the chorus, he says he can manage the "cats" by a prolonging or shortening of sounds. [This is obscure, but apparently each musician has ideas of his own about tempo.]

The "cats" must conform to him. The chorus is subject to the shite, or chief actor. A certain number of changes may have crept into the tradition. The art consists in not being mechanical. The "cats," the chorus, and the shite "feel out their own originality," and render their own emotions. Even during the last fifteen years some changes may have crept in unconsciously. Even in Tokugawa days there never was any general score bringing all the parts under a single eye. There is not and never has been any such score. There are independent traditions. [NOTE.—The privileges of acting as "cats" and as waki were hereditary privileges of particular families, just as the privilege of acting the chief parts pertained to the members of the five hereditary schools.] Minoru and other actors may know the parts [he means here the musical air] instinctively or by memory; no one has ever written them down. Some actors know only the arias of the few pieces of which they are masters.

Each "cat" of each school has his own traditions. When he begins to learn, he writes down in his note-book a note for each one of the twelve syllables. Each man has his own notation, and he has a more or less complete record to learn from. These details are never told to any one. The ordinary actors and chorus singers do not know them.

In singing, everything depends on the most minute distinction between "in" and "yo." Minoru was surprised to hear that this was not so in the West. In "yo" there must be "in," and in "in," "yo." This adds breadth and softness, "haba" he calls it.*

THE STAGE

The stage is, as I have said, a platform open on three sides and reached by a bridge from the green-room. The notes on the conversation of June 2 run as follows:

They have Hakama Noh in summer. The general audience does not like it, but experts can see the movements better as the actors sometimes wear no upper dress at all, and are naked save for the semi-transparent hakama. New servants are surprised at it.

Mr. Umewaka Minoru has tried hard not to change any detail of the old customs. In recent times many have urged him to change the

---

* This looks like a sort of syncopation. I don't know enough about music to consider it musically with any fullness, but it offers to the student of metric most interesting parallels, or if not parallels, suggestions for comparison with sapphics and with some of the troubadour measures (notably those of Arnaut Daniel), the chief trouble being that Professor Fenollosa's notes at this point are not absolutely lucid.

lights, but he prefers the old candles. They ask him to modernize the text and to keep the shite from sitting in the middle [of the stage? or of the play?], but he won't.

A pupil of his, a wood-dealer, says that a proper Noh stage could not be built now, for it is all of hinoten. The floor is in twenty pieces, each of which would now cost 250 yen. There must be no knots in the pillars, and all the large pillars and cross pieces are of one piece. This would cost enormously now even if it were possible at all.

Awoyama Shimotsuke no Kami Roju built this stage [the one now used by Minoru] for his villa in Aoyama more than forty years ago; it was moved to its present site in the fourth year of Meiji (1872). The daimyo sold it to a curio dealer from whom Umewaka Minoru bought it. Shimotsuke was some relation to the daimyo of Bishu, in Owari, and so he got the timbers for nothing. The best timber comes from Owari. So the stage had cost only the carpenter's wages (2000 yen?). Now the wood alone would cost 20,000 to 40,000 yen, if you could get it at all. You couldn't contract for it.

The form of the stage was fixed in the time of Hideyoshi and Iyeyasu. In Ashikaga (fourteenth century) the performances were in Tadasu ga wara, and the stage was open on all sides. The bridge came to the middle of one side (apparently the back) where the pine tree now is. The stage was square, as it now is, with four pillars. The audience surrounded it in a great circle "like Sumo" [whatever that may mean]. They had a second story or gallery and the Shogun sat in front. The roof was as it now is.

The roof should not be tiled, but should be like the roof of the shinto temples in Ise. Shimotsuke had had a tiled roof because he was afraid of fire. People had said that he (Minoru) was mad to set up a Noh stage [at the time when he was starting to revive the performance]; so he had made the roof small and inconspicuous to attract less notice.

Under the stage are set five earthen jars, in the space bounded by the pillars, to make the sound reverberate—both the singing and the stamping.* There are two more jars under the musicians' place and three under the bridge. This has been so since early Tokugawa times. The ground is hollowed out under the stage to the depth of four feet.†

The jars are not set upright, as this would obstruct the sound. They are set at 45 degrees. Sometimes they are hung by strings and sometimes set on posts. Minoru's are on posts.

---

* This stamping dates from the time when some mythological person danced on a tub to attract the light-goddess.

† The stage is in the open. Minoru says elsewhere, "Snow is worst for it blows on the stage and gets on the feet."

Some jars are faced right and some left; there is a middle one upright. Minoru says it is just like a drum, and that the curve of the jars has to be carefully made. The larger the jars the better.

Hideyoshi or Iyeyasu put the back on the stage. It is made of a double set of boards in order to throw the sound forward. They didn't like having the sound wasted. This innovation was, on that score, aesthetic.

"Social and palace" reasons have in some measure determined the form of the stage.

The floor is not quite level, but slopes slightly forward. The art of stage-building is a secret of "daiko." It is as difficult to build a Noh stage as to build a shinto temple, and there are no proper Noh stages built now.

The painting of the pine tree on the back is most important. It is a congratulatory symbol of unchanging green and strength.

On some stages they have small plum flowers, but this is incorrect; there should be no colour except the green. The bamboo is the complement of the pine. To paint these trees well is a great secret of Kano artists. When skilfully painted, they set off the musicians' forms.

The three real little pine trees along the bridge are quite fixed; they symbolize heaven, earth, and man. The one for heaven is nearest the stage, and then comes the one which symbolizes man. They are merely symbols like the painted pine tree. Sometimes when a pine is mentioned the actors look toward it.

The measurements of the stage have not changed since early Tokugawa days. It should be three ken square, but this measurement is sometimes taken inside, sometimes outside the pillars.

There is no special symbolism in the bridge; it is merely a way of getting across. The length was arbitrary under the Ashikaga; later it was fixed by rule. At the Shogun's court the bridge was 13 ken long, and one needed a great voice to act there. The middle palace bridge was 7 ken. Minoru's bridge is 5 ken. The bridge must be an odd number of ken, like 13, or like the "in" and "yo" numbers (7 and 5). The width is 9 "shaken" outside and 8 inside the pillars.

Part II

The reader, having perused thus far in patience or in impatience, will probably want to know what came of it all. Does the present Noh, saved from the ashes of the revolution, justify so minute an examination of its past? Believing, as I do, that the Noh is a very great art, I can heartily say that it does. I give here several further specimens of the text or libretto. The reader must remember that the words are only one part of this art. The words are fused with the music and with the ceremonial dancing. One must read or "examine" these texts "as if one were listening to music." One must build out of their indefiniteness a definite image. The plays are at their best, I think, an image; that is to say, their unity lies in the image—they are built up about it as the Greek plays are built up about a single moral conviction. The Greek plays are elaborate presentations of some incident of a story well known; so also the Japanese plays rely upon a certain knowledge of past story or legend. They present some more vivid hour or crisis. The Greek plays are troubled and solved by the gods; the Japanese are abounding in ghosts and spirits. Often the spirit appears first in some homely guise, as, in Catholic legend, we find Christ appearing as a beggar.

The spirit seems often an old man or old woman rapt in meditation. In Kumasaka we come upon a simple recluse. The plot is as follows:

The pilgrim priest is asked to pray for some anonymous soul. His interlocutor's hut has in it no shrine, no single picture of Buddha, nothing but a spear and an iron mace. The owner of the hut alludes to himself as "this priest." His gospel is the very simple one of protecting travellers from neighbouring bandits.

Suddenly both he and his hut disappear (vide the comments of the chorus). The pilgrim, however, having begun his prayer for the unknown dead man, goes on with the service.

He is rewarded. The second act opens with the reappearance of the spirit in splendid array. He is the spirit of Kumasaka, remembering the glory of his days, meditating upon them, upon his bowmen and deeds of arms. The final passage is the Homeric presentation of combat between him and the young boy, Ushiwaka. But note here the punctilio. Kumasaka's spirit returns to do justice to the glory of Ushiwaka and to tell of his own defeat. All this is symbolized in the dance climax of the play, and is told out by the chorus.

KUMASAKA

A Play in two Acts, by Ujinobu,
adopted son of Motokiyo

CHARACTERS

A PRIEST.

FIRST SHITE, or HERO, the apparition of KUMASAKA in the form of an old priest.

SECOND SHITE, the apparition of KUMASAKA in his true form.

CHORUS. This chorus sometimes speaks what the chief characters are thinking, sometimes it describes or interprets the meaning of their movements.

PLOT.—The ghost of Kumasaka makes reparation for his brigandage by protecting the country. He comes back to praise the bravery of the young man who had killed him in single combat.

PRIEST

Where shall I rest, wandering weary of the world? I am a city-bred priest, I have not seen the east counties, and I've a mind to go there. Crossing the hills, I look on the lake of Omi, on the woods of Awatsu. Going over the long bridge at Seta, I rested a night at Noji, and another at Shinohara, and at the dawn I came to the green field, Awono in Miwo. I now pass Akasaka at sunset.

SHITE
(*in the form of an old priest*)

I could tell that priest a thing or two.

PRIEST

Do you mean me? What is it?

SHITE

A certain man died on this day. I ask you to pray for him.

PRIEST

All right; but whom shall I pray for?

SHITE

I will not tell you his name, but his grave lies in the green field beyond that tall pine tree. He cannot enter the gates of Paradise, and so I ask you to pray.

PRIEST

But I do not think it is right for me to pray unless you tell me his name.

SHITE

No, no; you can pray the prayer, Ho kai shujo biodo ri aku; that would do.

PRIEST
(*praying*)

Unto all mortals let there be equal grace, to pass from this life of agony by the gates of death into law; into the peaceful kingdom.

SHITE
(*saying first a word or two*)

If you pray for him,——

CHORUS
(*continuing the sentence*)

—If you pray with the prayer of "Exeat" he will be thankful, and you need not then know his name. They say that prayer can be heard for even the grass and the plants, for even the sand and the soil here; and they will surely hear it, if you pray for an unknown man.

SHITE

Will you come in? This is my cottage.

PRIEST

This is your house? Very well, I will hold the service in your house; but I see no picture of Buddha nor any wooden image in this cottage—nothing but a long spear on one wall and an iron stick in place of a priest's wand, and many arrows. What are these for?

SHITE
(*thinking*)

Yes, this priest is still in the first stage of faith. (*Aloud.*) As you see, there are many villages here: Tarui, Awohaka, and Akasaka.

But the tall grass of Awo-no-gahara grows round the roads between them, and the forest is thick at Koyasu and Awohaka, and many robbers come out under the rains. They attack the baggage on horseback, and take the clothing of maids and servants who pass here. So I go out with his spear.

PRIEST

That's very fine, isn't it?

CHORUS

You will think it very strange for a priest to do this, but even Buddha has the sharp sword of Mida, and Aizen Miowo has arrows, and Tamon, taking his long spear, throws down the evil spirits.

SHITE

The deep love——

CHORUS

—is excellent. Good feeling and keeping order are much more excellent than the love of Bosatsu. "I think of these matters and know little of anything else. It is from my own heart that I am lost, wandering. But if I begin talking I shall keep on talking until dawn. Go to bed, good father, I will sleep too."

He seemed to be going to his bedroom, but suddenly his figure disappeared, and the cottage became a field of grass. The priest passes the night under the pine trees.

PRIEST

I cannot sleep out the night. Perhaps if I held my service during the night under this pine tree——

[*He begins his service for the dead man.*

PART SECOND

SECOND SHITE

There are winds in the east and south; the clouds are not calm in the west; and in the north the wind of the dark evening blusters; and under the shade of the mountain——

CHORUS

—there is a rustling of boughs and leaves.

SECOND SHITE

Perhaps there will be moonshine to-night, but the clouds veil the sky; the moon will not break up their shadow. "Have at them!" "Ho, there!" "Dash in!" That is the way I would shout, calling and ordering my men before and behind, my bowmen and horsemen. I plundered men of their treasure, that was my work in the world, and now I must go on; it is sorry work for a spirit.

PRIEST

Are you Kumasaka Chohan? Tell me the tale of your years.

SECOND SHITE
(*now known as* KUMASAKA)

There were great merchants in Sanjo, Yoshitsugu, and Nobutaka; they collected treasure each year; they sent rich goods up to Oku. It was then I assailed their trains. Would you know what men were with me?

PRIEST

Tell me the chief men; were they from many a province?

KUMASAKA

There was Kakusho of Kawachi, there were the two brothers Suriharitaro; they have no rivals in fencing.*

PRIEST

What chiefs came to you from the city?

KUMASAKA

Emon of Sanjo, Kozari of Mibu.

PRIEST

In the fighting with torches and in mêlée——

KUMASAKA

—they had no equals.

PRIEST

In northern Hakoku?

* "Omoteuchi," face-to-face attack.

KUMASAKA

Were Aso no Matsuwaka and Mikune no Kuro.

PRIEST

In Kaga?

KUMASAKA

No, Chohan was the head there. There were seventy comrades who were very strong and skilful.

CHORUS

While Yoshitsugu was going along in the fields and on the mountains, we set many spies to take him.

KUMASAKA

Let us say that he is come to the village of Akasaka. This is the best place to attack him. There are many ways to escape if we are defeated, and he has invited many guests and has had a great feast at the inn.

PRIEST

When the night was advanced the brothers Yoshitsugu and Nobutaka fell asleep.

KUMASAKA

But there was a small boy with keen eyes, about sixteen or seventeen years old, and he was looking through a little hole in the partition, alert to the slightest noise.

PRIEST

He did not sleep even a wink.

KUMASAKA

We did not know it was Ushiwaka.

PRIEST

It was fate.

KUMASAKA

The hour had come.

PRIEST

Be quick!

KUMASAKA

Have at them!

CHORUS
*(describing the original combat, now symbolized
in the dance)*

At this word they rushed in, one after another. They seized the torches; it seemed as if gods could not face them. Ushiwaka stood unafraid; he seized a small halberd and fought like a lion in earnest, like a tiger rushing, like a bird swooping. He fought so cleverly that he felled the thirteen who opposed him; many were wounded besides. They fled without swords or arrows. Then Kumasaka said, "Are you the devil? Is it a god who has struck down these men with such ease? Perhaps you are not a man. However, dead men take no plunder, and I'd rather leave this truck of Yoshitsugu's than my corpse." So he took his long spear and was about to make off——

KUMASAKA

—But Kumasaka thought——

CHORUS
(taking it up)

—What can he do, that young chap, if I ply my secret arts freely? Be he god or devil, I will grasp him and grind him. I will offer his body as sacrifice to those whom he has slain. So he drew back, and holding his long spear against his side, he hid himself behind the door and stared at the young lad. Ushiwaka beheld him, and holding his bill at his side, he crouched at a little distance. Kumasaka waited likewise. They both waited, alertly; then Kumasaka stepped forth swiftly with his left foot, and struck out with the long spear. It would have run through an iron wall. Ushiwaka parried it lightly, swept it away, left volted. Kumasaka followed and again lunged out with the spear, and Ushiwaka parried the spear-blade quite lightly. Then Kumasaka turned the edge of his spear-blade towards Ushiwaka and slashed at him, and Ushiwaka leaped to the right. Kumasaka lifted his spear and the two weapons were twisted together. Ushiwaka drew back his blade. Kumasaka swung with his spear. Ushiwaka led up and stepped in shadow.

Kumasaka tried to find him, and Ushiwaka slit through the back-chink of his armour; this seemed the end of his course, and he was wroth to be slain by such a young boy.

KUMASAKA

Slowly the wound——

CHORUS

—seemed to pierce; his heart failed; weakness o'ercame him.

KUMASAKA

At the foot of this pine tree——

CHORUS

—he vanished like a dew.

And so saying, he disappeared among the shades of the pine tree at Akasaka, and night fell.

THE END

SHOJO

This little dance-plan or eclogue is, evidently, one of the "opening or closing pieces in praise of the gods or the reign." It is merely a little service of praise to the wine-spirit. It is quite easy to understand, from such a performance as this, why one meets travellers who say, "Noh? I've seen Noh Dances; I know nothing about Noh Plays."

WAKI

I am a man called Kofu in a village by Yosu,* which is at the foot of Kane Kinzan in China, and because of my filial deference I dreamed a strange dream. And the dream told me that if I would sell saké in the street by Yosu I should be rich. I obeyed. Time passed. I am rich. And this is the strange thing about it: whenever I go to the market, there's the same man comes to drink saké. No matter how much he drinks, his face shows no change. It is curious. When I asked his name, he said, "Shojo." A shojo is a monkey. I waited for him where the river runs out at Jinyo, clipping chrysanthemum petals into the saké. I waited for him before moon-rise.

CHORUS

This is chrysanthemum water. Give me the cup. I take it and look at a friend.

HERO

O saké!

CHORUS

Saké is a word well in season. Saké is best in autumn.

HERO

Though autumn winds blow——

CHORUS

——I am not cold at all.

HERO

I will put cotton over——

* Yosu, i e Yang-tze.

CHORUS

—the white chrysanthemum flowers

> To keep in the smell.
> Now we'll take saké.

HERO

The guests will also see——

CHORUS

—the moon and the stars hung out.

HERO

This place is by Jinyo.

CHORUS

The feast is on the river.

HERO
(*who is in reality* SHOJO)

Shojo will dance now.

CHORUS

The thin leaves of ashi, the leaves of the river reeds, are like flute-notes. The waves are like little drums.

HERO

The voice sounds clear through the shore-winds.

CHORUS

It is the sound of autumn.

HERO

You are welcome. I have made this jar full of saké. Take it. It will never run dry.

CHORUS

No, it will never be empty—the saké of bamboo leaves; although you drink from the lasting cup of the autumn, the autumn evening remains ever the same.

The moon fades out of the river, and the saké weighs down my blood.

And I am shaking and falling; I lie down filled with wine, and I dream; and, awaking, I find the saké still flowing from the jar of Shojo, from the magical fountain.

THE END

TAMURA

This play is to be regarded as one of those dealing with the "pacification of the country and the driving out of evil spirits," although one might perhaps look upon it as a ceremonial play for the Temple founded by Tamura, or even less exactly a ghost play.

The notes are in fragments, or rather there are several long cuts, which do not, however, obscure the outline or structure of the play.

CHARACTERS

HERO, first apparition, a boy ("doji" or temple servant).
TAMURA MARO, second apparition.
WAKI, a priest.

(The opening may be thus summarized: The Waki comes on and says that he is going to Kioto to see the sights. It is spring, and he comes from Kiyomidzu. Sakura are blooming. He wants to ask questions about the place. The boy comes on, describes the flowers, and says that the light of the goddess Kwannon has made them brighter than usual. The Waki asks him who he is "to be standing there in the shade and sweeping up the fallen petals.")

WAKI
Are you the flower-keeper?

BOY
I am a man who serves the "Jinnushi Gongen." I always sweep in blossom season—so you may call me the flower-keeper, or the honorary servant; but, whatever name you use, you should think of me as some one of rank, though I am concealed in humble appearance.

WAKI
Yes, you look that. Will you tell me about this temple?

BOY

This temple is called Seisuiji; it was founded by Tamura
Maro. In Kojimadera of Yamato there was a priest named
Kenshin. He was always wishing to see the true light of
Kwannon. And one time he saw a golden light floating on the
Kotsu River. And he was going toward it, when he met an old
man who said to him, "I am Gioye Koji, and you must seek
out a certain patron and put up a great temple."

And the old man went off to the East, and he was Kwan-
non. And the patron was Maro, Sakanouye no Tamura Maro.

CHORUS

In this pure water, Kwannon with a thousand hands gives
blessing. She blesses this land and this people.

WAKI

Well, I have met some one interesting. Can you tell me of
other places about here?

BOY

The peak to the south is Nakayama Seikanji.

WAKI

And what is that temple to the northward where they are
ringing the nightfall bell?

BOY

That is the temple of Ashino-o. Look! the moon is lifting
itself over Mount Otoba,* and lights the cherry flowers. You
must look!

WAKI

It is an hour outweighing much silver.

> [*The* BOY *and the* PRIEST *together*
> *recite the Chinese poem.*

One moment of this spring night is worth a full thousand
    gold bars.
The flowers have a fine smell under the moon.[†]

> [*There is a break here in the notes.*
> *There should follow a chorus*
> *about cherries under the moon.*

* Otoba, "sounding-wings."
† Two lines from a poem by the Chinese poet Su Shih, A.D. 1036–1101.

CHORUS

Having seen these things with you, I know you are out of the common. I wonder what your name is.

BOY

If you want to discover my name, you must watch what road I take. You must see to what I return.

CHORUS

We cannot know the far or near of his route.

BOY

I go into the mountains.

CHORUS

He said: "Watch my path." And he went down in front of the Jinnushi Gongen temple, and to Tamura-do. He opened the door and went in.

END OF PART ONE

II

WAKI

I have watched all night under the cherries. I do service beneath the full moon.

[*He performs a service.*

HERO
(*in his second apparition, no longer the boy,
but* TAMURA MARO)

That is a very blessed scripture. Just because you have droned it over, I am able to come here and speak with the traveller. This is the blessing of Kwannon.

WAKI

How strange! A man appears, lit up by the light of the flowers. What are you?

TAMURA

To be open, I am none other than Sakano-Uye Tamura Maro, out of the time of Heijo Tenno. I conquered the eastern

wild men, beat down their evil spirit, and was an honest ser-
vant to my Emperor by the grace of this temple's Buddha.

> [*Here there follows a passage in*
> *which he describes his battles.*

CHORUS

The Emperor bade me beat down the evil spirits in Suzuka
in Ise, and to set the capital of that country in peace. I drew
up my forces, and then, before I set out, I came to this
Kwannon and prayed.

TAMURA

And then a strange sign appeared.

CHORUS

Having faith in the true smile of Kwannon, he went swiftly
to war, out past Osaka to the forest Awadzu. He passed
Ishiyamaji, and, thinking it one of the gods of Kiyomidzu, he
prayēd on the long bridge of Seta, as he was come nigh to Ise.

CHORUS
(changing from narrative of the journey
to description)

There the plum-trees were blossoming. All the scene
showed the favour of Kwannon and the virtue of the Emperor.

Then there was a great noise of evil voices, a shaking of
mountains.

TAMURA
(excitedly, and as if amid the original scene)

Hear ye the evil spirits! Once in the reign of Tenshi, the evil
spirit who served the bad minister Chikata died, and Chikata
fell. But you are near to Suzukayama; you are easy to kill.

CHORUS

Look to the sea of Ise, on the pine-moor of Anono the evil
spirits rain their black clouds. They pour down fires of iron;
they move like ten thousand footmen; they are piled like the
mountains.

TAMURA

Look forth on the carnage!

Chorus

The battle! Senju Kwannon pours lights on our banner. Her lights fly about in the air. She holds in her thousand hands the bow of "Great Mercy." Hers are the arrows of wisdom. Fly forth her thousand arrows. They harry the spirits; they fall in a swirl of hail. The spirits are dead from her rain.

How Great is the Mercy of Kwannon!*

* Tamura Maro had a special devotion to the Kwannon of the Seisui Temple. Her image, thousand-handed with an arrow in each hand, was woven on his battle-banners.

THE END

FOREWORD TO TSUNEMASA

The Noh, especially the Noh of spirits, abounds in dramatic situations, perhaps too subtle and fragile for our western stage, but none the less intensely dramatic. Kumasaka is martial despite the touch of Buddhism in the opening scene, where the spirit is atoning for his past violence.

Tsunemasa is gentle and melancholy. It is all at high tension, but it is a psychological tension, the tension of the séance. The excitement and triumph are the nervous excitement and triumph of a successful ritual. The spirit is invoked and appears.

The parallels with Western spiritist doctrines are more than interesting. Note the spirit's uncertainty as to his own success in appearing. The priest wonders if he really saw anything. The spirit affirms that "The body was there if you saw it."

As to the quality of poetry in this work: there is the favoured youth, soon slain; the uneasy blood-stained and thoughtless spirit; there are the lines about the caged stork crying at sunset, and they are as clear as Dante's.

"Era già l' ora che volge il disio."

TSUNEMASA

PRIEST

I am Sodzu Giokei, keeper of the temple of Ninnaji. Tajima no Kami Tsunemasa, of the house of Taira, was loved by the Emperor when he was a boy, but he was killed in the old days at the battle of the West Seas. And this is the Seizan lute that the Emperor gave him before that fighting. I offer this lute to his spirit in place of libation; I do the right service before him.
[*They perform a service to the spirit of Tsunemasa.*

PRIEST

Although it is midnight I see the form of a man, a faint form, in the light there. If you are spirit, who are you?

SPIRIT

I am the ghost of Tsunemasa. Your service has brought me.

PRIEST

Is it the ghost of Tsunemasa? I perceive no form, but a voice.

SPIRIT

It is the faint sound alone that remains.

PRIEST

O! But I saw the form, really.

SPIRIT

It is there if you see it.

PRIEST

I can see.

SPIRIT

Are you sure that you see it, really?

PRIEST

O, do I, or do I not see you?

CHORUS

Changeful Tsunemasa, full of the universal unstillness, looked back upon the world. His voice was heard there, a voice without form. None might see him, but he looked out from his phantom, a dream that gazed on our world.

PRIEST

It is strange! Tsunemasa! The figure was there and is gone, only the thin sound remains. The film of a dream, perhaps! It was a reward for this service.

SPIRIT

When I was young I went into the court. I had a look at life then. I had high favour. I was given the Emperor's biwa.* That is the very lute you have there. It is the lute called "Seizan." I had it when I walked through the world.

CHORUS

It is the lute that he had in this world, but now he will play Buddha's music.

PRIEST

Bring out what stringed lutes you possess, and follow his music.

* Lute.

SPIRIT

And I will lead you unseen.

[*He plays.*

PRIEST

Midnight is come; we will play the "midnight-play," Ya-banraku.

SPIRIT

The clear sky is become overclouded; the rain walks with heavier feet.

PRIEST

They shake the grass and the trees.

SPIRIT

It was not the rain's feet. Look yonder.

CHORUS

A moon hangs clear on the pine-bough. The wind rustles as if flurried with rain. It is an hour of magic. The bass strings are something like rain; the small strings talk like a whisper. The deep string is a wind voice of autumn; the third and the fourth strings are like the crying stork in her cage, when she thinks of her young birds toward nightfall. Let the cocks leave off their crowing. Let no one announce the dawn.

SPIRIT

A flute's voice has moved the clouds of Shushinrei. And the phœnix come out from the cloud; they descend with their playing. Pitiful, marvellous music! I have come down to the world. I have resumed my old playing. And I was happy here. All that is soon over.

PRIEST

Now I can see him again, the figure I saw here; can it be Tsunemasa?

SPIRIT

It's a sorry face that I make here. Put down the lights if you see me.

Chorus

The sorrow of the heart is a spreading around of quick fires. The flames are turned to thick rain. He slew by the sword and was slain. The red wave of blood rose in fire, and now he burns with that flame. He bade us put out the lights; he flew as a summer moth.

> His brushing wings were a storm.
> His spirit is gone in the darkness.

PART III

FENOLLOSA ON THE NOH

THE Japanese people have loved nature so passionately that they have interwoven her life and their own into one continuous drama of the art of pure living. I have written elsewhere* of the five Acts into which this life-drama falls, particularly as it reveals itself in the several forms of their visual arts. I have spoken of the universal value of this special art-life, and explained how the inflowing of such an Oriental stream has helped to revitalize Western Art, and must go on to assist in the solution of our practical educational problems. I would now go back to that other key, to the blossoming of Japanese genius, which I mentioned under my account of the flower festivals, namely, the national poetry, and its rise, through the enriching of four successive periods, to a vital dramatic force in the fifteenth century. Surely literature may be as delicate an exponent of a nation's soul as is art; and there are several phases of Oriental poetry, both Japanese and Chinese, which have practical significance and even inspiration for us in this weak, transitional period of our Western poetic life.

We cannot escape, in the coming centuries, even if we would, a stronger and stronger modification of our established standards by the pungent subtlety of Oriental thought, and the power of the condensed Oriental forms. The value will lie partly in relief from the deadening boundaries of our own conventions. This is no new thing. It can be shown that the freedom of the Elizabethan mind, and its power to range over all planes of human experience, as in Shakespeare, was, in part, an aftermath of Oriental contacts—in the Crusades, in an intimacy with the Mongols such as Marco Polo's, in the discovery of a double sea-passage to Persia and India, and in the first gleanings of the Jesuit missions to Asia. Still more clearly can it be shown that the romantic movement in En-

* "Epochs of Chinese and Japanese Art," by Ernest Fenollosa. London: Heinemann, 1911.

glish poetry, in the later eighteenth century and the early nineteenth, was influenced and enriched, though often in a subtle and hidden way, by the beginnings of scholarly study and translation of Oriental literature. Bishop Percy, who afterwards revived our knowledge of the mediaeval ballad, published early in the 1760's the first appreciative English account of Chinese poetry; and Bishop Hood wrote an essay on the Chinese theatre, seriously comparing it with the Greek. A few years later Voltaire published his first Chinese tragedy, modified from a Jesuit translation; and an independent English version held the London stage till 1824. Moore, Byron, Shelley, and Coleridge were influenced by the spirit, and often by the very subject, of Persian translations; and Wordsworth's "Intimations of Immortality" verges on the Hindoo doctrine of reincarnation. In these later days India powerfully reacts upon our imagination through an increasingly intimate knowledge. . . .

I

A form of drama, as primitive, as intense, and almost as beautiful as the ancient Greek drama at Athens, still exists in the world. Yet few care for it, or see it.* In the fifth century before Christ the Greek drama arose out of the religious rites practised in the festivals of the God of Wine. In the fifteenth century after Christ, the Japanese drama arose out of religious rites practised in the festivals of the Shinto gods, chiefly the Shinto god of the Kasuga temple at Nara. Both began by a sacred dance, and both added a sacred chorus sung by priests. The transition from a dance chorus to drama proper consisted, in both cases, in the evolving of a solo part, the words of which alternate in dialogue with the chorus. In both the final form of drama consists of a few short scenes, wherein two or three soloists act a main theme, whose deeper meaning is interpreted by the poetical comment of the chorus. In both the speech was metrical, and involved a clear organic structure of separate lyrical units. In both music played an important part. In both action was a modification

* The Noh has been "popularized" since Fenollosa wrote this.

of the dance. In both rich costumes were worn; in both, masks. The form and tradition of the Athenian drama passed over into the tradition of the ancient Roman stage, and died away in the early middle ages fourteen centuries ago. It is dead, and we can study it from scant records only. But the Japanese poetic drama is alive to-day, having been transmitted almost unchanged from one perfected form reached in Kioto in the fifteenth century.

It has been said that all later drama has been influenced by the Greek; that the strolling jugglers and contortionists, who wandered in troupes over Europe in the middle ages, constitute an unbroken link between the degenerate Roman actors and the miracle plays of the church, which grew into the Shakespearean drama. It is even asserted that, as the Greek conquest gave rise to a Greco-Buddhist form of sculpture on the borders of India and China, Greek dramatic influence entered also into the Hindoo and Chinese drama, and eventually into the Noh of Japan. But the effect of foreign thought on the Noh is small in comparison with that of the native Shinto influences. It is as absurd to say that the Noh is an offshoot of Greek drama as it would be to say that Shakespeare is such an offshoot.

There is, however, beside the deeper analogy of the Japanese Noh with Greek plays, an interesting secondary analogy with the origin of Shakespeare's art. All three had an independent growth from miracle plays—the first from the plays of the worship of Bacchus, the second from the plays of the worship of Christ, the third from the plays of the worship of the Shinto deities and of Buddha. The plays that preceded Shakespeare's in England were acted in fields adjoining the churches, and later in the courtyards of nobles. The plays that preceded the Noh, and even the Noh themselves, were enacted, first in the gardens of temples or on the dry river-beds adjoining the temples, and later in the courtyards of the daimio. On the other hand, the actual modus of the Shakespearean drama is practically dead for us. Occasional revivals have to borrow scenery and other contrivances unknown to the Elizabethan stage, and the continuity of professional tradition has certainly been broken. But in the Japanese Noh, though it arose one hundred years before Shakespeare, this continuity has never been broken. The same plays are to-day enacted in the same manner as then; even the leading actors of to-day are blood descendants of the very men who created this drama 450 years ago.

This ancient lyric drama is not to be confounded with the modern realistic drama of Tokio, with such drama, for instance, as Danjuro's. This vulgar drama is quite like ours, with an elaborate stage and scenery, with little music or chorus, and no masks; with nothing, in short, but realism and mimetics of action. This modern drama, a ghost of the fifth period, arose in Yedo some 300 years ago. It was amusement designed by the common people for themselves, and was written and acted by them. It therefore corresponds to the work of Ukiyo-ye in painting, and more especially to the colour prints; and a large number of these prints reproduce characters and scenes from the people's theatre.

As the pictorial art of the fifth period was divisible into two parts—that of the nobility, designed to adorn their castles, and that of the common people, printed illustration,—so has the drama of the last 200 years been twofold, that of the lyric Noh, preserved pure in the palaces of the rich; and that of the populace, running to realism and extravagance in the street theatres. To-day, in spite of the shock and revolution of 1868, the former, the severe and poetic drama, has been revived, and is enthusiastically studied by cultured Japanese. In that commotion the palaces of the daimios, with their Noh stages, were destroyed, the court troupes of actors were dispersed. For three years after 1868 performances ceased entirely. But Mr. Umewaka Minoru, who had been one of the soloists in the Shogun's central troupe, kept guard over the pure tradition, and had many stage directions or "tenets" preserved in writing along with the texts. In 1871 he bought an ex-daimio's stage for a song, set it up on the banks of the Sumida river in Tokio, and began to train his sons. Many patient pupils and old actors flocked to him; the public began their patronage; he bought up collections of costumes and masks at sales of impoverished nobles; and now his theatre is so thronged that boxes have to be engaged a week beforehand, and five other theatres have been built in Tokio. . . .

For the last twenty years I have been studying the Noh, under the personal tuition of Umewaka Minoru and his sons, learning by actual practice the method of the singing and something of the acting; I have taken down from Umewaka's lips invaluable oral traditions of the stage as it was before 1868; and have prepared, with his assistance and that of native scholars, translations of some fifty of the texts.

II

The art of dance has played a richer part in Chinese and Japanese life than it has in Europe. In prehistoric days, when men or women were strongly moved, they got up and danced. It was as natural a form of self-expression as improvised verse or song, and was often combined with both. But the growing decorum of a polite society tended to relegate this dancing to occasions of special inspiration and to professional dancers. These occasions were roughly of two sorts—formal entertainments at Court and religious ceremonial. The former, which survives to this day in the Mikado's palace, represented the action of historic heroes, frequently warriors posturing with sword and spear. This was accompanied by the instrumental music of a full orchestra. The religious ceremonial was of two sorts—the Buddhist miracle plays in the early temples and the god dances of the Shinto.

The miracle plays represented scenes from the lives of saints and the intervention of Buddha and Bodhisattwa in human affairs. Like the very earliest forms of the European play, these were pantomimic, with no special dramatic text, save possibly the reading of appropriate scripture. The Japanese miracle plays were danced with masks; and the temples of Nara are still full of these masks, which date from the eighth century. It is clear that many popular and humorous types must have been represented; and it is barely possible that these were remotely derived, through Greco-Buddhist channels, from the masks of Greek low comedy. In these plays the god is the chief actor, sometimes in dramatic relation to a human companion. The god always wears a mask. The solo part is established; and herein the play differs from the Greek, where the original rite was performed by a group of priests, or (in the comedy) by goats or fauns.

The most certainly Japanese element of the drama was the sacred dance in the Shinto temples. This was a kind of pantomime, and repeated the action of a local god on his first appearance to men. The first dance, therefore, was a god dance; the god himself danced, with his face concealed in a mask. Here is a difference between the Greek and Japanese beginnings. In Greece the chorus danced, and the god was represented by an altar. In Japan the god danced alone.

The ancient Shinto dance or pantomime was probably, at first, a story enacted by the local spirit, as soloist—a repetition, as it were, of the original manifestation. Shintoism is spiritism, mild, nature-loving, much like the Greek. A local spirit appeared to men in some characteristic phase. On the spot a Shinto temple was built, and yearly or monthly rites, including pantomime, perpetuated the memory of the event. Such things happened all over the country; and thus thousands of different stories were perpetuated in the dances—hence the wealth of primitive material. The thing can be seen to-day in every village festival. Even in great cities like Tokio, every district maintains its primitive village spirit-worship, that of some tutelary worthy who enacts the old story once a year on a specially made platform raised in the street, about which the people of the locality congregate. The plays are generally pantomime without text.

In the Shinto dance the soloist has no chorus. He performs some religious act of the spirit, though this is often turned into rude comedy. This dance takes the form of a dignified pantomime. It is not an abstract kicking or whirling, not a mere dervish frenzy, but is full of meaning, representing divine situations and emotions, artistically, with restraint and with the chastening of a conventional beauty, which makes every posture of the whole body—head, trunk, hands, and feet—harmonious in line, and all the transitions from posture to posture balanced and graceful in line. A flashlight glimpse across such a dance is like a flashlight of sculpture; but the motion itself, like a picture which moves in colour, is like the art of music. There is an orchestral accompaniment of flutes, drums, and cymbals, slow, fast, low, passionate, or accented, that makes a natural ground-tone. Akin to these are the moving street pageants, which are like early European pageants, or even those of to-day in Catholic countries.

Thus the three sources of the Noh, all belonging to the first period, are, in the order of their influence, (1) the Shinto god dance, (2) the warrior court dance, (3) the Buddhist sacred pantomime.

As the old Chinese court dances were modified in the aristocratic life of the second period, it was natural that lovers of poetry should begin to add poetical comment to the entertainment. Thus the next step consisted in the addition of a text for a chorus to sing during the solo dance. They were already used to accompany their verses with the lute.

In the first of the five periods, Japanese lyric poetry reached its height. It was quite different from the Chinese, as the language is polysyllabic, the sentences long and smooth, the tone gently contemplative. About the year 900, when the capital had been removed to Kioto, the longer and straggling verse structure went out of fashion. A tense stanzaic form had come into almost universal use. This fashion may be referred to Chinese influence. Rhyme, however, was not introduced. The lines, usually of five or seven syllables, are rich and sonorous. Soon afterwards the passion for composing and reciting this Japanese poetry became so powerful among the educated classes, especially in the cultured aristocracy at Kioto, where men and women met on equal terms, that the old court entertainments of dance and music had to be modified to admit the use of poetic texts. At first the nobles themselves, at their feasts or at court ceremonies, sang in unison songs composed for the occasion. The next step was to write songs appropriate to the dances; finally the chorus of nobles became a trained chorus, accompanied by court musicians. Thus by the end of the ninth century there was a body of performers definitely associated with the court, with a minister in charge of it. There were two divisions. The composition of the texts and the composition of the music and dances were allotted to different persons. At this stage the old Chinese subjects fell into the background, and subjects of Japanese historical interest, or of more national and lyric nature, were substituted.

Thus arose the court entertainment called Saibara, which ceased to be practised after the twelfth century. Most of the details of it are hopelessly lost, though a few texts remain from a manuscript collection compiled about the year 900. The music and dance are utterly lost, except so far as we can discern a trace of what they must have been, in the later practices of the Noh. It is interesting to find that the very names of some of the pieces in Saibara are identical with those used in Noh five centuries later. The Saibara pieces are very short, much like the lyric poems of the day; and they are often so lyrical or so personal as hardly to suggest how they may have been danced. It is also uncertain whether these brief texts were repeated over and over, or at intervals during the long dance, or whether they were a mere introduction to a dance which elaborated their thought.* The following Saibara will serve as example:

> O white-gemmed camelia and you jewel willow,
> Who stand together on the Cape of Takasago!
> This one, since I want her for mine,
> That one, too, since I want her for mine—
> Jewel willow!
> I will make you a thing to hang my cloak on,
> With its tied-up strings, with its deep-dyed strings.
> Ah! what have I done?
> There, what is this I am doing?
> O what am I to do?
> Mayhap I have lost my soul!
> But I have met
> The lily flower,
> The first flower of morning.

This new combination of dance and song soon spread from the court ceremonies to the religious rites of the god dances in the Shinto temples, not, however, to the Buddhist, which were too much under the influence of Hindu and Chinese

---

* Professor Fenollosa, in an earlier half-sentence which I have omitted, would seem to underestimate the effect of the dance on European art forms. It was from the May-day dance and dance-songs that the Provençal poetry probably arose. By stages came strophe and antistrophe tenzone, the Spanish loa and entremes. See also W. P. Ker, "English Mediaeval Literature," pp. 79 et seq., for the spread of the dance through Europe and the effect on the lyric forms. Compare also the first Saibara given in the text with the Provençal "A l'entrada del temps clar."

thought to care for Japanese verse. In Shinto dances the subject was already pure Japanese and fit for Japanese texts; and it may very well have occurred to some priest, in one of the thousand Shinto matsuris (festivals) going on all over the land, to sing a poem concerning the subject of the dance. By the end of the ninth century, in the second period, this custom had become common in the great Shinto festivals, in the Mikado's private chapel, and at Kasuga. The texts were sung by a trained chorus, and here is a second difference from the line of Greek advance. In Greece the chorus not only sang but danced; in Japan the chorus did not dance or act, but was merely contemplative, sitting at the side. The songs so sung were called Kagura.

A few examples of these ancient Shinto texts for Kagura have come down to us. They are not exactly prayers; they are often lovely poems of nature, for, after all, these Shinto gods were a harmless kind of nature spirit clinging to grottoes, rivers, trees, and mountains. It is curious to note that the structure of the texts is always double, like the Greek strophe and antistrophe. They were probably sung by a double chorus; and this is doubtless the basis of the alternation or choric dialogue.

Here is a kagura, sung by a priestess to her wand:

Strophe.   As for this mitegura,
              As for this mitegura,
              It is not mine at all;
              It is the mitegura of a god,
              Called the Princess Toyooka,
              Who lives in heaven,
              The mitegura of a god,
              The mitegura of a god.

Antistrophe. O how I wish in vain that I could turn myself
                 into a mitegura,
              That I might be taken into the hand of the
                 Mother of the Gods,
              That I might come close to the heart of a god,
                 close to the heart of a god!

III

We have now come to the point where we can deal with this mass of playwriting as literature. The plays are written in a mixture of prose and verse. The finest parts are in verse; ordinary conversation lapses into prose; the choruses are always in verse.

It appears that the first period of Japanese civilization supplied the chance elements for the Noh, that is, the dances and certain attitudes of mind. The second period supplied the beginnings of literary texts. The third period, dating from the end of the twelfth century, is marked by the rise of the military classes and supplied naturally a new range of dramatic motives. The land was filled with tales of wild achievement and knight-errantry and with a passionate love for individuality, however humble. The old court customs and dances of the supplanted nobles were kept up solely in the peaceful enclosures of the Shinto temples. New forms of entertainment arose. Buddhism threw away scholarship and mystery, and aimed only at personal salvation. As in contemporary Europe, itinerant monks scoured the country, carrying inspiration from house to house. Thus arose a semi-epic literature, in which the deeds of martial heroes were gathered into several great cycles of legend, like the Carolingian and the Arthurian cycles in Europe. Such were the Heike epic, the Soga cycle, and a dozen others. Episodes from these were sung by individual minstrels to the accompaniment of a lute. One of the most important effects of this new epic balladry was to widen greatly the scope of motives acceptable for plays.

As for comedy, another movement was growing up in the country, from farmers' festivals, the spring sowing of the rice, and the autumn reaping. These were at first mere buffooneries or gymnastic contests arranged by the villagers for their amusement. They were called Dengaku, a rice-field music. Later, professional troupes of Dengaku jugglers and acrobats were kept by the daimios in their palaces, and eventually by the authorities of the Buddhist and Shinto temples, in order to attract crowds to their periodic festivals. Such professional troupes began to add rude country farces to their stock of entertainments, at first bits of coarse impromptu repartee, con-

sisting of tricks by rustics upon each other, which were prob-
ably not out of harmony with some of the more grotesque
and comic Shinto dances. About the twelfth and thirteenth
centuries these two elements of comedy—the rustic and the
sacred—combined at the Shinto temples, and actors were
trained as a permanent troupe. Such farces are called Kiogen.
In the later part of the fourteenth century, towards the end,
that is, of the third period, Dengaku troupes of Shinto
dancers advanced to the incorporating of more tragic sub-
jects, selected from the episodes of the balladry. The god
dancer now became, sometimes, a human being, the hero of
a dramatic crisis—sometimes even a woman, interchanging
dialogue with the chorus, as the two ancient Shinto choruses
had sung dialogue in the Kagura.

It was not till the fourth period of Japanese culture, that is
to say, early in the fifteenth century, when a new Buddhist civ-
ilization, based upon contemplative and poetic insight into
nature had arisen, that the inchoate Japanese drama, fostered
in the Shinto temples, could take on a moral purpose and a
psychologic breadth that should expand it into a vital drama
of character. The Shinto god dance, the lyric form of court
poetry, the country farces, and a full range of epic incident, in
short, all that was best in the earlier Japanese tradition, was
gathered into this new form, arranged and purified.

The change came about in this way. The Zen parish priests
summoned up to Kioto the Dengaku troupe from Nara, and
made it play before the Shogun. The head actor of this Nara
troupe, Kwan, took the new solo parts, and greatly enlarged
the scope of the music of the other acting. During the life-
time of his son and grandson, Zei and On, hundreds of new
plays were created. It is a question to what extent these three
men, Kwan, Zei, and On, were the originators of the texts of
these new dramas, and how far the Zen priests are responsi-
ble. The lives of the former are even more obscure than is
Shakespeare's. No full account exists of their work. We have
only stray passages from contemporary notebooks relating to
the great excitement caused by their irregular performances.
A great temporary circus was erected on the dry bed of the
Kamo river, with its storeys divided into boxes for each noble
family, from the Emperor and the Shogun downwards. Great

priests managed the show, and used the funds collected for building temples. The stage was a raised open circle in the centre, reached by a long bridge from a dressing-room outside the circus.

We can now see why, even in the full lyric drama, the god dance remains the central feature. All the slow and beautiful postures of the early dramatic portion invariably lead up to the climax of the hero's dance (just as the Greek had planned for the choric dances). This often comes only at the end of the second act, but sometimes also in the first. Most plays have two acts. During the closing dance the chorus sings its finest passages, though it will have been already engaged many times in dialogue with the soloist. Its function is poetical comment, and it carries the mind beyond what the action exhibits to the core of the spiritual meaning. The music is simple melody, hardly more than a chant, accompanied by drums and flutes. There is thus a delicate adjustment of half a dozen conventions appealing to eye, ear, or mind, which produces an intensity of feeling such as belongs to no merely realistic drama. The audience sits spellbound before the tragedy, bathed in tears; but the effect is never one of realistic horror, rather of a purified and elevated passion, which sees divine purpose under all violence.

The beauty and power of Noh lie in the concentration. All elements—costume, motion, verse, and music—unite to produce a single clarified impression. Each drama embodies some primary human relation or emotion; and the poetic sweetness or poignancy of this is carried to its highest degree by carefully excluding all such obtrusive elements as a mimetic realism or vulgar sensation might demand. The emotion is always fixed upon idea, not upon personality. The solo parts express great types of human character, derived from Japanese history. Now it is brotherly love, now love to a parent, now loyalty to a master, love of husband and wife, of mother for a dead child, or of jealousy or anger, of self-mastery in battle, of the battle passion itself, of the clinging of a ghost to the scene of its sin, of the infinite compassion of a Buddha, of the sorrow of unrequited love. Some one of these intense emotions is chosen for a piece, and, in it, elevated to the plane of universality by the intensity and purity of treatment. Thus the drama became a storehouse of history, and a great moral force for the whole social order of the Samurai.

After all, the most striking thing about these plays is their marvellously complete grasp of spiritual being. They deal more with heroes, or even we might say ghosts, than with men clothed in the flesh. Their creators were great psychologists. In no other drama does the supernatural play so great, so intimate a part. The types of ghosts are shown to us; we see great characters operating under the conditions of the spirit-life; we observe what forces have changed them. Bodhisattwa, devas, elementals, animal spirits, hungry spirits or pseta, cunning or malicious or angry devils, dragon kings from the water world, spirits of the moonlight, the souls of flowers and trees, essences that live in wine and fire, the semi-embodiments of a thought—all these come and move before us in the dramatic types.

These types of character are rendered particularly vivid to us by the sculptured masks. Spirits, women, and old men wear masks; other human beings do not. For the 200 plays now extant, nearly 300 separate masks are necessary in a complete list of properties. Such variety is far in excess of the Greek types, and immense vitality is given to a good mask by a great actor, who acts up to it until the very mask seems alive and displays a dozen turns of emotion. The costumes are less carefully individualized. For the hero parts, especially for spirits, they are very rich, of splendid gold brocades and soft floss-silk weaving, or of Chinese tapestry stitch, and are very costly. In Tokugawa days (1602–1868) every rich daimio had his own stage, and his complete collection of properties. The dancing is wonderful—a succession of beautiful poses which make a rich music of line. The whole body acts together, but with dignity. Great play is given to the sleeve, which is often tossed back and forth or raised above the head. The fan also plays a great part, serving for cup, paper, pen, sword, and a dozen other imaginary stage properties. The discipline of the actor is a moral one. He is trained to revere his profession, to make it a sacred act thus to impersonate a hero. He yields himself up to possession by the character. He acts as if he knew himself to be a god, and after the performance he is generally quite exhausted.

IV

In Dojoji a girl is in love with a priest, who flees from her and takes shelter under a great bronze temple bell, which falls over him. Her sheer force of desire turns her into a dragon, she bites the top of the bell, twists herself about the bell seven times, spits flame from her mouth, and lashes the bronze with her tail. Then the bell melts away under her, and the priest she loves dies in the molten mass. In Kumasaka the boy-warrior, Ushiwaka, fights a band of fifteen giant robbers in the dark. They fight with each other also. One by one, and two by two, they are all killed. At one time all are dancing in double combat across stage and bridge. The Noh fencing with spear and sword is superb in line. In the conventional Noh fall, two robbers, facing, who have killed each other with simultaneous blows, stand for a moment erect and stiff, then slowly fall over backward, away from each other, as stiff as logs, touching the stage at the same moment with head and heel.

In the play of Atsumori there is an interesting ghost, taken from the epic cycle of the Yoritomo. Atsumori was a young noble of the Heike family who was killed in one of Yoshitsumi's decisive battles. The priest who opens the final scene tells the story thus:

I am one who serves the great Bishop Homeri Shonini in Kurodain temple. And that little one over there is the child of Atsumori, who was killed at Ichinotani. Once when the Shonini was going down to the Kamo river, he found a baby about two years old in a tattered basket under a pine tree. He felt great pity for the child, took it home with him, and cared for it tenderly. When the boy had grown to be ten years of age and was lamenting that he had no parents, the Shonini spoke about the matter to an audience which came to his preaching. Then a young woman came up, and cried excitedly, "This must be my child." On further enquiry he found it was indeed the child of the famous Atsumori. The child, having heard all this, is most desirous to see the image of his father, even in a dream, and he has been praying devoutly to this effect at the shrine of Kamo Miojin for seven days. To-day the term is up for the fulfilment of his vow, so I am taking him down to Kamo Miojin for his last prayer. Here we are at Kamo. Now, boy! pray well!

During his prayer the boy hears a voice which tells him to

go to the forest of Ikuta; and thither the priest and the boy journey. On arrival they look about at the beauty of the place, till suddenly nightfall surprises them. "Look here, boy, the sun has set! What, is that a light yonder? Perhaps it may be a house? We will go to take lodging there." A straw hut has been set at the centre of the stage. The curtain in front of it is now withdrawn, and the figure of a very young warrior is disclosed, in a mask, and wearing a dress of blue, white, and gold. He begins to speak to himself:

Gowun! Gowun! The five possessions of man are all hollow. Why do we love this queer thing—body? The soul which dwells in agony flies about like a bat under the moon. The poor bewildered ghost that has lost its body whistles in the autumn wind.

They think him a man, but he tells them he has had a half-hour's respite from hell. He looks wistfully at the boy, who wishes to seize him, and cries, "Flower child of mine, left behind in the world, like a favourite carnation, how pitiful to see you in those old black sleeves!" Then the spirit dances with restraint, while the chorus chants the martial scene of his former death. "Rushing like two clouds together they were scattered in a whirlwind." Suddenly he stops, looks off the stage, and stamps, shouting:

Who is that over there? A messenger from hell?
Yes, why do you stay so late? King Enma is angry.

Then the grim warriors frantically rush across the stage like Valkyrie, and Atsumori is forced to fight with a spear in a tremendous mystic dance against them. This is a vision of his torment transferred to earth. Exhausted and bleeding he falls; the hell fires vanish; and crying out, "Oh, how shameful that you should see me thus," he melts away from the frantic clutches of the weeping boy.

Among the most weird and delicately poetic pieces is Nishikigi, in which the hero and heroine are the ghosts of two lovers who died unmarried a hundred years before. Their spirits are in the course of the play united near a hillside grave where their bodies had long lain together. This spiritual union is brought about by the piety of a priest. Action, words, and music are vague and ghostly shadows. The lover, as a young man, had waited before the girl's door every night for months, but she, from ignorance or coquetry, had refused to notice him. Then he died of despair. She repented of her cruelty and died also.

The play opens with the entrance of the travelling priest, who has wandered to the ancient village of Kefu in the far north of the island. He meets the two ghosts in ancient attire. At first he supposes them to be villagers. He does not seem to notice their dress, or, if he does, he apparently mistakes it for some fashion of the province. Then the two ghosts sing together, as if muttering to themselves:

We are entangled—whose fault was it, dear?—tangled up as the grass patterns are tangled in this coarse cloth, or that insect which lives and chirrups in dried seaweed. We do not know where are to-day our tears in the undergrowth of this eternal wilderness. We neither wake nor sleep, and passing our nights in a sorrow, which is in the end a vision, what are these scenes of spring to us? This thinking in sleep of some one who has no thought for you, is it more than a dream? And yet surely it is the natural way of love. In our hearts there is much and in our bodies nothing, and we do nothing at all, and only the waters of the river of tears flow quickly.

Then the priest says:

It is strange, seeing these town-people here. I might suppose them two married people; and what the lady gives herself the trouble of carrying might be a piece of cloth woven from bird's feathers, and what the man has is a sword, painted red. It is indeed queer merchandise.

Gradually they tell him the story—they do not say at first that it is their own story. Two people had lived in that village, one of whom had offered the nishikigi, the charm-sticks, the "crimson tokens of love," night after night for three years. That was the man, of course; and the girl, apparently oblivious, had sat inside her house, weaving long bands of cloth. They say that the man was buried in a cave and all his charm-sticks with him. The priest says it will be a fine tale for him to tell when he gets home, and says he will go see the tomb, to which they offer to guide him. Then the chorus for the first time sings:

The couple are passing in front and the stranger behind, having spent the whole day until dusk, pushing aside the rank grass from the narrow paths about Kefu. Where, indeed, for them is that love-grave? Ho! you farmer there, cutting grass upon the hill, tell me clearly how I am to get on further. In this frosty night, of whom shall we ask about the dews on the wayside grass?

Then the hero, the man's ghost, breaks in for a moment: "Oh how cold it is in these evening dusks of autumn!" And the chorus resumes:

Storms, fallen leaves, patches of the autumn showers clogging the feet, the eternal shadow of the long-sloped mountain, and, crying among the ivies on the pine tree, an owl! And as for the love-grave, dyed like the leaves of maple with the tokens of bygone passion, and like the orchids and chrysanthemums which hide the mouth of a fox's hole, they have slipped into the shadow of the cave; this brave couple has vanished into the love-grave.

After an interval, for the changing of the spirits' costumes, the second act begins. The priest cannot sleep in the frost, and thinks he had better pass the night in prayer. Then the spirits in masks steal out, and in mystic language, which he does not hear, try to thank him for his prayer, and say that through his pity the love promise of incarnations long perished is now just realized, even in dream. Then the priest says:

How strange! That place, which seemed like an old grave, is now lighted up from within, and has become like a human dwelling, where people are talking and setting up looms for spinning, and painted sticks. It must be an illusion!

Then follows a wonderful loom song and chorus, comparing the sound of weaving to the clicking of crickets; and in a vision is seen the old tragic story, and the chorus sings that "their tears had become a colour." "But now they shall see the secret bride-room." The hero cries, "And we shall drink the cup of meeting." Then the ghostly chorus sings a final song:

How glorious the sleeves of the dance
That are like snow-whirls.

But now the wine-cup of the night-play is reflecting the first hint of the dawn. Perhaps we shall feel awkward when it becomes really morning. And like a dream which is just about to break, the stick and the cloth are breaking up, and the whole place has turned into a deserted grave on a hill, where morning winds are blowing through the pines.

ERNEST FENOLLOSA.
(? about 1906.)

NISHIKIGI*

A Play in two Acts, by Motokiyo

CHARACTERS

THE WAKI, a priest.
THE SHITE, or HERO, ghost of the lover.
TSURE, ghost of the woman; they have both been long dead, and
have not yet been united.
A CHORUS.

PART FIRST

WAKI

There never was anybody heard of Mt. Shinobu but had a
kindly feeling for it; so I, like any other priest that might want
to know a little bit about each one of the provinces, may as
well be walking up here along the much-travelled road.

I have not yet been about the east country, but now I have
set my mind to go as far as the earth goes, and why should-
n't I, after all? seeing that I go about with my heart set upon
no particular place whatsoever, and with no other man's flag
in my hand, no more than a cloud has. It is a flag of the night
I see coming down upon me. I wonder now, would the sea be
that way, or the little place Kefu that they say is stuck down
against it.

SHITE AND TSURE

Times out of mind am I here setting up this bright branch,
this silky wood with the charms painted in it as fine as the
web you'd get in the grass-cloth of Shinobu, that they'd be
still selling you in this mountain.

SHITE
(*to* TSURE)

Tangled, we are entangled. Whose fault was it, dear? tangled
up as the grass patterns are tangled in this coarse cloth, or as
the little Mushi that lives on and chirrups in dried seaweed.

---

* The "Nishikigi" are wands used as a love-charm. "Hosonuno" is the
name of a local cloth which the woman weaves.

406

We do not know where are to-day our tears in the under-growth of this eternal wilderness. We neither wake nor sleep, and passing our nights in a sorrow which is in the end a vision, what are these scenes of spring to us? this thinking in sleep of some one who has no thought of you, is it more than a dream? and yet surely it is the natural way of love. In our hearts there is much and in our bodies nothing, and we do nothing at all, and only the waters of the river of tears flow quickly.

CHORUS
Narrow is the cloth of Kefu, but wild is that river, that torrent
of the hills, between the beloved and the bride.
The cloth she had woven is faded, the thousand one hundred
nights were night-trysts watched out in vain.

WAKI
(*not recognizing the nature of the speakers*)
Strange indeed, seeing these town-people here,
They seem like man and wife,
And the lady seems to be holding something
Like a cloth woven of feathers,
While he has a staff or a wooden sceptre
Beautifully ornate.
Both of these things are strange;
In any case, I wonder what they call them.

TSURE
This is a narrow cloth called "Hosonuno,"
It is just the breadth of the loom.

SHITE
And this is merely wood painted,
And yet the place is famous because of these things.
Would you care to buy them from us?

WAKI
Yes, I know that the cloth of this place and the lacquers are famous things. I have already heard of their glory, and yet I still wonder why they have such great reputation.

TSURE
Well now, that's a disappointment. Here they call the wood "Nishikigi," and the woven stuff "Hosonuno," and yet you

come saying that you have never heard why, and never heard the story. Is it reasonable?

SHITE

No, no, that is reasonable enough. What can people be expected to know of these affairs when it is more than they can do to keep abreast of their own?

BOTH
(*to the* PRIEST)

Ah well, you look like a person who has abandoned the world; it is reasonable enough that you should not know the worth of wands and cloths with love's signs painted upon them, with love's marks painted and dyed.

WAKI

That is a fine answer. And you would tell me then that Nishikigi and Hosonuno are names bound over with love?

SHITE

They are names in love's list surely. Every day for a year, for three years come to their full, the wands Nishikigi were set up, until there were a thousand in all. And they are in song in your time, and will be. "Chidzuka" they call them.

TSURE

These names are surely a byword.
As the cloth Hosonuno is narrow of weft,
More narrow than the breast,
We call by this name any woman
Whose breasts are hard to come nigh to.
It is a name in books of love.

SHITE

'Tis a sad name to look back on.

TSURE

A thousand wands were in vain.
A sad name, set in a story.

SHITE

A seed pod void of the seed,
We had no meeting together.

TSURE

Let him read out the story.

CHORUS

At last they forget, they forget.
The wands are no longer offered,
The custom is faded away.
The narrow cloth of Kefu
Will not meet over the breast.
'Tis the story of Hosonuno,
This is the tale:
These bodies, having no weft,
Even now are not come together.
Truly a shameful story,
A tale to bring shame on the gods.

Names of love,
Now for a little spell,
For a faint charm only,
For a charm as slight as the binding together
Of pine-flakes in Iwashiro,
And for saying a wish over them about sunset,
We return, and return to our lodging.
The evening sun leaves a shadow.

WAKI

Go on, tell out all the story.

SHITE

There is an old custom of this country. We make wands of
mediation and deck them with symbols, and set them before
a gate when we are suitors.

TSURE

And we women take up a wand of the man we would meet
with, and let the others lie, although a man might come for a
hundred nights, it may be, or for a thousand nights in three
years, till there were a thousand wands here in the shade of
this mountain. We know the funeral cave of such a man, one
who had watched out the thousand nights; a bright cave, for
they buried him with all his wands. They have named it the
"Cave of the many charms."

WAKI

I will go to that love-cave,
It will be a tale to take back to my village.
Will you show me my way there?

SHITE

So be it, I will teach you the path.

TSURE

Tell him to come over this way.

BOTH

Here are the pair of them
Going along before the traveller.

CHORUS

We have spent the whole day until dusk
Pushing aside the grass
From the overgrown way at Kefu,
And we are not yet come to the cave.
O you there, cutting grass on the hill,
Please set your mind on this matter.
    "You'd be asking where the dew is
    "While the frost's lying here on the road.
    "Who'd tell you that now?"
Very well, then, don't tell us,
But be sure we will come to the cave.

SHITE

There's a cold feel in the autumn.
Night comes. . . .

CHORUS

And storms; trees giving up their leaf,
Spotted with sudden showers.
Autumn! our feet are clogged
In the dew-drenched, entangled leaves.
The perpetual shadow is lonely,
The mountain shadow is lying alone.
The owl cries out from the ivies
That drag their weight on the pine.
Among the orchids and chrysanthemum flowers
The hiding fox is now lord of that love-cave,

Nishidzuka,
That is dyed like the maple's leaf.
They have left us this thing for a saying.
That pair have gone into the cave.

> [*Sign for the exit of* SHITE *and* TSURE.

PART SECOND

(The Waki has taken the posture of sleep. His respectful visit to the cave is beginning to have its effect.)

WAKI
(*restless*)

It seems that I cannot sleep
For the length of a pricket's horn.
Under October wind, under pines, under night!
I will do service to Butsu.

> [*He performs the gestures of a ritual.*

TSURE

Aïe, honoured priest!
You do not dip twice in the river
Beneath the same tree's shadow
Without bonds in some other life.
Hear soothsay,
Now is there meeting between us,
Between us who were until now
In life and in after-life kept apart.
A dream-bridge over wild grass,
Over the grass I dwell in.
O honoured! do not awake me by force.
I see that the law is perfect.

SHITE
(*supposedly invisible*)

It is a good service you have done, sir,
A service that spreads in two worlds,
And binds up an ancient love
That was stretched out between them.

I had watched for a thousand days.
I give you largess,
For this meeting is under a difficult law.
And now I will show myself in the form of Nishikigi.
I will come out now for the first time in colour.

CHORUS

The three years are over and past:
All that is but an old story.

SHITE

To dream under dream we return.
Three years. . . . And the meeting comes now!
This night has happened over and over,
And only now comes the tryst.

CHORUS

Look there to the cave
Beneath the stems of the Suzuki.
From under the shadow of the love-grass,
See, see how they come forth and appear
For an instant. . . . Illusion!

SHITE

There is at the root of hell
No distinction between princes and commons;
Wretched for me! 'tis the saying.

WAKI

Strange, what seemed so very old a cave
Is all glittering-bright within,
Like the flicker of fire.
It is like the inside of a house.
They are setting up a loom,
And heaping up charm-sticks. No,
The hangings are out of old time.
Is it illusion, illusion?

TSURE

Our hearts have been in the dark of the falling snow,
We have been astray in the flurry.
You should tell better than we

How much is illusion,
You who are in the world.
We have been in the whirl of those who are fading.

SHITE

Indeed in old times Narihira said
(And he has vanished with the years),
"Let a man who is in the world tell the fact."
It is for you, traveller,
To say how much is illusion.

WAKI

Let it be a dream, or a vision,
Or what you will, I care not.
Only show me the old times over-past and snowed under;
Now, soon, while the night lasts.

SHITE

Look, then, for the old times are shown,
Faint as the shadow-flower shows in the grass that bears it;
And you've but a moon for lanthorn.

TSURE

The woman has gone into the cave.
She sets up her loom there
For the weaving of Hosonuno,
Thin as the heart of Autumn.

SHITE

The suitor for his part, holding his charm-sticks,
Knocks on a gate which was barred.

TSURE

In old time he got back no answer,
No secret sound at all
Save . . .

SHITE

. . . the sound of the loom.

TSURE

It was a sweet sound like katydids and crickets,
A thin sound like the Autumn.

SHITE

It was what you would hear any night.

TSURE

Kiri.

SHITE

Hatari.

TSURE

Cho.

SHITE

Cho.

CHORUS
(*mimicking the sound of crickets*)

Kiri, hatari, cho, cho,
Kiri, hatari, cho, cho.
The cricket sews on at his old rags,
With all the new grass in the field; sho,
Churr, isho, like the whirr of a loom: churr.

CHORUS
(*antistrophe*)

Let be, they make grass-cloth in Kefu,
Kefu, the land's end, matchless in the world.

SHITE

That is an old custom, truly,
But this priest would look on the past.

CHORUS

The good priest himself would say:
Even if we weave the cloth, Hosonuno,
And set up the charm-sticks
For a thousand, a hundred nights;
Even then our beautiful desire will not pass,
Nor fade nor die out.

SHITE

Even to day the difficulty of our meeting is remembered,
And is remembered in song.

CHORUS

That we may acquire power,
Even in our faint substance.
We will show forth even now,
And though it be but in a dream,
Our form of repentance.

[*Explaining the movement of the* SHITE *and* TSURE.

There he is carrying wands,
And she has no need to be asked.
See her within the cave,
With a cricket-like noise of weaving.
The grass-gates and the hedge are between them,
That is a symbol.
Night has already come on.

[*Now explaining the thoughts of the man's spirit.*

Love's thoughts are heaped high within him,
As high as the charm-sticks,
As high as the charm-sticks, once coloured,
Now fading, lie heaped in this cave;
And he knows of their fading. He says:
I lie a body, unknown to any other man,
Like old wood buried in moss.
It were a fit thing
That I should stop thinking the love-thoughts,
The charm-sticks fade and decay,
And yet,
The rumour of our love
Takes foot, and moves through the world.
We had no meeting.
But tears have, it seems, brought out a bright blossom
Upon the dyed tree of love.

SHITE

Tell me, could I have foreseen
Or known what a heap of my writings
Should lie at the end of her shaft-bench?

CHORUS

A hundred nights and more
Of twisting, encumbered sleep,

And now they make it a ballad,
Not for one year or for two only,
But until the days lie deep
As the sand's depth at Kefu.
Until the year's end is red with autumn,
Red like these love-wands,
A thousand nights are in vain.
I, too, stand at this gate-side:
You grant no admission, you do not show yourself
Until I and my sleeves are faded.
By the dew-like gemming of tears upon my sleeve,
Why will you grant no admission?
And we all are doomed to pass
You, and my sleeves and my tears.
And you did not even know when three years had come to
    an end.
Cruel, ah, cruel!
The charm-sticks . . .

Shite

                    . . . were set up a thousand times;
Then, now, and for always.

Chorus

Shall I ever at last see into that secret bride-room, which no
    other sight has traversed?

Shite

Happy at last and well-starred,
Now comes the eve of betrothal:
We meet for the wine-cup.

Chorus

How glorious the sleeves of the dance,
That are like snow-whirls!

Shite

Tread out the dance.

Chorus

Tread out the dance and bring music.
This dance is for Nishikigi.

SHITE

This dance is for the evening plays,
And for the weaving.

CHORUS

For the tokens between lover and lover:
It is a reflecting in the wine-cup.

CHORUS

Ari-aki,
The dawn!
Come, we are out of place;
Let us go ere the light comes.

[*To the* WAKI.

We ask you, do not awake,
We all will wither away,
The wands and this cloth of a dream.
Now you will come out of sleep,
You tread the border and nothing
Awaits you: no, all this will wither away.
There is nothing here but this cave in the field's midst.
To-day's wind moves in the pines;
A wild place, unlit, and unfilled.

FINIS

KINUTA

CHARACTERS

WAKI, a country gentleman.
TSURE, the servant-maid YUGIRI.
SHITE, the wife.
SECOND SHITE, ghost of the wife.

In Kinuta ("The Silk-board") the plot is as follows:
The Waki, a country gentleman, has tarried long in the capital. He at last sends the Tsure, a maid-servant, home with a message to his wife. The servant talks on the road. She reaches the Waki's house and talks with the Shite (the wife). The chorus comments. Finally, the wife dies. The chorus sing a death-song, after which the husband returns. The second Shite, the ghost of the wife, then appears, and continues speaking alternately with the chorus until the close.

HUSBAND

I am of Ashiya of Kinshu, unknown and of no repute. I have been loitering on in the capital entangled in many litigations. I went for a casual visit, and there I have been tarrying for three full years. Now I am anxious, over-anxious, about affairs in my home. I shall send Yugiri homeward; she is a maid in my employ. Ho! Yugiri! I am worried. I shall send you down to the country. You will go home and tell them that I return at the end of this year.

MAID-SERVANT

I will go, Sir, and say that then you are surely coming. (*She starts on her journey.*) The day is advancing, and I, in my travelling clothes, travel with the day. I do not know the lodgings, I do not know the dreams upon the road, I do not know the number of the dreams that gather for one night's pillow. At length I am come to the village—it is true that I was in haste—I am come at last to Ashiya. I think I will call out gently. "Is there any person or thing in this house? Say that Yugiri is here in the street, she has just come back from the city."

418

WIFE

Sorrow!—
Sorrow is in the twigs of the duck's nest
And in the pillow of the fishes,
At being held apart in the waves,
Sorrow between mandarin ducks,
Who have been in love
Since time out of mind.
Sorrow—
There is more sorrow between the united
Though they move in the one same world.
O low "Remembering-grass,"
I do not forget to weep
At the sound of the rain upon you,
My tears are a rain in the silence,
O heart of the seldom clearing.

MAID-SERVANT

Say to whomsoever it concerns that Yugiri has come.

WIFE

What! you say it is Yugiri? There is no need for a servant.
Come to this side! in here! How is this, Yugiri, that you are
so great a stranger? Yet welcome. I have cause of complaint.
If you were utterly changed, why did you send me no word?
Not even a message in the current of the wind?

MAID-SERVANT

Truly I wished to come, but his Honour gave me no
leisure. For three years he kept me in that very ancient city.

WIFE

You say it was against your heart to stay in the city? While
even in the time of delights I thought of its blossom, until
sorrow had grown the cloak of my heart.

CHORUS

As the decline of autumn
In a country dwelling,
With the grasses failing and fading—
As men's eyes fail—
As men's eyes fail,

Love has utterly ceased.
Upon what shall she lean to-morrow?
A dream of the autumn, three years,
Until the sorrow of those dreams awakes
Autumnal echoes within her.
Now former days are changed,
They have left no shadow or trace;
And if there were no lies in all the world
Then there might come some pleasure
Upon the track of men's words.
Alas, for her foolish heart!
How foolish her trust has been.

WIFE

What strange thing is it beyond there that takes the forms of sound? Tell me. What is it?

MAID-SERVANT

A villager beating a silk-board.

WIFE

Is that all? And I am weary as an old saying. When the wandering Sobu* of China was in the Mongol country he also had left a wife and children, and she, aroused upon the clear cold nights, climbed her high tower and beat such a silk-board, and had perhaps some purpose of her heart. For that far-murmuring cloth could move his sleep—that is the tale—though he were leagues away. Yet I have stretched my board with patterned cloths, which curious birds brought through the twilit utter solitude, and hoped with such that I might ease my heart.

MAID-SERVANT

Boards are rough work, hard even for the poor, and you of high rank have done this to ease your heart! Here, let me arrange them, I am better fit for such business.

WIFE

Beat then. Beat out our resentment.

* So Wu.

MAID-SERVANT

It's a coarse mat; we can never be sure.

CHORUS

The voice of the pine-trees sinks ever into the web!
The voice of the pine-trees, now falling,
Shall make talk in the night.
It is cold.

WIFE

Autumn it is, and news rarely comes in your fickle wind,
the frost comes bearing no message.

CHORUS

Weariness tells of the night.

WIFE

Even a man in a very far village might see. . . .

CHORUS

Perhaps the moon will not call upon her, saying: "Whose
night-world is this?"

WIFE

O beautiful season, say also this time is toward autumn,
"The evening moves to an end."

CHORUS

The stag's voice has bent her heart toward sorrow,
Sending the evening winds which she does not see,
We cannot see the tip of the branch.
The last leaf falls without witness.
There is an awe in the shadow,
And even the moon is quiet,
With the love-grass under the eaves.

WIFE

My blind soul hangs like a curtain studded with dew.

CHORUS

What a night to unsheave her sorrows—
An hour for magic—
And that cloth-frame stands high on the palace;
The wind rakes it from the north.

WIFE

They beat now fast and now slow—are they silk-workers down in the village? The moon-river pours on the west.

CHORUS
(*strophe*)

The wandering Sobu is asleep in the North country,
And here in the East-sky the autumnal wind is working
    about from the West.
Wind, take up the sound she is beating upon her coarse-
    webbed cloth.

CHORUS
(*antistrophe*)

Beware of even the pines about the eaves,
Lest they confuse the sound.
Beware that you do not lose the sound of the travelling
    storm,
That travels after your travels.
Take up the sound of this beating of the cloths.

Go where her lord is, O Wind; my heart reaches out and can be seen by him; I pray that you keep him still dreaming.

WIFE

Aoi! if the web is broken, who, weary with time, will then come to seek me out? If at last he should come to seek me, let him call in the deep of time. Cloths are changed by recutting, hateful! love thin as a summer cloth! Let my lord's life be even so slight, for I have no sleep under the moon. O let me go on with my cloths!

CHORUS

The love of a god with a goddess
Is but for the one night in passing,
So thin are the summer cloths!
The river-waves of the sky
Have cut through our time like shears,
They have kept us apart with dew.
There are tears on the Kaji leaf,
There is dew upon the helm-bar
Of the skiff in the twisting current.

Will it harm the two sleeves of the gods
If he pass?
As a floating shadow of the water grass,
That the ripples break on the shore?
O foam, let him be as brief.

WIFE

The seventh month is come to its seventh day; we are hard on the time of long nights, and I would send him the sadness of these ten thousand voices—the colour of the moon, the breath-colour of the wind, even the points of frost that assemble in the shadow. A time that brings awe to the heart, a sound of beaten cloths, and storms in the night, a crying in the storm, a sad sound of the crickets, make one sound in the falling dew, a whispering lamentation, hera, hera, a sound in the cloth of beauty.

MAID-SERVANT

What shall I say to all this? A man has just come from the city. The master will not come this year. It seems as if . . .

CHORUS

The heart, that thinks that it will think no more, grows fainter; outside in the withered field the crickets' noise has gone faint. The flower lies open to the wind, the gazers pass on to madness, this flower-heart of the grass is blown on by a wind-like madness, until at last she is but emptiness.

[*The wife dies. Enter the husband, returning.*

HUSBAND

Pitiful hate, for my three years' delay, working within her has turned our long-drawn play of separation to separation indeed.

CHORUS

The time of regret comes not before the deed,
This we have heard from the eight thousand shadows.
This is their chorus—the shadowy blades of grass.
Sorrow! to be exchanging words
At the string-tip—
Sorrow! that we can but speak
With the bow-tip of the adzusa!

The way that a ghost returns
From the shadow of the grass—
We have heard the stories,
It is eight thousand times, they say,
Before regret runs in a smooth-worn groove,
Forestalls itself.

GHOST OF THE WIFE

Aoi! for fate, fading, alas, and unformed, all sunk into the river of three currents, gone from the light of the plum flowers that reveal spring in the world!

CHORUS

She has but kindling flame to light her track . . .

GHOST OF THE WIFE

. . . and show her autumns of a lasting moon.* And yet, who had not fallen into desire? It was easy, in the rising and falling of the smoke and the fire of thought, to sink so deep in desires. O heart, you were entangled in the threads. "Suffering" and "the Price" are their names. There is no end to the lashes of Aborasetsu, the jailor of this prison. O heart, in your utter extremity you beat the silks of remorse; to the end of all false desire Karma shows her hate.

CHORUS

Ah false desire and fate!
Her tears are shed on the silk-board,
Tears fall and turn into flame,
The smoke has stifled her cries,
She cannot reach us at all,
Nor yet the beating of the silk-board
Nor even the voice of the pines,
But only the voice of that sorrowful punishment.

                                        Aoi! Aoi!

Slow as the pace of sleep,
Swift as the steeds of time,
By the six roads of changing and passing
We do not escape from the wheel,

* I.e. a moon that has no phases.

Nor from the flaming of Karma,
Though we wander through life and death;
This woman fled from his horses
To a world without taste or breath.

GHOST OF THE WIFE
Even the leaves of the katsu-grass show their hate of this underworld by the turning away of their leaves.

CHORUS
The leaves of the katsu show their hate by bending aside; and neither can they unbend nor can the face of o'ershadowed desire. O face of eagerness, though you had loved him truly through both worlds, and hope had clung a thousand generations, 'twere little avail. The cliffs of Matsuyama, with stiff pines, stand in the end of time; your useless speech is but false mocking, like the elfish waves. Aoi! Aoi! Is this the heart of man?

GHOST OF THE WIFE
It is the great, false bird called "Taking-care."

CHORUS
Who will call him a true man—the wandering husband—when even the plants know their season, the feathered and furred have their hearts? It seems that our story has set a fact beyond fable. Even Sobu, afar, gave to the flying wild-duck a message to be borne through the southern country, over a thousand leagues, so deep was his heart's current—not shallow the love in his heart. Kimi, you have no drowsy thought of me, and no dream of yours reaches toward me. Hateful, and why? O hateful!

CHORUS
She recites the Flower of Law; the ghost is received into Butsu; the road has become enlightened. Her constant beating of silk has opened the flower, even so lightly she has entered the seed-pod of Butsu.

FINIS

HAGOROMO

A Play in one Act

CHARACTERS

CHIEF FISHERMAN, HAKURYO.
A FISHERMAN.
A TENNIN.
CHORUS.

The plot of the play Hagoromo, the Feather-mantle, is as follows: The priest finds the Hagoromo, the magical feather-mantle of a Tennin, an aerial spirit or celestial dancer, hanging upon a bough. She demands its return. He argues with her, and finally promises to return it, if she will teach him her dance or part of it. She accepts the offer. The Chorus explains the dance as symbolical of the daily changes of the moon. The words about "three, five, and fifteen" refer to the number of nights in the moon's changes. In the finale, the Tennin is supposed to disappear like a mountain slowly hidden in mist. The play shows the relation of the early Noh to the God-dance.

HAKURYO

Windy road of the waves by Miwo,
Swift with ships, loud over steersmen's voices.

Hakuryo, taker of fish, head of his house, dwells upon the barren pine-waste of Miwo.

A FISHERMAN

Upon a thousand heights had gathered the inexplicable cloud. Swept by the rain, the moon is just come to light the high house.

A clean and pleasant time surely. There comes the breath-colour of spring; the waves rise in a line below the early mist; the moon is still delaying above, though we've no skill to grasp it. Here is a beauty to set the mind above itself.

CHORUS

I shall not be out of memory
Of the mountain road by Kiyomi,

Nor of the parted grass by that bay,
Nor of the far seen pine-waste
Of Miwo of wheat stalks.

Let us go according to custom. Take hands against the wind here, for it presses the clouds and the sea. Those men who were going to fish are about to return without launching. Wait a little, is it not spring? will not the wind be quiet? This wind is only the voice of the lasting pine-trees, ready for stillness. See how the air is soundless, or would be, were it not for the waves. There now, the fishermen are putting out with even the smallest boats.

HAKURYO

I am come to shore at Miwo-no; I disembark in Matsubara; I see all that they speak of on the shore. An empty sky with music, a rain of flowers, strange fragrance on every side; all these are no common things, nor is this cloak that hangs upon the pine-tree. As I approach to inhale its colour, I am aware of mystery. Its colour-smell is mysterious. I see that it is surely no common dress. I will take it now and return and make it a treasure in my house, to show to the aged.

TENNIN

That cloak belongs to some one on this side. What are you proposing to do with it?

HAKURYO

This? this is a cloak picked up. I am taking it home, I tell you.

TENNIN

That is a feather-mantle not fit for a mortal to bear,
Not easily wrested from the sky-traversing spirit,
Not easily taken or given.
I ask you to leave it where you found it.

HAKURYO

How! Is the owner of this cloak a Tennin? So be it. In this downcast age I should keep it, a rare thing, and make it a treasure in the country, a thing respected. Then I should not return it.

TENNIN

Pitiful, there is no flying without the cloak of feathers, no return through the ether. I pray you return me the mantle.

HAKURYO

Just from hearing these high words, I, Hakuryo, have gathered more and yet more force. You think, because I was too stupid to recognize it, that I shall be unable to take and keep hid the feather-robe, that I shall give it back for merely being told to stand and withdraw?

TENNIN

A Tennin without her robe,
A bird without wings,
How shall she climb the air?

HAKURYO

And this world would be a sorry place for her to dwell in?

TENNIN

I am caught, I struggle, how shall I . . . ?

HAKURYO

No, Hakuryo is not one to give back the robe.

TENNIN

Power does not attain . . .

HAKURYO

. . . to get back the robe. . . .

CHORUS

Her coronet,* jewelled as with the dew of tears, even the flowers that decorated her hair, drooping and fading, the whole chain of weaknesses† of the dying Tennin can be seen actually before the eyes. Sorrow!

---

* Vide examples of state head-dress of kingfisher feathers in the South Kensington Museum.

† The chain of weaknesses, or the five ills, diseases of the Tennin: namely, the Tamakadzura withers; the Hagoromo is stained; sweat comes from the body; both eyes wink frequently; she feels very weary of her palace in heaven.

TENNIN

I look into the flat of heaven, peering; the cloud-road is all hidden and uncertain; we are lost in the rising mist; I have lost the knowledge of the road. Strange, a strange sorrow!

CHORUS

Enviable colour of breath, wonder of clouds that fade along the sky that was our accustomed dwelling; hearing the sky-bird, accustomed, and well accustomed, hearing the voices grow fewer, the wild geese fewer and fewer, along the high-ways of air, how deep her longing to return! Plover and sea-gull are on the waves in the offing. Do they go or do they return? She reaches out for the very blowing of the spring wind against heaven.

HAKURYO
(*to the* TENNIN)

What do you say? Now that I can see you in your sorrow, gracious, of heaven, I bend and would return you your mantle.

TENNIN

It grows clearer. No, give it this side.

HAKURYO

First tell me your nature, who are you, Tennin? Give payment with the dance of the Tennin, and I will return you your mantle.

TENNIN

Readily and gladly, and then I return into heaven. You shall have what pleasure you will, and I will leave a dance here, a joy to be new among men and to be memorial dancing. Learn then this dance that can turn the palace of the moon. No, come here to learn it. For the sorrows of the world I will leave this new dancing with you for sorrowful people. But give me my mantle, I cannot do the dance rightly without it.

HAKURYO

Not yet, for if you should get it, how do I know you'll not be off to your palace without even beginning your dance, not even a measure?

TENNIN

Doubt is fitting for mortals; with us there is no deceit.

HAKURYO

I am again ashamed. I give you your mantle.

CHORUS

The young sprite now is arrayed, she assumes the curious mantle; watch how she moves in the dance of the rainbow-feathered garment.

HAKURYO

The heavenly feather-robe moves in accord with the wind.

TENNIN

The sleeves of flowers are being wet with the rain.

HAKURYO

All three are doing one step.

CHORUS

It seems that she dances.
Thus was the dance of pleasure,
Suruga dancing, brought to the sacred east.
Thus was it when the lords of the everlasting
Trod the world,
They being of old our friends.
Upon ten sides their sky is without limit,
They have named it, on this account, the enduring.

TENNIN

The jewelled axe takes up the eternal renewing, the palace of the moon-god is being renewed with the jewelled axe, and this is always recurring.

CHORUS
(*commenting on the dance*)

The white kiromo, the black kiromo,
Three, five into fifteen,
The figure that the Tennin is dividing.
There are heavenly nymphs, Amaotome,*
One for each night of the month,
And each with her deed assigned.

---

* Cf. "Paradiso," xxiii. 25:
  "Quale nei plenilunii sereni
  Trivia ride tra le ninfe eterne."

TENNIN

I also am heaven-born and a maid, Amaotome. Of them there are many. This is the dividing of my body, that is fruit of the moon's tree, Katsura.* This is one part of our dance that I leave to you here in your world.

CHORUS

The spring mist is widespread abroad; so perhaps the wild olive's flower will blossom in the infinitely unreachable moon. Her flowery head-ornament is putting on colour; this truly is sign of the spring. Not sky is here, but the beauty; and even here comes the heavenly, wonderful wind. O blow, shut the accustomed path of the clouds. O, you in the form of a maid, grant us the favour of your delaying. The pine-waste of Miwo puts on the colour of spring. The bay of Kiyomi lies clear before the snow upon Fuji. Are not all these presages of the spring? There are but few ripples beneath the piny wind. It is quiet along the shore. There is naught but a fence of jewels between the earth and the sky, and the gods within and without,† beyond and beneath the stars, and the moon unclouded by her lord, and we who are born of the sun. This alone intervenes, here where the moon is unshadowed, here in Nippon, the sun's field.

TENNIN

The plumage of heaven drops neither feather nor flame to its own diminution.

CHORUS

Nor is this rock of earth overmuch worn by the brushing of that feather-mantle, the feathery skirt of the stars: rarely, how rarely. There is a magic song from the east, the voices of many and many: and flute and sho, filling the space beyond the cloud's edge, seven-stringed; dance filling and filling. The red sun blots on the sky the line of the colour-drenched mountains. The flowers rain in a gust; it is no racking storm that comes over this green moor, which is afloat, as it would seem, in these waves.

---

* A tree something like the laurel.
† "Within and without," gei, gu, two parts of the temple.

Wonderful is the sleeve of the white cloud, whirling such snow here.

TENNIN

Plain of life, field of the sun, true foundation, great power!

CHORUS

Hence and for ever this dancing shall be called "a revel in the East." Many are the robes thou hast, now of the sky's colour itself, and now a green garment.

SEMI-CHORUS

And now the robe of mist, presaging spring, a colour-smell as this wonderful maiden's skirt—left, right, left! The rustling of flowers, the putting on of the feathery sleeve; they bend in air with the dancing.

SEMI-CHORUS

Many are the joys in the east. She who is the colour-person of the moon takes her middle-night in the sky. She marks her three fives with this dancing, as a shadow of all fulfilments. The circled vows are at full. Give the seven jewels of rain and all of the treasure, you who go from us. After a little time, only a little time, can the mantle be upon the wind that was spread over Matsubara or over Ashitaka the mountain, though the clouds lie in its heaven like a plain awash with sea. Fuji is gone; the great peak of Fuji is blotted out little by little. It melts into the upper mist. In this way she (the Tennin) is lost to sight.

FINIS

KAGEKIYO

A Play in one Act, by Motokiyo

CHARACTERS

SHITE, KAGEKIYO old and blind.
TSURE, a girl, his daughter, called HITOMARU.
TOMO, her attendant.
WAKI, a villager.
The scene is in HIUGA.

GIRL AND ATTENDANT
(*chanting*)

What should it be; the body of dew, wholly at the mercy of wind?

GIRL

I am a girl named Hitomaru from the river valley Kamegaye-ga-Yatsu,
My father, Akushichi-bioye Kagekiyo,
Fought by the side of Heike,
And is therefore hated by Genji.
He was banished to Miyazaki in Hiuga,
To waste out the end of his life.
Though I am unaccustomed to travel,
I will try to go to my father.

GIRL AND ATTENDANT
(*describing the journey as they walk
across the bridge and the stage*)

Sleeping with the grass for our pillow,
The dew has covered our sleeves.

[*Singing.*

Of whom shall I ask my way
As I go out from Sagami province?
Of whom in Totomi?
I crossed the bay in a small hired boat
And came to Yatsuhashi in Mikawa;
Ah, when shall I see the City-on-the-cloud?

433

ATTENDANT

As we have come so fast, we are now in Miyazaki of Hiuga. It is here you should ask for your father.

KAGEKIYO
(*in another corner of the stage*)

Sitting at the gate of the pine wood I wear out the end of my years. I cannot see the clear light, I do not know how the time passes. I sit here in this dark hovel, with one coat for the warm and the cold, and my body is but a framework of bones.

CHORUS

May as well be a priest with black sleeves. Now having left the world in sorrow, I look upon my withered shape. There is no one to pity me now.

GIRL

Surely no one can live in that ruin, and yet a voice sounds from it. A beggar, perhaps. Let us take a few steps and see.

KAGEKIYO

My eyes will not show it me, yet the autumn wind is upon us.

GIRL

The wind blows from an unknown past, and spreads our doubts through the world. The wind blows, and I have no rest, nor any place to find quiet.

KAGEKIYO

Neither in the world of passion, nor in the world of colour, nor in the world of non-colour, is there any such place of rest; beneath the one sky are they all. Whom shall I ask, and how answer?

GIRL

Shall I ask the old man by the thatch?

KAGEKIYO

Who are you?

GIRL

Where does the exile live?

KAGEKIYO

What exile?

GIRL

One who is called Akushichi-bioye Kagekiyo, a noble who fought with Heike.

KAGEKIYO

Indeed? I have heard of him, but I am blind, I have not looked in his face. I have heard of his wretched condition and pity him. You had better ask for him at the next place.

ATTENDANT
(*to girl*)

It seems that he is not here, shall we ask further?

[*They pass on.*

KAGEKIYO

Strange, I feel that woman who has just passed is the child of that blind man. Long ago I loved a courtesan in Atsuta, one time when I was in that place. But I thought our girl-child would be no use to us, and I left her with the head man in the valley of Kamegaye-ga-yatsu; and now she has gone by me and spoken, although she does not know who I am.

CHORUS

Although I have heard her voice,
The pity is, that I cannot see her.
And I have let her go by
Without divulging my name.
This is the true love of a father.

ATTENDANT
(*at further side of the stage*)

Is there any native about?

VILLAGER

What do you want with me?

ATTENDANT

Do you know where the exile lives?

VILLAGER

What exile is it you want?

ATTENDANT

Akushichi-bioye Kagekiyo, a noble of Heike's party.

VILLAGER

Did not you pass an old man under the edge of the mountain as you were coming that way?

ATTENDANT

A blind beggar in a thatched cottage.

VILLAGER

That fellow was Kagekiyo. What ails the lady, she shivers?

ATTENDANT

A question you might well ask, she is the exile's daughter. She wanted to see her father once more, and so came hither to seek him. Will you take us to Kagekiyo?

VILLAGER

Bless my soul! Kagekiyo's daughter. Come, come, never mind, young miss. Now I will tell you, Kagekiyo went blind in both eyes, and so he shaved his crown and called himself "The blind man of Hiuga." He begs a bit from the passers, and the likes of us keep him; he'd be ashamed to tell you his name. However, I'll come along with you, and then I'll call out, "Kagekiyo!" and if he comes, you can see him and have a word with him. Let us along. (*They cross the stage, and the villager calls*) Kagekiyo! Oh, there, Kagekiyo!

KAGEKIYO

Noise, noise! Some one came from my home to call me, but I sent them on. I couldn't be seen like this. Tears like the thousand lines in a rain storm, bitter tears soften my sleeve. Ten thousand things rise in a dream, and I wake in this hovel, wretched, just a nothing in the wide world. How can I answer when they call me by my right name?

CHORUS

Do not call out the name he had in his glory. You will move the bad blood in his heart. (*Then, taking up* KAGE-KIYO's *thought*) I am angry.

KAGEKIYO

Living here . . .

CHORUS
(going on with KAGEKIYO'S *thought)*

I go on living here, hated by the people in power. A blind man without his staff. I am deformed, and therefore speak evil; excuse me.

KAGEKIYO

My eyes are darkened.

CHORUS

Though my eyes are dark I understand the thoughts of another. I understand at a word. The wind comes down from the pine trees on the mountain, and snow comes down after the wind. The dream tells of my glory. I am loath to wake from the dream. I hear the waves running in the evening tide, as when I was with Heike. Shall I act out the old ballad?

KAGEKIYO
(to the villager)

I had a weight on my mind, I spoke to you very harshly; excuse me.

VILLAGER

You're always like that, never mind it. Has any one been here to see you?

KAGEKIYO

No one but you.

VILLAGER

Go on! That is not true. Your daughter was here. Why couldn't you tell her the truth, she being so sad and so eager? I have brought her back now. Come now, speak with your father. Come along.

GIRL

Oh, Oh, I came such a long journey, under rain, under wind, wet with dew, over the frost; you do not see into my heart. It seems that a father's love goes when the child is not worth it.

KAGEKIYO

I meant to keep it concealed, but now they have found it all out. I shall drench you with the dew of my shame, you who are young as a flower. I tell you my name, and that we are father and child, yet I thought this would put dishonour upon you, and therefore I let you pass. Do not hold it against me.

CHORUS

At first I was angry that my friends would no longer come near me. But now I have come to a time when I could not believe that even a child of my own would seek me out.

[*Singing.*

Upon all the boats of the men of Heike's faction
Kagekiyo was the fighter most in call,
Brave were his men, cunning sailors,
And now even the leader
Is worn out and dull as a horse.

VILLAGER
(*to* KAGEKIYO)

Many a fine thing is gone, sir, your daughter would like to ask you. . . .

KAGEKIYO

What is it?

VILLAGER

She has heard of your fame from the old days. Would you tell her the ballad?

KAGEKIYO

Towards the end of the third month, it was in the third year of Juei. We men of Heike were in ships, the men of Genji were on land. Their war-tents stretched on the shore. We awaited decision. And Noto-no-Kami Noritsune said: "Last year in the hills of Harima, and in Midzushima, and in Hiyo-dorigoye of Bitchiu, we were defeated time and again, for Yoshitsune is tactful and cunning. Is there any way we can beat them?" Kagekiyo thought in his mind: "This Hangan Yoshitsune is neither god nor a devil, at the risk of my life I might do it." So he took leave of Noritsune and led a party against the shore, and all the men of Genji rushed on them.

Chorus

Kagekiyo cried, "You are haughty." His armour caught every turn of the sun. He drove them four ways before them.

Kagekiyo
(*excited and crying out*)

Samoshiya! Run, cowards!

Chorus

He thought, how easy this killing. He rushed with his spear-haft gripped under his arm. He cried out, "I am Kagekiyo of the Heike." He rushed on to take them. He pierced through the helmet vizards of Miyonoya. Miyonoya fled twice, and again; and Kagekiyo cried: "You shall not escape me!" He leaped and wrenched off his helmet. "Eya!" The vizard broke and remained in his hand and Miyonoya still fled afar, and afar, and he looked back crying in terror, "How terrible, how heavy your arm!" And Kagekiyo called at him, "How tough the shaft of your neck is!" And they both laughed out over the battle, and went off each his own way.

Chorus

These were the deeds of old, but oh, to tell them! to be telling them over now in his wretched condition. His life in the world is weary, he is near the end of his course. "Go back," he would say to his daughter. "Pray for me when I am gone from the world, for I shall then count upon you as we count on a lamp in the darkness . . . we who are blind." "I will stay," she said. Then she obeyed him, and only one voice is left.

We tell this for the remembrance. Thus were the parent and child.

FINIS

NOTE

Fenollosa has left this memorandum on the stoicism of the last play: I asked Mr. Hirata how it could be considered natural or dutiful for the daughter to leave her father in such a condition. He said, "that the Japanese would not be in sympathy with such sternness now, but that it was the old Bushido spirit. The personality of the old man is worn out, no more good in this life. It would be sentimentality for her to remain with him. No good could be done. He could well restrain his love for her, better that she should pray for him and go on with the work of her normal life."

Part IV

I GIVE the next two plays, Awoi no Uye and Kakitsubata, with very considerable diffidence. I am not sure that they are clear; Japanese with whom I have discussed them do not seem able to give me much help. Several passages which are, however, quite lucid in themselves, seem to me as beautiful as anything I have found in Fenollosa's Japanese notes, and these passages must be my justification. In each case I give an explanation of the story so far as I understand it. In one place in Kakitsubata I have transferred a refrain or doubled it. For the rest the plays are as literal as the notes before me permit.

AWOI NO UYE

A Play by Ujinobu

INTRODUCTION

The story, as I understand it, is that the "Court Lady Awoi" (Flower of the East) is jealous of the other and later co-wives of Genji. This jealousy reaches its climax, and she goes off her head with it, when her carriage is overturned and broken at the Kami festival. The play opens with the death-bed of Awoi, and in Mrs. Fenollosa's diary I find the statement that "Awoi, her struggles, sickness, and death are represented by a red, flowered kimono, folded once length-wise, and laid at the front edge of the stage."

The objective action is confined to the apparitions and exorcists. The demon of jealousy, tormenting Awoi, first appears in the form of the Princess Rakujo, then with the progress and success of the exorcism the jealous quintessence is driven out of this personal ghost, and appears in its own truly demonic ("hannya") form—"That awful face with its golden eyes and horns revealed." The exorcist Miko is powerless against this demon, but the yamabushi exorcists, "advancing against it, making a grinding noise with the beads of their rosaries and striking against it," finally drive it away.

The ambiguities of certain early parts of the play seem mainly due to the fact that the "Princess Rokujo," the concrete figure on the stage, is a phantom or image of Awoi no Uye's own jealousy. That is to say, Awoi is tormented by her own passion, and this passion obsesses her first in the form of a personal apparition of Rokujo, then in demonic form.

This play was written before Ibsen declared that life is a "contest with the phantoms of the mind." The difficulties of the translator have lain in separating what belongs to Awoi herself from the things belonging to the ghost of Rokujo, very much as modern psychologists might have difficulty in detaching the personality or memories of an obsessed person from the personal memories of the obsession. Baldly: an obsessed person thinks he is Napoleon; an image of his own thought would be confused with scraps relating perhaps to St. Helena, Corsica, and Waterloo.

The second confusion is the relation of the two apparitions. It seems difficult to make it clear that the "hannya" has been cast out of the ghostly personality, and that it had been, in a way, the motive force in the ghost's actions. And again we cannot make it too clear that the ghost is not actually a separate soul, but only a manifestation made possible through Awoi and her passion of jealousy. At least with this interpretation the play seems moderately coherent and lucid.

Rokujo or Awoi, whichever we choose to consider her, comes out of hell-gate in a chariot, "because people of her rank are always accustomed to go about in chariots. When they, or their ghosts, think of motion, they think of going in a chariot, therefore they take that form." There would be a model chariot shown somewhere at the back of the stage.

The ambiguity of the apparition's opening line is, possibly, to arouse the curiosity of the audience. There will be an air of mystery, and they will not know whether it is to be the chariot associated with Genji's liaison with Yugawo, the beautiful heroine of the play Hajitomi, or whether it is the symbolic chariot drawn by a sheep, a deer, and an ox. But I think we are nearer the mark if we take Rokujo's enigmatic line, "I am come in three chariots," to mean that the formed idea of a chariot is derived from these events and from the mishap to Awoi's own chariot, all of which have combined and helped the spirit world to manifest itself concretely. Western students of ghostly folk-lore would tell you that the world of spirits is fluid and drifts about seeking shape. I do not wish to dogmatize on these points.

The Fenollosa-Hirata draft calls the manifest spirit "The Princess Rokujo," and she attacks Awoi, who is represented by the folded kimono. Other texts seem to call this manifestation "Awoi no Uye," i.e. her mind or troubled spirit, and this spirit attacks her body. It will be perhaps simpler for the reader if I mark her speeches simply "Apparition," and those of the second form "Hannya."

I do not know whether I can make the matter more plain or summarize it otherwise than by saying that the whole play is a dramatization, or externalization, of Awoi's jealousy. The passion makes her subject to the demon-possession. The demon first comes in a disguised and beautiful form. The prayer of the exorcist forces him first to appear in his true shape, and then to retreat.

But the "disguised and beautiful form" is not a mere abstract sheet of matter. It is a sort of personal or living mask, having a ghost-life of its own; it is at once a shell of the princess, and a form, which is strengthened or made more palpable by the passion of Awoi.

AWOI NO UYE

Scene in Kioto

DAIJIN

I am a subject in the service of the Blessed Emperor Shujakuin. They have called in the priests and the high priests for the sickness of Awoi no Uye of the house of Sadaijin. They prayed, but the gods give no sign. I am sent to Miko, the wise, to bid him pray to the spirits. Miko, will you pray to the earth?

MIKO

Tenshojo, chishojo,
Naigeshojo, Rakkonshojo.

Earth, pure earth,
Wither, by the sixteen roots
(Wither this evil)!

APPARITION

It may be, it may be, I come from the gate of hell in three coaches. I am sorry for Yugawo and the carriage with broken wheels. And the world is ploughed with sorrow as a field is furrowed with oxen. Man's life is a wheel on the axle, there is no turn whereby to escape. His hold is light as dew on the Basho leaf. It seems that the last spring's blossoms are only a dream in the mind. And we fools take it all, take it all as a matter of course. Oh, I am grown envious from sorrow. I come to seek consolation. (*Singing.*) Though I lie all night

hid for shame in the secret carriage, looking at the moon for
sorrow, yet I would not be seen by the moon.
> Where Miko draws the magical bow,
> I would go to set my sorrow aloud.

(*Speaking.*) Where does that sound of playing come from? It
is the sound of the bow of Adzusa!

MIKO

Though I went to the door of the square building, Adzu-
maya——

APPARITION

—you thought no one came to knock.

MIKO

How strange! It is a lady of high rank whom I do not
know. She comes in a broken carriage, a green wife clings to
the shaft. She weeps. Is it——

DAIJIN

Yes, I think I know who it is. (*To the Apparition.*) I ask you
to tell me your name.

APPARITION

In the world of the swift-moving lightning I have no ser-
vant or envoi, neither am I consumed with self-pity. I came
aimlessly hither, drawn only by the sound of the bow. Who do
you think I am? I am the spirit of the Princess Rokujo,* and
when I was still in the world, spring was there with me. I
feasted upon the cloud with the Sennin,† they shared in my
feast of flowers. And on the Evening of Maple Leaves I had
the moon for a mirror. I was drunk with colour and perfume.
And for all my gay flare at that time I am now like a shut
Morning-glory, awaiting the sunshine. And now I am come
for a whim, I am come uncounting the hour, seizing upon no
set moment. I would set my sorrow aside. Let some one else
bear it awhile.

---

* As in Western folk-lore, demons often appear first in some splendid dis-
guise.
† Spirits not unlike the Irish "Sidhe."

CHORUS

Love turns back toward the lover, unkindness brings evil return. It is for no good deed or good purpose that you bring back a sorrow among us, our sorrows mount up without end.

APPARITION

The woman is hateful! I cannot keep back my blows.

[*She strikes.*

MIKO

No. You are a princess of Rokujo! How can you do such things? Give over. Give over.

APPARITION

I cannot. However much you might pray. (*Reflectively, as if detached from her action, and describing it.*) So she went toward the pillow, and struck. Struck.

MIKO

Then standing up——

APPARITION

This hate is only repayment

MIKO

The flame of jealousy——

APPARITION

—will turn on one's own hand and burn.

MIKO

Do you not know?

APPARITION

Know! This is a just revenge.

CHORUS

Hateful, heart full of hate,
Though you are full of tears
Because of others' dark hatred,
Your love for Genji
Will not be struck out
Like a fire-fly's flash in the dark.

APPARITION

I, like a bush——

CHORUS

—am a body that has no root.
I fade as dew from the leaf,
Partly for that cause I hate her,
My love cannot be restored . . .
Not even in a dream.

It is a gleam cast up from the past. I am full of longing. I would be off in the secret coach, and crush her shade with me.

DAIJIN

Help. Awoi no Uye is sinking. Can you find Kohijiri of Tokokawa?

KIOGEN

I will call him. I call him.

WAKI (KOHIJIRI)

Do you call me to a fit place for prayer? To the window of the nine wisdoms, to the cushion of the ten ranks, to a place full of holy waters, and where there is a clear moon?

KIOGEN

Yes, yes.

WAKI

How should I know? I do not go about in the world. You come from the Daijin. Wait. I am ready. I will come.

> [*He crosses the stage or bridge.*

DAIJIN

I thank you for coming.

WAKI

Where is the patient?

DAIJIN

She is there on that bed.

WAKI

I will begin the exorcism at once.

DAIJIN

I thank you. Please do so.

WAKI
(*beginning the ritual*)

Then Gioja called upon En no Gioja, and he hung about
his shoulders a cloak that had swept the dew of the seven jew-
els in climbing the peaks of Tai Kou and of Kori in Riobu. He
wore the cassock of forbearance to keep out unholy things.
He took the beads of red wood, the square beads with hard
corners, and whirling and striking said prayer. But one prayer.
Namaku, Samanda, Basarada.

[*During this speech the* APPARITION *has disap-
peared. That is, the first* SHITE, *the* PRINCESS OF
ROKUJO. *Her costume was "The under kimono
black satin, tight from the knees down, embroi-
dered with small, irregular, infrequent circles of
flowers; the upper part, stiff gold brocade, just shot
through with purples, greens, and reds."*

[*The* HANNYA *has come on. Clothed in a scarlet
hakama, white upper dress, and "The terrible mask
with golden eyes." She has held a white scarf over
her head. She looks up. Here follows the great
dance climax of the play.*

HANNYA
(*threatening*)

Oh, Gioja, turn back! Turn back, or you rue it.

WAKI

Let whatever evil spirit is here bow before Gioja, and know
that Gioja will drive it out.

[*He continues whirling the rosary.*

CHORUS
(*invoking the powerful good spirits*)

On the east stand Gosanze Miowo.

HANNYA
(*opposing other great spirits*)

On the south stand Gundari Yasha.

CHORUS

On the west stand Dai Itoku Miowo.

Hannya

On the north stand Kongo——

Chorus

—Yasha Miowo.

Hannya

In the middle Dai Sei——

Chorus

Fudo Miowo
Namaku Samanda Basarada!
Senda Makaroshana Sowataya
Wun tarata Kamman,
Choga Sessha Tokudai Chiye
Chiga Shinja Sokushin Jobutsu.

Hannya
(*overcome by the exorcism*)

O terrible names of the spirits. This is my last time. I cannot return here again.

Chorus

By hearing the scripture the evil spirit is melted. Bosatsu came hither, his face was full of forbearance and pity. Pity has melted her heart, and she has gone into Buddha. Thanksgiving.

FINIS

KAKITSUBATA

By Motokiyo

Either Motokiyo or Fenollosa seems to have thought that the old sage Narihira was in his day the incarnation of a certain Bosatsu or high spirit. Secondly, that the music of this spirit was known and was called "Kohi" or "Gobusaki's" music. Narihira seems, after favour, to have been exiled from the court, and to have written poems of regret.

In the play a certain priest, given to melancholy, and with a kindliness for the people of old stories, meets with the spirit of one of Narihira's ladies who has identified herself with the Iris, that is to say, the flowers are the thoughts or the body of her spirit.

She tells him of her past and of Narihira's, and how the music of Gobusaki will lift a man's soul into paradise. She then returns to her heaven.

The rest is, I hope, apparent in the play as I have set it.

CHARACTERS

The Scene is in Mikawa

SPIRIT OF THE IRIS, KAKITSUBATA.
A PRIEST.
CHORUS.

PRIEST

I am a priest who travels to see the sights in many provinces; I have been to Miyako city and seen all the ward shrines and places of interest; I will now push on to the east country. Every night it is a new bed and the old urge of sorrow within me. I have gone by Mino and Owari without stopping, and I am come to Mikawa province to see the flowers of Kakitsubata in the height of their full season. Now the low land is before me, I must go down and peer closely upon them.

Time does not stop and spring passes,
The lightfoot summer comes nigh us,
The branching trees and the bright unmindful grass

Do not forget their time,
They take no thought, yet remember
To show forth their colour in season.

SPIRIT

What are you doing here in this swamp?

PRIEST

I am a priest on my travels. I think these very fine iris. What place is this I am come to?

SPIRIT

Eight Bridges, Yatsubashi of Mikawa, an iris plantation. You have the best flowers before you, those of the deepest colour, as you would see if you had any power of feeling.

PRIEST

I can see it quite well; they are, I think, the Kakitsubata iris that are set in an ancient legend. Can you tell me who wrote down the words?

SPIRIT

In the Ise Monogatari you read, "By the eight bridges, by the web of the crossing waters in Kumode, the iris come to the full, they flaunt there and scatter their petals." And when some one laid a wager with Narihira he made an acrostic which says, "These flowers brought their court dress from China."

PRIEST

Then Narihira came hither? From the far end of Adzuma?

SPIRIT

Here? Yes. And every other place in the north, the deep north.

PRIEST

Though he went through many a province, what place was nearest his heart?

SPIRIT

This place, Yatsubashi.

PRIEST

Here with the wide-petalled iris
On the lowlands of Mikawa.

SPIRIT

Throughout the length and width of his journeys——

PRIEST

Their colour was alive in his thought.

SPIRIT

He was Narihira of old, the man of the stories.

PRIEST

Yet this iris. . . .

SPIRIT
(*still standing by the pillar and bending sideways*)
These very flowers before you——

CHORUS

—are not the thing of importance. She would say:
"The water by the shore is not shallow.
The man who bound himself to me
Returned times out of mind in his thought
To me and this cobweb of waters."
   It was in this fashion he knew her, when he was strange in
this place.

SPIRIT

I should speak.

PRIEST

What is it?

SPIRIT

Though this is a very poor place, will you pass the night in
my cottage?

PRIEST

Most gladly. I will come after a little.

[*Up to this point the spirit has appeared as a simple
young girl of the locality. She now leaves her pillar
and goes off to the other side of the stage to be*

dressed. She returns in her true appearance, that is, as the great lady beloved of old by Narihira. She wears a black hoshiben crest or hat, an over-dress of gauze, purple with golden flowers, an under-dress of glaring orange with green and gold pattern. This shows a little beneath the great enveloping gauze.

SPIRIT
(*to tire-women*)

No, no. This hat, this ceremonial gown, the Chinese silk, Karaginu, . . . Look!

PRIEST

How strange. In that tumble-down cottage; in the bower, a lady clad in bright robes! In the pierced hat of Sukibitai's time. She seems to speak, saying, "Behold me!"
What can all this mean?

KAKITSUBATA

This is the very dress brought from China,
Whereof they sing in the ballad,
'Tis the gown of the Empress Takago,
Queen of old to Seiwa Tenno,*
She is Narihira's beloved,
Who danced the Gosetsu music.
At eighteen she won him,
She was his light in her youth.

This hat is for Gosetsu dancing,
For the Dance of Toyo no Akari.
Narihira went covered in like.
A hat and a robe of remembrance!
I am come clothed in a memory.

PRIEST

You had better put them aside. But who are you?

---

* Emperor of Japan, A.D. 859–876.

THE LADY

I am indeed the spirit, Kakitsubata, the colours of remembrance.

And Narihira was the incarnation of the Bosatsu of Gokusaki's music. Holy magic is run through his words and through the notes of his singing, till even the grass and the flowers pray to him for the blessings of dew.

PRIEST

A fine thing in a world run waste,
To the plants that are without mind,
I preach the law of Bosatsu.

LADY

This was our service to Buddha,
This dance, in the old days.

PRIEST
(*hearing the music*)

This is indeed spirit music.

LADY

He took the form of a man.

PRIEST

Journeying out afar
From his bright city.

LADY

Saving all——

PRIEST

—by his favour.

CHORUS

Going out afar and afar
I put on robes for the dance.

LADY

A robe for the sorrow of parting.

CHORUS

I send the sleeves back to the city.

LADY

This story has no beginning and no end,
No man has known the doer and no man has seen the deed.
In the old days a man
Wearing his first hat-of-manhood
Went out a-hunting
Toward the town of Kasuga in Nara.

CHORUS

We think it was in the time
Of the reign of Nimmio Tenno.

He was granted by Imperial Decree
Reading: "About the beginning of March,
When the mists are still banked upon Ouchiyama the
        mountain. . . ."
He was granted the hat-insignia, sukibitai,
As chief messenger to the festival of Kasuga.

LADY

An unusual favour.

CHORUS

It was a rare thing to hold the plays and Genbuku ceremony
in the palace itself. This was the first time it had happened.
The world's glory is only for once,
Comes once, blows once, and soon fades,
So also to him: he went out
To seek his luck in Adzuma,
Wandering like a piece of cloud, at last
After years he came
And looking upon the waves at Ise and Owari,
He longed for his brief year of glory:
        The waves, the breakers return,
        But my glory comes not again,
            Narihira, Narihira,
        My glory comes not again.
He stood at the foot of Asama of Shinano, and saw the
smoke curling upwards.

LADY

The smoke is now curling up
From the peak of Asama.
                  Narihira, Narihira,
                  My glory comes not again.

CHORUS

Strangers from afar and afar,
Will they not wonder at this?
He went on afar and afar
And came to Mikawa, the province,
To the flowers Kakitsubata
That flare and flaunt in their marsh
By the many-bridged cobweb of waters.

"She whom I left in the city?" thought Narihira. But in the
long tale, Monogatari, there is many a page full of travels . . .
and yet at the place of eight bridges the stream-bed is never
dry.
He was pledged with many a lady.
The fire-flies drift away
From the jewelled blind,
Scattering their little lights
And then flying and flying:

Souls of fine ladies
Going up into heaven.

And here in the under-world
The autumn winds come blowing and blowing,
And the wild ducks cry: "Kari! . . . Kari!"

I who speak, an unsteady wraith,
A form impermanent, drifting after this fashion,
Am come to enlighten these people.
Whether they know me I know not.

SPIRIT

A light that does not lead on to darkness.

CHORUS
(*singing the poem of Narihira's*)
No moon!
The spring

Is not the spring of the old days,
        My body
Is not my body,
But only a body grown old.
            Narihira, Narihira,
        My glory comes not again.

CHORUS

   Know then that Narihira of old made these verses for the
Queen of Seiwa Tenno. The body unravels its shred, the
true image divides into shade and light. Narihira knew me in
the old days. Doubt it not, stranger. And now I begin my
dance, wearing the ancient bright mantle.
                        [*Dance and its descriptions.*

SPIRIT

The flitting snow before the flowers:
The butterfly flying.

CHORUS

The nightingales fly in the willow tree:
The pieces of gold flying.

SPIRIT

The iris Kakitsubata of the old days
Is planted anew.

CHORUS

With the old bright colour renewed.

SPIRIT

Thus runs each tale from its beginning,
We wear the bright iris crest of Azame.

CHORUS

What are the colours of the iris?
Are they like one another, the flower,
Kakitsubata, Ayame.
      [*The grey and olive robed chorus obscure the bright dancer.*
What is that that cries from the tree?
                  [*The spirit is going away, leaving its*
                  apparition, which fades as it returns
                                  to the aether.

SPIRIT

It is only the cracked husk of the locust.

CHORUS
(*closing the play*)

The sleeves are white like the snow of the Uno Flower
Dropping their petals in April.
Day comes, the purple flower
   Opens its heart of wisdom,
It fades out of sight by its thought.
The flower soul melts into Buddha.

NOTE

I have left one or two points of this play unexplained in the
opening notice. I do not think any one will understand the
beauty of it until he has read it twice. The emotional tone is
perhaps apparent. The spirit manifests itself in that particular
iris marsh because Narihira in passing that place centuries be-
fore had thought of her. Our own art is so much an art of
emphasis, and even of over-emphasis, that it is difficult to
consider the possibilities of an absolutely unemphasized art,
an art where the author trusts so implicitly that his auditor
will know what things are profound and important.

The Muses were "the Daughters of Memory." It is by
memory that this spirit appears, she is able or "bound" be-
cause of the passing thought of these iris. That is to say, they,
as well as the first shadowy and then bright apparition, are the
outer veils of her being. Beauty is the road to salvation, and
her apparition "to win people to the Lord" or "to enlighten
these people" is part of the ritual, that is to say, she demon-
strates the "immortality of the soul" or the "permanence or
endurance of the individual personality" by her apparition—
first, as a simple girl of the locality; secondly, in the ancient
splendours. At least that is the general meaning of the play so
far as I understand it.

E.P.

CHORIO

By Nobumitsu
(who died in the 13th year of Yeisho, A.D. 1516)

CHARACTERS

The Scene is in China

FIRST SHITE, an old man.
SECOND SHITE, KOSEKKO.
WAKI, CHORIO.

PART I

WAKI

I am Chorio,* a subject of Koso of Kan, though I am busy
in service I had a strange dream that there was in Kahi an
earthen bridge, and that as I leaned on the bridge-rail there
came an old man on horseback. And he dropped one of his
shoes and bade me pick up the shoe. I thought this uncivil,
yet he seemed so uncommon a figure and so gone on in old
age that I went and picked up the shoe. "You've a true
heart," he said, "come back here in five days' time, and I will
teach you all there is to know about fighting."

He said that, and then I woke up, and now it's five days
since the dream, and I am on my way to kahi.

Dawn begins to show in the sky. I am afraid I may be too
late. The mountain is already lit, and I am just reaching the
bridge.

SHITE

Chorio, you are late, you have not kept your promise. I came
quite early, and now it is much too late. Hear the bell there.

CHORUS

Too late now. Come again. Come in five days' time if you
carry a true heart within you. And I shall be here, and will
teach you the true craft of fighting. Keep the hour, and keep

---

* Chinese. Chang Liang died 187 B.C. Koso of Kan = Kao Tsu, first Em-
peror of the Han dynasty. Kahi = Hsia-p'ei, in the north of Kiangsu. Kosekko
= Huang Shih Kung, Yellow Stone Duke.

truc to your promise. How angry the old man seemed. How suddenly he is gone. Chorio, see that you come here in time.

CHORIO

He is angry. I am sorry. Why do I follow a man wholly a stranger? Foolish. Yet, if he would teach me his secrets of strategy. . . .

CHORUS

I think that he will come back. He does not like wasting his time. Still, he will come back again. See, he has gone away happy.

PART II

CHORIO

"Frost tinges the jasper terrace,
A fine stork, a black stork sings in the heaven,
Autumn is deep in the valley of Hako,
The sad monkeys cry out in the midnight,
The mountain pathway is lonely."

CHORUS

The morning moonlight lies over the world
And flows through the gap of these mountains,
White frost is on Kahi bridge, the crisp water wrinkles
    beneath it,
There is no print in the frost on the bridge,
No one has been by this morning.
Chorio, that is your luck. That shadow shows a man urging
    his horse.

OLD MAN

I am the old man, Kosekko. Since Chorio is loyal in service, no fool, ready at learning . . .

CHORUS

Since he cares so much for the people . . .

KOSEKKO

His heart has been seen in high heaven.

CHORUS

The Boddisatwa are ready to bless him.

KOSEKKO

I will teach him the secrets of battle.

CHORUS

He says he will teach Chorio to conquer the enemy, and to rule well over the people. He urges his horse, and seeing this from far off, seeing the old man so changed in aspect, with eye gleaming out and with such dignity in his bearing, Chorio has knelt down on the bridge awaiting Kosekko.

KOSEKKO

Chorio, you are come in good time. Come nearer and listen.

CHORIO

Chorio then stood up and smoothed out his hat and his robe.

KOSEKKO

I know quite well he is wise, but still I will try him.

CHORUS

Kosekko kicked off his shoe so it fell in the river. Then Chorio leapt in for the shoe, but the river flowed between rocks; it was full of currents and arrow-like rapids. He went diving and floating and still not reaching the shoe.*

See how the waves draw back. A thick mist covers the place, a dragon moves in darkness, ramping among the waves, lolling its fiery tongue. It is fighting with Chorio; see, it has seized on the shoe.

CHORIO

Chorio drew his sword calmly.

CHORUS

He struck a great blow at the dragon; there was terrible light on his sword. See, the dragon draws back and leaves Chorio with the shoe. Then Chorio sheathed his sword and brought up the shoe to Kosekko, and buckled it fast to his foot.

KOSEKKO

And Kosekko got down from his horse.

* One must consider this as dance motif.

CHORUS

He alighted, saying, "Well done. Well done." And he gave a scroll of writing to Chorio, containing all the secret traditions of warfare. And Kosekko said, "That dragon was Kwannon. She came here to try your heart, and she must be your goddess hereafter."

Then the dragon went up to the clouds, and Kosekko drew back to the highest peak, and set his light in the sky; was changed to the yellow stone.

FINIS

GENJO

By Kongo

Story from Utai Kimmō Zuye

In China, under the Tō dynasty (A.D. 604–927), there was a biwa player named Renjōbu, and he had a biwa called Genjō. In the reign of Nimmyō Tennō (A.D. 834–850) Kamon no Kami Sadatoshi met Renjōbu in China, and learnt from him three tunes, Ryūsen (The Flowing Fountain), Takuboku* (The Woodpecker), and the tune Yōshin. He also brought back to our court the biwa named Genjō.

Murakami Tennō (947–967) was a great biwa player. One moonlit night, when he was sitting alone in the Southern Palace, he took the biwa Genjō and sang the old song:

> Slowly the night draws on
> And the dew on the grasses deepens.
> Long after man's heart is at rest
> Clouds trouble the moon's face—
> Through the long night till dawn.

Suddenly the spirit of Renjōbu appeared to him and taught him two new tunes, Jōgen and Sekishō (the Stone Image). These two, with the three that Sadatoshi had brought before, became the Five Biwa Tunes.

These five tunes were transmitted to Daijō Daijin Moronaga, who was the most skilful player in the Empire.

Moronaga purposed to take the biwa Genjō and go with it

---

* The words of "Takuboku" are—
> In the South Hill there's a bird
> That calls itself the woodpecker.
> When it's hungry, it eats its tree;
> When it's tired, it rests in the boughs.
>
> Don't mind about other people;
> Just make up your mind what you want.
> If you're pure, you'll get honour;
> If you're foul, you'll get shame.
> > By Lady Tso, A.D. 4th cent.

463

to China in order to perfect his knowledge. But on the way the spirit of Murakami Tennō appeared to him at Suma under the guise of an old salt-burner.*

GENJO

PART I

The Scene is in Settsu

CHARACTERS

FIRST SHITE, an old man.
TSURE, an old woman.
TSURE, Fujiwara no Moronaga.
SECOND SHITE, the Emperor Murakami.
TSURE, Riujin, the Dragon God.
WAKI, an attendant of Moronaga.

WAKI
What road will get us to Mirokoshi,† far in the eight-folded waves?

MORONAGA
I am the Daijo Daijin Moronaga.

WAKI
He is my master, and the famous master of the biwa, and he wishes to go to China to study more about music, but now he is turning aside from the straight road to see the moon-light in Suma and Tsu-no-Kuni.‡

MORONAGA
When shall I see the sky-line of Miyako, the capital? We started at midnight. Yamazaki is already behind us.

WAKI
Here is Minato river and the wood of Ikuta; the moon shows between the black trees, a lonely track. But I am glad to be

* Note supplied by A. D. W.
† China.
‡ Tsu-no-Kuni is the poetical name for Settsu province.

going to Mirokoshi. The forest of Koma is already behind us. Now we are coming to Suma.

Now we have come to the sea-board, Suma in Tsu-no-Kuni. Let us rest here a while and ask questions.

OLD MAN AND OLD WOMAN
It's a shabby life, lugging great salt tubs, and yet the shore is so lovely that one puts off one's sorrow, forgets it.

OLD MAN
The setting sun floats on the water.

OLD MAN AND OLD WOMAN
Even the fishermen know something grown out of the place, and speak well of their sea-coast.

OLD WOMAN
The isles of Kii show through the cloud to the southward.

OLD MAN
You can see the ships there, coming through the gateway of Yura.

OLD WOMAN
And the pine-trees, as far off as Sumiyoshi.

OLD MAN
And the cottages at Tojima, Koya, and Naniwa.

OLD WOMAN
They call it the island of pictures.

OLD MAN
Yet no one is able to paint it.

OLD MAN AND OLD WOMAN
Truly a place full of charms.

CHORUS
The air of this place sets one thinking. Awaji, the sea, a place of fishermen, see now their boats will come in. The rain crouches low in the cloud. Lift up your salt tubs, Aie! It's a long tramp, heavy working. Carry along, from Ise Island to the shore of Akogi. There is no end to this business. The salt

at Tango is worse. Now we go down to Suma. A dreary time at this labour. No one knows aught about us. Will any one ask our trouble?

OLD MAN

I will go back to the cottage and rest.

WAKI

(*at the cottage door*)

Is any one home here? We are looking for lodging.

OLD MAN

I am the man of the place.

WAKI

This is the great Daijin Moronaga, the master of biwa, on his way to far Mirokoshi. May we rest here?

OLD MAN

Please take him somewhere else.

WAKI

What! you won't give us lodging. Please let us stay here.

OLD MAN

The place isn't good enough, but you may come in if you like.

OLD WOMAN

When they were praying for rain in the garden of Shin-sen (Divine Fountain), he drew secret music from the strings of his biwa——

OLD MAN

—and the dragon-god seemed to like it. The clouds grew out of the hard sky of a sudden, and the rain fell and continued to fall. And they have called him Lord of the Rain.

OLD WOMAN

If you lodge such a noble person——

OLD MAN

—I might hear his excellent playing.

BOTH

It will be a night worth remembering.

CHORUS
The bard Semimaru played upon his biwa at the small house in Osaka, now a prince will play in the fisherman's cottage. A rare night. Let us wait here in Suma. The pine-wood shuts out the wind and the bamboo helps to make stillness. Only the little ripple of waves sounds from a distance. They will not let you sleep for a while. Play your biwa. We listen.

WAKI
I will ask him to play all night.

MORONAGA
Maybe it was spring when Genji was exiled and came here into Suma, and had his first draught of sorrow, of all the sorrows that come to us. And yet his travelling clothes were not dyed in tears. Weeping, he took out his small lute, and thought that the shore wind had in it a cry like his longing, and came to him from far cities.

CHORUS
That was the sound of the small lute and the shore wind sounding together, but this biwa that we will hear is the rain walking in showers. It beats on the roof of the cottage. We cannot sleep for the rain. It is interrupting the music.

OLD MAN
Why do you stop your music?

WAKI
He stopped because of the rain.

OLD MAN
Yes, it is raining. We will put our straw mats on the roof.

OLD WOMAN
Why?

OLD MAN
They will stop the noise of the rain, and we can go on hearing his music.

BOTH
So they covered the wooden roof.

CHORUS

And they came back and sat close to hear him.

WAKI

Why have you put the mats on the roof?

OLD MAN

The rain sounded out of the key. The biwa sounds "yellow bell," and the rain gives a "plate" note. Now we hear only the "bell."

CHORUS

We knew you were no ordinary person. Come, play the biwa yourself.

OLD MAN AND OLD WOMAN

The waves at this side of the beach can play their own biwa; we did not expect to be asked.

CHORUS

Still they were given the biwa.

OLD MAN

The old man pulled at the strings.

OLD WOMAN

The old woman steadied the biwa.

CHORUS

A sound of pulling and plucking, "Barari, karari, karari, barari," a beauty filled full of tears, a singing bound in with the music, unending, returning.

MORONAGA

Moronaga thought——

CHORUS

——I learned in Hi-no-Moto all that men knew of the biwa, and now I am ashamed to have thought of going to China. I need not go out of this country. So he secretly went out of the cottage. And the old man, not knowing, went on playing the biwa, and singing "Etenraku," the upper cloud music, this song:

"The nightingale nests in the plum tree, but what will she
    do with the wind?
Let the nightingale keep to her flowers."
    The old man is playing, not knowing the guest has gone
out.

OLD WOMAN
The stranger has gone.

OLD MAN
What! he is gone. Why didn't you stop him?

BOTH
So they both ran after the stranger.

CHORUS
And taking him by the sleeve, they said, "The night is still
only half over. Stay here."

MORONAGA
Why do you stop me? I am going back to the capital now,
but later I will return. Who are you? What are your names?

BOTH
Emperor Murakami, and the lady is Nashitsubo.

CHORUS
To stop you from going to China we looked on you in a
dream, by the sea-coasts at Suma. So saying, they vanished.

PART II

THE EMPEROR MURAKAMI
I came up to the throne in the sacred era of Gengi,* when
the fine music came from Mirokoshi, the secret and sacred
music, and the lutes Genjo, Seizan,† and Shishimaru. The last
brought from the dragon world. And now I will play on it.
    And he looked out at the sea and called on the dragon god,
and played on "Shishimaru."
    The lion-dragon floated out of the waves, and the eight
goddesses of the dragon stood with him, and he then gave

* A.D. 901–923.
† The lute Seizan. See first speech of "Tsunemasa."

Moronaga the biwa. And Moronaga took it, beginning to play. And the dragon king moved with the music, and the waves beat with drum rhythm. And Murakami took up one part. That was music. Then Murakami stepped into the cloudy chariot, drawn by the eight goddesses of the dragon, and was lifted up beyond sight. And Moronaga took a swift horse back to his city, bearing that biwa with him.

FINIS

APPENDIX I

SHUNKWAN, by Motokiyo (b. 1374, d. 1455).

Plot.—When Kiyomori* was at the height of his power three men plotted against him. They were detected and exiled to Devil's Island; "for many years they knew the spring only by the green new grass, and autumn by the turning of the leaves."

Then when Kiyomori's daughter was about to give birth to a child, many prisoners and exiles were pardoned in order to propitiate the gods, and among them Shunkwan's companions, but not the chief conspirator Shunkwan.

On the ninth day of the ninth month, which day is called "Choyo" and is considered very lucky, because Hosō of China drank ceremonial wine on that day and lived 7000 years, the two exiled companions of Shunkwan are performing service to their god Kumano Gongen. They have no white prayer cord, and must use the white cord of their exile's dress; they have no white rice to scatter, and so they scatter white sand. With this scene the Noh opens. Shunkwan, who alone is a priest, enters, and should offer a cup of saké, as in the proper service for receiving pilgrims, but he has only a cup of water.

While this ceremony is in progress, the imperial messengers arrive with the emperor's writ; they pronounce the names of Yasuyori and Naritsune, but not Shunkwan's. He thinks there must be some error. He seizes the paper and reads, and is frenzied with grief. He tries to detain his companions, but the messengers hurry them off. Shunkwan seizes the boat's cable. The messenger cuts it. Shunkwan falls to earth, and the others go off, leaving him alone.

This is, of course, not a "play" in our sense. It is a programme for a tremendous dance.

Modus of Presentation (Asakusa, October 30, 1898).—The companions wear dull blue and brown. Shunkwan's mask is of a dead colour, full of wrinkles, with sunken cheeks and eyes. His costume is also of blue and brown. The finest singing and dancing are after the others have entered the boat. Everything is concentrated on the impression of a feeling.

The scene is in "an island of Stasuma."

---

* Kiyomori, 1118–81.

KOI NO OMONI ("THE BURDEN OF LOVE"), said to be by the Emperor Gohanazono (1429–65).

Plot.—Yamashina Shoshi was the emperor's gardener, and as the court ladies were always walking about in the garden, he fell in love with one of them. He wished to keep this secret, but in some way it became known. Then a court officer said to him, "If you can carry this light and richly brocaded burden on your back, and carry it many thousand times round the garden, you will win the lady you love." But for all its seeming so light and being so finely ornamented, it was a very heavy load, and whenever he tried to lift it he fell to the ground, and he sang and complained of it, and at last he died trying to lift it.

And the court officer told the lady, and she was filled with pity and sang a short and beautiful song, and the ghost of Shoshi came and sang to her of the pain he had in this life, reproaching her for her coldness.

Modus.—From the very first the burden of love lay in the centre front of the stage, thus "becoming actually one of the characters." It was a cube done up in red and gold brocade and tied with green cords. The hero wore a mask, which seemed unnecessarily old, ugly, and wrinkled. His costume subdued, but rich. The court lady gorgeously dressed, with smiling young girl's mask and glittering pendant, East-Indian sort of head-dress.

The lady sat at the right corner, immobile, rather the lover's image of his mistress than a living being. He sings, complains, and tries several times to lift the burden, but cannot. The court officer sits a little toward the right-back. Shoshi dies and passes out.

The officer addresses the lady, who suddenly seems to come to life. She listens, then leaves her seat, half-kneels near the burden, her face set silently and immovably toward it. This is more graphic and impressive than can well be imagined. All leave the stage save this silent figure contemplating the burden.

The Shoshi's ghost comes in, covered with glittering superb brocades, he uses a crutch, has a mane of flying grey hair, and a face that looks like an "elemental."

KANAWA, THE IRON RING, by Motokiyo.

Story.—In the reign of Saga Tenno there was a princess who loved unavailingly, and she became so enraged with jealousy that she went to the shrine of Kibune and prayed for seven days that she might become a hannya. On the seventh day the god had pity, and appeared to her and said, "If you wish to become a hannya go to the Uji river and stay twenty-five days in the water." And she returned rejoicing to Kioto, and parted her hair into five strands and painted her face and her body red, and put an iron ring on her head with three candles in it. And she took in her mouth a double fire-stick, burning at both ends. And when she walked out in the streets at night people thought her a devil.

From this it happens that when Japanese women are jealous they sometimes go to a temple at night wearing an iron ring (Kanawa) with candles in it. Sometimes they use also a straw doll in the incantation.

Modus.—First comes Kiogen, the farce character, and says he has had a god-dream, and that he will tell it to the woman who is coming to pray.

Then comes the woman. Kiogen asks if she comes every night. He tells her his dream, and how she is to become a hannya by the use of Kanawa. She goes. Her face changes en route. Enter the faithless husband, who says he lives in Shimokio, the Lower City, and has been having very bad dreams. He goes to the priest Abē, who tells him that a woman's jealousy is at the root of it, and that his life is in danger that very night. The husband confesses his infidelity. The priest starts a counter exorcism, using a life-sized straw doll with the names of both husband and wife put inside it. He uses the triple takadana and five coloured "gohei,"* red, blue, yellow, black, white. Storm comes with thunder and lightning. The woman appears. She and the chorus sing, interrupting each other—she complaining, the chorus interpreting her thoughts. She approaches her husband's pillow with the intention of killing him. But the power of the exorcism prevails, and she vanishes into the air.

MATSUKAZE, by Kiyotsugu.

A wandering priest sees the ghost of the two fisher girls, Matsukaze and Murasame, still gathering salt on the seashore at Suma. They still seem to feel the waves washing over them, and say, "Even the shadows of the moon are wet," "The autumn wind is full, full of thoughts, thoughts of the sea." They seem to wish to be back in their old hard life, and say the moon is "envious" of the ghost life, and will only shine on the living; that the dews are gathered up by the sun, but that they lie like old grass left to rot on the sea-beach. "How beautiful is the evening at Summa for all the many times we have seen it and might be tired with seeing it. How faint are the fishermen's voices. We see the fisher boats in the offing. The faint

* Generally called mitegura; see p. 396.

moon is the only friend. Children sing under the field-sweeping wind; the wind is salt with the autumn. O how sublime is this night. I will go back to shore, for the tide is now at its full. We hang our wet sleeves over our shoulders, salt dripping from them. The waves rush to the shore, a stork sings in the reeds. The storm gathers in from all sides; how shall we pass through this night. Cold night, clear moon, and we two in deep shadow."

APPENDIX II

Fenollosa's notes go into considerable detail as to how one must place large jars under the proper Noh stage for resonance: concerning the officials in the ministry of music in the reign of some emperor or other; concerning musical instruments, etc.; concerning special ceremonies, etc. A part of this material can, I think, be of interest only to scholars; at least I am not prepared to edit it until I know how much or how little general interest there is in the Japanese drama and its methods of presentation. Many facts might be extremely interesting if one had enough knowledge of Noh, and could tell where to fit them in. Many names might be rich in association, which are, at the present stage of our knowledge, a rather dry catalogue.

Still, I may be permitted a very brief summary of a section of notes based, I think, on a long work by Professor Ko-haka-mura.

Certain instruments are very old (unless we have pictures of all these instruments, a list of Japanese names with the approximate dates of their invention will convey little to us). Music is divided roughly into what comes from China, from Korea, and what is native. "Long and short songs, which sang out the heart of the people, were naturally rhythmic." Foreign music . . . various schools and revolutions . . . priests singing in harmony (?) with the biwa. Puppet plays (about 1596, I think, unless the date 1184 higher on the page is supposed to be connected with "the great genius Chikamatsu"). Chikamatsu, author of 97 jōruri plays, lived 1653–1724. Various forms of dancing, female dancing, "turning piece," some forms of female dancing forbidden. Music for funerals and ceremonies.

"The thoughts of men, when they are only uttered as they are, are called 'tada goto,' plain word. But when they are too deep for 'plain word' we make 'pattern decoration' (aya), and have fushi (tones) for it."

An emperor makes the first koto from "decayed" wood; the sound of it was very clear and was heard from afar.

Field dances, shield dances, etc. "In the ninth month of the fourteenth year of Temmu (A.D. 686), the imperial order said: 'The male singers and female flute blowers must make it their own profession, and hand it down to their descendants and make them learn.' Hence these hereditary professions."

"In the festival of Toka, court ladies performed female dancing, ceremony of archery, wrestling (so the note seems to read). In the Buddhist service only foreign music was used."

More regulations for court ceremonies, not unlike the general meticulousness of "Leviticus."

Buddhism, growing popularity of Chinese music. "In Daijosai, the coronation festival, it was not the custom to use Chinese music. But in this ceremony at Nimmio Tenno's coronation, on the day of the dinner-party, they collected pebbles before the temple, planted new trees, spread sheets on the ground, scattered grain to represent the seashore, and took out boats upon it, and a dance was performed imitating fishermen picking up seaweed.

In the festival of the ninth month, literary men offered Chinese poems, so it may be that the music was also in Chinese style.

In the time of Genkio (1321–23), mention of a troupe of 140 dancers.

Udzumusa Masena (?) gives a list of pieces of music brought over from China. "Sansai Zuye," an old Japanese encyclopedia, certainly gives this list. Some of these names may be interesting as our knowledge of Noh increases. At any rate, I find already a few known names, notably the sea-wave dance mentioned in the Genji play already translated. I therefore give a partial list, which the reader may skip at his pleasure:

Brandish dancing, breaking camp music, virtue of war, whirling circle music, spring nightingale singing, heaven head jewel life, long life, jewel tree, back-garden flower (composed by a princess of China), King of Rakio (who always wore a mask on his face when he went into battle), congratulation temple, 10,000 years (Banzai), black-head music, Kan province, five customs, courtesy and justice music, five saints' music, pleasant spring, pleasant heart, playing temple, red-white peach pear flower, autumn wind, Rindai (a place in the out-of-the-way country of To), green sea-waves (sei kai ha), plucking mulberry old man, King of Jin breaking camp, divine merit, great settling great peace, returning castle music, turning cup, congratulation king benevolence. Three pieces for sword-dancing: great peace, general music, the palace of Komon; beating ball, music of (?) Ringin Koku. "A wild duck curving her foot is the dancing of Bosatsu mai." Kariobinga bird,* barbaric drinking wine, dinner drinking, "Inyang"† castle peace. Music of Tenjiku‡ in which the dancers are masked to look like sparrows, scattering hands, pluck off head, Princess of So, perfumed leaves, 10,000 autumns' music.

---

* The Kariobinga bird belongs to the Gyokuraku Jodo or Paradise of Extreme Felicity. The name is Sanskrit, the thing Indian.

† The name Inyang is wrong, but I cannot find the correct name.

‡ Tenjiku = India.

APPENDIX III

CARE AND SELECTION OF COSTUMES
(From another talk with Umewaka Minoru)

The clothes are put away in tansos (?), the costly ones on sliding boards, only a few at a time. Ordinary ones are draped in nagmochi (oblong chests). The best ones are easily injured, threads break, holes come, etc.

Costumes are not classified by the names of the rôles, but by the kind of cloth or by cut or their historic period, and if there are too many of each sort, by colour, or the various shape of the ornamental patterns. The best are only used for royal performances. The costume for Kakitsubata is the most expensive, one of these recently (i.e. 1901) cost over 500 yen. (*Note.*—I think they are now more expensive.—E.P.)

One does not always use the same combination of costumes; various combinations of quiet costumes are permitted. His sons lay out a lot of costumes on the floor, and Umewaka makes a selection or a new colour scheme as he pleases. This does not take very long.

ARNAUT DANIEL

Chansson Doil Mot Son Plan e Prim

A song where words run gimp and straight
I'll make for buds flaunt out their state,
And tips dilate
With floral sheen
Where many a green
Leaf cometh forth for viewing,
While 'neath dark shade
In grass and glade
I hear the birds are construing.

In copse I hear their chirp debate,
And lest any man me berate
At Love's dictate
I file and preen
And cut words clean
And cease not him pursuing.
'Spite his aid
I do not evade
Whate'er spites he be brewing.

To lover pride's not worth a bean.
Bad horse doth its lord demean as
Pride showeth spleen
Like swinger jade
And hath low laid
Proud man in glastre strewing,
For 'tis good fate
None miserate
Him who 'gainst love foe's mewing.

No mew nor yape shall me prevene
Nor turn me from my walwit queen;
Tho' for a screen
Being afraid
Gossips unbraid,
I feign not to be suing.
If 'spite their prate

Men fill their plate,
I'd have their swift undoing.

Though waith o'er wide ways I have strayed,
Thee alway doth my thought invade.
My song is stayed
By joys cognate
Ere separate
I went, with tears bedewing
Mine eyes; in teen
I sing amene
That joy should bring such rueing.

N'er leave I love tho' my sleep's frayed
Me; by no measure my love's weighed.
But have me brayed
If since the date
Of Cain the great
Was ere such trusty wooing
As mine hath been;
I am well seen
With her; 'tis joy's renewing.

Dear, despite men's hallooing
My heart is keen
And I bedene
Proclaim thee fame's renewing.

Can Chai la Fueilla

When sere leaf falleth
        from the high forkèd tips,
And cold appalleth
        dry osier, haws and hips,
Coppice he strips
        of bird, that now none calleth.
Fordel my lips
        in love have, though he galleth.

Though all things freeze here,
  I can naught feel the cold,
For new love sees, here
  my heart's new leaf unfold;
So am I rolled
  and lapped against the breeze here:
Love, who doth mould
  my force, force guarantees here.

Aye, life's a high thing,
  where joy's his maintenance,
Who cries 'tis wry thing
  hath danced never my dance,
I can advance
  no blame against fate's tithing
For lot and chance
  have deemed the best thing my thing.

Of love's wayfaring
  I know no part to blame,
All other pairing,
  compared, is put to shame,
Man can acclaim
  no second for comparing
With her, no dame
  but hath the meaner bearing.

I'ld ne'er entangle
  my heart with other fere,
Although I mangle
  my joy by staying here
I have no fear
  that ever at Pontrangle
You'll find her peer
  or one that's worth a wrangle.

She'd ne'er destroy
  her man with cruelty,
'Twixt here 'n' Savoy
  there feeds no fairer she,

Than pleaseth me
  till Paris had ne'er joy
In such degree
  from Helena in Troy.

She's so the rarest
  who holdeth me thus gay,
The thirty fairest
  can not contest her sway;
'Tis right, par fay,
  thou know, O song that wearest
Such bright array,
  whose quality thou sharest.

Chançon, nor stay
  till to her thou declarest:
'Arnaut would say
  me not, wert thou not fairest.'

Lancan Son Passat li Giure

When the frosts are gone and over,
And are stripped from hill and hollow,
When in close the blossom blinketh
From the spray where the fruit cometh,
  The flower and song and the clarion
Of the gay season and merry
Bid me with high joy to bear me
  Through days while April's coming on.

Though joy's right hard to discover,
Such sly ways doth false Love follow,
Only sure he never drinketh
At the fount where true faith hometh;
  A thousand girls, but two or one
Of her falsehoods over chary,
Stabbing whom vows make unwary
  Their tenderness is vilely done.

The most wise runs drunkest lover,
Sans pint-pot or wind to swallow,
If a whim her locks unlinketh,
One stray hair his noose becometh
     When evasion's fairest shown,
Then the sly puss purrs most near ye,
Innocents at heart beware ye
     When she seems colder than a nun.

See I thought so highly of her!
Trusted, but the game is hollow,
Not one piece soundly clinketh;
All the cardinals that Rome hath,
     Yea, they all were put upon.
Her device is 'Slyly Wary.'
Cunning are the snares they carry,
     Yet while they watched they'd be undone.

Whom Love makes so mad a rover,
'Ll take a cuckoo for a swallow,
If she say so, sooth! he thinketh
There's a plain where Puy-de-Dome is.
     Till his eyes and nails are gone,
He'll throw dice and follow fairly
—Sure as old tales never vary—
     For his fond heart he is foredone.

Well I know, sans writing's cover,
What a plain is, what's a hollow.
I know well whose honor sinketh,
And who 'tis that shame consumeth.
     They meet. I lose reception.
'Gainst this cheating I'd not parry
Nor mid such false speech tarry,
     but from her lordship will be gone.

CODA

Sir Bertran, sure no pleasure's won
Like this freedom naught so merry
'Twixt Nile 'n' where the suns miscarry
     To where the rain falls from the sun.

Lanquan Vei Fueill' e Flors e Frug

When I see leaf and flower and fruit
    Come forth upon light lynd and bough,
And hear the frogs in rillet bruit,
    And birds quhitter in forest now,
Love inkirlie doth leaf and flower and bear,
And trick my night from me, and stealing waste it,
Whilst other wight in rest and sleep sojourneth.

Love conducted me by fast route
    Into his resset derne, I trow,
Where without feod or tribute
    Doth me in freehold endow;
Nor could nor would I turn me otherwhere.
For breed of mind is there, none hath defaced it
In this bailey, whereon rich worth returneth.

Love, in thee am I grown astute;
    Long on thy book I bent my brow.
Without back-veerings or dispute,
    Love pleased me alway well enow.
And in ill-faring, Love, hast played me fair;
Thanks for so much, and for the honey tasted
From down-go of the day, till sunrise burneth.

From treacheries and boredoms dilute
    Love that I troop with, turns my prow.
Naught can the slack culrouns impute
    But I with truth-speaking disavow.
Those leak-mouth blabbards give me little care.
I not gainsay my word, have not debased it,
But will what she wills, whom my choice discerneth.

You'd know, if fear held me not mute,
    My heart lifts past Elwand and Plow.
Such be the treasuries and loot
    To me her charities allow.
Mine Esperance hath doubled me my fare.
Who hath most grace, were last to have disgraced it,
Where gaiety and youth she nothing spurneth.

Backers and fillers I refute;
    By steadfastnesse in love I cow.
These jacks that quality uproot,
    Being so quaint to bend and bow,
For all their yape so sturdy I repair
And so tread in Love's track as he hath traced it.
I find no stead wherefrom my joy adjourneth.

Get gone, my song, unto that Debonaire;
If loved he else, declare he hath effaced it,
But in her hue, his parsement naught turneth.

Autet e Bas Entrels Prims Fuoills

Now high and low, where leaves renew,
Come buds on bough and spalliard pleach
And no beak nor throat is muted;
Auzel each in tune contrasted
Letteth loose
Wriblis spruce.
Joy for them and spring would set
Song on me, but Love assaileth
Me and sets my words t'his dancing.

I thank my God and mine eyes too,
Since through them the perceptions reach.
Porters of joys that have refuted
Every ache and shame I've tasted;
They reduce
Pains, and noose
Me in Amor's corded net.
Her beauty in me prevaileth
Till bonds seem but joy's advancing.

My thanks, Amor, that I win through;
Thy long delays I naught impeach;
Though flame's in my marrow rooted
I'd not quench it, well 't hath lasted,

Burns profuse,
Held recluse
Lest knaves know our hearts are met,
Murrain on the mouth that aileth,
So he finds her not entrancing.

He doth in Love's book misconstrue,
And from that book none can him teach,
Who saith ne'er 's in speech recruited
Aught, whereby the heart is dasted.
Words' abuse
Doth traduce
Worth, but I run no such debt.
Right 'tis if a man over-raileth
He tear tongue on tooth mischancing.

That I love her, is pride, is true,
But my fast secret knows no breach.
Since Paul's writ was executed
Or the forty days first fasted,
Not Christus
Could produce
Her similar, where one can get
Charm's total, for no charm faileth
Her who's memory's enhancing.

Grace and valor, the keep of you
She is, who holds me, each to each,
She sole, I sole, so fast suited,
Other women's lures are wasted,
And no truce
But misuse
Have I for them, they're not let
To my heart, where she regaleth
Me with delights I'm not chancing.

Arnaut loves, and ne'er will fret
Love with o'er-speech. His throat quaileth,
Braggart voust is naught t'his fancy.

L'Aura Amara

I

The bitter air
Strips panoply
From trees
Where softer winds set leaves,
And glad
Beaks
Now in brakes are coy,
Scarce peep the wee
Mates
And un-mates.
    What gaud's the work?
    What good the glees?
What curse
I strive to shake!
Me hath she cast from high,
In fell disease
I lie, and deathly fearing.

II

So clear the flare
That first lit me
To seize
Her whom my soul believes;
If cad
Sneaks,
Blabs, slanders, my joy
Counts little fee
Baits
And their hates.
    I scorn their perk
    And preen, at ease.
Disburse
Can she, and wake
Such firm delights, that I
Am hers, froth, lees
Bigod! from toe to earring.

III

Amor, look yare!
Know certainly
The keys:
How she thy suit receives;
Nor add
Piques,
'Twere folly to annoy
I'm true, so dree
Fates;
No debates
    Shake me, nor jerk,
    My verities
Turn terse,
And yet I ache;
Her lips, not snows that fly
Have potencies
To slake, to cool my searing.

IV

Behold my prayer,
(Or company
Of these)
Seeks whom such height achieves;
Well clad
Seeks
Her, and would not cloy.
Heart apertly
States
Thought. Hope waits
    'Gainst death to irk:
    False brevities
And worse!
To her I raik,
Sole her; all others' dry
Felicities
I count not worth the leering.

V

Ah, fair face, where
Each quality
But frees
One pride-shaft more, that cleaves
Me; mad frieks
(O' thy beck) destroy,
And mockery
Baits
Me, and rates.
    Yet I not shirk
    Thy velleities,
Averse
Me not, nor slake
Desire. God draws not nigh
To Dome, with pleas
Wherein's so little veering.

VI

Now chant prepare,
And melody
To please
The king, who'll judge thy sheaves.
Worth, sad,
Sneaks
Here; double employ
Hath there. Get thee
Plates
Full, and cates,
    Gifts, go! Nor lurk
    Here till decrees
Reverse,
And ring thou take
Straight t'Arago I'd ply
Cross the wide seas
But 'Rome' disturbs my hearing.

CODA

At midnight mirk
In secrecies
I nurse
My served make
In heart; nor try
My melodies
At other's door not mearing.

En Cest Sonet Coind' e Leri

As this light, gay air repasses
Words, I plane and shave and twine them,
That the song may truth assert
    Ere my file hath featly embossed it;
Bedene Amor gilds and faces;
This comes so swiftly dealt
From her in whom is glory's meeting.

I serve the pride of golden lasses;
In her praise my words refine them;
Let my boasting stand apert:
    Hers I am. Who dares accost it?
Tho' the cold wind racks and races,
Love's rains in my heart a-pelt
Warm me 'spite winter's ill-treating.

Heard and paid a thousand masses,
Buy wax-lights and lamps, align them,
That God lift up my desert
    Higher than my fence hath tosst it,
Or the burnet hair that laces
'Cross her brows, and her gay, svelte
Form, pass Lucerne's dower competing.

Such desires my flame amasses
Much I fear lest she decline them,

(True love ere wrought man's hurt);
        Flooded heart where hers o'er crossed it
Flooded stays, with no dry places,
Such herb springs where she hath dwelt
Field and fold's hers, escheating.

Pope and Emp'ror I count asses;
Let See and Domain combine them;
From them to her I'd revert
        Who doth burn my heart and frost it,
Yet if she mend not her paces,
Kiss me ere New Year and melt
For my death to hell she's fleeting.

Tho' I'm brought to sorry passes
By love's aches, I not resign them;
E'en by wilderness engirt
        Have I made song and gloss't it
Worse than hand-work love's disgraces,
And ne'er pains as I have felt
Sir Mnalcas for his sweeting.

Aye, I, Arnaut, pluck wind's traces,
On ox, hunt hare, helter-skelt,
And I swim 'gainst torrent's beating.

En Breu Brisaral Temps Braus

Briefly bursteth season brisk,
Blasty north breeze racketh branch,
Barren rasps each branch on each
Tearing twig and tearing leafage,
        Chirmes now no bird nor cries querulous;
So Love demands I make outright
A song that no song shall surpass
        For freeing the heart of sorrow.

Love is glory's orchard close,
And is a pool of prowess staunch,
Whence comes every goodly peach,
If true heart come but to gather.
        Dies none frost-bit nor yet snowily,
For good sap forletteth blight;
Tho' culroun hack the base
        Leal heart saineth it on morrow.

If a mended fault shine best,
Know that I've in either haunch
More love without thought or bruit
Than one who speaks out and braggeth.
        It pains my heart worse than blistering
The while she shows me her despite,
Rather, in desert, pain I'd face,
        Where n'is nest of bird nor sparrow.

Gracious thinking and the frank,
Clear, and quick perceiving heart
Have love-led me to the fort,
Of her whose gesning most availeth.
        If she'th been harsh or quarrelsome,
Now we brief time with delight.
Finer she is and I more traist
        Than ere Atalant' and Meleagro.

Yet I shake from fear-to-risk
And turn oft from black to white;
So the longing raids my sense,
Know not if heart leaps or mourneth;
        Pleasure gives me hope that trembleth,
Blames me that I set not in flight,
To prayers, since I've such skill in them.
        On lyt else doth my will tarry.

The thought of her is my rest
And both my eyes are strained wry
Till she come into their reach;

Believe not my heart turns from her,
  Neither prayers nor games nor violing
Can turn 't a reed's breadth left or right
From her . . . What speak? God overwhelm
  Me, and let sea-wave be my barrow.

Where sound of "agre" turns the word,
Song of mine see thou cry "haro."

Doutz Brais e Critz

Sweet cries and cracks
  and lays and chants inflected
By auzels who, in their Latin belikes,
Chirm each to each, even as you and I
Pipe toward those girls on whom our thoughts attract;
Are but more cause that I, whose overweening
Search is toward the noblest, set in cluster
Lines where no word pulls wry, no rhyme breaks gauges.

No culs de sacs
  nor false ways me deflected
When first I pierced her fort within its dykes,
Hers for whom my hungry insistency
Passes the gnaw whereby was Vivien wracked;
Day-long I stretch, all times, like a bird preening,
And yawn for her, who hath o'er others thrust her
As high as true joy is o'er ire and rages.

Welcome not lax,
  and my words were protected
Not blabbed to other, when I set my likes
On her. Not brass but gold was 'neath the die.
That day we kissed, and after it she flacked
O'er me her cloak of indigo, for screening
Me from all culvertz' eyes, whose blathered bluster
Can set such spites abroad; win jibes for wages.

God who did tax
    not Longus' sin, respected
That blind centurion beneath the spikes
And him forgave, grant that we two shall lie
Within one room, and seal therein our pact,
Yes, that she kiss me in the half-light, leaning
To me, and laugh and strip and stand forth in the lustre
Where lamp-light with light limb but half engages.

The flowers wax
    with buds but half perfected;
Tremble on twig that shakes when the bird strikes—
But not more fresh than she! No empery,
Though Rome and Palestine were one compact,
Would lure me from her. But if kings could muster
In homage similar, you'd count them sages.

Mouth, now what knacks!
    What folly hath infected
Thee? Gifts, that th'Emperor of the Salonikes
Or Lord of Rome were greatly honored by,
Or Syria's lord, thou dost from me distract;
O fool I am! to hope for intervening
From Love that shields not love! Yea, it were juster
To call him mad, who 'gainst his joy engages.

(POLITICAL POSTSCRIPT)

The slimy jacks
    with adders' tongues bisected,
I fear no whit, nor have; and if these tykes
Have led Galicia's king to villeiny—
His cousin in pilgrimage hath he attacked—
We know—Raimon the Count's son—my meaning
Stands without screen. The royal filibuster
Redeems not honor till he unbar the cages.

CODA

I should have seen it, but I was on such affair,
Seeing the true king crown'd here in Estampa.

Er Vei Vermeills, Vertz, Blaus, Blancs, Groucs

Vermeil, green, blue, peirs, white, cobalt,
    Close orchards, hewis, holts, hows, vales,
And the bird-song that whirls and turns
    Morning and late with sweet accord
Bestir my heart to put my song in sheen,
And match that flower which hath such properties
It seeds in joy, bears love, and pain ameises.

Within my thought love's fires halt
    And inwardly desire assails,
With a soft flame where it most burns:
    Pain with a sweet savour to record.
For Love would have his liegemen be amene;
Traist, franke, mansuet, thankers, forgive with ease,
In court where fair speech wins, and pride debases.

Nor time nor place set me in fault,
    Nor right nor left thought me avails,
And if I lie in these concerns
    Then may her fine eyes ne'er turn toward
Me who am hers, awake, asleep, between.
And when I think upon her qualities
With Alexander's self would not change places.

To be her cook would so exalt
    My sprite, that one such day prevails
With me against twenty years. Heart spurns
    The twenty years, for the one day's hoard
Lifts up his joy. O fool to slide and lean,
Toward aught else. And hadst thou her treasuries
Naught wouldst thou seek amid Meander's traces.

Pleasure oft falleth in default,
    If she come not to turn the scales,
Yet, dunce I am, that cannot learn
    To say in brief, and get it scored,
"I will not leave you, and there have not been
Others than thou, the savour of all courtesies.
Gray distance hath no power to efface this."

If to pretending joys I vault
  The day seems a year long. It ails
Me, God gives me no art to kern
  And shorten time when I am bored,
For long delay doth make good lovers lean.
Moon and sun, be murrain on your ease,
That crush me with the leisure of your paces.

To her, who hath me whole, be gone bedene,
Arnaut counts up all her argosies
But needs surplus of wit to name these graces.

Amors e Jois e Liocs e Tems

Love, the season, joy, and place
Turn off my wits; woolgathering
From pain that bit me yesteryear
  When I hunted my hare with an ox.
My luck is now both better and worse:
I love (this much good star commands),
Unloved (set on wax my fate),
But until her hard heart to my prayers defer.

The man must seek rich lord apace,
Who hath run through his everything,
Thus to repair his flinder'd gear,
  For a poor sege's not worth a pox;
But I sought her, to reimburse
My love-loss open eyed, where stands
Open my heart, and will dictate
Truce to all other girls, if conquerer.

A dour man makes a poor face.
My loss 'tis, such face I bring
Shaken with my excess of fear,
  Who am in griefs unorthodox.
For if this girl lift not my curse,
Folk will have me mad on their hands,

Who am in love so wild insatiate,
Who would grow old and white her worshipper.

No man is so set on God's grace,
Hermit nor monk nor shaveling,
As I upon my lovely dear.
    'Twill show ere this year's off the stocks
I am her liege, nor would reverse
This had I king's lands or duke's lands.
So much to her my heart is dedicate
With no other dame, no doncel I confer.

But if I cover my disgrace
Of sighs and fears and caviling
As in the town song we hear:
    thunder enough upsets rain-crocks;
With six or five years blameless verse
I have gone on with my demands,
And when I'm gone bald on my pate,
Then maybe long love will have melted her.

She could my sighs and groans replace
Where love the deepest plants his sting,
For one look on her face, I veer
    And set myself to new song-locks.
I go up hill (no whit averse),
For my thought turns him pleasant strands.
Go up, my heart, in pain elate,
And follow thy desire without demur.

Base iron shall clear gold outrate
Ere Arnaut cease to be her follower.

Ans Quel Cim Reston de Branchas

Ere the winter recommences
And the leaf from bough is wrested,
On Love's mandate will I render
A brief end to long prolusion:

So well have I been taught his steps and paces
That I can stop the tidal-sea's inflowing.
My stot outruns the hare; his speed amazes.

Me he bade without pretences
That I go not, through requested;
That I make no whit surrender
Nor abandon our seclusion:
'Differ from violets, whose fear effaces
Their hue ere winter; behold the glowing
Laurel stays, stay thou. Year long the genet blazes '

'You who commit no offences
'Gainst constancy; have not quested;
Assent not! Though a maid sent her
Suit to thee. Think you confusion
Will come to her who shall track out your traces?
And give your enemies a chance for boasts and crowing?
No! After God, see that she have your praises.'

Coward, shall I trust not defences!
Faint ere the suit be tested?
Follow! till she extend her
Favour. Keep on, try conclusion
For if I get in this naught but disgraces,
Then must I pilgrimage past Ebro's flowing
And seek for luck amid the Lernian mazes.

If I've passed bridge-rails and fences,
Think you then that I am bested?
No, for with no food or slender
Ration, I'd have joy's profusion
To hold her kissed, and there are never spaces
Wide to keep me from her, but she'd be showing
In my heart, and stand forth before his gazes.

Lovelier maid from Nile to Sences
Is not vested nor divested,
So great is her bodily splendor
That you would think it illusion.

Amor, if she but hold me in her embraces,
I shall not feel cold hail nor winter's blowing
Nor break for all the pain in fever's dazes.

Arnaut hers from foot to face is,
He would not have Lucerne, without her, owing
Him, nor lord the land whereon the Ebro grazes.

Sim Fos Amors de Joi Donar Tant Larga

Had Love as little need to be exhorted
To give me joy, as I to keep a frank
And ready heart toward her, never he'd blast
My hope, whose very height hath high exalted,
And cast me down . . . to think on my default,
And her great worth; yet thinking what I dare,
More love myself, and I know my heart and sense
Shall lead me to high conquest, unmolested.

I am, spite long delay, pooled and contorted
And whirled with all my streams 'neath such a bank
Of promise, that her fair words hold me fast
In joy, and will, until in tomb I am halted.
As I'm not one to change hard gold for spalt,
And no alloy's in her, that debonaire
Shall hold my faith and mine obedience
Till, by her accolade, I am invested.

Long waiting hath brought in and hath extorted
The fragrance of desire; throat and flank
The longing takes me . . . and with pain surpassed
By her great beauty. Seemeth it hath vaulted
O'er all the rest . . . them doth it set in fault
So that whoever sees her anywhere
Must see how charm and every excellence
Hold sway in her, untaint, and uncontested.

Since she is such; longing no wise detorted
Is in me . . . and plays not the mountebank,
For all my sense is her, and is compassed
Solely in her; and no man is assaulted
(By God his dove!) by such desires as vault
In me, to have great excellence. My care
On her so stark, I can show tolerance
To jacks whose joy's to see fine loves uncrested.

Miels-de-Ben, have not your heart distorted
Against me now; your love has left me blank,
Void, empty of power or will to turn or cast
Desire from me . . . not brittle, nor defaulted.
Asleep, awake, to thee do I exalt
And offer me. No less, when I lie bare
Or wake, my will to thee, think not turns thence,
For breast and throat and head hath it attested.

Pouch-mouthed blubberers, culrouns and aborted,
May flame bite in your gullets, sore eyes and rank
T'the lot of you, you've got my horse, my last
Shilling, too; and you'd see love dried and salted.
God blast you all that you can't call a halt!
God's itch to you, chit-cracks that over bear
And spoil good men, ill luck your impotence!!
More told, the more you've wits smeared and congested.

Lo Ferm Voler Qu'el Cor M'intra

The firm wishing that gets ingress
To my heart fears no cad's beak or nail-tip
Of cad who by false speech doth lose his soul's hope,
And if I dare assail hm not with bough or osier
On quiet I, where one admits no uncle,
Will get my joy in garden or in bower.

When I remember the bower
Where to my spite I know that no man gets ingress,

But do no more than may brothers and uncles,
I tremble all length, all save my nail-tips,
As does a child before a switch of osier,
So fear I lest I come not near my soul's hope.

Of body 'twas not of soul's hope
That consenting she hid me in her bower.
Now it hurts my heart worse than strokes of osiers
That where she now is, her slave gets no ingress.
I cling mam to her as is the flesh to the nail-tip
And take warning of neither friend nor uncle.

Ne'er love I sister of uncle
As I love her I love, by my soul's hope.
Close cling I as doth the finger to nail-tip
And would be, and it please her, in her bower;
Love that in my heart gets ingress
Can shake me, as strong man not an osier.

Since flower sprang on dry osier,
Since Adam began this line of nephews and uncles,
Such fine love as to my heart hath ingress
Was not to my belief in body or soul's hope.
If she be in piazza nor bower,
My heart leave not by a nail-tip.

The heart roots and clings like the nail-tip
Or as the bark clings that clings to the osier,
For she is joy's palace, she is joy's bower
Nor love I so father, nor kinsman, nor kind uncle.
Double joy in Paradise, by my soul's hope,
Shall I have if ere true love there win ingress.

Arnaut sends the song of nail and uncle
With thanks to her the soul of his osier,
Son Dezirat, who to some purpose hath ingress in bower.

PAVANNES AND DIVISIONS

L'Homme Moyen Sensuel *

"I hate a dumpy woman"
—*George Gordon, Lord Byron.*

'Tis of my country that I would endite,
In hope to set some misconceptions right.
My country? I love it well, and those good fellows
Who, since their wit's unknown, escape the gallows.
But you stuffed coats who're neither tepid nor distinctly boreal,
Pimping, conceited, placid, editorial,
Could I but speak as 'twere in the "Restoration"
I would articulate your perdamnation.
This year perforce I must with circumspection—
For Mencken states somewhere, in this connection:
"It is a moral nation we infest."
Despite such reins and checks I'll do my best,
An art! You all respect the arts, from that infant tick
Who's now the editor of *The Atlantic*,
From Comstock's self, down to the meanest resident,
Till up again, right up, we reach the president,
Who shows his taste in his ambassadors:

---

*[*Note:* It is through no fault of my own that this diversion was not given to the reader two years ago; but the commercial said it would not add to their transcendent popularity, and the vers-libre fanatics pointed out that I had used a form of terminal consonance no longer permitted, and my admirers (*j'en ai*), ever nobly desirous of erecting me into a sort of national institution, declared the work "unworthy" of my mordant and serious genius. So a couple of the old gentlemen are dead in the interim, and, alas, two of the great men mentioned in passing, and the reader will have to accept the opusculus for what it is, some rhymes written in 1915. I would give them now with dedication "To the Anonymous Compatriot Who Produced the Poem 'Fanny,' Somewhere About 1820", if this form of centennial homage be permitted me. It was no small thing to have written, in America, at that distant date, a poem of over forty pages which one can still read without labour. *E.P.*]

A novelist, a publisher, to pay old scores,
A novelist, a publisher and a preacher,
That's sent to Holland, a most particular feature,
Henry Van Dyke, who thinks to charm the Muse you pack
    her in
A sort of stinking diliquescent saccharine.
The constitution of our land, O Socrates,
Was made to incubate such mediocrities,
These and a taste in books that's grown perennial
And antedates the Philadelphia centennial.
Still I'd respect you more if you could bury
Mabie, and Lyman Abbot and George Woodberry,
For minds so wholly founded upon quotations
Are not the best of pulse for infant nations.
Dulness herself, that abject spirit, chortles
To see your forty self-baptized immortals,
And holds her sides where swelling laughter cracks 'em
Before the "Ars Poetica" of Hiram Maxim.
All one can say of this refining medium
Is "*Zut! Cinque lettres!*" a banished gallic idiom,
Their doddering ignorance is waxed so notable
'Tis time that it was capped with something quotable.

Here Radway grew, the fruit of pantosocracy,
The very fairest flower of their gynocracy.
Radway? My hero, for it will be more inspiring
If I set forth a bawdy plot like Byron
Than if I treat the nation as a whole.
Radway grew up. These forces shaped his soul;
These, and yet God, and Dr. Parkhurst's god, the N.Y.
    Journal
(Which pays him more per week than The Supernal).
These and another godlet of that day, your day
(You feed a hen on grease, perhaps she'll lay
The sterile egg that is still eatable:
"Prolific Noyes" with output undefeatable).
From these he (Radway) learnt, from provosts and from
    editors unyielding
And innocent of Stendhal, Flaubert, Maupassant and
    Fielding.

They set their mind (it's still in that condition)—
May we repeat; the Centennial Exposition
At Philadelphia, 1876?
What it knew then, it knows, and there it sticks.
And yet another, a "charming man," "sweet nature," but
    was Gilder,
De mortuis verum, truly the master builder?

From these he learnt. Poe, Whitman, Whistler, men, their
    recognition
Was got abroad, what better luck do you wish 'em,
When writing well has not yet been forgiven
In Boston, to Henry James, the greatest whom we've seen
    living.
And timorous love of the innocuous
Brought from Gt. Britain and dumped down a'top of us,
Till you may take your choice: to feel the edge of satire or
Read Bennett or some other flaccid flatterer.
Despite it all, despite your Red Bloods, febrile concupiscence
Whose blubbering yowls you take for passion's essence;
Despite it all, your compound predilection
For ignorance, its growth and its protection
(Vide the tariff), I will hang simple facts
Upon a tale, to combat other facts,
"Message to Garcia," Mosher's propagandas
That are the nation's botts, collicks and glanders.
Or from the feats of Sumner cull it? Think,
Could Freud or Jung unfathom such a sink?

My hero, Radway, I have named, in truth,
Some forces among those which "formed" his youth:
These heavy weights, these dodgers and these preachers,
Crusaders, lecturers and secret lechers,
Who wrought about his "soul" their stale infection.
These are the high-brows, add to this collection
The social itch, the almost, all but, not quite, fascinating,
Piquante, delicious, luscious, captivating:
Puffed satin, and silk stockings where the knee
Clings to the skirt in strict (vide: *"Vogue"*) propriety.
Three thousand chorus girls and all unkissed,

O state sans song, sans home-grown wine, sans realist!
"Tell me not in mournful wish-wash
Life's a sort of sugared dish-wash"!
Radway had read the various evening papers
And yearned to imitate the Waldorf capers
As held before him in that unsullied mirror
The daily press, and monthlies nine cents dearer.
They held the very marrow of the ideals
That fed his spirit; were his mental meals.
Also, he'd read of christian virtues in
That canting rag called *Everybody's Magazine*,
And heard a clergy that tries on more wheezes
Than e'er were heard of by Our Lord Ch . . . . J . . . .
So he "faced life" with rather mixed intentions,
He had attended country Christian Endeavour Conventions,
Where one gets more chances
Than Spanish ladies had in old romances.
(Let him rebuke who ne'er has known the pure Platonic
        grapple,
Or hugged two girls at once behind a chapel.)
Such practices diluted rural boredom
Though some approved of them, and some deplored 'em.
Such was he when he got his mother's letter
And would not think a thing that could upset her. . . .
Yet saw an "ad." "To-night, THE HUDSON SAIL,
With forty queens, and music to regale
The select company: beauties you all would know
By name, if named." So it was phrased, or rather somewhat so
I have mislaid the "ad.," but note the touch,
Note, reader, note the sentimental touch:
His mother's birthday gift.   (How pitiful
That only sentimental stuff will sell!)

Yet Radway went. A circumspectious prig!
And then that woman like a guinea-pig
Accosted, that's the word, accosted him,
Thereon the amorous calor slightly frosted him.
(I burn, I freeze, I sweat, said the fair Greek,
I speak in contradictions, so to speak.)

I've told his training, he was never bashful,
And his pockets by ma's aid, that night with cash full,
The invitation had no need of fine æsthetic,
Nor did disgust prove such a strong emetic
That we, with Masefield's vein, in the next sentence
Record "Odd's blood! Ouch! Ouch!" a prayer, his swift
    repentance.

No, no, they danced. The music grew much louder
As he inhaled the still fumes of rice-powder.
Then there came other nights, came slow but certain
And were such nights that we should "draw the curtain"
In writing fiction on uncertain chances
Of publication; "Circumstances,"
As the editor of *The Century* says in print,
"Compel a certain silence and restraint."
Still we will bring our "fiction as near to fact" as
The Sunday school brings virtues into practice.

Soon our hero could manage once a week,
Not that his pay had risen, and no leak
Was found in his emloyer's cash. He learned the lay of
    cheaper places,
And then Radway began to go the paces:
A rosy path, a sort of vernal ingress,
And Truth should here be careful of her thin dress—
Though males of seventy, who fear truths naked harm us,
Must think Truth looks as they do in wool pyjamas.
(My country, I've said your morals and your thoughts are
    stale ones,
But surely the worst of your old-women are the male ones.)

Why paint these days? An insurance inspector
For fires and odd risks, could in this sector
Furnish more date for a compilation
Than I can from this distant land and station,
Unless perhaps I should have recourse to
One of those firm-faced inspecting women, who
Find pretty Irish girls in Chinese laundries,
Up stairs, the third floor up, and have such quandaries

As to how and why and whereby they got in
And for what earthly reason they remain. . . .
Alas, eheu, one question that solely vexes
The serious social folk is "just what sex is."
Though it will, of course, pass off with social science
In which their mentors place such wide reliance.
De Gourmont says that fifty grunts are all that will be prized
Of language, by men wholly socialized,
With signs as many, that shall represent 'em
When thoroughly socialized printers want to print 'em.
"As free of mobs as kings"? I'd have men free of that
    invidious,
Lurking, serpentine, amphibious and insidious
Power that compels 'em
To be so much alike that every dog that smells 'em,
Thinks one identity is
Smeared o'er the lot in equal quantities.
Still we look toward the day when man, with unction,
Will long only to be a *social function*,
And even Zeus' wild lightning fear to strike
Lest it should fail to treat all men alike.
And I can hear an old man saying: "Oh, the rub!
"I see them sitting in the Harvard Club,
"And rate 'em up at just so much per head,
"Know what they think, and just what books they've read,
"Till I have viewed straw hats and their habitual clothing
"All the same style, same cut, with perfect loathing."

So Radway walked, quite like the other men,
Out into the crepuscular half-light, now and then;
Saw what the city offered, cast an eye
Upon Manhattan's gorgeous panoply,
The flood of limbs upon Eighth Avenue
To beat Prague, Budapesth, Vienna or Moscow,*
Such animal invigorating carriage
As nothing can restrain or much disparage. . . .
Still he was not given up to brute enjoyment,
An anxious sentiment was his employment,

* Pronounce like respectable Russians: "*Mussqu.*"

For memory of the first warm night still cast a haze o'er
The mind of Radway, whene'er he found a pair of purple
    stays or
Some other quaint reminder of the occasion
That first made him believe in immoral suasion.
A temperate man, a thin potationist, each day
A silent hunter off the Great White Way,
He read *The Century* and thought it nice
To be not too well known in haunts of vice—
The prominent haunts, where one might recognize him,
And in his daily walks duly capsize him.
Thus he eschewed the bright red-walled cafés and
Was never one of whom one speaks as "brazen'd."

Some men will live as prudes in their own village
And make the tour abroad for their wild tillage—
I knew a tourist agent, one whose art is
To run such tours. He calls 'em . . . . . house parties.
But Radway was a patriot whose venality
Was purer in its love of one locality,
A home-industrious worker to perfection,
A senatorial jobber for protection,
Especially on books, lest knowledge break in
Upon the national brains and set 'em achin'.
('Tis an anomaly in our large land of freedom,
You can not get cheap books, even if you neeed 'em).
Radway was ignorant as an editor,
And, heavenly, holy gods! I can't say more,
Though I know one, a very base detractor,
Who has the phrase "As ignorant as an actor."

But turn to Radway: the first night on the river,
Running so close to "hell" it sends a shiver
Down Rodyheaver's prophylactic spine,
Let me return to this bold theme of mine,
Of Radway. O clap hands ye moralists!
And meditate upon the Lord's conquests.
When last I met him, he was a pillar in
An organization for the suppression of sin . . . .
Not that he'd changed his tastes, nor yet his habits,

(Such changes don't occur in men, or rabbits).
Not that he was a saint, nor was top-loftical
In spiritual aspirations, but he found it profitable,
For as Ben Franklin said, with such urbanity:
"Nothing will pay thee, friend, like Christianity."
And in our day thus saith the Evangelist:
"Tent preachin' is the kind that pays the best."

'Twas as a business asset *pure an' simple*
That Radway joined the Baptist Broadway Temple.

I find no moral for peroration,
He is the prototype of half the nation.

Pierrots

From the French of Jules Laforgue
(Scene courte mais typique)

Your eyes! Since I lost their incandescence
Flat calm engulphs my jibs,
The shudder of *Vae soli* gurgles beneath my ribs.

You should have seen me after the affray,
I rushed about in the most agitated way
Crying: My God, my God, what will she say?!

My soul's antennæ are prey to such perturbations,
Wounded by your indirectness in these situations
And your bundle of mundane complications.

Your eyes put me up to it.
I thought: Yes, divine, these eyes, but what exists
Behind them? What's there? Her soul's an affair for oculists.

And I am sliced with loyal æsthetics.
Hate tremolos and national frenetics.
In brief, violet is the ground tone of my phonetics.

I am not "that chap there" nor yet "The Superb"
But my soul, the sort which harsh sounds disturb,
Is, at bottom, distinguished and fresh as a March herb.

My nerves still register the sounds of contra-bass',
I can walk about without fidgeting when people pass,
Without smirking into a pocket-looking-glass.

Yes, I have rubbed shoulders and knocked off my chips
Outside your set but, having kept faith in your eyes,
You might pardon such slips.
Eh, make it up?
                    Soothings, confessions;
These new concessions
Hurl me into such a mass of divergent impressions.

QUIA PAUPER AMAVI

Orfeo

Alba

When the nightingale to his mate
Sings day-long and night late
My love and I keep state
> *In bower,*
> *In flower,*
> *'Till the watchman on the tower*
Cry:
>> *"Up! Thou rascal, Rise,*
>> *I see the white*
>>> *Light*
>>> *And the night*
>>> *Flies."*

I

Compleynt of a gentleman who has been waiting
outside for some time

"O Plasmatour and true celestial light,
Lord powerful, engirdlèd all with might,
Give my good-fellow aid in fools' despite
Who stirs not forth this night,
            And day comes on.

"Sst! my good fellow, art awake or sleeping?
Sleep thou no more. I see the star upleaping
That hath the dawn in keeping,
            And day comes on!

"Hi! Harry, hear me, for I sing aright
Sleep not thou now, I hear the bird in flight
That plaineth of the going of the night,
            And day comes on!

"Come now! Old swenkin! Rise up from thy bed,
I see the signs upon the welkin spread,
If thou come not, the cost be on thy head.
            And day comes on!

"And here I am since going down of sun,
And pray to God that is St. Mary's son,
To bring thee safe back, my companion.
                    And day comes on.

"And thou out here beneath the porch of stone
Badest me to see that a good watch was done,
And now thou'lt none of me, and wilt have none
Of song of mine."

(*Bass voice from within.*)
"Wait, my good fellow. For such joy I take
With her venust and noblest to my make
To hold embracèd, and will not her forsake
For yammer of the cuckold,
                    Though day break."

                              (*Girart Bornello.*)

II
Avril

When the springtime is sweet
And the birds repeat
Their new song in the leaves,
'Tis meet
A man go where he will.

But from where my heart is set
No message I get;
My heart all wakes and grieves;
Defeat
Or luck, I must have my fill.

Our love comes out
Like the branch that turns about
On the top of the hawthorne,
With frost and hail at night
Suffers despite
'Till the sun come, and the green leaf on the bough.

I remember the young day
When we set strife away,
And she gave me such gesning,
Her love and her ring:
God grant I die not by any man's stroke
'Till I have my hand 'neath her cloak.

I care not for their clamour
Who have come between me and my charmer,
For I know how words run loose,
Big talk and little use.
Spoilers of pleasure,
We take their measure.

(Guilhem de Peitieu.)

III
Descant on a Theme by Cerclamon

When the sweet air goes bitter,
And the cold birds twitter
Where the leaf falls from the twig,
I sough and sing
    that Love goes out
  Leaving me no power to hold him.

Of love I have naught
Save troubles and sad thought,
And nothing is grievous
     as I desirous,
Wanting only what
No man can get or has got.

With the noblest that stands in men's sight,
If all the world be in despite
  I care not a glove.
Where my love is, there is a glitter of sun;
God give me life, and let my course run
   'Till I have her I love
    To lie with and prove.

I do not live, nor cure me,
Nor feel my ache—great as it is,
For love will give
                    me no respite,
Nor do I know when I turn left or right
                                        nor when I go out.
        For in her is all my delight
        And all that can save me.

I shake and burn and quiver
From love, awake and in swevyn,
Such fear I have she deliver
                            me not from pain,
        Who know not how to ask her;
        Who can not.
Two years, three years I seek
And though I fear to speak out,
        Still she must know it.
If she won't have me now, Death is my portion
        Would I had died that day
        I came into her sway.
God! How softly this kills!
When her love look steals on me.
Killed me she has, I know not how it was,
        For I would not look on a woman.

Joy I have none, if she make me not mad
        Or set me quiet, or bid me chatter.
Good is it to me if she flout
        Or turn me inside out, and about.
        My ill doth she turn sweet.
        How swift it is. Pleasure is 'neath her feet.

        For I am traist and loose,
        I am true, or a liar,
        All vile, or all gentle,
        Or shaking between,
                        as she desire,

I, Cerclamon, sorry and glad,
    The man whom love had
                    and has ever;
    Alas! whoe'er it please or pain,
    She can me retain.

I am gone from one joy,
From one I loved never so much,
    She by one touch
    Reft me away;
    So doth bewilder me
    I can not say my say
                nor my desire,
    And when she looks on me
    It seems to me
              I lose all wit and sense.

    The noblest girls men love
    'Gainst her I prize not as a glove
    Worn and old.
    Though the whole world run rack
    And go dark with cloud,
    Light is
    Where she stands,
    And a clamour loud
           in my ears.

IV
Vergier

In orchard under the hawthorne
She has her lover till morn,
Till the traist man cry out to warn
Them. God how swift the night,
         And day comes on.

O Plasmatour, that thou end not the night,
Nor take my belovèd from my sight,

Nor I, nor tower-man, look on daylight,
'Fore God, How swift the night,
　　　　　　　And day comes on.

"Lovely thou art, to hold me close and kisst,
　Now cry the birds out, in the meadow mist,
　Despite the cuckold, do thou as thou list,
　So swiftly goes the night
　　　　　　　And day comes on.

"My pretty boy, make we our play again
　Here in the orchard where the birds complain,
　'Till the traist watcher his song unrein,
　Ah God! How swift the night
　　　　　　　And day comes on."

"Out of the wind that blows from her,
　That dancing and gentle is and pleasanter,
　Have I drunk a draught, sweeter than scent of myrrh.
　Ah God! How swift the night.
　　　　　　　And day comes on."

Venust the lady, and none lovelier,
For her great beauty, many men look on her,
Out of my love will her heart not stir.
By God, how swift the night.
　　　　　　　And day comes on.

V

Canzon

I only, and who elrische pain support
Know out love's heart o'erborne by overlove,
For my desire that is so firm and straight
And unchanged since I found her in my sight
And unturned since she came within my glance,
That far from her my speech springs up aflame;
Near her comes not. So press the words to arrest it.

I am blind to others, and their retort
I hear not. In her alone, I see, move,
Wonder. . . . And jest not. And the words dilate
Not truth; but mouth speaks not the heart outright:
I could not walk roads, flats, dales, hills, by chance,
To find charm's sum within one single frame
As God hath set in her t'assay and test it.

And I have passed in many a goodly court
To find in hers more charm than rumour thereof . . .
In solely hers. Measure and sense to mate,
Youth and beauty learnèd in all delight,
Gentrice did nurse her up, and so advance
Her fair beyond all reach of evil name,
To clear her worth, no shadow hath oppresst it.

Her contact flats not out, falls not off short. . . .
Let her, I pray, guess out the sense hereof
For never will it stand in open prate
Until my inner heart stand in daylight,
So that heart pools him when her eyes entrance,
As never doth the Rhone, fulled and untame,
Pool, where the freshets tumult hurl to crest it.

Flimsy another's joy, false and distort,
No paregale that she springs not above . . .
Her love-touch by none other mensurate.
To have it not? Alas! Though the pains bite
Deep, torture is but galzeardy and dance,
For in my thought my lust hath touched his aim.
God! Shall I get no more! No fact to best it!

No delight I, from now, in dance or sport,
Nor will these toys a tinkle of pleasure prove,
Compared to her, whom no loud profligate
Shall leak abroad how much she makes my right.
Is this too much? If she count not mischance
What I have said, then no. But if she blame,
Then tear ye out the tongue that hath expresst it.

The song begs you: Count not this speech ill chance,
But if you count the song worth your acclaim,
Arnaut cares lyt who praise or who contest it.

(Arnaut Daniel, a.d. about 1190.)

Moeurs Contemporaines

I
Mr. Styrax

1

Mr. Hecatomb Styrax, the owner of a large estate
                    and of large muscles,
A "blue" and a climber of mountains, has married
                    at the age of 28,
He being at that age a virgin,
The term "virgo" being made male in mediaeval latinity;
        His ineptitudes
Have driven his wife from one religious excess to another.
She has abandoned the vicar
For he was lacking in vehemence;
She is now the high-priestess
Of a modern and ethical cult,
            And even now Mr. Styrax
            Does not believe in aesthetics.

2

His brother has taken to gipsies,
But the son-in-law of Mr. H. Styrax
Objects to perfumed cigarettes.
            In the parlance of Niccolo Machiavelli,
            "Thus things proceed in their circle";
            And thus the empire is maintained.

II
Clara

At sixteen she was a potential celebrity
With a distaste for caresses.
She now writes to me from a convent;
Her life is obscure and troubled;
Her second husband will not divorce her;
Her mind is, as ever, uncultivated,
And no issue presents itself.
She does not desire her children,
Or any more children.
Her ambition is vague and indefinite,
She will neither stay in, nor come out.

III
Soiree

Upon learning that the mother wrote verses,
And that the father wrote verses,
And that the youngest son was in a publisher's office,
And that the friend of the second daughter

                      was undergoing a novel,

The young American pilgrim
Exclaimed:
      "This is a darn'd clever bunch!"

IV
Sketch 48 b. 11

At the age of 27
Its home mail is still opened by its maternal parent
And its office mail may be opened by

                  its parent of the opposite gender.

It is an officer,
         and a gentleman,
                  and an architect.

V

"Nodier raconte . . ."

1

At a friend of my wife's there is a photograph,
A faded, pale, brownish photograph,
Of the times when the sleeves were large,
Silk, stiff and large above the *lacertus*,
That is, the upper arm,
And décolleté. . . .

It is a lady,
She sits at a harp,
Playing,

And by her left foot, in a basket,
Is an infant, aged about 14 months,
The infant beams at the parent,
The parent re-beams at its offspring.
The basket is lined with satin,
There is a satin-like bow on the harp.

2

And in the home of the novelist
There is a satin-like bow on an harp.

You enter and pass hall after hall
And conservatory follows conservatory,
Lilies lift their white symbolical cups,
Their symbolical pollen is excerpted,
Near them I noticed an harp
And the blue satin ribbon,
And the copy of "Hatha Yoga"
And the neat piles of unopened, unopening books,

And she spoke to me of the monarch,
And of the purity of her soul.

VI
Stele

After years of continence
      he hurled himself into a sea of six women.
Now, quenched as the brand of Meleagar,
      he lies by the poluphloisboious sea-coast.

Παρὰ Θῖνα Πολυφλοίσβοιο Θαλάσσης.

SISTE VIATOR.

VII
I Vecchii

They will come no more,
The old men with beautiful manners.

Il était comme un tout petit garçon
With his blouse full of apples
And sticking out all the way round;
Blagueur! "Con gli occhi onesti e tardi,"

And he said:
        "Oh! Abelard," as if the topic
Were much too abstruse for his comprehension,
And he talked about "the Great Mary,"
And said: "Mr. Pound is shocked at my levity,"
When it turned out he meant Mrs. Ward.

And the other was rather like my bust by Gaudier,
Or like a real Texas colonel,
He said: "Why flay dead horses?
"There was once a man called Voltaire."

And he said they used to cheer Verdi,
In Rome, after the opera,
And the guards couldn't stop them

And that was an anagram for Vittorio
Emanuele Re D' Italia,
And the guards couldn't stop them.

      Old men with beautiful manners,
Sitting in the Row of a morning,
Walking on the Chelsea Embankment.

VIII
Ritratto

And she said:
      "You remember Mr. Lowell,
"He was your ambassador here?"
And I said: "That was before I arrived."
And she said:
      "He stomped into my bedroom. . . .
(By that time she had got on to Browning.)
". . . stomped into my bedroom. . . .
"And said: 'Do I,
"'I ask you, Do I
"'Care too much for society dinners?'
"And I wouldn't say that he didn't.
"Shelley used to live in this house."

She was a very old lady,
I never saw her again.

Homage to Sextus Propertius

I

Shades of Callimachus, Coan ghosts of Philetas
It is in your grove I would walk,
I who come first from the clear font
Bringing the Grecian orgies into Italy,
            and the dance into Italy.

Who hath taught you so subtle a measure,
                              in what hall have you heard it,
What foot beat out your time-bar,
                    what water has mellowed your whistles?

Out-weariers of Apollo will, as we know, continue their
     Martian generalities.
          We have kept our erasers in order,
A new-fangled chariot follows the flower-hung horses;
A young Muse with young loves clustered about her
                         ascends with me into the aether, . . .
And there is no high-road to the Muses.

Annalists will continue to record Roman reputations,
Celebrities from the Trans-Caucasus will belaud Roman
     celebrities
And expound the distentions of Empire,

But for something to read in normal circumstances?
For a few pages brought down from the forked hill
     unsullied?
                    I ask a wreath which will not crush my head.
                         And there is no hurry about it;
I shall have, doubtless, a boom after my funeral,
Seeing that long standing increases all things
                              regardless of quality.

And who would have known the towers
                         pulled down by a deal-wood horse;
Or of Achilles withstaying waters by Simois
Or of Hector spattering wheel-rims,

Or of Polydmantus, by Scamander, or Helenus and
     Deiphoibos?
Their door-yards would scarcely know them, or Paris.
Small talk O Ilion, and O Troad
                         twice taken by Oetian gods,
If Homer had not stated your case!

And I also among the later nephews of this city
                    shall have my dog's day
With no stone upon my contemptible sepulchre,
My vote coming from the temple of Phoebus in Lycia,
                            at Patara,
And in the mean time my songs will travel,
And the devirginated young ladies will enjoy them
                  when they have got over the strangeness,
For Orpheus tamed the wild beasts—
                     and held up the Threician river;
And Citharaon shook up the rocks by Thebes
            and danced them into a bulwark at his pleasure,
And you, O Polyphemus? Did harsh Galatea almost
Turn to your dripping horses, because of a tune, under
    Aetna?
We must look into the matter.
Bacchus and Apollo in favour of it,
There will be a crowd of young women doing homage to
    my palaver,
Though my house is not propped up by Taenarian columns
      from Laconia (associated with Neptune and Cerberus),
Though it is not stretched upon gilded beams;
My orchards do not lie level and wide
                      as the forests of Phaecia,
                  the luxurious and Ionian,
Nor are my caverns stuffed stiff with a Marcian vintage,
           (My cellar does not date from Numa Pompilius,
Nor bristle with wine jars)
Yet the companions of the Muses
               will keep their collective nose in my books,
And weary with historical data, they will turn to my dance
    tune.

Happy who are mentioned in my pamphlets
       the songs shall be a fine tomb-stone over their beauty.
                         But against this?
Neither expensive pyramids scraping the stars in their route,
Nor houses modelled upon that of Jove in East Elis,
Nor the monumental effigies of Mausolus,
                  are a complete elucidation of death.

Flame burns, rain sinks into the cracks
And they all go to rack ruin beneath the thud of the years.

Stands genius a deathless adornment,
                    a name not to be worn out with the years.

II

I had been seen in the shade, recumbent on cushioned Helicon,
                    the water dripping from Bellerophon's horse,
Alba, your kings, and the realm your folk
                    have constructed with such industry
Shall be yawned out on my lyre—with such industry.
My little mouth shall gobble in such great fountains
"Wherefrom father Ennius, sitting before I came, hath drunk."

I had rehearsed the Curian brothers, and made remarks on
     the Horatian javelin
(Near Q.H. Flaccus' book-stall).
          "Of" royal Aemilia, drawn on the memorial raft,
"Of" the victorious delay of Fabius, and the left-handed
                    battle at Cannae,
Of lares fleeing the "Roman seat" . . .
                    I had sung of all these
And of Hannibal,
          and of Jove protected by geese.
And Phoebus looking upon me from the Castalian tree,
Said then "You idiot! What are you doing with that water;
"Who has ordered a book about heroes?
                    You need, Propertius, not think
"About acquiring that sort of a reputation.
          "Soft fields must be worn by small wheels,
"Your pamphlets will be thrown, thrown often into a chair
"Where a girl waits alone for her lover;
          "Why wrench your page out of its course?
"No keel will sink with your genius
          "Let another oar churn the water,
"Another wheel, the arena; mid-crowd is as bad as mid-sea."

He had spoken, and pointed me a place with his plectrum.

Orgies of vintages, an earthen image of Silenus
Strengthened with rushes, Tegaean Pan,
The small birds of the Cytharean mother
                    their Punic faces dyed in the Gorgon's lake.
Nine girls, from as many countrysides
                    bearing her offerings in their unhardened hands:

Such my cohort and setting. And she bound ivy to his thyrsos;
Fitted song to the strings;
                         Roses twined in her hands.
And one among them looked at me with face offended,
Calliope:
          "Content ever to move with white swans!
"Nor will the noise of high horses lead you ever to battle;
"Nor will the public criers ever have your name
                              in their classic horns,
"Nor Mars shout you in the wood at Aeonium,
                    Nor where Rome ruins German riches,
"Nor where the Rhine flows with barbarous blood,
                    and flood carries wounded Suevi.
"Obviously crowned lovers at unknown doors,
"Night dogs, the marks of a drunken scurry,
"These are your images, and from you the sorcerizing
                    of shut-in young ladies,
"The wounding of austere men by chicane."
          Thus Mistress Calliope,
          Dabbling her hands in the fount, thus she
Stiffened our face with the backwash of Philetas the Coan.

III

Midnight, and a letter comes to me from our mistress:
                    Telling me to come to Tibur, *At* once!!:
Bright tips reach up from twin towers,
          Anienan spring water falls into flat-spread pools.

What *is* to be done about it?
                    Shall I entrust myself to entangled shadows,
Where bold hands may do violence to my person?

Yet if I postpone my obedience
                        because of this respectable terror
I shall be prey to lamentations worse than a nocturnal
    assailant.
And I shall be in the wrong,
                     and it will last a twelve month,
For her hands have no kindness me-ward,

Nor is there anyone to whom lovers are not sacred at
    midnight
And in the Via Sciro.

If any man would be a lover
                 he may walk on the Scythian coast,
No barbarism would go to the extent of doing him harm,
The moon will carry his candle,
                 the stars will point out the stumbles,
Cupid will carry lighted torches before him
                 and keep mad dogs off his ankles.
Thus all roads are perfectly safe
                 and at any hour;
Who so indecorous as to shed the pure gore of a suitor?!
    Cypris is his cicerone.

What if undertakers follow my track,
                 such a death is worth dying.
She would bring frankincense and wreathes to my tomb,
            She would sit like an ornament on my pyre.

Gods' aid, let not my bones lie in a public location
           with crowds too assiduous in their crossing of it;
For thus are tombs of lovers most desecrated.

May a woody and sequestered place cover me with its foliage
Or may I inter beneath the hummock
                 of some as yet uncatalogued sand;
At any rate I shall not have my epitaph in a high road.

IV
Difference of Opinion with Lygdamus

Tell me the truths which you hear of our constant young
    lady,
        Lygdamus,
And may the bought yoke of a mistress lie with
                        equitable weight on your shoulders;
For I am swelled up with inane pleasurabilities
                        and deceived by your reference
        To things which you think I would like to believe.

No messenger should come wholly empty,
                    and a slave should fear plausibilities;
        Much conversation is as good as having a home.
    Out with it, tell it to me, all of it, from the beginning,
I guzzle with outstretched ears.
Thus? She wept into uncombed hair,
                        And you saw it,
Vast waters flowed from her eyes?
                        You, you Lygdamus
Saw her stretched on her bed,—
                        it was no glimpse in a mirror;
No gawds on her snowy hands, no orfevrerie,
Sad garment draped on her slender arms.
Her escritoires lay shut by the bed-feet.
Sadness hung over the house, and the desolated female
    attendants
Were desolated because she had told them her dreams.

She was veiled in the midst of that place,
Damp woolly hankerchiefs were stuffed into her undryable
    eyes,
And a querulous noise responded to our solicitous
    reprobations.

    For which things you will get a reward from me,
                        Lygdamus?
To say many things is equal to having a home.

And the other woman "has not enticed me
                   by her pretty manners,
"She has caught me with herbaceous poison,
                she twiddles the spiked wheel of a rhombus,
"She stews puffed frogs, snake's bones, the moulded feathers
    of screech owls,

"She binds me with ravvles of shrouds.
                 "Black spiders spin in her bed!
"Let her lovers snore at her in the morning!
                "May the gout cramp up her feet!
        "Does he like me to sleep here alone, Lygdamus,?
        "Will he say nasty things at my funeral?"

And you expect me to believe this
               after twelve months of discomfort?

V

I

Now if ever it is time to cleanse Helicon;
              to lead Emathian horses afield,
And to name over the census of my chiefs in the Roman
    camp.
If I have not the faculty, "The bare attempt would be praise-
    worthy."
"In things of similar magnitude
              the mere will to act is sufficient."

The primitive ages sang Venus,
              the last sings of a tumult,
And I also will sing war when this matter of a girl is
    exhausted.
I with my beak hauled ashore would proceed in a more
    stately manner,
My Muse is eager to instruct me in a new gamut, or
    gambetto,
Up, up my soul, from your lowly cantilation,
              put on a timely vigour,

Oh august Pierides! Now for a large-mouthed product.
Thus:
"The Euphrates denies its protection to the Parthian
and apologizes for Crassus,"
And "It is, I think, India which now gives necks to
your triumph,"
And so forth, Augustus. "Virgin Arabia shakes in her inmost
dwelling."
If any land shrink into a distant seacoast,
it is a mere postponement of your domination,
And I shall follow the camp, I shall be duly celebrated,
for singing the affairs of your cavalry.
May the fates watch over my day.

2

Yet you ask on what account I write so many love-lyrics
And whence this soft book comes into my mouth.
Neither Calliope nor Apollo sung these things into my ear,
My genius is no more than a girl.

If she with ivory fingers drive a tune through the lyre,
We look at the process
How easy the moving fingers; if hair is mussed on her
forehead,
If she goes in a gleam of Cos, in a slither of dyed stuff,
There is a volume in the matter; if her eyelids sink into
sleep,
There are new jobs for the author,
And if she plays with me with her shirt off,
We shall construct many Iliads.
And whatever she does or says
We shall spin long yarns out of nothing,

Thus much the fates have alloted me, and if, Maecenas,
I were able to lead heroes into armour, I would not,
Neither would I warble of Titans, nor of Ossa
spiked onto Olympus,
Nor of causeways over Pelion,

Nor of Thebes in its ancient respectability,
                  nor of Homer's reputation in Pergamus,
Nor of Xerxes two barreled kingdom, nor of Remus and his
    royal family,
Nor of dignified Carthaginian characters,
Nor of Welsh mines and the profit Marus had out of them.
I should remember Caesar's affairs . . .
                       for a background,
Although Callimachus did without them,
                    and without Theseus,
Without an inferno, without Achilles attended of gods,
Without Ixion and without the sons of Menoetius and the
    Argo and without Jove's grave and the Titans.

And my ventricles do not palpitate to Caesarial *ore rotundos*,
Nor to the tune of the Phrygian fathers.

Sailor, of winds; a plowman, concerning his oxen;
Soldier, the enumeration of wounds; the sheep-feeder, of
    ewes;
We, in our narrow bed, turning aside from battles:
Each man where he can, wearing out the day in his manner.

3

It is noble to die of love, and honourable to remain
                       uncuckolded for a season.
And she speaks ill of light women,
                  and will not praise Homer
Because Helen's conduct is "unsuitable."

VI

When, when, and whenever death closes our eyelids,
Moving naked over Acheron
        Upon the one raft, victor and conquered together,
Marius and Jugurtha together,
                one tangle of shadows.

Caesar plots against India
Tigris and Euphrates shall from now on, flow at his bidding,

Tibet shall be full of Roman policemen,
The Parthians shall get used to our statuary
                and acquire a Roman religion;

One raft on the veiled flood of Acheron,
         Marius and Jugurtha together.
Nor at my funeral either will there be any long trail,
                bearing ancestral lares and images;
No trumpets filled with my emptiness,
Nor shall it be on an Atalic bed;
        The perfumed cloths shall be absent.
A small plebeian procession.
          Enough, enough and in plenty
There will be three books at my obsequies
Which I take, my not unworthy gift, to Persephone.

You will follow the bare scarified breast
Nor will you be weary of calling my name, nor too weary
      To place the last kiss on my lips
When the Syrian onyx is broken.

              "He who is now vacant dust
              "Was once the slave of one passion:"
Give that much inscription
            "Death why tardily come?"

You, sometimes, will lament a lost friend
      For it is a custom:
This care for past men,

Since Adonis was gored in Idalia, and the Cytharean
Ran crying with out-spread hair,
        In vain, you call back the shade,
In vain, Cynthia. Vain call to unanswering shadow,
        Small talk comes from small bones.

VII

Me happy, night, night full of brightness;
Oh couch made happy by my long delectations;
How many words talked out with abundant candles;
Struggles when the lights were taken away;
Now with bared breasts she wrestled against me,
Tunic spread in delay;
And she then opening my eyelids fallen in sleep,
Her lips upon them; and it was her mouth saying: Sluggard!

In how many varied embraces, our changing arms,
Her kisses, how many, lingering on my lips.
"Turn not Venus into a blinded motion,
Eyes are the guides of love,
Paris took Helen naked coming from the bed of Menelaus,
Endymion's naked body, bright bait for Diana,"
—such at least is the story.

While our fates twine together, sate we our eyes with love;
For long night comes upon you
and a day when no day returns.
Let the gods lay chains upon us
so that no day shall unbind them.

Fool who would set a term to love's madness,
For the sun shall drive with black horses,
earth shall bring wheat from barley,
The flood shall move toward the fountain
Ere love know moderations,
The fish shall swim in dry streams.

No, now while it may be, let not the fruit of life cease.

Dry wreathes drop their petals,
their stalks are woven in baskets,
To day we take the great breath of lovers,
to morrow fate shuts us in.

Though you give all your kisses
               you give but a few."

Nor can I shift my pains to other
        Hers will I be dead,
If she confers such nights upon me,
              long is my life, long in years,
If she give me many,
        God am I for the time.

VIII

Jove, be merciful to that unfortunate woman
        Or an ornamental death will be held to your debit,
The time is come, the air heaves in torridity,
        The dry earth pants against the canicular heat,
But this heat is not the root of the matter:
        She did not respect all the gods;
Such derelictions have destroyed other young ladies afore-
    time,
        And what they swore in the cupboard
              wind and wave scattered away.

Was Venus exacerbated by the existence of a comparable
    equal?
        Is the ornamental goddess full of envy?
Have you contempted Juno's Pelasgian temples,
        Have you denied Pallas good eyes?
Or is it my tongue that wrongs you
             with perpetual ascription of graces?
There comes, it seems, and at any rate
           through perils, (so many) and of a vexed life,
The gentler hour of an ultimate day.

Io mooed the first years with averted head,
        And now drinks Nile water like a god,
Ino in her young days fled pell mell out of Thebes,
        Andromeda was offered to a sea-serpent
            and respectably married to Perseus,

Callisto, disguised as a bear,

                    wandered through the Arcadian prairies

      While a black veil was over her stars,

What if your fates are accelerated;

                        your quiet hour put forward,

You may find interment pleasing,

You will say that you succumbed to a danger identical,

                    charmingly identical, with Semele's,

      And believe it, and she also will believe it,

                  being expert from experience,

And amid all the gloried and storied beauties of Maeonia

      There shall be none in a better seat, not one denying

          your prestige,

Now you may bear fate's stroke unperturbed,

               Or Jove, harsh as he is, may turn aside your

             ultimate day,

Old lecher, let not Juno get wind of the matter,

Or perhaps Juno herself will go under,

                    If the young lady is taken?

There will be, in any case, a stir on Olympus.

IX

I

The twisted rhombs ceased their clamour of accompaniment.

The scorched laurel lay in the fire-dust,

And the moon still declined wholly to descend out of heaven.

But the black ominous owl hoot was audible,

And one raft bears our fates

                  on the veiled lake toward Avernus

Sails spread on Cerulean waters, I would shed tears for two;

I shall live, if she continue in life,

      If she dies, I shall go with her.

Great Zeus, save the woman,
>   or she will sit before your feet in a veil,
>   and tell out the long list of her troubles.

2

Persephone and Dis, Dis, have mercy upon her,
There are enough women in hell,
>   quite enough beautiful women
Iope, and Tyro, and Pasiphae, and the formal girls of Achaia,
And out of Troad, and from the Campania,
Death has its tooth in the lot,
>   Avernus lusts for the lot of them,
Beauty is not eternal, no man has perennial fortune,
Slow foot, or swift foot, death delays but for a season.

3

My light, light of my eyes,
>   you are escaped from great peril,
Go back to great Dian's dances bearing suitable gifts,
Pay up your vow of night watches
>   to Dian goddess of virgins,
And unto me also pay debt,
>   the ten nights of your company you have promised me.

X

Light, light of my eyes, at an exceeding late hour I was
>   wandering,
And intoxicated,
>   and no servant was leading me,
And a minute crowd of small boys came from opposite,
>   I do not know what boys,
And I am afraid of numerical estimate,
And some of them shook little torches,
>   and others held onto arrows,
And the rest laid their chains upon me,
>   and they were naked, the lot of them,
And one of the lot was given to lust.

"That incensed female has consigned him to our pleasure."
So spoke. And the noose was over my neck.

And another said "Get him plumb in the middle!
    "Shove along there, shove along!"
And another broke in upon this:
           "He thinks that we are not gods."

"And she has been waiting for the scoundrel,
          and in a new Sidonian night cap,
And with more than Arabian odours,
          god knows where he has been,
She could scarcely keep her eyes open
          enter that much for his bail.
          Get along now!"

We were coming near to the house,
          and they gave another yank to my cloak,
And it was morning, and I wanted to see if she was alone,
    and resting,
And Cynthia was alone in her bed.
          I was stupified.
I had never seen her looking so beautiful
    No, not when she was tunick'd in purple.

Such aspect was presented to me, me recently emerged from
    my visions,
You will observe that pure form has its value.

"You are a very early inspector of mistresses.
"Do you think I have adopted your habits?"
    There were upon the bed no signs of a voluptuous
      encounter,
    No signs of a second incumbent.

She continued:
      "No incubus has crushed his body against me,
      "Though spirits are celebrated for adultery.
      "And I am going to the temple of Vesta . . ."
          and so on.

Since that day I have had no pleasant nights.

XI

1

The harsh acts of your levity!
                        Many and many.
I am hung here, a scare-crow for lovers.

2

Escape! There is, O Idiot, no escape,
Flee if you like into Ranaus,
                            desire will follow you thither,
Though you heave into the air upon the gilded Pegasean
    back,
        Though you had the feathery sandals of Perseus
To lift you up through split air,
          The high tracks of Hermes would not afford you
            shelter.

Amor stands upon you, Love drives upon lovers,
                        a heavy mass on free necks.

It is our eyes you flee, not the city,
You do nothing, you plot inane schemes against me,
Languidly you stretch out the snare
                     with which I am already familiar,
And yet again, and newly rumour strikes on my ears.

Rumours of you throughout the city,
                 and no good rumour among them.

"You should not believe hostile tongues,"
    "Beauty is slander's cock-shy,"
"All lovely women have known this,"
    "Your glory is not outblotted by venom,"
"Phoebus our witness, your hands are unspotted,"

A foreign lover brought down Helen's kingdom
              and she was lead back, living, home;
The Cytharean brought low by Mars' lechery
             reigns in respectable heavens, . . .

Oh, oh, and enough of this,
                              by dew-spread caverns,
The Muses clinging to the mossy ridges;
                                   to the ledge of the rocks;
Zeus' clever rapes, in the old days,
                              combusted Semele's, of Io strayed.
Of how the bird flew from Trojan rafters,
        Ida has lain with a shepherd, she has slept between
        sheep.

                                        Even there, no escape
Not the Hyrcanian seaboard, not in seeking the shore of Eos.

All things are forgiven for one night of your games. . . .
Though you walk in the Via Sacra, with a peacock's tail for a
        fan.

                                XII

Who, who will be the next man to entrust his girl to a friend?
Love interferes with fidelities;
The gods have brought shame on their relatives;
        Each man wants the pomegranate for himself;
Amiable and harmonious people are pushed incontinent into
        duels,
A Trojan and adulterous person came to Menelaus under
        the rites of hospitium,
And there was a case in Colchis, Jason and that woman in
        Colchis;
And besides, Lynceus,
                        you were drunk.

Could you endure such promiscuity?
        She was not renowned for fidelity;
But to jab a knife in my vitals, to have passed on a swig of
        poison,
Preferable, my dear boy, my dear Lynceus,
Comrade, comrade of my life, of my purse, of my person;

But in one bed, in one bed alone, my dear Lynceus.
      I deprecate your attendance;
I would ask a like boon of Jove.

And you write of Achelöus, who contended with Hercules,
You write of Adrastus' horses and the funeral rites of
    Achenor,
And you will not leave off imitating Aeschylus
      Though you make a hash of Antimachus,
You think you are going to do Homer.
      And still a girl scorns the gods,
Of all these young women
               not one has enquired the cause of the world,
Nor the modus of lunar eclipses
      Nor whether there be any patch left of us
After we cross the infernal ripples,
         nor if the thunder fall from predestination;
Nor anything else of importance.

Upon the Actian marshes Virgil is Phoebus' chief of police,
      He can tabulate Caesar's great ships.
He thrills to Ilian arms,
      He shakes the Trojan weapons of Aeneas,
And casts stores on Lavinian beaches.

Make way, ye Roman authors,
              clear the street O ye Greeks,
For a much larger Iliad is in the course of construction
              (and to Imperial order)
Clear the streets O ye Greeks!

And you also follow him "neath Phrygian pine shade:
      Thyrsis and Daphnis upon whittled reeds,
And how ten sins can corrupt young maidens;
      Kids for a bribe and pressed udders,
Happy selling poor loves for cheap apples.

Tityrus might have sung the same vixen;
      Corydon tempted Alexis,

Head farmers do likewise, and lying weary amid their oats
They get praise from tolerant Hamadryads."

Go on, to Ascraeus' prescription, the ancient,
                            respected, Wordsworthian:
"A flat field for rushes, grapes grow on the slope."

And behold me, small fortune left in my house.
        Me, who had no general for a grandfather!
I shall triumph among young ladies of indeterminate
    character,
My talent acclaimed in their banquets,
        I shall be honoured with yesterday's wreaths.

And the god strikes to the marrow.

        Like a trained and performing tortoise,
I would make verse in your fashion, if she should command it,
With her husband asking a remission of sentence,
        And even this infamy would not attract numerous
        readers
Were there an erudite or violent passion,
For the nobleness of the populace brooks nothing below its
    own altitude.
One must have resonance, resonance and sonority . . .
                            like a goose.

Varro sang Jason's expedition,
        Varro, of his great passion Leucadia,
There is song in the parchment; Catullus the highly
    indecorous,
Of Lesbia, known above Helen;
And in the dyed pages of Calvus,
        Calvus mourning Quintilia,
And but now Gallus had sung of Lycoris.
        Fair, fairest Lycoris—
The waters of Styx poured over the wound:
And now Propertius of Cynthia, taking his stand among
    these.

HUGH SELWYN MAUBERLEY

BY

E. P.

"*Vocat æstus in umbram*"
NEMESTANUS Ec. IV.

H. S. MAUBERLEY

(LIFE AND CONTACTS)

E.P.

Ode Pour L'Élection de Son Sépulchre

For three years, out of key with his time,
He strove to resuscitate the dead art
Of poetry; to maintain "the sublime"
In the old sense. Wrong from the start—

No hardly, but, seeing he had been born
In a half savage country, out of date;
Bent resolutely on wringing lilies from the acorn;
Capaneus; trout for factitious bait;

ʼΊδμεν γάρ τοι πάνθ᾽, δ᾽σ᾽ ἐνὶ Τροίη
Caught in the unstopped ear;
Giving the rocks small lee-way
The chopped seas held him, therefore, that year.

His true Penelope was Flaubert,
He fished by obstinate isles;
Observed the elegance of Circe's hair
Rather than the mottoes on sun-dials.

Unaffected by "the march of events,"
He passed from men's memory in *l'an trentiesme
De son eage;* the case presents
No adjunct to the Muses' diadem.

II

The age demanded an image
Of its accelerated grimace,
Something for the modern stage,
Not, at any rate, an Attic grace;

Not, not certainly, the obscure reveries
Of the inward gaze;
Better mendacities
Than the classics in paraphrase!

The "age demanded" chiefly a mould in plaster,
Made with no loss of time,
A prose kinema, not, not assuredly, alabaster
Or the "sculpture" of rhyme.

III

The tea-rose tea-gown, etc.
Supplants the mousseline of Cos,
The pianola "replaces"
Sappho's barbitos.

Christ follows Dionysus,
Phallic and ambrosial
Made way for macerations;
Caliban casts out Ariel.

All things are a flowing,
Sage Heracleitus says;
But a tawdry cheapness
Shall reign throughout our days.

Even the Christian beauty
Defects—after Samothrace;
We see το καλόν
Decreed in the market place.

Faun's flesh is not to us,
Nor the saint's vision.
We have the press for wafer;
Franchise for circumcision.

All men, in law, are equals.
Free of Peisistratus,

We choose a knave or an eunuch
To rule over us.

O bright Apollo,
τίν' ἀνδρα, τίν' ἥρωα, τίνα θεὸν,
What god, man, or hero
Shall I place a tin wreath upon!

IV

These fought, in any case,
and some believing, pro domo, in any case . .

Some quick to arm,
some for adventure,
some from fear of weakness,
some from fear of censure,
some for love of slaughter, in imagination,
learning later . . .

some in fear, learning love of slaughter;
Died some pro patria, non dulce non et decor . .

walked eye-deep in hell
believing in old men's lies, then unbelieving
came home, home to a lie,
home to many deceits,
home to old lies and new infamy;

usury age-old and age-thick
and liars in public places.

Daring as never before, wastage as never before.
Young blood and high blood,
Fair cheeks, and fine bodies;

fortitude as never before

frankness as never before,
disillusions as never told in the old days,
hysterias, trench confessions,
laughter out of dead bellies.

V

There died a myriad,
And of the best, among them,
For an old bitch gone in the teeth,
For a botched civilization,

Charm, smiling at the good mouth,
Quick eyes gone under earth's lid,

For two gross of broken statues,
For a few thousand battered books.

Yeux Glauques

Gladstone was still respected,
When John Ruskin produced
"Kings Treasuries"; Swinburne
And Rossetti still abused.

Fœtid Buchanan lifted up his voice
When that faun's head of hers
Became a pastime for
Painters and adulterers.

The Burne-Jones cartons
Have preserved her eyes;
Still, at the Tate, they teach
Cophetua to rhapsodize;

Thin like brook-water,
With a vacant gaze.

The English Rubaiyat was still-born
In those days.

The thin, clear gaze, the same
Still darts out faun-like from the half-ruin'd face
Questing and passive. . . .
"Ah, poor Jenny's case" . . .

Bewildered that a world
Shows no surprise
At her last maquero's
Adulteries.

"Siena Mi Fe', Disfecemi Maremma"

Among the pickled fœtuses and bottled bones,
Engaged in perfecting the catalogue,
I found the last scion of the
Senatorial families of Strasbourg, Monsieur Verog.

For two hours he talked of Gallifet;
Of Dowson; of the Rhymers' Club;
Told me how Johnson (Lionel) died
By falling from a high stool in a pub . . .

But showed no trace of alcohol
At the autopsy, privately performed—
Tissue preserved—the pure mind
Arose toward Newman as the whiskey warmed.

Dowson found harlots cheaper than hotels;
Headlam for uplift; Image impartially imbued
With raptures for Bacchus, Terpsichore and the Church.
So spoke the author of "The Dorian Mood",

M. Verog, out of step with the decade,
Detached from his contemporaries,
Neglected by the young,
Because of these reveries.

Brennbaum

The sky-like limpid eyes,
The circular infant's face,
The stiffness from spats to collar
Never relaxing into grace;

The heavy memories of Horeb, Sinai and the forty years,
Showed only when the daylight fell
Level across the face
Of Brennbaum "The Impeccable".

Mr. Nixon

In the cream gilded cabin of his steam yacht
Mr. Nixon advised me kindly, to advance with fewer
Dangers of delay. "Consider
        "Carefully the reviewer.

"I was as poor as you are;
"When I began I got, of course,
"Advance on royalties, fifty at first", said Mr. Nixon,
"Follow me, and take a column,
"Even if you have to work free.

"Butter reviewers. From fifty to three hundred
"I rose in eighteen months;
"The hardest nut I had to crack
"Was Dr. Dundas.

"I never mentioned a man but with the view
"Of selling my own works.
"The tip's a good one, as for literature
"It gives no man a sinecure."

And no one knows, at sight a masterpiece.
And give up verse, my boy,
There's nothing in it.

* * *

Likewise a friend of Bloughram's once advised me:
Don't kick against the pricks,
Accept opinion. The "Nineties" tried your game
And died, there's nothing in it.

X

Beneath the sagging roof
The stylist has taken shelter,
Unpaid, uncelebrated,
At last from the world's welter

Nature receives him,
With a placid and uneducated mistress
He exercises his talents
And the soil meets his distress.

The haven from sophistications and contentions
Leaks through its thatch;
He offers succulent cooking;
The door has a creaking latch.

XI

"Conservatrix of Milésien"
Habits of mind and feeling,
Possibly. But in Ealing
With the most bank-clerkly of Englishmen?

No, "Milésien" is an exaggeration.
No instinct has survived in her
Older than those her grandmother
Told her would fit her station.

XII

"Daphne with her thighs in bark
Stretches toward me her leafy hands",—
Subjectively. In the stuffed-satin drawing-room
I await The Lady Valentine's commands,

Knowing my coat has never been
Of precisely the fashion
To stimulate, in her,
A durable passion;

Doubtful, somewhat, of the value
Of well-gowned approbation
Of literary effort,
But never of The Lady Valentine's vocation:

Poetry, her border of ideas,
The edge, uncertain, but a means of blending
With other strata
Where the lower and higher have ending;

A hook to catch the Lady Jane's attention,
A modulation toward the theatre,
Also, in the case of revolution,
A possible friend and comforter.

*   *   *

Conduct, on the other hand, the soul
"Which the highest cultures have nourished"
To Fleet St. where
Dr. Johnson flourished;

Beside this thoroughfare
The sale of half-hose has
Long since superseded the cultivation
Of Pierian roses.

Envoi (1919)

Go, dumb-born book,
Tell her that sang me once that song of Lawes;
Hadst thou but song
As thou hast subjects known,
Then were there cause in thee that should condone
Even my faults that heavy upon me lie
And build her glories their longevity.

Tell her that sheds
Such treasure in the air,
Recking naught else but that her graces give
Life to the moment,
I would bid them live
As roses might, in magic amber laid,
Red overwrought with orange and all made
One substance and one colour
Braving time.

Tell her that goes
With song upon her lips
But sings not out the song, nor knows
The maker of it, some other mouth,
May be as fair as hers,
Might, in new ages, gain her worshippers,
When our two dusts with Waller's shall be laid,
Siftings on siftings in oblivion,
Till change hath broken down
All things save Beauty alone.

1920

(*Mauberley*)

I

Turned from the "eau-forte
Par Jaquemart"
To the strait head
Of Messalina:

"His true Penelope
Was Flaubert",
And his tool
The engraver's

Firmness,
Not the full smile,
His art, but an art
In profile;

Colourless
Pier Francesca,
Pisanello lacking the skill
To forge Achaia.

II

"Qu'est ce qu'ils savent de l'amour, et qu'est ce qu'ils peuvent comprendre?
S'ils ne comprennent pas la poésie, s'ils ne sentent pas la musique, qu'est ce qu'ils peuvent comprendre de cette passion en comparaison avec laquelle la rose est grossière et le parfum des violettes un tonnerre?"   CAID ALI

For three years, diabolus in the scale,
He drank ambrosia,
All passes, ANANGKE prevails,
Came end, at last, to that Arcadia.

He had moved amid her phantasmagoria,
Amid her galaxies,
NUKTOS ÁGALMA

– – –

Drifted . . . . drifted precipitate,
Asking time to be rid of . . . .
Of his bewilderment; to designate
His new found orchid. . . .

To be certain . . . . certain . . .
(Amid ærial flowers) . . time for arrangements—

Drifted on
To the final estrangement;

Unable in the supervening blankness
To sift TO AGATHON from the chaff
Until he found his sieve . . .
Ultimately, his seismograph:

—Given, that is, his urge
To convey the relation
Of eye-lid and cheek-bone
By verbal manifestation;

To present the series
Of curious heads in medallion—

He had passed, inconscient, full gaze,
The wide-banded irises
And botticellian sprays implied
In their diastasis;

Which anæsthesis, noted a year late,
And weighed, revealed his great affect,
(Orchid), mandate
Of Eros, a retrospect.

.   .   .

Mouths biting empty air,
The still stone dogs,
Caught in metamorphosis were
Left him as epilogues.

"The Age Demanded"

Vide Poem II. Page 549

For this agility chance found
Him of all men, unfit
As the red-beaked steeds of
The Cytheræan for a chain-bit.

The glow of porcelain
Brought no reforming sense
To his perception
Of the social inconsequence.

Thus, if her colour
Came against his gaze,
Tempered as if
It were through a perfect glaze

He made no immediate application
Of this to relation of the state
To the individual, the month was more temperate
Because this beauty had been
     . . . . . .

        The coral isle, the lion-coloured sand
        Burst in upon the porcelain revery:
        Impetuous troubling
        Of his imagery.
     . . . . . .

Mildness, amid the neo-Nietzschean clatter,
His sense of graduations,
Quite out of place amid
Resistance to current exacerbations

Invitation, mere invitation to perceptivity
Gradually led him to the isolation
Which these presents place
Under a more tolerant, perhaps, examination.

By constant elimination
The manifest universe
Yielded an armour
Against utter consternation,

A Minoan undulation,
Seen, we admit, amid ambrosial circumstances
Strengthened him against
The discouraging doctrine of chances

And his desire for survival,
Faint in the most strenuous moods,
Became an Olympian *apathein*
In the presence of selected perceptions.

A pale gold, in the aforesaid pattern,
The unexpected palms
Destroying, certainly, the artist's urge,
Left him delighted with the imaginary
Audition of the phantasmal sea-surge,

Incapable of the least utterance or composition,
Emendation, conservation of the "better tradition",
Refinement of medium, elimination of superfluities,
August attraction or concentration.

Nothing in brief, but maudlin confession
Irresponse to human aggression,
Amid the precipitation, down-float
Of insubstantial manna
Lifting the faint susurrus
Of his subjective hosannah.

Ultimate affronts to human redundancies;

Non-esteem of self-styled "his betters"
Leading, as he well knew,
To his final
Exclusion from the world of letters.

IV

Scattered Moluccas
Not knowing, day to day,
The first days end, in the next noon
The placid water
Unbroken by the Simoon;

Thick foliage
Placid beneath warm suns,
Tawn fore-shores
Washed in the cobalt of oblivions;

Or through dawn-mist
The grey and rose
Of the juridical
Flamingoes;

A consciousness disjunct,
Being but this overblotted
Series
Of intermittences;

Coracle of Pacific voyages,
The unforecasted beach:
Then on an oar
Read this:

"I was
And I no more exist;
Here drifted
An hedonist."

Medallion

Luini in porcelain!
The grand piano
Utters a profane
Protest with her clear soprano.

The sleek head emerges
From the gold-yellow frock
As Anadyomene in the opening
Pages of Reinach.

Honey-red, closing the face-oval
A basket-work of braids which seem as if they were

Spun in King Minos' hall
From metal, or intractable amber;

The face-oval beneath the glaze,
Bright in its suave bounding-line, as
Beneath half-watt rays
The eyes turn topaz.

UMBRA

Oboes

From *Poetry and Drama* for February 1912

I
FOR A BEERY VOICE

Why should we worry about to-morrow,
When we may all be dead and gone?
Haro! Haro!
    Ha-a-ah-rro!
There'll come better men
Who will do, will they not?
The noble things that we forgot.
If there come worse,
     what better thing
Than to leave them the curse of our ill-doing!
Haro! Haro!
    Ha-a-ah-rro!

II
AFTER HEINE

And have you thoroughly kissed my lips?
 There was no particular haste,
And are you not ready when evening's come?
 There's no *particular* haste.

You've got the whole night before you.
 Heart's-all-belovèd-my-own;
In an uninterrupted night one can
 Get a good deal of kissing done.

Phanopoeia

I
ROSE WHITE, YELLOW, SILVER

The swirl of light follows me through the square,
The smoke of incense
Mounts from the four horns of my bed-posts,
The water-jet of gold light bears us up through the ceilings;
Lapped in the gold-coloured flame I descend through the
    aether.
The silver ball forms in my hand,
It falls and rolls to your feet.

II
SALTUS

The swirling sphere has opened
    and you are caught up to the skies,
You are englobed in my sapphire.
                Io! Io!

You have perceived the blades of the flame
The flutter of sharp-edged sandals.

The folding and lapping brightness
Has held in the air before you.

You have perceived the leaves of the flame.

III
CONCAVA VALLIS

The wire-like bands of colour involute mount from my fingers;
I have wrapped the wind round your shoulders
And the molten metal of your shoulders
    bends into the turn of the wind,

AOI!
The whirling tissue of light
    is woven and grows solid beneath us;
The sea-clear sapphire of air, the sea-dark clarity,
    stretches both sea-cliff and ocean.

The Alchemist
Chant for the Transmutation of Metals

Sail of Claustra, Aelis, Azalais,
As you move among the bright trees;
As your voices, under the larches of Paradise
Make a clear sound,
Sail of Claustra, Aelis, Azalais,
Raimona, Tibors, Berangèrë,
'Neath the dark gleam of the sky;
Under night, the peacock-throated,
Bring the saffron-coloured shell,
Bring the red gold of the maple,
Bring the light of the birch tree in autumn
Mirals, Cembelins, Audiards,
                    Remember this fire.
Elain, Tireis, Alcmena
'Mid the silver rustling of wheat,
Agradiva, Anhes, Ardenca,
From the plum-coloured lake, in stillness,
From the molten dyes of the water
Bring the burnished nature of fire;
Briseis, Lianor, Loica,
From the wide earth and the olive,
From the poplars weeping their amber,
By the bright flame of the fishing torch
                    Remember this fire.
Midonz, with the gold of the sun, the leaf of the poplar, by
    the light of the amber,
Midonz, daughter of the sun, shaft of the tree, silver of the
    leaf, light of the yellow of the amber,

Midonz, gift of the God, gift of the light, gift of the amber
    of the sun,
                      Give light to the metal.
Anhes of Rocacoart, Ardenca, Aemelis,
From the power of grass,
From the white, alive in the seed,
From the heat of the bud,
From the copper of the leaf in autumn,
From the bronze of the maple, from the sap in the bough;
Lianor, Ioanna, Loica,
By the stir of the fin,
By the trout asleep in the gray-green of water;
Vanna, Mandetta, Viera, Alodetta, Picarda, Manuela
From the red gleam of copper,
Ysaut, Ydone, slight rustling of leaves,
Vierna, Jocelynn, daring of spirits,
By the mirror of burnished copper,
                O Queen of Cypress,
Out of Erebus, the flat-lying breadth,
Breath that is stretched out beneath the world:
Out of Erebus, out of the flat waste of air, lying beneath the
    world;
Out of the brown leaf-brown colourless
                Bring the imperceptible cool.
Elain, Tireis, Alcmena,
                Quiet this metal!
Let the manes put off their terror, let them put off their
    aqueous bodies with fire.
Let them assume the milk-white bodies of agate.
Let them draw together the bones of the metal.

Selvaggia, Guiscarda, Mandetta,
                Rain flakes of gold on the water,
Azure and flaking silver of water,
Alcyon, Phætona, Alcmena,
Pallor of silver, pale lustre of Latona,
By these, from the malevolence of the dew
                Guard this alembic.
Elain, Tireis, Allodetta
                Quiet this metal.

Cantus Planus

The black panther lies under his rose tree
And the fawns come to sniff at his sides:

Evoe, Evoe, Evoe Baccho, O
ZAGREUS, *Zagreus*, Zagreus,

The black panther lies under his rose tree.

||Hesper   adest.   Hesper || adest.
Hesper || adest.||

Poem
Abbreviated from the Conversation of Mr T. E. H.

Over the flat slope of St Eloi
A wide wall of sandbags.
Night,
In the silence desultory men
Pottering over small fires, cleaning their mess-tins:
To and fro, from the lines,
Men walk as on Piccadilly,
Making paths in the dark,
Through scattered dead horses,
Over a dead Belgian's belly.

The Germans have rockets. The English have no rockets.
Behind the lines, cannon, hidden, lying back miles.
Before the line, chaos:

My mind is a corridor. The minds about me are corridors.
Nothing suggests itself. There is nothing to do but keep on.

PERSONÆ (1926)

Salutation the Third

Let us deride the smugness of "The Times": GUFFAW!
      So much for the gagged reviewers,
It will pay them when the worms are wriggling in their vitals;
These are they who objected to newness,
Here are their tomb-stones.
      They supported the gag and the ring:
A little BLACK BOX contains them.
      So shall you be also,
You slut-bellied obstructionist,
You sworn foe to free speech and good letters,
You fungus, you continuous gangrene.

Come, let us on with the new deal,
      Let us be done with pandars and jobbery,
Let us spit upon those who pat the big-bellies for profit,
Let us go out in the air a bit.

Or perhaps I *will* die at thirty?
Perhaps you will have the pleasure of defiling my pauper's
      grave;
I wish you joy, I proffer you all my assistance.
It has been your habit for long
      to do away with good writers,
You either drive them mad, or else you blink at their suicides,
Or else you condone their drugs,
      and talk of insanity and genius,
But I will not go mad to please you,
      I will not flatter you with an early death,
Oh, no, I will stick it out,
      Feel your hates wriggling about my feet
As a pleasant tickle,
      to be observed with derision,

Though many move with suspicion,
   Afraid to say that they hate you;
The taste of my boot?
   Here is the taste of my boot,
Caress it,
   lick off the blacking.

Monumentum Aere, Etc.

You say that I take a good deal upon myself;
That I strut in the robes of assumption.

In a few years no one will remember the *buffo*,
No one will remember the trivial parts of me,
The comic detail will be absent.
As for you, you will rot in the earth,
And it is doubtful if even your manure will be rich enough

To keep grass
Over your grave.

Come My Cantilations

Come my cantilations,
Let us dump our hatreds into one bunch and be done with
  them,
Hot sun, clear water, fresh wind,
Let me be free of pavements,
Let me be free of the printers.
Let come beautiful people
Wearing raw silk of good colour,
Let come the graceful speakers,
Let come the ready of wit,
Let come the gay of manner, the insolent and the exulting.
We speak of burnished lakes,
Of dry air, as clear as metal.

Before Sleep

1.

The lateral vibrations caress me,
They leap and caress me,
They work pathetically in my favour,
They seek my financial good.

She of the spear stands present.
The gods of the underworld attend me, O Annubis,
These are they of thy company.
With a pathetic solicitude they attend me;
Undulent,
Their realm is the lateral courses.

2.

Light!
I am up to follow thee, Pallas.
Up and out of their caresses.
You were gone up as a rocket,
Bending your passages from right to left and from left to right
In the flat projection of a spiral.
The gods of drugged sleep attend me,
Wishing me well;
I am up to follow thee, Pallas.

Post Mortem Conspectu

A brown, fat babe sitting in the lotus,
And you were glad and laughing
With a laughter not of this world.
It is good to splash in the water
And laughter is the end of all things.

Fratres Minores

With minds still hovering above their testicles
Certain poets here and in France
Still sigh over established and natural fact
Long since fully discussed by Ovid.
They howl. They complain in delicate and exhausted metres
That the twitching of three abdominal nerves
Is incapable of producing a lasting Nirvana.

FROM *Instigations* (1920):

Cantico del Sole

The thought of what America would be like
If the Classics had a wide circulation
        Troubles my sleep,
The thought of what America,
The thought of what America,
The thought of what America would be like
If the Classics had a wide circulation
        Troubles my sleep.
Nunc dimittis, now lettest thou thy servant,
Now lettest thou thy servant
        Depart in peace.
The thought of what America,
The thought of what America,
The thought of what America would be like
If the Classics had a wide circulation . . .
            Oh well!
            It troubles my sleep.

FROM

GUIDO CAVALCANTI RIME

EDIZÌONE RAPEZZATA FRA LE ROVINE

Who is she that comes, makyng turn every man's eye
And makyng the air to tremble with a bright clearenesse
That leadeth with her Love, in such nearness
No man may proffer of speech more than a sigh?

Ah God, what she is like when her owne eye turneth, is
Fit for Amor to speake, for I can not at all;
Such is her modesty, I would call
Every woman else but an useless uneasiness.

No one could ever tell all of her pleasauntness
In that every high noble vertu leaneth to herward,
So Beauty sheweth her forth as her Godhede;

Never before was our mind so high led,
Nor have we so much of heal as will afford
That our thought may take her immediate in its embrace.

———

A breath of thy beauty passeth through mine eyes
And rouseth up an air within my mind
That moves a spirit so to love inclined
It breedeth, in all air, nobilities.

No vile spirit to discern his vertu is able
So great is the might of it,
He is the spryte that putteth a trembling fyt
On spirit that maketh a woman mercyable.

And then from this spirit there moveth about
Another yet so gentle and soft that he
Causeth to follow after him a spirit of pity

From the which a very rain of spirits poureth out,
And he doth carry upon him the key
To every spirit, so keen is his breath to see.

———

Surely thy wit giveth not welcome place
To that which this morn madeth thine honour to want,
Fye, how swiftly art thou shown mendicaunt
By that red air that is suffusing thy face.

Perhaps thou art let on rampage
By love of what is caught in Sesto's ring
Or some vile beam is come here to engage
Thee to make merry, whereof I am sorrowing,

Aye, sorrowing, so much as thou mayst see
In that before my Lady I dare not to flaunt,
Whereby I lose all of love's agrement;

The key brok'n off before me, her disdeign
Stuck in my heart to turn, making me
To love confusion, or to be gaye, or playne.

Tondo di Sesto, printed *tondo sesto* and unexplained or atrociously explained
in previous editions.
"Taken in an empty hoop of sophistries."
I find in Fr. Florentino's "Manuale di Storia della Filosofia":
Sesto Empirico. . . . Ogni, sillogismo è per lui un circolo vizioso, perchè
la premessa maggiore dovrebbe essere assicurata da una induzione completa:
ora, affinchè possa dirsi completa, è evidente che vi si debbia trovar com-
pressa anche la conclusione del sillogismo che ancora si ha da dimostrare etc.
The application here must be considered in relation to the whole philo-
sophic and scholastic background, the attribution of "Da più a uno fece sil-
logismo" etc.

This fayre Mistress, whereby Love maketh plain
How full he is of prowesse, adornèd to a marvel,
Tuggeth the heart out of thy masking-shell,
The which enhaunceth his life in her domain.

For her quadrangle is guarded with such a sweet smell
Every unicorn of India smelleth it out,
But her vertue against thee in jousting-bout
Turneth against us for to be cruel.

She is, certes, of such great avail
Nothing of all perfectness in her lacketh
That can be in creature subject to death,

Neither in this mortality did foresight fail.
'Tis fitting thy wit make known
Only that which it can take, or mistake, for its own.

With other
texts this is:
Hath of
itself, or
hath by
clarity as it
floweth
clearing
itself, its
savour my
friend, from
the one en-
chanteresse.

Every fresh and sweet-flavoured water-spring
Hath in Galicia its taste and its clearness,
Bernardo, my friend, from but the one
    enchanteresse;
It was she that answered thy sharp rhyming.

And in that Court where Love himself fableth
Telling of beauties he hath seen, he saith:
This pagan and lovely woman hath in her
All strange adornments that ever were.

Though I be heavy with the pain of that sigh
That maketh my heart burn but as a light
In shipwracke, I send Pinella a river in full
    flood

Mi pare che
questo
sonetto
accompagnava
un com-
mento o
traduzione
di qualche
filosofo arabo,
diciamo
Avicenna,
del quale
parla allegori-
camente.
    E.P.

Stockéd with Lamia-nymphs, that are foreby
Served each with her slave hand-maids, fair
    to sight
And yet more fair by manner of gentlehood.

Donna mi Prega

*(Dedicace—To Thomas Campion his ghost, and
to the ghost of Henry Lawes, as prayer
for the revival of music)*

BECAUSE a lady asks me, I would tell
   Of an affect that comes often and is fell
And is so overweening: Love by name.
E'en its deniers can now hear the truth,
I for the nonce to them that know it call,
Having no hope at all
                    that man who is base in heart
Can bear his part of wit
                    into the light of it,
And save they know't aright from nature's source
I have no will to prove Love's course
                                or say
Where he takes rest; who maketh him to be;
Or what his active *virtu* is, or what his force;
Nay, nor his very essence or his mode;
What his placation; why he is in verb,
Or if a man have might
           To show him visible to men's sight.

IN memory's locus taketh he his state   *Place*
   Formed there in manner as a mist of light   *La o've*
Upon a dusk that is come from Mars and stays.   *e*
Love is created, hath a sensate name,   *chi lo*
His modus takes from soul, from heart his will;   *fa*
From form seen doth he start, that, understood,   *creare*
Taketh in latent intellect—
As in a subject ready—
                    place and abode,
Yet in that place it ever is unstill,
Spreading its rays, it tendeth never down
By quality, but is its own effect unendingly
Not to delight, but in an ardour of thought
That the base likeness of it kindleth not.

IT is not *virtu*, but perfection's source   *Virtú*
Lying within perfection postulate   *e*
Not by the reason, but 'tis felt, I say.   *potenza*
Beyond salvation, holdeth its judging force
Maintains intention reason's peer and mate;
Poor in discernment, being thus weakness' friend,
Often his power meeteth with death in the end
Be he withstayed
                    or from true course
                                        bewrayed
E'en though he meet not with hate
                                  or villeiny
Save that perfection fails, be it but a little;
Nor can man say he hath his life by chance
Or that he hath not stablished seigniory
Or loseth power, e'en lost to memory.

HE comes to be and is when will's so great   *essenza*
It twists itself from out all natural measure;   *e*
Leisure's adornment puts he then never on,   *movimento*
Never thereafter, but moves changing state,
Moves changing colour, or to laugh or weep
Or wries the face with fear and little stays,
Yea, resteth little
                    yet is found the most
Where folk of worth be host.
And his strange property sets sighs to move
And wills man look into unformèd space
Rousing there thirst
                      that breaketh into flame.
None can imagine love
                        that knows not love;
Love doth not move, but draweth all to him;
Nor doth he turn
                  for a whim
                              to find delight
Nor to seek out, surely,
                          great knowledge or slight.

L OOK drawn from like,
              delight maketh certain in seeming   *piacimento*
Nor can in covert cower,
              beauty so near,
Not yet wild-cruel as darts,
So hath man craft from fear
              in such his desire
To follow a noble spirit,
              edge, that is, and point to the dart,
Though from her face indiscernible;
He, caught, falleth
              plumb on to the spike of the targe.
Who well proceedeth, form not seeth,
              following his own emanation.
There, beyond colour, essence set apart,
In midst of darkness light light giveth forth
Beyond all falsity, worthy of faith, alone
That in him solely is compassion born.

S AFE may'st thou go my canzon whither thee pleaseth
     Thou art so fair attired that every man and each
Shall praise thy speech
So he have sense or glow with reason's fire,
To stand with other
              hast thou no desire.

The Canzone

As it appears in the manuscript "Ld," Laurenziana 46–40
folio 32 verso, with a few errors corrected. Accents added
from the Giuntine edition.

Edizione Giuntina 1527.

D ONNA mi priegha
      perch'i volglio dire   *io*
   D'un accidente   *uno*
     che sovente
       é fero
Ed é sí altero
    ch'é chiamato amore   *Amore*

S ICCHE chi l negha   *Si chì lo*
     possa il ver sentire
Ond a'l presente   *Ed a'l*
    chonoscente
      chero
Perch' i no spero   *io nò*
    ch om di basso chore   *e'huom*

A TAL ragione portj chonoscenza   *raggio ne*
  Chè senza
    natural dimostramento
Non o talento   *hó*
    di voler provare   Ld. *mostrare*
Laove nascie e chì lo fá criare   *Lá dove ei posa, è*

E QUAL è sua virtu e sua potenza   *sia . . vertute, è potenza*
  L'essenza
     e poi ciaschun suo movimento   ms. *per*
E' l piacimento
    che'l fá dire amare
E se hom per veder lo puó mostrare:-   *huomo*

IN quella parte
              dove sta memoria   *memora*
Prende suo stato   *ms. su*
              sí formato
                        chome
Diafan dal lume
              d' una schuritade   *oscuritate*

LA qual da Marte   *Loqual*
              viene e fá dimora
Elgli é creato
              e a sensato   *ed há*
                        nome
D' alma chostume
              di chor volontade   *è di cor*

VIEN da veduta forma ches s'intende   *chè s'*
      Che 'l prende   Giuntine and Ld.
                        nel possibile intelletto   *Chè prende*
Chome in subgetto
              locho e dimoranza
E in quella parte mai non a possanza   *há posanza*
              ms. ca. pesança

PERCHÈ da qualitatde non disciende
      Risplende   *ms. risprende*
                  in sé perpetuale effecto
Non a diletto   *há*
              mà consideranza
Perche non pote laire simiglglianza:−   *Si, ch'ei non puote*
                                                            largir simiglianza

on é virtute
           mà da questa vene   *dà quella*
  Perfezione   *Perchè perfettion sì*
      ches si pone
           tale
Non razionale
     mà che si sente dicho   *omits si*

Fuor di salute
       giudichar mantene
E l antenzione   *Chè lá intenzion*
     per ragione   *per ragion*
        vale
Discerne male   ms. *Diserue*
     in chui é vizio amicho

Di sua virtu seghue ispesso morte   *sua potenza . . . spesso*
  Se forte
      la virtú fosse impedita
La quale aita
      la contrara via   *contraria*
Nonche opposito natural sia   *Non perchè opposta naturale*

Mà quanto che da ben perfett e torte   *buon perfetto tort'é*
  Per sorte   ms. *forte*
     non po dir om ch abbi vita   *puó . . . c' baggia*
Che stabilita
     non a singnioria   *há*
A simil puó valer quant uom l obblia:– *valor quando s'oblia*

Lʙssᴇʀ é quando
         lo volere a tanto
     Ch oltre misura
         di natura
            torna
Poi non si addorna
         di riposo maj

Mᴏᴠᴇ changiando
         cholr riso in pianto
E lla fighura
      con paura
         storna
Pocho soggiorna
       anchor di lui vedraj

Cʜᴇ n gente di valore il piu si trova
  La nova
       qualità move a sospirj
E vol ch om mirj
        in un formato locho
Destandos'ira la qual manda focho

Iɴᴍᴀɢɪɴᴀʀ nol puo hom che nol prova
  E non si mova
       perch' a llui si tirj
E non si aggirj
      per trovarvi giocho
E certamente gran saver nè pocho:–

ms. *omits* é
é
oltra

s'adorna

core, è riso, è pianto

i sospiri

ms. Ld.
Destandositj loqual

puote
Giá non
ms. ca. *Ne mo'va gia*
giri

Nè certamente

DA ssimil tragge   *Di*
            complessione e sghuardj   ms. *comprenssione*
    Che fá parere   *sguardo. omits e*
            lo piacere
                    piu certo   *omits piu*
Non puó choverto
            star quand é si giunto

NON giá selvagge
            la biltá son dardj   *le. . . dardo*
Ch a tal volere   *Chè tal*
        per temere
                sperto   *esperto*
Hom seghue merto   *Consegue*
            spirito che punto   *ch'é*

E Non si può chonosciere per lo viso
    Chompriso
                biancho in tale obbietto chade   *,bianco,*
E chi ben aude   *vade*
            forma non si vede   *Ca. in forma*
Perchè lo mena chi dallui procede   *dà lei*

FUOR di cholore essere diviso   *d'essere*
    Asciso   *Assiso*
            mezzo schuro luce rade   *in mezzo oscura luci*
Fuor d'ongni fraude
                dice dengno in fede
Chè solo da chostui nasce merzede:–   *di*

TU puoj sichuramente gir chanzone
    Dove ti piace ch i t o sí ornata   *ch'io t'hó si adornata*
    Ch assa lodata   *assai*
            sará tua ragione
Dalle persone
            ch anno intendimento
Di star con l' altre tu non aj talento:–

ALFRED VENISON'S POEMS

Social Credit Themes

By
The Poet of Titchfield Street

"Only Social Credit could have produced this poet."
E. POUND

TO
S. C. N.

The Charge of the Bread Brigade

Half a loaf, half a loaf,
Half a loaf? Um-hum?
Down through the vale of gloom
Slouched the ten million,
  Onward th' 'ungry blokes,
  Crackin' their smutty jokes!
We'll send 'em mouchin' 'ome,
Damn the ten million!

There goes the night brigade,
They got no steady trade,
Several old so'jers know
  Monty has blunder'd.
Theirs not to reason why,
Theirs but to buy the pie,
Slouching and mouching,
  Lousy ten million!

Plenty to right of 'em,
Plenty to left of 'em,
  Yes, wot is left of 'em,
Damn the ten million.
Stormed at by press and all,
How shall we dress 'em all?
  Glooming and mouching!

See 'em go slouching there,
With cowed and crouching air
  Dundering dullards!
How the whole nation shook
While Milord Beaverbrook
  Fed 'em with hogwash!

Alf's Second Bit

Sir,—Your printing of my little piece about the Hunger Marchers has encouraged me to send you another. They come to me while I'm pushing my rabbit-barrow down Titchfield Street. I don't claim to be as educated as some of your other poets; but I attend night schools and pick up a bit of the dictionary that way. It would tickle my missus to see this new bit in print.   A.V.

The Neo-Commune

Manhood of England,
Dougth of the Shires,
      Want Russia to save 'em
And answer their prayers.
Want Russia to save 'em;
Lenin to save 'em; Trotsky to save 'em
(And valets to shave 'em)
The youth of the Shires!

Down there in Cambridge
Between auction and plain bridge,
      Romance, revolution 1918!
An idea between 'em
I says! 'ave you seen 'em?
The flower of Cambridge,
The youth of the Shires?

Alf's Third Bit

Sir,—Lumme, I was pleased, and so was the missus, to see my bit in your paper last week. Any luck this time?   A.V.

Dole the Bell! Bell the Dole!

Whom can these duds attack?
Soapy Sime? Slipp'ry Mac?
Naught but a shirt is there

Such as the fascists wear,
Never the man inside
Moving a nation-wide
　　Disgust with hokum.

Plenty to right of 'em,
Plenty to left of 'em,
Yeh! What is left of 'em,
　　Boozy, uncertain.
See how they take it all,
Down there in Clerkenwall
Readin' th' pypers!

Syrup and soothing dope,
Sure, they can live on hope,
　　Ain't yeh got precedent?
Ten years and twelve years gone,
Ten more and nothing done,
　　GOD save Britannia!

Alf's Fourth Bit

Sir,—That looked to me all right last week, though I didn't
think you'd print my letter as well. How's this?　　A. V.

Rudyard the dud yard,
Rudyard the false measure,
Told 'em that glory
Ain't always a pleasure,
But said it wuz glorious nevertheless
To lick the boots of the bloke
That makes the worst mess.

Keep up the grand system
Don't tell what you know,
Your grandad got the rough edge.
Ain't it always been so?

Your own ma' warn't no better
Than the Duchess of Kaugh.
My cousin's named Baldwin
An' 'e looks like a toff.

You 'ark to the sargent,
And don't read no books;
Go to God like a sojer;
What counts is the looks.

Alf's Fifth Bit

Sir,—I've tried a bit of fancy-work this time; and I hope to
see it in print like the rest.   A. V.

The pomps of butchery, financial power,
Told 'em to die in war, and then to save,
Then cut their saving to the half or lower;
When will this system lie down in its grave?

The pomps of Fleet St., festering year on year,
Hid truth and lied, and lied and hid the facts.
The pimps of Whitehall ever more in fear,
Hid health statistics, dodged the Labour Acts.

All drew their pay, and as the pay grew less,
The money rotten and more rotten yet,
Hid more statistics, more feared to confess
C.3, C.4, 'twere better to forget

How many weak of mind, how much tuberculosis
Filled the back alleys and the back to back houses.
"The medical report this week discloses . . ."
"Time for that question!" Front Bench interposes.

Time for that question? and the time is NOW.
Who ate the profits, and who locked 'em in
The unsafe safe, wherein all rots, and no man can say how
What was the nation's, now by Norman's kin
Is one day blown up large, the next, sucked in?

Alf's Sixth Bit

Sir,—I've put the names in, but you can leave them out if
they're friends of yours. It's what I think.   A. V.

Let some new lying ass,
Who knows not what is or was,
          Talk economics,
Pay for his witless noise,
Get the kid nice new toys,
          Call him "professor."

Lies from the specialist
Give t'old ones a newer twist
          Harder to untie.
Here comes the hired gang
Blood on each tired fang
          Covered with lip-stick.

"Oh, what a charming man,"—
That's how the press blurb ran,—
          "Professor K———s is."
Now they can't fire him.
NO! they won't hire him.
          Still Dr. S———'s
Not tied to the ring around,
Not quite snowed under.
          Being a physicist
They can't quite bribe him.
Oh, what a noise they made
          Those parliamentarians.

Oh what a fuss they made
Stirring the marmalade
          These parliamentarians
Never an honest word
In their dim halls was heard
          For more than a decade.

Alf's Seventh Bit

Sir,—If the Co-ops want my address, you can give it to them. I guess they ought to be grateful to you and me for showing up the game.   A. V.

Did I 'ear it 'arf in a doze:
The Co-ops was a goin' somewhere,
Did I 'ear it while pickin' 'ops;
How they better start takin' care,

That the papers were gettin' together
And the larger stores were likewise
Considering something that would, as you
Might say, be a surprise

To the Co-ops, a echo or somethin'?
They tell me that branded goods
Don't get a discount like Mr. Selfridge
Of 25 per cent. on their ads., and the woods

Is where the Co-ops are goin' to,
And that Oxford Street site
Is not suited to co-operation—
A sort of Arab's dream in the night.

"We have plenty, so let it be."
The example of these consumers in co-operation
Might cause thought and be therefore
A peril to Selfridge and the nation.

Alf's Eighth Bit

Sir,—I've been reading some of the other fellers' poetry lately; and, lumme, if I don't think I can do it as well as any of them; and with real meat in mine, not just my own rabbits. What say you?   A. V.

Vex not thou the banker's mind
  (His *what?*) with a show of sense,
Vex it not, Willie, his mind,
  Or pierce its pretence
On the supposition that it ever
Was other, or that this cheerful giver
Will give, save to the blind.

Come not anear the dark-browed sophist
  Who on the so well-paid ground
Will cheerfully tell you a fist is no fist,
  Come not here
With 2 and 2 making 4 in reason,
Knowest thou not the truth is never in season
  In these quarters or Fleet St.?

In his eye there is death,—I mean the banker's,—
  In his purse there is deceit,
It is he who buys gold-braid for the swankers
  And gives you Australian iced rabbits' meat
In place of the roast beef of Britain,
And leaves you a park bench to sit on
If you git off the Embankment.

This is the kind of tone and solemnity
  That used to be used on the young,
My old man got no indemnity
  But he swaller'd his tongue.
Like all his class was told to hold it in those days,
To mind their "p"s and their "q"s and their ways
An' be thankful for occasional holidays.

I don't quite see the joke any more,
  Or why we should stand to attention
And lick the dirt off the floor
  In the hope of honourable mention
From a great employer like Selfridge
Or a buyer of space in the papers.
I'm getting too old for such capers.

Alf's Ninth Bit

Sir,—Here's another improvement on a worn-out model. I
did it very nearly in my sleep. A bit of genius, what?

A. V.

Listen, my children, and you shall hear
The midnight activities of Whats-his-Name,
Scarcely a general now known to fame
Can tell you of that famous day and year.

When feeble Mr. Asquith, getting old,
The destinies of England were almost sold
To a Welsh shifter with an ogling eye,
And Whats-his-name attained nobility.

The Dashing Rupert of the pulping trade,
Rough from the virgin forests inviolate,
Thus rose in Albion, and tickled the State
And where he once set foot, right there he stayed.

Old 'Erb was doting, so the rumour ran,
And Rupert ran the rumour round in wheels,
And David's harp let out heart-rending squeals:
"Find us a harpist!! DAVID is the man!!"

Dave was the man to sell the shot and shell,
And Basil was the Greek that rode around
On sea and land, with all convenience found
To sell, to sell, to sell, that's it, to SELL

Destroyers, bombs and spitting mitrailleuses.
He used to lunch with Balfour in those days
And if the papers seldom sang his praise,
The simple Britons never knew he was,

Until a narsty German told them so.
Listen, my children, and you shall hear
Of things that happened very long ago,
And scarcely heed one word of what you hear.

Bury it all, bury it all well deep,
And let the blighters start it all over again.
They'll trick you again and again, as you sleep;
But you shall know that these were the men.

Alf's Tenth Bit

Sir,—Seems to me that at this rate I shall have written
enough to make a book before long. But I'm beginning to be
guessed in Titchfield Street; and a lady asked me the other
day if I sold venison! Is this what they call fame?   A. V.

Wind

Scarce and thin, scarce and thin
    The government's excuse,
Never at all will they do
    Aught of the slightest use.
Over the dying half-wits blow,
Over the empty-headed, and the slow
    Marchers, not getting for'arder,
While Ramsay MacDonald sleeps, sleeps.

Fester and rot, fester and rot,
    And angle and tergiversate
One thing among all things you will not
    Do, that is: *think*, before it's too late.
Election will not come very soon,
And those born with a silver spoon,
    Will keep it a little longer,
Until the mind of the old nation gets a little stronger.

Alf's Eleventh Bit

Sir,—I've had a go this week at the big bugs; and don't I know 'em! My little kid is one of their victims, and a proper mess they'd make of him if I didn't watch out.   A. V.

Sir Launcelot Has a Newspaper Now

My great press cleaves the guts of men,
My great noise drowns their cries,
My sales beat all the other ten,
Because I print most lies.

I get the kids out on the street
To sell the papers early,
At one o'clock I go to lunch,
Looking so big and burly.

I wear a fine fur coat and gloves
And spats above my shoes,
They have to do the dirty work,
I do whatever I choose.

They have to stand about in mud
And cold fit for despair,
But I have made a ruddy pile
From profits on hot air.

I pump the market up and down
By rigging stock reports,
And get my pickings on the side
From dress goods ads, and sports.

The King was once the biggest thing
In England? I'll say YES!
But knights and Lords to-day respect
The power of the Press.

Alf's Twelfth Bit

Sir,—Can I bring rabbits out of the hat as well as off my barrow? Watch me! How's this for the rabbit in Mr. Montague's hat? Didn't know it was there, did he?   A. V.

Ballad for the "Times" Special Silver Number

Sez the *Times* a silver lining
Is what has set us pining,
               Montague, Montague!

In the season sad and weary
When our minds are very bleary,
               Montague, Montague!

There is Sir Hen. Deterding
His phrases interlarding,
               Montague, Montague!

With the this and that and what
For putting silver on the spot,
               Montague, Montague!

Just drop it in the slot
And it will surely boil the pot,
               Montague, Montague!

Gold, of course, is solid too,
But some silver set to stew
               Might do, too. Montague!

With a lively wood-pulp "ad."
To cheer the bad and sad,
               Montague, Montague!

Another Bit—and an Offer

Sir,—I reckon the apparatus is punctured, what with the Budget and all. With your kind permish, I'll make my tens of thousands of readers a sporting offer. The first that sends you £10 shall have the twelve poems dedicated to him and printed in a book to sell off my barrer with the rabbits. And you, kind Sir, will see fair play as between patron and poet. Now, then, who's going to be the lucky first?

I see by the morning papers
That America's sturdy sons
Have started a investigation
Of the making of guns.

The morning paper tells me
They have asked the senate to guess
Whether Mr. Dupont and the gun-sharks
Have influence with the press.

I sit alone in the twilight
After my work is done
And wonder if my day's three and eight-pence
Would count on the price of a gun.

Was I started wrong as a kiddie,
And would my old man have been smarter
To send me to work in Vickers
Instead of being a carter?

Safe and Sound

My name is Nunty Cormorant
And my finance is sound,
I lend you Englishmen hot air
At one and three the pound.

I lend you Englishmen hot air
And I get all the beef
While you stalwart sheep of freedom
Are on the poor relief.

Wot oh! my buxom hearties,
What ain't got work no more
And don't know what bug is a-bitin'
To keep your feelin's sore,

There is blokes in automobiles
And their necks sunk into fur
That keep on gettin' usury
To make 'em cosier.

I read these fellers puts it
Most tidily away
And then lends out their printed slips
To keep the wolf away

From their vaults and combination
Safes in Thread and Needle street.
I wouldn't 'ave the needle
If I had more grub to eat.

Oh the needle is your portion,
My sufferin' fellow men,
Till the King shall take the notion
To own his coin again.

                                        A. V.

Song of Six Hundred M.P.'s

"We yare 'ere met together
    in this momentuous hower,
Ter lick th' bankers' dirty boots
    an' keep the Bank in power.

We are 'ere met together
    ter grind the same old axes
And keep the people in its place
    a'payin' us the taxes.

We are six hundred beefy men
    (but mostly gas and suet)
An' every year we meet to let
    some other feller do it."

I see their 'igh 'ats on the seats
    an' them sprawlin' on the benches
And thinks about a Rowton 'ouse
    and a lot of small street stenches.

"O Britain, muvver of parliaments,
    'ave you seen yer larst sweet litter?
Could yeh swap th' brains of orl this lot
    fer 'arft a pint o' bitter?"

"I couldn't," she sez, "an' I aint tried,
    They're me own," she sez to me,
"As footlin' a lot as was ever spawned
    to defend democracy."

                                        A. V.

Ole Kate

When I was only a youngster,
    Sing: toodle doodlede oot!
Ole Kate would git her 'arf a pint
    An wouldn't giv' a damn hoot.

"Them stairs! them stairs, them gordam stairs
Will be the death of me"
I never heerd her say nothin'
About the priv'lege of liberty.

She'd come a sweatin' up with the coals
An a-sloshin' round with 'er mop,
Startin' in about 6 a.m.
And didn't seem never to stop.

She died on the job they tells me,
Fell plump into her pail.
Never got properly tanked as I saw,
And never got took to jail,

Just went on a sloshin'
And totin' up scuttles of coal,
And kissin' her cat fer diversion,
God rest her sloshin' soul.

"Gimme a kissy-cuddle"
She'd say to her tibby-cat,
But she never made no mention
Of this here proletariat.

The Baby

The baby new to earth and sky
Has never until now
Unto himself the question put
Or asked us if the cow

Is higher in the mental scale
Than men like me and you,
Or if the cow refrains from food
Till she finds work to do.

"The baby new to earth and sky,"
As Tennyson has written,
Just goes ahead and sucks a teat
Like to-day's great men in Britain.

A. V.

National Song (E.C.)

There is no land like England
Where banks rise day by day,
There are no banks like English banks
To make the people pay.

There is no such land of castles
Where an Englishman is free
To read his smutty literature
With muffins at his tea.

Chorus:

For the French have comic papers—
Not that nice Britons read 'em,
But the bawdy little Britons
Have bank sharks to bleed 'em
And to keep an eye on their readin' matter
Lest they should overhear the distressing chatter
Of the new economical theories
And ask inconvenient queeries.

GUIDE TO KULCHUR

The Lioness Warns Her Cubs

Ware of one with sharp weapons
Who carries a tiger-tail tuft
Ware of one who comes with white dogs,
O son of the shorthaired lioness,
Thou my child with short ears,
Son of the lion, that I feed on raw meat,
Carnivore,
Son of the lioness whose nostrils are red with bloody-booty,
Thou with the bloodred nostrils,
Son of the lioness who drinkest swampwater,
Water-lapper my son.

Praise Song of the Buck-Hare

I am the buck-hare, I am,
The shore is my playground
Green underwood is my feeding.

I am the buck-hare, I am,
What's that damn man got wrong with him?
Skin with no hair on, that's his trouble.

I am the buck-hare, I am,
Mountaintop is my playing field
Red heather my feeding.

I am the buck-hare, I am,
What's wrong with the fellow there with his eyes on a girl?
I say, is his face red!

I am the buck-hare, I am,
Got my eyes out ahead
You don't lose me on a dark night, you don't.

I am the buck-hare, I am,
What's wrong with that bloke with a poor coat?
Lice, that's what's he got, fair crawlin' he is.

I am the buck-hare, I am,
I got buck teeth.
Buck-hare never gets thin.

I am the BUCK-HARE, I am,
What's that fool got the matter with him?
Can't find the road! Ain't got no road he CAN find.

I am the buck-hare, I am,
I got my wood-road,
I got my form.

I am the buck-hare, I am,
What ails that fool man anyhow?
Got a brain, won't let him set quiet.

I am the buck-hare, I am,
I live in the big plain,
There's where I got my corral.

I am the buck-hare, I said so.
What's wrong with that loafer?
He's been to sleep in a bad place, he has.

I am the buck-hare,
I live in the bush, I do,
That's my road over yonder.

I am the buck-hare, I said so,
Women that don't get up in the morning,
I know how they look by the chimney.

I am the buck-hare, I said it,
I can tell any dumb loafer
Lying along by the hedge there.

I am the buck-hare,
Women don't love their men?
I can tell by what their cows look like.

PERSONÆ
(enlarged version, 1949)

To Whistler, American
On the loan exhibit of his paintings at the Tate Gallery.

You also, our first great,
Had tried all ways;
Tested and pried and worked in many fashions,
And this much gives me heart to play the game.

Here is a part that's slight, and part gone wrong,
And much of little moment, and some few
Perfect as Dürer!
"In the Studio" and these two portraits,* if I had my choice!
And then these sketches in the mood of Greece?

You had your searches, your uncertainties,
And this is good to know—for us, I mean,
Who bear the brunt of our America
And try to wrench her impulse into art.

You were not always sure, not always set
To hiding night or tuning "symphonies";
Had not one style from birth, but tried and pried
And stretched and tampered with the media.

You and Abe Lincoln from that mass of dolts
Show us there's chance at least of winning through.

* "Brown and Gold—de Race."
  "Grenat et Or—Le Petit Cardinal."

(*Poetry, 1912*)

Middle-Aged

"'Tis but a vague, invarious delight
As gold that rains about some buried king.

As the fine flakes,
When tourists frolicking
Stamp on his roof or in the glazing light
Try photographs, wolf down their ale and cakes
And start to inspect some further pyramid;

As the fine dust, in the hid cell
Beneath their transitory step and merriment,
Drifts through the air, and the sarcophagus
Gains yet another crust
Of useless riches for the occupant,
So I, the fires that lit once dreams
Now over and spent,
Lie dead within four walls
And so now love
Rains down and so enriches some stiff case,
And strews a mind with precious metaphors,

And so the space
Of my still consciousness
Is full of gilded snow,

The which, no cat has eyes enough
To see the brightness of."

(Poetry, 1912)

Abu Salammamm—A Song of Empire

*Being the sort of poem I would write if King George V should have me
chained to the fountain before Buckingham Palace, and should give me all
the food and women I wanted.*

To my brother in chains Bonga-Bonga.

Great is King George the Fifth,
     for he has chained me to this fountain;
He feeds me with beef-bones and wine.
Great is King George the Fifth—
His palace is white like marble,
His palace has ninety-eight windows,
His palace is like a cube cut in thirds,
It is he who has slain the Dragon
         and released the maiden Andromeda.
Great is King George the Fifth;
For his army is legion,
His army is a thousand and forty-eight soldiers
         with red cloths about their buttocks,
And they have red faces like bricks.
Great is the King of England and greatly to be feared,
For he has chained me to this fountain;
He provides me with women and drinks.
Great is King George the Fifth
         and very resplendent is this fountain.
It is adorned with young gods riding upon dolphins
And its waters are white like silk.
Great and Lofty is this fountain;
And seated upon it is the late Queen, Victoria,
The Mother of the great king, in a hoop-skirt,
   Like a woman heavy with a child.

Oh may the king live forever!
Oh may the king live for a thousand years!
For the young prince is foolish and headstrong;
He plagues me with jibes and sticks,
And when he comes into power
He will undoubtedly chain someone else to this fountain,
And my glory will
Be at an end.

                                        (Poetry, 1912)

M. Pom-POM

*(Caf' Conc' song
The Fifth, or Permanent International)*

M. Pom-POM allait en guerre
      Per vendere cannoni
Mon beau grand frère
Ne peut plus voir
      Per vendere cannoni.

M. Pom-POM est au scnat
      Per vendere cannoni
Pour vendre des canons
Pour vendre des canons
      To sell the god damn'd frogs
      A few more canon.

                    (Townsman, 1938)

CONFUCIUS
THE GREAT DIGEST &
UNWOBBLING PIVOT

An edition for Walter de Rachewiltz

Ta Hsio
The Great Digest

NOTE

Starting at the bottom as market inspector, having risen to be Prime Minister, Confucius is more concerned with the necessities of government, and of governmental administration than any other philosopher. He had two thousand years of documented history behind him which he condensed so as to render it useful to men in high official position, not making a mere collection of anecdotes as did Herodotus.

His analysis of why the earlier great emperors had been able to govern greatly was so sound that every durable dynasty, since his time, has risen on a Confucian design and been initiated by a group of Confucians. China was tranquil when her rulers understood these few pages. When the principles here defined were neglected, dynasties waned and chaos ensued. The proponents of a world order will neglect at their peril the study of the only process that has repeatedly proved its efficiency as social coordinate.

TERMINOLOGY

The light descending (from the sun, moon and stars.) To be watched as component in ideograms indicating spirits, rites, ceremonies.

The sun and moon, the total light process, the radiation, reception and reflection of light; hence, the intelligence. Bright, brightness, shining. Refer to Scotus Erigena, Grosseteste and the notes on light in my *Cavalcanti*.

"Sincerity." The precise definition of the word, pictorially the sun's lance coming to rest on the precise spot verbally. The right-hand half of this compound means: to perfect, bring to focus.

The eye (at the right) looking straight into the heart.

What results, i.e., the action resultant from this straight gaze into the heart. The "know thyself" carried into action. Said action also serving to clarify the self knowledge. To translate this simply as "virtue" is on a par with translating rhinoceros, fox and giraffe indifferently by "quadruped" or "animal."

The man in two successive positions.
Serves as prefix to indicate motion or action.

The will, the direction of the will, *directio voluntatis*, the officer standing over the heart.

To succeed in due hour. Prefix action taking effect at the sun's turn.

Fidelity to the given word. The man here standing by his word.

Humanitas, humanity, in the full sense of the word, "manhood." The man and his full contents.

道

The process. Footprints and the foot carrying the head; the head conducting the feet, an orderly movement under lead of the intelligence.

保
佑
命

This phrase—nourishing, supporting the destiny—should be compared with the *Odyssey*, I, 34.

鬼

This ideogram for a spirit contains two elements to be watched.

厶

One readily sees the similarity of this element to the bent heraldic arm of Armstrong and Strongi'tharm. I have never found it in composition save where there is indication of energy, I think we may say, a source of personally directed energy.

儿

The running legs indicate rapid motion or at least the capacity for motion.

CHU HSI'S PREFACE

My master the Philosopher Ch'eng says: The Great Learning, Great Digest, is the testament of Confucius, transmitted, the initial study for whomso would pass the gate into virtue. If we today can see how the men of old went about their study, it is due solely to the conservation of these strips of bamboo; the Analects and the Book of Mencius are subsequent.

He who studies must start from this meridian and study with warm precision; cutting to this homely pattern he will not botch.

CONFUCIUS' TEXT

1. The great learning [adult study, grinding the corn in the head's mortar to fit it for use] takes root in clarifying the way wherein the intelligence increases through the process of looking straight into one's own heart and acting on the results; it is rooted in watching with affection the way people grow; it is rooted in coming to rest, being at ease in perfect equity.

2. Know the point of rest and then have an orderly mode of procedure; having this orderly procedure one can "grasp the azure," that is, take hold of a clear concept; holding a clear concept one can be at peace [internally], being thus calm one can keep one's head in moments of danger; he who can keep his head in the presence of a tiger is qualified to come to his deed in due hour.

3. Things have roots and branches; affairs have scopes and beginnings. To know what precedes and what follows, is nearly as good as having a head and feet.

Mencius' epistemology starts from this verse.

4. The men of old wanting to clarify and diffuse throughout the empire that light which comes from looking straight into the heart and then acting, first set up good government in their own states; wanting good government in their states, they first established order in their own families; wanting order in the home, they first disciplined themselves; desiring

self-discipline, they rectified their own hearts; and wanting to rectify their hearts, they sought precise verbal definitions of their inarticulate thoughts [the tones given off by the heart]; wishing to attain precise verbal definitions, they set to extend their knowledge to the utmost. This completion of knowledge is rooted in sorting things into organic categories.

5. When things had been classified in organic categories, knowledge moved toward fulfillment; given the extreme knowable points, the inarticulate thoughts were defined with precision [the sun's lance coming to rest on the precise spot verbally]. Having attained this precise verbal definition [*aliter*, this sincerity], they then stabilized their hearts, they disciplined themselves; having attained self-discipline, they set their own houses in order; having order in their own homes, they brought good government to their own states; and when their states were well governed, the empire was brought into equilibrium.

6. From the Emperor, Son of Heaven, down to the common man, singly and all together, this self-discipline is the root.

7. If the root be in confusion, nothing will be well governed. The solid cannot be swept away as trivial, nor can trash be established as solid. It just doesn't happen.

"Take not cliff for morass and treacherous bramble."

明

The preceding is the first chapter of the canon containing Confucius' words as Tseng Tsze has handed them down. Now follow ten chapters of Tseng's thoughts as his disciples recorded them. In the oldest copies there was a certain confusion due to the shuffling of the original bamboo tablets. Now, basing myself on Ch'eng's conclusions, and having reexamined the classic text, I have arranged them as follows. ("On the left," in the Chinese method of writing.)—Chu Hsi.

TSENG'S COMMENT

I

1. It is said in the K'ang Proclamation: He showed his intelligence by acting straight from the heart.

2. It is said in the Great Announcement: He contemplated the luminous decree of heaven, and found the precise word wherewith to define it.

3. It is said in the Canon of the Emperor (Yau): His intelligence shone vital over the hill-crest, he clarified the high-reaching virtue, *id est*, that action which is due to direct self-knowledge.

4. All these statements proceed from the ideogram of the sun and moon standing together [that is, from the ideogram which expresses the total light process].

This is the first chapter of the comment giving the gist (sorting out the grist) of the expressions: Make clear the intelligence by looking straight into the heart and then acting. Clarify the intelligence in straight action.

II

1. In letters of gold on T'ang's bathtub:

AS THE SUN MAKES IT NEW
DAY BY DAY MAKE IT NEW
YET AGAIN MAKE IT NEW.

2. It is said in the K'ang Proclamation:

He is risen, renewing the people.

3. The *Odes* say:

> *Although Chou was an ancient kingdom*
> *The celestial destiny*
> *Came again down on it NEW.*
> —*Shi King*, III, 1, 1, 1.
> (*Decade of King Wen*)

4. Hence the man in whom speaks the voice of his forebears cuts no log that he does not make fit to be roof-tree [does nothing that he does not bring to a maximum, that he does not carry through to a finish].

This is the second chapter of the comment containing and getting the grist of the phrase: Renew the people. Ideogram: axe, tree and wood-pile.

III

1. The *Book of Poems* says:

> *The royal domain is of 1000 li*
> *Thither the people would fly to its rest*
> [*would hew out its resting place*].
> —*Shi King*, IV, 3, 3, 4.

2. The *Book of Poems* says:

> *The twittering yellow bird,*
> *The bright silky warbler*
> *Talkative as a cricket*
> *Comes to rest in the hollow corner of the hill.*
> —*Shi King*, II, 8, 6, 2.

Kung said: comes to its rest, alights, knows what its rest is, what its ease is. Is man, for all his wit, less wise than this bird of the yellow plumage that he should not know his resting place or fix the point of his aim?

3. The *Odes* say:

> *As a field of grain*
> *White-topped in even order,*
> *The little flowing ears of grain*

Bending in white, even order,
So glorious was King Wan,
Coherent, splendid and reverent
In his comings to rest, in his bournes.
                    —*Shi King*, III, 1, 1, 4.

As prince he came to rest in humanity, in the full human
      qualities, in his manhood;
As a minister, in respect;
As a son, in filial devotion;
As a father in carrying kindliness down into particular acts,
      and in relation to the people, in fidelity to his given word.

4.   The *Odes* say:
Cast your eye on Ch'i river,
The slow water winding
Bright reflecting the shaggy bamboo;
Shaggy green are the flowing leaves,
Shaggy the bamboo above it,
Our Lord has so many talents
As we cut,
As we file,
As we carve the jade and grind it,
Firm in decision, Oh!
On guard against calumny and its makers, oh!
Splendid, oh! oh!
His voice our impulse, Aye!
A prince of many talents, who will carry through to the end,
Who will not go back on his word.
                    —*Shi King*, I, 5, 1, 1.

"As we cut, as we file," refers to the intelligent method of
study; "As we carve the jade and grind it" refers to the self-
discipline; "Firm in decision, on guard against calumny and
its makers" indicates his anxiety to be fair; "Splendid, his
voice our impulse" indicates his stern equity in the halls of
judgment; "A prince of many talents, who will carry through
to the end, who will not go back on his word" indicates that
style of conduct offered as the grain to the gods, without
blemish, total in rectitude, and this the people cannot forget.

5. The *Odes* say:

> *In our ceremonial plays,*
> *In the ritual dances with tiger masks and spears*
> *The archetype kings are not forgotten.*
>
> —*Shi King*, IV, 1, 4, 3.

The great gentlemen honor the worth they honored and hold in attentive affection the growing and ordered things which they held in affection; the lesser folk delight in that wherein the ancient kings delighted and profit by what profited them [their canals and good customs]; thus the generations pass like water and the former kings are not forgotten.

This is the third chapter of the comment sifting out the grist of the phrase: be at ease in total rectitude.

Whether the ideogram indicating distinctions, which Legge translates "former," starts out by indicating a cutting of meat after hunting or a measuring of the different slices of the moon astronomically, I cannot say, nor do I remember whether Karlgren has an opinion on it.

IV

Kung said: In hearing law-suits I am no worse than anyone else, but one should eliminate law-suits. If the not quite candid were unable to pour out their rhetoric to the full, a greater awe and respect [for government justice] would prevail in the popular mind. This is called knowing the root.

This is the fourth chapter of the comment giving the gist of the remark (in the Confucian canon) about the root and the branch.

V

This is called knowing the root.
This is called completing the cognitions.

知
之
至

There is here a lacuna in place of the fifth chapter of the comment. Ch'eng's speculation about it was not essential to E. P.'s earlier edition and is not in the Stone-Classics as the reader can see for himself.

VI

1. Finding the precise word for the inarticulate heart's tone means not lying to oneself, as in the case of hating a bad smell or loving a beautiful person, also called respecting one's own nose.

On this account the real man has to look his heart in the eye even when he is alone.

2. There is, for the small man living unobserved, no iniquity that he will not carry through to the limit; if he sees a true man he turns and takes cover, hides his iniquities, sticks out his merits, but the other fellow sees the significance of this as if he saw into his lungs and liver; what is the good of his faking, what dish does it cover?

That is the meaning of the saying: the true word is in the middle inside and will show on the outside. Therefore the man of real breeding who carries the cultural and moral heritage must look his heart in the eye when alone.

3. Tseng Tsze said: what ten eyes gaze at, what ten hands point to should preserve a certain decorum [ought to be mentionable, discussable].

4. You improve the old homestead by material riches and irrigation; you enrich and irrigate the character by the process

of looking straight into the heart and then acting on the results. Thus the mind becomes your palace and the body can be at ease; it is for this reason that the great gentleman must find the precise verbal expression for his inarticulate thoughts.

This is the sixth chapter of the comment, sorting out the grist of the sentence about finding precise verbal expression for the heart's tone, for the inarticulate thoughts.

The dominant ideograms in the chapter are the sun's lance falling true on the word, and the heart giving off tone.

VII

1.   In the phrase, "Self discipline is rooted in rectification of the heart," the word rectify (*cheng*) can be illustrated as follows: if there be a knife of resentment in the heart or enduring rancor, the mind will not attain precision; under suspicion and fear it will not form sound judgment, nor will it, dazzled by love's delight nor in sorrow and anxiety, come to precisions.

2.   If the heart have not stable root, eager for justice, one looks and sees not [looks and sees phantoms]; listens and hears not [listens internally and does not hear objectively]; eats and knows not the flavors.

That is what we mean by saying: self-discipline is rooted in rectifying the heart.

This is the seventh chapter of the commentary giving the gist of: "rectifying the heart disciplines the character."

As to the frequent lack of tense indications, the ideogramic mind assumes that what has been, is and will be. Only the exception, or the sequence of events requires further indications. See also verse 3 of the canon.

VIII

1. The phrase, "Regulation of the family is rooted in self-discipline," can be understood by observing that men love what they see growing up under their own roof, and show partiality; if they have something in contempt and hate it, they are partial; if they are filled with reverence and respect, they are partial; if they feel sorrow and compassion, they are partial; and then someone comes arrogantly along paying no attention to us, and our judgment of them is thereby influenced. There are, thus, few men under heaven who can love and see the defects, or hate and see the excellence of an object.

2. Hence the shaggy proverb: No man knows his son's faults, no one knows the stone-hard grain in the stalk's head from the first sprouts.

3. That is the meaning of the saying: If a man does not discipline himself he cannot bring order into the home.

This is the eighth chapter of the comment dealing with self-discipline and domestic order.

IX

1. What is meant by saying, "To govern a state one must first bring order into one's family," is this: the man who, being incapable of educating his own family, is able to educate other men just doesn't exist. On which account the real man perfects the nation's culture without leaving his fireside. There, at home, is the filial sense whereby a prince is served; there the fraternal deference that serves in relations to one's elders and to those in higher grade; there the kindness in matters of detail that is needed in dealing with the mass of people.

2. The K'ang Proclamation says: "As if taking care of an infant." If the heart sincerely wants to, although one may not hit the mark precisely in the center, one won't go far wrong. No girl ever yet studied suckling a baby in order to get married.

3. One humane family can humanize a whole state; one courteous family can lift a whole state into courtesy; one grasping and perverse man can drive a nation to chaos. Such are the seeds of movement [*semina motuum*, the inner impulses of the tree]. That is what we mean by: one word will ruin the business, one man can bring the state to an orderly course.

4. Yau and Shun led the empire by their humanity and the people followed; Chieh and Chou governed the empire with overweening violence and the people copied their conduct, their imperial orders being in contradiction to their likes, the people did not follow the orders.

Whence we note that the prince must have in himself not one but all of the qualities that he requires from others, and must himself be empty of what he does not want from others in reflex. No one has ever yet been able to induct others into a style of conduct not part of his own viscera.

5. That is why the government of a state is rooted in keeping order in one's own family.

6. The *Odes* say:

> *Delicate as the peach-tree in blossom*
> *The leaves abundant as grass-blades,*
> *Fragile fair she goes to the house of her husband,*
> *The bride who will bring harmony to it*
> *As an altar raised on earth under heaven.*
> —*Shi King*, I, 1, 6, 3.

As an altar bringing harmony and order into the home. Given that, one can teach the people throughout the state.

7. The *Odes* say:

> *In harmony with heaven above*
> *And with earth below*
> *The elder and younger brothers*
> *About an altar, in harmony.*
> —*Shi King*, II, 2, 9, 3.

When there is this harmony between elder and younger brothers you can educate the men of the nation.

8.   The *Odes* say:
  He practiced equity without its making him feel
  That a javelin were being thrust into his heart.
                              —*Shi King*, I, 14, 3, 3.

[*Aliter*, faultlessly.] On these lines he rectified the state to its four angles. When right conduct between father and son, between brother and younger brother, has become sufficiently instinctive, the people will follow the course as ruled.

9.   That is the meaning of: The government of the state is rooted in family order.

This is the ninth chapter of the comment giving the gist of: Put order in the home in order to govern the country.

X

1.   The meaning of, "World Order [bringing what is under heaven into equilibrium] is rooted in the good government of one's own state," is this: If those in high place respect the aged, the people will bring filial piety to a high level; if those in high place show deference to their elders, the people will bring their fraternal deference to a high level; if those in high place pity orphans, the people will not do otherwise; it is by this that the great gentlemen have a guide to conduct, a compass and square of the process.

2.   If you hate something in your superiors, do not practice it on those below you; if you hate a thing in those below you, do not do it when working for those over you. If you hate something in the man ahead of you, do not do it to the fellow who follows you; if a thing annoy you from the man at your heels, do not push it at the man in front of you. Do not in your relations with your left-hand neighbor what annoys you

if done at your right, nor in your relations to your right-hand neighbor what annoys you if done at your left. This is called having a compass and T-square of the process.

3. The *Odes* say:

> *What a joy are these princes*
> *At once father and mother of their people.*
>
> —*Shi King*, II, 2, 5, 3.

To love what the people love and hate what is bad for the people [what they hate] is called being the people's father and mother.

4. The *Odes* say:

> *South Mountain*
> *Cutting the horizon, fold over fold,*
> *Steep cliffs full of voices and echoes,*
> *Towering over the echoes,*
> *Towering;*
> *Resplendent, resplendent, Yin, Lord Conductor,*
> *The people gaze at you, muttering under their breath.*
>
> —*Shi King*, II, 4, 7, 1.
> (Chia-fu's invective against Yin)

Those who have rule over states and families cannot but look themselves straight in the heart; if they deviate they bring shame on the whole empire.

5. The *Odes* say:

> *Until the Yin had lost the assembly . . .*
> *They could offer the cup and drink with*
> *The Most Highest.*
>
> —*Shi King*, III, 1, 1, 6.

We can measure our regard for equity by the Yin. High destiny is not easy. Right action gains the people* and that gives one the state. Lose the people, you lose the state.

---

* I think this ideogram has an original sense of the people gathered at its tribal blood rite.

6.   Therefore the great gentleman starts by looking straight into his heart to see how he is getting on with the process of acting on the basis of such direct observation. When he can see and act straight in this, he will have the people with him; having the people, he will have the territory; having the land, the product will be under his control, and controlling this wealth he will have the means to act and make use of it.

7.   The *virtu*, i.e., this self-knowledge [looking straight into the heart and acting thence] is the root; the wealth is a by-product.

8.   If you leave the root in the open and plant the branch, you will merely embroil the people and lead them to robbing hen-roosts.

9.   Rake in wealth and you scatter the people. Divide the wealth and the people will gather to you.

10.   Words that go out a-wry, pettishly, will return as turmoil, and as for money: ill got, ill go.

11.   The K'ang Proclamation has said: Heaven's decree is not given in permanence: Proceeding with rightness you attain it, and with unrightness spew it away.

12.   In the Ch'u History it is said: The Ch'u state does not go in for collecting wealth [treasuring porcelain, jewels and money] but counts fair-dealing* its treasure.

13.   Uncle Fan (refusing an offer of bribery) said: The lost man [King Wen in exile] does not treasure jewels and such wealth, counting his manhood and the love of his relatives the true treasure.

14.   It is said in the Ch'in Declaration: If I had but one straight minister who could cut the cackle [ideogram of the ax and the documents of the archives tied up in silk], yes, if

* Legge says "its good men."

without other abilities save simple honesty, a moderate spender but having the magnanimity to recognize talent in others, it would be as if he himself had those talents; and when others had erudition and wisdom he would really like it and love them, not merely talk about it and make a show from the mouth outward but solidly respect them, and be able to stand having talented men about him; such a man could sustain my sons and descendents and the black-haired people, and benefits would mount up from him.

But if, when others have ability, he acts like a jealous female sick with envy, and hates them; and if, when others have knowledge and sage judgment, he shoves them out of the way and prevents their promotion and just can't stand 'em when they have real worth, he will *not* preserve my sons and grandsons and the Chinese people, in fact he can be called a real pest.

15.   Only the fully humane man will throw out such a minister and send him off among the barbarians of the frontiers. He will not associate with him in the Middle Kingdom; that is what is meant by: Only the fully humane man can love another; or can really hate him.

16.   To see high merit and be unable to raise it to office, to raise it but not to give such promotion precedence, is just destiny; to see iniquity and not have the capacity to throw it out; to throw it out and not have the capacity to send it to distant exile, is to err.

17.   To love what the people hate, to hate what they love is called doing violence to man's inborn nature. Calamities will come to him who does this [definite physical calamities], the wild grass will grow over his dead body.

18.   Thus the true man has his great mode of action which must be from the plumb center of his heart, maintaining his given word that he come to his deed in due hour. Pride and jactancy lose all this.

19.   And there is a chief way for the production of wealth, namely, that the producers be many and that the mere

consumers be few; that the artisan mass be energetic and the consumers temperate, then the constantly circulating goods will be always a-plenty.*

20.   "Good king is known by his spending, ill lord by his taking." The humane man uses his wealth as a means to distinction, the inhumane becomes a mere harness, an accessory to his takings.

21.   There has never been in high place a lover of the human qualities, of full manhood, but that those below him loved equity. Never have such lovers of equity failed to carry through their work to completion, nor have the treasures in such a ruler's libraries and arsenals not been used to his benefit and stayed his.

22.   The official, Meng Hsien, said: Men who keep horses and carriages do not tend fowls and pigs; a family that uses ice in its ancestral ceremonies does not run a cattle and sheep farm; one having a fief of a hundred war chariots does not maintain a minister to clap people into the Black Maria [for non-payment of unjust taxes]. Rather than have a minister who claps people into the police van [nefariously] it would be better to have one who robs the state funds. That is the significance of the phrase: a country does not profit by making profits, its equity is its profit.

23.   When the head of a state or family thinks first of gouging out an income, he must perforce do it through small men; and even if they are clever at their job, if one employ such inferior characters in state and family business the tilled fields will go to rack swamp and ruin and edged calamities will mount up to the full; and even if, thereafter, an honest man be brought into the administration he will not be then able to find remedy for these ills.

* I think the ideogram indicates not only a constant circulation of goods but also a sort of alluvial deposit all along the course of the circuit.

That is the meaning of:
A state does not profit by profits.
Honesty is the treasure of states.

The old commentator ends by saying: "Despise not this comment because of its simplicity."

The translator would end by asking the reader to keep on re-reading the whole digest until he understands HOW these few pages contain the basis on which the great dynasties were founded and endured, and why, lacking this foundation, the other and lesser dynasties perished quickly.

D.T.C., Pisa;
5 October—5 November, 1945.

"We are at the crisis point
of the world."

—*Tami Kume, 1924.*

"Equity

is

the

Treasure

of

States"

Chung Yung
The Unwobbling Pivot

NOTE

The second of the Four Classics, Chung Yung, *THE UN-WOBBLING PIVOT*, contains what is usually supposed not to exist, namely the Confucian metaphysics. It is divided into three parts: the axis; the process; and sincerity, the perfect word, or the precise word; into

Metaphysics:
Only the most absolute sincerity under heaven can effect any change.

Politics:
In cutting an axe-handle the model is not far off, in this sense: one holds one axe-handle while chopping the other. Thus one uses men in governing men.

Ethics:
The archer, when he misses the bullseye, turns and seeks the cause of the error in himself.

CHU HSI'S PREFACE

My master the philosopher Ch'eng says: The word *chung* signifies what is bent neither to one side nor to the other. The word *yung* signifies unchanging. What exists plumb in the middle is the just process of the universe and that which never wavers or wobbles is the calm principle operant in its mode of action.

The spirit of this work comes from the door of Confucius, the heart's law transmitted *viva voce* from master to pupil, memorized and talked back and forth as mutual control of the invariable modus of action. Tsze Sze, fearing that with the passage of time the tradition might be distorted, wrote it out on the bamboo tablets and thus it came down to Mencius.

At its start the book speaks of the one principle, it then

spreads into a discussion of things in general, and concludes by uniting all this in the one principle. Spread it out and its arrows reach to the six ends of the universe, zenith and nadir; fold it again and it withdraws to serve you in secret as faithful minister. Its savour is inexhaustible. It is, all of it, solid wisdom. The fortunate and attentive reader directing his mind to the solid, delighting in it as in a gem always carried, penetrating into its mysterious purity, when he has come to meridian, to the precise understanding, can use it till the end of his life, never exhausting it, never able to wear it out.

PART ONE

TSZE SZE'S FIRST THESIS

I

1. What heaven has disposed and sealed is called the inborn nature. The realization of this nature is called the process. The clarification of this process [the understanding or making intelligible of this process] is called education.

Note by Chu Hsi, an eleventh century commentator: The preceding is the first chapter in which Tsze Sze presents the tradition of the thought as the basis of his discourse. The main thing is to illumine the root of the process, a fountain of clear water descending from heaven immutable. The components, the bones of things, the materials are implicit and prepared in us, abundant and inseparable from us.*

Tsze Sze then speaks of the necessity of watching, nourishing, examining and re-examining them seriously and concludes by speaking of the way in which the spiritual nature of the sage carries his transmuting and operant power to its utmost; his work to effect changes (land improvements, bettering of seed for example); all this stretching to an efficient life. The author wants the student to seek not a surface or single stratum of himself but to find his plumb center making use of himself.

Thus he would abandon every clandestine egoism and letch toward things extraneous to the real man in order to realize to the full the true root.

* Cf. Shi King, III, 3, 6, 7.

2. You do not depart from the process even for an instant; what you depart from is not the process. Hence the man who keeps rein on himself looks straight into his own heart at the things wherewith there is no trifling; he attends seriously to things unheard.

3. Nothing is more outwardly visible than the secrets of the heart, nothing more obvious than what one attempts to conceal. Hence the man of true breed looks straight into his heart even when he is alone.

4. Happiness, rage, grief, delight. To be unmoved by these emotions is to stand in the axis, in the center; being moved by these passions each in due degree constitutes being in harmony. That axis in the center is the great root of the universe; that harmony is the universe's outspread process [of existence]. From this root and in this harmony, heaven and earth are established in their precise modalities, and the multitudes of all creatures persist, nourished on their meridians.

Yang Shih calls this chapter the essential marrow, the true meridian of the work. In the ten following chapters Tsze Sze cites certain phrases of Confucius in order to bring out the full sense of this initial statement.

II

1. Chung Ni (Confucius) said: The master man finds the center and does not waver; the mean man runs counter to the circulation about the invariable.

The two ideograms chung *and* yung *represent most definitely a process in motion, an axis round which something turns.*

2. The master man's axis does not wobble. The man of true breed finds this center in season, the small man's center is rigid, he pays no attention to the times and seasons, precisely because he is a small man and lacking all reverence.

III

He said: Center oneself in the invariable: some have managed to do this, they have hit the true center, and then?
Very few have been able to stay there.

IV

1. Kung said: People do not move in the process. And I know why.

Those who know, exceed. (The intelligentzia goes to extremes). The monkey-minds don't get started. The process is not understood. The men of talent shoot past it, and the others do not get to it.

2. Everyone eats and drinks. Few can distinguish the flavors.

V

The Philosopher said: They do not proceed according to the process. No, people do not use the main open road.

VI

Kung said: Shun, for example, understood; he was a great and uprising knower. He liked to ask questions of people, and to listen to their simple answers. He passed over the malice and winnowed out the good. He observed their discordant motives and followed the middle line between these inharmonic extremes in governing the people, thus he deserved his name. [That is the significance of the ideogram "Shun" the hand which grasps, the cover that shields the discordant extremes.]

Further examination of the 136th radical might find a root for "the discordant opposites," in the signs of the waning and new-horned moon.

VII

Kung said: All men say: "Yes, I know." And in their excitement they run wildly into every net and snare, falling plumb bang into the trap and none knows how to extricate himself therefrom. Everyone says: "Yes, we know." But if they manage to lay hold of the unwavering axis they can not keep a grip on it for a month.

VIII

Kung said: Hui's mode of action was to seize the unwavering axis, coming to an exact equity; he gripped it in his fist, and at once started using it, careful as if he were watching his chicken-coop, and he never let go or lost sight of it.

IX

Kung said: The empire, kingdoms, families can be governed harmoniously; honors and salaries can be refused, you can tread sharp weapons and bright steel underfoot, without being able to stand firm in the unwavering center.

X

TSZE LU'S QUESTION

1. Tsze Lu asked about energy.

2. Kung answered: Do you mean the energy of the South or do you mean Nordic energy, or your own, that which you ought to have yourself and improve?

3. To teach with kindly benevolence, not to lose one's temper and avenge the unreasonableness of others, that is the energy of the South. The wellbred man accumulates that sort of energy.

4. To sleep on a heap of arms and untanned skins, to die unflinching and as if dying were not enough, that is Nordic energy and the energetic accumulate that sort of energy.

5. Considering which things, the man of breed, in whom speaks the voice of his forebears, harmonizes these energies with no loss of his own direction; he stands firm in the middle of what whirls without leaning on anything either to one side or the other, his energy is admirably rectificative; if the country be well governed, he does not alter his way of life from what it had been during the establishment of the regime; when the country is ill governed, he holds firm to the end, even to death, unchanging. His is an admirably rectificative energy.

XI

1. To seek mysteries in the obscure, poking into magic and committing eccentricities in order to be talked about later; this I do not.

2. The man of breed comes into harmony with the process and continues his way. Go half way and then stop, I can't let it go at that.

3. The man of breed pivots himself on the unchanging and has faith. To withdraw from the world, unseen and unirritated by being unseen, his knowledge ignored: only the saint or the sage can compass this.

PART TWO

TSZE SZE'S SECOND THESIS

XII

1. The ethic of the man of breed implies a great deal, but is not showy; it is fecund, distributive, tranquil, secret and minute.

2. Quite humble or simple people can participate in this ethic, but in its utmost not even the sage can know all of the process; the simple and sub-mediocre can follow some of the precepts, but in its utmost not even the sage can realize all of it. Great as are heaven and earth men find something to say against them in criticism; when the man of breed uses the word "great" he means something which nothing can contain; when he defines the minute he means something which nothing can split.

3. In the *Book of Poems* it is said:
   The falcon comes out like a dog
   From the high-arched gate of heaven;
   The fish moves on wing-like foot in the limpid deep.

This is to evoke the thought of height and depth.

4.   The ethic of the man of high breed has its origin in ordinary men and women, but is, in its entirety, a rite addressed to heaven and earth.

This chapter refers to the phrase in the first chapter: "One does not depart from the process." There now follow eight chapters to back up this one.

XIII

1.   Kung said: The process is not far from man, it is not alien from him. Those who want to institute a process alien to mankind [at variance with human nature] cannot make it function as an ethical system.

2.   The *Book of Poems* says:
> *Cutting axe-handle*
> *Cutting an axe-handle,*
> *The model is not far off.*

One seizes one axe-handle in cutting the other. One can, at a glance, note a divergence from the model. Thus the man of breed uses men in governing men. Having eliminated the defects, he stops.

3.   If a man have good will at his center [sympathy in his midheart] the process is not far from him: Do not to another what you would not like to have happen to you.

4.   The ethics of the man of true breed contain four things and I have not been able to perform one of them. I have not been able to serve my father as I would have a son serve me; nor my prince as I would have a minister serve me; nor to treat my elder brother as I would have a younger treat me; nor a friend as I would have a friend treat me. No. These things I have not attained to.

The honest man looks into himself and in his daily acts maintains constant respect to his given word that his deeds fall not below it. If he have failed in something, he dare not slacken in the attempt toward it; if he have erred, he dare not carry the error to the extreme; his words accord with his acts and his conduct with his words as of one who turns to compare them with scruple.

The essence of honesty is that it springs from the heart.

XIV

1. The man of breed looks at his own status, seeing it in clear light without trimmings; he acts, and lusts not after things extraneous to it.

2. Finding himself rich and honored he behaves as befitting one who is rich and honored; finding himself of low estate he behaves as is fitting for a man of low estate; be he among barbarian tribes he acts as one should act where men and dogs sleep round the camp fire; in sadness and difficulty he acts as man should in sadness and straits. The man of breed can not be split in such a way as to be shut off and unable to rejoin himself.

3. In high office he does not ill-treat his subordinates; in lower post he does not flatter his seniors. He corrects himself and seeks nothing from others, thus he is not disappointed; and has no resentments toward heaven above, nor rancors against other men here below.

4. The man of probity is therefore calm and awaits his destiny. The small man takes risks, walking on the edge of the precipice, trying to fool his luck and outwit the hazard.

5. Kung said: there is an analogy between the man of breed and the archer. The archer who misses the bulls-eye turns and seeks the cause of his failure in himself.

XV

1. In the honest man's ethic we find analogy to the traveler to a far country: he has first to cross the near; likewise to the high climber who must first start at the bottom.

2. The *Book of Poems* says:
> *Union of affection with wife and children*
> *Is like the sound of drums and lutes,*
> *The music of the* sih *lute*
> *Measured by that of the* ch'in *lute;*
> *The harmony between elder and younger brother*
> *Is like that at the holy altar*
> *When the grain is offered up to the gods.*
> *Bring your family thus into order*
> *That you may have joy under your roof;*
> *Therein is the treasure,*
> *There are the silk and the gold.*
>   —*Shi King*, II, 1, 4, 7, 8.

The Ode beginning:
> *Glorious and abundant*
> *The cherry trees are in flower*
> *In all the world there is nothing*
> *Finer than brotherhood.*

3. Kung said: The parents are in harmony, their wills harmonize, do they not?

> *Translator's Note: I think he means that the actual generative power is due precisely to this harmony. Harmony of will and of all else.*

XVI

1. Kung said: The spirits of the energies and of the rays have their operative *virtu*.

The spirits of the energies and the rays are efficient in their *virtu*, expert, perfect as the grain of the sacrifice.

2. We try to see them and do not see them; we listen and nothing comes in at the ear, but they are in the bones of all things and we can not expel them, they are inseparable, we can not die and leave them behind us.

3. They impel the people of the whole empire to set in order and make bright the vessels for the sacred grain, to array themselves for the rites, to carry human affairs to the cog-

nizance of the gods with their sacrifice, they seem to move above (the heads of the officiants) as water wool-white in a torrent, and to stand on their right hand and left hand.

4.   These verses are found in the *Odes*:

> *The thought of the multitude*
> *Can not grasp the categories*
> *Of the thoughts of the spirits*
> *Circumvolving, but the tense mind*
> *Can shoot arrows toward them.*
> —*Shi King*, III, 3, 2, 7.

Intangible and abstruse the bright silk of the sunlight
Pours down in manifest splendor,
You can neither stroke the precise word with your hand
Nor shut it down under a box-lid.

XVII

1.   Kung said: Shun was a son in the great pattern, that is his glory; in knowing himself he was a sage and he acted on the clarity of his self-knowledge; for honors he had the Empire, possessing all inside the four seas; he offered the sacrifices in the ancestral temple and his descendents offered them there to him.

2.   One would say that having this capacity for seeing clearly into himself and thereby directing his acts, he perforce came to the throne, perforce had these high honors, perforce this enduring fame, and longevity.

3.   From of old, Heaven, in creating things, of necessity concentrates their materials in them, with energy and in due proportions, and thence it comes that it nourishes the vigorous tree and fells that which is ready to fall.

4.   The *Book of Poems* says:

> *Our joy is the Honest Prince*
> *Worthy of affection*
> *Ornament of our culture*
> *True hearted and a good magistrate.*

His virtues have coordinated the people
And brought them into harmony with nature
His happiness and prosperity are from heaven
And he has nourished this heavenly fortune;
He has augmented his destiny
And reinforced the beneficence of the elements.
                    —*Shi King*, III, 2, 5, 1.
                    (Cf. Odyssey I, 34.)

5. Who has this great power to see clearly into himself without tergivisation, and act thence, will come to his destiny (that is a high destiny).

XVIII

1. Kung said: King Wen alone of men had no cause for regrets. His father was King Chi, his son Wu; the first laid the sound basis for the Empire and the second transmitted it with honor.

2. King Wu completed the work of the Kings T'ai, Chi and Wen. He buckled on his armour but once, and with that once conquered the Empire, without losing his spotless reputation in the world. His title was "Son of Heaven," he had what lies within the four seas, he offered the sacrifices in the ancestral temple and his descendants maintained him with the same rites. So they nourished his spirit.

3. King Wu received the "Decree" [was confirmed by heaven as Emperor] in his old age; the Duke of Chou completed the just and splendid labors of the Kings Wen and Wu, and established posthumous titles for the Kings T'ai and Chi, he honored the earlier Dukes with Imperial ceremonies, and extended the order of ceremonies to the princes and great officers, to the rest of the officers and scholars and to the people. Thus if the father was a grand officer and the son a scholar, the funeral was of a grand officer and the sacrifice that of a scholar; if the father was a scholar and the son a great officer the funeral was of a scholar and the sacrifice of a great officer.

Mourning for a great officer was for one year; for the Emperor three; in wearing mourning for one's father or mother there was no difference because of rank; in this noble and plebs were the same.

XIX

1. Kung said: How high was the filial sense [sensibility] carried by King Wen and the Duke of Chou.

2. Filial piety is shown in the rectitude and precision wherewith one executes the will and completes the work of one's forebears.

3. In the Spring and Autumn they set in order and adorned the sacred halls of their forebears. They set out the sacred vessels, donned the ceremonial robes and offered the sacred fruits of the season.

4. With the rites in the ancestral temple they distinguished the degrees of the Imperial family, disposing the participants according to rank, they indicated also the worth of services rendered. The subalterns presented the cup in the general toast, and thus even the most humble had their part in the rites. In the banquets that followed the guests were arranged "according to hair" [as to color, i.e., according to age.]

5. They sat in the seats of their forebears, they followed their ceremonies, they executed their classic music. They honored those whom their forebears had honored, showed love to those whom their forebears had held in affection, and greeted the dead as though they were present in person.

6. With the rites to earth and heaven they honored the God of Heaven; with the ceremonies in the ancestral temples they paid homage to their forebears.

He who understands the meaning and the justice of the rites to Earth and Heaven will govern a kingdom as if he held it lit up in the palm of his hand.

DUKE NGAI'S QUESTION
XX

1. The Duke Ngai asked about government.

2. Kung replied: The government of Wen and Wu is clearly recorded on the square wooden tablets and on the strips of bamboo. Produce such men and a government will spring up in their style, forget such men and their form of government will shrivel.

3. If men proceed in sane manner, government will spring up quickly, you will see how swift is the process of earth that causes straight plants to rise up; an eminent talent for government will cause government to rise as rushes along a stream.

> *Pauthier notes that the bamboo is both hard and supple.*

4. Government is rooted in men, it is based on man. And one reaches men through oneself.

You discipline yourself with ethics, and ethics are very human; this *humanitas* is the full contents of man, it is the contents of the full man.

One orders a system of ethics with human qualities.

5. This good will, *humanitas*, ethics, is man. The great thing is affection for relatives, the watching them with affection. Equity is something that springs up from the earth in harmony with earth and with heaven.

> *Translator's Note: The ideogram represents the sacrificial vase. Ethics are born from agriculture; the nomad gets no further than the concept of my sheep and thy sheep.*

The great thing [in a system] is to render honor to the honest talent. The rites and forms of courtesy derive from the divers degrees of affection for our relatives and the proportionate honors due to the worthy.

6. *Legge rejects the next verse and Pauthier translates it:* "If the subalterns have not the confidence of their superiors they cannot govern the people." *Legge finds that this does not lead to verse 7.*

The ideogram in dispute shows a hunting dog and a bird under the grass. The hunting dog is a dog in whom one trusts, but he is also a dog who trusts and has confidence in the judgment of the hunter. As the phrase recurs in verse 17, I translate it tentatively in that place.

7. Thence the man of breed can not dodge disciplining himself. Thinking of this self-discipline he cannot fail in good acts toward his relatives; thinking of being good to his blood relatives he cannot skimp his understanding of nature and of mankind; wanting to know mankind he must perforce observe the order of nature and of the heavens.

8. There are five activities of high importance under heaven, and they are practiced with three virtues. I mean there are the obligations between prince and minister; between father and son; between husband and wife; between elder and younger brothers; and between friends. Those are the five obligations that have great effects under heaven. The three efficient virtues are: knowledge, humanity and energy; and they are to be united in practice, do not attempt to split them apart one from the other.

9. Some are born with instinctive knowledge, others learn by study, others are stupid and learn with great difficulty but the scope of knowing is one, it does not matter how one knows, the cult of knowledge is one.

Some proceed calmly setting themselves in harmony with the process [of nature, without doing violence to themselves] others behave well in the hope of profit, others forcing themselves against the grain, but the finished labor is one.

10. Confucius said: Love of study is near to knowledge; energy is near to benevolence; to feel shame is near to boldness.*

*Intrepidity. Morrison says that the Chinese soldiers in the XIXth Century had this ideogram embroidered on the back and front of their jackets.

11.   He who knows these three (virtues) knows the means to self-discipline, he who can rule himself can govern others, he who can govern others can rule the kingdoms and families of the Empire.

12.   All who have families and kingdoms to govern have nine rules to follow, to wit: to control themselves, to honor men of honest talent, to treat their relatives with affection, to respect the great ministers, to maintain the *esprit de corps* of the rest of the officers and officials, to treat the people as children, to attract the artisans of the hundred trades to the country, to show courtesy to those who come from afar, and to show tact in dealing with the princes and great feudal chiefs of the states.

13.   By self-discipline one establishes the model of conduct; by honoring and promoting honest men of talent one guards against being deceived [i.e. one sets up as a model men who do not try to show superlative cleverness in deceiving others]; kindness to relatives prevents rancor between the [imperial or royal] uncles and brothers; he who respects the great ministers will not be led astray by vain rumors [by false news]; maintaining the *esprit de corps* among the officers civil and military will conduce to their good conduct according to custom; treating the mass of the people as children will mean that the "hundred families" [the whole people] will stimulate each other [in good conduct] from a simple tendency toward imitation; attracting the artisans of the hundred trades will mean that the empire's raw materials will be utilized continually and efficiently; courtesy to foreigners [merchants, etc.] will bring them from the four corners of the earth, and cordial relations with the princes and feudatories will have beneficent repercussions everywhere.

14.   Discriminate; illuminate; use abundantly all things available; do not drive toward anything that is contrary to the rites: these are the modes of self-discipline, the instruments of self-discipline.

Keep calumny afar off, get rid of viscid show, hold material riches in low esteem and in high esteem that conduct which comes from the straight gaze into the heart, from the inner clarity: that is the way to stimulate worthy ministers; giving positions of honor and high salaries and sharing in their loves and hates is the way to lead the imperial relatives to treat you with parental affection; giving them plenty of subordinate officers properly and seriously to carry out confidential orders and missions of trust is the way to encourage the great ministers; cordial confidence and good pay are the means of keeping up the officers' *esprit de corps*; requiring service in due seasons only, and keeping the taxes light, is the way to encourage the people; daily supervision, monthly tests, food ration proportionate* to the work done, are the ways of encouraging the artisans; to go with the departing a bit of their way, and to go out to meet those who arrive, praise the capable, have compassion on the incompetent, are modes of establishing easy intercourse with foreigners from afar; to continue the line of succession in families where the direct line fades out, to restore ruin'd states, to bring order into confusions, to give support to weak states in their times of danger, taking hold of these perils well beforehand, to receive personally their ambassadors punctually at the appointed hour, constitute the ways of maintaining cordial relations with the great feudatories and chiefs.

15. All those who have the government of kingdoms and great families have these nine rules to observe, not separately one from another, but all together as a whole.

16. In all affairs those which are calmly prepared make a solid base, those which are not prepared run to ruin before they are ripe; speeches calmly prepared are not empty, affairs thought out in tranquility are not sabotaged later, and you do not get tired in carrying them out; action well considered beforehand does not bring anguish and a well thought mode of action is not interrupted from internal causes, it goes on without blocking obstacles and constrictions.

---

*The ideogram seems to indicate an order against the granary, a sort of mandate for grain, but may also contain the idea of giving the full pay as soon as the work is finished, not delaying the payment.

17. If there be not mutual trust between subalterns and their chief* you will not manage to govern the people. There is a way to obtain the confidence of one's superiors; if there be not fidelity to the given word between friends there will not be confidence between you and your chiefs; to attain confidence between friends there is a way or process to follow; if a man cannot get on with his relatives, his friends will not have confidence in him; there is a way to get on with your relatives; if, searching inside yourself, you cannot tell yourself the truth in plain words, you will not get on with your relatives; and for attaining this precision of speech with yourself there is a way; he who does not understand what the good is, will not attain a clear precision in defining himself to himself.

18. Sincerity, this precision of terms is heaven's process.
What comes from the process in human ethics. The sincere man finds the axis without forcing himself to do so. He arrives at it without thinking and goes along naturally in the midst of the process [*Ts'ung yung chung tao*], he is a wise man. He who is sincere seizes goodness, gripping it firmly from all sides.

19. He concentrates in a pervading study, searches benevolently as if he were watching over a rice field, he looks straight into his own thoughts, he clarifies the just distinctions [between one thing or category and another], and continues thus with vigor.

20. If there is something he have not studied, or having studied be unable to do, he does not file it away in the archives; if there be a question he have not asked, or to which, after research, he have not found an answer, he does not consider the matter at an end; if he have not thought of a problem, or, having thought, have not resolved it, he does not think the matter is settled; if he have tried to make a distinction but have not made it clear [as between things or categories] he does not sink into contentment; if there be a principle which he has been unable to put into practice, or if

* See note in place of verse 6, on the hunting dog.

practicing, he have not managed to practice with energy or vigor, he does not let up on it. If another man gets there with one heave, he heaves ten times; if another succeed with a hundred efforts, he makes a thousand.

21.   Proceeding in this manner even a fellow who is a bit stupid will find the light, even a weak man will find energy.

TSZE SZE'S THIRD THESIS
XXI

Intelligence that comes from sincerity is called nature or inborn talent; sincerity produced by reason is called education, but sincerity [this activity which defines words with precision] will create intelligence as if carved with a knife-blade, and the light of reason will produce sincerity as if cut clean with a scalpel.

Tsze Sze takes up the theme of this 21st chapter and reaffirms it in the chapters that follow.

XXII

Only the most absolute sincerity under heaven can bring the inborn talent to the full and empty the chalice of the nature.

He who can totally sweep clean the chalice of himself can carry the inborn nature of others to its fulfillment; getting to the bottom of the natures of men, one can thence understand the nature of material things, and this understanding of the nature of things can aid the transforming and nutritive powers of earth and heaven [ameliorate the quality of the grain, for example] and raise man up to be a sort of third partner with heaven and earth.

XXIII

He who does not attain to this can at least cultivate the good shoots within him, and in cultivating them arrive at precision in his own terminology, that is, at sincerity, at clear definitions. The sincerity will begin to take form; being formed it will manifest; manifest, it will start to illuminate, illuminating to function, functioning to effect changes.

Only the most absolute sincerity under heaven can effect any change [in things, in conditions].

XXIV

In the process of this absolute sincerity one can arrive at a knowledge of what will occur. Kingdoms and families that are about to rise will give, perforce, happy indications; kingdoms and families about to decay will give forth signs of ill augury. You look at the divining grass and at the turtle's shell; but look at the four limbs.

If ill fortune or good be on the way, one or the other, the good will be recognizable before hand, the ill will be evident before hand, and in this sense absolute sincerity has the power of a spiritual being, it is like a *numen*.

XXV

1. He who defines his words with precision will perfect himself and the process of this perfecting is in the process [that is, in the process par excellence defined in the first chapter, the total process of nature].

2. Sincerity is the goal of things and their origin, without this sincerity nothing is.

On this meridian the man of breed respects, desires sincerity, holds it in honor and defines his terminology.

3. He who possesses this sincerity does not lull himself to somnolence perfecting himself with egocentric aim, but he has a further efficiency in perfecting something outside himself.

Fulfilling himself he attains full manhood, perfecting things outside himself he attains knowledge.

The inborn nature begets this activity naturally, this looking straight into oneself and thence acting. These two activities constitute the process which unites outer and inner, object and subject, and thence constitutes a harmony with the seasons of earth and heaven.

XXVI

1. Hence the highest grade of this clarifying activity has no limit, it neither stops nor stays.

2. Not coming to a stop, it endures; continuing durable, it arrives at the minima [the seeds whence movement springs].

3. From these hidden seeds it moves forth slowly but goes far and with slow but continuing motion it penetrates the solid, penetrating the solid it comes to shine forth on high.

4. With this penetration of the solid it has effects upon things, with this shining from on high, that is with its clarity of comprehension, now here, now yonder, it stands in the emptiness above with the sun, seeing and judging, interminable in space and in time, searching, enduring, and therewith it perfects even external things.

5. In penetrating the solid it is companion to the brotherly earth [offers the cup of mature wine to the earth] standing on high with the light of the intellect it is companion of heaven persisting in the vast, and in the vast of time, without limit set to it.

6. Being thus in its nature; unseen it causes harmony; unmoving it transforms; unmoved it perfects.

7. The celestial and earthly process can be defined in a single phrase; its actions and its creations have no duality. [The arrow has not two points].
There is no measuring its model for the creation of things.

tse pu ts'e

8. The celestial and earthly process pervades and is substantial; it is on high and gives light, it comprehends the light and is lucent, it extends without bound, and endures.

9. In the heavens present to us, there shine separate sparks, many and many, scintillant, but the beyond [what is beyond them] is not like a corpse in a shut cavern.

Sun, moon and the stars, the sun's children, the signs of the zodiac measuring the times, warners of transience, it carries all these suspended, thousand on thousand, looking down from above the multitude of things created, it carries them, now here, now there, keeping watch over them, inciting them, it divides the times of their motions; they are bound together, and it determines their successions in a fixed order. The visible heaven is but one among many.

This earth that bears you up is a handful of sand, but in its weight and dusky large, it holds The Flower Mount and Dog Mountain without feeling the weight of them; Hoang Ho, the river, and the oceans surge and the earth loses not a drop of their waters, holding them in their beds, containing the multitude of their creatures.

Mount Upholder that you now look upon is but a fold of rock amid many, a pebble, and on its sides grow the grasses and trees, sheltering wild fowl and the partridge, the four-footed beasts and stags; gems are hidden within it abundantly that were for delight or for commerce.

This water is but a spoonful mid many; it goes forth and in its deep eddies that you can in no wise fathom there be terrapin and great turtles, monsters, crocodiles, dragons, fish and crustaceans to make rich whomso will seek with a bold eye into their perils.

10.   The *Book of the Odes* says:
   The decree of heaven takes the bird in its net.
   Fair as the grain white-bearded
   There is no end to its beauty.

The hidden meaning of these lines is: thus heaven is heaven [or this is the heavenly nature, co-involgent].

   As silky light, King Wen's virtue
   Coming down with the sunlight, what purity!
   He looks in his heart
   And does.
                  —*Shi King,* IV, 1, 2, 1.

Here the sense is: In this way was Wen perfect.

The *unmixed* functions [in time and in space] without bourne.

This unmixed is the tensile light, the Immaculata. There is no end to its action.

NOTE

Twenty-four centuries ago Tsze Sze needed to continue his comment with a profession of faith, stating what the Confucian idea *would* effect; looking back now over the millennial history of China there is need neither of adjectives nor of comment.

And for that reason I end my translation at this point, temporarily at least.

The dynasties Han, Tang, Sung, Ming rose on the Confucian idea; it is inscribed in the lives of the great emperors, Tai Tsong, Kao Tseu, Hong Vou, another Tai Tsong, and Kang Hi. When the idea was not held to, decadence supervened.

In the Occident Guicciardini wrote: "Nothing impossible to him who holds honor in sufficient esteem."

THE CONFUCIAN ANALECTS

PROCEDURE

The Root of Confucian teaching and its definition are given in The Adult Study (Confucius' summary and Tseng's comment) and the Pivot (Tsze Sze's three statements on Metaphysics, Politics and Ethics).

The Analects have no such coherence or orderly sequence; they are the oddments which Kung's circle found indispensable, and for 2,500 years the most intelligent men of China have tried to add to them or to subtract. After a millennium they found that Mencius' work could not be subtracted. And the study of the Confucian philosophy is of greater profit than that of the Greek because no time is wasted in idle discussion of errors. Aristotle gives, may we say, 90% of his time to errors, and the Occident, even before it went off for seven or more centuries into an otiose discussion of fads and haircuts (*vide* "The Venerable" Bede), had already started befuddling itself with the false dilemma: Aristotle OR Plato, as if there were no other roads to serenity.

Mencius never has to contradict Confucius; he carries the Confucian sanity down into particulars, never snared into rivalry by his flatterers.

Given the tradition that the Analects contain nothing superfluous, I was puzzled by the verses re length of the nightgown and the predilection for ginger. One must take them in the perspective of Voltaire's: "I admire Confucius. He was the first man who did *not* receive a divine inspiration." By which I mean that these trifling details were useful at a time, and in a world, that tended to myths and to the elevation of its teachers into divinities. Those passages of the Analects are, as I see it, there to insist that Confucius was a Chinaman, not born of a dragon, not in any way supernatural, but remarkably possessed of good sense.

He liked good music, he collected *The Odes* to keep his followers from abstract discussion. That is, *The Odes* give particular instances. They do not lead to exaggerations of dogma. Likewise he collected the *Historic Documents*, asserting, quite truly, that he had invented nothing. Without Kung no one would discover that his teaching, or at any rate the root and the seed, are there in the "History Classic."

The London *Times* has recently hit a new low in neglecting Kung's habit of summary. Anyone so unfortunate as to have the *Times'* critique of Kung's anthology thrust before them must, indeed, tingle with a slight warmth of irony. Kung said: "There are 300 Odes and their meaning can be gathered into one sentence: Have no twisty thoughts."

Some translators think of everything, positively of everything, save what the original author was driving at.

E. P.

Brief Concordance

Book   Chapter

Tactics I, 16.
No twisty thoughts: II, 2.
Government: II, 19; XII, 7; XII, 14; XIII, 1.
Veracity: II, 22; IX, 24.
Flattery: II, 24, I.
Arrangement of sequence of the ODES: IX, 14.
Men not horses: X, 12.
The Old Treasury: XI, 13.
VI, 11, cf/Agassiz.
The Official: VI, 12.

man standing by his word

respect for the kind of intelligence that enables grass
seed to grow grass; the cherry-stone to make cherries

After Confucius' death, when there was talk of regrouping, Tsang declined, saying: "Washed in the Keang and Han, bleached in the autumn sun's-slope,* what whiteness can one add to that whiteness, what candour?" (Mencius III, 1; IV, 13.)

The friend who hoped to find beauty in this translation will not find the beauty of the Odes, nor the coherence of the Pivot. The Analects are neither a continuous narrative, nor a collection of fancy ideas. It is an error to seek aphorisms and bright saying in sentences that should be considered rather as definitions of words, and a number of them should be taken rather as lexicography, as examples of how Kung had used a given expression in defining a man or a condition.

Points define a periphery. What the reader can find here is a set of measures whereby, at the end of a day, to learn whether the day has been worth living. The translation succeeds in its moderate aim if it gives the flavour of laconism and the sense of the live man speaking.

After finishing it I turned back to Pauthier's French, and have included a number of his phrases as footnotes (marked P), sometimes as alternative interpretation, sometimes for their own sake even when I do not think he is nearer the original meaning.

The few dictionary references [M] *are to* R. H. Mathews' Chinese-English Dictionary (*Cambridge, Harvard University Press, 1947, 4th ed.*), *that being the one most easily obtainable at the moment.*

*During the past half-century (since Legge's studies) a good deal of light has been shed on the subject by Fenollosa (*Written Character as a Medium for Poetry*), Frobenius (*Erlebte Erdteile*) and Karlgren (studies of sacrificial bone inscriptions).*

E. P.

---

* *yang²*: bright, positive. Definite illustration of why one wants a bilingual edition. The usage of terms by any great stylist is, or should be, determined by the Four Books.

BOOK ONE

I

1. He said: Study with the seasons winging past, is not this pleasant?

2. To have friends coming in from far quarters, not a delight?

3. Unruffled by men's ignoring him, also indicative of high breed.

II

1. Few filial and brotherly men enjoy cheeking their superiors, no one averse from cheeking his superiors stirs up public disorder.

2. The real gentleman goes for the root, when the root is solid the (beneficent) process starts growing, filiality and brotherliness are the root of manhood, increasing with it.

III

1. He said: Elaborate phrasing about correct appearances seldom means manhood.

IV

1. Tseng-tse said: I keep an eye on myself, daily, for three matters: to get to the middle of mind when planning with men; to keep faith with my friends; lest I teach and not practice.

V

1. He said: To keep things going in a state of ten thousand cars: respect what you do and keep your word, keep accurate accounts and be friendly to others, employ the people in season. [*Probably meaning public works are not to interfere with agricultural production.*]

VI

1. He said: Young men should be filial in the home, and brotherly outside it; careful of what they say, but once said, stick to it; be agreeable to everyone, but develop friendship (further) with the real men; if they have any further energy left over, let them devote it to culture.

VII

1. Hsia-tze said: Gives weight to real worth and takes beauty lightly [*or "amid changing appearances"*], puts energy into being useful to his father and mother, and his whole per-

sonality into serving his prince; keeps his word with his friends; call him unaccomplished, I say that he is accomplished.

VIII

1. He said: A gentleman with no weight will not be revered, his style of study lacks vigour.

2. First: get to the middle of the mind; then stick to your word.

3. Friendship with equals.

4. Don't hesitate to correct errors.

IX

1. Tseng-tse said: Look clearly to the end, and follow it up a long way; the people acting on conscience will get back to the solid.

X

1. Tze-Chin asked Tze-Kung: When the big man gets to a country he has to hear about its government, does he ask for what's given him or is it just given?

2. Tze-Kung said: The big man is easy-going and kindly, respectful in manner, frugal, polite, that's how he gets it. His mode of going after it differs from other men's.

XI

1. He said: During a father's life time, do what he wants; after his death, do as he did. If a man can go along like his father for three years, he can be said to be carrying-on filially.

XII

1. Yu-tze said: Gentleness (easiness) is to be prized in ceremony, that was the antient kings' way, that was beautiful and the source of small actions and great.

2. But it won't always do. If one knows how to be easy and is, without following the details of ceremony, that won't do.

XIII

1. Yu-tze said: When keeping one's word comes near to justice one can keep it; when respect is almost a ceremony it will keep one far from shame and disgrace. Starting with not losing one's relatives, one can found a line with honour. [*This reading will be disputed and is perhaps too bold.*]

XIV

1. He said: A gentleman eats without trying to stuff himself, dwells without seeking (total) quietude, attends to busi-

ness, associates with decent people so as to adjust his own decencies; he can be said to love study.

XV

1. Tze-King said: Poor and no flatterer, rich and not high-horsey, what about him?

He said: Not like a fellow who is poor and cheerful, or rich and in love with precise observance.

2. Tze-King said: It's in the Odes "as you cut and then file; carve and then polish." That's like what you mean?

3. Ts'ze here, one can begin to discuss the Odes with him; gave him the beginning and he knew what comes (after it).

XVI

1. He said: Not worried that men do not know me, but that I do not understand men.

BOOK TWO

I

1. Governing by the light of one's conscience is like the pole star which dwells in its place, and the other stars fulfill their functions respectfully.

II

1. He said: The anthology of 300 poems can be gathered into the one sentence: Have no twisty thoughts.

III

1. He said: If in governing you try to keep things leveled off in order by punishments, the people will, shamelessly, dodge.

2. Governing them by looking straight into one's heart and then acting on it (on conscience) and keeping order by the rites, their sense of shame will bring them not only to an external conformity but to an organic order.

IV

1. He said: At fifteen I wanted to learn.

2. At thirty I had a foundation.

3. At forty, a certitude.

4. At fifty, knew the orders of heaven.

5. At sixty was ready to listen to them.

6. At seventy could follow my own heart's desire without overstepping the t-square.

V

1. Mang-I-tze asked about filiality. He said: Don't disobey.*

2. Fan Ch'ih was driving him and he said: Mang-Sun asked me about filiality, I said: it consists in not disobeying (not opposing, not avoiding).

3. Fan Ch'ih said: How do you mean that? He said: While they are alive, be useful to them according to the proprieties, when dead, bury them according to the rites, make the offerings according to the rites.

VI

1. Mang Wu the elder asked about filiality. He said: A father or mother is only worried as to whether a child is sick.

VII

1. Tze-Yu asked about filiality. He said: Present day filial piety consists in feeding the parents, as one would a dog or a horse; unless there is reverence, what difference is there?

VIII

1. Tze-Hsia asked about filiality. He said: The trouble is with the facial expression. Something to be done, the junior takes trouble, offers food first to his elders, is that all there is to filiality?

IX

1. He said: I have talked a whole day with Hui and he sits quiet as if he understood nothing, then I have watched what he does. Hui is by no means stupid.

X

1. He said: Watch a man's means, what and how.

2. See what starts him.

3. See what he is at ease in.

4. How can a man conceal his real bent?

XI

1. If a man keep alive what is old and recognize novelty, he can, eventually, teach.

XII

1. The proper man is not a dish.

* P. expands the single word *wei* to mean: *s'opposer aux principes de la raison*, making the sentence equivalent to Gilson's statement of Erigena: Authority comes from right reason—anticipating the "rites" (light and dish of fecundity) a few lines further down.

XIII

1. Tze-Kung said: What is a proper man? He said: He acts first and then his talk fits what he has done.

XIV

1. He said: A proper man is inclusive, not sectary; the small man is sectarian and not inclusive.

XV

1. He said: Research without thought is a mere net and entanglement; thought without gathering data, a peril.

XVI

1. He said: Attacking false systems merely harms you.

XVII

1. He said: Yu, want a definition of knowledge? To know is to act knowledge, and, when you do not know, not to try to appear as if you did, that's knowing.

XVIII

1. Tze-Chang was studying to get a paid job.

2. He said: Listen a lot and hide your suspicions; see that you really mean what you say about the rest, and you won't get into many scrapes. Look a lot, avoid the dangerous and be careful what you do with the rest, you will have few remorses. Salary is found in a middle space where there are few words blamed, and few acts that lead to remorse.

XIX

1. Duke Ai asked how to keep the people in order. He said: Promote the straight and throw out the twisty, and the people will keep order; promote the twisty and throw out the straight and they won't.

XX

1. Chi K'ang asked how to instill that sincere reverence which would make people work. He said: Approach them seriously [*verso il popolo*], respectful and deferent to everyone; promote the just and teach those who just cannot, and they will try.

XXI

1. Some one asked Confucius why he was not in the government.

2. He said: The Historic Documents say: filiality, simply filiality and the exchange between elder and younger brother, that spreads into government, why should one go into the government?

> [P. turns this admirably: Pourquoi considérer seulement ceux qui occupent des emplois publics, comme remplissant des fonctions publiques.]

XXII

1. He said: Men don't keep their word, I don't know what can be done for them: a great cart without a wagonpole, a small cart and no place to hitch the traces.

XXIII

1. Tze-Chang asked if there were any knowledge good for ten generations.

2. He said: Yin, because there was wisdom in the rites of Hsia, took over some and added, and one can know this; Chou because it was in the rites of Yin took some and added; and one can know what; someone will thread along after Chou, be it to an hundred generations one can know.

XXIV

1. He said: To sacrifice to a spirit not one's own is flattery.

2. To see justice and not act upon it is cowardice.

BOOK THREE
Pa Yih
The Eight Rows

I

1. Corps de ballet eight rows deep in Head of Chi's courtyard. Kung-tze said: If he can stand for that, what won't he stand for?

II

1. The Three Families used the Yung Ode while the sacrificial vessels were cleared away. He said: "The Princes are facing the Dukes, the Son of Heaven is like a field of grain in the sunlight," does this apply to their family halls?

III

1. A man without manhood, is this like a rite? Is there any music to a man without manhood?

IV

1. Lin Fang asked what was the root of the rites?

2. He said: That is no small question.

3. Better to be economical rather than extravagant in festivities and take funerals sorrowfully rather than lightly. [Poignancy rather than nuances (of ceremony).]

V

1. He said eastern and northern tribes have princes not like this Hsia country has lost. [*Or:* which has lost them.]

VI

1. The head of the Chi sacrificing to T'ai Shan (the Sacred East Mountain) Confucius said to Zan Yu: Can't you save him? The reply was: I cannot. Kung said: Too bad, that amounts to saying that T'ai Shan is below the level of Lin Fang. [*Vide supra*, IV, 1.]

VII

1. He said: The proper man has no squabbles, if he contends it is in an archery contest, he bows politely and goes up the hall, he comes down and drinks (his forfeit if he loses) contending like a gentleman.

VIII

1. Tze-Hsia asked the meaning of:
"The dimpled smile, the eye's clear white and black,
   Clear ground whereon hues lie."

2. He said: The broidery is done after the simple weaving.

3. (Hsia) said: You mean the ceremonial follows . . . ?

4. He said: Shang's on, I can start discussing poetry with him.

IX

1. He said: I can speak of the Hsia ceremonial but you can't prove it by Chi (data); I can speak of the Yin ceremonies but Sung (data) won't prove it. The inscribed offerings are insufficient to argue from, were they adequate they could bear me out. [*I should think this* hsien 4. M. 2699, *might refer to the inscribed sacrificial bones, which Karlgren has done so much work on.*]

X

1. He said: When the Emperor has poured the libation in the Sacrifice to the Source of the dynasty, I have no wish to watch the rest of the service.

XI

1. Someone said: What does the sacrifice mean? He said: I do not know. If one knew enough to tell that, one could govern the empire as easily as seeing the palm of one's hand.

XII

1. He sacrificed as if he had taken root-hold in the earth, he sacrificed to the circumvolent spirits as if they took root.

2. He said: If I do not enter into this light, it is as if I did not sacrifice. [*Or*, if I do not give, *i.e.* myself, to it.]

XIII

"stove versus altar"

1. Wang-sun Chia asked the meaning of: It is better to pay court to the hearth [*present lexicons*: stove] than to the mysterious (the household gods).

2. He said: It simply isn't. Who sins against heaven has nothing to pray to. [No means of getting light with the seasons.]

XIV

1. He said: Chou revised the two dynasties, how full and precise was its culture, I follow Chou.

XV

1. Entering the Great Temple he asked about every detail. Someone said: Who says the Man from Tsau knows the rites? He goes into the Great Temple and asks about everything. He said: That is the etiquette.

XVI

"bullseye better than shooting thru the target"

1. He said: In archery the going clean thru the leather is not the first requisite. Men aren't equally strong. That was the old way [? when they were expected to be all of them fit for it].

XVII

1. Tze-Kung wanted to eliminate the sheep from the sacrifice to the new moon.

2. He said: You, Ts'ze, love the sheep, I love the rite.

XVIII

1. He said: Some people consider it sycophancy to serve one's prince with all the details of the rites.

XIX

1. The Duke of Ting asked how a prince should employ his ministers, and how ministers should serve their prince. Kung-tze answered. The prince uses his ministers according to the prescribed ceremonial, ministers serve the prince by their sincerity. [The prince to judge the propriety, the ministers (middle-heart) not to fake in the execution.]

XX

1. He said: The fish-hawk song [*the first of the folk-songs in the anthology*] is pleasant without being licentious, its melancholy does no hurt (does not wound).

XXI

1. The Duke Ai asked Tsai Wo about the chthonian altars.* Tsai Wo replied: The Hsia dynasty's clans planted pines, the Yin cypress, and the men of Chou chestnut trees (*li*) in order to instill awe (*li*) in the populace.

2. Kung heard this and said: Perfect acts do not use words, prolonged customs are not sentenced, what formerly was is not to be blamed.

XXII

1. He said: Kwan Chung is a small dish, and how!

2. Someone said: Is Kwan Chung stingy?

3. He said: Kwan Chung had the Triple-Return (pagoda), court functionaries did not work overtime, how can he have been stingy?

4. "Did Kwan Chung, then, know the ceremonies?"

5. (He) said: Princes of States plant gate-screens; Kwan Chung also set up a gate-screen. When State-Princes meet they have a small table for inverted cups; Kwan also had a small table, if Kwan knew how to behave who doesn't?

XXIII

1. Talking with the superintendent of music in Lu, he said: One can understand this music; a rousing start in unison, then the parts follow pure, clear one from another, (brilliant) explicit to the conclusion.

---

* P. *autels ou tertres de terre*; rather than P's "*autour*", I should take "amid" pines, etc.

XXIV

1.   The Border Warden at I asked to see him, saying when gentlemen come here I have always seen them. (Kung's) escort introduced him. He came out saying: Small group of friends [*lit:* you two three gentlemen] how can you regret his loss of office. The empire has long been in anarchy. Heaven will use the big man as a watchman's rattle. [L. (*Legge*): bell with wooden tongue. M.: with clapper.]

XXV

1.   He said: The Shao (songs) are completely beautiful and wholly good. The Wu are beautiful, completely, but not completely good (morally proportioned).

XXVI

1.   He said: Dwelling on high without magnanimity, performing the rites without reverence, coming to funerals without regrets; why should I bother about 'em?

BOOK FOUR

I

1.   He said: A neighborhood's humanity is its beauty. If a man doesn't settle among real people, how can he know.

II

1.   He said: without manhood one cannot stand difficulties, nor live for long amid pleasures. The real man is at rest in his manhood, the wise man profits by it.

III

1.   He said: only the complete man can love others, or hate them.

IV

1.   He said: if the will is set toward manhood, there is no criminality. [*The graph of* kou³ *suggests grass-root cf/mustard seed.*]

V

1.   He said: Riches with honour are what men desire; if not obtained in the right way, they do not last. Poverty and penny-pinching are what men hate, but are only to be avoided in the right way.

2. If a gentleman give up manhood, what does his title really mean, what does the complete name gentle-man mean?

3. A proper man doesn't merely lay off his manhood after dinner. He must have it to make a sequence, he must have it in sudden disasters.

VI

1. He said: I have not seen anyone who loves whole-humanity and who hates un-whole manhood, if he love this whole-manhood (humanity) he cannot rise above it; if he hate the un-whole manhood, he would go to work on his own manhood, he would not try to get incomplete men to heighten his character for him.

2. If a man can direct his energy for one day toward manhood, eh? I have not seen anyone's energy insufficient.

3. A case may exist, but I have not seen it.

VII

1. He said: A man's errors, every one of 'em belong to his environment (clique, party, gang he associates with), watch his faults and you can judge his humanity.

VIII

1. He said: hear of the process at sun-rise, you can die in the evening. [*Word order is*: morning hear process, evening die can? may, you may, it is possible that you may.]

IX

1. He said: A scholar with his will on learning the process, who is ashamed of poor clothes, and fusses over bad food, is not worth talking to.

X

1. He said: a proper man is not absolutely bent on, or absolutely averse from anything in particular, he will be just.

XI

1. The proper man is concerned with examining his consciousness and acting on it, the small man is concerned about land; the superior man about legality, the small man about favours.

XII

1. He said: always on the make: many complaints.

XIII

1. He said: Can with ceremony and politeness manage a state, what difficulty will he have; unable to govern a state with ceremonies and courtesy; what ordered enlightenment has he?

XIV

1. He said: Not worried at being out of a job, but about being fit for one; not worried about being unknown but about doing something knowable.

XV

1. He said: Shan, my process is unified, penetrating, it holds things together and sprouts. Tsang said: Only?

2. (Kung)²-tze went out. A disciple asked: what does he mean? Tsang-tze said: the big man's way consists in sincerity and sympathy, and that's all.

XVI

1. He said: The proper man understands* equity, the small man, profits.

XVII

1. He said: See solid talent and think of measuring up to it; see the un-solid and examine your own insides.

XVIII

1. He said: In being useful to father and mother, one can almost reprove them; but if they won't do what one wants one must respect them and not oppose† them, work and not grumble.

XIX

1. He said: during their lifetime one must not go far abroad, or if one does, must leave an address.

XX

1. He said: To carry on in a father's way for three years, can be called continuing as a son.

XXI

1. He said: one must recognize the age of one's father and mother both as a measure of good, and of anxiety.

---

* *yu*: mouth answering in the affirmative, parable: responds to, all out for.
† *wei cf*/II. v. i.

XXII

1.   He said: The men of old held in their words for fear of not matching them in their character.

XXIII

1.   Those who consume their own smoke seldom get lost. The concise seldom err.

XXIV

1.   He said: the proper man wants to put a meaning into his words (or to be slow in speech), ready in action.

XXV

1.   He said: candidness is not fatherless, it is bound to have neighbours.

XXVI

1.   Tze-Yu said: Harping on things with a prince brings disgrace, and between friends estrangement.

BOOK FIVE

Kung-Ye Ch'ang

I

1.   He described Kung-Ye Ch'ang as a suitable husband: although he was fettered with the black (criminal's) rope he was not guilty; completing the idea he gave him his daughter to wife.

2.   Of Nan Yung he said: if the country were well governed he would not be out of office; if the country were in chaos he would escape punishment and disgrace; he gave him his elder brother's daughter to wife.

II

1.   He said of Tze-Chien: a proper man, and how! If there weren't proper men in Lu, where did he get it from?

III

1.   Tze-Kung said: What about me, Ts'ze? Confucius said: You're a dish. "What kind?" Confucius said: Oh, a jewelled one for the altar.

IV

1.   Someone said: Yung is a full man but not eloquent. [Persuasive, *ideogram: man tranquillizing a woman.*]

2.   He said: How would he use verbal cleverness? Resist men with glibness, it will get you constant detestations from them; how would he use clever talk?

V

On not wishing to be forced into insincerity

1.   He was urging Ch'i-tiao to go into government employ, who answered: I couldn't keep my word (if I did). Confucius was pleased. [*Word order*: I this, or thus, is not can stand by my word.]

VI

1.   He said: The process is not acted upon [*old style: "the way is not trodden"*]. I will get onto a raft and float at sea and . . . eh . . . Yu will follow me. Tsze-lu (Yu) was pleased to hear this. Confucius said: Yu likes audacity more than I do, he wouldn't bother to get the logs (to make his raft).

VII

1.   Mang Wu the elder asked if Tze-Lu was a whole man. Confucius said: I don't know.

2.   He (Mang) asked again, and Confucius said: In a state of a thousand cars he could manage military enrollment, but I do not know if he is a total man.

3.   "What about Ch'iu?" Confucius said: He could govern a city of a thousand families, or a clan mounting a hundred war cars, I do not know if he is all one can ask of a man.

4.   "What about Ch'ih?" Confucius said: Ch'ih, in an immaculate sash, could be used to talk to visitors and court guests, I do not know if he is all one can ask of a man.

VIII

1.   He asked Tze-Kung: who comprehends most, you or Hui?

2.   The answer: No comparison, Hui hears one point and relates it to ten (understands its bearing on ten, I on one only); I hear one point and can only get to the next.

3.   He said: Not the same, I agree you are not alike.

IX

1.   Tsai Yu was sleeping in day-time. Confucius said: Rotten wood cannot be carved; a wall of dung won't hold plaster, what's the use of reproving him?

2. He said: When I started I used to hear words, and believe they would be acted on; now I listen to what men say and watch what they do. Yu has caused that adjustment.

X

1. He said: I do not see anyone constant. Someone answered: Shan Ch'ang. He said: Ch'ang is moved by his passions, how can he achieve constancy?

XI

1. Tze-Kung said: What I don't want done to me, I don't want to do to anyone else. Confucius said: No, Ts'ze, you haven't got that far yet.

XII

1. Tze-Kung said: The big man's culture shows, one can manage to hear about that; the big man's words about the inborn-nature and the process of heaven, one cannot manage to hear. [They don't go in through the ear.]

XIII

1. When Tze-Lu had heard of anything he couldn't practice he was only worried about having heard it. [*Doubtful reading*].

XIV

1. Tze-Kung asked how Kung-Wan got to be called "Wan," the accomplished. Confucius said: He was active, loved study and was not ashamed to question his inferiors, therefore described as "the accomplished."

XV

1. He said to Tze-Ch'an: there are four components in a proper man's doing: He is reverent in his personal conduct, scrupulously honourable in serving his prince, considerate in provisioning the people, and just in employing them.

XVI

1. He said: Yen P'ing understood friendship, however long the intercourse his scruples remained as at first.

XVII

1. He said: Tsang Wan the elder kept a large tortoise; his capitals showed depicted mountains, and the little columns were adorned as if with duckweed; just what sort of knowledge had he? [*Legge's punctuation. Shift the comma and it cd/mean*, dwelt on Tsan (Tortoise) mountain.]

XVIII

1.   Tze-Chang asked about Tsze-Wan made minister three times and his face showed no pleasure, retired three times and his face showed no displeasure, felt constrained to tell the new minister about the old minister's (mode of) governing? Confucius said: a sincere man. (Chang) said: and as to his being the total man? Confucius said: I don't know how he can be called fully human.

2.   Ch'ui-tze killed the Ch'i prince, Ch'an Wan had forty teams of horses, he abandoned them and went abroad, coming to another state he said: "They are like the great officer Ch'ui" and departed from that first state, to a second, and again saying: "They are like the great officer Ch'ui," he departed. What about him? Confucius said: pure. (Chang) said: total manhood? Confucius said: I do not know how this can amount to being total manhood.

XIX

1.   Chi Wan thought three times before taking action. Confucius heard it and said: Twice might be enough.

XX

1.   He said: Ning Wu when the country was well governed behaved as a savant; when the country was in chaos he acted as a simple rustic; one can attain this wisdom but not this simplicity.

XXI

1.   When he was in Ch'an he said: Return, let me return. My associates are little children, uppish, shortcutters, versatile and accomplished up to the end of the chapter, but do not know how to moderate.

XXII

1.   He said: Po-i and Shu-ch'i did not think about antient hates (birds hidden under the grass), you might say they moulted off their resentments.

XXIII

1.   He said: Who calls Wei-shang Kao straight? Somebody begged a little vinegar, and he begged it from a neighbour and gave it him.

XXIV

1.   He said: elaborate phrases and expression to fit [L. insinuating, pious appearance] self-satisfied deference; Tso

Ch'iu-ming was ashamed of; I also am ashamed of 'em. To conceal resentment while shaking* hands in a friendly manner, Tso-Ch'iu-ming was ashamed to; I also am ashamed to.

XXV

1. Yen Yuan and Tze Lu were with him, he said: Let each of you say what he would like.

2. Tze-Lu said: I would like a car and horses, and light fur clothes that I could share with my friends. They could spoil 'em without offense.

3. Yen Yuan said: I should like goodness without aggressiveness and to put energy into doing a good job without making a show of it.

4. Tze-Lu said: Now, boss, I should like to hear your bent. Confucius said: that the aged have quiet, and friends rely on our words, and that the young be cherished.

XXVI

1. He said: is this the end of it? I have seen no one who can see his errors and then go into his own mind and demand justice on them in precise, just, discriminating words.

XXVII

1. He said: a village with ten homes will contain sincere men who stand by their word quite as well as I do, but no one so in love with study.

BOOK SIX

I

1. He said: Yung could be appointed to a throne [*idiom*: south face].

2. Ching-kung asked about Tze-sang Po-tze. Confucius said: Can do. [Able, handy.]

3. Chang-kung said: if a man's home address is reverence he can be easy going, and thereby come near the people, that's permissible? But if his basic address is: take it easy and he carries that into action, it will be too much of a take-it-easy.

---

* This is the picture, L. and P. stick to the dictionary simply, *appearing friendly*.

4. Confucius said: Yung has the word for it.

[*Note: the terminology in some of these very short verses must be discussed between students, no one version can be just swallowed.*]

II

1. The Duke Ai asked which of the young fellows loved study.

2. Confucius replied: There was Yen Hui who loved to study, he didn't shift a grudge or double an error [L. repeat a fault]. Not lucky, short life, died and the pattern is lost, I don't hear of anyone who likes to study.

III

1. Tze Hwa was commissioned to Ch'i, Mr. Zan asked grain for his mother. He said: give a fu. He asked for more. He said give a bushel. Zan gave five ping. [*L. note figures it may have been the whole of his own grain allowance.*]

2. Ch'ih was going to Ch'i, with a team of fat horses, and wearing light fox fur, I have heard that gentlemen aid the distressed, not that they tie up with riches. [L.M.: add to wealth of rich.]

3. Yuan Sze being made governor, declined 900 measures of grain given him.

4. Confucius said: Don't, they could be given to your big and little hamlets, villages, towns.

IV

1. He said in reference to Ching-kung: if the spotted cow's calf be red with the right sort of horn, though men won't want to use it, will the mountains and rivers reject it?

V

1. He said: Hui, now, a mind that for three months wouldn't transgress humanity; the rest of 'em, can reach this pattern for a day or a month, and that's all. [*L. probably better:* get to it in a day or a moon, and that's all, *i.e.*, get there but not stick.]

VI

1. Chi K'ang asked if Chung-yu could be appointed as colleague in government. Confucius said: Yu's a determined fellow, what would be the trouble about his carrying on the government work? (K'ang) asked if Ts'ze could be given a

government appointment. Said: Ts'ze's intelligent (penetrating) why not? (K'ang) said: and Ch'iu? Said: Ch'iu's versatile, what's against his doing government work?

VII

(On declining to serve an evil overlord.)

1. The Head of Chi appointed Min Tze-chien governor of Pi. Min Tze-chien said: Kindly decline for me, and if they come back for me I shall have to (go) live up over the Wan.

VIII

1. Po-niu was ill. Confucius went to ask after him and took hold of his hand through the window. Said: he's lost, it is destiny, such a man, and to have such a disease. Such a man, such a disease.

IX

1. He said: Hui had solid talent (merit). One bamboo dish of rice, one ladle full of drink, living in a wretched lane, others couldn't have stood it. Hui continued to enjoy (life) unaltered, that's how solid his talent was.

X

1. Yen Ch'iu said: It's not that I don't like your system, I haven't the strength for it. He said: If a man isn't strong enough he stops half way, you shut yourself in (draw your own limit. M. 2222).

XI

1. He said to Tze-Hsia: Observe the phenomena of nature as one in whom the ancestral voices speak, don't just watch in a mean way.

XII

1. When Tze-Yu was governor of Wu-ch'ang, he said to him: Got any men there, what about 'em? Answered: Got Tan-t'ai Mieh-ming who never takes a short cut and never comes to my office except when he has government business.

XIII

1. He said: Mang Chih-fan doesn't brag. He was in the rear of a retreat, but when nearing the (city) gate, whipped up his horse and said: not courage keeping me back, horse wouldn't go.

XIV

1. He said: if you haven't the smooth tongue of T'o the prayer-master, or Sung Chao's beauty, it's hard to get away with it in this generation.

XV

1.   He said: The way out is via the door, how is it that no one will use this method.

XVI

1.   He said: More solidity than finish, you have the rustic; more finish than solid worth, the clerk; accomplishment and solidity as two trees growing side by side and together with leafage and the consequence is the proper man.

XVII

1.   He said: men are born upright, if they tangle this in-born nature, they are lucky to escape.

XVIII

1.   He said: Those who know aren't up to those who love; nor those who love, to those who delight in.

XIX

1.   He said: One can talk of high things (or, of the better things) with those who are above mediocrity, with those below mediocrity one cannot.

XX

1.   Fan Ch'ih asked about knowing. He said: put your energy into human equities, respect the spirits and powers of the air and keep your distance, that can be called knowing. He asked about humanitas. (Confucius) said: the real man goes first for the difficulty, success being secondary. That you can call manhood.

XXI

1.   He said: the wise delight in water, the humane delight in the hills. The knowing are active; the humane, tranquil; the knowing get the pleasure, and the humane get long life.

XXII

1.   He said: If Ch'i could make one change it would come up to Lu; if Lu could achieve one change it would arrive at the right way to do things.

XXIII

1.   He said: a cornered dish without corners; what sort of a cornered dish is that?

XXIV

1.   Tsai Wo said: If you yell: "well-hole" [*Both L. and M. say: meaning, "a man down it"*], will the proper man go down after him? He said: why? a proper man would come to the edge, he can't (be expected to) sink; he can be cheated, but not entrapped.

> [It is not up to him to go down it. *Why not the literal:* If they tell him manhood is at the bottom of the well, will he go down after it? *a simple pun on the spoken word* jen[2] *without the graph.*]

XXV

1.   He said: A proper man extends his study of accomplishment, he brings it into close definition for the rites, and that may enable him to keep from divagations (from overstepping the edge of the field).

XXVI

1.   He went to see (the duchess) Nan-tze. Tse-Lu was displeased. The big man said: Well I'll be damned, if there's anything wrong about this, heaven chuck me.

XXVII

1.   He said: the pivot that does not wobble (what it's all about, always); looking into the mind and then doing; attain this? Few men have for long.

XXVIII

1.   Tze-Kung said: if a man extend wide benefits to the people and aid them all [*pictorially:* sees that they all get an even or constant water supply] would you call that manhood? He said: why attribute that to manhood, he would have to be a sage, Yao and Shun were still worried about such things. [*Or:* at fault, unable to accomplish all that.]

2.   The complete man wants to build up himself in order to build up others; to be intelligent (see through things) in order to make others intelligent.

3.   To be able to take the near for analogy, that may be called the square of humanitas, and that's that.

BOOK SEVEN

Shu Erh

I

1. He said: Transmitting not composing, standing by the word and loving the antient [L. antients]. I might get by in old P'ang's class.

II

1. He said: like a dog by a spent camp-fire (i.e., silent or dark) remembering, studying and not satiate [*pictogrammically same dog under shelter. The "remembering" is specifically keeping the right tone of the word. Various signs containing dog cover the various emotions of dog in given conditions, and are oriented by context*], teaching others without being weary, how can these things apply to me?

III

1. He said: To see into one's mind and not measure acts to it; to study and not analyse [*rt/hand component also in verb "to plough"*], to hear equity and not have the gumption to adjust (oneself to it), to be wrong and unable to change, that's what worries me.

IV

1. When dining at home, he was unbent, easy-like, with a smile-smile. [*P. charmingly; ses manières étaient douces et persuasives! que son air etait affable et prévenant!*]

V

1. He said: deep my decadence, I haven't for a long time got back to seeing the Duke of Chou in my dreams.

VI

1. He said: keep your mind (will, directio voluntatis) on the process (the way things function).

2. Grab at clarity in acting on inwit as a tiger lays hold of a pig.

3. That outward acts comply with manhood.

4. Relax in the cultural arts.

VII

1. He said: from the fellow bringing his flitch of dried meat upward, I have never refused to teach (anyone).

VIII

1. He said: not zeal not explain [*slightly more inclusive than L.'s* I do not explain to anyone who is not eager], not wishing to speak, not manifesting. [*L. M. slant it to equivalents of:* I don't show it to anyone who won't put his own cards on the table.] I hold up one corner (of a subject) if he cannot turn the other three, I do not repeat (come back to the matter).

IX

1. When eating beside someone in mourning he did not stuff himself.

2. He did not sing on the same day he had mourned.

X

1. He said to Yen Yuan: When in office keep to the edge of its duties; when out, don't meddle (keep under the grass), only I and you have this sense.

2. Tze-Lu said: if you were in charge of the three army corps whom would you take for associate?

3. He said: Not someone who would tackle a tiger bare-handed or cross a stream without boats and die without regret. Not on the staff; but a man who keeps both eyes open when approaching an action, who likes to plan and bring to precision.

XI

1. He said: If I could get rich by being a postillion I'd do it; as one cannot, I do what I like.

XII

1. The things he looked very straight at, were the arrangement of altar dishes, war and disease.

XIII

1. In Ch'i he heard the "Shao" sung, and for three months did not know the taste of his meat; said: didn't figure the performance of music had attained to that summit.

XIV

1. Yen Yu said: is the big man for the Lord of Wei? Tze-Kung said: I'll ask him.

2. Went in and said: What sort of chaps were Po-i and Chu-Ch'i? Confucius said: Antients of solid merit.

"(Did they) regret it?"

(Confucius) said: they sought manhood, and reached manhood, how could they regret after that?

(Tze-Kung) came out and said: He's not for him. (No go. Not business, won't work.)

XV

1. He said: a meal of rough rice to eat, water, to drink, bent arm for a pillow, I can be happy in such condition, riches and honours got by injustice seem to me drifting clouds.

XVI

1. He said: If many years were added to me, I would give fifty to the study of The Book of the Changes, and might thereby manage to avoid great mistakes.

XVII

1. [L.: What he constantly talked of, *but ya³ means also* elegant.] He frequently spoke of (and kept refining his expression about) the Odes, the Historic Documents, the observance of rites (ceremonial, correct procedure) all frequently (or polished) in his talk.

XVIII

1. The Duke of Sheh asked Tze-Lu about Confucius; Tze-Lu did not answer.

2. He said: Couldn't you have said: He's so keen and eager he forgets to eat, so happy he forgets his troubles and doesn't know age is coming upon him?

XIX

1. He said: I wasn't born knowing; love antiquity (the antients), actively investigating.

XX

1. He did not expatiate on marvels, feats of strength, disorder or the spirits of the air.

XXI

1. He said: three of us walking along, perforce one to teach me, if he gets it right, I follow, if he errs, I do different.

XXII

1. He said: Heaven gave me my conscience, what can Hwan T'ui do to me.

XXIII

1. He said: You two or three, do I hide anything from you? I do not hide anything from you, I don't go along and

not give it you, that's me. (You are getting the real Ch'iu, Confucius-Hillock.)

XXIV

1. He taught by four things: literature, procedure, sincerity (middle-heart) and standing by his word. [P. *rather better:* employait quatre sortes d'enseignements. Taught by means of four things.]

XXV

1. He said: I have not managed to see a sage man. If I could manage to see a proper man (one in whom the ancestral voices function) that would do.

2. He said: A totally good man, I have not managed to see. If I could see a constant man (consistent, a "regular fellow") that would do.

3. To lack and pretend to have, to be empty and pretend to be full, to be tight and pretend to be liberal: hard to attain consistency (in that case).

XXVI

1. He fished but not with a net; shot but not at sitting birds.

XXVII

1. If there are men who start off without knowledge, I don't. I listen a lot and pick out what is balanced, see a lot and keep the tone of the word, and so manage to know.

XXVIII

1. It was bothersome to talk with Hu-hsiang folk, the disciples were worried when Kung received a boy.

2. He said: I give to those who approach, not to those who go away; who is so deep; if a man wash and approach, I give to the clean (or, to his cleanliness) I don't uphold his past (or his future).

XXIX

1. He said: Manhood, how is it something afar off; I want to be human, and that humanity I get to.

XXX

1. The Minister of Crimes in Ch'an asked Confucius if the Duke Chao knew the correct procedure. Confucius said: he knew the procedure.

2. Confucius went out, and (the Minister) beckoned to Wu-ma Ch'i saying: I hear the gentleman is not prejudiced

(partisan) yet he is partisan. The prince married a Wu, of the same surname as (himself) and called her Wu-elder. If that's knowing proper procedure, who don't know procedure?

3. Wu-ma Ch'i reported this. Confucius said: Ch'iu's lucky (i.e., I am lucky). If I make a mistake it's bound to be known.

XXXI

1. If he was with a man who sang true, he would make him repeat and sing in harmony with him.

XXXII

1. He said: I am about up to anyone else in education, it's the personal conduct of a proper man, that's what I don't come up to.

XXXIII

1. He said: As sage, as full man, can I set myself up as a model? I try and don't slack when tired, I teach men without weariness, that's the limit of what you can say of me. Kung-hsi Hwa said: Exactly what we younger chaps can't get by study.

XXIV

1. He was very ill. Tze-Lu asked to pray. He said: Does one? Tze-Lu answered: one does. The Eulogies say: We have prayed for you to the upper and lower spirits venerable. He said: I, Ch'iu, have been praying for a long time.

XXXV

1. He said: extravagance is not a pattern for grandsons; parsimony is pattern of obstinacy; better be obstinate than break the line to posterity.

XXXVI

1. He said: the proper man: sun-rise over the land, level, grass, sun, shade, flowing out; the mean man adds distress to distress.

XXXVII

1. He was both mild and precise; grave and not aggressive, reverent and tranquil.

BOOK EIGHT
T'ai Po

I

1. He said of T'ai Po: It can be said that he completely brought his acts up to the level of his inwit; three times refusing the empire, the people could not arrive at weighing the act.

> *Note: T'ai Po abdicated in favour of his younger brother, Wan's father, in order that Wan might inherit. This because he considered Wan the member of the family capable of delivering the state from the Yin dynasty.*

[*Syntactical trouble re/"three times." Wan's father was the third son. The three might mean "in three ways"; for himself, his second brother, and their heirs?*]

II

1. He said: respect without rules of procedure becomes laborious fuss; scrupulosity without rules of procedure, timidity (fear to show the thought); boldness without such rules breeds confusion; directness without rules of procedure becomes rude.

2. Gentlemen "bamboo-horse" to their relatives [*The bamboo is both hard on the surface and pliant*] and the people will rise to manhood; likewise be auld (acquaintance) not neglected, the people will not turn mean (pilfer).

III

1. Tsang-tze was ill; called his disciples saying: uncover my feet, my hands, the Odes say: cautious, tread light as on the edge of a deep gulph, or on thin ice. And now and for the future I know what I am escaping, my children.

IV

1. Tsang-tze was ill, Mang Chang-tze went to enquire.

2. Tsang said: When a bird is about to die, its note is mournful, when a man is about to die, his words are balanced.

3. There are three things a gentleman honours in his way of life: that in taking energetic action he maintain a calm exterior at far remove from over-bearing and sloth, that his facial expression come near to corresponding with what he says, that the spirit of his talk be not mean nor of double-talk. The sacrificial covered splint fruit baskets and altar platters have assistants to look after them.

V

1.   Tsang-tze said: Able yet willing to ask those who were not talented, possessed of many things, but enquiring of those who had few, having as though he had not, full and acting as if empty, not squabbling when offended, I once had a friend who followed that service.

VI

1.   Tsang-tze said: Fit to be guardian of a six cubits orphan (a prince under 15) in governing a state of an hundred *li* who cannot be grabbed by the approach of great-tallies [ta chieh 795 (e) 6433.30 *must mean something more than L's "any emergency," i.e., must indicate not getting rattled either at nearing the annual report to the overlord, or by the coming near it, i.e., to the chance of appropriating to himself the symbol of power*] a proper man? aye, a man of right breed.

VII

1.   Tsang-tze: An officer cannot lack magnanimous courage (boldness of bow-arm) he carries weight on a long journey.

2.   Full manhood in fulfilling his personal duties, is that not weighty, death and then it ends, is not that long?

VIII

1.   He said: Aroused by the Odes.

2.   Stablished by the rites.

3.   Brought into perfect focus by music.

IX

1.   He said: People can be made to sprout (produce, act, follow) they cannot be commissioned to know.

X

1.   He said: In love with audacity and loathing (sickened at) poverty: (leads to) confusion; when a man's lack of manly qualities is excessively deep that also means disorder.

XI

1.   He said: Though a man have the Duke of Chou's brilliant ability, if he be high-horsey and stingy, the rest is not worth looking at.

XII

1.   He said: It is not easy to study for three years without some good grain from it.

> [*Ideogram* ku; *interesting us meaning both corn and good, or good luck.*]

XIII

1. He said: strong and faithfully loving study [strong, *again the "bamboo-horse"*: hard and supple] maintaining till death the balanced, radiant process.

2. As for looking for troubled waters to fish in. Not enter a province on the brink, nor live in a disorganized province; when the empire has the process (is functioning) will be looked at; when it is without organization, will be out of sight.

3. When a state is functioning, poverty and meanness are shameful; when a state is in chaos (ill governed) riches and honours are shameful. [*Let us say:* under a corrupt government.]

XIV

1. He said: not being in (an) office; not plan its functioning.

XV

1. He said: when Music Master Chih began [L. entered office] the ensemble finale of the fish-hawk song, came wave over wave an ear-full and how!

XVI

1. He said: Uppish and not straight, ignorant and dishonest, [*let us say:* not spontaneous], quite simple and still not keeping their word; I don't make 'em out. [Empty-headed, and not keeping their word.]

XVII

1. He said: study as if unattainable, as if fearing to lose (grip on it).

XVIII

1. He said: lofty as the spirits of the hills and the grain mother, Shun and Yu held the empire, as if not in a mortar with it. [M. 7615, e: as if unconcerned.]

XIX

1. He said: How great was Yao's activity as ruler lofty as the spirits of the hills; only the heavens' working is great, and Yao alone on that pattern, spreading as grass, sunlight and shadow, the people could not find it a name.

2. How marvellous the way he brought his energies to a focus. Brilliant-gleaming? the perfect expression of his statutes.

XX

1. Shun had five men [*emphasis on "men", I think*] for ministers and the empire was governed.

2. King Wu said: I have ten able ministers [*vide* L. *and* M. 4220. a 3.]. [*Unorthodox reading:* King Wu said: I have ten men to serve me in this chaos. M. 4220. 27. I have ten obstreperous, wrong-headed ministers.]

3. Kung-tze said: Talents are really hard to find. The houses of T'ang (Yao) and Yu (in the person of Shun). At the time of (Yao of the house of) T'ang and (Shun of) Yu in their plenitude, there was a woman and nine men only.

4. Having two thirds of the empire, by keeping them in service (in the uniform) of Yin, the conscientiousness of Chou can be said to have attained its maximum in action.

XXI

1. He said: I find Yu without flaw, frugal in drinking and eating, showing the utmost filial continuity with the spirits and powers of air, badly dressed ordinarily, but absolutely elegant in sacrificial black and blue robes and sovran-cap (mortar board), an inferior palace for a house, he put all his energy into the irrigation and drainage (aqueducts and ditches), I find him utterly flawless.

BOOK NINE

Tze Han

I

1. He seldom spoke of profits, destiny, and total manhood.

II

1. A villager from Ta-Hsiang said: Great man, Kung-tze extends his studies but does nothing to bring his reputation to a point.

2. Confucius heard this and asked his young students: what should I do, take up charioteering or take up archery? I'll take up charioteering.

III

1. He said: The ceremonial hemp cap is now silk; that's an economy, I conform.

2. Bowing as you enter the hall is according to the rites, they now bow when they have come up the hall, cheeky; although against the common usage, I conform [or continue (to bow)] at the lower end of the hall.

IV

1.   He was cut off from four things; he had no prejudices, no categoric imperatives, no obstinacy or no obstinate residues, no time-lags, no egotism.

V

1.   He was alarmed in Kwang.

2.   Said: King Wan has passed on, the wan (the precise knowledge) is rooted here?

3.   If heaven were about to destroy that spirit of precision, after Wan's death, it would not have lasted on and been given to me. If heaven is not about to destroy that spirit, what are the people of Kwang to me? [L.: what can they do to me?]

VI

1.   A great minister said to Tze-kung: your big man is a sage, how versatile he is.

2.   Tze-kung said: Aye, by heaven's indulgence is almost a sage, and also very versatile.

3.   Confucius heard, and said: does the great minister know me? I was poor when young and therefore can do many things, humble jobs. Need a proper man, a gentleman, be versatile? He need not.

4.   Lao says He said: I was not trained (educated to the examinations)* and therefore learned the various arts.

VII

1.   He said: How do I grasp knowledge? I am not wise, but if a plain man ask me, empty as empty [like? work in a cave?], [L:] I set it forth from one end to the other and exhaust it.

[*"Knock at double,"* or at both starts or principles, suggests the meaning: investigate the paradox, or the two principles, the conjunction, apparent contradiction, and then exhaust the question.]

VIII

1.   He said: the miracle bird has not arrived, the river gives forth no map (of turtle-shell), I've only myself to rely on.

IX

1.   Seeing anyone in mourning or in full ceremonial dress and cap, or a blind man (one of the blind musicians) even though they were young he would rise, or, passing, pass quickly.

---

* L.: having no official job.

X

1. Yen Yuan sighed heavily and said: I looked up, they filled the aloft; I bored in to them and they were totally solid; respectfully standing before them, they suddenly took root-hold in consequence.

2. The big man, orderly, one point tied to another, with perfect balance induces men (words that grow as easily as weed, but are good, grain-words), he enlarges us with literature, and keeps us in bound by the rites.

> *"Rites": This word* li³ *contains something of the idea in the French "il sait vivre," though it would be an exaggeration to say that one can always render it by that phrase.*

3. Wishing to finish, I cannot; having exhausted my talent, it is as if something was built up lofty; although I wish to comply with it, there is no way (to do so completely) (branch causes stop).

XI

1. He was very ill, Tze-Lu wanted the students to act as ministers.

2. In an interval of the fever He said: Yu (Tze-lu) has been being too-clever for a long time, whom would I fool by pretending to have ministers when I haven't: fool heaven?

3. Wouldn't it be better to die among two or three intimates than in ministers' hands? Might not have a big funeral, but I wouldn't just die in a ditch [*lit:* going along a road].

XII

1. Tze-kung said: I have a beautiful gem here; put it in a case and hoard it, or try to get a good price and sell it? He said: sell it, sell it, I wait for its price.

XIII

1. He was wanting to live among the wild tribes.

2. Someone said: Rough, vulgar, how do you mean? He said: if the right kind of man lived there, how would they stay so?

XIV

(Arrangement of the Song book)

1. He said: From Wei I came back to Lu and the music was put in order, the Elegantiae and the Lauds were each put in its proper place.

XV

1. He said: In public to be useful to the Dukes and Ministers, in private to be useful to one's father and elder brothers, not daring to neglect the service of dead; not to be obstinate with drink; how does this apply to me?

XVI

1. Standing on a river-bank he said: it is what passes like that, indeed, not stopping day, night.

XVII

1. I do not see love of looking into the mind and acting on what one sees there to match love of someone having beauty.

XVIII

I do not in the least understand the text of this chapter. Only guess at it I can make is:

1. He said: As a mountain (grave-mound) is not made perfect by one basket of earth; yet has position, I take position. If you dump one basket of earth on a level plain it is a start (toward the heap?), I make that start.

> *The chapter might conceivably refer to determining the proper site for a tumulus even if one could not complete it. L. unsatisfied as to meaning, and P. unsatisfactory.*

XIX

1. He said: Never inert in conversation, that was Hui.

XX

1. He described Yen Yuan: Alas, I see him advance, I never see him stop (take a position).

> *Putting the accent on the hsi (2-5), "a pity?" as Legge does not.*

> *There is no more important technical term in the Confucian philosophy than this chih (3) the hitching post, position, place one is in, and works from. Turn back also to the difficult chap. xviii. above.*

XXI

1. He said: There are sprouts that do not flower; flowers that come not to fruit, oh yes.

XXII

1. He said: You can respect 'em soon after birth, how can one know what will come up to present record; at forty or fifty and not heard (or if they don't hear sense) that (maturity) just isn't enough to respect.

XXIII

1.   He said: can one help agreeing with talk of sound doctrine? It's the altering to enact that matters; can one fail to be pleased with south-east gentleness of discourse, it's the elucidation that matters. To be pleased and not elucidate (not understand), to assent but not act on. I just don't know how to take (that sort).

XXIV

1.   He said: put first getting to the centre of the mind, and keeping one's word; no friends not like one; when a mistake is made, not fearing to change.

XXV

1.   He said: the commander of three army corps can be kidnapped, you cannot kidnap a plain man's will.

XXVI

1.   Standing by a man dressed in furs, unembarrassed, Yu could do that?

2.   No hates, no greeds, how can he use evil means?

3.   Tze-lu kept repeating this to himself. Confucius said: How can that be enough for complete goodness?

XXVII

1.   He said: when the year goes a-cold we know pine and cypress, then you can carve them.

XXVIII

1.   He said: the wise are not flustered, the humane are not melancholy, the bold are not anxious.*

XXIX

1.   He said: there are some we can study with, but cannot accompany in their mode of action; there are some we can collaborate with, but cannot build sound construction with, some we can construct with but not agree with as to the significance of what we are doing.

XXX

1.   The flowers of the prunus japonica deflect and turn, do I not think of you dwelling afar?

2.   He said: It is not the thought, how can there be distance in that?

---

* These are definitions of words.

BOOK TEN

Heang Tang
(*villeggiatura*)

I

1. Kung-tze in his village, looking as if he were too simple-hearted to utter.

2. In the dynastic temple, or court, speaking with easy pertinence; answering with prompt respect.

II

1. At court with the Lower-great officers straight from the shoulder; with the Upper-great officials with gentle courtesy.

2. With the sovran present, level alertness, grave readiness.

III

1. On the Prince calling him to receive a visitor, his face registered a change and his legs flexed.

2. He saluted (the officers whom he was standing with), left and right hand, his robe fore and aft evenly adjusted.

3. Swiftly advanced as if winged.

4. The visitor gone, it was his duty to report saying: the guest does not look back.

IV

1. Entering the ducal gate he hunched up like a ball as if there wasn't room.

2. Did not stand in the middle of the gateway, nor tread on the threshold-stone door-sill in going out.

3. Passing the sovran's standing place his expression changed and his legs seemed to flex, he spoke as if short of breath.

4. He went up the hall, he held his breath as if not breathing.

5. Coming out, when he had descended one step, his face relaxed to a pleasant expression, from the bottom of the steps he moved quickly, as if winged, to his place, still cagey on his feet.

V

1. Carrying the sceptre his body was bent as if it were too heavy to lift, the upper part at the level of the salute, the lower as when handing over something. His face grim, and his feet as if tethered.

2.   Giving the ceremonial gifts, his face placid.

3.   In private audience, as if enjoying it.

VI

1.   Gentlemen do not (or the gentleman did not) wear dark purple puce ornaments.

2.   Nor red purple in undress [*can also mean "mourning clothes"*].

3.   Approximately in hot weather an unlined dress of linen or grass cloth must show and appear [L. over his underwear].

4.   Black silk dress, lambskin; white dress fawn-skin; yellow dress fox fur.

5.   Undress fur coat long with short sleeve [L. short right sleeve].

6.   Had to have night gown half again as long as his body.

7.   At home thick fox and badger fur.

8.   Discarding mourning put all the gadgets on his belt.

9.   Lower garments, except aprons, cut in (to the waist).

10.   Lamb skin and black cap not used on visits of condolence.

11.   At beginning of the month would always go to court in court dress.

VII

1.   When fasting insisted on bright linen clothes.

2.   For fasting had to change his diet, sit in a different place.

VIII

1.   Couldn't get rice too clean or mince too fine for him.

2.   Would not eat mouldy rice or fish or meat that had gone off, nor would he eat anything that had changed colour, stank, was ill cooked or out of season.

3.   Did not eat meat badly cut or with the wrong sauce.

4.   When there was a lot of meat he would not take more than what properly went with the rice, only in matter of wine was no blue nose (set no limit) but didn't get fuddled.

5.   Did not take wine or eat dried meat from the market.

6.   Always had ginger at table.

7.   Didn't eat a great deal [or a lot of different things at a time?].

8.   Did not keep the meat from the ducal sacrifices over night; nor that of the domestic sacrifice more than three days. It is not eaten after three days.

9.   Did not talk while eating nor in bed.

10.   Although but coarse rice or vegetable broth he would offer decorously a gourd (ladle-full) in sacrifice.

IX

1.   Not sit on a mat askew.

X

1.   With villagers drinking, when the old fellows with canes went out, he followed.

2.   When the villagers drive out the devils in winter, he put on court robes and stood on his east steps.

XI

1.   On occasion of messengers from another state (or to it) he bowed twice and escorted the messenger out.

2.   Chi K'ang made him a present of medicine, he bowed and accepted it, saying: I don't know how far it goes, I don't dare take it.

XII

1.   The stable burned while he was away at court, he said: Any of the men hurt? not asking about the horses.

XIII

1.   On the prince sending food, he would adjust his mat and taste it before anyone else; the prince sending raw food he would cook it and set it before the spirits inviting them; if the prince sent him a live animal he would put it to pasture.

2.   In service of the prince at a feast, the prince sacrificed, first tasting.

> *Not clear, but L. evidently correct that Confucius acted as taster, either for prince, or for the spirits.*

3.   Being ill, the prince came to see him, he set his head to the east and had his court robes spread over him, his belt across them.

4.   When summoned by sovran order, he did not wait for the team to be hitched, he went on foot.

XIV

1.   Entering the great dynastic temple he asked about all details of the service.

XV

1.   When a friend died with no one to return (the body to its home for burial) he said: I will see to the funeral.

2.   If a friend sent a present, though it were a carriage and pair, he did not bow, but only for a present of sacrificial meat.

XVI

1.   In bed did not lie in the pose of a corpse; at home no formal manners.

2.   Seeing anyone in mourning, although a familiar, he would change (his expression); seeing anyone in ceremonial cap, or blind, although he himself were in slops, he would salute with ceremony.

3.   To a person in mourning he would bow over the dash-board. He would bow over the dash-board to anyone carrying the census tablets.

4.   He would rise and bow with different expression at a feast with a loaded table.

5.   He would change expression at sudden thunder or a keen gust of wind.

XVII

1.   To get into the carriage he would stand plumb and take hold of the cord.

2.   In the carriage he did not twist his head around, gabble, or point.

XVIII

1.   "Beauty: That which arises, hovers, then comes to nest."

2.   He said: Mountain ridge, the hen pheasant, the ringed pheasant the season, how! It is the season! Tze-lu [??] showed respect [3709 a?], thrice smelled and rose. [? thrice inhaled the mountain air?]

> *Difficult as to the number of times the hen pheasant "hsiu" scented. Commentators in general give it up.*
>
> *P. apparently tries to connect the verse with the yellow bird that knows where to rest.* Great Learning III, 2.

BOOK ELEVEN
Hsien Tsin
The Earlier Approach

I

1.   He said: Earlier approach to the rites and to music was the countryman's, the latter the gentleman's; I come at 'em the earlier way.

II

1. He said: None of those who followed me to Ch'an and Ts'ai now come to my door.

2. Showing *virtu* in act: Yen Yuan, Min Tze-ch'ien, Zan Po-niu, Chung-King; valued for their conversation: Tsai Wo, Tze-Kung; for administrative services: Zan Yu, Chi Lu; for their literary studies: Tze-yu, Tze-hsia.

III

1. He said: Hui's no help, he's pleased with everything I say.

IV

1. He said: Min Tze-ch'ien most certainly filial, no one disagrees with what his father, mother and all his brothers say (differs from what they say of him).

V

1. Nan Yung thrice came back to (quoting) "The White Sceptre"; Kung-tze gave him his elder brother's daughter to wife.

VI

1. Chi K'ang asked which of the disciples loved study. Kung-tze answered: There was Yen Hui who loved study, unfortunately he died young, and the model's lost.

VII

1. Yen Yuan died and (his father) Yen Lu wanted Confucius to sell his carriage to pay for the coffin.

2. Confucius said: Talents or no talents every man calls his son, son. Li died and had a coffin but no outer shell. I did not go on foot to get him an outer shell; having ranked just below the Great Officers, it was not fitting to go on foot.

VIII

1. Yen Yuan died, Confucius said: Heaven destroys me, destroys me.

IX

1. Yen Yuan died, and He mourned greatly; disciples said: This is excessive.

2. He said: Excessive?

3. If I do not greatly lament him, whom should I?

X

1. Yen Yuan died, the disciples wanted a big funeral. Confucius said: You may not.

2. The disciples gave a great funeral.

3.   Confucius said: Hui treated me as a father. I have not managed to treat him as a son, not my fault but yours.

XI

1.   Chi Lu asked about the service for ghosts and spirits. Confucius said: You cannot be useful to the living, how can you be useful to (serve) ghosts?

"Venture to ask about death."

Said: Not understanding life, how can you understand death? [*Or "the living, how understand the dead?"*]

XII

1.   Min-tze was waiting on him looking respectful, Tze-Lu looking active, Zan Yu and Tze-Kung, frank and easy. He was pleased.

2.   (Said): The Sprout, there, (Yu) won't die a natural death.

XIII

1.   Lu folk in the matter of the new long Treasury building:

2.   Min Tze-ch'ien said: What about repairing the old one? Why change and build?

3.   He said: Great man for not talking, when he does it's mid target. [*Chung*, the middle, what it's all about.]

XIV

1.   He said: What's Yu's lute doing at my door?

   [*Commentator's guess that "Sprout's" music was too warlike. Might distinguish "campaign" lute from scholar's lute? Must-lute and Now-lute.*]

2.   The disciples did not revere Tzu-lu (Yu). He said: The Sprout has come up the hall, but not entered the inner apartment.

XV

1.   Tze-Kung asked: Who's the better man, Shih or Shang? He said: Shih goes past the mark, Shang don't get there.

(Tze-King) said: "So Shih's the better?"

He said: It's as bad to overdo as not to get there.

XVI

1.   The Chi chief was richer than the Duke of Chau, yet Ch'iu went on raking in taxes and piling up wealth for him.

2.   Confucius said: No disciple of mine. The kids can beat drums and go after him (for all I care).

   "Taxes" is from Legge, Mathews follows it, but with no other illustration to back it up. (Lien [M. 3999] *is not*

among the different sorts of legalized tax mentioned by Mencius III.i, iii. 6. Han⁺ (2052) must be a misprint in some editions.) Could be: went on raking it in, piling it up, supplementing his profits, his increase.

XVII

1. Ch'ai is simple.
2. Shan is coarse.
3. Shih, deflected.
4. Yu ("the Sprout") is unkempt.

All these adjectives unsatisfactory. Probably defined by the quality of the men described when *they were used.*

It is assumed (by L. etc.) that they are pejorative. I cannot feel that the assumption is proved.

XVIII

1. He said: Hui's not far from it, frequently hard up. [K'ung *can mean also:* blank.]

2. Ts'ze does not receive (accept) destiny (? take orders) [L.: accept the decrees of Heaven], his riches fatten, his calculations are often correct.

XIX

1. Tze-Chang asked: How does a "shan⁴" man [*dictionary:* good man] act? He said: He does not trample footsteps [*note 502.7 combine, as "feelings"*], he does not enter the (inner) apartment.

This verse can only be taken as a definition of the word shan,⁺ *which pictogrammically suggests symmetry, over a mouth. Goodness of the solar Ram, or what will you? L. takes it "inner chamber of the sage."*

XX

1. He said: Firm orderly discourse, we accept a fellow, but is he the real thing, or is it just gravity?*

XXI

1. Tze-Lu asked if he should act [L. immediately] on what he heard.

He said: Your father and elder brother are alive, why should you act on what you hear?

---

* Sterne: a mysterious carriage of the body, to conceal the defects of the mind. *Chuang*¹, sedateness, dressed-up-ness.

Zan Yu asked if he should act on what he heard. He said: When you hear it, do it.

Kung-hsi Hwa said: (Tze-Lu) Yu asked if he should act when he heard a thing, and you said: Your father and brother are alive. Ch'iu asked if he should act on what he heard, you said: Go to it. I am perplexed and venture. . . . Confucius said: Ch'iu is slow, therefore I prodded him; "the Sprout" too active, so I tried to slow him down.

XXII

1. He was in dread in Kwang, Yen Yuan came after him. He said: I thought you were dead.

(Yen) said: You are alive, how should I venture to die?

XXIII

1. Chi Tze-zan asked whether Chung Yu and Zan Ch'iu could be called great ministers.

2. He said: I thought you would ask about someone out of the ordinary, and you ask about Yu and Ch'iu.

3. You call a man a great minister when he serves his prince honestly, and retires when he cannot.

4. You can call Yu and Ch'iu "ministers" and that's all.

> [*Or perhaps better "tool-ministers,"* 1556.b.] *Pauthier with neat irony* "considerés comme ayant augmenté le nombre des ministres."

5. (Tze-zan) said: Aye, they'll always follow along.

6. He said: They would not follow along to parricide or regicide.

XXIV

1. Tze-Lu got Tze-Kao made governor of Pi.

2. He said: You are injuring somebody's son.

3. Tze-Lu said: There are men of the people, there are land altars and altars of the grain spirits, why do we need to read books and go on with study?

4. He said: That's why I hate big smart talk [fluency, L. glib-tongued people].

XXV

1. Tze-Lu, Tsang Hsi, Zan Yu, and Kung-hsi Hwa were sitting with him.

2. He said: I am a day older than you, but pay no attention to that.

3. You sit round saying: We are unknown, if somebody should recognize you, what would you do [L. like to do]?

4. Tze-Lu replied straight off the bat: "Thousand chariots' state. Shut in between large states, and armies of invasion, grain and provision famine, I could give the people courage if I had three years' run, and teach 'em the rules, put 'em on the square." The big man smiled (or grinned).

5. "Ch'iu, how about you?"

Replied: "Give me the job of a sixty, seventy or fifty li square district. I could give 'em abundant crops in three years. It would need a superior man to teach 'em the rites and music." [*"Abundant crops"—probably more literal:* there would be enough (for the) people.]

6. "What about you, Ch'ih?"

Replied: I don't say I could do that sort of thing, should like to study, serve in the ancestral temple, at audience of the princes, ceremonial chapter style [L. & M. dark square-made robe, black linen cap] to be lesser assistant.

7. "Chieh (clever-boy), what about you?" Struck his *se* (25-string lute) with curious jingling, laid down the lute and got up, answering: Differ from the three of 'em in what they grasp at.

Confucius said: What harm, let each say what he wants (*directio voluntatis*).

(Chieh) said: Toward the end of spring, in nice spring clothes, with five or six fellows who have been capped, and six or seven kids, go bathe in I river (Shantung) with the wind over the rain dance [*probably*, wind for the rain dance, *could be*: wind suitable for the rain dance] to chant (through the service) and go home.

The big man heaved a sigh of assent: I am with Chieh.

[*L. calls this young man Tien.*]

8. The three went out, Tsang Hsi delaying, and said: What about these three men's words? Confucius said: Each one expressed his preference, that's all.

9. (Hsi) said: Boss, why did you grin at "The Sprout"?

10. He said: A state is managed with ceremony, his words were not polite, so I grinned.

11.   "But Ch'iu didn't ask for a state."

"Calmly, did you ever see a district fifty, sixty or seventy li square that wasn't a state?"

12.   "Only Ch'ih, was he asking for a state?"

"Together in ancestral temple, who save nobles would be there; if Ch'ih were a lesser acolyte, who'd be the big ones?"

BOOK TWELVE

I

1.   Yen Yuan asked about full manhood. He said: Support oneself and return to the rites, that makes a man.

> [*The "support oneself" is fairly literal. It cannot be limited to superficial idea of making a living, but certainly need not be taken ascetically. "Determine the character" might render one side of the phrase.*]

If a man can be adequate to himself for one day and return to the rites, the empire would come home to its manhood. This business of manhood sprouts from oneself, how can it sprout from others?

2.   Yen Yuan said: Wish I had the eye to see it, may I ask?

If something is contrary to the rites, don't look at it; don't listen to it, don't discuss it, if it is contrary to the rites don't spend energy on it. Yen Yuan said: I am not clever but I would like to act on that advice.

II

1.   Chung-kung asked about full manhood. He said: Out of doors look on men as if you were receiving great guests; put men to work as if you were performing the Great Sacrifice, what you don't want (done to you) don't do to another, settle in a district without fault-finding, take root in the home without fault-finding.

Chung-kung said: I'm not clever, but I'd like to put those words into practice.

III

1.   Sze-ma Niu asked about manhood. He said: The full man's words have an edge of definition. [*L. merely:* slow of speech.]

2. (Niu) said: [*as L.*] Cautious and slow of speech, is that a definition of manhood? He said: Difficult business to reach one's verbal manifest in one's actions unless the words are defined [L.: unless the speech be slow].

[*The right hand component of this* jen⁺ *is clearly shaped as* jen (4) 3110; *not as in M.'s* 3117, *but not in all printed editions.*]

IV

1. Sze-man Niu asked about (the term) gentleman. He said: The man of breed has neither melancholy nor fears.

2. (Niu) said: Being without retrospective melancholy or fear, is that being the gentleman? [Or: How does that constitute the *chun tzu*?]

3. He said: On introspection nothing wrong (diseased), how would he have regrets or fears?

V

1. Sze-ma Niu said in worry (or regret): Everyone has brothers except me. I haven't (or have lost 'em).

2. Tze-Hsia said: "I've heard said:

3. "Death and life have their sealed orders, riches and honours are from heaven."

4. The man with the voices of his forebears within him is reverent; he gives men respect, and holds to the right usage, all men within the four seas are elder and younger brothers. How can the proper man be distressed for lack of brothers?

VI

1. Tze-chang asked about light. He said: He whom slow soaking slander, and

tiger-stomach receive inform

[*L. "statements that startle"*]

have no effect on (are no go with) can be called enlightened [*bis* can be called perspicuous, far-seeing].

VII

1. Tze-Kung asked about government. He said: Enough food, enough weapons, and that the people stand by their word [L. have confidence in their ruler].

2. Tze-Kung said: If you can't manage this, which do you omit first? He said: The armaments.

3. Tze-Kung: If you can't manage the other two, which do you omit first? He said: The food. All must die, but if the people be without faith (fail of their word) nothing stands.

VIII

1. Chi Tze-ch'ang said: A proper man needs the solid qualities, that's enough, what's the use of higher culture?

2. Tze-kung said: Pity the great philosopher's words, he is a superior man (but) four horses cannot overtake the tongue.

3. The finish is as the substance, the solid, the substance like the polish it takes; tiger-skin, leopard-skin are like dog-skin and goat-skin if you take the hair off.

IX

1. The Duke Ai said to Yu Zo: Bad year, scant harvest, what's to be done?

2. Yu Zo: Why not tithe?

3. "Two tenths not enough, how would I manage with one?"

4. Answered: If the hundred clans have enough, who won't give enough to the prince, if the hundred clans are in want who will give enough to the prince?

> *The great discussion of the tenth tithe vs/fixed charge, is given in Mencius III.1. iii, 6.*

X

1. Tze-chang asked about raising the level of conscience and detecting illusions (delusions). He said: The first thing is: get to the centre (what it is all "about"), stand by your word, respect the meum and tuum, that will elevate your virtue (level of conscious acts).

2. Love a man, you wish he may live; hate and you wish him to die; then you wish him to live, and turn round and want him to die, that is a muddle.

3. "Really it is not on account of the wealth, and yet you note a difference." [*This refers to Odes* II, IV, 4, 3, *the brother of the first wife, taking leave of brother-in-law remarried to a rich woman.*]

XI

1. Duke Ching of Ch'i asked Kung-tze about government.

2. Kung-tze replied: Prince to be prince; minister, minister; father, father; son, son.

3. The Duke said: Good. I stand by that, if the prince be not prince; minister not minister; father not father; son not son, although there is grain can I manage to eat it all?

> L. *"Although I have my revenue, can I enjoy it?"* Possibly: *"although there is grain will I have time to eat it?"* M. gives no example of chu (1) *interrogative.*

XII

1. He said: Settle disputes with half a word, "the Sprout" could do that.

2. Tze-lu (the Sprout) never slept on a promise.

XIII

1. He said: In hearing litigations I am like another, the thing is to have no litigation, *n'est-ce pas?*

XIV

1. Tze-chang asked about government. He said: Not to lie down on it; to act from the middle of the heart.

XV

1. He said: Extensive study for accomplishments; restraint by the rites; by short-cuts across fields you lose the great road.

XVI

1. He said: The proper man brings men's excellence to focus, he does not focus their evil qualities; the mean man does the reverse.

XVII

1. Chi K'ang asked Confucius about government. Kung-tze replied; Government consists in correcting; if you lead by being correct, who will dare be incorrect?

XVIII

1. Chi K'ang worried about thieves, questioned Confucius. Kung-tze answered: If you weren't covetous, they wouldn't steal even if you paid 'em.

XIX

1. Chi K'ang asked Confucius about government: "What about killing the wayward for the benefit of the well behaved?"

Kung-tze answered: Why kill to govern? If you want the good, the people will be good; the proper man acting according to his conscience is wind, the lesser folk acting on conscience, grass; grass with wind above it must bend.

XX

1.   Tze-chang asked what an officer should be like to go far.

2.   He said: What do you call going far?

3.   Tze-chang said: To be heard of throughout the state, to be heard of in his clan.

4.   He said: That's notoriety not distinction (or perspicacity, making a wide noise not getting very far).

5.   The far-effective man is solid, upright, loves justice; examines people's words, looks into their faces, thinks how, in what way, he is inferior to them, roots in the state and goes far; roots in his family and effects things at a distance.

6.   The notorious bloke puts up a show of manhood, and acts counter to it, perfectly confident; is heard about to the end of the state, makes a noise throughout all his clan.

XXI

1.   Fan Ch'ih walking with him below the rain altars (or to celebration of the rain sacrifice pantomime) said: Venture to ask how to lift one's conscience in action; to correct the hidden tare, and separate one's errors?

2.   He said: An excellent question!

3.   Put first the action, second the success. Won't that raise the level of your conscious acts? Work on one's own faults, not on someone else's hatefulnesses, won't that comb out the hidden weeds?

For one morning's temper to jeopard one's life and even that of one's relatives, isn't that hallucination?

XXII

1.   Fan Ch'ih asked about humaneness. He said: Love men. Asked about knowledge. He said: To know men.

2.   Fan Ch'ih didn't get as far (see through to the end of that answer).

3.   He said: Promote the straight, and grind the crooked, that way you can straighten 'em.

4.   Fan Ch'ih retired, and seeing Tze-Hsia said: Just saw the big man and asked him about knowledge. He said: Promote the straight and grind the crooked, that way you can straighten the crooks, how did he mean it?

5.   Tze-Hsia said: That's a rich and ample saying.

6.   Shun had the Empire, picked out Kao-Yao from the multitude, promoted him, and wrong 'uns departed. T'ang

had the Empire, he picked out I Yin from all the hordes, pro-
moted him, and the wrong 'uns departed.

XXIII

1. Tze-Kung asked about friendship. He said: Speak out
from the centre of your mind, maintain the true process, if he
can't hitch to it, don't disgrace yourself.

XXIV

1. Tsang-tze said: The proper man makes friends on the
basis of culture, and by his friends develops his manhood (or
develops his manhood through this fluid exchange).

BOOK THIRTEEN

Tze-Lu, the Sprout

I

1. Tze-Lu asked about government. He said: Go ahead,
and work at it.

2. Asked further. Said: Don't lie down on it.

II

1. Chung-kung being minister of the Chi Head asked
about government. He said: First get your assistants, overlook
small faults and promote men of solid talent.

2. Said: How shall I know men of solid talent?

Said: Promote those you do know, will everybody then ne-
glect those whom you don't?

III

1. Tze-Lu said: The Lord of Wei is waiting for you to
form a government, what are you going to do first?

2. He said: Settle the names (determine a precise termi-
nology).

3. Tze-lu said: How's this, you're divagating, why fix 'em?

4. He said: You bumpkin! Sprout! When a proper man
don't know a thing, he shows some reserve.

5. If words (terminology) are not (is not) precise, they
cannot be followed out, or completed in action according to
specifications.

6. When the services (actions) are not brought to true fo-
cus, the ceremonies and music will not prosper; where rites

and music do not flourish punishments will be misapplied, not make bullseye, and the people won't know how to move hand or foot (what to lay hand on, or stand on).

7.   Therefore the proper man must have terms that can be spoken, and when uttered be carried into effect; the proper man's words must cohere to things, correspond to them (exactly) and no more fuss about it.

IV

1.   Fan Ch'ih asked to be taught agriculture. He said: I am not as good as an old peasant. Asked to study gardening. He said: I am not as good as an old gardener.

2.   Fan Ch'ih went out. He said: What a nit-wit, that Fan.

3.   If the men above love the rites no one of the people will dare be irreverent. If the men above love justice, none of the people will fail to conform, if the men above love veracity, none of the people will want to use mendacity, when the Great one is like this, the people of the Four Squares will come to him with their children on their backs, what does he need to know about farming?

V

1.   Reciting the three hundred odes, given a government mission and not understanding it, sent to the Four Coigns and not being able to give the answers, even with a lot of talk won't be able to carry it through. [L.: notwithstanding extent of his learning, what practical use is it?]

VI

1.   He said: When a prince's character is properly formed, he governs without giving orders (without orders, things go on). If his character is twisty he can give orders, but they won't be carried out.

VII

1.   He said: The governments (forms of government) of Lu and Wei: elder and younger brothers.

VIII

1.   He described Ching, a younger member of the Ducal family in Wei, by saying: He knew how to live (run a house). When he began to own something he said: what a lot. When he had a bit more, he said: this is enough. When rich, he said: how magnificent.

IX

1. When he went to Wei, Zan Yu drove.
2. He said: What's the population?
3. Zan Yu said: Well populated, what next? Said: Enrich them.
4. Said: They are rich, what next? Said: Educate.

X

1. He said: If anybody had used me for twelve months I'd have been able to do something, and in three years to have done something perfect.

XI

1. He said: Honest men govern a country a hundred years, they could vanquish the malevolent and get rid of the death penalty. I mean these precise words.

[*Possibly the first time anyone had thought of this.*]

XII

1. He said: With a real king, it would need a generation to produce the consequent humanization.

XIII

1. He said: If a man correct himself what difficulty will he have in consequent government, if he cannot correct himself, what's he doing in (or with) government, anyhow? [*P. comment pourrait-il rectifier la conduite des autres?*]

XIV

1. To Zan-tze, coming from court, he said: Why so late? Answered: There was official business. He said: May have been business *affaires du prince*, but if it were government business, even though I'm not in office, been very hard for me not to hear of it.

XV

1. Duke Ting asked if there were one sentence that could bring prosperity to a state. Kung-tze answered: One sentence could hardly put all that in motion.

[*cf*/Great Learning, Mature Study IX.3, *semina motuum.*]

2. There is a saying: it is difficult to be a prince, not easy to be a minister.
3. Knowing it is difficult to be prince, this one sentence might nearly bring prosperity to a state.

4.   Said: Is there one sentence that can ruin a state? Kung-tze answered: Hardly, but there's a saying: no pleasure in being prince save that no one can go counter to what I say.

5.   If good and unopposed that's all right? But if evil and no one oppose, that's almost enough to ruin a state? *N'est-ce pas?*

XVI

1.   The Duke of Sheh asked about government.

2.   He said: Those near, happy; those afar, attracted and come.

XVII

1.   Tze-Hsia, being governor of Chu-fu, asked about government. He said: Not want things rushed, and not on the lookout for small profits; If you want things rushed they won't go through to the end;* looking for small profits, the big jobs won't be done right.

XVIII

1.   The Duke of Sheh said to Kung-tze: There are honest characters in my village, if a man steals a sheep his son will bear witness to it.

2.   Kung-tze said: There are honest men in my village with this difference; a father will conceal his son's doing, and a son his father's. There's honesty (straight seeing) in that, too.

XIX

1.   Fan Ch'ih asked about full manhood. He said: When living in comfort to be modest, when taking hold of affairs to observe honest procedure.

If one is to distinguish the kung[1] *from the* ching[+] *I think we must take it as between stasis and kinesis, the* ching *containing the radical for beat, and going back, I take it, to beating on the earth to propitiate the grain spirits (grass on top left, and various meanings of the* chü *(1541, a, b)—both terms given in dictionary as reverent).*
With sincerity in what you give men, even among the wild tribes (bowmen, and with dogs at camp-fire) east and north, these qualities cannot be shed (cannot be wasted, *leaf fallen, from tree rad/*).

---

* P. *Alors vous ne les comprendrez bien.*

XX

1. Tze-kung asked for the definition of an officer. He said: He has a sense of shame, if you send him to the last corner of the realm, he will carry out the prince's decrees and not disgrace himself.

2. Said: What's the next thing to that? [*Or as L.:* What category next?] Said: His own temple group weigh him and find him filial, folk in his own village knowing his weight find him brotherly.

3. Said: May I ask what next? Said: When he speaks he must stick to his word; acts must be consequent, water-on-stone, water-on-stone (persistent) little men, mebbe they constitute the next lot.

4. Said: What about the lot now in government? He said: Pint-pots and bamboo baskets (or buckets, utensils), count 'em as that, it'll do. [*E poi basta.*] (*Aliter:* they can use an abacus, calculate their own advantage, *or simply "all told".*)

XXI

1. He said: Not being able to give to (be with) men who act on "what it is all about," I must (teach) the pushing and the cautious; the forward will go ahead and take hold; the cautious will stick to not doing what's not to be done. [P. *s'abstiennent au moins de pratiquer ce qui dépasse leur raison.*]

XXII

1. He said: The people of the South have a saying: an unconstant (inconsistent, inconsequent) man can't rise to be a wizard or doctor (better: can neither invoke nor cure), that's a good one.

2. Inconsistent (incoherent) in carrying his inwit into act, likely to meet disgrace.

3. He said: Not observing the signs, and that's all.

[*?* *a simple inattention enough to bring his downfall or:* he does not observe the signs, and that's all there is to be said about it; *for the doctor it would be symptoms, fails to diagnose, thus defining the word* heng², *consequent;* pu heng, *not consequent. One must insist on the nature of many verses as being set down in order to define particular words, as did Lorenzo Valla in his Elegantiae. Also Kung's laconism, highly pleasing to some readers.*]

XXIII

1. He said: The proper man is pleasant spoken but not just like everyone else. The small man is identical but not agreeable.

XXIV

1. Tze-kung said: What about a fellow that everyone in the village likes? He said: Won't do.

"What about a fellow everyone in his village hates?" He said: Won't do. Not up to the man whom the decent people in the village like and the wrong 'uns hate.

XXV

1. He said: The superior man is easy to serve and hard to please. Try to please him with something crooked and he won't be pleased. He employs men in accordance with their capacity. The mean man is easy to please and hard to work for. You can please him by doing wrong. He wants to get everything out of the same man.

XXVI

1. He said: The proper man is liberal and not high-horsey [*The* t'ai⁺. 6023 *liberal, hand grip over water rad/can also mean exalted, with the cross-light, lofty, high-minded and not proud*] (honoured and not proud). The mean man is proud and not high-minded (honoured, honourable).

XXVII

1. He said: The firm-edge, the persistent, the tree-like, those who hold in their speech, come near to full manhood.

> *No, reticent. And to combat anyone who thinks Karlgren a mere academic, cf/his note on "the impure light of fire that shines outward, the pure light of water that shines inward."*

XXVIII

1. Tze-lu said: What's the real definition of a scholar. He said: Urgent, quiet; [*M. gives the three terms:* earnest, pressing, pleased] standing by or looking at his own thought, his own mind-field or heart-field, easy to get on with (i^2) cheerful. [*I shd/ be inclined to add "spontaneous" to possible meanings of this* i^2.] He can be called a scholar (-officer), earnest with his friends, and stimulating; cheerful and spontaneous with his elder and younger brothers.

XXIX

1. If a good man teach the people for seven years, they can go to war.

XXX

1. He said: To send an untrained people to war is to throw them away.

BOOK FOURTEEN

Hsien Wan
Hsien asked

I

1. Hsien asked what is shameful. He said: When the country has a good government to be thinking only of salary; when the country has bad government, to be thinking only of salary: that is shameful.

II

1. "When the letch to get on, to make a show, when resentments and greeds aren't given way to; that makes manhood?"

2. He said: That constitutes doing what's difficult. As to its being full manhood (*humanitas*), I don't know.

III

1. He said: Loving comfort, cuddling domesticity, is not enough to make a scholar (scholar-officer, *shih*).

IV

1. He said: When the country is decently governed: daring words; daring acts. When the country is not decently governed, daring acts and conventional speech. [Sun *in first tone, a grandson; in 4th: Prudent, docile, reserved.*]

V

1. He said: He who has the *virtu* to act on his inwit must have words, but he who has words needn't necessarily act according to conscience. He who is manly must have courage, audacity, but he who is audacious needn't necessarily have full *humanitas*, manhood.

VI

1. Nan-kung Kuo said to Kung-tze: Yi was a good archer, Ao could drag a boat along on land, neither died a natural

death. Yu and Chi did their own farm-work and rose to be emperors. The big man didn't reply. Nan-kung Kuo went out. He said: A proper man, that! what a man ought to be like. Respects conscientious action as a man should.

VII

1.   He said: Superior men aren't always complete; no mean man has manhood.

> *The language is very close; one might say,* a man can have the voice of his ancestry within him, without attaining complete *humanitas*. No mean man has *humanitas*.

VIII

1.   He said: Love exists, can it be other than exigent? Where there is sincerity (mid-mind, mid-heart) can it refrain from teaching?

> [*"word-each."* 2338. hui⁺. *Again it is instruction by sorting out terms. Can you get the centre of the mind, without terminology?*]

IX

1.   He said: Drawing up the decrees (government orders) P'i Shan invented the straw (i.e., made the rough drafts), Shih-shu inched the words* and discussed them with the Chef du Protocole (the *Hsing jen*, official in charge of travelling envoys), Tze-Yu combed 'em out and polished 'em and Tze-Chan of Tung Li added the beauties.

X

1.   Someone asked about (this) Tze-Chan. He said: A kind man.

2.   Asked about Tze-Hsi. He said: That bloke! That one!

> [*If you accept Legge's interpretation, but the* pi tsai *might be perhaps taken as:* "just another, uomo qualunque." *There just isn't enough in the text to indicate tone of voice: query, alas? or what will you!*]

3.   Asked about Kwan Chung. He said: *Jen yeh*†, man who snatched from Po chief, P'ien, a city of three hundred (L. families), (L. the latter) ate coarse rice till his teeth were gone

---

  * P. (?) *les examinait attentivement et y plaçait les dits des anciens.*

  † Possibly wider reading wd/ enlighten as to bearing of Chinese equivalents of, Oh, ugh, and ah! and any flavour that might have been kept in a strictly oral tradition as to tone of voice used. Here it seems to be approbative, and the *tsai* seems pejorative in verse 2.

(L. and current, till death) without a grumbling word. [*L.'s note, that the dispossessed respected Kwan to this extent.*]

XI

1. He said: To be poor without grumbling or resentments is difficult; easy to be rich and not haughty.

XII

1. He said: Mang Kung-ch'o for being an elder (senex, senator) of the Chao or Wei, has it in abundance (easily more than fill the pattern requirements), couldn't make it as Great Officer of Tang or Hsieh.

XIII

1. Tze-Lu asked about the perfect man (the man of perfect focus).

He said: As if he had Tsang Wu-chung's knowledge, Kung-ch'o's freedom from greed, Chwang of Pien's bravery, Zan Ch'iu's versatile talents, culture enough for the rites and music, he'd have the wherewithal for human perfection.

2. Said: At present why need we such perfect humanity; to see chance of profit and consider equity, to see danger and be ready to accept one's fate, not to forget the level words of a compact made long ago, that also would make a focus'd man (a man brought to the point, perfect).

XIV

1. Asking about Kung shu Wan, he said to Kung-ming Chia: Do you stick by the statement that your big man doesn't talk, doesn't smile, doesn't accept anything?

2. Kung-ming Chia replied: That's from rumours (reports) overrunning the limit. My big man talks when it's the time, whereby he does not bore with his talking; smiles when pleased, thereby not boring with grins; when it is just to take, he accepts, thus he don't wear people out with taking. He said: Yes, does he really do that?

XV

1. He said: Tsang Wu-chung flowing thru Fang, asked Lu to appoint a successor; although you say this is not bringing pressure to bear on a prince, I won't stand by that definition.

XVI

1. He said: Duke Wan of Tsin was wily and not correct, [chüeh$^{2\cdot5}$; wily *from words and an awl, clouds of three colours, hypocrite. P. admirably:* un fourbe sans droiture.]

Duke Hwan of Ch'i was correct and not wily.

XVII

1. Tze-lu said: Duke Hwan executed the Ducal-son (his brother) Chiu; Shao Hu died [L. with his boss], Kwang Chung did not die, say, is that inhuman (unmanly?)?

2. He said: Duke Hwan gathered the princes, not with weapons and war cars: Kwan Chung's energy (strength) that was; is that manly? It is manly.

XVIII

1. Tze-Kung [*not to be confused with Kung* (*fu*) *tze*] said: I'd give it that Kwan Chung was lacking in humanity, Duke Hwan had his brother Chiu bumped off, and (Kwan Chung) couldn't die, but came back and worked with Hwan as (Prime Minister).

2. He said: Kwan Chung reciprocal'd, aided Duke Hwan as prime minister, overruling the princes; unified and rectified the empire, and people till today receive the benefits. But for Kwan Chung we'd be wearing our hair loose and buttoning our coats to the left.

3. You want him to behave like a common man or woman, who could end in a creek or ditch without anyone's being the wiser?

XIX

1. Kung-shu Wan's minister, the Great Officer Hsien, rose shoulder to shoulder with Wan in this Duke's (court).

2. Confucius hearing this said: Wan's the name for him [*Wan*, accomplished, having real culture] on that count.

XX

1. He was speaking of the evil government of the Duke Ling of Wei (Nan-tze's husband). K'ang-tze said: A man like that, how come he don't lose (his state)?

2. Kung-tze said: The second brother Yu looks after guests and strangers; the ecclesiastic T'o looks after the dynastic temple; Wang-sun Chia looks after the army corps and regiments, men like that, how lose his (state)?

XXI

1. He said: If a man don't say what he means, it's difficult to shape business to it, action to it. [*L. and M. take the* put se *as meaning immodest. Pictogrammic interpretation at least as interesting.*]

XXII

1. Chan Ch'ang murdered the Duke of Ch'i.

2. Confucius took a bath, went to court, and made formal announcement to the Duke Ai, in these words: Chan Ch'ang has murdered his prince; this invites punishment.

3. The Duke said: Inform the Three Great.

4. Kung-tze said: Coming (in rank) just after the Great Officers, I did not venture to leave my prince uninformed. (My prince) says inform the Three Great.

5. He announced it to the Three, (who pled) *non possumus*.

Kung-tze said: Coming just after the Great Officers, I did not dare omit the announcement.

XXIII

1. Tze-lu asked about serving a prince. He said: Don't cheat him, stand up to him [L. withstand him to his face].

XXIV

1. He said: A proper man progresses upward (far), a mean man progresses downward (far).

> *Might almost say:* goes far up, far down. All the way through, penetrates upward or downward. *Covers the meaning:* his mental penetration goes upward, or downward.

XXV

1. He said: In the old days men studied to make themselves, now they study to impress others.

XXVI

1. Chu Po-yu sent a man to Confucius.

2. Kung-tze sat with him and questioned him: What's your boss doing?
Replied: "My big man wants to diminish the number of his errors, and cannot." The messenger went out. Kung-tze said: Some messenger, isn't he?

XXVII

1. He said: Not in a particular government office, don't plan to run it.

XXVIII

1. Tsang-tze (his son-in-law) said: A proper man's thoughts do not go outside (the sphere of) his office. [Yi King *diagram 52, eight characters, here seven, omitting one.*]

XXIX

1.   He said: A proper man is ashamed of words [L. modest in speech], and goes beyond (them) in action. [*Also:* ashamed of words that exceed his action.]

XXX

1.   He said: A proper man's mode of life is three-ply. I can't make it: manhood without regrets; knowing, he is without suspicion; courageous and therefore without anxiety.

2.   Tze-Kung said: Boss, that's the way you go on yourself.

XXXI

1.   Tze-Kung square-measured men (one by another). Confucius said: Tze, you must have heavy talents, *n'est-ce pas?* Anyhow, I haven't got the spare time.

XXXII

1.   He said: Not worried that others don't know me, worried by my incapacities.

XXXIII

1.   He said: Not anticipating deceit or calculating on infidelity [L. anticipate attempts to deceive him, nor think beforehand of not being believed. *Might even be:* don't oppose deceit (to deceit) or calculate on a man's lies, or lying], but to be quick to spot a hoax when it happens, man who can do this must have solid sense?

XXXIV

1.   In course of conversation (old) Wei-shang Mau, said to him: Hummock, my boy, how do you manage to roost when there's a roost going, do you manage it by an oily tongue?

2.   He said: I don't dare oil the tongue, but I hate stick-in-a-rut-ness (hate being boxed in with frowst).

XXXV

1.   He said: A horse is grade A not because of strength but from a balance of qualities (proportionate ensemble).

> *This is another definition, directing thought to the composition of the ideogram itself. A "separate differences horse," extraordinary, yes, defined by the* ch'eng, *with sense of weighing of the grain, good grain, agreeable etc.* (383) vid. *also alternations* (3607).

XXXVI

1.   Someone said what about returning straight goodness for injury [L. kindness for injury]?

2.   He said: What do you do to repay someone who acts straight with you?

3.   See straight when someone injures you, and return good deeds by good deeds.

> *L. has the old:* justice for injury, kindness for kindness. *This does not exhaust the contents of the ideograms.* Yüan (4th): *murmur, harbour resentment. Allay resentment by straightness, watch a man who harbours resentment against you. Give frank act for frank act. Understanding of Confucius has been retarded by wanting to fit his thought into gross occidental cliches.*

XXXVII

1.   He said: The extent to which no one understands me!

2.   Tze-kung said: How do you make out no one understands you (knows you)?

He said: I do not harbour resentment against heaven, I study what is below and my thought goes on, penetrates upward. Is it heaven that knows me? [*Not id. but cf/Aristotle: generals* FROM *particulars.*]

XXXVIII

1.   Kung-po Liao slandered [*currently "smeared"*] Tze-Lu to Chi-sun [*cd. be:* definitely brought formal charge against him, *or:* laid an information, pejorative, or definitely false]. Tze-fu Ching-po told of it, saying: The big man is certainly having his intentions misled (direction of his will deflected) by Kung-po Liao, I have strength enough to have him executed in the market place or in court. [*i.e. as common criminal or great officer*].

2.   He said: If my mode of living is to make headway, or if my process is to go to waste, it is destined [*seal and mouth of heaven*]; what can Kung-po Liao do about that decree?

XXXIX

1.   He said: Some with solid talents get away from their generation.

2.   Those nearest (that solidity) retire from a particular locality.

3.   The next grade get away from dazzle (display).

4. Those next get away from words [the dominion of catch phrases. *Cd/ even be:* stop talking].

> 5172, *in various connotations.* (i): *look down upon. rad/ 160. "bitter". A cross under rad/ 117. looks not unlike a graph of a spinning-whorl.*

XL

1. He said: Seven men started this [L. have done this].

XLI

1. Tze-lu was passing the night at Stone Gate, the gate guard said: Where from?

Tze-lu said: The Kung clan.

Said: He's the man who knows there's nothing to be done, yet sticks with it (keeps on trying).

XLII

1. He was drumming on the musical stone in Wei, a man with a straw hamper on his back passed the door of the Kung family house, and said: What a mind he's got beating that stone, *n'est ce pas?*

2. That was that, then he said: How vulgar! Persistent, water on stone, water on stone. When one is not recognized that's the end of it, end it. "Over deep with your clothes on, pick 'em up when the water is shallow." (Odes I. iii. 9.)

3. He said: Certainly, no difficulty about that.

> [*The text does not give one sufficient to insist on the bearing of the* kuo, 3732, *fruit.*]

XLIII

1. In the History, Tze-chang said: What's the meaning of the statement: Kao-tsung observing the imperial mourning did not speak for three years?

2. He said: Why drag in Kao-tsung, in the old days everyone did. When the sovereign died, the hundred officers carried on, getting instructions from the prime minister for three years.

XLIV

1. He said: When men high up love the rites the people are easily governed.

XLV

1. Tze-lu asked about "right 'uns." He said: (The proper man) disciplines himself with reverence for the forces of vegetation.

Said: Is that all there is to it?

Said: Disciplines himself and quiets others (rests them, considers their quiet).

Said: Disciplines himself and brings tranquillity to the hundred clans. Discipline self and quiet the hundred clans, Yao and Shun were almost in agony over that (almost painfully anxious to do that).

XLVI

1. Yuan Zang remained squatting on his heels as Kung approached.

He said: Young and not deferentially (holding the line) fraternal, come to manhood and not transmitting, old and not dying, exactly a burglarious bum. Hit him over the shin with his cane.

XLVII

1. A young Ch'ueh villager ran errands for him, someone said: Up and coming?

2. He said: I see him sit in men's chairs, walk abreast of his elders, he's not trying to fill up, he's trying to finish in a hurry.

BOOK FIFTEEN

Wei Ling Kung
Duke Ling of Wei

I

1. Duke Ling of Wei asked Kung-tze about tactics. Kung-tze replied: I have heard a bit about sacrificial stands and dishes, I have not studied the matter of army arrangements. He left next morning.

2. In Chan, provisions cut off, those following him sickened so no one could get up.

3. Tze-Lu showing his irritation said: Does a gentleman have to put up with this sort of thing? He said: A gentleman gets obstinate when he has to; a small man dissolves (when he's up against it).

II

1. He said: Tz'u ("Grant"), you think I make a lot of studies and commit things to memory?

Replied: Aye, ain't it so?

Said: No, I one, through, string-together, sprout [*that is:* unite, flow through, connect, put forth leaf]. For me there is one thing that flows through, holds things together, germinates.

III

1. He said: Sprout, few know how to carry their inwit straight into acts.

IV

1. He said: Shun governed without working. How did he do it? He soberly corrected himself and sat looking to the south (the sovereign sat on a throne looking south), that's all.

V

1. Tze-chang asked about conduct.

2. He said: Speak from the plumb centre of your mind, and keep your word; bamboo-horse your acts [*that is*, have this quality of surface hardness, and suppleness] with reverence for the vegetative powers, even if you are among the wild men of the South and North (Man and Mo), that is the way to act. If you speak without this candour, and break your word; if you act without polish (honour) and reverence, how will it go even in your own bailiwick (department [*and*] neighbourhood)?

3. Standing (stablishing, building up a heap) let him form a triad looking at those two powers before him (*either* facing him, *or* existing there before him).

> Note the three "armstrongs," bent arms with biceps, in upper part of the ts'an ideogram, and use of same in The Pivot XXII, last line.

In his carriage let him see them hitched to the yoke [*from rad 144, as traces or reins. Contrast: "like a carriage with no place to hitch the traces"*], then he can proceed.

4. Tze-chang wrote these (words) on his belt.

VI

1. He said: Straight, and how! the historian Yu. Country properly governed, he was like an arrow; country in chaos he was like an arrow.

2.   Some gentleman, Chu Po-yu! country decently gov-
erned, he is in office; when the government is rotten he rolls
up and keeps the true process inside him.

VII

1.   He said: When you can talk to a man, and don't, you
lose the man; when it's no use talking to a man, and you talk
to him, you waste words. An intelligent man wastes (loses)
neither men nor words.

VIII

1.   He said: An officer (scholar) ruling his mind, a humane
man (man of full manhood) will not try to live by damaging
his manhood; he will even die to perfect his humanitas.

> *There are probably earlier expressions of this concept; I
> have not yet found an earlier statement as to abolition of
> the death penalty.* Vide supra XIII, xi.

IX

1.   Tze-kung asked about this business of manhood. He
said: The craftsman wanting to perfect his craft must first put
an edge on his tools (take advantage of implements already
there, the containers). Living in a country, take service with
the big men who have solid merit, make friends with the hu-
mane scholar-officers.

X

1.   Yen Yuan asked about governing.

2.   He said: Go along with the seasons of Hsia [*the Hsia
calendar, but probably including the dates for the markets, how-
ever computed*].

3.   *L. & M. both say:* Use Yin state carriages. [*I think it
may refer to the gauge, the wheel-spread, cf/ ref/ to uniform
gauge of wheel-ruts.*]

4.   Wear the Chou coronation cap [*mortar board with
fringe. I suppose this is related to four-squareness, Urzahl*].

5.   Music patterned to the Shao pantomimes.

6.   Banish the ear-noise* of Chang, and clear out the flat-
terers. The tonalities of Chang are slushy, and double-talkers
a danger (diddling, debauching).

---

* P. (excellently): *modulations.*

XI

1. He said: Man who don't think of the far, will have trouble near.

XII

1. He said: Can't get beyond the fact; I have not seen anyone who loves acting from inwit as they love a beautiful person.

XIII

1. He said: Tsang Wan-chung like a man who has purloined his position, he knew the solid merit of Hui of Lin-hsia, and did not get him for colleague.

XIV

1. He said: Requiring the solid from himself and the trifling from others, will keep one far from resentments.

XV

1. He said: When a man don't say, "What's it like, what's it like?" I don't (bother to) compare him to anything, and that's that (*aliter*: I don't know where he'll end up).

XVI

1. He said: Gabbling all day without getting to a discussion of equity (ethics, justice), in love with being clever in a small way; hard to do anything with 'em.

XVII

1. He said: The proper man gives substance (makes the substance of his acts equity) to his acts by equity.

   Cf/ final words of the Ta S'eu: *The treasure of a state is its equity,* or, better, as all Confucian statements treat of process not stasis: *What profits a state is its honesty.*

He proceeds according to the rites, puts them forth modestly, and makes them perfect by sticking to his word. That's the proper man (in whom's the voice of his forebears).

XVIII

1. He said: The proper man is irritated by his incapacities, not irritated by other people not recognizing him.

XIX

1. He said: The gentleman is irritated if his generation die without weighing the worth of his name.

   This sentence illustrates the inadequacy of "gent" as in current parlance of the last century, to translate chun

tzu. cf/ Dial *essay 25 years ago*. *L. gives:* name not men-
tioned after his death. *v. weak for ch'eng 383. from grain rad/*

XX

1.   The proper man seeks everything in himself, the small
man tries to get everything from somebody else.

XXI

1.   He said: The proper man is punctilious but not quar-
relsome, he is for exchange, not provincial.

XXII

1.   He said: The proper man does not promote a fellow for
what he says; nor does he throw out a statement because of
who says it.

XXIII

1.   Tze-kung asked if there were a single verb that you
could practice thru life up to the end.
He said: Sympathy [L. reciprocity], what you don't want
(done to) yourself, don't inflict on another.

XXIV

1.   He said: Whom have I run down or puffed up? If I've
overpraised any one he had something worth examining.
2.   This people had the stuff in 'em (the timber) which en-
abled the three dynasties to find the straight way and go along
it (the timber whereby, the wherewithal).

XXV

1.   Even I reach back to a time when historians left blanks
(for what they didn't know), and when a man would lend a
horse for another to ride; a forgotten era, lost.

XXVI

1.   He said: Elaborate sentences, worked up words confuse
the straightness of action from inwit, lack of forebearance in
small things, messes up greater plans.

XXVII

1.   He said: When the mob hate a man it must be examined;
when everybody likes a man, it must be examined, and how!

XXVIII

1.   He said: A man can put energy into the process, not the
process into the man. [*Ovvero:* a man can practice the right
system of conduct magnanimously, but the fact of there being
a right way, won't make a man use it.]

XXIX

1. He said: To go wrong and not alter (one's course) can be defined (definitely) as going wrong.

XXX

1. He said: I've gone a whole day without eating, (*or even:* I've tried going a whole day without eating) and a whole night without sleep, meditating without profit, it's not as useful as studying particular data (grinding it up in the head).

XXXI

1. He said: The proper man plans right action, he does not scheme to get food: he can plow, and there be famine: he can study, and perhaps get a salary; the proper man is concerned with the right action, he is not concerned with the question of (his possible) poverty.

XXXII

1. He said: Intelligent enough to arrive, not man enough to hang onto; though he succeed, he will fail.

2. Intelligent enough to get a job, man enough to keep it, not go through his work soberly, folk won't respect him.

3. Intelligent enough to get, man enough to hold, regular in his work but not following the correct procedure, no glory.

XXXIII

1. He said: You cannot know a proper man by small things, but he can take hold of big ones, a small man cannot take hold of great things, but you can understand him by the small.

XXXIV

1. He said: The folk's humanity is deeper than fire or water, I've seen people die from standing on fire or water. I have seen no one die from taking a stand on his manhood.

    (*Much of the raciness of Kung's remarks must lie in the click of a phrase, and the turning of different facets of the word.*) Shen 5724, tao 6140, *if in sense of violate, one can read the remark as deep irony.*

XXXV

1. He said: Manhood's one's own, not leavable to teacher. [*Tang, 6087, has very interesting complex of meanings, among which*: undertake, fill an office. *L. nearer meaning:* functioning of manhood cannot be handed over to teacher, *more ironically:* pedagogue.]

XXXVI

1.   He said: The proper man has a shell and a direction (*chen*[1]).

> *This* chen *is a key word, technical, from the "Changes" it is more than the ataraxia of stoics, the insensitivity, ability to "take it." It implies going somewhere. The Confucian will find most terms of Greek philosophy and most Greek aphorisms lacking in some essential; they have three parts of a necessary four, or four parts where five are needed, nice car, no carburetor, gearshift lacking.*

He does not merely stick to a belief [*pictogram: word and lofty, or capital*].

XXXVII

1.   He said: Serving a prince put reverence into the service, feeding comes second.

XXXVIII

1.   He said: See that education has no snob divisions.

XXXIX

1.   He said: Problem of style? Get the meaning across and then STOP.

XL

1.   Mien the (blind) musician called, when they reached the steps Confucius said: Steps; when they came to the mat, he said: Mat; when all were seated he said: So-and-so's there; so-and-so's over there.

2.   Master Mien went out. Tze-chang asked: Is it correct speak to the music master in that way?

3.   He said: That is correct when helping the blind.

BOOK SIXTEEN

Ke She
The Head of Chi

I

1.   The head of the Chi clan was about to attack Chwan-yu.

2.   Zan Yu and Chi-lu went to see Kung-tze, saying: The Chi Boss is going to give Chwan-yu the works.

3.   Kung-tze said: Ain't that your fault, Hook?

4.   It's a long time since one of the earlier kings appointed the headman of Chwan-yu to hold the sacrifices in East Mang, and it is in the middle of our own territory, the man who officiates at its chthonian and grain rites is one of our state servants, how can one attack it?

5.   Zan Yu said: Our big man wants to, we two ministers are both against it.

6.   Kung-tze said: Hook, Chau Zan used to say: While using your power, keep line; when you cannot, retire. How can one serve as guide to a blind man, if he do not support him, or help him up when he falls?

7.   Moreover, your words err, when a tiger or rhino [P. *buffle*] gets out of its stockade, when a turtle or jewel is broken in its casket, whose fault is that?

8.   Zan Yu said: But Chwan-yu is now strong, and near Pi, if he don't take it now it will make trouble for his sons and grandsons in coming generations.

9.   Kung-tze said: Hook, you make a proper man sick refusing to say: I want, and needing to make a discourse about it.

10.   Me, Hillock. I have heard that men who have states or head families are not worried about fewness, but worried about fairness [*potter's wheel ideogram: aliter as verb:* worried about ruling justly], not worried about scarcity, but worried about disquiet. If every man keeps to his own land, there will be no poverty, with harmony there will be no lack of population but tranquillity without upsets (subversions).

11.   It's just like that. Therefore if distant people do not conform, one should attract them by one's own disciplined culture, and by honest action, when they have come in, they will quiet down.

12.   You, Yu and Ch'iu, are now aides to your big man, distant tribes do not come in, and cannot come [L. he cannot attract them]. The state is divided and decadent, people are going away and splitting up, the state can't hold onto them [L. he cannot preserve it].

13.   And he plans to take up shield and lance inside the territory. I am afraid the Chi grandsons' trouble is not in Chwan-yu, it is inside their own door-yard, behind their own gate-screen. [Hsiao[1], troublesome, *or even* whistling round their gate-screen. M. *gives* ch'iang, *merely as* wall. 2620.]

II

1. Kung-tze said: When the empire is decently governed, the rites, music (musical taste), police work and punitive expeditions proceed from the Child of Heaven; when the empire is not governed, these proceed from the feudal chiefs. When they are decided by these princes, they usually lose (sovereignty) within ten generations. When these (rites, etc.) proceed from the great officers the loss usually occurs within five generations; when the subsidiary ministers in charge of the states give the orders, they usually smash within three generations.

2. When the empire is properly governed the government is NOT in the control of the great officers.

3. When the empire is properly governed, the folk don't discuss it.

III

1. Kung-tze said: For five generations the revenue has not come in to the ducal house. The government was seized by the great officers, four generations ago, the three lines of the Hwan (Dukes) are mere epigones.

IV

1. Kung-tze said: There are three valuable friendships, and three harmful. Friendship with the straight, with the faithful [Liang, 3947 b. *not in sense as above in* XV, xxxvi, *has also sense:* considerate] and with the well-informed are an augment; making a convenience of snobs, nice softies (excellent squshies), and of pliant flatterers does one harm.

V

1. Kung-tze said: There are three pleasures which augment a man, three that harm. The pleasure of dissociating perceptions of rites and music; pleasure in other men's excellence; the pleasure in having a lot of friends with talent and character, augment; the enjoyment of swank, loafing and debauchery, harm.

VI

1. Kung-tze said: When you manage to meet a proper man, there are three committable errors: to speak when it is not up to you to speak, *videlicet* hastiness; not to speak when you should, that's called covertness; and to speak without noting a man's expression, that is called blindness.

VII

1.   Kung-tze said: The proper man guards against three things; in youth before the blood and spirits have come to orderly course, he guards against taking root in luxurious appearances; at maturity when the blood and spirits are in hardy vigour, he guards against quarrelsomeness; and in old age when the blood and spirits have waned, against avarice.

VIII

1.   Kung-tze said: The proper man has three awes; he stands in awe of the decrees of destiny [*heaven's mouth and seal*], he stands in awe of great men, and of the words of the sages.

2.   The piker does not recognize the decrees of heaven, he is cheeky with great men, and sneers at the words of the sages.

IX

1.   Kung-tze said: Those who know instinctively (as at birth) are the highest; those who study and find out, come next; those who are hampered and study come next [k'un, *hampered, a tree boxed in, limited, in poverty, chance of growth. In distress, weary*]. Those who are boxed in [L. stupid] and do not study constitute the lowest people.

X

1.   Kung-tze said: The proper man has three subjects of meditation; in seeing, that he see with intelligence [*or* with his intelligence, *definite pictogram of moving eye and light from above, very strong and very inclusive phrase*], in hearing, that he hear accurately, i.e. apprehend [*the component mind in lower rt/ of ideogram*, get the meaning], that his appearance be serene, his bearing respectful, and that his speech come from the plumb centre of his mind (not slanty), that his affairs maintain reverence [*I do not think this ideogram can be too far separated from the original source, it has to do with vegetative order*]; when in doubt, that he ask questions, and when enraged that he think of troublesome consequence; when he sees the chance of gain, that he think of equity.

> *Up to now we have had many definitions of words, several chapters define or dissociate categories, ref/* Ta S'eu, *testament, verses 3, 4.*

XI

1.   Kung-tze said: Seeing the good as if unreachable; seeing evil as if it were boiling to the touch; I have seen such men, and heard such talk.

2.   Living in retirement to find out what they really want, practicing equity to carry into conduct. I have heard conversation about this, but have not seen such men.

XII

1.   Duke Ching of Ch'i had a thousand quadriga, on the day of his death (even at his funeral) the people did not praise his honesty [L. not praise for single virtue]. Po-i and Shu-ch'i died of hunger 'neath Southslope Head and the folk praise them down to this day.

2.   That illustrates what I was saying.

XIII

Kung-fu-tzu's son

1.   Ch'an K'ang asked Po-yu if he had heard anything "different" [i.e. *from what K. told the rest of them*].

2.   He replied: No, he was standing alone (one day) as I was passing the hall in a hurry (or going by the court-yard), he said: Studied the odes? (*Or* are you studying the odes?)

I replied: No.

"Not study the odes, won't be able to use words."

I went out and studied the Odes.

3.   Another day he was again standing alone, I went by the court in a hurry. Said: Studying the rites?

Replied: No.

"If you don't study the rites you won't be able to stand up" (build up a character).

I went out and studied the Rites.

4.   Those are the two things I've heard (from him).

5.   Ch'an K'ang retired saying delightedly: Asked one question and got to three things. I heard of the Odes, I heard of the Book of Rites, I heard that a proper man don't nag his son.

XIV

1.   The wife of the prince of a state is styled by the prince: The distinguished person; she calls herself: Small child; the people of the state call her: The Prince's distinguished person; those of other states style her: Little small sovran, and of (still) other states style her Prince's distinguished person.

BOOK SEVENTEEN

Yang Ho
(a minister who had usurped power)

I

1. Yang Ho wanted to see Confucius (Kung-tze), Kung-tze did not see him. He sent Kung-tze a pig. Kung-tze, timing to miss him, went out to pay his duty call, but met Yang on the road.

2. He said: I want to talk to you: keeping treasure inside you, country in chaos, call that manly?

Said: No.

"In love with work (in love with following the service) continually missing the time, call that intelligent?"

Said: No.

"Sun and moon move, the year don't wait for you."

Said: O.K. I'll take office.

II

He said: Men are born pretty much alike, it's practising something that puts the distance between them.

III

He said: Only those of highest intelligence, and lowest simplicity do not shift. [L. cannot be changed, *text probably includes both meanings.*]

IV

(On cultural persuasion)

1. At Battle-Wall he heard the sound of stringed instruments and singing.

2. The big man smiled with pleasure saying: Why use an ox knife to kill a fowl?

3. Tze-yu replied, I'm the man, sir, who once heard you say: If the gentleman studies the process and loves men, the lower people will study the process and be easy to rule. [*I suppose Yen Tze-yu was in charge of this frontier town on a crag.*]

4. He said: You fellows, Yen's words are on the line, I was just joking round it.

V

1. Kung-shan Fu-zao giving trouble in the passes [field paths, 4896, short cuts, *hence vb/* rebel] of Pi, invited him and he (Confucius) wanted to go.

2. Tze-lu was "not amused," said: Not to be done, that's that. Why must you poke into that Kung-shan gang?

3. He said: The man's invited me, suppose I go with him [*aliter*: is that empty, an empty gesture. *Depends on which sense one gives to* 6536 (*or c*) t'u], suppose he should make use of me, couldn't I create a Chou in the East?

VI

Tze-chang asked Kung-tze about manhood. Kung-tze said: To be able [neng², *power in union, as differing from* k'e, *power to support, hold up, carry*] to practice five things (all together) would humanize the whole empire.

(Chang) asked clarification.

Said: Sobriety (? *serenitas*), magnanimity, sticking by one's word, promptitude (in attention to detail), kindliness (*caritas*).

Serenity will shape things so that you will not be insulted.

With magnanimity you will reach the mass.

Keep your word and others will confide [*also*: trust you enough to employ you].

By promptitude you will get thru your jobs (meritorious work).

Kindliness is enough to get results from those you employ.

VII

1. Pi Hsi invited him and he wanted to go.

Tze-Lu said: I, Sprout, am the chap who heard you say, sir, "When a man personally does evil, a proper man won't enter [won't go into (it with him)].

Pi-Hsi is in rebellion in Chung-mau. If you go, what's that like?

2. He said: I said it. But isn't it said: You can grind a hard thing without making it thin.

Isn't it said: Some white things can be dipped and not blackened. [*Cf. G. Guinicelli*].

3. Am I like a bitter melon, to be hung up and not eaten?

VIII

1. He said: Sprout, have you heard the six terms (technical terms) and the six befuddlements (overgrowings)?

Replied: No.

2. "Sit down, I'll explain 'em to you."

3. Love of manhood minus love of study: befuddlement into naïveté.

Love of knowledge without love of study: runs wild into waste incorrelation.

Love of keeping one's word, without study runs amok into doing harm.

Love of going straight without studying where to, degenerates into bad manners.

Love of boldness without love of study, leads to chaos.

Love of hard edge (hardness, stiffness) leads to impertinence.

IX

1. He said: Mes enfants, why does no one study the great Odes? [*Or more probably*: these Odes.]

2. The Odes can exhilarate (lift the will).

3. Can give awareness (sharpen the vision, help you spot the bird).

4. Can teach dissociation. [*L. takes it as*: exchange, sociability.]

5. Can cause resentment (against evil).
    L. regulate feelings ?? katharsis ?? means of dealing with resentment. I mistrust a soft interpretation.

6. Bring you near to being useful to your father and mother, and go on to serving your sovran.

7. Remember the names of many birds, animals, plants and trees.

X

He said to (his son) Po-Yu: You go to work on the Chao-South and Shao-South poems. A man who hasn't worked on the Chao-nan and Shao-nan is like one who stands with his face to a wall.

XI

He said: Rites, they say, Rites! How do we place the jewels and the silk robes? Music, they say, Music! Where do the gongs and drums stand? [*Mind on instruments not on shape of the music.*]

XII

He said: Hard as a whetstone outside and wobbly as grass (or squshy) inside is rather like a picayune fellow who bores a hole in a wall to steal.

XIII   2556

He said: These (? lenient) village prototypes are purloiners (con men) acting on a conscience not their own [*L. takes*

yuan² (7725) *as equiv.*; 7727. ? *Rousseauequers*] good careful,
thieves of virtue. [*P. cherchent les suffrages des villageois.* Note
7725 a.]

XIV

He said: To pass on wayside gossip and smear with scold-
ing is to defoliate one's candour.

> T'u² *is primarily smear, secondarily road, with binome
> L. and M. tell what one has heard on the road.*

> *General sense perfectly clear, the verse is against careless
> gossip and ill-natured slander, "smear-scold" is there in
> the pictogram if one wants it.*

(To waste acts proceeding from clear conscience) is to stop
acting on one's own inner perceptions.

XV

1.   He said: How can one serve a prince along with these
village-sized (kinky) minds?

2.   Until they get on they worry about nothing else, and,
when they have, they worry about losing the advantages.

3.   When they are afraid of losing (advantages, privileges)
there is nothing, absolutely nothing they will not do to retain
(them) (no length they won't go to).

XVI

1.   He said: Men of old had three troubles which no
longer exist.

2.   The old uppishness was reckless (ostentatious), the
present uppishness, mere dissipation;

> [*Might say*, old was hearty, present dissolute. Excess
> vs. pettiness, petty leaks. Exuberance vs. license. *There is
> nothing in such brief statements unless they are taken as
> fixing the meaning and usage of the words.*]

the old punctilio [attention, *cd. almost be point of honour*] was
modest (implying consideration of values), the present is mere
peevishness; the old simplicity was direct, the present consists
in thinking you can fool others by simple wheezes, [*or simply:*
is faked] and that's that.

XVII

He said: Elaborate phrases and a pious expression (L.M. in-
sinuating) seldom indicate manliness.

XVIII

He said: I hate the way purple spoils vermilion, I hate the way the Chang sonority confuses the music of the Elegantiae, I hate sharp mouths (the clever yawp, mouths set on profits) that overturn states and families.

XIX

1. He said: I'd like to do without words.

2. Tze-kung said: But, boss, if you don't say it, how can we little guys pass it on?

3. He said: Sky, how does that talk? The four seasons go on, everything gets born. Sky, what words does the sky use?

XX

Zu Pei wanted to see Kung-tze. Kung-tze declined on account of illness. As the messenger was going out the front door, he took his lute and sang so that the latter could hear.

> *L. notes indicate that Zu had probably asked advice before and not taken it, and that the call was fake, try on.*

XXI

1. Tsai Wo asked about three years' mourning, wasn't one full year enough?

2. He said: If gentlemen do not observe the rites, the rites will go to ruin; if music is not played for three years the music will slip down.

3. The old (good) grain is exhausted, the new grain has risen; fire you kindle by twirling wood is a different fire, you can stop at the end of a year.

> *L. put in idea that "kindling by friction we go thru all the changes of wood" on the belief that they used different kinds of wood drills at different seasons, elm, willow, in spring, date, almond in summer. I should be more inclined to think that Kung indicates a break in continuity, but ends on the note:* but do it if you like. Cf. *verse 6 below.*

4. He said: You'd feel at ease eating your rice and wearing embroidered clothes?

Said: Quite.

5. He said: If you can feel easy, go ahead, but the proper man during the period of mourning does not savour sweet food, does not delight in hearing music, docs not feel easy in

cushy surroundings, and therefore does not indulge, but if you now feel easy about it, go ahead.

6. Tsai Wo went out.

He said: He is not fully humane, a child does not leave its parental arms till it is three; three years' mourning is observed everywhere under heaven, did (Tsai Wo) Yu have three years' parental affection?

I suggest that the mediaeval debate between active and contemplative life is moderated in the old Chinese disposition, the need of contemplative period being answered by the years of mourning.

XXII

He said: Stuffing in food all day, nothing that he puts his mind on, a hard case! Don't chess players at least do something and have solid merit by comparison?

XXIII

Tze-lu said: Does the proper man honour bravery?

He said: The proper man puts equity at the top, if a gentleman have courage without equity it will make a mess; if a mean man have courage without equity he will steal.

XXIV

1. Tze-kung said: Does the proper man have his hatreds also?

Said: He has hates, he hates those who proclaim the ill doing of others; he hates those who live below the current and slander those above; he hates those who are bold without observing the rites (don't use their courage rightly, audacious in outraging the proper procedures), he hates those who obstinately presume and obstruct* [*or*, who are satisfied to presume and obstruct.]

2. Said: Granty, have you any hates?

"Hate those who snoop and pretend they have found out by intelligence; hate those who think brashness is courage; hate blabbers who pretend they do it from honesty."

---

* P. v. interesting and probably right "*qui s'arrêtent*," plus the explanation (*au milieu de leurs entreprises sans avoir le coeur de les achever*), i.e. stop halfway because they haven't the guts to finish.

XXV

He said: Young women and small men [*L. in sense of: flappers and house boys*] are hard to rear, familiarity loses respect, and aloofness rouses resentment.

XXVI

He said: If a man is hateful at forty he'll be so to the end.

BOOK EIGHTEEN

Wei Tze
The Viscount of Wei

I

(*Decline of the Yin Dynasty*)

1. The Viscount of Wei retired. The Viscount of Chi became a slave. Pi-kan protested and died.

2. Kung-tze said: Yin had three men (with a capital M).

II

1. Hui of Liu-Hsia, chief criminal judge, was dismissed three times. Someone said: Isn't it about time for you to clear out?

Said: Going straight and being useful to others, where would I go and not be fired three times? If I want to go crooked, what need of leaving my parental country?

III

1. Duke Ching of Ch'i awaiting Kung-tze said: I can't treat him a Chi chief, but something between that and a Mang chief.

Said: I am an old man, I can't make use of his theories (can't use the Confucian procedure). [*Thus L. but hard to get from text strictly more than* cannot use. Employ him, give him office.] Kung-tze proceeded, traveled [L. took departure].

IV

1. Ch'i folk (? the man of Ch'i) sent a present of female musicians (corps de ballet), Chi Hwan accepted them and did not hold court for three days. Confucius traveled.

V

1. The madman of Ch'u, Chich-yu, passed Kung-tze, singing out: "Phoenix, oh Phoenix, how is your clarity fallen,

no use blaming what's past, you might look out for what's to come. There's danger to anyone who goes into this present government."

2.   Confucius got down (from his carriage) and wanted to talk with him but (Chieh) hurried away, so he could not.

VI

1.   Ch'ang-tsu and Chieh-ni were teamed plowing [*Plowmen worked in pairs* / vide Odes etc.]. Kung-tze going by, sent Tze-lu to ask about the ford.

2.   Ch'ang-tsu said: Who's that driving?
Tze-lu said: Kung Hillock.
Said: Kung Hillock of Lu?
Said: Yes.
Said: He knows the ford.

3.   (Tze-lu then) asked Chieh-ni.
Chieh-ni said: Who are you, sir?
Said: I'm Sprout, secundus.
Said: A pupil of Kung Hillock of Lu?
Replied: Yes . . .
Said: "Disorder overfloods all the empire, who has the means to change it? Moreover, rather than follow a man who leaves one chief after another, better follow a scholar who has given up the world (this generation) altogether." He did not stop covering up the seed in his furrow.

4.   Tze-lu went and reported, the big man sighed: One cannot collaborate with birds and beasts. If I don't work with these people whom can I work with? If the empire were on the right track, it would not need me, Hillock, to change it. [*Or* I would not give (myself, or effort) to change it.]

VII

1.   Tze-lu was lagging behind and met an old man carrying a basket of weeds, on a staff over his shoulder. Tze-lu asked: Have you seen my big man?

The old man said: See by your arms and legs you haven't done any work; don't know the five grains one from another, who is your big man? He put down his stave and started weeding.

2.   Tze-lu bowed and stood before him.

3.   He kept Tze-lu for the night, killed a chicken, fixed the millet and fed him, introduced his two sons.

4.   At sun-up Tze-lu went on and told of this.

He said: A recluse; sent Tze-lu back to see him again. When he arrived, the old man was gone.

5.   Tze-lu said: It's not right not to take office.

You can't neglect the relations between old and young, how can he neglect the right relation between prince and minister, wishing to conserve his personal purity, he lets loose chaos in the great order. A proper man takes a government job, goes straight. He knows perfectly well perfect principles are not followed [*or* he knows in the end that they aren't (universally) followed].

VIII

1.   The men who have retired: Po-i, Shu-ch'i, Yu-chung, I-yi, Chu-chang, Hui of Liu-hsia, Shao-lien.

2.   He said: Not lowering their aims, not disgracing themselves, Po-i, Shu-ch'i. I'd say.

3.   Can say Hui of Liu-hsia, and Shao-lien did lower their aims, did undergo personal shame, but their words were centred in reason and their acts worth consideration. That's all.

4.   Can say of Yu-chung and I-yi, they went to live in retirement and talked. They kept themselves pure [M:], in their retirement they hit the mean of opportunism (wasted in midbalance).

5.   I differ from these models, I have no categoric can and cannot.

IX
(*Dispersion of the musicians of Lu*)

1.   The grand music master Chih went to Ch'i.

2.   Kan, conductor for second meal, went to Ch'u.

Liao, "third meal," went to Ts'ai.

Chueh, "fourth meal," went to Ch'in.

3.   The drummer Fang Shu went into the Honan [L. north of the river].

4.   Wu, the hand drum, went to Han.

5.   Yang the assistant conductor, and Hsiang the musical stone went to the sea.

X

1. The Duke of Chau said to the Duke of Lu, a proper man does not neglect his relatives; he does not grieve his great ministers by keeping them useless; he does not cast off the old without great reason. [L. members of old families?]

XI

1. Chau had eight officers; Po-ta; Po-kwo, Chung-tu, Chung-hwu, Shu-ya, Shu-hsia, Chi-sui, Chi-kwa.

BOOK NINETEEN

Tze-Chang

I

1. Tze-Chang said: The scholar-gentleman* sees danger and goes thru to his fate [L. sacrifice life]; when he sees a chance of getting on he thinks of equity, at sacrifices his thoughts are full of reverence for the powers of vegetation; in mourning, of grief; that is perhaps a complete definition.

II

1. Tze-Chang said: To comprehend acting straight from the conscience, and not put energy into doing it, to stick to the letter of the right process and not be strong in it, can you be doing with that sort? Does it matter what becomes of them? To believe in the right course, and not maintain it.

III

1. Tze-hsia's pupils asked Tze-Chang about friendly association.

Tze-Chang said: What does Tze-hsia say?

Replied: Tze-hsia says share it with those who can and ward off those who cannot. [*L. adds "advantage you." The* chiao¹ *covers the meanings*: pay, exchange, communicate. *Say:* with whom there can be an exchange.]

Tze-chang said: Differs from what I've heard, i.e. the proper man honours solid merit and is easy on the multitude, praises the honest and pities the incompetent. If I have

*The *shih* might very well have been translated knight in the age of European chivalry on various counts.

enough solid talent what is there in men I can't put up with? If I haven't solid merit men will be ready enough to ward me off, why should I ward off others?

IV

1.   Tze-hsia said: If a mean contrivance functions there must be something in it worth attention, but carry it far: 'ware mud. That's why the proper man doesn't use it.

V

1.   Tze-hsia said: To be daily aware of what he lacks, not forgetting what he can make function (capacity due to what bits of knowledge he has put together), can be defined as loving study.

VI

1.   Tze-hsia said: Extending study, keeping the will hard yet supple; putting a fine edge on one's questions, and stickin' close to what one really thinks. Manhood takes root in the centre of these.

VII

1.   Tze-hsia said: Artificers (the hundred works) live in a market amid the outlay of their tools to perfect their technique. [*The* szu⁺ (? cf *Arab.* suk), *tools spread for use, also concurrence of shops of similar ware.*] The proper man studies so that he arrive at proceeding in the process. [*Very much:* pour savoir vivre. *Really learn how to live, up to the hilt.*]

VIII

1.   Tze-hsia said: The mean man just has to gloss his faults.

IX

1.   Tze-hsia said: The proper man undergoes three transformations, at a distance: stern; gentle to approach; his words firm as a grindstone.

X

1.   Tze-hsia said: A proper man keeping his word [*or:* whose word is believed] can make the people work hard; if he don't keep his word they will consider the same work an oppression. A man who keeps his word can remonstrate with his prince, if he do not keep it, the remonstrance will be taken for insult.

XI

1.   Tze-hsia said: If a man does not transgress the barriers of the great virtues, he can have leeway in small (go out and in).

XII

1. Tze-Yu said: Tze-hsia's door-men and little chaps are correct in sprinkling and sweeping, answer politely, make their entries and exits, all in a model manner, these are branches, without the root, what about it?

2. Tze-hsia heard it and said: Too bad, Tze-Yu is wrong. What does a proper man's method put first and teach and put second and loaf over? By analogy with plants and trees he divides (activities) into kinds, but how could the proper man's behaviour bring false accusation against any of them? Only the sage starts out knowing all the consequences.

XIII

1. Tze-hsia said: When the man in office has an abundance (of energy) he studies; when the studious man has an abundance he goes into office.

XIV

1. Tze-yu said: Lamentation ought to stop at the end of the mourning period.

XV

1. Tze-yu said: My friend Chang can do difficult things, oh yes, but he is not completely humane.

XVI

1. Master Tsang said: Magnificent! Chang is mag-nificent, but hard to be human with him [or: difficult to combine all that splendour with being really human].

XVII

1. Master Tsang said: I've heard our big man say you can't tell all there is in a man until he is mourning his relatives.

XVIII

1. Master Tsang said: I've heard our big man say Mang Chwang was a true son, others can be that, but when it comes to his not changing his father's ministers, nor his father's mode of government, that is hard for 'em to match.

XIX

1. The Mang chief having made him chief criminal judge, Yang Fu questioned Master Tsang. Master Tsang said: The high-ups have lost the way, the people have been in disorder for a long time, when you find it out, pity 'em, don't think yourself clever.

XX

"A bad name"

1. Tze-kung said: "Crupper's" uncleanness wasn't as low as all that. That's why the proper man hates living at the bottom of the drain-slope where all the rot flows down.

XXI

1. Tze-kung said: A superior man's errors are like solar and lunar eclipses, when he goes wrong everyone sees it, when he comes back to course again all lift their faces. [Yang *can also mean:* trust.]

XXII

1. Kung-sun Ch'ao of Wei asked Tze-kung: How did Chung-ni (Chung secundus, Confucius) study?

2. Tze-kung said: Wan and Wu's system hadn't completely collapsed, the men of solid talent conserved the great features (the great parts of it were rooted in their memory) and the minor items were rooted in the memories of the men without talents, no one was wholly without something of Wan and Wu's method, how could the big man help studying it, though without an ordinary teacher?

XXIII

1. Shu-sun Wu-shu said to a high court officer: Tze-kung is superior to Chung-ni.

2. Tze-fu Ching-po told Tze-kung, Tze-kung said: By analogy with a house wall, mine is shoulder high, one can look over it at the house and family, and what is good in them.

3. The big man's wall is many times the height of an eight-footer, if you don't find the door and go in, you can't see the splendour of the feudal temple, or the hundred officers' riches.

4. But how few find the door, wasn't that big chap's remark perfectly suited to him?

XXIV

1. Shu-san Wu-shu spoke ill of Chung-ni. Tze-kung said: It's no use, you can't break him down. It's the other men that are "hillocks" [*play on Confucius' familiar name Ch'iu "hillock"*] and hummocks that one can walk up. Chung-ni, the sun, the moon you cannot walk up stairs to. Though a man wants to cut himself off what harm does that do to the sun and moon, many people see them who cannot measure a

meridian. [*The pictogram is a measure of the sun-rise, rather than of capacity, as L.*]

XXV

1.   Ch'an Tze-ch'in said to Tze-kung, You are overdoing this respectfulness, how is Chung-ni more talented than you are?

2.   Tze-kung said: The proper man can be known from a single sentence and one sentence is enough to show what a man does not know. Can't neglect keeping the word aligned with the mind.

3.   You can't reach the big man, just as you can't get to heaven by walking up stairs.

4.   If the big man were in charge of a state or clan, what is properly called establishment would be established, the proper system would work, the traces would be hitched so that they would draw, energies would be harmonized. He would be splendid in life, lamented in death, how can one match him?

BOOK TWENTY

I

1.   Yao said: Attent! you Shun, heaven's calendar [*sun under grain under cover*] has now pulsed through in its count to take root in your personal strength, hang onto what it is all about, hand and foot (biceps and legs) if within the four seas there be dearth and exhaustion, the defining light of heaven [L. heaven's revenue] will come to perpetual end.

2.   Shun gave the same sealed order to Yü. [T'ang, *as in the* Shu IV, iii, 3.]

3.   Said: I, the little child Li ("Shoe") dare to use the black victim; dare clearly announce to the Whiteness above all Whiteness above all kings, to the Dynasty Overspreading; dare not pardon offences, nor let those who serve the spread cloth of heaven be overgrown; their report roots in the mind of the O'erspreading.

If in us, the emperor's person, be fault, it is not by the myriad regions, if the myriad regions have fault, it takes root from our person. [*Cf.* Wu, *in the* Shu V. iii.]

4.   Chao had a great conferring: honest men could be rich.

5. Although he had the Chao relatives, not a matter of someone else's manhood, if the hundred clans err, it is rooted in me the one man.

6. He kept watch over the balances (weights) and the measuring [*I shd/ say* taking the sun. L./ measures], he investigated the statutes and regulations [*or better:* the functioning of the regulations, how they worked, whether they worked. *La Vie du Droit*], he combed out the useless officials, and the government of the Four Coigns went ahead.

7. He built up wasted states, restored broken successions, promoted men who had retired, and the people of the empire returned to good sense.

8. What he put weight on was feeding the people, mourning and offerings.

9. By magnanimity reached to everyone; by keeping his word got their trust; got thru a lot of work by attention to detail and kept them happy by justice.

II

1. Tze-chang asked Kung-tze how one should carry on government.

He said: Honour the five excellences and throw out the four evils.

Tze-chang said: How do you define the five excellences?

He said: The proper man [*here*, man-in-authority] is considerate without being extravagant, energetic (or even urging) without grumbling, desires without greed, is honourable without hauteur, and boldly protective without ferocity.

2. Tze-chang said: What do you mean by being considerate not extravagant? He said: Cause the people to profit by what he profits by (their cut of grain), isn't that being considerate without extravagance? When he picks out the right work for them, they work, who will grumble; desiring manhood and attaining it, is that greed? Whether he is dealing with many or few, with small matter or great, the proper man does not venture to be churly, is not that being honourable and not haughty? The proper man adjusts his robe and cap, honours what is clearly worthy of honour, [Occhio per la mente. *If a strict stylist is distinguishing* chien (4) 860 M *and* shih (4) 5789, *the former wd / he* eye-sight *and the latter, I take it,* mind-sight, intellectual clarity] with dignity so that

others look up to him and even fear him, isn't that severity without ferocity?

3. Tze-chang said: How define the four evils? He said: Not to teach people and then put them to death is cruelty; not to warn people and then expect them to have things finished perfectly, is called oppression. [*L. admirably*: to require suddenly the full tale of work without having given warning.] To be dilatory (sloppy) in giving orders and exigent in expecting them carried out at the precise date is cheating.

> 6752. *This* tse (2–5) *certainly cannot be translated* thief *in all contexts, it is an abusive term, centre of meaning seems to be nearer to "cheat" though theft is certainly included. "Con game" with violence, any thieving trick.*

As in giving to others, to come out and give in a stingy manner

> *Thus L., but if we are getting down to brass tacks, I should think the* ch'u na: go out-insert, *might refer to the familiar "kick-back," getting personal repayment from an official payment to another.*

called having assistant-officers.

> *Unless it refers to* kick-back *or something more than manner, seems hardly great enough to be listed among the four hateful or evil things.* 4809. o (4–5). *That is to say it wd/ seem to be stretching the* o (4–5) *into a milder meaning than it usually has in the* Four Books. P. on appelle cela se comporter comme un collecteur d'impots.

III

1. He said: Not to know the decree [the sealed mouth. *L.* adds "of heaven," *not to recognize destiny*] is to be without the means of being a proper man (the ancestral voice incomplete).

2. Not to know the rites is to be without means to construct.

3. Not to know words (the meaning of words) is to be without the fluid needful to understand men.

THE CLASSIC ANTHOLOGY
DEFINED BY CONFUCIUS

Book 1. Chou and the South

I   (I)

"Hid! Hid!" the fish-hawk saith,
by isle in Ho the fish-hawk saith:
            "Dark and clear,
            Dark and clear,
So shall be the prince's fere."

Clear as the stream her modesty;
As neath dark boughs her secrecy,
            reed against reed
            tall on slight
as the stream moves left and right,
            dark and clear,
            dark and clear.
To seek and not find
as a dream in his mind,
            think how her robe should be,
            distantly, to toss and turn,
            to toss and turn.

High reed caught in *ts'ai* grass
            so deep her secrecy;
lute sound in lute sound is caught,
            touching, passing, left and right.
Bang the gong of her delight.

II   (2)

Shade o' the vine,
Deep o' the vale,
Thick of the leaf,
                    the bright bird flies
singing, the orioles
gather on swamp tree boles.

Shade of the vine,
Deep o' the vale,
Dark o' the leaf
                    here 'neath our toil
                    to cut and boil
stem into cloth, thick or fine
No man shall wear out mine.

Tell my nurse to say I'll come,
                    Here's the wash and here's the rince,
                    Here's the cloth I've worn out since,
Father an' mother, I'm comin' home.

III   (3)

She:
                    Curl-grass, curl-grass,
                    to pick it, to pluck it
                    to put in a bucket
                    never a basket load
Here on Chou road, but a man in my mind!
                    Put it down here by the road.

He:
                    Pass, pass
                    up over the pass,
a horse on a mountain road!
A winded horse on a high road,
give me a drink to lighten the load.
As the cup is gilt, love is spilt.
                    Pain lasteth long.

Black horses, yellow with sweat,
are not come to the ridge-top yet.
           Drink deep of the rhino horn
But leave not love too long forlorn.

Tho' driver stumble and horses drop,
we come not yet to the stony top.
Let the foundered team keep on,
How should I leave my love alone!

IV   (4)

    In the South be drooping trees,
    long the bough, thick the vine,
    Take thy delight,
    my prince, in happy ease.

    In the South be drooping boughs
    the wild vine covers,
    that hold delight, delight, good sir,
    for eager lovers.

    Close as the vine clamps the trees
    so complete is happiness,
    Good sir, delight delight in ease,
    In the South be drooping trees.

V   (5)

Locusts a-wing, multiply.
Thick be thy
           posterity.

Locusts a-wing with heavy sound;
strong as great rope may thy line
                     abound.

Wing'd locust, that seem to cease,
in great companies hibernate,
So may thy line last and be great
           in hidden ease.

VI   (6)
καλὴ κἀγαθή

O omen tree, that art so frail and young,
so glossy fair to shine with flaming flower;
that goest to wed
and make fair house and bower;

O omen peach, that art so frail and young,
giving us promise of such solid fruit,
going to man and house
to be true root;

O peach-tree thou art fair
as leaf amid new boughs;
going to bride;
to build thy man his house.

VII   (7)

To peg down the rabbit nets, observe his care;
good at this job, so also in warfare
                to be his prince's wall.

Neat to peg down the rabbit nets
where the runs cross
and to be duke's man at arms
                never at loss.

Deep in mid forest pegging the nets,
elegant in his art;
fit to be the duke's confidant,
                His very belly and heart.

VIII   (8)

Pluck, pluck, pluck, the thick plantain;
pluck, pick, pluck, then pluck again.

Oh pick, pluck the thick plantain,
Here be seeds for sturdy men.

Pluck the leaf and fill the flap,
Skirts were made to hide the lap.

IX   (9)

Tall trees there be in south countree
that give no shade to rest in
And by the Han there roam young maids
to whom there 's no suggestin'

that they should wade the Han by craft
or sail to Kiang's fount on a raft.

2

I've piled high her kindling wood
and cut down thorns in plenty;
to get the gal to go home with me.
I've fed the horse she lent me.

She will not wade the Han by craft
or sail to Kiang-fount on a raft.

3

I have piled high the kindling wood
and cut down sandal trees
to get this girl to take a man
and raise the colts at ease.

"One does not wade the Han by craft,
or reach the Kiang-fount on a raft."

X   (10)

By the levees of Ju
I cut boughs in the brake,
not seeing milord
to ease heart-ache.

I have seen him
by the levees of Ju, 'tis enough,
cutting the boughs, to know
he'll not cast me off.

Square fish with a ruddy tail,
though the king's house blaze, and though
thou blaze as that house, the faith
of thy forebears shall not fail.*

XI (11)
MYTHICAL BEAST

Kylin's foot bruiseth no root,
                    Ohé, Kylin.
In Kylin's path, no wrath,
                    Ohé, Kylin.
Kylin's tooth no harm doth,
                    Ohé, Kylin:
                    Wăn's line
                    and clan.

Book 2. Shao and the South

I (12)

Dove in jay's nest
to rest,
she brides
with an hundred cars.

Dove in jay's nest
to bide,
a bride
with an hundred cars.

---

* Note: bream's tail supposed to turn red in danger.

Dove in jay's nest
at last
and the hundred cars
stand fast.

II (13)

Pluck the quince
to serve a prince,
by isle, and pool.

Plucking quinces
in service of princes,
in vale, pluck again
and carry to fane.

In high wimple
bear to the temple
ere dawn light,
then home
for the night, leisurely, leisurely.

III (14)

"Chkk! chkk!" hopper-grass,
nothing but grasshoppers hopping past;
tell me how a lady can
be gay if she sees no gentleman?

But when I've seen a man at rest,
standing still, met at his post,
my heart is no more tempest-toss'd.

2

I climb South Hill to pick the turtle-fern,
seeing no man
such climb 's heart-burn

but to see a good man at rest,
standing still, met at his post,
I no more think this trouble lost.

3
To climb South Hill picking the jagged fern
and see no man, who shall not pine and yearn?

But to see good man at rest
standing still there at his post
is the heart's design's utmost.

IV   (15)

Some reeds be found by river's brink
and some by catchit pool
that she doth pull and pluck
to bring by basket-full;

Be her baskets round or square
she doth then all this catch prepare
in pots and pans of earthen-ware;

Then neath the light-hole of the shrine
she sets the lot in neat array
that all the family manes come
bless proper bride in ordered home.

V   (16)

Don't chop that pear tree,
Don't spoil that shade;

Thaar 's where ole Marse Shao used to sit,
Lord, how I wish he was judgin' yet.

VI   (17)

"Dew in the morning, dew in the evening,
          always too wet for a bridal day."

The sparrow has no horn to bore a hole?
Say you won't use your family pull!
       Not for the court and not for the bailiff,
       shall you make me a wife to pay with.

Toothless rat, nothing to gnaw with?
And a whole family to go to law with?
       Take me to court, see what will come.
       Never, never, never will you drag me home.

VII   (18)

In fleecy coats with five white tassels,
affable snakes, the great duke's vassals glide
from his hall
to tuck their court rations inside.

In lambskin coats with five wider tassels,
affable snakes, the duke's vassals all
glide out to dinner
on leaving the hall.

With quadruple tassels or seams to their coats,
lambskin and all, with that elegant look,
noble vassals, affable snakes
glide out to consume what they get from the Duke.

VIII   (19)

Crash of thunder neath South Hill crest,
how could I help it, he would not rest,
       Say shall I see my good lord again?

Crash of thunder on South Mount side,
how could I help it, he would not bide,
       And shall I see my good lord again?

Crash of thunder under South Hill,
a fighting man maun have his will,
       Say shall I see my true lord again?

IX (20)

"Oh soldier, or captain,
Seven plums on the high bough,
plum time now,
seven left here, 'Ripe,' I cry.

Plums, three plums,
On the bough, 'Plum time!' I cry.

'No plums now,' I cry, I die.
On this bough
Be no plums now."

X (21)

Three stars, five stars rise over the hill
We came at sunset, as was his will.
                                    One luck is not for all.

In Orion's hour, Pleiads small
Came with coverlets to the high hall.
Sun's up now
Time to go.
            One luck is not for all.

XI (22)

Divided Kiang flows back to Kiang again:
abide us she could not,
abide us she would not.

Isles in the Kiang there be,
she so disliked our company,
Divided Kiang flows back to Kiang again.

As the T'o flows back to Kiang,
First she pouted, then she flouted,
            Then, at last, she sang.

XII   (23)

Lies a dead deer on younder plain
whom white grass covers,
A melancholy maid in spring
                              is luck
                              for
                              lovers.

Where the scrub elm skirts the wood,
be it not in white mat bound,
as a jewel flawless found,
                dead as doe is maidenhood.

Hark!
Unhand my girdle-knot,
                stay, stay, stay
                or the dog
                may
                bark.

XIII   (24)
EPITHALAMIUM

Plum flowers so splendid be,
rolling, onrolling quietly,
a royal car with young royalty.

Flowers of plum abundantly,
Heiress of P'ing, heir of Ts'i,
to their wedding right royally.

Tight as strands in fisherman's line
may this pair in love combine,
heir and heiress loyally,
whereby P'ing is bound to Ts'i.

XIV (25)

THE GAMEKEEPER

(model game conservation or it lacks point)*

Of five young wild pig he shoots but one,
> Green grow the rushes, oh!
White-Tiger is a true forester's son.

Of five boneen he shot but one.
> Green grow the rushes, oh!
White-Tiger is a true forester's son.

SONGS OF THE THREE PARTS OF WEI

Pei, to the North
Yung, the Southern Section
Wei, to the East

Book 3. Airs of Pei

I (26)

Pine boat a-shift
on drift of tide,
for flame in the ear, sleep riven,
driven; rift of the heart in dark
no wine will clear,
nor have I will to playe.

Mind that 's no mirror to gulp down all 's seen,
brothers I have, on whom I dare not lean,
angered to hear a fact, ready to scold.

My heart no turning-stone, mat to be rolled,
right being right, not whim nor matter of count,
true as a tree on mount.

* Political allusion not to be ruled out.

Mob's hate, chance evils many, gone through,
aimed barbs not few;
at bite of the jest in heart
start up as to beat my breast.

O'ersoaring sun, moon malleable
alternately
lifting a-sky to wane;
sorrow about the heart like an unwashed shirt, I
clutch here at words,
having no force to fly.

II   (27)

Green robe, green robe, lined with yellow,
Who shall come to the end of sorrow?

Green silk coat and yellow skirt,
How forget all my heart-hurt?

Green the silk is, you who dyed it;
Antient measure, now divide it?

Nor fine nor coarse cloth keep the wind
from the melancholy mind;
Only antient wisdom is
solace to man's miseries.

III   (28)
LIMPIDITY

Swallows in flight
on veering wing,
she went to bridal so far over the waste,
my tears falling
like rain, as she passed from sight.

Head up, head down, throat straight the swallows fly
thru a haze
of tears, when she went to bridal
I stood at gaze.

I went with her toward the South;
up, down, left, right, the swallows cry.
I stood helplessly, as she passed from sight.

Chung Jen, deep of heart, taught
me in quietness the antient lordly thought:
sun's aid, in my littleness.

IV   (29)

Sun, neath thine antient roof, moon speaking antient speech,
Bright eyes, shall ye reach the earth, and find
a man who dwells not in antient right,
nor shall have calm, putting me from his sight!

Sun constant, and O moon, that art ever in phase,
shall ye pretend to move
over the earth
to find him who returns not my love,
nor shall have calm who makes no fair exchange!

Sun, neath thine antient roof, moon speaking antient speech,
shall ye range from the east
and find his like of evil reputation?
how should his course run smoothe,
forgetting love?

Sun constant, and O moon, that art ever in phase,
up from the east always; father and mother mine
that have of me no care,
shall ye not pine
that guard not my right!

V   (30)

THE MARQUISE CHUANG KIANG
against her husband

Cold parcheth the end wind, colder mockery,
Frigid the smile to my heart's misery.

Dust in the wind and sand; what should a promise be?
You promise and do not come, yet stand
in my heart constantly.

The wind has blown the sky
to one black solid cloud, all the day long
night long I sleep not
seeking to mutter this wrong.

Under black solid cloud,
thunder, thunder so loud I sleep not,
seeking to speak its thought.

VI   (31)

Bang, the drum. We jump and drill,
some folks are working on Ts'ao Wall still
or hauling farm loads in Ts'ao
but we're on the roads, south, on the roads

under Tsy Chung.
Sung and Ch'en come.
We've rolled 'em flat but
we'll never get home.

To stay together till death and end
for far, for near, hand, oath, accord:
Never alive
will we keep that word.

VII   (32)

Soft wind from South to find
what is in the thorn-tree's mind;
thorn-tree's mind, tender and fair,
our mother thorned down with care.

South wind on fagot
that was tree when
she thought of goodness,
yet made us not thoughtful men.

Smooth the cool spring of Tsün
flows to the lower soil,
seven sons had our mother
worn hard with toil;

Yellow bird's beauty
makes good in song,
seven sons
do her wrong.

VIII   (33)

Pheasant-cock flies on easy wing,
absent lord, to my sorrowing.

As the bright pheasant flies
wind lowers and lifts the tone;
sorrow: my lord gone out,
I am alone.

Look up to the sun and moon
in my thought the long pain,
the road is so long, how
shall he come again.

Ye hundred gentlemen, conscienceless
in your acts, say true:
He neither hates nor covets,
what wrong shall he do?

IX   (34)
BOTTLE-GOURD

Bitter the gourd leaf, passed the high-water mark,
"Let the deep drench, o'er shallows lift a sark!"

At the over-flooded ford: "Won't wet an axle block!"
Hen pheasant cries, seeking her pheasant-cock.

Tranquil the wild goose's note
at sunrise, ere ice gins thaw,

noble takes mate
observing the antient law.

Boatman cocks thumb, some go,
I do not so,
Waiting till my man come.

X (35)
THE EFFICIENT WIFE'S COMPLAINT

Wind o' the East dark with rain,
a man should not bring his olde wife pain
but should bide concordantly.
Gather *feng* gather *fei*,
man can eat and live thereby,
Now what fault is spoke against me
that I should not wedded die?

Slow road go I, mid-heart in pain,
You scarce came to my domain.
Who saith now the thistle scratches?
Soft as shepherd's-purse that matches
your new leman feasts with you
in full joy as brothers do.

King River 's muddied by the Wei
yet pools to clearness presently.
You feast your doxy now she 's new
and with me will naught to do.
So come not near my dam and weir,
let my fish-basket be,
In your hate what hold have I,
Indifferent all futurity!

Ready to raft the deep,
wade shallow or dive for gain—
sharing both had and lost—
and help the destitute
whate'er it cost

Not your heart's garden now,
an opponent,
you lower my market price
blocking my good intent.
I worked when we were poor and took no heed,
whom you, now rich, compare to poison weed.

I piled good store to last the winter through
so now you feast, and your new doxy 's new.
'Twas I who saved for winter and you who spent,
mine the real work, you now wax violent
forgetting all the past for good or best
when 'twas with me alone that you found rest.

XI   (36)

(KING CHARLES)

Why? why?

By the Lord Wei,
For the Lord Wei this misery
sleeping in dew.
Never pull through!

Worse, worse!
Say that we could
go home but for his noble blood.

Sleeping in mud,
why? why?

For Milord Wei.

XII   (37)

Mao Mount's vine-joints show their age,
Uncles and nobles, how many days?

Why delay here with no allies;
Why delay here in lack of supplies?

Fox furs worn thru, without transport,
Uncles and nobles, sorry sport!

We be the rump of Li with tattered tails,
a lost horde amid fears,
and your embroidered collars
cover your ears.

XIII (38)
GUARDSMAN IN BALLET

Élite (or ee-light) ready on the dot
for court theatrical
even at mid-day, by the upper loge
in the Duke's court, and I am tall,
strong as a tiger, to whom horse-reins are silk.

A flute in left hand, in my right a fan;
red as if varnished when the duke sends wine,
                              a man?

Hazel on hill, mallow in mead,
West Country men for prettiness, who guessed?
What ass would say: this beauty 's from the West?

XIV (39)
BRIDE'S NOSTALGIA FOR HOME FOLKS

Ware spring water that flows to the K'i,
flowing thought is jeopardy.
Every day my thought 's in Wei,
where pretty cousins would talk to me
we would devise right pleasantly.

To Tsy for the night, and farewell cup at Ni;
When a girl marries she goes out
far from her parents and close male kin;
there's a feast and she
asks her aunts and sisters all in.

Now I would night by Kan and Yen.
"Grease the axle and fix the lynch-pin"
anything to get quickly to Wei
without roadside calamity.

"By Fei-Ts'üan's winding stream"
of Sü and Ts'ao is all my dream,
and all I can get is a p.m. drive
to keep my inner life alive.

XV   (40)

North gate, sorrow's edge,
purse kaput, nothing to pledge.

I'll say I'm broke
none knows how, heaven's stroke.

Government work piled up on me.

When I go back where I lived before,
my dear relatives slam the door.
This is the job put up on me,
Sky's "which and how"?
or say: destiny.

Government work piled up on me.

When I come in from being out
my home-folk don't want me about;
concrete fruit of heaven's tree
not to be changed by verbosity.

XVI   (41)

Cold wind, and rain
North snows again.
                    Kindly who love me, take hands and go!
                    Make haste,
                    State 's waste!

Sougheth to North,
Sleeteth cold snow,
   Kindly who love me, take hands and go!

All red things foxes, each black a crow
(evils in omen) love me, and go
   State 's waste.
   Make haste
     and
     go.

XVII (42)
THE APPOINTMENT MANQUÉ

Lady of azure thought, supple and tall,
I wait by nook, by angle in the wall,
love and see naught; shift foot and scratch my poll.

Lady of silken word, in clarity
gavest a reed whereon red flower flamed less
than thy delightfulness.

In mead she plucked the *molu* grass,
fair as streamlet did she pass.

   "Reed, art to prize in thy beauty,
    but more that frail, who gave thee me."

XVIII (43)
"Satire on the marriage of Duke Süan"

New tower's sheen reflected full in Ho,
She sought a beau
with whom to curl at eve.

She sought a beau with whom to curl at eve
By tower, by Ho, by flow and got
His ruckling relative.

Goose to get in a fish-net set!
His ruckling relative.

XIX (44)
"Rumours as to the death of Süan's sons"

A boat floats over shadow, two boys were aboard.
There is a cloud over my thought
and of them no word.

The boat floats past the sky's edge, lank sail a-flap;
and a dark thought inside me: how had they hap?

Book 4. Yung Wind

I (45)

Pine boat a-drift in Ho,
dark drifts the tufted hair.
Mated we were till death,
   Shall no one keep faith?
   Mother of Heaven,
   Shall no one keep faith!

Boat drifts to the shore,
Dark tufts float in the waste.
My bull till death he were,
   Shall no one be traist?
   Mother of Heaven,
   Shall no one be traist!*

II (46)
(Three strophes with negligible variations)

The things they do and the things they say
   in the harem,
   in the harem,
There is no end to the things they say in the harem,
There is no shame in the things they say in the harem,
   So pull not the vine away.

---

* She refuses to marry again

III (47)
CAESAR'S WIFE

Go with him for a life long
with high jewelled hair-do,
Stately as a hill,
suave as a mountain stream
                Show gown,
                Show gown,
                        and yet?

Cloak like a pheasant,
Hair like a storm cloud, jade in her ears,
High comb of ivory set
white as her forehead,
                        Diva,
                        Diva,
                            and yet?

Splendour at court high guests to entertain,
erudite silk or plain flax in the grain,
above it all the clear spread of her brows:
"Surely of dames this is the cynosure,
the pride of ladies and the land's allure!"
                        and yet?

IV   (48)
THE CONSTANT LOVER

To gather the "gold thread" south of Mei,
Who saith 'tis fantasy?

Mid the mulberry trees of Sang Chung
said: "In Shang Kung," Miss Kiang to me,

        "And then a week-end on the K'i."

To take in wheat crop, north of Mei,
Who saith 'tis fantasy?

Mid the mulberry trees of Sang Chung
said: "In Shang Kung," to me the first Miss Yi

"And then a week-end on the K'i."

To get in mustard east of Mei,
Who saith 'tis fantasy?

Mid the mulberry trees of Sang Chung
said: "In Shang Kung," Miss Yung to me

"And then a week-end on the K'i."

V (49)

Quails and pies
show enmities,
but a man with *no* savoury quality
is my own brother apparently.

Pies and quails
tear each other's entrails
and there's a fair lady would do no less:
Let me present our Marchioness.

VI (50)

TING

the star of quiet course, marking the time
to end field work

The star of quiet being in mid-sky,
he reared up Bramble hall;
took sun to measure the wall;
planted abundantly
chestnut and hazel tree;
tung tree and varnish roots
whence wood to make our lutes.

He clomb the waste-land there to spy
how Ch'u and T'ang lands lie;
measured to fit the shadow's fall
mountain site for his capital,
orchard space lying under it all.
Then he took augury
of how things by right should be;
learned from the shell what was eventually,
that is, the event in its probity.

On timely rainfall in the starlit gloom,
would call his groom to hitch
ere day was come,
"To orchard and sown!" he'ld say,
so straight a man, the course
of heart so deep
that gave him three thousand tall horse.

VII (51)
NO TRUST IN RAINBOWS

Rainbow duplex in East
no one dares trust in,
girl going out must
leave afar her kin.

Cloud-flush in morning's west,
'twill rain until mid-day,
a girl leaves kin and best,
wedding away.

This haste to wed
by hap, 's for pretty fools,
men rather trust girls' wits
who know the rules.

VIII (52)
SANS EQUITY AND SANS POISE
"Dentes habet."

Catullus

A rat too has a skin (to tan)
A rat has a skin at least
But a man who is a mere beast
might as well die,
his death being end of no decency.

A rat also has teeth
but this fellow, for all his size, is beneath
the rat's level,
why delay his demise?

The rat also has feet
but a man without courtesy need not wait
to clutter hell's gate.

Why should a man of no moral worth
clutter the earth?
This fellow's beneath the rat's modus,
why delay his exodus?

A man without courtesy
might quite as well cease to be.

IX (53)

Ox tails flap from the pikes
outside the market dykes
at Tsün;
Yak tails with plain silk bands,
The quadriga stands to wait an honoured guest
whose fame deserves our best.

Let falcon banners fly by Tsün
and silken panoply

float beyond moat in capital.
Five horses wait;
is not this fitting state?

The plumed flags fold and fall
above Tsün's wall
with white silk bands.
Six horsemen in full state
stand to felicitate
a guest
whose fame deserves our best.

X (54)
Baroness Mu impeded in her wish to help
famine victims in Wei

I wanted to harness and go
share woe in Wei,
I would have made Ts'ao my first halt,
It was never my fault
that a deputy went to my brother
across grass and water,
could he carry my grief?

Without your visa I could not go,
I cannot honour your act
nor retract.
My sympathy was real, yours the offence
if I cannot carry my condolence.
Wrongly you wrought.
I cannot stifle my thought.

(Without your visa, does honour requite it so?)

Nor was my thought wrong in this
you would not approve.
I cannot take home my condolence,
If thus wrongly you wrought,
I cannot stifle my thought.

I climb the cornered hill seeking heart's ease,
If sorrow be real, let heart with sorrow's load
go its sole road.

The Hü crowd's vulgar cry
sounds out presumptuously.
I wanted to go to the plains
where the thick grain is.
I would have asked aid of great states,
their kings and great potentates;
some would deny, some do their most,
but I would have had no blame.

All your hundred plans come to naught,
none matched my thought.

Book 5. Wei Wind

1 (55)
πολύμητις
The bamboos grow well under good rule

Dry in the sun by corner of K'i
green bamboo, bole over bole:
Such subtle prince is ours
to grind and file his powers
as jade is ground by wheel;
he careth his people's weal,
stern in attent,
steady as sun's turn bent
on his folk's betterment
                              nor will he fail.

Look ye here on the coves of the K'i:
green bamboo glitteringly!
Of as fine grain our prince appears
as the jasper plugs in his ears

ground bright as the stars in his cap of state;
his acumen in debate
splendid, steadfast in judgement-hall
he cannot fail us
                    nor fall.

In coves of K'i,
bamboo in leaf abundantly.
As metal tried is fine
or as sceptre of jade is clean;
stern in his amplitude,
magnanimous to enforce true laws, or lean
over chariot rail in humour
as he were a tiger
                    with velvet paws.

II   (56)

Made his hut in the vale, a tall man stretched out
sleeps, wakes and says: no room for doubt.

Lean-to on torrent's brink, laughter in idleness,
sleeps, wakes and sings; I will move less.

In a hut on a butte, himself his pivot, sleeps,
wakes, sleeps again,
swearing he will not communicate
with other men.

III   (57)
EPITHALAMIUM
"Sidney's sister"

Tall girl with a profile,
broidery neath a simple dress,
brought from Ts'i her loveliness
to Wei's marquisat.

Younger sister of Tung-Kung
("Palace of the East," crown-prince)

One sister of hers is the darling
of the great lord of Hing,
the other's man, T'an's viscount is.

Hand soft as a blade of grass,
a skin like cream, neck like the glow-worm's light,
her teeth as melon seeds,
a forehead neat as is a katydid's,
her brows and lids, as when you see her smile
or her eyes turn, she dimpling the while,
clear white, gainst black iris.

Tall she came thru the till'd fields to the town,
her quadriga orderly
that four high stallions drew
with scarlet-tasselled bits, and pheasant tails
in woven paravant.
Thus to the court, great officers, retire,
and let our noble Lord assuage his fire.

Ho tumbles north, tumultuous, animate,
forking the hills;
sturgeon and gamey trout
swim and leap out
to spat of nets and flap of flat fish-tails,
with Kiang dames' high hair-dos flashing bright
above the cortège's armèd might.

IV   (58)
PEDLAR

Hill-billy, hill-billy come to buy
silk in our market, apparently?
toting an armful of calico.

Hill-billy, hill-billy, not at all
but come hither to plot my fall,
offering cloth for raw silk and all,
till I went out over the K'i
to Tun Mount, in fact, quite willingly,

and then I asked for a notary.
I said: It's O.K. with me,
we could be spliced autumnally,
                              be not offended.

Autumn came, was waiting ended?
I climbed the ruin'd wall, looked toward Kuan pass.
On the Kuan frontier no man was.
I wept until you came,
trusted your smiling talk.   One would.
You said the shells were good and the stalks all clear.
You got a cart
and carted off me and my gear.

> *Let doves eat no more mulberries*
> *While yet the leaves be green,*
> *And girls play not with lustful men,*
> *Who can play and then explain,*
> *   for so 'tis usèd,—*
> *   and girls be naught excusèd.*

The mulberry tree is bare,
yellow leaves float down thru the air,
Three years we were poor,
now K'i's like a soup of mud,
the carriage curtains wet, I ever straight
and you ambiguous
with never a grip between your word and act.

Three years a wife, to work without a roof,
up with the sun and prompt to go to bed,
never a morning off. I kept my word.
You tyrannize, Brothers unaware,
if told would but grin and swear
(with truth, I must confess):
If I'm in trouble, well, I made the mess.

"Grow old with you," whom old you spite,
K'i has its banks and every swamp an edge.
Happy in pig-tails, laughed to hear your pledge,

sun up, sun up, believing all you said,
who in your acts reverse
(as a matter of course)
all that you ever said
and for the worse,
an end.

V   (59)
SEHNSUCHT, LONG POLES

Slim poles to fish in the K'i
but no bamboo long
enough to reach you
save in a song;

To left is Yüan Spring,
to right, the K'i;
a girl flows out
leaving her family.

K'i River to right
at left flows Yüan Spring,
slow flash of a quiet smile, jangling
of the stones at your belt.

Oars (and are they of juniper?) lift and fall in the K'i
in my mind's eye the pine boat swerves
as I drive in the park
to quiet my nerves.

VI   (60)
WOLF

Feeble as a twig,
with a spike so big
in his belt, but know us he does not.
        Should we melt
at the flap of his sash ends?

Feeble as a gourd stalk (epidendrum)
to walk with an out-size ring

at his belt (fit for an archer's thumb
that might be an archer's,
as if ready for archery
which he is not)
we will not, I think, melt,
(complacency in its apogee)
at the flap of his sash ends.

VII   (61)

Wide, Ho?
A reed will cross its flow;
Sung far?
One sees it, tip-toe.

Ho strong?
The blade of a row-boat cuts it so soon.
Sung far? I could be there
(save reverence) by noon

                        (did I not venerate
                        Sung's line and state.)*

VIII   (62)

Baron at arms,
ten-cubit halbard to war is
in the front rank
of the king's forays
                        driving, driving:

Eastward,
Eastward.
Why oil my hair, that's like a bush flying,
Or pile it high
If he come not forbye.

* Said to be by the divorced wife of Huan of Sung, after her son's acces-
sion, decorum forbidding her to return to court.

Rain, oh rain,
in drought's time,
Or the bright sun quickens;
and a rhyme in my thought of him:
For sweetness of the heart
the head sickens.

How shall I find forgetting-grass
to plant when the moon is dark
that my sorrow would pass
or when I speak my thought? Alas.

IX (63)
(STRIP-TEASE?)

K'i dam, prowls fox,
a heart 's to hurt
and someone 's there has got no skirt.

By the K'i's deep on the prowl;
got no belt on, bless my soul.

Tangle-fox by K'i bank tall:
who says: got no clothes at all?

X (64)

Gave me a quince, a beryl my cover,
not as a swap, but to last forever.

For a peach thrown me, let green gem prove:
exchange is nothing, all time 's to love.

For a plum thrown me
I made this rhyme
with a red "ninth-stone"
to last out all time.

Book 6. Songs of Wang

Breviora (Lieder) of Kingsland or the Royal Domain

I (65)

THRU THE SEASONS

"O thou man."
Thos. Hardy in Under the Greenwood Tree

Black millet heeds not shaggy sprout,
Aimless slowness, heart's pot scraped out,
Acquaintance say: Ajh, melancholy!
Strangers: he hunts, but why?
        Let heaven's far span, azure darkness,
        declare what manner of man this is.

Black millet heeds not the panicled
ear in the forming.
Aimless slowness, heart in dead daze,
Acquaintance say: Ajh, melancholy!
Strangers say: he hunts, but why?
        Let heaven's far span, azure darkness,
        declare what manner of man this is.

Black millet recks not the heavy ears
of the temple grain.
Aimless slowness, heart choked with grief.
Acquaintance say: Ajh, melancholy!
Strangers say: he hunts, but why.
        Let heaven's far span, azure darkness,
        declare what manner of man this is.*

        "Tous je connais"
              Villon.

* According to tradition, a lament on the overgrown site of the old capital. Including parts of the commentary one would get the refrain:
    By the far heaven's dark canopy
    What manner of man hath wrought this misery?

ALITER

From the commentary: "Where once was palace now
is straggling grain."

Straggling millet, grain in shoot,
aimless slowness, heart's pot scraped out,
acquaintance say: He is melancholy;
Strangers: what is he hunting now?

Sky, far, so dark.
"This, here, who, how?"

Straggling millet, grain on the stalk,
walking aimless, heart drunk with grief.
Acquaintance say: Ah, melancholy.
Strangers: What is he hunting now?

Sky, slate, afar,
"This man, who, how?"

Straggling millet, grain heavy in ear
aimless slowness, choking in heart
my acquaintance say: How melancholy.
Strangers: What is he hunting now?

Sky never near:
"This, here, who, how?"*

II   (66)

He's to the war
for the duration;
Hens to wall-hole,
beasts to stall,
shall I not remember
him at night-fall?

---

* The heaven is far off, there is here a human agency. One very often
comes round to old Legge's view, after devious by-paths.

He's to the war
for the duration,
fowl to their perches,
cattle to byre;
is there food enough;
drink enough
by their camp fire?

III (67)

What a man! with a bamboo flute calls me out
to gad about and be gay
moreover!

What a man with a feather fan calls me out
to gad about to the stage play
and then some!

IV (68)

Troops transferred from one mountain area to another

Rapids float no fagot here
nor can she guard Shen frontier.
Heart, O heart, when shall I home?

Ripples float no thorn-pack thru
nor will she fight by us in Fu.
Heart, O heart, when shall I home?

Freshets float no osier here
nor can she guard Hü frontier.
Heart, O heart, when shall I home?

Ripples break no fagot band.*

* If at head waters, can receive no message token by water-post; cf/the
messages sent in this way in the Tristan legend.

V   (69)

Dry grass, in vale:
                    "alas!

"I met a man, I
                 met
                       a man.

"Scorched, alas, ere it could grow."
A lonely girl pours out her woe.

"Even in water-meadow, dry "
Flow her tears abundantly,
                    Solitude 's no remedy.

VI   (70)

Rabbit goes soft-foot, pheasant 's caught,
I began life with too much élan,
Troubles come to a bustling man.
                    "Down Oh, and give me a bed!"

Rabbit soft-foot, pheasant 's in trap,
I began life with a flip and flap,
Then a thousand troubles fell on my head,
                    "If I could only sleep like the dead!"

Rabbit goes soft-foot, pheasant gets caught.
A youngster was always rushin' round,
Troubles crush me to the ground.
                    I wish I could sleep and not hear a sound.

ALITER

Ole Brer Rabbit watchin' his feet,
Rabbit net 's got the pheasant beat;
          When I was young and a-startin' life
          I kept away from trouble an' strife

But then, as life went on,
Did I meet trouble?
                    Aye, my son;
Wish I could sleep till life was done.

VII   (71)

Vine over vine along the Ho,
thru the vine-clad wilderness I go
so far from home to call a stranger "Dad,"
                    who will not hear.

Vine over vine by edges of the Ho,
thru the tangled vines I go
so far to come to seek a stranger's care
Should I say "mother" to some stranger there?

Vine over vine upon the brinks of Ho,
entangled vine
so far from home. Say "brother" to some stranger?
                    Where none 's mine.

VIII   (72)
TAEDIUM

Plucking the vine leaves, hear my song:
"A day without him is three months long."

Stripping the southernwoods, hear my song:
"A day without him is three autumns long."

Reaping the tall grass hear my song:
"A day without him 's three years long."

IX   (73)

In stately chariot, robes a green flare,
think of you?
                    Do I dare?

In creaking car of state and fleecy gown,
as a cornelian bright in panoply,
Think of you?
             I dare not so high.

So different a house in life, and then to lie
in the one earthen cell, unendingly.
And my sincerity?
             As the sun's eye.

X   (74)

Hemp on hill,
tell me, pray:
What keeps young Tsy Tsie away?

On mid slope
wheat grows fine,
Why doesn't Tsy Kuo come to dine?

There blows a plum on yonder hill
who wants those young bucks for her own.
Shall I give up my girdle stone?

Book 7. Songs of Cheng

"Banish the songs of Cheng."
K'ung, the Anthologist

K'ung-fu-tsy seems to have regarded the tunes to these
verses as a species of crooning or boogie-woogie.

I   (75)

Live up to your clothes,
    we'll see that you get new ones.
You do your job,
    we'll bring our best food to you 'uns.

If you're good as your robes are good
We'll bring you your pay and our best food.

Nothing too good, bigosh and bigob
For a bureaucrat who will really

                          attend to his job.

II   (76)

Hep-Cat Chung, 'ware my town,
don't break my willows down.
The trees don't matter
but father's tongue, mother's tongue
           Have a heart, Chung,
                      it's awful.

Hep-Cat Chung, don't jump my wall
nor strip my mulberry boughs,
The boughs don't matter
But my brothers' clatter!
           Have a heart, Chung,
                      it's awful.

Hep-Cat Chung, that is *my* garden wall,
Don't break my sandalwood tree.
The tree don't matter
But the subsequent chatter!
           Have a heart, Chung,
                      it's awful.

III   (77)

Shu goes hunting, no one stays
in the town's lanes and by-ways
or if they do
there's not a he-man there like Shu.

Shu 's after game, no one at table or bottle now
to eat or drink, or if they do
they are not a patch on Shu.

Shu 's in the wild field, there's no hitched horse in town;
though if you might
find someone driving there
'twere no such knight.

IV (78)

Shu 's to the field, the reins of his double team
seem silken strands;
His outer stallions move
as in a pantomime. Thru thicket and marsh
flare beaters' fires.
Stript to the waist he holds a tiger down
for the Duke's smile and frown:
>   "This once, but not again.
>   I need such men."

Shu 's to the hunt,
his wheel-bays pull strong.
The other pair are as twin geese a-wing.
He comes to marsh, the beaters' fires flash out.
Good archer and good driver to control,
The envy of all, be it to drive or shoot.

Again to hunting, now with the grays,
Pole pair show even head,
Outer pair like a hand outspread.
Shu to the break,
thru thicket swamp flare the fires.
Then driving slow,
Quiver set down, shoot comes to end.
Envy of all, he cases his bow.

V (79)
MANOEUVRES
"D'un air bonasse."
Vlaminck

Ts'ing men in P'eng
having a fling,
staff car, tasselled spears, snorting

horses cavorting,
>   by Ho!

Ts'ing men in Siao, staff cars clank,
one spear higher than t'other,
as they meander
>   by Ho bank.

Ts'ing men in Chou,
drivers, guards, and a left turn, right draw,
space, a place,
as we observe the commander's
>   affable face.

VI   (80)

Lamb-skin for suavity, trimmed and ornate,
But a good soldier who will get things straight;

Note that lamb coat, fleecy to leopard cuff,
a dude, but he knows his stuff.

Who gave three buttons meant:
This chap 's no mere ornament.

VII   (81)

I plucked your sleeve by the way, that you should pause.
Cast not an old friend off without cause.

That a hand's clasp in the high road could thee move:
Scorn not an old friend's love.

VIII   (82)

"Cock crow!" she says.
He says: " 'Tis dark."
"Up, sir," she says,
"Up, see, get out
and shoot the geese that be flyin' about."

"You shoot, I cook, that is as it should be,
eat, drink, grow old in mutual amity,
guitars and lutes in clear felicity.

I knew you'd come, by the girdle stone,
I to obey for the second one.
Three stones at a girdle be
Signs of returned felicity."

IX   (83)

In chariot like an hibiscus flower at his side
ready to ride and go, with gemmèd belt
Kiang's eldest frail and beauty of the town, our capital;

Like an hibiscus spray to walk with him,
to sway, to hover
as that petal'd flower, with sound of pendants
swinging at her waist, Kiang's eldest loveliness,
say in that sound is her true nature traced,

Nor shall effacèd be,
once known, from memory.

X   (84)
THE ADORNED BUT IMMATURE GALLANT

On mount doth noble ilex grow
and marsh weed in the lowland low.

                  'Tis not Tsy-tu doth now appear;
                  No man, but a boy perks here.

High pine on hill,
in swamp the dragon flower,

                  Not lovers' twilight this,
                  but the children's hour.

XI (85)

Withered, withered, by the wind's omen,
a state lost for the soft mouth of a woman;

What the wind hath blown away,
can men of Cheng rebuild it in a day.*

ALITER

Withered, withered at the winds' call,
Uncles you lead, I follow you all;

Withered, withered, as the wind floats,
You pipe, my uncles, I but follow your notes.

XII (86)

So he won't talk to me when we meet?
Terrible!
     I still can eat.

So clever he won't even come to dinner;
Well, beds are soft,
         and I'm no thinner.

XIII (87)

Be kind, good sir, and I'll lift my sark
and cross the Chen to you,
But don't think you are the only sprig
     in all the younger crew.

Think soft, good sir, and I'll lift my sark
and cross the Wei to you;
But play the pretentious ass again, and
     some other young captain will do.

---

* Where the winds blow, withered leaves must.
  Folk under overloads are as blown dust.
  L. and K. completely at loggerheads. Following Mao the meaning would
be: The prince, overborne by his ministers, ironizes.

XIV   (88)

A handsome lad stood in the lane,
Alas, I asked him to explain.

A rich boy came for me to the hall
and I wasn't ready. How should it befall?
                    Who wants a lady?

Here in my hidden embroideries
with a plain dress over them down to my knees,
Junior or elder, harness and come,
come with a wagon and cart a girl home.

Top and skirt of embroideries
covered in plain silk down to my knees,
Junior or elder, harness and come,
bring on your wagon and take a girl home.

XV   (89)

East gate's level stretch of land,
madder on bank there, easy to hand,
so near his home, and he so far.

By the east gate chestnuts grow
over garden walls so low,
There I ever think of thee,
and thou comest ne'er to me.

XVI   (90)
"As on the last day of the moon"

Cold wind, and the rain,
cock crow, he is come again,
                    my ease.

Shrill wind and the rain
and the cock crows and crows,
I have seen him, shall it suffice
                    as the wind blows?

Wind, rain and the dark
as it were the dark of the moon,
What of the wind, and the cock's never-ending cry;
Together
again
he and I.

XVII   (91)
THE STUDENT'S BLUE COLLAR OR LAPEL

Blue, blue collar, my heart's delight,
I can't come out,
Why shouldn't you write?

Blue, blue sash, heart's misery.
I cannot come out, but you might come to me.

You swish about
between gates of the towered wall,
So far, no wrong.
One day without you
is three months long.

XVIII   (92)

Dashing waters untie not
the knot that binds a thorn fagot.
Elder and younger brothers we
in bonds of so small family,
Trust not men's idle tales
who use words to hide their thought.

Splashing unties no fagot bound,
elder and younger brothers we;
I say: trust not their perfidy.

XIX   (93)

At the great gate to the East
Mid crowds

be girls like clouds
who cloud not my thought in the least.

        Gray scarf and a plain silk gown
        I take delight in one alone.

Under the towers toward the East
be fair girls like flowers to test,

        Red bonnet and plain silk gown
        I take delight with one alone.

XX   (94)

Mid the bind-grass on the plain
that the dew makes wet as rain
I met by chance my clear-eyed man,
        then my
        joy began.

Mid the wild grass dank with dew
lay we the full night thru,
        that clear-eyed man and I
        in mutual felicity.

XXI   (95)
SAY IT WITH PEONIES

Chen and Wei
flow thereby
        touching together,
Man and girl, girl and man
        to pluck valerian:
"The play?" says she.
"Seen it," says he.
"If so, let's go
Over Wei
pleasantly."

        Playing there, girls and men
        Prescribe this mutual medicine.

Chen and Wei in alacrity
as pampas blades a-gleam
by bank and stream
come girls and a throng of officers.   .

She says: "Have you seen . . . ?"
He says: "I been."
"Let's again." Over Wei
Pleasantly,
                    Ready girl, ready man
                    offer mutual medicine.

Book 8. The Often Mildly Satirical Verses of Ts'i

I   (96)
NONDUM ORTO JUBARE.

Alba belingalis

"Cock's crow'd. The courtiers are all
crowding the hall."
Cock hasn't, she lies
but one hears some blue flies.

"East's bright. Court's met."
East's not, but the waning moon*
sends up some light.

"Flies fly high, but also hum,
'Twere sweet to dream, by side, but knights
who walk from court assembly also talk and might even rage
at innocent
concubinage."

* Waning moon,
   moon is about to set.

II   (97)
TOUJOURS LA POLITESSE

"That turn 'll get her." I said.
We were loafing about under Nao,
each in his hunting gig
after a brace of wild pig;
You bowed and replied: "Yours, better!"

"Some cut." I said.
We had come to the meet at Dog Hill,
two boar for the kill. You said,
with a bow: "And yours, now!"

We met on the south slope of Nao,
wolves the game this time,
the exchange of the same lightness,
save that you said bowing: "Majesterial!"
a huntsman not to be outdone in politeness.

III   (98)

He waited me by our gate-screen,
                come by, come by.
His ear-plugs shone so florally,
                come by,
on white silk tassels airily,
                come by, come by.

He came straight in to our court-yard,
                come by, come by.
His ear-plugs flamed so fiery,
                come by,
on silken thread like greenery,
                come by.

He stopped not till he reached the hall,
                come by, come by.
The yellow tassels airily
held two topaze right royally,
                come by, come by.

IV (99)

TOWN LIFE

Sun's in the East,
her loveliness
Comes here
To undress.

Twixt door and screen
at moon-rise
I hear
Her departing sighs.

V (100)

Still dark,
mistaking a kilt for a coat
upside down:
            "To the Duke, sir, since . . ."

It was not yet light,
mistaking a coat for a kilt,
down for up,
            and to audience!

Break thru the close garden fence
with staring eyes, a fool tries.
Milord 's lost all sense of tense
night, day, audience,
day, night,
and no time ever right.

VI (101)

South Mount soaring, cock fox sly,
Lu Road wide open as Miss Ts'i went to bride.
I said, to bride.
            Put it aside.

Five kinds of vine-rope shoes
by twos, cap-strings are mated.

And Lu Road was wide, when Miss Ts'i, as stated
went to bride, settled and fixed,
       Why push betwixt.

How sow hemp? Hemp goes by furrows,
formal wedding fix tomorrows.
    A girl is placed by those who breed her,
      Would you now still cuddle and feed her?

How 's kindling split?
By axe, and the fit
tool to arrange a marriage with decencies,
is the broker who sees
to the details and formalities.
And you'd move her?
Now the whole job is settled and over?

VII   (102)
"Their eyes are in the ends of the Earth."

    Field not too great a field
    lest weeds outproud thy grain;
    nor of foreign affairs
    lest 'ou break under strain.

    Field not too great a field
    lest the overgrowth break thee,
    nor foreigners
    lest worry unmake thee.

    The tufted babe
    that wriggles in thy lap,
    ere thou art ware
    will wear a grown man's cap.

VIII   (103)

With sound of the hounds, black hounds,
he is riding the bounds, a tall man, a real man.

"Ting-a-ding" sound the hounds, black hounds
on double ring.

A sporting man's fling, triple ring
to his hounds, when a man
thinks of his hunting.

(Some men think of the game or else
give attention to rings, hair-dos and bells.)

IX (104)

The wicker of the weir is broke,
loose fish are out again
as the Lady of Ts'i comes home
with a cloud in her train.

The wicker of the weir is broke
as ex-Miss Ts'i comes home again,
luce and perch be broken out
as many as drops of rain.

The wicker of the weir is broke
and these fish make a very great clatter.
The Lady of Ts'i comes home with a train,
all of them loose as water.*

X (105)
LA MADONE DES WAGONS-LITS

On comes her car with a rattle-de-bang,
woven leather like cinnabar,
Loose, loose, a flaming star,
id est, Miss Ts'i shooting the moon
to Lu,
      to Lu,
            started at sunset, none too soon.

---

* Legge says the satire is against her son the Duke of Lu for not keeping the dowager in order. Karlgren dissents. "Loose Fish," usual term for unattached males.

With a black flash of quadrigas
and the multitude of her chariots,
double teams matched, smooth-oiled reins,
Lu Road stretching across the plains.

Full be the waters of Wen
as we hear the whang of marching men,
Miss Ts'i and Lu Road we see
both wider than all liberality.

Across Wen water churning mud
a herd of travellers in flood
and, loose on Lu Road, Miss Ts'i
showing compassion abundantly.

XI (106)

"An ater an albus" . . .

Catullus

Compleat, alas, and prosperous,
profile'd and tall "to lower is as to raise."
His fine eyes blaze,
Clever of foot and great in archery.

Competent, alas, and of wide fame,
a dark pellucid eye;
Focussed in equity,
can shoot all day and never miss the dot,
        a nephew, a spread nephew, certainly.

Competent, alas, and of winning grace,
clearly with naught to learn *in feminis*
or in the dance and courtly pantomime,
bull's-eye each time,
four arrows on the dot:
        could he block civil war,
        or should he not?

Book 9. Songs of Ngwei

(*Under Tsin domination, presumably, the new ruling class
from seven points of view.*)

I (107)

Thin fibre shoes 'gainst frost,
At soft hands' cost a girl can make her clothes
or ply the needle with those same hands
to make her goodman's stiff belt and bands.

Goodman? or mean? we mean
good to accumulate and accumulate,
noted of late at her left hand
on formal occasions, meticulous
with an ivory pin in a belt*
which cramps him, we mean
the tightening has an inner cause

(if you take not the pin's point, but ours.)

II (108)
ENCROACHMENT
"Families who use ice, do not etc."
Ta Hio

To gather sorrel
in swamplands of Fen,
is a suitable act for local men,
but for a resplendent officer
who moves in charge of a ducal car?

Fen has one grove of mulberry trees
Fen folk were wont to use
till such a flowery officer,
a "button man," came to administer
and have charge of the public roads.

---

* Ivory pins or spikes carried in the belt for untying knots.

By one crook of the Fen ox-lip grows
that Fen folk once gathered to ease their woes
till wc got such a gem of an officer
of the Duke's household,
of the kind some dukes prefer.

III   (109)
JE BOIS DANS MON VERRE

Garden peach, in a dish ere long (my own)
as my worry goes into song.
Strangers say: "The scholar is proud.
Others fit in. Why 's he so loud?"
Those who know me, plumb not my thought.

Garden blackberry (my own) made to eat,
a heart worries for the state of the State;
Strangers find me utterly wrong
because "other men get along."
Friends, finding me distraught,
Plumb not my thought.

(Who can plumb another man's thought?)

IV   (110)

I climb the knoll;
gaze to my father's land from the knoll's shade,
and he will be saying, praying:
            "That boy's on hard service
            dawn to sundown, no end.
            Let him care for the flag, as I could commend.
            So he return in the end."

I climb bald rock, eyes seek
my mother's house, and she:
            "No rest, my bairn,
            That his bones lie not in the waste."

I climb the ridge
look to my brother's stead,
and he:
>"The kid is abroad,
>a file filled,
>If only he doesn't get killed
>(and an eye on the flag.)"

V (111)

In their ten-acre allotments, barons at ease
say: "These are surely our mulberry trees."

Outside their allotments, as I've heard tell,
they say just as calmly: ". . . and these as well."

VI (112)
"SILK-DINE"
that is, in idleness

K'an, k'an, sandalwood
planks are good by Ho
on clear water we float their weight.

Men of state
nor sow nor reap
yet keep grain to fill three hundred markets;
never hunt nor hear dogs bark, yet
never lack
badger skins to cover the back.
And I could name
some courtyards filled with a total district's game,
>where they dine in milk-white silk
>(Idle food to the nobleman!)

K'an, k'an,
axes clank.
From oak to spoke,
we pile the planks by Ho bank,
steady as the waters flow.

They never sow nor reap
nor hunt, yet keep
grain as much as three hundred krorcs
and have yards full of young, hung wild boars
    to help 'em dine in milk-white silk
    (Idle food for the nobleman!)

K'an, k'an, trim
and bend a wheel-rim
by whirling water we pile the logs
on bank; they never hunt or run with the dogs,
nor sow, nor reap, yet keep
grain to fill up three hundred bins,
and when they would stuff their skins
in their court one never fails
to see a string of good fat quails.
    So they dine in milk-white silk.
    (Idle food for a nobleman.)

VII (113)
RATS

RATS,
stone-head rats lay off our grain,
three years pain,
enough, enough, plus enough again.
More than enough from you, deaf you,
we're about thru and ready to go
where something will grow
untaxed.
Good earth, good sown,
and come into our own.

RATS,
big rats, lay off our wheat,
three years deceit,
and now we're about ready to go
to Lo Kuo, happy, happy land, Lo Kuo, good earth
where we can earn our worth.

RATS,
stone-head rats, spare our new shoots,
three years, no pay.
We're about ready to move away
to some decent border town.
Good earth, good sown,
and make an end to this endless moan.

Book 10. Songs of T'ang

the northernmost part of the great Tsin fief under the
Chou dynasty. Yao's country.

I (114)

Cricket in hall, the year runs to its close,
Rejoice and now, ere sun and moon subtract.
Exceed no bound, think what thine office is;
          Enjoy the good, yet sink not in excess.
          Hereto is good knight's true attentiveness.

Cricket in hall, the year is on the wain.
The sun and moon defend no man's delight.
Stretch not thy wish, know where stands outerness,
Right man is light of foot in banquet rite.

Cricket's in hall, the killers' carts put by,
Rejoice and now, tho' suns be insolent.
Too-much sires woe, be mindful of thine extent.
          Enjoy the good yet sink not in excess,
          True scholar stands by his steadfastness.

II (115)

Thorn-elm on mountain, white elm on slope,
the clothes you never wear,
carriages idle there
be another's fact or hope
     when you are dead, who now but mope.

Kao tree on crest, shrub in low-land,
dust in your courtly dancing place,
bells on rack and drums unlaced
shall be others' jollity
    when you've proved your mortality.

Terebinth stands high on the crest, chestnut in vale,
wine thou hast and lutes in array,
undrunk, unstruck today.
Who makest not carouse:
    another shall have thy house.*

III   (116)

Water dashing
on sharp-edged rocks;
silk robe and red lapel
followed to Wu
and saw Milord there,
                wasn't that a happy affair!

Swift water knocks
on the bright white rocks;
white silk robe and broidered axe
followed to Ku and saw the chief,
                who could say that was grief?

Water dashing
on white flare of stone;
We hear it is ordered and dare tell none.†

---

* Traditionally an admonition to Marquis Chao of Tsin, written between
744–738 B.C.

† Tradition that this concerns the conspiracy of Ch'eng-shy against Chao,
Marquis of Tsin; commentators at loggerheads as to its bearing: pro-rock,
pro-water, loyalty to legal insignia, warning, irony, incitement, taunt to
Ch'eng-shy who had illegally assumed the insignia. Which wd/ come to: We
hear you have the appointment (from heaven) but fear to proclaim (kao) it
openly. 744–738 B.C. The obscurity undoubtedly intentional.

IV   (117)
"Evviva la torre di Pisa!"

Oh, the pods keep a sproutin'
          upon the pepper tree,
the sprouts keep a risin'
and the big pods hangin' down,
the pods keep a growin'
        for a strong man on his own.

The big pods keep a hangin',
the sprouts keep a risin'
and the big pods hangin' down,
the new sprouts keep a growin'
          for a strong man on his own.*

V   (118)
TS'AN
the three stars of Orion

She says:
      I've tied the faggots round,
      Three stars are in the sky,
          a night, a night,
      to see my man, and hold him pleasantly.

      Now I've bundled up the grass,
      Three stars rise o'er the hill,
          a night to meet,
          a night to meet,
          by luck, not by our will.

He says:
      Now I've bound the thorns together,
      Three stars above the door
      have brought me to tie with such a lass
      as never I saw before.

---

* Traditionally refers to rising power of Huan-Shu, co-rebel with Ch'eng-shy.

VI   (119)

The pear tree stands alone, a-gleam with leaf,
I walk alone, my grief,
among men upon the road, none of my father's breed
                    lifts load, shares aim.

The pear tree stands alone, so green in leaf,
Bowed and alone, my grief
where no man shares my name
fraternal upon the road
                    lifts load, shares aim.

VII   (120)
(Meaning wholly conjectural)

Lamb-skin coat and a leopard cuff
goes on living beneath my roof.

There are others, I've been told
and this one is gettin' old.

Askin' and askin', now I hear
others are called and might appear
with a lambskin coat and leopard trim
although I am fond of him.*

VIII   (121)
PAO
That carrion crow has advantage.

Buzzards on oak, after neat flight,
King's work is never to slight,
Now we cannot tend our grain
What shall sustain father or mother, heaven say:
Is this our crime? shall we home again?

----

* Legge follows commentators who interpret it as complaint against a bad governor, personally liked. My translation probably wrong, and others' no better.

Buzzards fly and nest in thorns,
thick the thorns as the king's affairs.
Neglect of grain no man spares.
How shall a father and mother eat
with this deficient grain supply?
Shall the far archèd heaven defend
mankind from such an end?

Buzzards from sky come down mid mulberries,
In king's affairs is no ease,
As test?
Shall father or mother see
rice or spiked-grain harvest?

Such darkness the archèd heaven brings
as the common order of things.

IX   (122)

'Tis to lack seven robes
lacking thine,
which gift could a peace define.

As if losing the sixth coat
(if he lack thine)
leave peace remote.

X   (123)

At the road's bend
dare say he'd make a
nice gentleman-friend.

Lonely pear tree by the way side,
How shall I for my true-love provide?

Dare say he'd agree, but how feed him?

Russet pear at bend of the way,
Dare say he'd come play, but . . .

True love won't feed him.

XI (124)
ALBA

Creeper grows over thorn,
bracken wilds over waste, he is gone,
Gone, I am alone.

Creeper overgrows thorn,
bracken spreads over the grave, he is gone,
Gone, I am alone.

The horn pillow is white like rice,
the silk shroud gleams as if with tatters of fire.
In the sunrise I am alone.

A summer's day,
winter's night, a hundred years
and we come to one house together.

Winter's day, summer's night,
each night as winter night,
each day long as of summer,
                but at last to the one same house.

XII (125)

"Pick ling! Pick ling! on Shou-Yang's crest!"
Such words, a mere mare's-nest,
                would not stir credulity
                yet you believe the worst of me.
If you swallow such nonsense now
When will you find a way, or how?

"Go for thistles to South-Head's base."
Would you try in any case?
                Indeed you would not, why and how
                can you swallow such nonsense now?

"And for mustard? Shou-Yang's east side."
Would you try it, or have you tried?
                    Tell me truly, who but a fool
                    Believes such silly tales out of school.

Book II. Songs of Ts'in

Feudal state from 897–221, rising to dynasty after Chou.
As the Chou capital moved eastward, Ts'in subject to wild
infiltration from the West.

I   (126)

Chariots, rank on rank
with white-fronted horses;
You'd see Milord?
                    Eunuchs are bosses.

Terebinth on the hill, chestnuts in valley;
Once you're inside, there are lutes in each alley.
                    Delight, delight
                    and the long night
                                        coming.

Mulberries on the crest,
willows in marsh-land valley,
                    drum-beat and shamisan,
                                        dally, dally,
                    Death's up the alley.

II   (127)
WINTER HUNT

His sports-car leads with the iron-grays,
six reins are in his hand
and behind come all the hunt
to follow at his command,

Now boars rush from underbrush,
strong against spear,
young pigs of the year;
and the Duke's voice clear:
               "To the left,
               by the bounds,
               pull out the hounds."

Hallo and Hark
then to North Park
double teams
neat in their rounds
with the tinkling sounds
of bells, and the long and short-nosed hounds.

III   (128)

So have I seen him in his service car
who now in war afar,
five bands on the curving pole, side shields and silver'd trace,
bright mats and bulging hub;
dapple and white-foot pace
into my thought. I see him neat as jade
in service shack, and in my thought confused.

Great dapples held, and by six reins restrained,
black-maned,
the darker pair outside,
locked dragon shield and silver-ringèd rein
before my thought again
who now by border wall
moves suave as once in hall.

Team in an even block, gilt trident-haft
with silver-basèd butt, and emboss'd shields,
bow-case of tiger's fell, graved lorica;
the bows are bound to laths inside their case;

Shall he not fill my thought,
                    by day, by night,
whose mind and act are right,
whose fame, delight?

IV   (129)

PHANTOM

Dark, dark be reed and rush,
the white dew turns to frost;
                    what manner of man is this?
                                        lost?

                    Gin I rin up,
                    Gin I go down,
                    Up stream heavy, there he'd be
                    In mid water distantly.

Chill, chill be the reeds,
the white dew not yet dry;
                    What manner of man is he
                    under the hanging bank?

                    Up stream heavily.
                    gin I swim down,
                    on tufted isle
                    distantly.

Ever falls dew on bright reeds.
                    What manner of thing is he
                    who seems to be there on the marge

                    Up stream, to the West, at large?
                    Hard to go up, to swim, tho' he seem
                    there on the isle, mid-stream.

V   (130)

The outdoor chief establishes court

On South sky-line, white fir and plum
So the Prince come,
>   fox fur for broidery,
>   ruddy of face,
>   true lord, true race.

On South Mountain, vale and aisle
Tale of the hall he reared meanwhile,
Whose blue-black robe showed double axe displayed.
Hear, at his belt "tsiang-tsiang" of the pendant jade.*
>   To whom longevity
>   and fame always in memory.

VI   (131)

THE THREE SHAY BROTHERS
Funeral sacrifice for Duke Mu, 621 B.C.

Ever unstill, cross, cross,
yellow wings come to the thorn.

>   Who? with Duke Mu?
>   Shay Yen-Si. Who?
Shay Yen-Si, pick of an hundred men, shook at the grave's
>   edge then.

>   Dark heaven, you take our best men,
>   An hundred; to have him again.

Ever unstill, cross, the yellow birds
come to mulberry boughs.

>   Who? with Duke Mu?
>   Shay Chung-Hang. Who?
Shay Chung-Hang who'd block an hundred men
Moaned at the grave's brink then.

---

* The "tsiang-tsiang" is onomatopoeia but the lines could also be rendered:
>   Saith ever: "Shall and shall";
>   never: "oblivion."

Dark heaven, you take our best men,
An hundred to have him again.

Ever unstill, cross, cross,
The yellow wings come to the thorn,

Who? with Duke Mu?
Shay K'ien-Hu, who could hold an hundred men,
Shook at the grave's brink then.

Dark heaven, you wipe out our best men.
We'd give an hundred
To have him again.

VII   (132)
"Long wind, the dawn wind"

Falcon gone to the gloom
and the long wind of the forest
Forgetting the children I bore you,
North, North?

Thick oak on mount, six grafted pears in the low,
Whither, whither
North, north
forgetful so?

Plum trees of the mountain,
Peach blossoms of the plain
Whither, whither?
I am drunk with the pain.

VIII   (133)

What! No clothes?
Share my cloak, at the king's call
spear, lance and all
prepare
and advance
with axes, together.

What! no clothes?
My underwear is just your size.
Levies arise,
at the king's call
we rise all
      with lances and halbards, together.

What! no clothes?
Take my spare kilt. Shine mail-coat and axe!
    Lift we our packs
      and out together.

IX (134)

With him to say good-bye
To the north banks of the Wei,
      Uncle, my uncle,
I bless thy ways
I give thee four bays
      for thy car, at departing.

My thought within is deeper, uncle my own.
Take this jasper for girdle stone,
      departing.

X (135)
WELCOME OUTSTAYED

Alas, in Hia's house
where we made great carouse
Naught's now to spare.

The old tree bears no fruit
      for Milord's heir.

Once four great courses were
set for each visitor,
all different. And all now different here,

The old tree bears no fruit
      for Milord's heir.

SONGS OF THREE SMALL STATES
AND OF PIN
DUKE LIU'S OLD CAPITAL

Book 12. Songs of Ch'en

I   (136)

On Yüan hill, mutable, affable, candid, but
held of no account.

(Fluid as water that all tones reflects
of ten-day passion that no man respects.)

Under that hill to stand
tapping a hand-drum, waving an egret's feather,

Tapping an earthen pot on Yüan Road,
winter or summer, man
you weigh as much as your load:

                                        the egret fan.

II   (137)

HILARE DIE

White elm at East Gate,
Bent Hill's oaks are tall,
Middle Sir's daughter
dances under them all.

Grain dawn for the errand,
we see "South Lady" race
her hemp unspun
to dance in the market place.

Grain dawn for going
till over the cauldron's edge
we see you as the Sun's flower;
grant we hold pepper in pledge.*

* A ritual dance, conjecturally, for solar fecundation.

III (138)

Neath a patched door-flap,
no man to hurry me,
a spring of fresh water
and none to worry me.

There be bream that swim not in Ho;
Kiang girls of Ts'i
                    but others also.

More streams than Ho give fish
Tsy girls of Sung
                    be not the only dish.

There be bream that swim not in Ho;
Kiang-of-Ts'i girls
                    but others also.

More streams than Ho give fish,
Tsy-of-Sung girls be not the only dish.

IV (139)
THE THIRD DAUGHTER OF KI

Soak hemp in East Moat, can't go wrong,
By East Gate 's a girl who will answer a song.

You can limber the thickest hemp in that situation,
and pass the time in polite conversation
                    with Miss Ki the 3rd/

Soak mat-grass by East Gate moat,
Miss Ki the 3rd/ is no flash in the pan, Sir,
But a young lady, and pretty,
                    who knows the answers.

V   (140)

RENDEZ-VOUS MANQUÉ

Neath East Gate willows
'tis good to lie.
She said:
          "this evening."
          Dawn 's in the sky.

Neath thick willow boughs
          'twas for last night.
Thick the close shade there.
          The dawn is axe-bright.

VI   (141)

Thorns by the Campo Santo gate
need axe, and so does he, as most men know,
whose knowledge puts no end to his misdeeds.

Owls perch on cemetery trees,
plum trees, indeed, and hoot
and so do I, as were a warning and that gets no ear.
When he's knocked flat, he may hear.

ALITER

You can take an axe to the jujube trees
that clog the gates of cemeteries,
but to deal with this dirty cuss,
by courtesy only, anonymous?

To know is not to make an end
of his old habits, but of his friend.

Owl sits moody by graveyard gate
on the plum tree, to tell him to do this, that and t'other.
After he's down he may start to bother.

VII (142)

Magpies nest on the mound,
Sweet grass on higher ground,
　　　Who has lured my love away?
　　　　　　My wound!

Tiles on the temple path,
The high bank hath
many a blossom still.
　　　Who was it lured my love away?
　　　　　　My wound!

VIII (143)

The erudite moon is up, less fair than she
who hath tied silk cords about
　　　　　　a heart in agony,
She at such ease
　　　　so all my work is vain.

My heart is tinder, and steel plucks at my pain
so all my work is vain,
　　　　she at such ease
　　　　as is the enquiring moon.

A glittering moon comes out
less bright than she the moon's colleague
that is so fair,
　　　　of yet such transient grace,
at ease, undurable, so all my work is vain
　　　　torn with this pain.*

IX (144)
THE DIVERSIVE

Why to the broken forest?
He follows the Summer South,
He drives not to the broken forest
　　　But to Hia Nan's mouth.

* A few transpositions but I think the words are all in the text.

"Harness my team of horses, harness and say:
'We go to the plain past Chu Ye.'
That'll help me, and help the colts thru
to breakfast in Chu."*

X   (145)

Marsh bank, lotus rank
                    and a ladye;
Heart ache and to lie awake
                    and a-fevered.

Marsh edge, valerian in sedge
                    and a ladye;
Hard head she hath.
I lie a-bed
                afflicted.

Marsh bank, lotus rank,
                    a ladye,
straight as an altar stone her loveliness,
I lie in restlessness
                    all the night
                    comfortless.

ALITER

Graceful as acorus or lotus flower
what dame in bower
plagues me to wake from sleep?
I sweat from every vein.

As marsh hath rush or sharp valerian,
Tall formal beauty, and mid-heart my lack!

Marsh bank hath acorus to sway and flare,
Shall lily on lake compare
with a tall woman's loveliness
that though I wake or sleep
                    I turn and toss?

---

* Legge says: a satire on Duke Ling's intrigue with Hia Nan. I take it with
play on meaning of her name "Summer South."

Book 13. Songs of Kuei

I   (146)

Fine clothes for sport
and slops in court
and your intent
is to show talent
          for government?

Lamb's wool for sport,
fox fur in court and hall,
to me no festival.

Sure, the wool shines like fat
in the sun's rays; reflects the light
and is quite scintillant,
feathers of light in fact
          to my heart's blight.

II   (147)

Sad 'tis to see good customs in neglect,
Our mourners now be no more circumspect.

Saw I a white cap now,
it were as music mid thorns,
          Haro! the day.

Or a white robe?
Came such a robe in sight
methinks I would, outright,
go with the wearer miles upon his road.

Saw I white knee-pads decent misery
I'd know one man still feels and thinks as I.

III   (148)

Vitex in swamp ground,
branched loveliness,
would I could share that shrub's unconsciousness.

Vitex negundo, casting thy flowers in air,
thy joy to be, and have no family care.

Vitex in low marsh ground,
thy small fruit grows
in tenderness,
having no heavy house.

IV   (149)
THE KETTLE-DRUMS*

Not the wild wind
nor the roar of the chariots
            But the ruin of Chou's way
                        breaks me.

Not the storm's whirling
nor the war cars' surging
But the ruin of highways in Chou,
                        and unpitied.

If a man can boil fish
let him wash out his cauldron,
If a man would home West
let him cherish this tone.

* Vide Frobenius, the drums were made for temporary use by stretching
the cover over the nomad's pots.

Book 14. Songs of Ts'ao

I   (150)
POLONIUS ON OSTENTATION
(The banner-fly wears proper mourning in season?)

Trappings as bright as wings of the banner-fly
give me concern,
                            come back and live quietly.

Flashy your dress as light fly's moving wing
to my concern,
                            could you come home?

Grub digs out of its hole to see and spy
snow-white the hemp of its panoply,
to my concern,
                            could you come back and talk quietly.

II   (151)
OUTDOORS VERSUS THE COURT
(Conjecturally: country girl's advice to the guardsman)

Marquis' yeoman, oh so brave
to lift lance or show signal stave,
but the person living at ease
has three hundred footmen with red pads on their knees.

Pelican on the dam
wets not a wing,
she 's less important than
her furnishing.

Pelican on the weir will not stir
even to dip its beak,
and she whom you seek
cares less than you for her.

South Mount, East Slope, you scarce can see thru the mist
when the dawn 's half alight.
Pleasant, yes, ready, yes,
the youngest girl has an appetite.

III   (152)
THE YOUNG IN NEWFANGLENESSE

Dove in this mulberry tree
feeds seven young untiringly;
Our lord, a unit of equity
hath heart of such constancy.

He keeps to his old nest,
the young wings flap
over the plum tree.

Silk sash and deer-spot cap,
still in the old precinct of mulberries;
they to the jujube now; the old eye ever on right,
no whimsies, the four corners ever in sight.

Dove in mulberry, young 'uns now try the hazel bough;
Call 'em the hazeleers;
He to the state gives form;
Sets norm:

Why not ten thousand years?
How not ten thousand years?

IV   (153)

Down from the spring the knife-sharp waters run
flooding the wolf-grass;
By night I wake and sigh
for Chou's lost majesty.
                    Chou 's down.

Cold waters flood and rot the sandal root;
By night I wake and sigh:
                        Chou 's down.

Chill waters seep milfoil in overflow;
By night I wake and weep that capital.

Millet rose thick, by mothering rain on soil;
Then were the Four States ruled by Earl Sün's toil.

Book 15. Songs of Pin

1   (154)

August sees the heat break.
In October we take our winter wear
gainst New Year's wind and March' cold air,
lacking serge of wool and hair
how 'ld we last till harvest time?

Third month: out the plows;
fourth: toe to field, childer and spouse
carry our snacks to the south sectors
where we prepare to meet the inspectors.

2

Sinketh the fiery sign neath the seventh moon;
ninth, we get clothes; when spring 'gins quicken
orioles in broom and bracken
cry to basket-bearing girls
trapsing about field-paths in Wei
to strip leaves from the mulberry;

as the slow days lengthen out
they'll to the southernwood, no doubt, and
mid the crowds some maids will sigh

for fear of the Duke's boys passing by
(we mean shrinking prospective brides
who'd prefer their home firesides.)

3

August moon marks the heat's edge,
September is for reed and sedge
when the silkworms start to hatch
we'll go twig the mulberry patch
with little axe and small hatchet
lop the splay boughs, to keep she-trees tight set.
So in August shrilleth shrike,
in September they'll spin belike
to make such yellow, stark red and black
as befits young lordling's back.

4

May is for grass seed,
June, Cicada's joy;
September, harvest, November to destroy
dead leaves,
Badger's in season when the year goes out,
wild-cat can make a young lord's coat.
In great hunts (March) that ready men for wars,
commons get piglets; nobles, the full-size boars.

5

June's green hopper moves a thigh,
"sedge-cock" wings it in July,
cricket 's a-field one month,
next, neath our eaves, and ere two more be sped,
he's over lintel, and crawls beneath thy bed.

Plug up the chinks, smoke out the rats,
block the north-lights, replaster wattle-slats
and tell the wife: the year draws to its close,
bide we at home the while, in full repose.

6

July 's to eat red plums, start on wild-vine.
Sunflower and bean in August pot combine;
strip, next, the dates, and neath November moon
take rice for saki that in spring eftsoon
shall keep old age and eyebrows from all need.

Eat melons in August, trim thy calabash,
then take in hemp seed. Trash,
thistles and fagots from any stinking tree
our farmers get as their gratuity.

7

Ninth month; beat hard
the space that was thy summer garden-yard
and in the tenth bring here field-sheaves to stack.
Early millet and late, hemp, beans nor wheat shall lack,
so tell the farm-hands: all the harvest 's in,
lets to our town, that indoor work begin.
Get grass by day, twist this by night to rope the thatch
lest any roof lack patch against the rain
whereneath to bide, till we sow next year's grain.

8

d'iông, d'iông (clash, crash) chop ice neath the second moon,
store it neath third, and in fourth month
when dawn's claw scratcheth sky
offer young lamb and leek roots pungently
if thou 'ldst have sheep to kill come next still frost,
asperge the yard for the twin-bottle feast
and with killed beasts then move processional
to lift great horn in the high ducal hall
and toast:
                  ten thousand years, Milord, to time's utmost.

II   (155)

Great horned owl, thieved my young!
Owl. Owl, raze not a house upsprung
from kindness, toil; we say the anointed young
are for pity.

2

Ere the sky was dark with rain
I set my trees to provide and tithe mulberries,
and with silken skein
bound door and lattice frame,
O you, down there,
who shall despise my name?

3

Hand that laboured, worn to the bone
clutching at thistles to build up the rent
and with a sore mouth,
shall I not have roof of my own?

4

Wings unfeathered, my tail unplumed,
a house in fragments, doomed,
shaken with wind and rain,
            a-wash, afloat, *Aude me!**

III   (156)
GAG, said to have been used in night attack
to insure silence

From the long East Mount campaign
we came west, under a drizzle of rain
nor believed the news or their oaths,
but to be free of the gag and of army clothes.
Worms had filmed over the mulberry trees, under the stars
we guardsmen slept lonely, under our cars.

---

* The Duke of Chou against the uncles in the rebellion. *Mencius* II.i.IV,
3; *Shu* V.vi, 15.

Homesick we went to the East Mountain,
We come now west again under a spatter of rain,
slogging along.
Gourds over the eaves,
sowbug in chamber, spiders ply
web over door;
what was once field is now forest thereby,
wild deer for cattle, take no fright
of the glow-worms' eerie light
that can be
aid to one's memory.

From the long East Mount campaign
came back under a sousing rain,
cranes loud on ant-hill to drown our consorts' weeping,
worn out with sweeping,
sprinkling and plugging the walls;
levy comes home; bitter gourds over wood-pile
of chestnut boughs,
three years since the soldier has seen his house.

From the long East Mount campaign
we came west again under the rain.
Then the flash of an oriole's wing:
a new wife with dapple team come to meeting.
Her duenna has tied her formal sash, set
to the ninety rules of her etiquette;
piebal'd sorrels and bays a-dash to prove
a new love's glory—and no love
like an old love.

IV   (157)

Axes broken, hatchets lacking,
Eastward packing, the Duke of Chou gained
four states, and the Emperor reigned
over them all. He pitied our men,
Yet they were trained.

We have blunted our axes,
We lack work-tools,
Chou's Duke invades and rules as is fit
the four states of the East to their benefit;
Pity our men's condition,
his praise carries them on.

Axes broken, work-tools lacking,
Chou's Duke corrected
four states and connected
them all under one rule and test;
By his pity of fighting men
they now find rest.

V   (158)

How cut haft for an axe?

Who hacks
holds a haft.
To take a wife
properly
one gets a notary.

To hack an axe-haft
an axe
hacks;
the pattern 's near.

Let who weds never pass
too far
from his own class.

VI   (159)

Nine meshes of the net enclose
two sorts of fishes, bream, these, rudd, those:
Behold our Prince in his bright-broidered clothes.

Wild geese a-wing circle the isle;
The Duke's coming 's so short a while;

Wild geese seek land as but a pause in flight;
Return, and not to be here but a night;

The Dragon-Robe in so brief a stay,
Who'd neither cause us grief, nor stay away.

VII   (160)

Big bad wolf falls over his tail;
Dutiful Duke goes quiet along the trail
in his good red shoes so orderly?

Big bad wolf trips over his jowl,
let him fall on his tail and howl;
The Duke rings true.
Who'll carry thru?

HE.

PART TWO
IN EIGHT BOOKS

ELEGANTIAE
OR SMALLER ODES

Book 1. Deer Sing

I (161)

"Salt
lick!" deer on waste sing:
grass for the tasting, guests to feasting;
strike lute and blow
pipes to show how
feasts were in Chou,
    drum up that basket-lid now.

"Salt
lick!" deer on waste sing:
sharp grass for tasting, guests to feasting.
In clear sincerity,
here is no snobbery.
This to show how
good wine should flow
    in banquet mid true
    gentlemen.

"Salt
lick!" deer on waste sing,
k'in plants for tasting, guests to feasting;
beat drum and strumm
lute and guitar,
lute and guitar to get
deep joy where wine is set
mid merry din
let the guest in, in, in, let the guest in.

II (162)
REQUEST FOR FURLOUGH

Toiling stallions, winding road,
Would I were home, the king's load
is heavy as heart, on Chou Road,

Heavy team ever strains,
They be black with white manes;
would I were home, I am oppresst
by duty that gives a man no rest.

Doves can fly, then rest on oak
but the king's yoke heavy is
and my father in distress.

Weary pigeon can come to tree,
I cannot serve my mother fittingly.
There's no rest in
the king's livery.

By the black manes of my white horse
I yoke these words in remorse with this refrain:
Let me report to my mother again.

III (163)

Where the dunes come down from the lowland plain,
bright flowers, a legate's train
keen on their errand.

Bright flower in lowland
that gallops
fearing to lose its hour,
the legate's train
astrain, each:

Horses like fillies,
reins drenched with sweat
from hard driving
for what news they can get;

Dapples on silky rein
push hard to catch as can
what the folk
of this land plan.

With six drenched reins
the whites with black manes
surge over all the plains
to measure reports;

Light grays with an even pull
urge, surge. Reports must be full.

IV (164)

FRATERNITAS

Splendour recurrent
in cherry-wood,
in all the world there is
nothing like brotherhood.

Brothers meet
in death and sorrow;
broken line, battle heat,
Brothers stand by;

In a pinch they collaborate
as the ling bird's vertebrae
when friends of either
protractedly just sigh.

Wrangle at home, unite outside
when friends of either are ready of course
to help either with anything
"short of brute force."

And peril past, there be those who
let brothers stew
in their own juice
as unfriends born, of no immediate use.

Set out the dishes
serve the wine,
let brothers dine tonight
with boyhood appetite.

Wife and childer together be
as sound of lutes played concurrently;
there's a deeper tone in fraternity
when elder and younger rise to agree.

Calm over earth, under sky
so be thy hearth and house as they should be;
probe to the utmost plan,
here the sincerity to rest a man.

V (165)

"Takk! Takk!" axes smack
Birds sing "ying, ying"
From dank vale copse
to high tree tops
they fly and cry:
         a mate, mate, mate!

Shall we not seek cognate?
Spirits attend
him who seeketh a friend.
Air, hear our cry
concording harmony.

"Ugh! Ugh!" grunt woodmen all,
let the tree fall.
Wine strained, lamb fat, I call all
my dad's clan, if any come not, not
my fault, they were invited, all hereabout.
I've swept my court and washed it out,
for this meal:
eight courses and fatted veal.
None of my mother's folk have been slighted,
If they don't come they were, in any case, invited.

Hack tree on hill,
here's wine to fill
a whole line of cups and bowls;
When souls rot good food is wasted,
Sound wine 's here and to be tasted,
When it's gone we'll buy more.
Bang the pint-pot, foot dance, and dine,
use our leisure in circumstance!
Wine, wine, wine, WINE,
Wine after, and wine before.

VI   (166)
The nobles reply to one of the preceding "Deer Odes"

Heaven conserve thy course in quietness,
Solid thy unity, thy weal endless
that all the crops increase and nothing lack
in any common house.

Heaven susteyne thy course in quietness
that thou be just in all, and reap
so, as it were at ease, that every day
seem festival.

Heaven susteyne thy course in quietness
To abound and rise as mountain hill and range
constant as rivers flow that all augment
steady th' increase in ever cyclic change.

Pure be the victuals of thy sacrifice
throughout the year as autumns move to springs,
above the fane to hear "ten thousand years"
spoke by the manes of foregone dukes and kings.

Spirits of air assign felicity:
thy folk be honest, in food and drink delight;
dark-haired the hundred tribes concord
in act born of thy true insight.

As moon constant in phase; as sun to rise;
as the south-hills nor crumble nor decline;
as pine and cypress evergreen the year
be thy continuing line.

VII   (167)

Pick a fern, pick a fern, ferns are high,
"Home," I'll say: home, the year's gone by,
no house, no roof, these huns on the hoof.
Work, work, work, that's how it runs,
We are here because of these huns.

Pick a fern, pick a fern, soft as they come,
I'll say "Home."
Hungry all of us, thirsty here,
no home news for nearly a year.

Pick a fern, pick a fern, if they scratch,
I'll say "Home," what's the catch?
I'll say "Go home," now October's come.
King wants us to give it all,
no rest, spring, summer, winter, fall,
Sorrow to us, sorrow to you.
We won't get out of here till we're through.

When it's cherry-time with you,
we'll see the captain's car go thru,
four big horses to pull that load.
That's what comes along our road,
What do you call three fights a month,
and won 'em all?

Four car-horses strong and tall
and the boss who can drive 'em all
as we slog along beside his car,
ivory bow-tips and shagreen case
to say nothing of what we face
sloggin' along in the Hien-yün war.

Willows were green when we set out,
it's blowin' an' snowin' as we go
down this road, muddy and slow,
hungry and thirsty and blue as doubt
(no one feels half of what we know).

VIII (168)

We took out our carts to the fields beyond the wall.
Emperor's call. Told the teamsters to load.
The king's road is a hard road, a thorny road.

We took out our cars to the village beyond the walls,
our flags with the double snake and the ox-tails,
falcon and turtle flags flappin' about,
but the grooms are worn out.

Majesty ordered Nan Chung build the Fang wall;
we took out our cars lickety-clickety at the call,
plenty of flags with dragons and snakes—
Nan Chung give the Hien-yün the shakes
when he squared up the North Wall.

When we went out the grain was growin'
that 's on the mind now its drizzlin' and snowin',
sloggin' along in snow and mud,
king's work tough, however you look,
"Home?" we're afraid they'd chuck us the book.

Grasshoppers jumpin' chirruppy-churrp
"Not seen our men. Wish they'd come!"
That's what the women are sayin' at home.
Nan Chung 's a terror against the Jung.

Spring days gettin' long,
Now be the orioles in song,
Leaf-pickin' nearly done,
We pluckin' captives to learn what they know;
Goin' home, and the goin' is slow
But Nan Chung 's rolled out the rovin' hun.

IX (169)

There's fine fruit on
the lone pear-tree
and no rest for the king's armee.
One day, then another day,
Sun and moon wearin' away,
October now, let a torn heart grieve,
Will they ever get their winter leave?

Lonely pear-tree full of leaves,
Government work, no reprieves,
Heart can break here in the shade,
Will they ever come back from that raid?

I climb the hill north of the town
to get in twigs of *k'i* willows
as the government work goes on.
Hard on the old folks;
"Broken car?"
"Horses foundered?"
"They can't be far."

They haven't even loaded yet,
Can't be coming; never get set.
He hasn't started, he'll never come.
My heart sadder than I can tell
I tried my luck by straws and shell,
They both said he was nearing home.

X

SOUTH TERRACE, no text
One of the six "lost odes."

Book 2: The White Flower Decad

Title poem and four others lost, there being some discussion
as to whether texts once existed, or whether the titles refer to
the music only.

The "lost odes" have left their titles and numerals:

    I. The white flower (of a blameless life).

    II. The shu (panicled millet) flowers. A poem of the seasons.

    IV. The keng sprouts. That keng being a very interesting ideogram, seventh of the ten stems, a path or orbit, the evening star, and to change or restore. Production in kind, cyclic, each in its time.

    VI. The top of the pyramid, or mount veneration.

  VIII. The sprouting of equity, how men came to observe it.

Banquet and dance songs, some of them probably sung by troops of dancers, others by guests and host.

III   (170)

Fine fish to net,
ray, skate;
Milord's wine is
heavy and wet.

Fish to trap,
bream, tench,
Milord has wine
to drink and quench.

Fine fish to trap,
carp and mud-fish,
Milor' has' wine
in quantities'h.

Food in plenty
say good food
Plenty of food
all of it good,

This the song each guest agrees on:
Milor's good food all fits the season.

V (171)
(? ROUND IN CANON)

South lakes full of flickering fish,
Barbel make a pretty dish,
    jab down that top-net on 'em!
A gent by liquor gets good guests,
    blessings upon 'em!

Howk 'em up with a landing scoop,
He's got wine and a full troop,
    blessings upon 'em!

Sweet gourds climb on southern trees;
Right 'uns are the sort that please
    in gentleman's festivities.

Elegant doves,
good bottle-men,
Milord has wine,
Do come dine again.

VII (172)

South Mount's shrub, North Mount's grass,
all the joy that ever was
in any state or family
is founded on gentility,
    ten thousand years.

South Mount's berries, North Mount's willows
any state that gives light still owes
that lustre to its gentlemen
    ten
    thousand years.

South Mount's medlar, North Mount's plum,
a lord who keeps troth
is to his people both
    father and mother,
    fame without end.

South Mount's mangrove, North Mount's sloes
dark as nobles' aged brows,
age shall end not
joy of feasting
mid men of untarnished fame,

Vigour ever, South Mount's aspen
North Mount pine, wrinkled skin shall end not feasting,
loyal joy the hour outlasting
    gentlemen to proof in testing
    maintain and rule your after-line.

IX   (173)
THE SHINING DRAGON
(? of royal favour)

Thick southernwood
dew drenches,
the sight of Milord gives serenity,
on feasting benches
revelry;
lasting shall his praises be.

Thick southernwood
dew-soaked the night;
He's here all right
princely to sight;
tho' the dragon gleam
his eye stays straight
nor in old age
shall divagate
    (unswerving honesty
    not undermined in senility.)

Thick southernwood
dew-drenched the night;
he's here all right
dining fraternally.
When elder and younger brothers agree
age shall but strengthen their honesty.

Thick southernwood
dew-filled the night;
He's here all right.
To men of the gleaming rein
concord in every harness bell,
ten thousand lucks, and all's well.

X (174)

Dew, deep lying,
Till day no drying,
Calm night outstaying
Let no dry man away.

Dew deep in grass
as manes pass,
calm thru night all
in clan hall
                    feasting.

Dew on willow, dew on thorn;
as sun's head threadeth
each good knight treadeth,
of heart-sight, deed's born aright.

"Fellow-" and "trust-" tree fruit
nor think to do it;
true gentles so
do as they do.

(Gentle blood
breedeth rectitude.)

ALITER

Deep, deep the dew
that will not dry till day;
Drink deep the night,
let none go dry away.

Deep, deep the dew
in the abundant grass;
Beneath this roof
ancestral manes pass.
Out-drink the night.*

Book 3. Red Bows

Mainly songs of action, or dramatized dances recalling the
hunts and campaigns? The red ceremonial bow conferred
considerable authority on the recipient.

I   (175)

Unstrung red bow,
honour's token, honour'd guest,
from my heart's sincerity,
bang gong, bang drum
till the noon come,
     feast.

Red bow unstrung
for honoured guest
to carry away
by my heart's cordiality
bang gong, bang drum
at my right hand
     till the noon come.

Red bow unstrung,
case it, my guest.
By my heart's cordiality
bang gong, bang drum
till the noon come,
     toast.

* All of which ought to be got back into lyric form somehow.
 Grass receives dew, the courtiers an ethical or at least deportmental lead
from their prince. The rest as in the first version.

II (176)

As in mid-mount, sandal tree,
His delight is in equity.

By the stream's marge stands a tree,
to have but seen him is jollity.

As asters grow in hills and dells,
I have seen him, and got five hundred cowrie shells.

Willow boat bobs to wave's cup or crest,
Now I have seen him, my heart is at rest.

III (177)

When the sixth moon roosted, we got out the war-cars,
heavy equipment. Huns flamed raiding;
The king's command was: Peace in the kingdom.

Matched blacks in quadriga, trained and in order,
Ere that moon's end all was focus'd in our allotments,
So the king outed us to emperor's aid.

Great horses by fours, broad under fetlock
o'er-bore the hun dogs, doughty the duke's deed;
We stood to war's needs and order was in the kingdom.

Feckless huns town'd in Tsiao, seized Huo, lacking provisions,
scythed into Hao up to its border, unto King's north-bank.
Broidered our banners, bearing bird-signs,
bright white the pendants, ten ranks of war cars
van'd our advancing.

War-cars well-weighted; straight the stallions
trained to be trusty, struck at the Hien-yun;
drove to T'ai-Yüan; and Ki-fu
law'd all the states, in peace as in war time.

Ki-fu feasted then, much was afforded him.
From Hao homing our road ever long.
Wine to the worthy, minced carp and roast terrapin.
Chang Chung the filial is here.

                    IV   (178)

Ready to reap the millet stands,
where was unused land ere Fang Shu took command.
3000 cars went to his wars.

Fang Shu's black-dappled team of four
drew his red-screened car to the war,
shagreen quiver and hooked breast-plate,
his rein-ends of metal ornate.

New grain for our supplies,
where was waste, hamlets rise
since Fang Shu took command of what had been fallow land
with 3000 lacquered cars, dragon flag and snake banneret,
bells in bridles and bit-ends set,
red knee-shields flash
and, at his girdle, pale green gems clash.

Swift flying hawk in heaven's gate
droppeth to stance and state, Fang Shu
to command
3000 cars
by band, manned, trained;
wheeled under flag, turned,
and, as the sun draws, Fang Shu:
to the deep of the drum, to forward and then
drew back the men
scattered in raiding.

Ghing crawlers chirrp'd at a great state,
Fang Shu was old but met their weight
(Ghing horde counted his age, and lost
went down in holocaust).

Chiefs brought for question here,
then with sound as of breaking thunder
with snorting
with flashing
his cars plowed the huns under.
The Ghing and Mann tribes knew fear.

As by the sun's force, promised, Fang Shu
crashed thru.

v   (179)

By fours the great stallions, pair'd as to prize
Drew our assault cars toward the sun-rise.

But good light field cars with the bull horses, pull thru
to the grassland and parkage near Fu.

Chief-huntsmen sound the halloo
as over burnt grass
beaters pass, each to place, and shake
signal flags, yak-tail, turtle-and-snake,
to take
game in Ao.

Atta horse, atta horse,
teams move as in chess,
gilt shoes, red knee-caps,
a hunt in court dress.

Thumb-ring and wrist-shield, bows bent in the same
instant, one volley heaps up the game.

Four bays, no swerve of the outer pair,
none out of step under the yoke,
howe'er they gallop each volley
hits as with one, I say ONE, axe-stroke.

Whinney in order, as the flags sign, they run;
beaters contend not, nor goes all the game to one great
    kitchen.

Who hunts so without clamour is a king
to avail in the great focussing.

VI (180)

When the sun in his course
layed lance on the right mark of the dial
we bowed to the architype horse,
the senior, with rites of the season;
good hunting cars and good pullers
we went up the great dunes
to drive in the wild herds.

When the sun said it was cow day
we picked our ponies
and sought game in the plain,
antlered bucks, does. By the rivers of Shensi
                        was imperial hunting.

Game thick in that river land,
in covert or breaking it, grouped or turning
we charged right and left,
some herd 'em, some grapple
to make imperial banquet.

We bent our bows and aimed arrows,
let fly at young boars and big rhinos
so to serve guest and make meat for wine's wetting.
To every hunter and guest
at the evening meal shall come
the great horn
with wine of the best.

ALITER (and more briefly)

HILARE DIE, fifth in decade:
to the Ur-horse we prayed
with field-cars arrayed
bull horses tall chased the wild flocks
on high hill (malga) overall.

HILARE DIE, that of the seventh moon,
we picked our mounts to match game
(steeds swift as deer)
does and stags came thru
Ts'i and Tsii.
                          An Emperor's ado.

Mid plain crowded, to start up or wait,
bevy and pair. We darted out left and right
to our Lord's delight.

Bent our bows till arrows reached arm-pit
Then shot down
young boar and stot,
rhino as well, to feast all guests
with sweet wine
fit to the test.

VII   (181)

Wild geese with a "whish" of wing,
officers go to the waste.
            "Toil, you lone fish."

From wing, geese nest in marsh,
we scholars raise a wall,
5000 toise in all to each day's stint
where quiet homes shall rise
from our toiled agonies.

Wild geese cry harsh a-wing
(wise see the toil)
Fools call us proud
and say:
                    Too loud.

VIII   (182)

What hour is this? the court-yard flare burns bright,
we hear a chink of bit-bells thru the night.

We hear it faint: "chin-chink" across the night,
he comes not yet, the court-yard flare flicks bright.

What hour of dawn, the lanthorn wick smokes still
to greet his flag that crests yon eastward hill.

IX   (183)
CH'AO TSUNG*
Churning of water,
Homage to Thetis.

Churning waters pay court to Sea, in the East,
Swift-flying falcon cometh to rest
but who among you, brothers, countrymen, eldest or least
squarely faces this chaos,
                    having neither father nor mother?

Churning waters now overflowing all banks,
The hawk flies untamed and wild.
Bandits break ranks, there is no control,
They are not followed. Sorrow, not to assuage!

High hawk come to mid mount,
what the folk say is gone wrong
and no one opposes them. 'Ware friend, nor hold
their propaganda of no account.†

---

* The Tsung is the ancestral temple: pay court to, or come to the court.
† A mistranslation, but it may keep the student from coming to rest.

X (184)
ON DECLINING OFFICE

The cranes cry over the nine marshes
and their cry sounds over the waste,
Fish go dark through the deep
or lie at rest by the isles,

Delight is in a garden of sandal-woods
with withered leaves blown beneath them,
Let some other hill's rock serve you for whetstone.

The crane cries over the nine pools of the marshland
and its sound carries up toward the sky,
fishes lie by isles or go seaward;

There is delight in the closed garden of sandal-woods,
grain now in the alleys between them:
Let some other hill's rock grind your jade.

Book 4. Minister of War

I (185)

"Lord of the Light's axe,"* by what cause
should we, the king's teeth and claws
be cast into misery
'thout roof or stay?

Lord of the Light's axe, why should we officers
be cast into distress
that is
bottomless?

---

* The prayer ideogram composed of the two radicals: axe; and the light
descending. Last character in the song explained in commentary as meaning
that the old women would be worn out getting in kindling wood etc., work
properly done by the filial sons. Commentary cites tradition that the Palace
Guards were sent to the north frontier for defence after the disgraceful de-
feat of King Süan's regular forces there in 788 B.C.

Minister of War, aye slow in the ear,
how hast construed
that a mother's corpse
is soldier's food.

II (186)
SCALE ALTRUI

Garden sprouts for bright white colts,
tether and tie till mid-day,
nay, he's away
   to ramble.

Garden beans for these brilliant wee'uns,
tether and tie a welcome guest
   for a good night's rest.

He could be duke or a marquis rather
would he foregather
with peers in our capital
   but his delight
   is to be eremite.

In deep vale to chew a spare bale
of scant hay, that a king's jewel were,
could he but bear
high life on another's stair.

III (187)
HUANG NIAO

Yaller bird, let my corn alone,
Yaller bird, let my crawps alone,
These folks here won't let me eat,
I wanna go back whaar I can meet
the folks I used to know at home,
   I got a home an' I wanna' git goin'.

Yalla' bird, let my trees alone,
Let them berries stay whaar they'z growin',
These folks here ain't got no sense,

can't tell 'em nawthin' without offence,
Yalla' bird, lemme, le'mme go home.
I gotta home an' I wanna' git goin'.

Yalla' bird, you stay outa dem oaks,
Yalla' bird, let them crawps alone,
I just can't live with these here folks,
I gotta home and I want to git goin'
To whaar my dad's folks still is a-growin'.

IV (188)

I go the waste, weeds shade but to the knee;
Under thy roof alliance bade me come,
You do not feed me,
let me go home.

I walk the waste, these weeds my food;
I came invited, as I construed,
Let me go as I had come,
You do not feed me,
let me go home.

I walk the waste, with but rough weeds to taste;
off with the old kin, on with the new,
not for their riches,
yet change was due.

ALITER

I tread the waste, save bracken there's no shade,
I came your in-law
to an offered house, as you bade.

An ex-wife's no bond, you're wed anew,
to say she's rich, that were too much to say;
Just word: you see it now a different way.

V   (189)

By curvèd bank
in South Mount's innerest wood
clamped as the bamboo root, rugged as pine,
let no plots undermine
this brotherhood.

Heir'd to maintain the lines
carnal and uterine;
doors west and south,
reared up the mile-long house
wherein at rest to dwell,
converse and jest.

Tight bound the moulds wherein to ram down clay,
beaten the earth and lime gainst rain and rat,
no wind shall pierce to cold the Marquis' state
nor bird nest out of place,
here is he eaved,
who moves as on winged feet,
sleeves neat
as a pheasant's wing,
prompt as the arrow's point
to the bull's-eye.
And here the audience hall,

Rich court in peristyle
with columns high
their capitals contrived right cunningly;
cheery the main parts,
ample the recess
where he may have repose in quietness.

Mat over mat, bamboo on rush
so it be soft, to sleep, to wake in hush,
from dreams of bears and snakes?
                    Saith the diviner:

Which mean
Bears be for boys; snakes, girls.
Boys shall have beds, hold sceptres for their toys,
creep on red leather,
bellow when they would cry
in embroidered coats
ere come to Empery.

Small girls shall sleep on floor and play with tiles,
wear simple clothes and do not act amiss,
cook, brew and seemly speak,
conducing so the family's quietness.

VI   (190)

No sheep! Who says: No sheep?
300 to every flock.
Who says: No kine?
By nineties, of temple stock,
kink-horned the sheep, silk-ear'd the kine.

Some down to river-brink,
some drink pool'd streams;
to lie, to low.
Your hinds have thick leaf coats,
wide hats (bamboo), a-back their food-supplies.
Your beasts, by thirties, are ready for sacrifice.

Your herders rustle fagots, hens and cocks,
hemp-twigs to kindle fires; your flocks
'thout murrain, neck and neck,
sound mutton, solid,
rush to the pent-hold at the shepherd's beck,
such was their care.

The neat-herd dreams of fish, portending men;
of flags a-wind, turtle in toise, embannered falconry.
Many the fish?
Full shall the bushel be;
new homesteads rise
                              after such augury.

VII   (191)

Abacus against high cloud, crag over crag, Mount South
to echo with cry on cry;
O'er-towering Yin, thou proud
as people cower, burning with inner heat
daring no open jest, so soon an end,
the hour all-seen, save in thy mind.

Grade over grade, Mount South,
so thick thy gnarl of wood,
Lord Yin, thou proud,
unjust in tyranny, the corners of heaven reek death,
no man to praise thy chaos in disease,
you cast no fault aside.

Yin, viceroy
"foundation stone" of Chou
to judge and bind state's weal
as on a potter's wheel
the Emperor's "Next" defined
by title but not by fact,
Unmuddle the mass,
Make it possible for folk to be honest.
Fell glare of sky, pitiless
caving our troops to but a hollow shell,
this is unright.

Without presence, without affection:
among the people no faith, no word-keeping.
No enquiry, no appointments (no delegation of power).
With proper levels, proper dismissals
there would be no ambiguous minor officials,
nor your picayune in-laws in fat government jobs.

Heaven in dither
wrangles rain hither.
Glare sun's unkindness
sendeth great (moral) blindness.

When gentles attain,
people regain
quiet; be gentles just,
hates must
go out.

Dire sun over sky, no polar force;
no parts hold to calm course;*
'tis as if moon's fiat
wrought folk's unquiet.
Heart stupefied
drunk with grief, who 's to guide
the state straight, who hold plow-handle.†
If king rule
not himself, to all clans 'tis dule,
Four steeds take yoke
stretch necks to the four coigns and see
in every coign, misery.

Prodded of hate
lancing today who is
next day's cup-mate.

O Heaven un-level, this king unstill,
mending never a fault, hateth all ordered will.

Kia-Fu has raised this verse
to probe the King's evil mood;
let him work his heart to this form
and a thousand towns can have food.

VIII (192)
TRAHISON DES CLERCS;
against the perversion of language

Frost's nimble silk
beneath a summer moon
cuts heart, men's talk the more.

---

* New crops of woe each month.
† Quis clavum afferat?

Double-talk on the up,
I am alone,
My heart, ai! ai!
gnawed to the bone.

2

Begat me, you twain, to pain
in the mid cult of mouth-talk,
nor before, nor yet shall be
that grief, the more it's real,
draws more insult.

3

In doleful dumps, having no salary,
vacant in thought, this thought comes over me:
other non-criminals may soon be vexed
—hack-driving—to find paid jobs,
nor know where crow lights next.

4

Mid-wood now scrub and bare deforested,
mere fagot-twigs where once the tall trees stood;
the heaven 's in nightmare, yet it once was able
to run smooth course, to all men merciable,
none to withstand it. And it hates what man?

5

Call mountain mole-hill, the high crest says: you lie.
Double-talk runs, not even in jeopardy.
Call the diviners, and their vapid blocks
emit: We're wise, who knows crow-hens from -cocks?

6

"The heaven 's lid high," not dare to stand up straight;
"The earth's crust thick," not dare to not tread light;
and mark these words that have both order and spine,
while you chameleons turn more serpentine:

7

Thick wheat mid rocks upon the terraced hill,
The sky-shake knocks, as tho' it could not fix me,
seeking my style, and yet cannot annex me,
hating at length
yet using not my strength.

8

Sorrow at heart, as tho' by cords constricted;
grind of his reign whereby are all afflicted
to quench that lamp whereby wide earth was lit,
Proud hall of Chou.
                    Pao Sy 'll abolish it.

9

Thought's tread at end beneath the cold of rain,
knock off the cart-props till the load fall out,
and then cry: Lord, is there no help about?

10

not slip the cart poles, that be true spokes-men?
Keep eye on driver in perils, and you won't overturn
but reach hard track's end.
                    That's not your concern.

11

A shallow basin gives the fish no shade,
dive as they will, there's flash of fin's knife-blade;
Sorrow in heart for any shred or flaw
to see the state, and all, neath tiger's claw.

12

Good wine, good victuals;
neighbours, come to dine,
praise from feeding kin.
I've but my skin
alone, to keep grief in.

13

The low have houses and the mean get tips,
Folk with no salary
the heavens swat,
While ploots can manage
and the "outs" cannot.

IX (193)

Of Queen Pao Sy, Huang's town planning at Hiang,
and the Solar Eclipse of 29 August 776 B.C.

The sun was eaten
when the green moon-sprout
saw August out,
Sin-Mao, the day
(sky's acrid 8, earth's 4)
Ugly, and how.
Moon gnawed out, sun under yoke,
Pity the folk
          beneath.

2

Sun, moon, foretell
evil? run wild,
State without rule,
good men exiled.
Moon's gnawed out in normal course,
What imprecise force
swallows the sun?

3

Flame-flower flasheth
with dire lashing
of cloud's tail in all-quake;
no covered quiet,
no sky's seal.
The 100 rivers o'erflow,
mountains are fallen,

high crests become valleys,
vale reared into summit,
and as for man now:
none changeth a fault.

4

Not Huang-fu the Premier,
nor Fan at the Cultura Popolare,
nor Kia-Po of the Interior,
nor Chung-yün of Logistics,
nor Tsou the recorder,
nor Kuei at the War Office,
nor Kü of the Heavies;
But she?
flames away, dwelling in splendour.

5

Will Huang-fu say:
Not the moment?
Does he stir us without representation;
to shift our roofs and our house-walls?
Plow-land to bent and waste moor,
mid which vexations he says:
"I am not tyrannous,
These are the regulations."

6

Our prudent Huang has had a building scheme
and three contracting lords are now enriched,
There's no police chief left for royal guard,
the hunting set has been, all, led Huang-ward.
(To Huang's new town, that is.)

7

I dare not post a monthly works report,
knowing the mare's-nest it would raise in court.
It is not heaven has sent these torments down,
this devil's brew boils from the talk of town.*

* Gush of conversation, back biting and interoffice contentions come UP
out of men.

8

Far, far my village
in cark of care,
there 's a state surplus, I alone
worry, everyone else resigns.
Sole not to rest, impenetrable
word of the sky
that says not why I presume
not to copy these friends of mine:
Resign!
          Damn'd if I will, I were as ego'd as they.

                 X   (194)

Light, light aloft   slow in thy deed,
crystal thy flow   deadly our need,
swifter to earth   death, famine, dearth;
lopped off the state. Autumnal sky
awful thy might,   feckless, unplanned:
One eddying punishment
sinks guilty and innocent.

                      2

Chou's breed washed out,   nowt to hitch to,
The big shots quit,   there's none to know
if I do my bit; how I sweat.
The three top men cut short their office hours,
fief courts don't sit to hour or date,
All talk duty   and turn to hate.

                      3

Light over sky   if princes lie
what hath man to steer thereby?
An hundred lords respect themselves? Not even!
By that the less revere each other, or heaven.

                      4

From war learned nothing, nor from famine either,
two plagues to warn him and he learned from neither.
Will you hear truth from a poor worn-out groom

when coward princelings fear to use the broom,
nor dare speak truth when asked for their advice,
but at the least whisper vanish in a trice?

5

Ill 's beyond speech. Speak truth and suffer for it,
Fat jobs to those who, with flow of words, ignore it.

6

Accept an office? That is thorns and death,
that to refuse will be lèse-Emperor;
to take? a peril that even your friends incur.

7

And if I say to you: come back to court.
"No town house, I've no house," is your retort.
For tears and blood, and every word incur
hate. When you went out
Who followed as carpenter.

Book 5. Lesser Compleynts

1 (195)
"PLANNERS" RAW DEAL
770 B.C. approx.

Heaven's worry, scurries to earth;
twisty planning, what's to block it?
At sight of good plan, they turn to rotten again,
the sight of their planning
gives me a pain.

2

First say yes, then say no;*
good plan, no go,

* Aliter:
    Dirty water and slanders run
    together in yes-men and drain pits.

but a rotten they dress in flummery,
the sight of their planning worries me.

                    3
Tired turtles, clean petered out
decline to bother with human doubt
(poked hot sticks into tortoise shells*
which answer us no oracles)
planners and planners pullulate
concluding nothing (not even debate).
Worders are it
in the king's abode,
no one dares put his name on a chit;
all maps and no marching
                    covers no road.

                    4
Our active designers
don't like old ways—
irked by the solid symmetrical—
but let 'em hear the sound of a phrase,
they'll quarrel over it days and days
as builders who change for the last thing told 'em
never get a house to hold 'em.

                    5
State
all a wobble,
scanners and boobs—
a few left to gobble—
bright boys and planners,
some who'll "take trouble"
all of a bubble
down into quick-sand.

                    6
No tool 'gainst tiger,
no boat for river,
That much, no more,

* Answer given by the way the shell splits from the heat.

and they know it;
but above all to be precise
at the gulf's edge
or on thin ice.

II   (196)
GNOMIC VERSES

Ring-dove, my gentle, to sing and fly
Wingèd to circle, up and away
I think of antiquity, men of old gone,
And of those two, at wake of day.

2

The wise drink and hold their wine, but topers say
that to be drunk is to be rich for a day.
Yield men, all men, this advice:
Heaven speaks once and never twice.

3

Beans mid plain, plain folk pluck 'em,
Bug had a boy but the mud-wasp took him;
Better be careful to train your sons
to be clean, as your pattern runs.

4

Collaboration will never fail
between the two ends of the bright wag-tail,
first to sing and then to fly
as the days and the moons pass by
a slug-a-bed shames his family.

5

Orioles flicker across the sky
and then pick grain from the threshing floor,
We get jailed if we pick up more;
good and evil run nip and tuck
so I'll scatter this grain to try my luck.*
(responsus est?)

* Some form of divination answered by noting how the birds pick up the
scattered grain, or rice.

6

Man ought to sit quiet as bird on bough,
cagey as edging a precipice,
light-foot as treading on thin ice.

III   (197)

Capped crows flap in flock
home. I am alone to weather shock;
For what evil done to the sky
hath my heart misery?

2

Chou road that level was,
now hidden under wild grass,
heart-ache, unsleeping a-bed,
old before time, grieved body and head.

3

Mulberries and catalpas of farm-stead be to revere,
Father and mother more dear;
am I not carnal and uterine?
What birth-hour ill-chosen as mine?

4

Thick are the willows, the broad locust thin of voice,
cool are the reeds about the dark-deep pool,
I, like a boat a-drift, come to no rest;
sleep not for worry burrowing in my breast.

5

So easy a-foot in wild-wood the stags run,
Pheasant aloft seeks mate as moon fades from the sun,
I, like a sickened tree losing its boughs,
with ache at heart now dark as no man knows.

6

Men shelter the hunted hare,
bury the corpse by wayside,
but the prince (my father) has gripped his heart.
Tears, tears, never dried!

7

As if sworn on the wine cup
he gives credence to lies he has not examined,
compassionless. But men fell trees by their lean,
where they be thick; split fagots by grain.
He shelters the guilty,
Mine is the pain.

8

Naught stands higher than mount,
nor is hollow deeper than water-fount;
that the Prince have not light nor dark in his words—
ears be in echoing wall,
Let him keep from my weir and fish-trap who hath
neither examined my case
nor the aftermath.

IV   (198)

Ascribed to the time of King Li, circa 770 B.C.

Sky, my father, I have not sinned,
I am confused,
Terrible mother aloft,
I have not sinned,
Glare light,
                it is not my guilt.

2

Chaos in sperm
usurped submergedly
soaking in, secretly;
burst to twice life when Milord
believed calumny.
Would he show preference,
Joy, rage,
crooks would hence; it would all stop,
and speedily.

3

Multiple treaties drag confusion out,
belief in thieves adds violence to doubt,
Bandits' sweet talk but more enflames the blaze,
mid which incoherence
'twill be the King who pays.

4

A superior man
raised the great bric-a-brac,
the temple's apse and fore;
great plan needeth great architect.
I can but track
plain man, plain crook, hot-foot in plain affair
as hounds run a sly hare,
my similar.

5

Gentlemen, as I've heard tell
plant trees that are workable;*
many minds among wayfarers, mind 'ee,
on the high road North and South
twisty tall talk comes from the mouth
and words soft as the shamisan
distinguish the thick-faced man.

6

Which kind teeters here on the stream's brink,
no fist, no force, making mess
in already muddled offices?
Swollen legs give 'em acumen?
Planning lots of things they'll do when,
they get what they haven't, namely: men.

---

* "Il n'y a rien de plus désagréable que l'acajou."—French cabinet-maker
in 1924.

V (199)

What sort of chap—
twisty mind— 's come
to my dam, not to my door?
What now and how?
Ganged up with Pao.

2

There were two in this devilment,
to pass in silence evil meant and
There was a different tale to tell
before you found me "impossible."

3

What can he be, on my garden path
unseen, but heard talking as they went by,
no shame before men, no awe of sky.

4

Neither North nor South, can't blow straight,
but as whirl-wind
come to my dam to disturb my mind.

5

Travelling easy, that's the rub
and no time to come in. Hurried you'd stop to grease hub
and wheel, and you haven't called once
to see how I feel.

6

Would be pleased to see you and du'nno why
you take this notion of passin' me by,
never once in to ease the eye.

7

Old duets with flute and pipe,
we used to play 'em stripe by stripe;
Believe you don't know me? Dog, pig and cock
mark my oath on the chopping-block.

8

If you were a devil or water-sprite
one couldn't see you by daylight,
but looking you eye to eye
one can see all that there is to see
and get, in out and out prosody,
eh? a near-total silhouette.

VI   (200)

Such elegant streaky lines in brocade
till the solid shell is made;
liars by littles ply their trade.

2

Stitch a-sky, dot, the South Sieve's made.
Who loves to aid
these smearers in the smearing trade?

3

Winging,
gad about,
tittling, tattling
to be found out.

4

The quickness of the hand deceives the eye
and repetition suaves mendacity,
Non obstat, you'll be ousted bye and bye.

5

Proud men ride high to watch the workers sweat,
O'er-hanging heaven look down upon their pride
and pity those on whom the yoke is set.

6

Take therefore, I say, these smearers
and fellow travellers, chuck 'em
to wolves and tigers, and if the striped cats spew 'em forth,

offer 'em to the Furthest North.
If the old pole decline to spare 'em place,
kick 'em clean off it into stellar space.

7

And here's my address, I am still
at Willow Hollow Road by Acre Hill,
Meng Tsy has lost his balls but makes this verse,
let the administration heed it, or hear worse.

VII   (201)
EAST WIND

Soft wind of the vale
that brings the turning rain,
                peril, foreboding;
Come time of quiet and revelry
you'll cast me from your company.

2

Idle the valley wind, hot tempest then,
far in your pleasure, near in your pain.
Came time of quiet revelry
You cast me from your company.

3

Scorching breath on the height, grief,
all grass must die, no tree but loseth leaf
Soft is the valley wind, harsh on the crest,
You remember the worst of me
Forgetting the best.

VIII   (202)
THE ORPHAN

Waving ling? not ling but weed,
You two begat me, by labour to need.

Weed or plant that gives no grain,
you two begat me in toil and pain.

Shamed the jug that fills no cup;
orphan's life, proverb saith,
is worth less than early death.
Who sustaineth the fatherless?
Who stayeth the motherless?
Carry gagged grief beyond the court-yard wall,
In my house there is no one at all.

You who begat me, you who bore,
suckled and fed me long from your store,
embraced me at parting and when I came in,
by my candour I would have made return,
my luck runs ill, having no end nor bourne.

Harsh over South Mount
the whirl-winds moan,
all men have grain, I suffer alone.

Plod, plod, South Mount,
wind blows unceasingly,
I am the only grainless man
who does not die.

IX (203)

Of the old barbecues and a new plutocracy, adorned but
useless as the constellations. Ascribed to time of King Liu.

Heaped grain-platters, long thorn-wood spoon,
Chou road smooth as a whetstone
arrow-shaft-straight,
Gentles walking it, small folk, sedate, observe.
Looking back on this, it appears
in the mind. Define it? Save by my tears?

2

In small states of the East, and in great
no loom clicketh.
Shuttles are still, rollers turn not, the frost pricketh
thru the thin fibre of espadrilles.

Spindly duke's sons on Chou road now,
What hath been here, to and fro,
   to outlast it?
   The mind's sorrow.

3

Let not the flow of this chill melancholy
rot the cut wood;
tax on tax, tally on tally,
I wake and sigh for our poor folk,
small cut wood to pile and carry,
when can they rest from cart and yoke?

4

Down east the boys can't draw their service pay,
while western youth's a luxury display,
Where boatmen's sons are sporting bear-skin coats
the farm-boy bureaucrat tries, fails, and gloats.

5–6

Some will for wine who won't for broth
and wear great belt-gems, whose worth 's but froth.
A river of stars is lit across the heaven,
Trine Damsels* weave to the seventh house at even
with seven ply
for us nor cloth nor sign.
That eye-full of led oxen in the sky
draws not our farm carts here terrestrially.
Dawn's in the East, in West, Hyads nestle at ease.
East Venus, West Hesperus
to open and date the day,
Sky hath a rabbit-net that takes
    naught save its way.

7

South hath a Sieve that sifts us out no grain,
The northern Ladle dips us up no wine.

---

* Vega and the other two stars of the triangle.

As the unsieving sieve might give tongue to attest
The handle of the Ladle is in the west.

X   (204)

June 's mid-summer, August brings coolth again;
The ancestral spirits are harsh, were they not men?

2

Autumn sees the plants wither,
wild beauties decline together;
all things cold now as pain,
I turn to go home again.

3

Winter day sparkles with snow, turning winds moan,
Others have luck, all of them. I am alone.

4

There be fine growths a-mountain,
Lord of the Chestnut, Marquis Plum
by ruin of roof-tree come
to banditry, and none to guess
their curdle of bitterness.

5

Spring water floweth, both to clear and in mud,
my days are but built up calamity; how call this good?

6

Floods of the Kiang and Han,
churning, South States record.
Worn out with service
I get no reward.

7

The quail and kite take air,
sturgeon hath lair
in deep waters evading.

8

Bracken hath crest,
Willow its rest in marsh
taking no wrong,

           my rest:
           a song.

Book 6. North Mount

1   (205)

Officer and gentleman
sent to pluck medlars   on Mount Po Shan
all day, all day never to swerve
from the king's work, and my parents to serve
in grief.

2

Under the scattered sky all lands are fief,
all men to the sea's marge serve but one chief
and there is no justice known to the great,
I go alone   but straight.

3

Four stallions, bang, bang, hither and yon,
isn't it fine that I'm "not old"
and so few ready to do what I'm told
and my back still strong and straight
enough   for a border state.

4

That some men loll in banquet bout
and others work till clean worn out;
Some for the state in bed to lie,
others on road incessantly.

5

Some root mid ladies in luxury,
all in the king's cause naturally
and never hear a harsh command,
the rest of us sweating distractedly
in heavy harness incessantly
(from head to tail)
with both a pack and the martingale.

6

Some wine deep in rich luxury,
others be torn by anxiety;
fear blame, driven in, driven out
as the winds jerk,
year long, year long, nothing but work.

II   (206)

Let the Great Cart alone,
'ware dust.
Think not on sorrows
lest thy heart rust.

Push no great cart
lest dust enflame thine eye,
brood not on sorrows
lest joy pass by.

Push not the great wheel-spoke in moil and sweat
lest thou make thy troubles
                              heavier yet.

III   (207)

Light upon light that shines above the sky,
naught here on earth evades thy glittering eye;
We, who invade the West and pass
the steppe of K'iu over wild grass,
set out beneath a February moon
going thru cold and heat.

Now bitter poison rankles in the mind
thinking of courts and ease
we weep and would go home—
fearing the penalties.

2

Long, long ago we set out
thinking the sun and moon veering about
would see us home at the year's turn,
heavy in mood to brood that I alone
work for that crowd—
no furlough allowed,
longing for home,
fearing the price.

3

Sun and moon in their ingle
when we set out, now we'd about
in longing for home, work here piled on
more miserable
now's the year's end, to get harvest in,
of that harvest I pick not a bean
nor get southernwood;
think of their ease in offices
and go as far as the first night's inn,
lose nerve:
                "be sent back again."

4

Haro! ye gentles, think 'ee that ease endures
and that no quake shall shake your sinecures?
Best take an honest colleague now and then
to attract the favouring spirits of the air
and keep the official process in repair.

5

Ergo, milordlings, loaf not too much
but look upon your jobs as really such,
Show sometimes liking for clean government
that the airy powers concede your preferment.

IV (208)

Cl-ang, cl-ang go the bells,
turgid the Huai, clashing of waters
till sorrow has torn the mind
and the lords of old time go not out of heart.

2

Gong over gong, cold waters driven
till the heart is riven for the clear deeds
of the lords of old
     flawless.

3

Bells, drums, over the three isles of Huai
till the heart is moved that we see not their like
    who were here before us.

4

"Ch-in, ch-in" of the bells,
two lutes, organ and stone
in even tone,
so shall the "Elegantiae,"
so shall the "South" be sung,
    nor flutes shall mar.

V (209)

They have cleared the thorn from this place
how, here, in the old days? Here was grain sown in the old days
abundant, here was grain
for the rites, for the barns,
for distilling
that we offer up with corn and wine to the spirits
that they aid us aye and the more.

2

Here move we quiet in order
here be led cattle spotless and rams
for the rites of winter and autumn,
flayers, boilers and carvers

and they who lay out and make ready
to invoke the spirit of banners,
to invoke the spirit of light,
to the spirits outspaced like banners,
to the glory of brightness,
to the source of the dynasty
here in his cartouche
white-shining, our sovran.
May the spirits aid in the banquet,
may the filial line never fail,
all this in the aim of plenty
10,000 years and with no bound.

3

That they be alert at the pyres and ovens of barbecue
slow moving near the tall stands
for the baked meats and the grilled meats,
that they care for small trays,
no flaw, tho' they be many;
that the guests take the communion cup in due turn
each back to each, thus reciprocal
a rite for the observance of equity
that there be ease and good confidence
the word spoken smiling;
that the sustainers, spirits, also come in due order
that the end be abundance,
good vintage, 10,000 years.

4

We have gone thru with the fire rite
and no fault, the flamen has made the announcement,
he conveys this to the heir
          at the second stance by the altar,
the fumes of the filial incense are perfume,
the souls in the air lust after your drink and victuals,
your luck is an hundred fold.
As is the hidden so is the pattern,
as the service was orderly
there shall be early harvest.
There has been order,

there has been promptness
(we have beaten the ground for the grain spirit.)
You have brought basket-offering and in order
there shall be yield to the maximum
          thru time without end.

                              5
The service of the equities has been carried out in detail
gong and drum have alerted,
the heir sits to receive the augur's announcement
the airy spirits (the spirits who go upward)
have all drunk and stand upright (cease drinking)
The representative of the White Splendour (the halo'd)
has risen
drum and gong sound: (nunc dimittis)
the spirits, sustainers, have instantly ascended back to their
          dwelling.
All the servants and noble dames
clear away with celerity,
the men of the patronymic
repair to their private feast.*

                              6
Enter musicians playing adagio
quieting music for favours to follow.
Your victuals are served,
no one grumbles, all is congratulation (or jollity),
they have drunk and eaten their fill,
the airy souls lust for your drink and victuals,
may they give you years and old age,
very benevolent, very timely
and in totality, sons' sons and grandsons
that they go not out of lordship in leading.

                    VI   (210)
           YÜ'S CONTOUR FARMING, BONIFICA

      Aye by South Mount Yü began
      tilling for man

  * Karlgren admirably, "lay feast"; purely human, not haunted.

CLASSIC ANTHOLOGY

by dyke and drain
squared plain land and low.
His sons' sons' sons', have it so now
bound and townland south and east.

2

The heaven above stands as one arch of cloud,
falls snow, fine sleet
plus drizzle and soak
riching, by mulch, full favour the grain
of all our folk.

3

Field by field as feather by feather
with ditch and dykes
sleek millet spikes (shu and tsi)
high harvested
give the heir wine and bread,
aye, to ten thousand years
to honour the manes of his ancestors,
          they as guests to his offering,
          he in ripe age.

4

Huts in mid field and melons by the banks,
candy their pulp also for offering
to his line's source, our thanks
and this shall bring sky's grace in age.

5

Clear wine in sacrifice to heaven's light
an healthy bull, red, to the great tablet's lord
with tinkle of bells at the knife's hilt
parting the hair, fat and blood spilt.

6

An holy reek to rich the temple air
in honour of Brightness
and to ten thousand years, invoke

our halo'd sires: exchange
luck for this smoke,
unbroke by time.

VII   (211)

Fair fields outspread yield an hundred
measures for one.
High grain a-field, hundred-fold yield.
Old crop meets new. Our farmers here
be fed all the year,
aye, from of old, such yield hath been.
So shall we go to south lots now
to weed and hoe
millet enow (shu and tsi) shall abundant be
to aid and set homestead
for the best cadets we've bred.

2

By the brightness of the altar vessels arranged;
by the pureness of the victim ram;
by the power of Earth and the square
bean fields generous, and tillers prosperous
to strum lute, archilute; beat drum;
come processional* to meet the Lord of the Field,
so pray we rain be sweet
that millets twain (tsi and shu)
grain our yeomen
and women.

3

Antient of line, here now's the Heir.
Wives, weeuns, bear
lunch baskets out.
The inspector 's about
south fields now to see what's good
and dips his hand
in everyone's food,
left, right, he says, to taste

* ?Corpus Domini: "La procession va à travers les champs."

what is dainty and what waste.
Grain even high o'er all we scan.
Calm lord maketh a ready man.

4

Heir mid his crop,
Grain flows over the reapers' scythes
as water over dam's top, or as thatch
to stack like humpy islands in the field.
A thousand barnes be filled,
10,000 carts,
millet, rice, maize, reapers have taken
be thus 10,000 years' prosperity,
and unshaken.

VIII   (212)

Great plowlands need
many chores, seed,
tools and forecare.
Grind share and go
start with the plow on south slopes now.
Let the grain grow
then pile it high in courtyard where
As grandsire was, is now heir.

2

Come sprout, come ear,
hard grain and good
let every weed and tare,
gnaw-bug and worm,
caterpillar, slug
fall dead in flame,
honour to T'ien Tsu,
in fact and name,
                    God of the field.

3

Thickens the cloudy sky
that rain like a slanting axe

feed our Duke's field
then bless our yield,
We reap not miserly,
old women and poor follow our spoor.
To their relief
leave loosened sheaf,
short stock and unripe ear.

4

Now's come Greatgrandsire's heir,
women and youngsters bring
lunches to the men labouring
on the south slope, the overseer
does reverence to the four Corners of Air;
pours back the wine to earth (that gave the wine)
red bullock and black
pay for the millet crop;
by offer and sacrifice
funnel us further felicities.

IX   (213)

OLE MAN RIVER
keeps flowing in mid-channel

Waters of Lo swirling and bound,
our prince has found true measure
(that is, the norm, his rest,
plenty with regularity,
as reed or thatch)
As red leather covers the knee
so stand six army corps
neat in their panoply.

2

Glinting Lo with never a drought,
as sword fills the jewelled scabbard's mouth,
so is he fit to last ten thousand years
and pillar up his house.

3

Waters of Lo, never a break in your flow
or his equity; that he bring
10,000 years
to all his clans prosperity.

X   (214)

The year puts on her shining robe
of flowers and leaves in broidery
amid the flower of viscounts court-dressed
I can give praise to quietness.

The year puts on his shining robe
that is rue's yellowest pageantry
The flower of viscounts in orderliness
be as chapter and verse of happiness.

The year puts on her shining robe
of yellow flowers and flowers white,
so comes each lord holding six smooth reins;
his four white horses have jet black manes.

Left goes left where it should be,
right goes to right accordingly,
I therefore praise these gentlemen
who know and show both the how and when.*

---

* A prince welcomes or replies to the feudatories who may have spoken
the foregoing in fact or in pantomime.

Book 7. Sang Hu

The Haw Finch, or bird rather like an oriole that arrives
when the mulberry comes into leaf.

I   (215)
"Bright clothes hide not true virtue."
A king greets his princes

Criss-cross on flaming wing
may these orioles get full blessing;
and gentles who sing.

Criss-cross gleaming throat,
by orioles I mean
gentlemen who are
the whole state's screen,

A flying buttress, wings of the laws,
model to show how things be done;
to them happiness rightly won,

neither in rashness,
neither fearful of hardness,
neither boastful in the day of good fortune.

To them sound wine and gentle thought
when the great ivory horn is brought
each unto each in proper turn to all,
this luck, long, long to abide—
into pit of pride
ne'er may we fall.

II   (216)
The Nobles reply to the foregoing
"Kün tsy wan nien"
That the gentleman last 10,000 years

Big duck fly yellow over hand nets and wide nets spread even
"Kün tsy wan nien"
May his happiness flow in harmony with earth and with
heaven.

2

Big duck stand on the dam, and stretch left wings* in amity
                  "Kün tsy wan nien"
May we have, in leisure, felicity.

3

Teams in his stable, stall feed and war grain
                  "Kün tsy wan nien"
May his wealth be doubled again.

4

Steeds in his stable, war grain and stall feed
                  "Kün tsy wan nien"
That he have, ever, abundance over his need.

III   (217)

        Leather caps, sound wine, good food,
        where all be kin,
        Here is no outer man,
        all be of our father's clan
        as mistletoe to cypress tree
        to their chief in fealty—
        worried without him, glad he's here.

        Caps of leather, sound wine, good food in season,
        Where else? how else? for what reason
        could such a company foregather?
        As mistletoe to pine
        close knit to clan and line,
        no stranger here has part,
        and from thy face
        the movements of my heart.

        Leather on head, food good, wine sound,
        gathered round, so many a-kin;
        melting flakes fall ere hard snow sets in,
        sorrow and death attend no man's desire.

---

* Left wings: Legge says ducks head to tail. Similar defence manoeuvre of
bulls in ring, able to watch approach of attack from either direction.

Slake well thy thirst before the even come
while ye have brothers' eyes to see
and ere ye tire.
Princely is leisure,
no man drinks here for hire.

IV (218)

Hot axle, I drove, drove
to my love
        hasting,
neither food nor drink
        tasting.
I thought of her inwit,
No friends with me
        feasting.
Pheasant finds home
in flat forest,
My heart a nest
in her thought
        resting.

In with the lynch-pin, thought to a lady,
the youngest, the charmer, and go,
not by thirst, not for hunger,
the clear tone of her mind attests:
perfect feast needs no great guests.

2

In level forest pheasant makes nest
a level head to lesson me
how a model feast is laid
that long love unwearied be.

3

Our wine but vin ordinaire,
we share spare
food but with jollity
and my inferior character
will serve to sing and dance with her.

4

On ridge my stroke
lops bough from oak
fagots for fire wood
mid the thick underbrush where was leaves riot
if so thou come to eye
my heart hath quiet.

5

This I foresaw a-drive
when I went forth to wive, urging my horses
over mount, over hill, my six reins as lute-strings tight,
I drove aright
under Hesper, thee to meet,
so is my heart made suave with the heat.

V   (219)

Flies, blue flies on a fence rail,
should a prince swallow lies wholesale?

Flies, blue flies on a jujube tree,
slander brings states to misery.

Flies, blue flies on a hazel bough
even we two in slanderers' row
                    B'zz, b'zz, hear them now.

VI   (220)

Guests at mat in due order
left, right, big dish in centre,
sauces at border;
wine suave and sun'd as wine should be,
out of wine cometh unity,
                    bang the drum and strike the bell

After toast comes archery
all in due formality:

"Show your bow-skill!"
" 't's a hit if I do."
"The cup with three legs goes to you."

2

With six-holed flutes
that were bamboo shoots,
drum time, with pantomime
to our line's root:
         Noel! Noel! that fiery rite delight
         HIM, the flame, our light
in flow, in rite
till the hundred rites all
be done here in hall
to phallus' and forest's purity
that thy line enduring be
deep as all continuity;
so deep the lust
each man here must
         laud thy coherence.
      Rivals grasp hands, ere hence
      comes One from ingle:
         "Let no man drink single,
         but dip and pour
         great cup's honour
            welding thy seasons."

3

Guests start eatin', mild and even,
The sober sit an' keep behavin',
but say they've booz'd then they do not.
When they've booz'd they start a-wavin' an' a-ravin',
Yas' sir they rise up from the ground
and start dancin' an' staggerin' round
each to his own wild fairy fancy
as they never would when sober.
Sobers sit and drunks go gay
elegant or with display
in order or in indecency.
         Drunks never know sufficiency.

4

When they've drunk they'll stagger and yell
and upset their plates as well,
dancing like devil masks from hell,
don't know the post house (where to stop)
with their crooked caps a-top
they canna' dance, but stagger and flop.
They'd be welcome to their pleasure
if they'd go when wholly soused
but to be booz'd and not to go
we define as lèse virtù
(failure, that is, to correlate
outward act with mental state)
But drinkin' 's great
up to proper measure.

5

And as at every drinking bout
some can hold it and some pass out,
we appoint, at every rally,
a toast-master and his keep-tally
so that those who can't hold their liquor
or, as we say, run true to form,
are kept from worse enormity
of word or of activity;
after three cups cannot tell lamb
from hornèd ram, but still
want more liquor ardently.

VII   (221)
THE CAPITAL IN HAO
Not to stir trouble from down up, or vice-versa.

Fine fish in weed, that is their place.
And the king's good wine in his palace.

Fish in pond-weed wagging a tail
And the king in high Hao at his wassail.

While fish in pond-weed lie at ease
the kings of Hao may live as they please.

VIII   (222)
The fountain of honour is not the fountain of produce.

Princes coming to court the king
and I've nowt to give for the beans they bring,
be the baskets round or square
as they come with car and four.
A black or an ax-coat* to wear?

2
Mid hornéd bubbles at the spring's threshold
as the leaves of cress† unfold
nobles come, their flags a-flap
jangle of bells at bridle strap
of trace horse or pole horse in harness,
princes coming to pluck the cress.

3
Red leather (aprons) above the knees
and, below them, side-cut puttees,
and with cordial alacrities;
Sky's Son's command
can renew rents and titles to land.

4
Oak's thick-leaved boughs,
Welcome, welcome!
that shade this house
welcome!
ten thousand lucks alight
on ye, to left and right,
cohort and liegemen,
rear guard and flank
    Justice and order
    guard the Imperial House.

---

* Insignia of rank.
† Take cress, i.e. examination with prizes.

5

Willow boat by a mooring rope,
Welcome, Lords, to these assizes
in the hope of richer prizes,
easier rents that ever more
ye may lie snug as dog neath door.

IX   (223)

GNOMIC VERSES
Snow that is watery dust

Strong is the horn-tipped bow,
bend it again,
kith and kin should not
break under strain,
Lord as you do,
your folk will so
and follow as you teach.
If brother brother impeach,
        who will give aid?

Good red bow warps, be it not kept a-frame,
brothers strewn wide be 'n peril to do same.

2

So hast 'ou wrong to keep thy kin afar,
whom will they copy, if not their officer?

3

Elder to younger should indulgence show
and aid his brothers in their fortune also:
good brothers in their mutual relations
should not augment their cares and exacerbations.

4

Turgid is grutch
who clutching honours
learns no manners. One such will
ruin a canton to end all in ill.

5

Old horse plays colt,
old dolt steps out of line,
eats for three men
and is an ass in wine.

6

Teach not the ape to climb,
thou fling'st not mud
at whomso lies in mire, an thou but plan
decently
small men will swarm to thee.

7

Thick cloud moults snow
that melts before the sun
yet none
would stand aside from preferment
thinking to mount more high on falling pride.

8

Deep drifted snow the sun's eye melts away,
Man and Mao* had their day,
          My heart! their day!

X   (224)

'Neath the thick willow 'tis good to lie,
Let the Imperial foot pass by
If he gi' me a low job it would lift me too high.

2

Better stay 'neath the willow bough
than crush a toe beneath the Imperial car,
if he gave me a lift, it would take me too far.

* Tribes.

3

A bird can circle high over cloud,
a man's mind will lift above the crowd
reaching employ on high above us all
to dwell in deeper misery when he fall.

Book 8. The Old Capital

1   (225)

For an officer
in the old Capital, fox fur
(yellow) his manner without pretense;
his speech made sense
    Ergo ten thousand now
    yearn to return to Chou.

2

In the old Capital scholars all
wore wide plaited leaf hats and small
silk caps (black), the ladies' hair
was of a neatness that appeared unaided,
    the present hair-dos
    leave my heart unpersuaded.

3

In the old Capital officers wore ear-plugs fittingly
of seu stones (common jade) and the dames seemed
as to the manner born of Yin or Ki.
None such do we see pass
    today, and my heart is
    as smothered beneath wild grass.

4

The scholars' sash ends in the older court
had a certain grace in severity,
their ladies' side hair curved like a scorpion's tail,
something to follow, tho' we never see.

5

There was no fuss about the fall
of the sash ends, there was just that much to spare
and it fell, and ladies' hair
curved, just curved and that was all
the like of which, today, is never met;
And I therefore
express regret.

II   (226)

The morning 's over and I've picked less
than a handful of green *lu* grass.
My hair 's in a tangle, I'd better go wash.

2

The morning 's over and I have got
less than a skirt-full of indigo, five days to come;
sixth: he comes not.

3

When he wanted to hunt
I cased his bow,*
when he'd a-fishing go
I carded his fishing line also.

4

Then folk would stand to watch him pull out
tench or bream, bream or trout.

---

* Graph is "long leather" meaning presumably that she took the bow off
the rack where it had been tied to keep from warping, and put it in a leather
hunting sheath.

III   (227)
Soft rain
High grain.

Rain fats our millet sprout,
ours, who went on and out
under Earl's urging.

2

We pushed and heaved and prodded our oxen,
crowding the road, saying how home was good
to come back to.

3

Massed men about cars moved in close order
saying: this done, we'll go home from the border.

4

Close was the work at Sie under Shao's urging.
Shao's Earl planned it,
manned it, finished it all with due ardour.

5

We cleared the slope and the plain,
cleared streams and the springs, by Shao was the settlement;
the King's heart is now content.

IV   (228)

Berry leaves in marsh, thick as leaves can
be. 'tis joy to see a gentleman.

Mulberry in the low-land low
gloss of the leaf,   'tis so
much joy to see   a true man.

Mulberry covers the low-land glade with
shade that lets but small light through,
Honesty holds men together like glue.

I have held him in love so long,
from heart's midmost be it song
not to be lost.

V   (229)

White the marsh flower that white grass bindeth,
my love 's afar,
    I am alone.

2

White cloud and white dew shun,
amid all flowers, none.
Steep are the steps of heaven
    to him unknown.

3

The overflow seeps north from the pool,
rice hath its good therefrom;
singing I sigh
for a tall man far from home.

4

Are mulberries hacked to firewood for the stove?
A tall man, hard of head, wrecks my love.

5

Drums, gongs in the palace court
are heard by passers by,
yet if you think at all
of my pain, you think but scornfully.

6

Tall maribou stand at the dam,
cranes cry over dry forest
that a tall man teareth
the heart in my breast.

7

Drake at the weir spread a wing to the left in amity,
in man's unkindness his mind
is scattered as two against three.

8

These flat thin stones will not raise
me high enough to see
him who embitters my days.

VI (230)

The silky warble runs in the yellow throat,
never kept katydid to rote
                          unceasing so—
yet comes to rest in angle of the hill.
Roads to go,
loads how?
Drink, eat,
think as taught,
carts ought
          to carry us, carry us on.

The silky warble runs in the yellow throat,
bird comes to rest by angle of the hill,
a road 's to go, needs must
that never comes to end,
drink, eat,
think as taught,
carts ought to carry us, carry us on.

The silky warble runs in the yellow throat,
birds in hillside abide,
dare we not go? Needs must
fear dust, bars end, but on,
drink, eat,
think as taught,
cars ought
          to carry us on.

VII (231)

The host pours, tastes, offers, and then receives back the
drinking cup in his turn.

Take and boil but a melon leaf
so be good wine is to pour,

be but one rabbit head to grill or roast,
amid gentlemen the taste 's in the toast.

Be but one rabbit head to roast or grill
if for the toast wine there be,
taste, offer, and take back the cup. Good company
maketh all the feast savoury.

VIII (232)

Where the torrent bed breaks our wagon wheels,
            up, up, the road,
the mountain stream runs far;
            toil, toil, toil, to the East is a war
and no leisure.

Where the torrent bed breaks our wagon wheels
            up, up, the road steep
and the mountain stream runs far;
            toil, toil, toil, to the East is a war
and we to it.

Pig wades in wave, full ford; rump 's white
            as moon in the Hyades.
That means yet heavier rain; we, levied East
            get no white ease.

IX (233)

Lily bud floating, yellow as sorrow,
grief today, what of tomorrow?

Gone the bud, green the leaf,
better unborn than know my grief.

Scrawny ewes with swollen heads,
the fish traps catch but stars.

What man has food now
after these many wars?

X   (234)

Yellow, withered all flowers, no day without its march,
who is not alerted?
Web of agenda over the whole four coigns.

Black dead the flowers,
no man unpitiable.
Woe to the levies,
are we not human?

Rhinos and tigers might do it, drag it out
over these desolate fields, over the sun-baked waste.
Woe to the levies,
morning and evening no rest.

Fox hath his fur, he hath shelter in valley grass,
Going the Chou Road, our wagons our hearses, we pass.

PART THREE
IN THREE BOOKS

THE GREATER ODES

Book 1. Decade of King Wen

I (235)

The simplicity and written civilization of Chou supersedes
the bronze and luxury of Yin-Shang.

Glare King Owen, rooted above,
light as the light of heaven.
Chou, though old, had
the decree, twice-given.

Bright, aloft, Wen, glitteringly,
Chou, tho' an old regime, gat new decree;
Had not Chou been there like the sun's fountainhead
the supernal seals had never caught sun's turn
that King Wen tread
up, down, to stand
with the heavenly veils to left hand and right hand.

2

Untiring Wen that hath untiring fame,
such order and such resource by him came
to Chou with sons and grandsons of Wen,
to sons of grandsons and collateral,
root, branch, an hundred generations; and all
Chou's officers; is it not said:
Such source is as of light a fountainhead?

3

Is he not so the sun above his clan,
and they the radiant wings gleaming to flank?
Think on the lustre of our officers
born in the kingly state,

whom this state bred and holds; Chou's pace
orders them all—to King Wen's quietness.

4

Wen, like a field of grain beneath the sun
when all the white wheat moves in unison,
coherent, splendid in severity,
Sought out the norm and scope of Heaven's Decree
till myriad Shang were brought under fealty.
Shang and his line in all their opulence

5

Now stand in livery for Chou's defence, that all
may know Sky's favour is not perpetual,
so no man's luck shall hold.
Yin men, now, when we pour
wine to our manes, stand about the door
with tiger's grace and ease,
clad in their antient splendid broideries,
faithful at court and in the battle line,
mindful what NUMEN stands within the shrine.

6

Mindful what manes stand here to preside;
what insight to what action is conjoint,
long may we drink the cup of fellowship,
Yin's pride in mind, always to show the point,
a tub of water wherein to note
thy face. Had Yin not lost the full assembly's vote
He had long held to drink with the Most High,
yet mistook fate for mere facility.

7

High destiny 's not borne without its weight
(equity lives not save by constant probe)
Be not thy crash as Yin's from skies, foreseen.
The working of Heaven hath neither sound nor smell,
Be thy cut form of justice as Wen's was, shall rise
ten thousand states, thine, and with candour in all.

II (236)
Referring to Yin-Shang as Yin to avoid confusion with Ta-
Sheng, names having very different ideograms which do
not confuse the eye in the Chinese text.

O light that shineth neath dire power aloft
(mind was below, above: blood-might to harm)
The heaven 's not solid, and to reign 's not soft.
Yin could not hold th' inherited empire neath his arm.

2

When of Yin-Shang, Jen, Chy's second daughter
wed into Chou and was brought up to court,
by lucid insight, honest in her deed, she
made in her body Wen, of King Ki's seed.

3

And this King Wen, attentive in his mind,
wide-soaring in observation,
so clear in serving the power that is on high,
designing in his heart felicity
from inwit to his act moved ever so straight
he got in sovereignty the whole Quadrate.

4

The Skies looked down and two fates came to nest,
Wen began action, Heaven raised up his mate
on the North Banks where Hia meets with the Wei,
Wen laudable in his stance and she
                    heraldric heiress of the Palatinate,

5

of that great House, who seemed
a younger sister of Heaven. Wen after smooth augury
went out to meet her at the ferry of Wei,
bridging that stream with boats and pageantry.

6

The seal was from heaven, to Wen this destiny
in Chou's high seat, and Hsin's first born his queen

who in her strength bore Wu, the augmenter of fate
who, after the "Flame of Words"* laid Yin prostrate.

7

The hosts of Yin
were as a forest in route.
For the oath at Mu spoke out: I begin this
and well. Shang-Ti is near you now,
let no man doubt.

8

Then the plain overflowed with the flashing of hard-wood
    cars,
black manes and the dash of the bays,
Shang-Fu in the van always
as a crested eagle soars,
And Wu, the King, fluid cool†
layed out so towering Yin
and in the clear light of the morning
inspected his men.

III   (237)

As gourd-vines spread, man began
leaf after leaf and no plan
overgrowing the Tsü and Ts'i,
living in caves and in stone hives
ere ever they knew a house with eaves.

2

Old Duke T'an Fu galloped his horses‡
along the western water courses
along their banks to the slopes of K'i
and took Lady Kiang for his company
to set up the House of Dynasty.

---

* I take it, the Great Declaration. *Shu* V.1(3).
  † The battle order to the troops at Mu (*Shu* V.2) was to stop and reform
after a maximum of six or seven steps forward and at most four, five, six, or
seven blows struck.
  ‡ 1326 B.C.

3

Dark violets filled the Chou plain
and thistles sweet as an artichoke*
where T'an 'gan plan
and to invoke
the scorched divining shell.
"Time: now; place: here; all's well,"
said the shell, "Build wall ad hoc."

4

Gave men comfort and quietness;
settled, right, left, with boundaries;
with laws, drainage and harvesting,
from West to East all was to his ordering.

5

He called assistants for all this,
called a proctor of prentices
to build him a house, to build them a home;
with plummet, tightened frame boards, and line,
raised a temple to his forebears
with wings wide to the moving airs.

6

Earth in baskets for the wall, lime at call;
whacked it with paddles, scraped and beat,
scrape and repeat,
each day 5000 feet,
moving faster than the drum beat.

7

Reared they a great draw-bridge and gate
and a gate of state with a portcullis;
built also the great chthonian altar
for hecatomb ere they went to war
or did any other large business,

* "as a dumpling," what other thistle?

8

Some trash T'an could not annihilate
but held to his honour at any rate;
cleared out the bushy thorn and oak
to make road for travelling men
and so discouraged the hunting hun.

9

Then King Wen brought to civility
the lords of Yü and of Ju-i;
taught 'em to bow and stand aside,
say: after you, and: if you please,
and: this is no place for barbarities.

IV (238)

This oak, scrub oak men pile
for fagots; order in government
hath power, to left and right, tensile
to zest men's interest.

And order is held by the split seal and mace,
His honourers are long-haired suitable officers.

Many and many oars take boats on Ghing
to meet the king of Chou's six army corps.

And as

The Milky Way sets rule aloft in sky,
in his longevity the king of Chou
has raised up men distantly.

To make true form as metal or jade he grinds;
as needle that draws on silk,
draws on the whole nation's mind.

V (239)

For deep deer-copse beneath Mount Han
hazel and arrow-thorn make an even, orderly wood;
A deferent prince
seeks rents in fraternal mood.

2

The great jade cup holds yellow wine,
a fraternal prince can pour
blessing on all his line.

3

High flies the hawk a-sky,
deep dives the fish,
far, far, even thus amid distant men
shall a deferent prince have his wish.

4

The red bull stands ready, and
clear wine is poured,
may such rite augment the felicity
of this deferent lord.

5

Thick oaks and thorn give folk fuel to spare,
a brotherly prince shall energize
the powers of air.

6

And as no chink is between vine-grip and tree
thick leaf over bough to press,
so a fraternal lord seeks abundance
only in equity;
in his mode is no crookedness.*

* Last line is echo'd in the Tennin's speech in Hagoromo.

VI (240)
Three generations to make a gent

T'ai Jen Wen's mother, by her orderliness
won grace of Chou Kiang, dowager
of the Royal House.
T'ai Sy made triple ply, as chord to their tone
of fame; we count
her an hundred sons as if her own.

2

Kind to the manes of the ducal hall,
He nagged not against their timing,
gave no offence at all in any season;
patterned his mate,
which pattern his brothers caught;
thru whom he managed clans and the state.

3

In court suave concord,
at rites, reverence;
presence invisible,   as the sun draws up
effortless support.   the vapour's thread
                                       tho' unseen

4

Mid swirl of great evils not to be set aside,*
had courage to respect perfection,
a pattern till then that none
had heard tell of; and to investigate
abuses not codified.

5

Therefore focussed men even now
fit acts to inwit; youth starts,
but men of old had stamina to carry it thru;
their glory: elegance
asserted officially.†

* Not till his son Wu won the victory of Mu plains.
† The ode is full of terms that become technical in Confucian ethics.
Analects XVI.xiv; *Chung Yung* XV; *Mencius* I.1.7, 12. "Don't lie down on it."

VII (241)

How King Wen received the succession, his attack
on Ch'ung. All this before the battle of Mu.

White God above,
thine eye in awe
looked down and saw
neither Hia nor Yin
trusted of men;
probed the great states,
their walls, their hates,
and only to West
one clan stood test.
He therefore led
Chou to kingstead.

2

Raised up a screen,
cleared brush and vine,
levelled the land's lay
(terraced the slopes)
dug ditch, set hedge trees,
whip-stalk and tamarisk;
drove out the Kuan horde
(the "string tribes")
Light to lead action
heaven shifted,
Drinking with heaven
Chou had the lordship;

3

Neath Sky's eye on hill,
cut oak and thorn tree,
lined pine and cedar,
A state he founded
And men to king it
from T'ai's time to Ki.
King Ki, kind of heart

took his brother's part and rent
so to apply it
that with glory
the Four Coigns had quiet.*

4

Sky gauged the mind of Ki,
silently fame
marked out his straightness,
which then shone out
and shining knew to choose;
advanced in technique
lordly to attend the voices,
then was king,
ruled a great state, obeyed
and knew proportions.
And so we come to Wen—
inwit and act conjoint—
anointed of the sky;
sons of his grandsons
still hold empery.

5

Out of the Welkin
came the word to Wen:
Burn not to deviate,
to kindle and grab
at every lust's desire.

First to the Mount, saw Mi in jactancy
daring so great a state,
invading Yüan, raiding as far as Kung;
Blazed in his anger, mobilized, blocked out the horde;
made Chou secure and so qualified
to take the empire in his stride.

* T'ai convinced that his nephew Wen was most fit to rule, abdicated in
favour of Wen's father Ki, presumably the third brother of T'ai, not next in
seniority. Thus eliminating both his own sons and senior nephews.

6

His base the capital;
invaders from Yüan's edge
climbed to high crag and ridge
but got no slopes
or upland pasture dales,
neither our springs to be their water supply.
Pools, springs, ours, south of Mount K'i
the pick of the plain
measured in homestead, in land made fit by the river Wei;
Wen suzerain
over the ten thousand fiefs of the plain
(and measuring square).

7

Then God to Wen: I mind me the equipoise
bright in thy act and thought,
a decor without great noise,
neither mnemonic nor as a lesson taught
but following fluid the pattern cut aloft.
Sky then to Wen, the king:
Ware of thine enemy; bring
brethren, hooks,
battering rams, all
great carrochs and go
against Ch'ung wall.

8

Great carrochs and the arbalasts creaked slow,
giving Ch'ung time to parley beneath the wall;
Questioned the prisoners, slow, one by one,
almost in silence the left ears fall,
seeking the sanction from the Father of War
that all in the four squares be rightly done,
first in the camp-site; second, before the town.
Then to the catapults! and Ch'ung is down.
High Ch'ung is down and hath no exequies,
her rites are out
and to land's end no man defies.

VIII   (242)

When he planned to begin a spirit tower
folk rushed to the work-camp and overran
all the leisure of King Wen's plan;
old and young with never a call
had it up in no time at all,

The king stood in his "Park Divine,"
deer and doe lay there so fine,
so fine so sleek; birds of the air
flashed a white wing while fishes splashed
on wing-like fin in the haunted pool.

Great drums and gongs
hung on spiked frames
sounding to perfect rule and rote
about the king's calm crescent moat,

Tone unto tone, of drum and gong.

About the king's calm crescent moat
the blind musicians beat lizard skin
as the tune weaves out and in.

IX   (243)
WU, AS THE GREAT FOOT-PRINT

King Wu in their spoor,
three wise kings were set over Chou,
Avatars now they be in heaven over all
while he drinks with them in capital.

2

Drinking King's cup in capital,
seeks their insight where right to drink must
hatch from folk's trust, he
builds for long dynasty.

3

Perfect the trust.
A map to man,
thinking what sonship could be,
he taught all sons filiality.

4

Men sought him as man to man,
his deeds done from heart-sight
taught men how right is done
when paternal nature lasts into son.

5

Lasting light is ours like a great rope
from Wu "the spoor"
unto ten thousand years, while skies endure.

6

Luck down from heaven,
homage from the four coigns in, to pack
ten thousand years. Shall he lack
acolytes?

X   (244)
WANG HOU CHENG TSAI

Praise to King Wen for his horse-breeding,
that he sought the people's tranquility
and saw it brought into focus.
                WEN! Avatar, how!

2

Wen had the Decree and war-merit;
when he carried the attack against Ch'ung
he made Feng capital of the province.
                Wen! avatar, how!

3

He solidified the walls of its moat;
He raised Feng on the pattern
not hasting at whim, but in conformity, filial,
A sovran, avatar, how!

4

The king's justice was cleansing
and the low-walls were four-square at Feng
even throughout the kingdom
the kingly house was their-bulwark,
A sovran, avatar, how!

5

Feng water flowed east
that was Yü's spinning,
the four squares were even,
Splendid the rule over princes,
Emperor, avatar, how!

6

In Hao was the capital and the half-circlet of water,*
From West from East from South from North
none thought to break order
(no man but wore Wu's insignia)
Emperor, avatar, how!

7

He divined, to the 9th straw of ten in the casting
that Hao be the capital for his dwelling;
The tortoise confirmed it; Wu brought it to finish,
WU, avatar, how!

8

Feng water makes the white millet;
Did Wu not choose his officials?
He bequeathed the design to his dynasty
that their line feast and at leisure.
Wu, avatar, how!

* 1134 B.C.

Book 2. Decade of Sheng Min

THE CREATION (of mankind, or of the Chou clan)

HOU TSI, John Barleycorn, settles in T'ai.

DUKE LIU, the magnanimous, in Pin (allegedly about
1796 B.C.).

THE DUKE SHY OF SHAO addresses King Ch'eng
(possibly 1109 B.C. or thereabouts).

DUKE MU OF SHAO, in time of disorder under King Li
(the "changed odes" IX, X) 877–841.

THE EARL OF FAN, idem.

1   (245)
"Prince Millet," J. Barleycorn, Hou Tsi

Mankind began when Kiang Yüan poured wine
to the West sun and circling air
and, against barrenness, trod the Sky's spoor.
Then, as a sudden fragrance funnelled in
and to its due place,
a thunder-bolt took body there to be
and dawn Hou Tsi, whom she bare on his day
and suckled presently.

2

Saith legend: was full moon, and effortless
the first birth was as a lamb's, no pain, no strain,
slit, rent, in auspice of the happy spirit in the child;
the upper sky unstill, unslaked by sacrifice?   lamb,
intent on this kindling birth.   burning
                                                        babe

3

And, by tradition, he was "Cast-away"
in narrow lane to lie
suckled between the legs of kine and ewes.
There be to attest
that he was Cast-away in flat forest
wherein the woodmen found

(hacking at trees) Hou Tsi upon the ground
and on cold ice, warmed by a bird's plumes
till the bird took flight
whereon he howled to welkin with such might of sound
it filled the wood-paths and the forest around.

the
snow
bird

4

Then crept aloft to the hill-paths of K'i
and to High Crag
whereon, to eat and mouth, planted broad beans
which gave leaf suddenly.
Rice was his servant, ripe, more ripe;
hemp and wheat stood
over the fields like tent cloths,
melons gat laughing brood.

5

Was Hou Tsi's harvest mutual process?
Howkt out thick choking grass,
put in the sound yellow grain
that squared to husk, filled out its sleeve to full
as it would burst the ears, unmoulding and tasteable
bent there with weight of head
durable; so had in T'ai his stead.

6

From him we have first-class seed, our classic grain:
blacks, doubles, reds and whites.
To keep blacks, doubles, they be stacked a-field.
Red and white yield
we bear a-back to barn
or shoulder high,
wherefore Hou made the rite yclept "return."

7

What is our rite, become traditional?
Some hull, some take from mortar, winnow or tread,
some soak (or sift with ever shifting sound)
and boil till steam and rising fumes abound.
Some turn to augury or plunge in thought

and kindle southern-wood with moon-like fat
leading the ram to cross-road sacrifice
on spit to turn, heating the seeds a-field
so to insure next year full harvest-yield.

8

From heaped plate and clay dish the odours rise
to please, in season, the power above the skies
by their far-searching smell that fits the time.
Hou Tsi began these rites. The folk of Chou
unblemished have maintained them until now.

II   (246)

FESTAL

Tough grow the rushes, oh!
No passing kine break down
their clumpy wads, and blades so glossy growin'.
Our brothers all be here at call
assembled as to rule
wherefore lay down the mat, the mat
and bring the old man his stool.

2

Put a soft straw mat on a bamboo mat
let lackeys bring in the stools,
toast against toast, wine against wine
observant of all the rules,
then rinse the cups and bring catsups*
with pickles, roast and grill,
trype and mince-meat and while drums beat
let singers show their skill.

3

The trusty bows are tough, my lads,
each arrow-point true to weight
and every shot hits plumb the spot
as our archer lines stand straight.

---

* Karlgren fancies a bit of tongue in the menu and someone else has a
note on kidney sausage.

They shoot again and four points go in
as if they were planting trees,
For a tough wood bow and the archers row
attest the gentilities.

4

An heir to his line is lord of this wine
and the wine rich on the tongue.
But by the great peck-measure, pray in your leisure
that when you're no longer young
your back retain strength to susteyne
and aid you kin and clan.
Luck to your age! and, by this presage,
joy in a long life-span.

III (247)
"Per plura diafana"

strophe 3

Drunk with thy wine, but with thy candour filled,
Prince, to ten thousand years, felicity.

2

Drunk is thy wine and ready is thy food,
May'st 'ou for ten thousand years give light to thy brood,

3

With a clarity that doth as vapour rise,
Good moon enjoin such ends
as be from planting the ghost's voice commends.

4

What such commending?

"Thy dishes here be clean."
Friends lend an extra ear
to whom, in awe, maketh his justice seen.

5

Who honoureth right order, timely,
His line shall last
filial, enduring, not to be declassed.

olim de
Malatestis

6

What thing is class?

House, garden, lady's path,
let them stand for ten thousand years,
dignified aftermath.

7

What is succession, what posterity?
May heaven quilt soft thy rent
and for ten thousand years let there be
cortège and host to follow thy decree.

8

How shall be cortège?

Heirs to thy consort,
Consorts and heirs be theirs
to fill thy court.

IV (248)
ON WEI NEAR HAO

Ducks on the river King
the dukes' ghosts come to hall
for banqueting
quiet and all
Clear wine, good food for manes set,
their mood at this banquet
that joy be more perfect yet.

2

Ducks land on sand,
Dukes' ghosts in hall,
where all is as all should be
many wines make much revelry,
and who eats as the Sire's ghost
shall know prosperity's utmost.

3

Ducks by isle,
the dukes' ghosts come to hall
to have quiet withal,
clear wine, thin sliced smoked meat,
where the ghosts of nobles eat
felicity shall be complete.

4

Ducks there where the rivers meet,
the ducal manes come to eat,
wherefore in templed hall
Felicity makes festival.

5

Ducks in the gorge, as thru the fragrant fume
the ghost is come,
Wine to taste, baked meats to nose,
where ghosts feed come no future woes.

V   (249)

THE SUN SPIDER
in the Ideogram Hien

At leisure to take delight,
Tensile his virtu is
who leads his folk aright,
and their officers; his rents
from heaven, he augments
fate that the skies renew.

2

A thousand rents, an hundred luck's intake;
his grandsons multiply.
White wheat a-field and glory upon high,
fit prince, fit king
errs not, forgets not, but leads men by
antient legality.

3

Respect for equity keeps well defined the crown,
fame of clear conscience fructifies the deed.
No grudge, no hate,
leading as though on parity
with the multitude, luck comes unboundedly.
He makes, to the four coigns, all orderly.

4

Holding the end threads
over his dinner table in amity.
Appointed ministers, princes of birth
all watch his eyebrows, and the work goes on,
the official work.
Of common men everyone
has his own earth.

VI   (250)

Duke Liu, the frank,
unhoused, unhapped,
from bound to bourne
put all barned corn in sacks
and ration bags
for glorious use, stretched bow
showed shield, lance, dagger-axe
and squared to the open road.

2

Duke Liu, the frank
looked to the plain afar
to help his many and multitude,
conforming (to geography)
he issued an order accordingly.
They grumbled a bit and then clomb high
to the ridge and echo of Yen Mount and then
came down to the plain beneath.
His only boat was of green jaspar
that gleamed at the tip of his sword-sheath.

3

Frank Duke Liu
passed by the Hundred Founts,
saw the wide watershed,
clomb to the South Mount's head;
scanned site for capital
to o'erhang the wild:
a time to dwell in house, a time is meant
to live in bivouac, a time to tell
tales and make argument.

4

Duke Liu, the frank,
based on his capital
spread order thru
that land as on swift foot,
gave mat and stool
to whom should mount or lean in cenacle.
Sent to the cattle-fold,
pork was from sty
and wine from calabash
for all the templed line
to drink and eat.

5

Duke Liu, the frank,
measured the hills to know the light and shade,
dark female and light male, the wide and long,
where land would answer, where to prod in seed;
how the springs drained, and to three army corps
measured the marsh and plain
all to be channelled fields for tithe and grain,
measured the South West slope,
so dwelt in Pin
where desert waste had been.

6

So lodged, in Pin, Duke Liu
fixed fords on Wei,
whetstone and anvil rock (for stepping stones).
Gave them based house and laws,
assembly and land-tenure
even to Huang Vale and the torrents of Kuo
both banks, to river bend,
many were housed and all was made secure.

VII   (251)

Cleared by its flowing, dip the flood water up
and it will steam thy rice or other
grain; a deferent prince is
to his people both father and mother.

Rain-water cleared by its overflood
if thou ladle it out will wash thy altar jar;
To a fraternal prince will his folk
return, as to home from afar.

In a fraternal prince his folk have rest,
as from rain water
cleared by its flowing thou hast
a pure house, or thy garden is blest.

VIII   (252)

Around the hill-bend the south wind whirling,
Prince, in your brotherliness
coming at ease to sing
unhurried, let these notes fit your turn.

2

Say is friendship leisure's test,
best of leisure giveth rest,
Prince, for your young-brotherliness
in such life as rest confers
may you live and drink wine with your ancestors
and so your life reach term.

3

May you to earth and sky at crux of winter,
Prince in all deference
reply, and set firm the calendar
when, turning beneath his cliff, the sun goes hence.
May an hundred spirits of the air allied
gather to banquet where you preside
and so your life reach term.

4

You have received it: dynasty
for how long? To enjoy great rent?
Prince deferent,
the candour of a House is its longevity.

5

(Rashness is, fortitude is)
There are the filial,
there are those who see straight
to take action to lead;
to shelter. Young and fraternal prince, be thy pattern
such that the four coigns heed.

6

O source and height,
jade sceptre, bright fountainhead,
Think what your fame can be
and what men hope, Prince brotherly, that hold
the square of the realm on guiding rope.

7

Hark to the phoenix wings astir in the air,
Here is their bourne, here is their place of rest,
Old and tried officers crowd round the throne
to know thy will, now thou art Heaven's son.

8

Old and tried officers crowd round the throne,
Hark to the phoenix-wings at heaven's gate,
Let him appoint such as will keep touch
with the folk of his state.

9

Hark to the phoenix' song
o'er the high ridge amid dryandra boughs
that face the rising sun,
thick, thick the leaves,
so calm serene that song.

CODA

The Lord's wagons be many,
his fast horses trained better than any,
And a few verses will make a song
when there's a tune to drag it along.*

---

* I see no reason not to take this as a coronation ode in three parts. St/
1–3; 4–6; 7–10. Or 7–9 and 10 as coda. Circa 1109 or 1116 B.C. No one will
deny the presence of ambiguous passages in the original. The chapter in the
Shu (V.12) is of particular interest in bearing directly on the tradition.

IX   (253)

Duke Mu to his colleagues in the ministry, avoiding
lèse majesté in the form. First of the "changed odes,"
in King Li's time. 877–841 B.C.

Folk worn out, workin' so late,
Kind rule at centre hauls on a state.
Pitch out the slimers and scare off worse,
Thieves and thugs see a light and curse;
Easy on far men, do with what's near,
And the king can sit quiet the rest of the year.

2

Folk worn out need support,
Men gather round a kindly court;
Throw out the punks who falsify your news,
scare off the block-heads, thugs, thieves and screws.
Don't shove it off on the working man,
But keep on doing what you can
              for the king's support.

3

Folk worked out need time for breath,
Kindness in capital
draws on the four coigns withal;
Sweep out the fakes and scare the obsequious
thugs, thieves and screws
and don't promote the snots to sin on sly.
Respect men who respect the right
and your own honesty may heave into sight.

4

Folk burnt out need a vacation,
Kind court alleviates people's vexation;
Throw out the flattering fakes,
scare blighters and crushers,
Don't ruin folk pretending it's government,
tho' you're mere babes in this business
and the job bigger than you can guess.

5

Folk burnt out need a little peace,
Kindness in middle causes no injuries.
Turn out the oily tongues and parasites,
thieves, squeezing governors; don't upset honest men.
The king wants jewels and females,
I therefore lift up these wails.

X   (254)
Attributed to the Earl of Fan in King Li's time,
877–841 B.C.

The sky's course runs a-foul and in reverse,
a jaundiced people sink beneath the curse.
Given to untruth plotting never a-right,
You say, and lie, that no sage sees the light.
                    Against your nearsightedness
                    I employ this reproving verse.

2

The heavens send down the hard, pull in your smirk
Gainst sky's square kick, no man has time to shirk.
Words fit to fact
folk will enact;
Calm discourse
needeth no force.

3

From a different line of work, my colleagues,
I bring you an idea. You smirk.
It's in the line of duty. Wipe off that smile, and
as our grandfathers used to say:
Ask the fellows who cut the hay.

4

There is no joke in heaven's severity,
Old men clear ditches and young men step high.
My word 's not moss-grown. Your frivolity

is a muck heap's blaze.
Fagots, not to be saved, blaze higher,
Medicine grass puts out no fire.

5

Dour heaven 's not cogged to fit your jactancy,
Good men sit corpse-like still, perversity
is your line. The people groan,
none dares ask why
all 's wrack, no charity.

6

Light's lattice, the sky aloft, tunes man
as flute or pitch pipe can;
easy to lift as half
the jade tally-mace, none tries to enlarge his half to tune.
Prone to untune, be not yourselves the base
of their untunedness.

7

True men a fence, and serried ranks a wall,
Great states a buffer, clans as a flank bulwark.
Straightness in action gives calm. That meditate,
Clan-chiefs shall be as solid thy stronghold,
let it not moulder here till solitude
be not thy worst to fear.

8

Revere the anger of heaven
nor count it vain stage-play;
Revere the motion of heaven, bawl not thy jactancy,
The light of heaven is clear enough to see
the king going out, and at sunrise there's light
enough to show
the revel's remnant, idleness' overflow.

Book 3. Decade of T'ang

I   (255)

Wide, wide aloft, Sky's overhanging power,
Fearing the curse, divers the fates and many.
Man's multitude
is of heaven, all born, and none
can trust to fate alone.

                  They be few who conclude.

2

King Wen said: So!
Towering on high
Yin-Shang, taxers run wode beneath your tyranny,
oppressors unbounded beneath your tyranny
by you hold office and in uniform
Heaven made them evil, but you hoist their power.

3

King Wen said: So!
Yin-Shang insatiate,
one honest appointment arouses hate,
The over-steppers of boundaries answer
with a flux of debate.
You set thieves in the core of your state,
Then wait in wishful thinking
and make no move to investigate.

4

King Wen said: So!
You brawl in the middle kingdom;
collect resentments and call it sincerity.
There is no light in your conscience
and your acts shed, therefore, no light
in your inwit and you are left without ministers,

                              without party.

5

King Wen said: So!
Yin-Shang not tanned of wind but of wine
red. Not in virtue's line
moving, wrong in your stance,
You have taken a tiger's roaring for pattern
and think that mere noise is a form.
Having neither light nor darkness to norm,
neither darkness nor light,
You bed at dawn and rise up with the coming of night.

6

King Wen said: Huh,
Yin-Shang aloft there,
Your noise is like bugs in the grass,   cicada,
as the bubbling of soup in a cauldron.   broad
                                                         locust
Great and small are near to destruction,
your arrogance sprouts by the roadside,
You enter the middle kingdom to tyrannize
and the pest spreads to the Devil's dominion.

7

King Wen said: So,
Woe to proud Yin up aloft,
It is not that skies are unseason'd,
Yin useth not the old wisdom.
Even tho' there are no old men and perfect,
the antient statutes remain and he does not hear them,
                    The great seal is broken, cast down.

8

King Wen said: So!
Damned Yin, there is a saying:
                    Utter destruction is knowable
Tho' branch and leaf be unwithered
                    the root is rotted away.

Yin's reflecting tub was not far distant,
It was in the generations of the dynasty of the Hia.*

* Presumed to be by Duke Mu, in the time of King Li's disorders, 877–
841 B.C. recalling great precedent.

II (256)

Ascribed to Duke Wu of Wei, who reigned 811–756 B.C.
He reproves himself, at the age of 95. Vide also Ode 220.

Control, control, in awe of ownership
That angle be clear twixt what is mine and thine.
Anal. corner XVII.16;
Mencius I.i.V.1.

Show of respect is held as virtu's sign,
Thus the old saw was meant:
No man 's all-wise, plain
men are fools as of their natural bent,
the sage's nonsense runs against the grain.

2

First seek out manhood,
four coigns will follow this, give thee assent
in word; study thine inwit to shape thy business,
four realms will agree in mind 'thout argument.
Lofty ambition is reached by calm decree
so be the far scope is proclaimed seasonably.
Revere all straightness, respecting thine and mine,
thy pattern shall the whole folk's form define.

3

How stand we now? Confusion in government,
bemusèd chaos up, and conscience down,
flat down, be it on back or front,
but sunk at any rate—thou art so drunk
and deep in nothing save it be merriment.
Severed continuance, thou dunce,
shallow in law of antient kingly light
that might, in this darkness, tow thy bark aright.

With false diffuseness
in seeking precedent,
losing the clear
and penal laws intent.

4

Disorder hath no preferment from the sky;
as the spring's seepage that runs wallowing down
with no clear channels, it but sinks, is lost.
Wake with the sun and go thou late to bed,
dust out thy court-yard and sprinkle, folk will take
order. Attend to thy carts and nags,
bows, arrows and weapons, for the land's defence
'gainst the wild Mann and crude South's insolence.

5

Weigh your appointees to their natural weight,
measure your feudal lords attentively
lest ructions come upon you unaware.
Mean from the heart what flows out from the tongue;
respect your own respect for equity
nor lack true tenderness.
Flaw in jade sceptre can be ground away,
'gainst word ill-spoke there is no remedy.

6

Glib not with facile speech,
no man can gate thy tongue vicarious.
Words cannot die and pass,
every fool speech begets its argument,
unright begets reply in unright's zone.
Be just in recompense, stand by thy friends,
be father to all folk of little means
and your wee'uns' wee'uns shall be
a line grown to a rope: posterity,
none without heritor.

7

Meet not thy friends with scowls,
Error 's yclept almost vicinity,
and when thou art thine own sole company
say not: No man can see thru the roof's air-hole,
In my north-west ingle is naught can make shame,
here is no eye.
The spirits have their own divisions of thought
not to our measure wrought,
that ours yet shoot toward.

8

Prince, 'tis thy job to keep thy conscience clean
inducing so a probity
laudable.
Care for the place you're in, plant there your tree,
defect not toward men's rights in property
either by theft or gentler usurpation
and you'll be followed, almost, by the nation;
Peach thrown to me, shall net a plum for thee
and . . . lambs will have horns, my son,
when rainbows turn to stone.

9

Tough wood will bend
if silk 's to make the string,
Calmness curves men and conscience is their base.
Wise, at these words, mere words, old saws,
do right, while fools deny,
run to reverse, and call them my tyranny
to prove: *quot homines, tot sententiae*
                    (each man, his mind).

10
[*still himself to himself*]

I took thy paw ere thou knew'st fair from base;
Showed thee the how, which when thou wouldst not face,
grabbed at thine ear. Dost thou plead ignorance?

And a father of grown-up brats? We fear . . .
We fear that men are incomplete,
Cock-sure at cock-crow and naught done by night.

II

Bright is the light that gleams in over-sky
yet leaves me grumped in black stupidity,
grinding it out, over and over again,
the self-same lesson, which, if thou dost hear,
art bored contemptuous, not bored to tears.
Dost 'ou plead ignorance?

After these ninety years?

12

This is the spot, the old stand is not changed,
but can'st 'ou act? can'st do it? That 's the rub,
to keep the people from yet greater woe,
tho' heaven frowns pestilence and state 's to wrack?
Take parallel, thou hast not far to go
nor doth sky err.
Defilement of inner light
brings blight,
and dire, on all thy folk.

III   (257)
Ascribed to the Earl of Jui, who died 827 B.C.

Soft shade of these mulberries
was a fit place for ten days' ease
but they keep hackin' away,
people's itch is no comfort to me,
heart levelled up with misery
I look to the burnished sky
that might look down again pityingly.

2

Here be four hefty nags
with a flutter and flap of falcon flags
and an unendable hullabaloo,
every state government fallen thru,

nobody left wearing black hair,
jinx on the remnants everywhere,
howling and mourning and every grief
and the kingdom rotten to its last leaf.

3

Also the state's money has given out,
given out and flowed away
and heaven has nothing to say;
under suspicion, nowhere to stand.
Jump off? nowhere to land.
Gentlemen could of course combine to run the state
without acrimony and party line.
Well, who started it anyhow?
And who the devil can stop it now?

4

I brood on the land's woe and house woe
born out of date
to early grief,
from west to east no relief,
no quiet, and as for thorns round the gate!

5

Think, damn it, on the brink
of ruin, I tell you to think,
and appoint solid officers, wet hand
for hot iron (you can drown
in a stream while discussing the best way to filter it)
even hot iron will sink.

6

North wind blows breath down the throat,
the people are decent, you head 'em off;
love hay-ricks because they are power
over the people, not because they are food stuff.
You treat grain
as if it were jewels and porcelain,
it is hoarded in silos instead of being used
for food in good will.

7

Death rains and chaos from heaven down
swamping the king and throne,
worms gnaw thru root and joint of the grain,
woe to the Middle Land, murrain and mould.
Prospect of plenty is sudden emptiness,
no strength for the troops in this distress
to think of over-arched nothingness.

8

A kind prince hath men's respect
for his mind's grip, plans' scopes,
and for the care he sets to select
right men to aid him.
But this cantankerous top
thinks he alone is right
and guided by his own sole liver and lights
ascribes the trouble to the folk's uppishness,
grown uppish (and from him) over night.

9

Observe in the middle wood pair'd herds of deer
in contrast to false friends among us here.
Slander grows no good grain
and, as the old saw says:
Roads both ways
run thru valleys
(such is their natural route).

10

A wise man's words
are heard an hundred *li*,
A fool delights
in his own jactancy.
Sans words, no power,
Why fear, why jealousy?

11

The good man is not wanted, is not pushed on,
The tough guy 's on the make from dawn to dawn,
with folk always a-letch for stress and storm
although rank poison would be better for 'em.

12

Great winds move clear
thru the great hollow vales,
Good men avail likewise
as if thought's form made the grain rise.
Dirty dog must
perforce find dust.

13

Great wind to tomb,
Greed, so, is doom.
Could he hear and reply
to what I mutter drunkenly
for his good,
utterly misunderstood?

14

And will you, friends, say that I sing
in ignorance, that I know nothing, yet sing?
Beasties on wing
time's dart shall touch presently.
I was your goodly shade,
and your rage turns against me.

15

There is no limit to what some people will do,
Cool officials' shifty backs
do not make-good popular lacks.
They say they can't help what goes on,
alleging that people are twisty naturally
they seek force to enforce their authority.

16

The "people" are not in the least perverse
the high-ups rob, cheat 'em and do worse,
then tell you they haven't sufficient power,
polite while you're there, jip you next hour,
and then say calmly: It wasn't me.

I have therefore compiled
this balladry.

IV (258)

DROUGHT

The Milky Dragon twists bright across heaven
and the King says: What wrong has been done in this time?
(that the rain comes not neither is promised)
but sorrow, confusion, famine,
again, yet again, neither do the spirits of air sustain us
though I have prayed to them all, grudging no victim.
The sceptre and pierced jade lie here lifeless*

> Aude me, Domine
> Assuage, O assuage!

2

The great drought is come as parching,
quilted with locusts and swollen,
there is no sacrifice I have not offered
neither have I neglected the bournes nor their altars,
Above, below, I have offered up offering
and I have buried.
There is no power I have not honoured,
The Lord Tsi does not uphold us
Nor the power of heaven approach us,
Waste, devast the earth,
would that it fell upon me, on my person only!

---

* Or simply that he has buried all he has, to propitiate the powers of earth.

3

For the great drought I offer no self-exculpation,
I quake as under the thunder,
that there be no whole man left in Chou,
God over heaven, neither that I survive.
Why will none join me in reverence
that the spirit of the ancestral cartouche,
                    the founder, the cult, come not to end?

4

The great drought! None can withstay it,
It is impetuous fire against which I have no recourse.
The great destiny draws to an end,
we find neither awe nor shelter,
nor do the pastoral lords of aforetime
                    bring us their aid,
O source of my founders, carnal and uterine,
                    How can you bear this in quiet?

5

Great the drought, the high hills are parched
and their rivers withered away,
without and within the fire-demons consume us,
My heart is made barren with the sorrow of burning,
The pastoral dukes of aforetime will not hear us
neither will the bright god over heaven
permit me to lay down my charge.

6

The drought has parched into the depth,
I struggle, I labour and dare not retire.
Why comes this affliction upon us, mad with the heat,
We know not the reason.
We prayed early that there be harvest,
we have neglected no bourne of the Square,
O light that is high over welkin
this is not what we expected,
By my reverence for the bright spirits of air

they ought not to hate me.
I have had awe for the intelligence of the spirits
for the light in the air circumvolvent
they should not hold me under their anger.

7

The drought has parched deep into the earth,
the people are dispersed leaving no records,
the local governments are fallen to pieces,
the prime minister, the head of the horse-guards,
the head of the commissariat have broken down,
The great officers have done their utmost, no one has funked,
I look up to heaven, saying.
                              Where is the bourne?

8

I look up with awe to heaven,
the stars are like broom-straws and holes;
the great officers and the princes
shine as idly, giving no profit.
The great decree comes near to its term.
Do not cast off your precisions,
why seek in me the causes of local government troubles,
I look up with awe to heaven. How should it grant me rest?

V   (259)
SUNG, IN HONAN,
highest of the Five Peaks*

High, pine-covered peak full of echoes,
Proud ridge-pole of Heaven, roof-tree
whence descended the whirl of spirits
begetters of Fu and Shen,
Out of the echoing height, whirling spirits of air descended.
To sires of Chou were given in vassalage, bulwarks,
under the bright wings of the sun
a square kingdom against invasion,
Strong as the chamber of winds.

---

* To celebrate King Süan's appointment of the Marquis of Shen to defend
the South Border, Ode by Yin Ki-fu. Süan's time 826–781 B.C.

2

The King set task to Lord Shen
        who is as a full altar
to carry on in his service; to set city at Sie;
to be pattern to all the South States.
To the Earl of Shao he commanded saying:
Make smooth the way of Lord Shen
that he set house in the South Land
there to form the South state
and that coming ages maintain this labour.

3

And the King said to Lord Shen:
Be thou pattern to all the lands of the South,
make use of these men of Sie;
lift a pivot that shall not shake.
And to Earl Shao: Mark out the lands of Lord Shen
into fields.
And to the Master of Stewards:
settle men in these homesteads.

4

To Lord Shen the labour, and to Earl Shao
the building construction
to begin the town wall and the inner temple
(to roof perfectly temple and fane)
And when this labour was ended
he gave to Lord Shen four horses,
high steppers with gleaming harness and breast-hooks,

5

and a car of state with the horses, saying:
Our plan is your shelter,
there is no land like the South
I give you this sceptre whereon to raise up your treasure,
Go forth, Uncle Royal,
and maintain the lands of the South.

6

At Mei was the feast valediction
and the Lord Shen turned south
to form true homestead in Sie
And to Earl Shao he commanded
that he lay out Lord Shen's land divisions
and set provision stations in mountain passes
that there be no undue delay.

7

So the Lord Shen came to Sie
in due order with cohorts
with footmen and charioteers
and through all Chou was united rejoicing
for such solid defence and good bulwark.
Was not the Lord Shen as a sun drawing vapours,
the Royal Uncle, ensample in peace as in war?

8

And the Lord Shen acted on conscience
by mildness and probity bending the thousand states,
Be he famed to the four coigns of all things.
Ki-fu has made this song
the tune and the text of it
to be as a wind of healing
As his gift to the Lord Earl of Shen.

VI   (260)

Heaven of fire and water
making man
had stuff and plan;
put there matter and sheaf
took grip in seed
to natural good disposed.

Water above, fire beneath
so man had, from heaven, his breath,
                              a vapour,

matter and form compact,
seed and cord held intact

> to love

natural heart
> shown in act.

Sky saw the holder of Chou
clearly attent
on humble folk's betterment,
so made and sent
Chung Shan-fu
to maintain this Child of Nature
> in Chou.

2

Chung Shan was pattern of praise
handsome of face as of ways,
with a mind for the antient laws
ever detailed. In vigour of equity,
By his concord with the Sky's Child
an enlightened destiny prevailed.
> (And Chou's rule spread).

3

This was the King's command:
Chung Shan set hand
to form the hundred princes, and—
as from Chung's Source it was, and heritage—
to guard the king's body, promulgate, report;
be the king's tongue and throat;
levy, and govern outer borders and palatine,
that the four coigns keep line.

4

System in Royal decree,
in Chung Shan, aptitude
to know the states, good and not good,

astute to use his light,
to keep himself himself, uninterruptedly*
day, night,
serving the Monarchy.

5

"Eat soft, spit hard out," so the proverb says,
In Chung Shan's case, the rule was put in doubt.
Poor widows and fatherless were not insulted
Nor to encroaching bojars indulgence granted.

6

Men have a saying: 'Ware,
virtue is light as a hair,
few can lift it, most gaze
(contemplatively) at honour's ways.
Chung lifted it, and wd/ rely
on no man's affectionate partiality,
where failed straight letter of the King's decrees
Chung Shan-fu filled in the deficiencies
                                        (patched up the royal robe).

7

Cross-road sacrifice when
Chung Shan set out,
strong his teams.

Light of foot, in his battalions,
every man eager to pace the stallions,
"pang, pang" and
rein bells chink when Chung Shan-fu began
the great East wall
at the King's command.

8

Four fleet stallions on rein the
eight rein bells jangled away

---

* *Ta Hio*, K'ung 4.

when Chung Shan-fu went out to Ts'i,
Here 's a hope for his quick return,
Ki Fu lifts this neat bordone
with clear sound as wind over wheat
That Chung Shan's mind from labour long
may come to quiet at least in a song.

VII (261)

On Balk-hill high Yü began
terracing fields. That road, his way, still manifest,
so the Lord Han had his charge from the king direct:
"Ancestral right, but waste it not,
ever alert, by day, by night,
not easy to fence lands of the sort
whose lords come not to court,
thereby giving Us support."

2

With four great stallions tense
on rein, the Marquis of Han went to audience,
By royal grace held tally-mace, flag, palio;
got chequered car-screen and embossed brass yoke,
black robe, red shoes, and for his team,
breast hooks and frontlets engraved,
a leathered front-board with tiger-fell
and metal rein-rings as well.

3

At the cross-roads Han sacrificed,
nighted at T'u. Hien gave him the parting feast,
clear wine in an hundred jars, and large menu:
roast turtle and rare fish with garnishings,
sweet sprouts of young bamboo,
and, as a parting gift, team, chariot
and paraphernalia plates, as fits clan feast.

4

Kuei-fu's daughter, King Fen's niece,
Han had by hand such royal piece
to meet at Kuei's with an hundred teams,
bells a-din, catching the light.
The escort girls about her were like clouds
unto the Marquis' eye,
and the great wall-gate flamed with
that splendour of pageantry.

5

Kuei-fu by war, then, had passed thru
all states, none missed, and, when he sought
site for his daughter's homestead, knew
none to match Han in pleasauntness.
Rivers tend great greenness to send there,
fish in abundance be mid this fertility,
bream, tench. Doe and deer cry mating where
roams many a bear and great bear,
lynxes and tigers there be. His child Han Ki
could have, thus, home there delightfully.

6

Wide be the walls of Han,
Yen troops had capped them tight.
Font of this dynasty got charge
in causal time, mid hundred tribelets, to be lord,
Marquis of Han, over the Chui and Mo horde
and great lands North, to be
their Earl because of solid wall and moat,
ploughed lot and register
and pay tribute in pelts
of the white fox, red pard and yellow bear.

VIII   (262)
How Hugh Tiger of Shao went against the South Tribes,
over the Kiang (825 B.C.)

Kiang and Han
                    crashing along,

A river of men
        flowing as strong,
Never a stop,
        never astray,
When we went out a-hunting
        the wild tribes of the Huai,
Out with our cars
falcon-flags clack,
never a halt,
no broken rank,
when we marched to outflank
        the wild tribes of the Huai.

2

Turgid the waters of Kiang and Han,
a glitter of men
        flow rank upon rank.
As threads on a loom
        done as to plan,
We sent dispatches up to the throne:
"The four coigns are quiet,
in four coigns no riot,
Let the King's commons live quiet."
There was, so, for a time no unsettlement
and the King's mind was content.

3

By green Kiang banks,
By green Han banks
The King ordered Shao Tiger
to make model state administration:
open it all four square
for cultivation,
tithe and define,
with no sudden demands, no extortion,
but as Royal Domain to perfection utmost
set there bounds, forms and laws
even to the south sea-coast.

4

And the King commanded Hugh Shao:
Ten days, wide proclamation:
Wen and Wu received the Decree, and the Duke of Shao
was their bulwark.
Count me as a child, be thou like him,
go into function; judge;
make use of your fortune (the grant)
the light come to rest upon you.

5

"Measured to you that you should measure in turn
by sceptre-spoon, wine from the holy urn,
clear jade to lift out the black-millet's breath
that Wen above (spirits above) may know in Earth beneath
hills, lands and fields are set in your account
as from the ancestral fount in just accrue
take up this charge from Chou (in Chou)."
And as the grain bows, Hugh bowed then:
"Ten thousand years, Sky's son, to be thy span."

6

Low as the grain falls, with his head to ground
bowed Hugh: "Royal grace manifest,
let it so rise that the Great Duke may attest
it unto ten thousand years, Sky's Son,
in the brightness of his mentality
may the fame of his mind know no end;
as an arrow may his civilized insight penetrate
by act the four realms of the state."

IX   (263)

THE CONTINUING VALOR
Concerning King Süan's expedition against the Huai
further North, ode attributed to Earl Shao, Duke Mu,
hero of the preceding. The aim being comfort of the
border states of the Sü.

SPLENDOUR ON SPLENDOUR, LIGHT OF THE MIND TO
    ENLIGHTEN:
The King to his Minister,

Huang-fu of the line of Nan Chung*
High Commander:
That he set in order the six army corps;
That My weapons be sharpened;
That there be awe and a warning
as a kindness
to the States of the South (to defend them).

2

The King said to the Head of the Yin clan:
Order Hiu-fu Earl of Ch'eng to make flank defence
left bank and right bank,
to alert (police) all my regiments
that march by the reaches of Huai,
that he keep eye (care for) the lands of the Sü
that there be no dawdling and no billeting
and in the Three Services most exact coöperation
to the one end.

3

Splendid, dire, terrible in magnificence
the Imperial operation royally
stretched out, supported, aroused
with no gaps and no straggling,
ever deploying and prodding.
Sü land was shaken by the hooves of the cavalry
as sky under wings of thunder.

4

The King lifted his war might as a bird from a field nest,
as anger of thunder;
he sent out his tiger-dragoons
growling and roaring like tigers
they moved out ever more thickly by the sluices of Huai.

With captives ever more under paw
the Huai banks were sectioned
and King's arms there to hold them.

* For Nan Chung, vide Ode 168.

5

Many and thick moved the king's troops
as the wings of birds flying
(as the red plumes of the pheasant);
as flood of the Kiang and Han,
as the gnarled roots of the mountains,
as rivers o'erflowing
undulant as bright wheat, and continuous.
None could measure them, none could stay them
and they cleaned up Sü-land.

6

The king's candour was clear and continuous,
Sü land came into the kingdom
therein to have equal equities
by the work of Heaven's anointed,
Sü land was quiet,
The Sü came to the court-yard:
"In Sü there would be no twisting."
Whereon the King said they could go home.

X   (264)
Ascribed to the Earl of Fan, against King Yu, 780–770 B.C.

I look up with awe to the exigeant heaven
which hath no kindness to me-ward,
my unquiet is come to the full.
The sky presses down heavy as whetstone
nothing moves calm in this country
officers and folk are afflicted
boll-weevils in root and joint
gnaw, spread pestilence
and there is no end to this evil,
criminals are not apprehended,
there is no easy reform.

2

The Royal Domain has over-run private holdings;
if the feudal lords had retainers, you have usurped them;
the people are as birds in a net,

the innocent lie in the sprung trap of the stocks,
and the criminals walk up and down boasting.

3

Wise man rears a wall
and a sly bitch downs it,
so nice to look at, elaborate in contriving?
No. Dirty, an owl, her tongue long as a dust-storm.
The stair-way, confusion not descended from heaven
but up-sprung from women and eunuchs
from whom never good warning nor lesson.

4

They attack willful to injure, in this wise:
Their first slander passes unnoticed,
there is no bourne to their tattle,
as if a nobleman did not know the nature of usury
at three hundred per cent ("in the manner of trade")!
Keep the hens out of public business,
let 'em stick to silk-worms and weaving.

5

Why is the welkin thorny
that the powers of air do not bless us?
you even shelter the wild tribes of the North
and turn hate against me,
you do not look to the signs of the times,
you disregard justice,
men resign from their offices
and the uprooted state is worn out.

6

Heaven is come down like a net
all-taking, and men go dolorous into exile,
heaven is come down like a net
hardly-visible,
and men go into exile heart-broken.

7

High spouts the water, from the hornèd spring;
deep grief.
Neither before nor after but come now
that sky should work as mole beneath the grass
and nothing is
beyond its power to thong.
Wrong not the light that brought thy line to be
and might save, still, sons coming after thee.

XI   (265)
Attributed to the Earl of Fan

Compassionate heaven, O thou autumnal sky
hasty to awe, famine is here, now surely death draws nigh,
Folk die and flow to exile in the waste,
dead homes and stables are hidden beneath wild grass.

2

Heaven has let down a drag-net of ill-doing,
the locusts have gnawed us with word-work,
they have hollowed our speech,
Perverse alliances and continuing crookedness have divided us,
evil men are set above us, in ease.

3

Amid slanders and vain disputations
they see themselves flawless,
they know not their errors
they count on their not being seen,
emulous, ostentatious, cantankerous in their ostentation
by long disorder
the high offices are brought down.

4

As grass in a drought year
with nothing to water its shoots,
as cress in dry tree fork, dry as a bird's nest
so in this state
there is none not given to sabotage.

5

Former prosperity stood not on a chance of weather,
nor does calamity now.
They have dredged up their rice,
why don't they retire from office,
and the older ones first?

6

Pool dry without inflow,
Fountain dry without inner spring,
they have overflowed wide with their injuring,
they have engrossed and expanded their functions,
may they not overwhelm me.

7

When the king (Süan) got the Decree here before you
he had a Duke of Shao to uphold him
who brought the state an hundred *li* in one day;
Today they lose daily similar holding,
and as to the nature of sorrow
there are men who do not strive to grasp the antique.

PART FOUR

ODES OF THE TEMPLE AND ALTAR

Book 1. The Temple Odes of Chou
i. Ts'ing Miao

I (266)

Wholesome and clean the temple space
with health and clarity of the grain;
ordered the harmony and pace
that gentlemen sustain assembled,
gathering what King Wen's virtue sowed,
that is frankness of heart,
straight act that needs no goad.

He who is gone beyond is now the norm in sky,
the map and movement whereto these conform;
as is above, below,
not manifest, incarnate from our sires in span;
needs not dart forth, but is here present in man.

II (267)

Tensile is heaven's decree
in light and grain without end.
As the pure silk (that tears not)
was the insight of Wen,
and he acted upon it.
In its beauty are we made clear,
its beauty is our purification
              as we bow at the altar.
Be strong his line to the fourth generation,
may his great-grandsons be strong.

III   (268)

Clear, coherent and splendid,
King Wen's dissociations,
continuing use hath perfected,
they are bound in the felicitous program of Chou.

ALITER

Fluid in clarity,
from mouth to ear binding, scintillant;
scrupulous, enkindling,
King Wen's classifications initially
tracing the lines of our worship,
the spirit moves in their use;
hath brought them to focus.
Chou maintained their enlightenment.

IV   (269)

Ardent in refinement Lords-dividers, Lords-justices,
source of felicity, chthonian, and of abundant
kindness to us without bourne;
great-grandsons sustain this.

No tally-mace but to your state,
kings and clans think of merit and prowess
continuing solid this empery
effortless, binding humanity
that the four coigns obey.

Most manifest the insight that goes into action
in forming the whole state service,
thus the kings of old pass not into oblivion.

ALITER

The unviolent (or unwrangling) man
shall the four coigns obey,
whose lucid thought is in act, not in display.
On his instruction many princes form,
nor shall oblivion wreck this norm.

V   (270)

Sky raised this hill, high hill
T'ai Wang found waste, dressed (ruled).
Wen had his rest,
    beat its rocked trails to roads, K'i's roads
that his sons' sons maintain.*

VI   (271)

Dawn, dark, he laid the covert, close-packed foundation
            in coherence, in splendour
            twisted the cord of brightness;
            by his mind's oneness he
            built calm into Dynasty.

Light above heaven focussed the decree
doubly on dynasty (in Wen and Wu) then came
King Ch'eng, who daring never to rest
early or late, bulked in the bases,
close-knit, intimate,
coherent, splendid in ardour,
by his heart's singleness
spread order to the land's utmost recess.

VII   (272)

Hymn for princes at audience in the Hall of Light, end of
Autumn, sacrifice to God and King Wen.

            We bring, we give
            a ram and bull alive,
            Let heav'n stand right.
            King Wen's law is our light;
            Sun clears four coigns,
            that is Wen's joy.
            He's accepted.

            Day, night, in fear
            of heaven's majesty,
            our bread shall he be.

* K'i means a hill trail. The K'i are the dalesmen, alpini.

VIII   (273)

As spoken by the Duke of Chou on tour of inspection
after Wu's overthrow of Shang, and thence afterward
at commemorations (?)

"The legality of his kingship binds in
the continuity of the sovereignty."

In season to ride the bounds:
Light over sky through sky
       this son is its leaf.

Solid and dexter order holdeth Chou
at his light word to shake
and none shake not,
three fields (T'ien, Hao and Wei)
spirits awake; comply
as in his breast
so in hill crest
the powers of air attest
concord
to Huang Ho utterward;
Light to the mind from Chou
forming to all men that shall sit on thrones.

King in legality
continues his sov'reignty
"Lay down your weapons now
put by shield, lance and bow,
arrows also.

"I seek to nourish all,   (? considered as the
as my mind sees   King's words)
       may my deed fall."

"Hia outseasoning   (? oath in response, both
I swear to uphold the king."   by the Duke, or later
                                           commemorators, and the
                                           chief assistants?)

IX (274)

Great	hand	King	Wu
vied	not,	made	heat.
He	drew	not as	sun
rest	from	work	done.

Shang-	Ti	(over	sky)
king'd	our	Ch'eng and	K'ang;
bound	all	four	coigns;
hacked	clear	their	light.

Gong,	drum,	sound	out,
stone,	flute,	clear in	tone
ring	in	strong	grain;
bring	here	hard	ears.

Work,	true,	shall	pay.
As we've	drunk	we are	full,
Luck	ev-er	is and	shall
Come	with	new	grain.

X (275)

Think to thine art, Lord Grain.
By thy power to drink down
cup for cup of heaven's own
stablish thou us by damp and heat.
Without thee is naught complete,
barley and wheat from thee we cull,
Over-sky gave thee the rule
how to feed us. Lead us,
not by this field bourne held in,
that the fruitage ever run
in seasons of the Hia's sun.

The Temple Odes of Chou
ii. Ch'en Kung

I   (276)

Wards of the fields   respect the laws of grain
see that the tithe be just (as king, so laws)

Come test, come eat.

Aids of the wards   now is the end of spring,
what more's to seek
tho' field be old or new?

White's on the wheat,   come now 'tis clear as day
bright is the sky above
at last's to use the strong and quiet year.

Fate of our multitude, so tell them fate:
who readies his spud and hoe
shall not reap late. They mow beneath your eye
and light's aloft, packed tight
wheat grains are in ear.

Imperial wheat
receive their intelligence.

II   (277)

Augur, oh King Complete, by thy light's point,
gleam of the ray that falls from thee, at ease,
(We from the altar call)
lead on thy peasants all;
show sowing day.

Swift then and up in every family field,
grant that each thirty *li* of this tilled land yield
ten thousand rationings.
We plow by twos.

III (278)

Egrets to fly
to this West Moat,
guests at my portal
be such cause for joy.

No hate roots there,
and here in court no irk,
but as the seeds of motion are
to all their folk, early and late
cause praise.*

IV (279)

Full be the year, abundant be the grain,
high be the heaps composed in granaries,
robust the wine for ceremonial feast
and lack to no man be he highest or least,
neither be fault in any rite here shown
so plenteous nature shall inward virtue crown.

V (280)

Blind making sound,
much sound
in the temple court,
Chou's court,
carved frames
and tiger-stands,
high teeth
and rangèd plumes

Drum sound shall make the "field,"
stone gong, the "stall,"
with bamboo's ordered tones to "left" it all.
Lordly voice, played,
over-played
processional of sound

---

* *Ta Hio* IX.3.

reaching the shades
as their audition is
in this sound's mysteries.

Sound, blind sound,
teach our ancestral shades
where guests outside the gate
insatiate remain
desiring perfect sound
last,

Guest facing ghost
to time's utmost.

VI   (281)

CONSERVATION HYMN,
for the first month of winter

. . . θεῷ ἱερὸν ἰχθύν,
ὃν λεῦκον καλέουσιν, ὃ γάρ θ' ἱερτατος ἄλλων.

Lo, how our love of god is shown in fish,
here be all sorts in sacrificial dish
such as our grandsires' sires offered of old,
we have conserved them, manifold
blessings, held from age to age
by men who shun all forms of sacrilege.*

VII   (282)

Quiet as waters flowing in a moat
before great tripods princes move about.
The Son of Welkin stands as a field of grain.

Here is the great bull brought for sacrifice,
assistant manes round the altar rise,
O great white Source, O thou great sire of all
see how thy sons and theirs are filial.

---

* Icthyological dictionaries available to Karlgren give two kinds of stur-
geon. Legge ventures further: thryssa, mud-fish and yellow-jaws.

The constant voice shall all thy temple fill
for peace, for war, our conduct thy delight
as former Kings and latter wrought aright.

Bushy the brows of venerable age,
grant they be ours, O far, great spirit assuage!
Father and maker, that the spirits come
To prove they be not sundered in the tomb.

VIII   (283)

They come for talley-rods,
bright dragon-flags display'd
glittering, jangling
rein-bells, and dash boards.
Here be the princes
led to the fane,
Bright shone the ancestral eye,
filial this majesty.

Thick be the brows of age
so long sustain'd,
mind ye the imperial luck:
ardour, and skill, princes and dukes,
strands twined to felicity,
given coherence, given zeal
pure wealth and common weal be one
clear light on agèd altar stone.

IX   (284)
Welcome to the representative of the former dynasty,
Shang; this is shown by the dynastic colour of the horses

A guest, a guest and a white stallion,
his escort a battalion
honest to stand there as cut in stone,
guest for a night and a night, and twice,
right (whom we can trust, trust.)

Give him a tether to tether his team.
Left, right, courtiers gleam,
easy to say: reflect, recall,
go with him further on his course, meditate:
all quiet throughout the state—

that on his line, once loud in majesty
the heavens pour down untimed felicity.

X   (285)

Wu royal,
if we inherit
age-old quiet
'tis by his merit.

Not by envy in his zeal
Wu king'd the Imperial rule;

Wen by his learning won
what has been from that time on.

Wu had the heritage;
layed low Yin-Shang's rage by arms
and left to us our world of quiet farms.

The Temple Odes of Chou
iii. Tho' I be lytl (Min yü siao tsy)

I   (286)
KING CH'ENG

Tho' I be lytl, alas, come soon to care,
sick with its weight I hie
to the ancestral majesty
duty that lasts with lasting line for aye.

Tho' I be lytl, reverent I am
from dawn till night
of the high king's light,
the threads that he as our first preface wrought

shall not pass out of our thought
if so that thought
stand by the altar stone
where first it shone.*

II   (287)

I seek a bourne and stop mid river grass,
led by the gleam that my dead father lit;
follow the time's divisions that he set
and find no magic herb no *molu* yet.

I am not deep to rule such family cares,
move thou, my father's spryte,
up, down this court: bulk of my aid,
so be my body in bail to assure thy light.

III   (288)
CH'ENG, THE YOUNG KING,
on the monarch's duty to observe the seasons
and calendar

Awe is upon me,
thought from heaven pours down,
No light fate his who comes young to the crown,

Nor may I say that heaven is there, remote,
high there, unreached, aloft above my head
to mount and sink, star after star's scrutiny
enters our destiny.

I, but a child, must choose whereon to stand,
by sun, by moon, counting the sky's command;
study to know how men of old caught stars
and by their light
saw time to act, cleaving the wrong from right.

* 1116 B.C. *Shu* V.xiii; V.vii.

IV   (289)

Whenas my heart is filled with kings and deeds
seeking avoid the cause of new regret,
take not a wasp for bird that has no sting.
To see what moves, and snatch, solves nothing yet.
Wall built sans plan is wall soon over-set,
neither can rest who would always show wing.

V   (290)

Gainst high scrub oak and rathe to plow the marsh
pair'd plowmen went, attacking gnarl and root;
pacing low slough and ordered boundry dyke
what crowd is here: the master and his son,
aids, wives and food; strong ready neighbour men
sharpened the plows, so came south fields a-grain.

A power from far and silent in the shoot
see how the spirit moves within the corn
strong as a stallion, quiet as water on tongue.
Here be the stalks a-row, silky and white;
wave as a cloth beneath the common sun.

Ordered the grain and rich beyond account,
fit to distil to drink in sacrifice.
Let manes come to taste what we devise
agnate and cognate. As pepper to ease old age
here without altar shall be holiness
not now for new, but as it was of old
tho' tongue be light against the power of grass.

VI   (291)

Speed, speed the plow
on south slopes now
grain is to sow
                    lively within.

Here come your kin,
baskets round
baskets square,
millet 's there.

With a crowd of rain-hats
and clicking hoes
out goes the weed
to mulch and rot
on dry and wet,
crop will be thicker on that spot.

Harvest high,
reapers come by
so they mow
to heap it like a wall
comb-tooth'd and tall

an hundred barns to fill
till wives and childer fear no ill.

At harvest home kill a yellow bull,
by his curved horn is luck in full
(be he black-nosed seven foot high,
so tall 's felicity.)

Thus did
men of old
who left us this land
to have and to hold.

VII   (292)
Probably for the day after sacrifice to the representatives
of the ancestors

Let robes be of bright silk,
caps reverent worn.
From hall to gate-house base,
from ram to bull,
from great tripod to small

bear the great rhino-horn of holy curve.
Sweet the wine,
be gentler still thy mind. If now
thy thought be sage
it shall sustain thee in thine old age.

VIII   (293)
δικαιοσύνη
To conclude a dance in honour of Wu

A delight of metal was the king's host,

he obeyed the seasons,
he provisioned when the sun lay dark in the matrix.

In the day of purity and of ardour
he used the Great Intervention
when the sun lay plumb on the dial.

We dragoons receive (favoured) what the high king built,
may we use his dissociations.

Be justice the basis of faith
in this army.

IX   (294)
Sung in connection with a dance to Wu, and, in
declarations of war, to the war god. Said to date from
the time of King K'ang.

Tranquil'd* ten thousand states,
year after year of abundance,
that the heavenly ukase change not,
the horn was not cut off.

O dawn in the forest,
steady sun amid boughs,
Wu,

* *Shu* V.vii.

King,
guaranteed there should be such officers,
the four coigns to have quiet.

Calm was
in his house
that its light gleamed up to heaven,
filling the space between. He was Emperor
as if at his ease.*

X   (295)

Said to contain the formula used by Wu in
granting fiefs in the Dynastic Temple

> When the season was full
> to the sun's turn
> the silk was unravelled.

King Wen worked where he was
(established position)

We properly answer; receive.

Spread with the sun's turn
due order of thought into the uttermost.

We go out to seek the quiet procedure,

the time of Chou is of destiny
to the utmost order of thought.

XI   (296)

"THE P'AN," that is, the "transport song,"
which I take to mean the one used
when carrying the talley-jades
to Wu and to his successors
in his capital

> In bright season
> Chou was risen;
> mounting High Mount,

* *Analects* VIII.xvii (VIII.xxi).

passing Proud Mount
crag to echo on peak of Mount Yo.

Wings of water in Ho
packed thick, ever to flow
over all spread
neath Heaven's lid.

Gather the talleys at turn of the sun.
Time, Chou, and fate are one.*

Book 2. The Horse Odes of Lu
εὔιππος

I   (297)
KIUNG KIUNG MU MA

Wild at grass the bull horses
move over moor-land,
black-rump'd and roans,
all-blacks and bays,
a splendour for wagons, unwinded.
Phang! Phang! I'll say some horses!!

2

Strong, sleek, move wide over moor-land, bull horses
dapple, piebald and bay,
strong on the traces
mixed white hair and yellow,
there is no end to his thinking of horse power.

3

At graze over moor-land strong stallions
whites and bays with black manes
and white-maned black stallions

---

* *Shu* V.xiii, 24; "in response to the people."

pull with due order, unwinded;
Our lord's thought is unflagging
for the breeding of horses.

4

Wide over moor-land at grass the bull horses
iron-grey, sleek, calico, dapple
fish-eyed great stallions for cars,
So our lord's thoughts bite
and his cavalry charges.

II   (298)

YU PI

Strong sleek   roan teams
That seek   the duke
To light his government,
day, night,
so do the egrets wheel ere they alight.
Drum beat and dance
maintain delight with wine.

2

Sleek stallions   and strong
early and late   to court
bring men, drums, wine. Men
come, go, come yet again
as egrets on the wing
and take their firm delight.

3

Strong sleek   gray teams
that seek   the duke,
stand near the banquet hall.
Be this inaugural: vintage to plenteous years
and to the prince sound grain
that his line maintain
for sons unto sons in ever firm delight.

III (299)
P'AN SHUI

Joy by the sickle-pool, cress there to gather,
Lord Lu approaches, his flags together, the dragon banners
wave as the cress-leaves; horse bells clear sounding,
none seeking precedence, pell-mell yet orderly
all for long riding.

2

As thought delights in water
by the half-circling pool
picking pond-weed,
hooves clicking clearly
high feet of horses:
clear his fame, clear his face,
clear his laugh is, to teach without anger
in this place.

3

Mallows beside the pool are light to gather,
Lord Lu approaches for wine and feasting.
Heavy the wine to lighten age,
by the long pilgrimage
wild tribes were bent to the sage.

4

As a white field of grain, Lord Lu
acting by light
of his insight
respecting straightness
in awe of the equities, the people's canon and rule,
loyal in peace, in war
before the fane brilliant to carry on,
a filial son,
what the Lord of the Cartouche began,
seeking in himself felicity,
antient lucidity.

5

Clear was the mind of Lu, his insight
guided his acts aright;
raised then this college by the crescent pool.
The wild Huai came neath his rule.
Tiger dragoons bring trophies here;
captive by pool-brink risketh an ear;
as by Kao-Yao the questioning,
brought to the water's encircling.

6

Officers to assembly defined
spread Lu's type of mind,
inwit to act; so, when they attacked,
swept out to East and South
by zeal and clarity o'erthrowing barbary,
neither with shouting nor with splurging
nor with recourse to military tribunals
as faithful retrievers brought their deeds to this pool.

7

The long, horned bows
volley compact,
in the cars' manège war-skill appears
uniting unwinded
infantry and charioteers, overswept Huai.
Till here
be now tillers who were vagrant rebels aforetime,
as solidly planned, the Huai are now faithful dependents.

8

Wild flapping owls flock'd to the crescent's trees
eating their fill of the grove's mulberries,
have now our tone proper at heart.
The Huai, that is, learnt civilities, in art
and in exchange bring rarities,
tusk and tooth ivories
and tortoise shells
with southern metal for crucibles.

IV   (300)
LORD GRAIN

The secret temple is still and consecrate,
solid the inner eaves.
From limpid thought to act
Kiang Yüan moved straight
till the awesome sky
filled her with its progeny.
Nor ill, nor hurt, nor distant moon's delay
hindered, so she brought forth Hou Tsi.

The hundred boons descend by Tsi:
millet and grain by him do multiply,
thick grain and panicled, the early and late
(early for bread, the late for sacrifice).

By pulse and wheat
Tsi got a state
tho' small, he taught the people all
to sow and reap
the early grain and the late, the rice, the black
the whole earth through;
followed the work of Yü.

2

Of Hou Tsi's line came T'ai,
king on south slopes of K'i,
first to trim jactancy
of overweening Shang.
Then Wen and Wu concluded that King T'ai began,
neath heaven's governance and hour
by Wu's ado:
"Have no split aim, nor doubt"
in Mu
plain polished off Shang:
"God's eye, and Shang's at end."

In this work all had part*
and the King said: Shu Fu, unkle,

* *Chung Yung* XXVI.7.

your eldest son
shall be Marquis of Lu
and your great opening house shall be
wheel-aid to Chou.

3

Thus was the Marquis made lord of the East,
to him the hills and streams in lasting fief.
Now Duke Chuang's son
of Chou duke's line
comes with the dragon-flags to sacrifice,
holding the six tough reins.

Spring, Autumn, there is no break
nor ever error in this sacrifice
to the holy sky, its power
and to Hou Tsi, first ancestor.
Red bulls are slain, unsplotched, approved
by the high powers, moved
to light and plenty, and is
Chou's spirit here adjoint
to Sky and Tsi.

4

For the Autumnal rite,
in summer, bulls, one white
two red, wear boards across their horns
to keep them whole.
The great libation jars
are prepared and one 's shaped like a bull.
Boil'd and roast pig, minced meat and soup
are set on stand in great and little trays.
A thousand dancers in maze
assert the heir prosperous.
Thus, eager, in fane, wave after wave
of the dance portrays:

long life and steadfastness,
stay of the Eastern State
That Lu be regulate

'thout fail or fall
'thout shake or quake
three antient friends shall stand
solid as crags and balks
to uphold thy hand.

5

So the Duke has a thousand cars,
Red the tassel, green the bow-band,
heavy the bows, two lances stand
upright in every car,
thirty thousand of infantry,
casques with red strings of cowries' shells
in regiments compact, act;
breast the wild tribes, the dogs,
north, west, King, Shu, and war
none dares before
Chou's arms.

6

Honour and glory and long years to fleck
hair faded yellow, the plump round back
and old cronies for argument,
who still know what that glory meant,
to be old with you in governance
endless years as a thousand pass
and in those years
under old brows, no injuries.

High holy T'ai-Shan mounts o'er craggy Lu,
"Turtle-" and "Cover-heights" we passed through
overgrowing the waste Great East
till we came to the salt sea coast,
There the wild Huai were evened out,
nowhere the allegiance left in doubt.
Lord Lu worked it so.

7

Upholder of Yi and Fu, both,
overlord of the House where had fallen Sü

and so came to the salt sea coast
Huai and the wild men of Man and Mo
and yet further the southern hordes
acknowledged these overlords, Lu.

8

Heaven assigned him such unmixed rule,
and in his age, that he uphold Lu state
to live in Shang and Hü, resume Chou Duke's domain,
Lord Lu
that he feasts in joy
with mother grown old and spouse,
his proper great lords and officer corps
of states and lands to have and bequeath
that many and all have felicity
with old men's hair and children's teeth.

9

Pines of Tsu-lai,
Cypress of Sin
were trimmed to measure and brought in,
cut to eight feet by one foot square,
with their pine beam-horns and carven heads
lofty in chamber and corridor.
The new sun temple intricate
Hi Sy raised it, high and great,
ten thousand may it accommodate.

Book 3. The Odes of Shang
This being the oldest part of the Anthology

I   (301)

NA

Thick, all in mass
bring drums, bring drums
bring leather drums and play

to T'ang, to T'ang
source of us all, in fane
again, again, pray, pray:
Tang's heir, a prayer
that puts a point to thought.

With thud of the deep drum,
flutes clear, doubling over all,
concord evens it all, built on
the stone's tone under it all.
T'ang's might is terrible
with a sound as clear and sane
as wind over grain.

Steady drum going on,
great dance elaborate,
here be guests of state
to us all one delight.

From of old is this rite
former time's initiate,
calm the flow
early and late
from sun and moon concentrate
in the heart of every man
since this rite began.

Attend, attend, bale-fire and harvest home,
T'ang's heir at the turn of the moon.

II   (302)

KYRIE ELEISON
father of all our line
KYRIE ELEISON!

Vintage in autumn, light of old,
iterate and no end,
be this in every man, and be thou here.

We have brought clear wine,
reward our exact thought;
our broth's to taste,

cut herbs in proper blend,
set on the stand in silence utterly,*
set in the dish and no word spoke the while:
peace in our time,

let our brows age with the years
nor be our death when they be wrinkled with time.

Muffled the axles, studded the yokes,
eight bells with little strokes
sound the approaching sacrifice.
We had our fate of sky, ready to wide.

Calm came from sky,
abundance by aiding grain,
year after year full grain.

Come to the fane and feast
that plenty ever descend, attend,
Bale fire and harvest home,
T'ang's heir at the turn of the moon.

III (303)
BLACK SWALLOW

At heaven's command
came the black swallow down
and Shang was born;
came the black swallow down
that Shang should wear the crown
in Yin, mid bearded grain, Yin plenteous.

Of old Sky told war's T'ang
to build up walls (measure the land) four square
that was the "square decree" and
thru the Nine Parts utterly
all things were squared.

---

* *Chung Yung* XXIII.4.

Shang, the first dynasty,
never in jeopardy
stood here to Wu Ting's heir,
in Wu Ting's heirs, war's kings
having no overlords.

Ten dragon banners ride
to our high altar side
for great grain rite, father to son.

The king's domain is of a thousand *li*
that is the people's rest
and their fixed point,
all lands are measured thence
to the four seas' defence,
whence come to fane
to serve the surrounding airs
in Capitol, by Ho the bounding stream, true officers.

Yin had the high decree
rightly, as things should be
The hundred rents pour in
rightly to Yin.

IV   (304)

Out of the deep Shang's wisdom was,
long urged of stars.
Yü alone stood
gainst the great flood, and spread
it wide by the long watershed;
bounded great outer states.
Sung waits, meanwhile, its moon
till heaven chose girl to bear
Shang for an heir.

2

Dark king of the ready hand
had statc with little land,
made that great, and, in the greater state
trod down on no man's right;
followed the light with deeds.
Siang-T'u in those days
swept back the wild sea's Malays.

3

The Sky's decree inviolate
stood until T'ang all orderly.
T'ang, not a day too late
came, sage, full of awe to trace
footsteps of the measuring sun
till to the very altar stone
came light deliberate.
As sky respects this order processional
so be it model, in fate,
to the earth's nine parts in all.

4

Received a small state's talley and then the great
split jade of office. Lesser fiefs
hung there like tassels on his falcon flag.
Neither contending
nor with covetousness
neither too hard
nor lax in softness,
spread his rule, tranquilly
an hundred rents flowed to his treasury.

5

Had tribute jade in lesser and great assess,
stud stallion of lesser states, a favouring dragon cloud
spread round his power
not by the thunder shock
nor heaving abrupt
but with calm confidence in his mind's use
augmented an hundred-fold his revenues.

6

The warrior king set flag upon his car,
had pity, gripped his axe and blazed to war.
None dared
stand our shock.
Three sucking shoots clamped round the King of Hia,
a stump (a block, dead wood)
None moved, none understood
(had news) in Hia.
So all the nine great holds were ours utterly,
Wei, Ku, cut down; K'un's Wu and Hia's Kie.

7

Once with time's leaf half grown
came quake and shake
whereon the heavens sent down
A-Heng* to aid the Imperial Crown,
Shang's bulwark and defence to be
solid at all points dexterously.

V   (305)

Of Yin-Wu the swift scourge,
How he fell upon King-Ch'u;
passed thru the gorges and blocked them;
bottled the King hordes and trimmed them,
thread of Shang's line, a successor,
                    OYEZ!

"O ye of King-Ch'u
that dwell in the south parts of my kingdom,
whom T'ang of old set in true order
so that even unto Ti-Kiang (the far tribes)
none dared not come to the cauldron of sacrifice
nor avoid the king's judgement:
Say now that Shang endures."

* Yi-Yin. *Shu* IV.4, 5, 6.

Heaven has ordained many princes,
with capitals as Yü span (and defined)
the year's works be brought to the fold
"Forfend calamity,
we have sowed and stored without interruption."

Sky ordered decent and inspection:
Attend to the folk below
without usurpations, without extravagance,
nor venture to loll back in leisure.
He commanded the lower states,
and the feudal states by seal, there was happiness.

Shang's capital high in the air and quiet,
ridge-pole to the four coigns,
Splendour of fame to Shang,
clear, washed clear in his sensitivity to prognostic
as of wings and of water;
his old age was contentment
that he sustain our kind of posterity.

They went up the King mountain,
straight trunks of pine and cypress
they cut and brought here,
hewed pillars and rafters
carved pine beam-horns ornate
contrived pillars and sockets
to the inner shrine, perfect
that his ray come to point in this quiet.

ELEKTRA

A PLAY BY
EZRA POUND
AND
RUDD FLEMING

DRAMATIS PERSONAE

TUTOR	*to Orestes*
ORESTES	*son of Agamemnon and Klytemnestra*
ELEKTRA	*daughter of Agamemnon and Klytemnestra*
CHORUS	*of Mycenean women*
CHRYSOTHEMIS	*sister of Elektra and Orestes*
KLYTEMNESTRA	*Queen of Argos and widow of Agamemnon*
AEGISTHUS	*Klytemnestra's lover and accomplice*
PYLADES	*silent friend to Orestes*

Scene: *at Mycenae, in front of Agamemnon's palace*

TUTOR

Well, here's where your father landed when he
got back from the Trojan war, this is where you
wanted to come to;
Old Argos over there
where the gad-fly chased Miss Inachus,
and that's the Lukeum, named after the wolf-god,
the wolf-killer, market place now;
and Hera's church on the left
everybody's heard about that.
Down below there: Mycene,
centre of the gold trade,
and Pelop's palace, the throne room
where the dirty murder was done.
That's where I picked you off your dad's
bloody body,
that is to say your kind sister
did, and give you to me to take off and raise
like a proper avenger.

And now, Orestes, it's up to you
and your dear friend Mr Pilades, stranger in these parts.
Get goin' quickly.
Sun's risin', birds are a singin',
stars going down, darkness broken,
Get going before people start moving about
and be clear in your own minds what you're up to.

ORESTES

All right, old Handy,
you sure have stuck with us
like a good ole horse rarin' for battle,
urgin' on and keepin' right forward
up in front every time.
This is what we're agoin' to do,
listen sharp and check up if
I miss any bullseyes.

When I went off to the Pythoness
to ask about doin' right by my father
Phoebus answered:

Dont start a war,
take a chance, do it yourself:
Kinky course, clean in the kill.

Now as that's the oracle that we heard
the first chance you get
you nip into this building, find out everything that's
going on there, and keep us wise to the lot of it. Snap.
Nobody'll recognize your old block
after all these years, under all this herbage
Make yr cock-crow
You've come here from their best pal Phanoteus
first time you've ever been out of Phocia.
Swear that Orestes was killed in a chariot race
at the Pythians. Put in the details.

We'll go to dad's tomb, as ordered
with libations an' all my pretty curls
we'll bring back that nice brass urn
we hid in the underbrush
to back up the yarn that I'm dead
and buried
and this dust all that is left of me.
They'll like that.
I dont mind being dead that way
if I can live on into honour.
I dont suppose the lie will ruin our luck
not the first time a wise guy
has said he was dead
in order to get a warm welcome;
and if it lets me bust out afterward
and explode 'em.

Earth of the fatherland
bless the roads we have come by
for the old home and this clean up,

the gods are in me to do this,
clean the old home
that I be not sent back into exile dishonoured
give back the heritage
that I bring back the old rule of abundance
and make it solid.

Nuff talk. Get in there, old buck, and
keep steady
We'll be out here and watch for the moment,
the time.
            Best leader men have.

ELEKTRA
Oh, oh, I'm so unhappy.

TUTOR
Some slavey howling, inside there

ORESTES
Poor Elektra, might be,
wanna stay and listen?

TUTOR
Certainly not. Get our bearings first
as Loxias ordered. Holy water to wash up
the tomb-stone.
That's the way to win out.

ELEKTRA
OO PHAOS HAGNON
                    Holy light
Earth, air about us,
                    THRENOON OODAS
                    POLLAS D'ANTEREIS AESTHOU
tearing my heart out
when black night is over
all night already horrible
been with me
my father weeping

there in that wretched house
weeping his doom
Not killed abroad in the war
but by mother and her bed-boy Aegisthus.
Split his head with an axe as
a woodcutter splits a billet of oak,
and that killed him
and nobody else in this house seems to mind.
Well I'm not going to forget it
and the stars can shine on it, all of them
tears of hate
all flaming rips of the stars
tide
destiny
and the day can look on it
I wont stand it and just keep quiet
                    ALL' OU MEN DE
                    LAEXOO THRENOON
You cant stop a nightingale crying, for her young, or me
on this house porch
let everyone hear it
Hell and Persephone
                    OO DOOM' AIDOU
OO CHTHONI' Hermes, Oh Queen of Avenging
                    ARA, O Vengeance
Hear me
ye that watch over shed blood,
over murder, over the usurping of beds
CURSE, and hear me
god seed, ye Erinnys, of doom
aid and defend us, avenging our father's death

HAI TOUS ADIKOOS THNEISKONTAS HORATH'
HAI TOUS EUNAS HUPOKLEPTOMENOUS
ELTHET' AREXATE TISASTHE PATROS
PHONON HEMETEROU
KAI MOI TON EMON PEMPSAT' ADELPHON

MOUNE GAR AGEIN OUKETI SOOKOO
LUPES ANTIRROPON ACHTHOS

   (*sinks onto step*)

and
send me my brother
I can do no more on my own
this grief is too heavy

   CHORUS
OO PAI PAI DUSTANOTATAS
ELEKTRA MATROS TIN' AEI
TAKEIS OOD' AKORESTON OIMOOGAN
TON PALAI EK DOLERAS ATHEOOTATA
MATROS HALONT' APATAIS AGAMEMNONA
KAKAI TE CHEIRI PRODOTON HOOS HO TADE
   POROON
OLOIT' EI MOI THEMIS TAD' AUDAN

Poor Elektra
you had a curse for a mother
and are withered with weeping,
Agamemnon was tricked and murdered.
That was a long time ago,
but a dirty hand did it, maternal,
and to breed their destruction
if my deem is heard in dooming.
            EI MOI THEMIS TAD' AUDAN

      ELEKTRA (*quasi sotto voce*)
Yes, you are come nobly to help me,
I can feel that,
But I must go on.
DEAD, he is dead, I must go on
OO GENETHLA GENNAIOON
HEKET' EMOON KAMATOON PARAMUTHION
OIDA TE KAI XUNIEMI TAD' OU TI ME

PHUNGANEI OUD' ETHELOO PROLIPEIN TODE
ME OU TON EMON STENACHEIN PATER' ATHLION
ALL' OO PANTOIAS PHILOTETOS AMEIBOMENAI
   CHARIN
EATE M' OOD' ALUEIN
AIAI HIKNOUMAI
(*to Chorus*) It's my job,
I have never asked to neglect it
let me go on alone

   CHORUS
But you wont get him back out of black hell
by praying and groaning,
you wear yourself out with too much of it,
no harm to let up for a little

   (*emphatic and explicit with meaning to ram it in*)

ALL' OU TOI G' EX AÏDA
PANKOINOU LIMNAS PATER' AN-
STASEIS OUTE GOOISIN OUT' EUCHAIS
ALL' APO TOON METRIOON EP' AMECHANON
ALGOS AEI STENACHOUSA DIOLLUSAI
EN HOIS ANALUSIS ESTIN OUDEMIA KAKOON
TI MOI TOON DUSPHOROON EPHIEI
nothing to be DONE AMEXANON about it
why do you want to make it all the harder?

   ELEKTRA
It wd/ be childish just to forget him,
I'd be a ninny. Carried off that way
          a ITUN aien Itun.
NEPIOS HOS TOON OIKTROOS
OICHOMENOON GONEOON EPILATHETAI
ALL' EME G' HA STONOESS' ARAREN PHRENAS
HA ITUN AIEN ITUN OLOPHURETAI
ORNIS ATUDZOMENA DIOS ANGELOS
IOO PANTLAMOON NIOBA SE D' EGOOGE NEMOO
   THEON

HAT' EN TAPHOOI PETRAIOOI
AIEI DAKRUEIS
I think my mind groans as the sound of Itys
lamenting, terrified,
bringing the news from Zeus
Niobe weeping in a stone tomb
has a better portion from heaven
weeping forever.
AT EN TAPHO PETRAIOO
AIEI DAKRUEIS.

CHORUS
OUTOI SOI MOUNAI TEKNON
ACHOS EPHANE BROTOON
Not only you, dear,
everyman alive's got his load
PROS HO TI SU TOON ENDON EI PERISSA
HOIS HOMOTHEN EI KAI GONAI XUNAIMOS
HOIA CHRUSOTHEMIS DZOOEI KAI IPHIANASSA
poor Chrysothemis, Iphianassa
KRUPTAI T' ACHEOON EN HEBAI
and yr/ boy brother
in exile
god send 'un back to Mycenae
OLBIOS HON HA KLEINA
GA POTE MUKENAIOON
DEXETAI EUPATRIDAN DIOS EUPHRONI
BEMATI MOLONTA TANDE GAN ORESTAN

(*English echo*)

till Orestes come to the t h r o n e

ELEKTRA
whom I keep on expecting,
childless, wretched,
unwed, in a dither of fear
muddly with tears,
one thing after another, unending, and always worse;
and he's forgotten all

that's ever happened to him or been told him
every message I get is a cheat
always he wants to come
and never shows up

    CHORUS (*chorus moving/ clear cut position: pause/ move*)
THARSEI MOI THARSEI TEKNON
ETI MEGAS OURANOOI
ZEUS HOS EPHORAI PANTA KAI KRATUNEI
HOOI TON HUPERALGE CHOLON NEMOUSA
METH' HOIS ECHTHAIREIS HUPERACHTHEO MET'
    EPILATHOU
CHRONOS GAR EUMARES THEOS
OUTE GAR HO TAN KRISAN
BOUNOMON ECHOON AKTAN
PAIS AGAMEMNONIDAS APERITROPOS
OUTH' HO PARA TON ACHERONTA THEOS
    ANASSOON

    ELEKTRA
Hopeless and there's no help,
wasted already, gone by in despair
no going back on that
fatherless
loverless
housed neath my father's bed
kenneled and fed on trash
in a shapeless sack.

    CHORUS (*chorus moving/ pause/ move*)
THARSEI MOI etc. . . . . ANASSOON.

    ELEKTRA
gone, gone so much,
hopeless and no redress
gainst time that's gone, nothing to ward that off
fatherless, loverless, without stand-bye
a worthless waif,

roofed where my father wed;
in a shapeless sack,
to stand around the empty tables
and to be fed on their trash.

CHORUS

She'd a gloomy voice when he came;
and a gloomy sound when the brass axe hit him,
on the couch there in his dining-room.
A twisty idea
and a letch that killed him,
one vehemence led to another
procreating the form
whether god or man did it.

ELEKTRA

That was the vilest of all days
and that night at dinner was worse,
beyond speakable language,
horrible
I saw my father killed by the pair of 'em,
and insulted.
Bitched my life, that did, that betrayal.
Zeus avenger, don't let 'em enjoy it unpunished,
make it hurt. Them in their luxury! Agh!

CHORUS

Hush. Stop sounding off or talk sense,
Quit piling troubles one on top of the other
always making a row with that grouch of yours
Dont take the discussable to the powerful

only give 'em a handle.

ELEKTRA (*starts as if muttering*)

DEINOIS ENANKASTHEN
It's too horrible, I cant keep it in
I know you mean well, it's no use.
Go away and leave me alone,
let me have my cry out.

CHORUS

But, dearie, you only make it all worse,
I'm talkin' to you like a mother,
                    you can trust me

ELEKTRA

Is there any limit to the nature of misery?
Is there anything pretty about neglecting the dead?
Has that idea cropped up anywhere among men?
If so I dont want their respect
and if I come near to getting any good from it
may I not live tranquil among 'em
by smothering my keening for the shame of this house.
For if the dead lie down—earth and then—nothing,
wretched
and there be no death for a death
shame wd go wrack,
all duty wd end & be nothing

CHORUS

I rushed out here for your sake as well as mine
if you dont like what I say, have it yr/ own way
we'll stick by you.

ELEKTRA

I'm sorry, I oughtn't to let 'em get me down,
but I am driven.
They've got the power, all I can do is yammer
and make too much noise.
I'm ashamed of this clatter.
How cd/ any decently brought up girl
see that done to her father, and act any different?
I see it day and night getting thicker, not dying down,
and my own mother the most loathsome of all
and I have to live in the same house with
the people who murdered my father
and have 'em pushing me round
WHACK, take it, WHACK, leave it,
always the same, which ever way they've hexed it.
How do you think I pass my time, anyhow?

when I see Aegisthus sitting there
in my father's chairs
even wearing his clothes
pouring libations
right by where he killed him
then havin' mother right there in the same bed
just to show off, a whore, a mother? call it
a concubine
she's got so used to the dirty slob,
no longer scared of the curse
celebrates with a dance once a month
with a whole sheep for "his" dinner.
Joke that is
         but it gets me down all the same.
And I go moulder in an attic
and blubber over "Agamemnon's bean-O," yes
they call it by old pop's name.
can't even have my cry out in peace
with that old big-talk bawling me out:
"You the only slut ever lost a father,
nobody else has any troubles,
go rot and keep on yowling in hell."
That's how she goes on
EXCEPT when someone says Orestes is comin'
then she gets scared and blows her top proper
goes shoutin' frantic:
"You got him away, it's all your fault,
you cheated me out of Orestes, you sneak,
mark my word,
you'll get your come-uppence."
That's her bark, and her ponce sicks her on,
         marvelous,
of all the dastardly yellow pests,
fightin' from under her skirts
and me rotting away, waiting here for Orestes
to put a stop to it all.
and he's worn out all hope, by waiting,
dither and dally,
yes, my dears, a nice place for moderation and decency
and with all this rot I've gone rotten.

CHORUS
Is Aegisthus here, while you're talkin'?

ELEKTRA
Naturally NOT. Think I could get out, with him in?

CHORUS
Well then, I can say what I think.

ELEKTRA
He's out, you can say what you like.

CHORUS
Well about yr/ brother, is he coming or not?

ELEKTRA
Sez he will an' he dont.

CHORUS
A man's likely to take his time on a big job.

ELEKTRA
If I'd gone slow, he wdn't be there to take it.

CHORUS
Hang on, he was born honest,
he wont let you down, cares too much

ELEKTRA
If I didn't think that, I'd be dead.

CHORUS
Sshh, here comes yr/ sister.
I see she's carrying . . . eh. . . . offerings,
like for DOWN THERE (*points downward*) all very proper.

CHRYSOTHEMIS (*tone of thorough weariness, and
        discouragement*)
Oh Dear, are you out here again, sounding off,
never learn, makes it worse

let out every fool feeling you got in yr/ gizzard.
I dont like the mess any better than you do,
If I could get hold of the power
I'd show 'em what I think,
but for the present I'm going to let down my sail
pipe down, and not think I'm hurting 'em when I'm not.
and I advise you to do the same
What I say to 'em isn't so, and what you think is,
but I've got to obey in order to keep my freedom of action.

ELEKTRA

It's just awful the way you take her part
and forget him.
YOU didn't think of any of that
it's just what she told you.
you can do one of two things: be honest and speak out,
or play dumb and forget your friends
You just said if you had the power
you'd show how you hate 'em
but when I'm all out to do right by my father,
will you come in on it? No. You try to put me off it.

(*pause: very clearly enunciated: different tempo: pausing
between each word*)

Need we add cowardice to all the rest of this filth?

Tell me, or lemme tell you what good it cd/ do me
to stop objecting out loud
I'm not dead yet, it's a dirty life
but my own.
It annoys 'em. That honours the dead,
if the dead get any joy out of *that*.
You say you hate 'em, but
you play ball with our father's assassins
Well I wdn't knuckle under, not for one minute
nor for all this stuff they have given you

*(takes hold of Chrysothemis' bangles or bracelet, or what-
ever ornament, or fine dress—some smallish ornament, in
contrast to Klytemnestra's overload)*

that you swank about in.
　　　Have yr/ big dinners, comforts
and everything easy,
　　　your lie-down flow-about life.
If I don't eat, I don't make myself spew with disgust.
Keep my self-respect anyhow
I wouldn't want to have a sense of honour like yours
nor wd/ you if you understood it
you're even called by your mother's name
when you cd/ use father's
　　　　　　　　and he was some good
best of the lot of 'em.
It dont look nice.
most people wd. say you are going back
on yr/ dead father, and the people you care for.

CHORUS
For the gods' sake, keep your tempers,
there's something to be said on both sides
if either of you cd/ learn from the other.

CHRYSOTHEMIS
Oh, I'm used to the way she goes on.
I wouldn't have come here now, but she's in worse danger,
in fact they want to stop her howls once and for all.

ELEKTRA
Well what can be worse? If you'll tell me
anything worse, I'll shut up.

CHRYSOTHEMIS
All I know is that if you dont quit bawling
they'll shut you up where you'll never see daylight
in some black jail outside the country,
do stop to think, and dont blame me
whcn it's too latc.

ELEKTRA
So that's what they're up to.

CHRYSOTHEMIS
As soon as Aegisthus gets back

ELEKTRA
The sooner the better

CHRYSOTHEMIS
So he can?
You're off yr/ poor head. What for?

ELEKTRA
To get away from the lot of you
as far as possible

CHRYSOTHEMIS
But at least you're alive here?

ELEKTRA
A beautiful life, something for me to admire

CHRYSOTHEMIS
Might have been if you'd learned to adjust yourself

ELEKTRA
Don't educate me up to double crossing my friends.

CHRYSOTHEMIS
I'm only telling you to bend and not break
when you come up against power.

ELEKTRA
Slobber over 'em. Not my way.

CHRYSOTHEMIS
It's perfectly respectable not to fail
out of sheer stupidity.

ELEKTRA
All right I'll fail, for my father's honour
if it's so ordered.

CHRYSOTHEMIS
I am sure he'd excuse one.

ELEKTRA
You commend everything nasty.

CHRYSOTHEMIS
Well I suppose you wont listen to anything I say
let alone agree with it.

ELEKTRA
Probably NOT. Not yet such a zero.

CHRYSOTHEMIS
Well, I'll be moving along.

ELEKTRA (*noticing the offerings for the first time, having
been up to now absorbed in her own fury*)
Goin' far?
What you carrying THAT for,
　　　　all roasted?

CHRYSOTHEMIS
Mother told me to go water the grave.

ELEKTRA
What!! and nobody whom she hates worse?

CHRYSOTHEMIS
You mean the one she murdered

ELEKTRA
Where did she get THAT fancy?

CHRYSOTHEMIS
Had a nightmare, I think, and it scared her.

ELEKTRA
God help us. Whatever next!

CHRYSOTHEMIS
That's cheered you up, now she's scared.

ELEKTRA
You tell me about that dream, then I'll talk.

CHRYSOTHEMIS
I dont really know much about it.

ELEKTRA
Spill it. a little word often counts for a lot,
down or up

CHRYSOTHEMIS
What they say is that it was like as if dad
stood there right by her, and a second time
in plain daylight. And took hold of his sceptre,
the one Aegisthus uses now, and planted it by the altar
and a branch grew right out of it

and spread over all Mycenae.

That's what one of the girls says, who was there
while she was telling it before Helios.
That's all I know except that she was so scared
she sent me out. Now listen
you pray to the gods. Dont be a fool
listen to me, before it's too late.

ELEKTRA
Don't put a bit of it on the tomb
It's not clean before man or gods that you
plant gifts or carry lustrations
from that hating woman, to dirty his grave.
throw 'em away, bury 'em, hide 'em deep
so long as none of 'em gets near his grave.

Let 'em stay and wait for HER till she dies
let her find 'em in hell, when she dies,
a little deposit.
The crust she's got, wanting to put flowers
on the grave of the man she murdered,
you think the dead from his grave is goin' to
reach up a lovin' right hand for these ornaments?

Killed him like any damn foreigner,
and wiped 'er bloody 'ands on his 'air,
cut off his hands and feet to keep the
ghost from walkin and grabbin her.
But dont YOU think of carrying that
stuff to purge her of murder.
Chuck it away.
Cut off the tip of one of yr/ curls
and this hank of mine

    (*jerks out a lock of her own* [*wig*] *violently*)

and my belt, it's not much,
just a plain belt without ornaments.
But kneel and beg him to come up out of the earth
to protect us,
and that young Orestes get the upper hand of his enemies
and stay alive till he's got 'em under his feet,
so that we can crown him with something better
than what we give now

I think mebbe he's troubling her dreams
Anyhow, you do this for me, and for him
even if he is dead, we still love him.

    CHORUS
She's on the right track now, dear,
you do what she says.

CHRYSOTHEMIS

I certainly will, it's what ought to be done
and no sense in arguing it.
But keep quiet about it for gods' sake
if the old screw gets wind of it
she'll make me pay for the risk.

CHORUS

You can say that I never guess right
a fool born without second sight,
that my head was never screwed tight
But if Justice don't win just this once
I'm a dunce
            and before a great time has gone by
My heart's risin now
and my dreams are breathin deep
with a free and airy sound:
the greek king wont forget you
but he'll be comin yet
and the double headed axe
be payin back the smacks

and the bloody blood be flowin' once again.

And Vengeance will come out
from her hiding bush no doubt
she will come with brazen tread
to their adulterous bed
to wipe out all the stain
as they wrestle there unwed;
ever with lock and sign
ill doer and ill do's mate
shall never dodge out of fate
ill done hath ill do won
black ends that which black began
fate shall out run any man
Nothing foretells tomorrow to man
neither horrors in dreams nor in oracles
ef thet night-sight dont damn well smash 'em.

(*SING the GREEK*)

OO PELOPOS HA PROSTHEN
POLUPONOS HIPPEIA
HOOS EMOLES AIANES
TADE GA
EUTE GAR HO PONTISTHEIS
MURTILOS EKOIMATHE
PANCHRUSEOON DIPHROON
DUSTANOIS AIKIAIS
PRORRIDZOS EKRIPHTHEIS
OU TI POO
ELEIPEN EK TOUD' OIKOI
POLUPONOS AIKIA

(*Chorus Leader speaks*)

For Myrtil's curse
when he was drowned after that crooked horse-race
chucked out of his gilded car into the sea

and the curse has continued
on the house of Pelops
rotting the earth.

KLYTEMNESTRA (*entering*)
Out here again making trouble, might have known it,
now Aegisthus' not here,
he keeps you from making dirt on your friends' doorstep.
he's away and you pay no attention to me
you've shot off a lot of brash talk
to a lot of people
a lot more than was so
about how forward I am, how unjust
insulting you and your gang

Nobody ever insulted me? Eh??
Bad, eh?
well I've heard 'em from you often enough

just as bad.
Your father, eh? always that, never different
that's your excuse
I killed him,
yes, me, and a good job, dont I know it,
'ave I ever denied it?
with Justice on my side, I wasn't alone
as you'll have to admit if you think straight

This "father" you're always crying about
was the only one of the greeks who wd/ stand for
sacrificing your own sister to the gods,
he didn't have as much trouble in makin' her as I had
he put her in, I got her out
Well, who did he sacrifice her FOR?
you tell me, for whom an' for what?
The greeks. You say for the greeks?
which of two greeks was it?
it wasn't up to them to kill my girl
and if he killed her for his brother
hadn't I got any rights?
Hadn't Menelaus two children of his own
wasn't it up to them to die, if it was
their father and mother who were cause of the sailing.
Did Hell want mine more than hers?
or had the rotter less paternal affection
than Menelaus?
Signs of a gutless and dirty father? I say
they are, even if we split on it.

And it's what your dead sister wd/ say if she cd/ manage a
    voice
I'm not peeved about what I've done
and if you want to sling abuse
try slinging it at somebody else in the family
get on the right track, put the blame where it belongs.

ELEKTRA (*calm*)
Well this time you can't say I started it.
but if you'll let me, I'll give you the rights of it
about my father and sister

KLYTEMNESTRA
Of course I'll let you, and if you
had always used that tone of voice
no one wd/ have objected to listening.

ELEKTRA
All right, you admit you killed him,
can anyone say anything worse?
legally or illegally?
Well justice didn't come into it.
it was your letch for that bounder you're living with.
Go ask Artemis and her dogs why she
shut up the winds in Aulis
all of them, for what vengeance.
and as she wont tell you, I will:
He was hunting away thru her forest
and not only started a spotted buck with 8 points
but made smutty jokes about it, it was
a kill
not according to hunting rites.
And Artemis didn't like it
she held up the Achaeans
to make my father pay
for the buck with his own daughter.
that's why and how she was killed.
she went to the altar smokes
a sacrifice,
the troops couldn't get either home or to Ilion
no other way out.
He did it against his own nature
not in favour of Menelaus.
But even if he had done it for Menelaus, to take it your way,
ought you to have killed him?

What law was that?
You'd better be careful setting up that sort of law
for the rest of the world, you'll get into trouble
and wish you hadn't.
for if blood for blood makes justice,
you'll be the first to go.
And what you say is all sophistry anyhow,
fake,
say what you like, you get into bed with the murderer
and breed to put out the true heirs,
expect me to like it?
Call that avenging a daughter? If that's your excuse?
a dirty job to marry an enemy
for the sake of a daughter?
And nobody aint allowed to warn you
without your puttin up a squawk about slandering mama.
Slave-driver more than a mother I'd call you
and a rotten life I have with you and your fellow-feeder
put all the low jobs onto me

And poor Orestes who got away by the skin of his teeth
wearing away out of luck
You always accuse me of saving him
to come back and clean up the dirt
and you know damn well I would have too, if I could.
So if I'm a dirty scold, impudent,
completely impertinent,
looks like it runs in the family,
from your side at least.

CHORUS
Gheez, she's a-goin' it fierce,
right or not she dont care a hang.

KLYTEMNESTRA
Why should I bother what she thinks
spittin' out at her mother that way, at her age,
Bi god there's nothing she'd stop at,
no sign of shame

ELEKTRA (*suddenly perfectly calm*)
Well now I think I have got a sense of shame
I distinguish between suitable conduct
and what I am driven to by yr/ hate and yr/ devilments.
dirty workers teach dirty work.

KLYTEMNESTRA
You beastly whelp, it's what I've said
and NOT done, that makes you talk a great deal too much.

ELEKTRA
Now you're talkin',
you did the job, not me,
and things done get names
            nomina sunt consequentia rerum

KLYTEMNESTRA
By the Virgin you'll pay for this
when Aegisthus gets home.

ELEKTRA
Nice nature comin' out, ain't it?
temperamental, tells me to say what I like
and hasn't got brains enough to hear it.

KLYTEMNESTRA
You'd even spoil the sacrifice, shouting
now I've let you get it all out.

ELEKTRA (*coldly*)
go along, yes, DO sacrifice, please
and dont say my noise is jinxing you,
I wont say anything more.

KLYTEMNESTRA (*to maid*)
Here, you, pick up all this fruit and incense,
so I can pray and get rid of these worries

(*sotto voce*)

Hear me Apollo, Patron,
keep down this scandal
don't answer so these spies can get it
(I am not speaking this among friends)
cant spill it all out with her here
ready to yatter
and spread mean silly nonsense all thru the town
envious little bitch
But do hear me, let me explain
this ghost in the shifty vision of a dream
O Apollo Lykeios, if it's lucky let the luck come to me
and if it's evil, let it fall on my enemies,
if anybody's trying to cheat me out of my money
don't let 'em.
Let me run the house of Atreides as long as I live
and keep hold of the sceptre. Preserve me
to live comfortably with these friends,
and with children who like me
and who aren't gone bitter with spite and gloom
O Phoibos Lyceios hear me, with favour
give to us all that we ask,
and you know all the rest I dont say
for the sons of God see all that there is.

TUTOR
I'm a stranger in these parts, can
any of you kind ladies tell me
ef that's Milord Aegisthus's palace?

CHORUS
Yes, stranger, you've hit it, bullseye.

TUTOR
Would I be right in sayin that woman there is the queen?
She looks it.

CHORUS
She's it

TUTOR

Gruss Gott, your Highness, I've got good
news for you and Aegisthus, Come from a friend of his.

KLYTEMNESTRA

That's nice.
(*dropping voice*) wonder who the deuce that can be.

TUTOR

Phanoteus, of Phocia. It's a serious matter.

KLYTEMNESTRA

Well, what is it? go on, stranger
must be good if it comes from him.

TUTOR

Orestes is dead. That's the short of it.

ELEKTRA

Oooh, that's the end. I'm finished.

KLYTEMNESTRA

What, what, don't bother with her.

TUTOR

He's dead. Orestes, finish! na poo.

ELEKTRA

Ruin, ruin, I can't go on.

KLYTEMNESTRA

(*to Elektra*) Mind your own business.
Now, stranger, tell me about it,
how did it happen?

TUTOR

That's what I'm here for. He went up for the big Delphic
        proize
that's the biggest greek games

and when he heard the herald yellin' out for the first race
the foot race, he came out shining
admired of all beholders
an' he got the proize uv the first race
I never see a man like him, from start to finish
the crown he had for the victory
I'm only tellin' the part of it.
He took all the foive proizes, you could hear the umpires
tellin' it: Agamemnon's son, young Orestes.
Win for Argos. Old general's son licked the lot of 'em.

(*change tone, and shaking head*)

There's no lickin' the god's bad temper
An' the next day toward sundown
he entered, there were all of the charioteers,
Sparta, Achaia, and two boys from Libya:
drivers, and one team of thessalian mares;
an Aeolian, young chestnut fillies, and another from Megara.
A white Aneian, and the Athenian, number nine,
the city the gods put up, and last and tenth the Beotian.
And the umpires ranged 'em up as the lot fell
and they sounded off with the brazen horn
shakin' the reins and a-lickin' the horrses
and a yellin' till you couldn't hear over the plain
and the track wuz narrow, the lot of 'em drivin' togedder
and a-lammin' the horses, each one tryin' to git out of
the bunches
and the wheels a-rollin', and the horses a-snortin'
and their sweat spattered over the cars,
and their breath steamin' on the droivers in front of 'em
and Orestes come round at the turn, at the turns
all of 'em, shavin' the pillars
loosin' the off horse and pullin' in on the nigh,
And the Anenian's bolted between the sixth and the 7th
        round
and foul'd the Barcaen's, and they all piled up then
the lot of 'em.
except the Athenian
                who slowed up

and then Orestes
                    pulled in on his team
nothin' left but the two of 'em
all RIGHT, till the very last turn, when his
axle-tip hit the pillar
                    and busted
and he got t'rown over the rail
and caught in the reins of his horses
                    wid the crowd yellin' for pity
now seein' him bumped on the ground and now lifted
wid his feet in the air
                    till the other charioteers
got hold of his horses
and found him
                    broke beyond recognition,
his best friend wouldn't have known him.

        (*pauses*)

And the Phoceans burnt it then and there on a pyre
and the envoys are comin', bringin' what's left in an urn
to lay his dust in his fatherland.
It's a sad story, madam, I
saw it wid me own eyes.
Never a worse one.

    CHORUS
Ah, ah, that's the end of the dynasty
        TO PAN DE DESPOTAISI TOIS PALAI
They are blotted out root and branch.
        HOOS EOIKEN, EPHTHARTAI.

    KLYTEMNESTRA
Oh god. what, which, I dunno if it's lucky.
Terrible, if it's terrible, it's, it's useful anyhow
it's a miserable state of things when
nothing but my own sorrows save my own life.

TUTOR
What, lady, am I gettin you down with this news?

KLYTEMNESTRA
That's the worst of being a mother,
can't hate a child no matter how badly they treat you.

TUTOR
Seems I came on a useless errand.

KLYTEMNESTRA
No, not useless, if you've got sure proof of his death
born of my life, forgetful of the breasts that suckled him
banished himself to get away from me
never seen me since he left the country
accused me of killing his father
and he was threatening
                    what awful things he wd/ do
till I cdn't get a night's sleep or a cat nap
thinking I was going to die every minute
and now, eh, now I needn't be scared of him any more
nor of that worse little bloodsucker living here with me,
the pest,
now we'll get a day's peace somewhere
in spite of her threats.

ELEKTRA
Ooooh, he's dead. and it fits her book
motherly excitement
very pretty

KLYTEMNESTRA
Not for you. I dare say He's better off.

ELEKTRA
Holy vengeance—god hear her,
and him not cold in the grave.

KLYTEMNESTRA
Fate HAS heard, and managed it very nicely.

ELEKTRA
Go on, keep it up. You're top dog,
you've hit the jack-pot.

KLYTEMNESTRA
You and Orestes can't spoil it now.

ELEKTRA
Spoil it! No, this is *our* finish.

KLYTEMNESTRA (*to Tutor*)
You'd deserve more than a good fat tip
if you'd make her hush and finish her yatter.

TUTOR
Well, m'am, I'll be goin', if everything is in good shape.

KLYTEMNESTRA
No, no, can't treat a friend's messenger that way.
Come in, do, and let her yowl
out here about her friends' troubles, and hers.

ELEKTRA
Looks like she's grief-stricken, weepin an' wailin
about her poor son being wiped out that way?
went out bursting with laughter.
   poor me
    OO TALAIN' EGOO
   not ever
I'll lie down at the gate here
and die here, got no friends anyhow.

 (*sinks onto step*)

And if anybody kills me, because he dont like it
any of them inside, be a favour,
got no wish to live anyhow.

CHORUS
God, where the hell are you? Zeus,
Apollo, no light and no lightening,
is there no one to show these things up?

ELEKTRA
AI AI

CHORUS (*gesticulating*)
No use in crying.

ELEKTRA
AIH

CHORUS
SHHH.

ELEKTRA
you are killing me

CHORUS
what?

ELEKTRA
don't tell me about life after death
that's only another kick when I'm down.
they're dead forever

CHORUS (*sings*)
OIDA GAR ANAKT' AMPHIAREOON CHRUSODETOIS
    HERKESI
KRUPHTHENTA GUNAIKOON
KAI NUN HUPO GAIAS
Nay but King Amphiarion
that died for a golden chain
caught in a false wife's net
under the earth reigns yet

ELEKTRA (*disgusted and bored with the song*)
Ajhh

CHORUS (*singing*)
He reigns and lords his mind
PAMPSUCHOS ANASSEI

ELEKTRA (*beginning to cheer up, still dubious, but singing
now and echoing the tone of the Chorus*)
AHI

CHORUS
and bodes no good at all
for her who slew him

ELEKTRA
slain

CHORUS
aye, slain

ELEKTRA
known, over known,
mid grief, an avenger.
OID' OID' EPHANE GAR MELETOOR
AMPHI TON EN PENTHEI.
I have none.
He was, and is not.
HOS GAR ET' EN
PHROUDOS ANARPASTHEIS
vanished away, torn from me.

CHORUS
sorrow attains thee, sorrow.

ELEKTRA
known, dont I know, over known,
day after day, moon over moon,
overfull, pain over pain
horrors of hate abate not
ever.

CHORUS
our eyes be witness

ELEKTRA
then do not deceive me
neither lead me astray

CHORUS
thou say'st?

ELEKTRA
not into emptiness
      where there is no one at *all*

CHORUS (*the two "alls" simultaneously*)
all men must die

ELEKTRA
but to die so, so clawed in whirling doom
torn in the track, if so that death must come. . . .

CHORUS
mid tortures so
whose death was unforeseen

ELEKTRA
How not? and him so far
no hand to lay . . . .

CHORUS (*here strong AHI*)
AHI

ELEKTRA
his mangled limbs
in decent grave,
unwept to meet strange clay.

CHRYSOTHEMIS (*very pretty, blonde, just a shade plump showing heredity from fat, tubby, shortish mama, trots in puffing*)

Oh dearest. . . . so happy. . . . such news . . .
I'm all out of breath from running . . . . .
your troubles are over

ELEKTRA (*voice of complete sceptical weariness*)
what? you with a cure-all?

(*after a pause, and looking her up and down*)

where did you find what ain't?

CHRYSOTHEMIS
He's here . . . Orestes is here . . .
I'm tellin you, just as sure as you see me.

ELEKTRA
You're CRAZY, poor dear, plumb crazy
don't joke about horrors.

CHRYSOTHEMIS
I'm not, I swear by the hearth-stone
he's come for the two of us.

ELEKTRA (*sigh*)
Oh dear, poor dear, has anyone LIVING
put that nonsense into your head?

CHRYSOTHEMIS
No, but me, ME, what I've seen,
me, with my own eyes, seen.

ELEKTRA
WHAT proof? you poor fool
you're blotto delirious.

CHRYSOTHEMIS
For gods' sake wait till I finish telling you,
and then decide whether I'm batty

ELEKTRA

All right, go on, if you like to talk.

CHRYSOTHEMIS

It was like this
I was goin' to father's old grave
and there was milk newly spashed over it
running down from the top of the mound
and all sorts of wreathes all around it
put there for father
like as if

> (*Elektra masked, at first not even looking at Chrysothemis*
> *but boredly into distance, gradually grows attentive.*
> *Slowness in turning of head, as per Noh*)

and I was wondering, and looking to see who,
who on earth cd/ —
and looking to see if anyone might be coming
and when I saw everything quiet
I sneaked up nearer the mound
and there was a new lock of hair on it
right on the edge
and, oh dear, it came over me while I was looking at it
that Orestes had put it there,
dear Orestes, put it there for a sign
almost as if I had seen him
and I picked it up and burst out crying,
I was so happy,
    it can't be ill omen.
and I'm perfectly sure nobody else cd/ have put it there
who'd have cared? except us,
I didn't put it there, and you didn't
cause you couldn't get out of the house,
SHE wouldn't have, she's not taken that way
and she cdn't have, without being seen.
No, NO, my dear, Orestes put that stuff on the grave,
you buck up.
The same devils can't always run things,
ours have been pretty bad,

But the luck's changing,
happen a really good day might come in

ELEKTRA
Poor thing, you always were soft in the head.

CHRYSOTHEMIS
But aren't you glad?

ELEKTRA
you dont know whether you're on earth, or raving.

CHRYSOTHEMIS
dont I know what I've seen with my own eyes, SEEN.

ELEKTRA
He's dead, and the dead wont help you and he cant.
god help you, poor you.

CHRYSOTHEMIS
Oh, o, O, but who told you.

ELEKTRA
A man who was there and saw it. Killed.

CHRYSOTHEMIS (*in tone of complete puzzlement*)
Where is he, the man? It's very peculiar.

ELEKTRA (*pointing with thumb over shoulder*)
In THERE, and mother's so glad to see him.

CHRYSOTHEMIS
Oh dear . . . but whoever can have put all those wreathes
on the tomb?

ELEKTRA
Somebody must have put 'em there for Orestes.

CHRYSOTHEMIS

O. O, and me running to make you happy
and not knowing we'd only come into more trouble
besides what we had.

ELEKTRA

Well that's how it is. And now you turn to and help me,
at least this much with the load.

CHRYSOTHEMIS

You want me to raise the dead?

ELEKTRA

That's not what I said. At least I wasn't born crazy.

CHRYSOTHEMIS

well what do you want me to do, that I can do?

ELEKTRA

Dont break down, and do what I tell you.

CHRYSOTHEMIS

I'll do anything that can be the least use.

ELEKTRA

You can't do a good job without work.

CHRYSOTHEMIS

I know that. I'll do everything that I can.

ELEKTRA

Well then listen.
I'm going to finish it up.
We got no more friends to stand by us
Hell's grabbed the lot
and left us
you can see that. nobody left but us.
As long as HE was alive I went on
hoping he'd come and put things right about father,

wipe out the murder.
Now he's gone, not there any more,
I rely on you
we've got to kill Aegisthus ourselves.
you're not scared?
It's *our* father was murdered.
we've only got our own hands.
might as well look at it straight.
wont get anywhere sittin still,
what hope is left standing
here you are crying and grousing about being cheated out
of father's fortune, that's that,
and we're not getting any younger
Dont think they'll ever let you get married,
Aegisthus wont let us have children,
he's too cagey for that,
          not to put him out of the running
But you do what I tell you
FIRST: you'd be showing respect for your dead father down
      under
AND for your brother as well
SECONDLY you could live like a free woman, free born, as
      you were,
for the rest of your life,
and you'd get a fit man to marry.
People recognize quality, everybody does.
You listen to me, and we'd both be respected,
anybody from here or abroad wd/ say:
there they are, those girls saved the dynasty
risked their lives doing it
threw out the crooks, settled the murderers' hash.
You just got to like 'em
everybody's got to respect 'em

    (*dreamy half-tranced voice merging into greek*)

we'd have our proper place of honour
in processions and in assemblies
on account of our courage

(*sing greek*)

IDESTHE TOODE TOO KASIGNETOO PHILOI
HOO TON PATROOION OIKON EXESOOSATEN
HOO TOISIN ECHTHROIS EU BEBEKOSIN POTE
PSUCHES APHEIDESANTE PROUSTETEN PHONOU
TOUTOO PHILEIN CHRE TOODE CHRE PANTAS
    SEBEIN
TOOD' EN TH' HEORTAIS EN TE PANDEMOOI
    POLEI
TIMAN HAPANTAS HOUNEK' ANDREIAS CHREOON
we'd have a reputation everywhere
and it wd/ last even when we are dead.

Trust me, my dear, and stand by your father,
work with me for your brother, get me out of my misery
get yourself out of yours,
and remember this, the free born ought not to
sink into slavery.

> CHORUS
Well I guess
lookin forward is about the best ally one cd
have, if you're talking or listenin'
to things like this

> CHRYSOTHEMIS
No, girls, if she weren't on the wrong track
she'd have had a little caution before she sounded off
and she just hasn't got any.

> (*to Elektra*)

where do you look to get the nerve to fight
or get me into the ranks?
cant you see you were born a *woman* not a *man*
you haven't got the physical strength
of these people you're up against.

their gods, their luck is comin' up every day
and ours going out, *not* comin' in at all.

(*Chrysothemis repetitive and very patient*)

You try to break a man like that?
who cd/ get away with it
& not break;
not make a complete mess of it
Dont make it worse
if anybody heard you talkin this way
you'd get into more trouble.
We wont get OUT of anything that way,
and fine talk's no use if we're dirty dead
Death's not the worst that can happen
but not to be able to die when you want to.
I put it to you, before we're completely wiped out
us two and all of the family
keep your temper, hold in.
I'll keep my mouth shut about what you've said
cause I think it's, all of it, useless.
BUT do hang on to your wits, from now on
dont go up against the people in power.

CHORUS (*to Elektra*)
You better listen, there's nothing more useful
to a human being than forethought, and a prudent mind.

ELEKTRA
Just as I thought . . . . .
all right, I'll do it alone,
it's got to be done—or have a try at it anyhow.

CHORUS
Ooooh, Lord
I wish you'd taken the chance the day he died!
anything was possible then

ELEKTRA
Not that I didn't want to; I hadn't the sense.

CHRYSOTHEMIS
I wish you still had as much

ELEKTRA
that means you won't help me at all.

CHRYSOTHEMIS
It CAN'T be lucky.

ELEKTRA
Nice mind, no guts!

CHRYSOTHEMIS
I can bear up even under that compliment.

ELEKTRA
You wont have to stand any more.

CHRYSOTHEMIS (*blandly*)
That remains to be seen.

ELEKTRA
Oh get out, you're no use at all.

CHRYSOTHEMIS (*a bit peeved*)
I am so, but you can't see it.
you'll never learn.

ELEKTRA
Go tell it all to mama.

CHRYSOTHEMIS (*explanatory*)
But I don't hate you that way.

ELEKTRA
No, but think how you'd lead me to shame.

CHRYSOTHEMIS
No I would NOT.
I'm only asking you to think forward.

ELEKTRA
and accept YOUR values?

CHRYSOTHEMIS
When you get untangled, I'll take to yours,
you can think for us both, then.

ELEKTRA
That's talking, too bad you mean it the wrong way on.

CHRYSOTHEMIS
That's just the trouble with you.

ELEKTRA
What? you mean what I say isn't perfectly true?

CHRYSOTHEMIS
EVEN JUSTICE CAN BE A PEST.

ELEKTRA
Anyhow, I dont want to go by your standards of conduct.
I'd rather die.

CHRYSOTHEMIS
But if you did you'd probably find I'm right.

ELEKTRA
I'm going on, anyhow. You can't scare me.

CHRYSOTHEMIS (*very soberly*)
You're serious? you wont think it over?

ELEKTRA
Nothing stinks worse than bad advice.

CHRYSOTHEMIS
You just dont understand what I'm saying.

ELEKTRA

I've been thinking this way a long time.

CHRYSOTHEMIS (*resignedly*)
Well, I'll go now.
You can't stand my talk, and I dont think
you're going the right way about it.

ELEKTRA
Yes, go along, but I'll never trail after you
for the urging
It's useless to chase after shadows,

(*mezzo voce, as if reflecting*)

such a lot of them,
all of them void.

CHRYSOTHEMIS
If you ever aim to teach yourself to think straight,
think about it now. You'll think of what I'm saying.
Too . . . . . late.

CHORUS

Strophe

TI TOUS ANOOTHEN PHRONIMOOTATOUS
    OIOONOUS
ESOPOOMENOI TROPHAS
KEDOMENOUS APH' HOON
TE BLASTOOSIN APH' HOON T' ONASIN
    HEUROOSI
TAD' OUK EP' ISAS TELOUMEN
ALL' OU TAN DIOS ASTRAPAN
KAI TAN OURANIAN THEMIN
DARON OUK APONETOI
OO CHTHONIA BROTOISI PHAMA
KATA MOI BOASON OIKTRAN
OPA TOIS ENERTH' ATREIDAIS
ACHOREUTA PHEROUS' ONEIDE

Shall not justice be done
by Zeus among men,
Shall a sound be borne under earth
to the sons of Atreus?
              All
              is not well in his hall.
              His line dies out.

Antistrophe

HOTI SPHIN EDE TA MEN EK DOMOON NOSEI [DE]
TA DE PROS TEKNOON DIPLE PHU-
LOPIS OUKET' EXISOUTAI PHILOTASIOOI DIAITAI
PRODOTOS DE MONA SALEUEI
ELEKTRA TON AEI PATROS
DEILAIA STENACHOUS' HOPOOS
HA PANDURTOS AEDOON
OUTE TI TOU THANEIN PROMETHES
TO TE ME BLEPEIN HETOIMA
DIDUMAN HELOUS' ERINUN
TIS AN EUPATRIS HOODE BLASTOI

from above   be wise birds of omen
Tossed and alone
              Elektra
                  mourns
constant aid hath she none
As Philomel in grief
              her sire's shade
              so shamed of all the world
nor cares to live or die,
were he avenged.

A child, indeed, of what race!   *Strophe β*
Of what breed! heed, heed
Nor would she live in shame

(*Greek crescendo*)

OUDEIS TOON AGATHOON YAR
DZOON KAKOOS EUKELIAN AISCHUNAI THELEI
NOONUMOS OO PAI PAI

So fame's all-hovering   wing
shall bear her praise
for beauty of heart and mind
                for constant faith

      Nay, ere she die   *Antistrophe β*
      may power come
to lift her high,
      may yet her house be strong
as Zeus gave law.

DZOOIS MOI KATHUPERTHEN
CHEIRI KAI PLOUTOOI TEOON ECHTHROON
    HOSON
NUN HUPOCHEIP NAIEIS
EPEI S' EPHEUREKA MOIRAI MEN OUK EN
    ESTHLAI
BEBOOSAN HA DE MEGIST' EBLASTE NOMIMA
    TOONDE PHEROMENAN
ARISTA TAI DZENOS EUSEBEIAI

ORESTES
Eh, can any of you ladies
tell me: did we hear right and
are we gettin' to where we wanted to come to?

CHORUS (*more or less automatically, mechanically
answering*)
Where do you want to get to?

(*turning suddenly suspicous*)

    AND WHY??
What are you here for?

ORESTES

Aegisthus. Where does he live,

  (*with morgue and double entente*)

I been looking for him for SOME time.

CHORUS (*gruffly*)

Well yuh can't blame the fellow that told you

  (*thumb over shoulder, pointing*)

you got here.
This is it.

ORESTES

Well, eh . . . will any of you go in and . . . eh . . .
say politely that we have respectfully got here.

                    eh . . . on foot

CHORUS

This unfortunate girl should
              She's of the family.

ORESTES (*dubiously*)

Yes, lady? would you go say that some Phocaeans

  (*accent and tone, a bit grim and deliberate*)

. . . have come for Aegisthus. . . .

ELEKTRA (*half-sob*)

Oh God, I spose you've got the proof with you.

ORESTES

Proof of what? Old Stroffy
told us to bring the news of Orestes.

ELEKTRA (*sort of gasp*)
eeh, I was afraid so.

(*in sort of glaze noticing her own hands*)

I'm all of a tremble.

ORESTES
We've got it here, all that is left of him
in this little jug, as you can see if you want to.

ELEKTRA
O. O it's all I can bear.

ORESTES
If it's Orestes you're crying for,
If it's for his troubles,
he's all there in the urn.

ELEKTRA
Oh give it me, for god's sake, give it to ME

(*hardly pause, but spoken staccato dividing the clauses*)

It's the end of the line.
we're all there together:
ashes.

(*Elektra clutching at the urn which Pylades is carrying*)

ORESTES
Give it to her, let her have it, whoever she is
She's not asking from spite,
must be a friend or one of the family

ELEKTRA'S KEENING
All that is left me
my hope was Orestes

dust is returned me
in my hands nothing, dust that is all of him,
flower that went forth

would I had died then
ere stealing thee from the slaughter
died both together
lain with our father

Far from thy homeland
died far in exile
no hand was near thee
to soothe thy passing,
corpse unanointed
fire consumed thee,
all now is nothing,
strangers have brought thee
small in this urn here
Sorrow upon me
fruitless my caring

I as mother and sister both
thy nurse also ere thou hadst thy growth
this was my past
and swept away with thee
ever to me
thy summons came.

all in a day
and is no more.
Dead Agamemnon, dead now my brother
I am dead also, the great wind in passing
bears us together.
Mirth for our foemen.

(*anger now stronger than grief, for a moment: SPOKEN*)

And that bitch of a mother is laughing
and they haven't sent back even the shape of him,
but a ghost that cant do its job.

Ajnn.   ajhn.

(*SINGS*)

thou the avenger, no more avenging
born to misfortune, ashes avail not
shadows avail not

ahi,   ahi,
bodiless
brother that art not.

(*SPOKEN*)

The spirits love me no longer.
you kept sending messages
secretly, you would take vengeance.

(*SINGS*)

thy death, my dying
dred road thou goest
brother, my slayer
as ever above earth
let death divide not

(*singing to the urn*)

Oimoi   Oimoi

take me in with you
I now am nothing, make place beside thee
naught into naught, zero to zero
to enter beside thee
our fortune equal
death endeth pain.

CHORUS (*sings*)
Mortal thy father, all men are mortal
Mortal Orestes,
All men must die.

ORESTES (*speaks*)
I can't stand much more of this

ELEKTRA (*speaks*)
What's it to you

ORESTES
Good god, are you Elektra?

ELEKTRA
I am, and in misery.

ORESTES
Heaven help me.

ELEKTRA
What do you care about me?

ORESTES (*very quick & angry*)
what in hell have they done to you?

ELEKTRA
But are you sorry for ME

ORESTES
Unmarried, and such a life

ELEKTRA
what are you lookin' at?
what you got to be sad about?
it isn't YOUR funeral

ORESTES
I didn't know the half of it

ELEKTRA
What's that got to do with ANYTHING?
with anything we have said?

ORESTES
seeing you in this condition . . .

ELEKTRA
but you haven't seen anything yet
not the least part

ORESTES
Amn't I seeing enough, can there be anything more,
more, worse?

ELEKTRA
Yes, living here with these assassins.

ORESTES
Whose assassins?

ELEKTRA
My father's, and me a slave.

ORESTES
Who compels you?

ELEKTRA
They *say* she's my mother.

ORESTES
How? beats you, starves you?

ELEKTRA
Yes, and everything else.

ORESTES
And there's no one to help you, or stop her?

ELEKTRA
Nobody. Nothing but the dust that you've got there.

ORESTES
Poor dear, I've been sorry for you, a long time.

ELEKTRA
Well you're the first man that ever WAS.
and the only one.

ORESTES
Cause I've got the same trouble.

ELEKTRA
You mean you're a relative?

(*after pause*)

where from?

ORESTES
Can you trust these people?

ELEKTRA
They're all right. You can trust 'em.

ORESTES
Give me back that jug, and I'll tell you.

ELEKTRA
No, don't cheat me that way, for god's sake.

ORESTES
Come on, you won't miss it.

ELEKTRA
Oh gosh, don't rob me, it's all I've got.

ORESTES
I wont. Give it here.

ELEKTRA
Oh poor Orestes, if I can't even bury you.

ORESTES
Watch what you're saying.
you oughtn't to weep.

ELEKTRA
What when my brother's dead.

ORESTES
You oughtn't to talk that way about him.

ELEKTRA
What! Amn't I fit to

ORESTES (*admiringly*)
You're fit for anything, but that isn't your job.

ELEKTRA
Not when I'm carrying his body here in my hands?

ORESTES
They're not his. That's a fairy tale.

ELEKTRA
Well where IS his grave.

ORESTES
It aint. you dont bury people while they're alive.

ELEKTRA
What are you talking about?

ORESTES
Only the truth.

ELEKTRA
He's alive?

ORESTES
As I am.

ELEKTRA
YOU?

ORESTES
Here's dad's ring.

ELEKTRA
O PHILTATON PHOS

ORESTES
what a day. I'll say it is.

ELEKTRA
And I hear you talking.

ORESTES
Yes. we're agreed on that.

ELEKTRA
and I can hold onto you.

(*embraces*)
ORESTES
never let go.

ELEKTRA
Oh my dears, this is Orestes
he wasn't really dead after all
he was just pretending, so he could get here.

CHORUS
Yes we can see him. makes one cry this does.

ELEKTRA (*singing starts sotto-voce, trembly; asides spoken
rhythmically with kettle drum accompaniment*)
heart, heart, heart thou art come

ORESTES
yes, but keep quiet
for a bit just keep quiet

ELEKTRA
what for

ORESTES
somebody might hear there inside.

ELEKTRA (*sings greek like Carmagnole. THIS song can be burst into. Like wild Sioux injun war dance with tommy hawks*)
ALL' OU MA TEN
ADMETON AIEN
ARTEMIN

Oh to hell with all the hens
in the old hen house

I aint afraid of hens
cause they aint a bit of use.

ORESTES
bi god when the women get goin' it's Mars,

ELEKTRA
OTOTOTOTOI
clear again, not to be ended,
not to be forgotten,
how our ill started, trouble began.

ORESTES
Don't I know it but
    to tell in its time
        when the DEED recalls it

ELEKTRA
any time's right, now, I've hardly got my mouth free.

ORESTES
I'll say it is. And you damn well keep it free.

ELEKTRA

How?

ORESTES

By not talking too much at the wrong time.

ELEKTRA

You came when I'd given up hope
I got to keep quiet now?

ORESTES

I came as the gods moved me

ELEKTRA

That's the best the gods have done yet.

ORESTES

Dont want to hold down on yr/ whoopee
But afraid you're overdoing it.

ELEKTRA

It's been so long, long, but the road's right,
you "deign" deign to show up here
now I can see you
& you see my troubles
but not me
                    DONT. . . . .

ORESTES

Dont what?

ELEKTRA

Dont defraud me
of the pleasure of seeing you here

ORESTES

damn well let anybody else try it

ELEKTRA
you dont mind?

ORESTES
Of course not how cd/ I

ELEKTRA
Oh dearest friends
if now's to ear
a voice I ne'er
had hoped to hear

If joy shall not
burst forth at this
then ever dumb in wretchedness
shd/ one live on in deep distress.

Now thou art here
                in full daylight
                shall I not pour
                forthmy delight,
who ne'er in deepest woe
                had forgot thee.

ORESTES (*probably holding onto her, and trying to stop her
    gentle, but to get his hand on her jaw or mouth*)
Yes, yes, but lay off the talk,
You don't have to tell me how that bitch and Aegisthus
are running all dad's place to ruin
sluicin' it out in extravagance, luxury
no time now for all that
got to get on with the job
tell me the best way to get to it,
so I can fit the time,
where to show, and where to hide
to put an end to these bumptious bastids, and *how*.

And dont look so damn happy
that when we go in, she'll twig something is up

Keep yr/ face mum, keep on weepin and bawlin'
so she wont guess what we're up to,
and laugh when we've finished the business
and have got to some sort of freedom.

    ELEKTRA (*breathlessly eager*)
Ye'ss, my dear, I just love it
it's all yours and not mine
I wont get in the way, I wont bother.
You know Aegisthus is out, she's alone in the house now
don't worry about my lookin' happy
I loathe her,
                And I've been weeping and crying
(for joy, but she needn't know that.)
for the dead come alive
to do what I'd never have believed
so incredible that if father himself shd/ come
here alive I'd believe it
since you've got here this way
tell me what you want done and I'll follow
since even alone I'd have done one or two things,
I'd have damn well thrown 'em out
or gone bust, been decently dead.

    ORESTES (*puts hand over her mouth*)
But HUSH
              sounds as if someone
was coming out.

    ELEKTRA
Yes, gentlemen, this is the way
nobody in this house will object to what you're bringing

    TUTOR (*furious*)
You BLOODY fools shut up
aint you got ANY sense whatever
no more care for your lives
you aint on the brink of trouble,
you arc plumb bang in the middle
dont you know you're in danger

real danger, damn it.
If I hadn't been here keepin watch in this doorway
they'd already know what you're at before you get
to it, before you get in there yourselves.
I've saved you that, anyhow,
and now if you've got thru with your gabble
& your blasted roaring
go in, But quiet,
no good wasting time, either,
                    get it over.

     ORESTES
What does it look like in there.

     TUTOR
All jake, especially as nobody knows you

     ORESTES
you've told 'em I'm dead?

     TUTOR
You're a ghost in hell as far as they go

     ORESTES
And
     they're
          DEElighted.
What do they say about that?

     TUTOR
We'll go into THAT later.
and the worse they do, the better . . .

     ELEKTRA
For gods' sake, who's this?

     ORESTES
Can't you see

ELEKTRA
Haven't the foggiest . . .

ORESTES
Well you handed me over to him.

ELEKTRA
What, what?

ORESTES
Well he sneaked me out of here
and got me to Phocis

ELEKTRA (*gasps—tone of voice covers omitted words*)
The only one of the lot
who stood by me when father was murdered.

ORESTES
that's him. now hush.

ELEKTRA (*to Tutor*)
What a day
YOU've done it alone.
You've saved the line. How did you get here
You've saved him and me
in all this misery, bless your hands

(*grabs em, and presses them to her booZUM or cheeks*)

Oh gods bless the feet that brought you

(*bit hysterical still*)

how could you go on and not tell me,
and telling us all of those lies
and yet brought him.
You seem more like a father,
OOH how I hated you.
                    What a dear.

TUTOR
Yes, yes, but now hush.
there's enough to fill nights and days
we can go into that when the time comes

(*then noticing Orestes and Pylades are still standing there*)

What the hell are you doing here
Get on with it, she's alone
if you lose time, she'll have all the slaves up to fight you
not only the servants but the palace guards
the whole corps of them,
                          and no pikers.

ORESTES (*to Pylades who hasn't said a damn word.*)
Come on, Pylades, cut the cackle.
May the gods of the door be with us.

ELEKTRA (*does the praying/ sings, sort of sing-song*)
O King Apollo,
                    HILEOOS
Favour us, favour us
oft have I prayed thee
my little I gave thee
Phoibos, Lukeios
aid the right now
              let the gods show their godhead

CHORUS
                    Mars breathing blood
              hounds that miss never their prey
miss never their spring, under the roof,
seeking the doers of ill, all ill, by stealth, by guile,
              Mars, breatheth blood,
          dogs that never miss their prey,
              the palace roof,
nor yet under-long to wait for the proof, of my presage.
              will, heart, and all.

ELEKTRA (*emerging from door, or slowly turning as part of a pivoted door*)

Oh my dears, my dears. . . . . .

        It's coming. . . . . .

            sh hh hhh

(*arm bent, hand level with shoulder, turns body sixty degrees very slowly*)

SIGA PROSMENE

CHORUS (*gt/ agitation*)

What? what?

        whataretheydoing?

ELEKTRA

She's putting the wreath on the urn . . .

        and . . . and they're waiting.

CHORUS

Whatchu come out for?

ELEKTRA

To keep watch for Aegisthus

        so he dont catch 'em

KLYTEMNESTRA

AiHIII, nobody left,

        oohhhh assassins.

ELEKTRA

Hear that?

        Yes. dears, it's a noise.

CHORUS

It's awful. Gimme the creeps.

KLYTEMNESTRA

aaaaah, Aegisthus. AE-gis-thus

ELEKTRA
Hear it, that's it again.

KLYTEMNESTRA
Pity your mother

ORESTES (*grim*)
Did you pity father or me?

CHORUS (*now SINGS/ cry of misery/ keening on one note
or minimum rise and fall but monotonous and legato*)
O city, o WRETCHED house
and the curse's tooth gnaws
        day after day

KLYTEMNESTRA
That's done it.

ELEKTRA
Hit her again.

KLYTEMNESTRA
Twice, twice.
always twice.

ELEKTRA (*between her teeth*)
Ajh. GOD, I wish it was Aegisthus.

CHORUS
In the end, weight unto weight
fate works out to its end
They live who lie under ground
the blood of the dead, long dead
overfloods their slayers.
The dead hand drips Mars
and the slain,
            I can't blame 'em.

ELEKTRA
Orestes, how'd it go?

ORESTES
All right
The house is cleaned up
if that oracle was on the square.

ELEKTRA
The bitch is dead?

ORESTES (*sobered tone vs. Elektra's exultation*)
You wont have any more trouble with mother.

CHORUS
Sshh. Here comes Aegisthus.

ELEKTRA
Back, can't you get back . . .

ORESTES
Where is the bloke?

ELEKTRA
Comin' up from the lower town, very chesty . . .

CHORUS
Quick, get into that vestibule, Hop!!
Good job so far. Now the next one.

ORESTES
We'll do it. Don't worry.

ELEKTRA
Hurry, hurry.

ORESTES
Exit.

ELEKTRA
Now mine.

CHORUS
Now just a few polite words wd/ come in handy,
so he won't guess he's rushin'
plumb bang into ruin,
                    an' he damn well deserves it.

AEGISTHUS (*rather sissy voice, even a slight lisp*)
Say you, where can I find these chappies from Phocis
They say Orestes got killed in a chariot race
all messed up.

(*to Elektra*)

Here YOU, always so full of lip
it's mostly your business,
                    you ought to know.

ELEKTRA
Sure I know. Think I dont care
about the last relative left me

AEGISTHUS
Well where are these chaps. Spit it out.

ELEKTRA
Inside, she's SO pleased to see 'em.

AEGISTHUS
They said he was dead? How do they know.

ELEKTRA
They don't. They've only got the corpse with 'em.

AEGISTHUS
Can I get a look at it.

ELEKTRA (*spoken slowly*)
Yes.

(*slight pause*)

It's an awful mess.

AEGISTHUS
Taint often you say anything to please me.

ELEKTRA
Go on and enjoy it, if that's the kind of thing you enjoy.

AEGISTHUS
Shut up.

(*to Chorus*)

Get these doors open
so everybody in Mycene, and ARGOS
can see

(*they open the big portone doors, slowly*)

if anybody had hopes of this man
they can now see him dead

(*smacks his thigh*)

and do what I tell 'em
and not wait till they're dead to find out.

ELEKTRA
Oh, I've learned that.
No use goin' up against people in power.

AEGISTHUS
O Zeus, that's a shape
looks as if the gods didn't like him
Here, I take that back. it aint lucky.
Lift that napkin off his face, I'm one of the family
in mourning.

ORESTES
Lift it yourself. It's not my place
to show these signs of love and devotion.

AEGISTHUS
That's right.

(*to Elektra*)

go call Klytemnestra
if she's at home.

ORESTES (*as Aegisthus lifts napkin*)
She's right there. You needn'y look any further.

AEGISTHUS
Gaaaaa!

ORESTES
Whazza matter? haven't you seen her before?

AEGISTHUS (*in fury*)
Who th' HELL. Damn, damn
I'm trapped.

ORESTES
Haven't
        you
                ever learned
That the
        DEAD
                don't
                        DIE?

AEGISTHUS
Ajh. you're Orestes.

ORESTES
Ain't you clever. And it took you so LONG to find out.

AEGISTHUS
Here now, wait a minute, just let me

ELEKTRA

DON'T
            don't let him get a word in
the brute's caught, what good's a half hour
Kill him. Kill him.
            and let the sextons cart him out
get the stuff out of sight,
            and let me forget it.

ORESTES (*snarling*)
GET ON IN THERE, stow the gab
you're in for it.

AEGISTHUS
Why have I got to go in

    (*breaking*)

and die in the dark
Why can't you do it here?

ORESTES
None of your business. You'll die
where you killed my father.

AEGISTHUS
Fate. fate, under this damned roof of Pelops
everything happens here.

ORESTES
You'll get YOURS here at any rate.
I can tell you that much.

AEGISTHUS
You didn't get that from your father.

ORESTES
Make a song about it?
            sing IN.

AEGISTHUS
I follow

ORESTES (*patient dragging voice, but sword point in small of Aegisthus' back*)
after you

AEGISTHUS
Hah. Fraid I'll give you the slip.

ORESTES
No, but you aren't dying for pleasure
you've got to go thru with it ALL.
It's a pity you can't all of you die like this
and as quickly, everyone like you.
it wd/ save a lot of unpleasantness.

CHORUS (*sings*)
O SPERM' ATREOOS
                    Atreides, Atreides
come thru the dark.

(*speaks*)

my god, it's come with a rush

(*sings*)

Delivered, Delivered.
                    TEI NUN HORMEI TELEOOTHEN
swift end
                    so soon.

SOPHOKLES
WOMEN OF TRACHIS

A VERSION BY
EZRA POUND

The Trachiniae *presents the highest peak of Greek sensibility registered in any of the plays that have come down to us, and is, at the same time, nearest the original form of the God-Dance.*

A version for KITASONO KATUE, hoping he will use it on my dear old friend Miscio Ito, or take it to the Minoru if they can be persuaded to add to their repertoire.

PERSONAE

The Day's Air, DAIANEIRA, *daughter of Oineus.*

HERAKLES ZEUSON, *the Solar vitality.*

AKHELOÖS, *a river, symbol of the power of damp and darkness, triform as water, cloud and rain.*

HYLLOS, *son of Herakles and Daysair.*

LIKHAS, *a herald.*

A messenger.

A nurse, or housekeeper, old and tottery, physically smaller than Daysair.

IOLE, *Tomorrow, daughter of Eurytus, a King.*

Captive women.

Girls of Trachis.

Women of Trachis

DAYSAIR:
"No man knows his luck 'til he's dead."
They've been saying that for a long time
but it's not true in my case. Mine's soggy.
Don't have to go to hell to find that out.

I had a worse scare about getting married than any
girl in Pleuron, my father's place in Aetolia.
First came a three-twisted river, Akheloös,
part bullheaded cloud, he looked like,
part like a slicky snake with scales on it
shining, then it would look like a bullheaded man
with water dripping out of his whiskers, black ones.

Bed with that! I ask you!

And Herakles Zeuson got me out of it somehow,
I don't know how he managed with that wet horror,
you might find out from some impartial witness
who could watch without being terrorized.

Looks are my trouble. And that
wasn't the end of trouble.

Herakles never gets sight of his children,
like a farmer who sows a crop and doesn't
look at it again till harvest.
Always away on one assignment or another
    one terror after another,
        always for someone else.

We been outlawed ever since he kill'd Iphitz,
living here in Trachis with a foreigner,
and nobody knows where he is.

Bitter ache of separation brought on me,

ten months then five, and no news,
bitter childbirth in separation
worried for some awful calamity.
Black trouble may be connected with
    this memo he left me.

I keep praying it doesn't
                mean something horrible.

    NURSE:
If a slave be permitted, milady?
I've heard you worrying time and again about Herakles . . .
If I'm not speaking out of my turn, ma'am, you got
a fine lot of sons here, why not Hyllos
    go look for his father?

He's coming now. There, hurrying!
If you felt like to tell him,
    if. . . .

    DAYSAIR:
See here, son, this slave talks sense,
    more than some free folks.

    HYLLOS:
What's she say? Lemme hear.

    DAYSAIR:
No credit to you, that you haven't gone to look for your
    father.

    HYLLOS:
I've just heard . . . if it's true.

    DAYSAIR:
Heard what? That he's sitting around
                    somewhere or other.

    HYLLOS:
Farmed out last year to a woman in Lydia.

DAYSAIR:
He's capable of anything, if . . .

HYLLOS:
Oh, I hear he's got out of *that*.

DAYSAIR:
Do they say he's alive or dead?

HYLLOS:
They *say* he's in Eubœa,
                              besieging Eurytusville
        or on the way to it.

DAYSAIR:
You know he left some sort of forecast
        having to do with that country?

HYLLOS:
No, I didn't know that.

DAYSAIR:
That it would be the end of him,
                              or that when he got
through with the job, he would live happy ever after.
It's on the turn of the wheel.
Don't you want to go and work with him?
If he wins we're saved,
        if he doesn't we're done for.

HYLLOS:
Of course I'll go. I'd have gone before now
        if I had known.
I've never worried very much about him
one way or the other. Luck being with him.
But now I'll go get the facts.

DAYSAIR:
Well, get going. A bit late,
        but a good job's worth a bonus.

KHOROS: *Str. 1* (*accompaniment strings, mainly cellos*):
PHOEBUS, Phoebus, ere thou slay
and lay flaked Night upon her blazing pyre,
Say, ere the last star-shimmer is run:
Where lies Alkmene's son, apart from me?
Aye, thou art keen, as is the lightning blaze,
Land way, sea ways,
in these some slit hath he
found to escape thy scrutiny?

Ant. 1
DAYSAIR is left alone,
    so sorry a bird,
For whom, afore, so many suitors tried.
And shall I ask what thing is heart's desire,
Or how love fall to sleep with tearless eye,
So worn by fear away, of dangerous road,
A manless bride to mourn in vacant room,
Expecting ever the worse,
    of dooms to come?

Str. 2
NORTH WIND or South, so bloweth tireless
wave over wave to flood.
Cretan of Cadmus' blood, Orcus' shafts err not.
What home hast 'ou now,
    an some God stir not?

Ant. 2
PARDON if I reprove thee, Lady,
To save thee false hopes delayed.
Thinkst thou that man who dies,
Shall from King Chronos take
    unvaried happiness?
Nor yet's all pain.

(*drums, quietly added to music*)
The shifty Night delays not,
Nor fates of men, nor yet rich goods and spoil.
Be swift to enjoy, what thou art swift to lose.

Let not the Queen choose despair.
Hath Zeus no eye (who saith it?)
     watching his progeny?

DAYSAIR:
You've found out, I suppose, and want to help me stop
     worrying.
Hope you'll never go through enough to understand how.
One grows up, gets fed. "Don't get sun-burnt."
"Don't get wet in the rain. Keep out of draughts,"
that's a girl's life till she's married.
Gets her assignment at night: something to think about,
that is, worry about her man and the children.
You've seen my load, while it's been going on.
Well, here's another to wail about:
before King Herakles rushed off the last time,
he left an old slab of wood with sign writing on it.
Never could get a word out of him about it before,
for all the rough jobs he went out on,
he just couldn't bear to speak of it,
talked as if he were going to work, not to his funeral.
Now? not a bit of it:
all about my marriage property,
what land each of the children was to get from the entail.
Time to work out in three months,
either he would be dead, or come back and spend
the rest of his life without trouble,
all fixed by the gods, end of Herakles' labours,
as stated
     under an old beech-tree in Dodona
where a pair of doves tell you.
Time up,
     see how much truth was in it.
I started from a sound sleep, shaking,
in terror I should have to live on
robbed of the best man ever born.

KHOROS:
Hush. Here comes a man with a wreath on.
     That means good news.

MESSENGER:
Queen Daysair,
let me be the first to calm your anxiety.
Alkemene's son is alive, and has won,
and is carrying the spoils to the gods
                                        of our country.

DAYSAIR:
What are you talking about?

MESSENGER:
You'll soon see him, the man you want,
crowned with Victory. He's looking splendid.

DAYSAIR:
You get this from some local bloke, or a foreigner?

MESSENGER:
There in the summer pastures
Likhas the herald is telling a whole crowd of people
I came on ahead, thought I might get
    a tip for the news.

DAYSAIR:
Why doesn't he come himself, if there's anything to it?

MESSENGER:
He can't for the crowd, ma'am.
They're all jammed round him
    wanting the details.
He can't move a step. They want it.
But you'll see him here pretty soon.

DAYSAIR:
Zeus in the long grass of Oeta,
joy hast Thou given me with its season.

Tune up, you there, you women, inside
and out here.
      I had given up hope.
Never thought I would see it.
Let's sing and be happy.

      KHOROS:
APOLLO
      and Artemis, analolu
                              Artemis,
Analolu,
Sun-bright Apollo, Saviour Apollo
                  analolu,
Artemis,
Sylvan Artemis,
Swift-arrowed Artemis, analolu
By the hearth-stone
                  brides to be
Shout in male company:
                  APOLLO EUPHARETRON.
Sylvan Artemis,
            torch-lit Artemis
With thy Ortygian girls,
                  Analolu
Artemis,
      Io Zagreus,
Join now, join with us
            when the great stag is slain,
Lord of hearts, Artemis,
Ivied Zagreus,
            Analolu,
Dancing maid and man,
Lady or Bacchanal
                  dancing toe to toe
By night,
By light shall show
                  analolu
                        Paian.

DAYSAIR:
Yes, my dear girls, I make out the crowd
and finally and at last and at leisure
the herald, to be received,
                              and,
if his news is good,
                    welcomed.

LIKHAS:
That it is, Milady,
                   and worth hearing,
and paying for.

DAYSAIR:
Is Herakles alive?

LIKHAS:
Sound in wind and limb, mind and body.

DAYSAIR:
Where? In Greece or in some damn foreign desert?

LIKHAS:
On the cliff of Eubœa,
setting up altars to Zeus Kaenean.

DAYSAIR:
A vow, or to stave off evil?

LIKHAS:
A vow, made when he went to conquer
        these women's country.

DAYSAIR:
Good God! What are these poor devils?
        Where do they come from?

LIKHAS:
These are the ones he picked for the gods (and
        himself) when he sacked Eurytus.

DAYSAIR:

And he's been waiting all this time
  to conquer a city?

LIKHAS:

No, most of the time he was in Lydia,
that's what he says, sold into bondage,
and you can't blame it on anyone except Zeus.
Says he was in servitude to the barbarian Omphale
  (that's what he says).
So disgusted he swore to get back at the man
     who'd double-crossed him;
chuck him and his whole house into slavery,
wife, child and the lot of 'em.
Swore in foreign troops and went to Eurytus' place
  as he blamed it all on Eurytus.
Well, he was drunk, and he killed a man,
threw him off a cliff, and was punished.
Zeus wouldn't stand it,
  and Herakles blamed it on 'Rytus
who had insulted him
  and had him thrown out of the dining hall,
which was how he came to be on the cliff
  up at Tirunth
when Iphytz was there hunting lost horses,
and he killed him, and so on,
and Zeus wouldn't stand it.
So when he'd done his time, he got a gang together
and sacked 'Rytus' city.
  These are the captives.
That's what comes of big talk.
Said Herakles couldn't shoot as well as his kids, 'Rytus's.
Hell's full of big talkers.
He'll be along as soon as he's finished
  the celebration. All very fine—
Sacrifice, captives.
  C'est très beau.

KHOROS:

Yes, isn't it, Your Majesty.
Everything will now be all right.

DAYSAIR:

If it lasts, yes. Looks all right, why can't I feel easy about it?
My luck runs with his. I wonder.
I'm sorry for those poor girls,
                in a strange country,
orphans, slaves,
I hope no child of mine ever—
    or that I don't live to see it.
    (*to* IOLE)
You look as if you were taking it worse
    than any of the others.
Girl, wife, young; no, you can't have been
married yet. And good family.

Who is she, Likhas?
I'm sorrier for her than for the rest of them.
She seems to feel it.

LIKHAS:

How do I know? She might be top drawer,
   why ask me?

DAYSAIR:

Royal? Had Eurytus a daughter?

LIKHAS:

I dunno. I haven't asked her.

DAYSAIR:

Didn't anyone tell you?

LIKHAS:

I had plenty else to do, without asking that kind of
   question.

DAYSAIR: (*to* IOLE)
Well then, you tell me.
What's happened? Who are you?

LIKHAS:
It'll be a change if she does,
hasn't uttered a pip-squeak
since she came down
                    from the windy country
Tears, tears, tears,
       but it's excusable,
she's had pretty bad luck.

DAYSAIR:
Let her alone, let her go in,
I don't want to add to her troubles,
       she's had enough.
Everybody in!
Have to hurry to get things in order.
                         [*Exeunt Likhas and captives.*]

MESSENGER:
'Arf a mo' Ma'am! Better find out
what you're taking in there. I know
       a bit more about that.

DAYSAIR:
What's this? What are you stopping me for?

MESSENGER:
Jus' lis'en a bit,
if what I told you before was worth hearing . . .

DAYSAIR:
Shall I call 'em back?

MESSENGER:
We're enough. There's enough of us here.

DAYSAIR:
They're all gone. Don't talk riddles.

MESSENGER:
That fellow was lying, one time or the other,
one heck of a messenger!

DAYSAIR:
Put it on the line, what do you know?
    Get it out clearly.

MESSENGER:
All started when he had a letch for the girl,
and when her pro-eh-Genitor 'Rytus wouldn't
        let him put her to bed on the Q.T.
Wasn't about Iphytz or Omphale
he sacked the town, and killed 'Rytus to get her.
He's not bringing her here as a slave. Too het up.
So I thought I would be telling Your Majesty,
this is what Likhas was saying,
        and plenty of Trachinians heard him.
I'm sorry to worry you. But the facts . . .

DAYSAIR:
What have I done, what have I done!
Just a nobody, and he took oath that she was.
    What a mess.

MESSENGER:
She's somebody, all right, all right.
Name's Iole, and 'Rytus her father.
And Likhas hadn't found that out
    'cause he hadn't troubled to ask her.

KHOROS:
To hell with all double-crossers,
    they are the last of all dirtiness.

DAYSAIR:
What shall . . . what shall . . . my dear girls,
    what, what. . . .

MESSENGER:
You might start by questioning Likhas,
scare the lights out of him, and he might tell you.

DAYSAIR:
I'll do that. You're talking sense.

MESSENGER:
Want me to go, or . . ?

DAYSAIR:
You stay here. There he comes, without being asked.

LIKHAS:
What do you want me to tell Herakles, Madam?
    I'm leaving.

DAYSAIR:
Not in quite such a hurry. You were
    in no hurry to get here.
Let's have a little conversation.

LIKHAS:
Yours to command, Ma'am.

DAYSAIR:
Have you any respect for the truth?

LIKHAS:
So help me God. Nothing but . . .

DAYSAIR:
Who was the woman you brought here?

LIKHAS:
I don't know about her family, she comes from Eubœa.

MESSENGER:
Look at her. You know who this is?

LIKHAS:
Who are you?

MESSENGER:
Don't mind that.
Answer my question, if you've got sense enough.

LIKHAS:
Her most Gracious Majesty, Queen of Herakles,
Daughter of Oineus, Daysair.

MESSENGER:
Right for once! She's your Queen.

LIKHAS:
To whom my most faithful service . . .

MESSENGER:
Service, duty, yes duty, my dicky-bird
and if you don't . . .

LIKHAS:
What's this screw-ball?
                    If I don't . . .

MESSENGER:
Do your duty, do you get that?
        It sounds fairly clear.

LIKHAS:
Silly to stop for this nonsense, I'm off.

MESSENGER:
One little question.

LIKHAS:
Get on with it. Not the quiet type, are you?

MESSENGER:
That girl, you know which one,
  you took into the house?

LIKHAS:
What about her?

MESSENGER:
Don't know her by sight, eh, you don't?
and you said she was 'Rytus's daughter,
  the Princess Iole.

LIKHAS:
Nobody ever heard me say anything of the sort.

MESSENGER:
Oh yes they did. Plenty of us, us Trachinians,
  a whole agora heard it.

LIKHAS:
Just talk, a mere rumour.

MESSENGER:
Just an opinion? eh? rumour? eh?
And you swore pink they were bringing her
  to be Herakles' wife.

LIKHAS:
Wife? Good God, Your dear Majesty,
  who is this outsider?

MESSENGER:
Just somebody heard you talking.
Not the Lydian army, and its queen.
He sacked a whole town cause he liked the
            look in her eyes. Took a fancy.

LIKHAS:
Beg to differ, Your Majesty. No use
    bothering with this screw-ball.

DAYSAIR:
THUNDER of God! By the black vale of Oeta,
    don't weasel to me.
                    And
                        besides
you're not going to tell it to a bad woman,
or to one that doesn't know that men
just naturally don't want the same thing all the time.
How's any slugger going to stop Love with his hands?
That's a nice way to think of it?
He starts off the gods, as he fancies.
Me, am I going to win at it?
Be perfectly silly to blame the man while he's crazy,
    or the girl they're blaming.
No shame to me . . . . no harm.
It's not that at all. BUT . . . .
    if he taught you to lie,
the lesson you learned is
                    not
                        a nice one.
And if you taught yourself to lie,
    thinking some good would come of it,
    you saw cross-eyed.
You come out with the truth, the whole
truth. Now.
It's no compliment to call a free man a liar,
when a free man is called a liar it's no pretty compliment
and it'll all come out anyhow,
    how are you going to hide it?
Plenty of people heard you, and will certainly tell me.
And if you think . . . not nice to be in terror of me . . .
not to find out, would pain me, mightn't it?
And what's so awful to know?
    That man Herakles! hasn't he
had plenty of others on me?
Ever driven me to nag him, or blame him?

And if he was overflowing with passion for her,
will I but pity her greatly, and the more.
Her looks have ruin'd her life,
  and ruin'd the land of her fathers,
not knowing, wretched,
  didn't know what it was all about.
All this gone under the wind.
I'm telling you: do dirt to others but . . .
  Don't weasel to me.

KHOROS:
Better do as she says.
  She won't blame you, in the long run,
  and I will be grateful.

LIKHAS:
Oh Majesty, Your Dear Majesty, I see you understand
  that human beings are human
I'll tell the truth, I won't hold back on you.
It's as that chap there says it was.
Herakles was hit by a tremendous passion,
it swept over him,
  and he seized all Oechalia
and gave it over to pillage, her fatherland,
but I'll say this much for him,
he never denied it, or told me to conceal it.
It was me, your Majesty, who was afraid it
      would pain you,
me who did wrong, eh, if, eh, you
  think it was wrong of me,
and now you know all of it, for his sake
and for your sake, both of your sakes together,
do put up with the girl.
He beat all the champions into subjection
and now Eros throws him down with all his inferiors.

DAYSAIR:
Yes, We think that's what's to be done
  and just that way.
This imported trouble won't be got rid of

by a losing fight versus the gods.
Let's go in, and I'll get you something for Herakles
and a note to take with it.
Got to send him something suitable in return.
Wouldn't be right for you to go back
without something, having come with all this.

KHOROS: *Str.*
KUPRIS bears trophies away.
Kronos' Son, Dis and Poseidon,
There is no one
                    shaker unshaken.
Into dust go they all.
Neath Her they must
                    give way.

Ant.
TWO gods fought for a girl,
Battle and dust!
Might of a River with horns
                    crashing.
Four bulls together
                    Shall no man tether,
Akheloös neither,
                    lashing through Oneudai
As bow is bent
                    The Theban Cub,
Bacchus' own, spiked is his club,
HE is God's Son.
                    Hurled to one bed,
Might of waters like a charge of bulls crashing.
Get a dowsing rod.
Kupris decides
To whom brides
                    fall.

ROCK and wrack,
Horns into back,
Slug, grunt and groan,
                    Grip through to bone.

Crash and thud
Bows against blood
            Grip and grind
            Bull's head and horn.
BUT the wide-eyed girl on the hill,
Out of it all,
        frail,
Who shall have her?
To stave her and prove her,
Cowless calf lost,
Hurtled away,
          prized for a day?

    [*Music in this Khoros fifes, kettle drums, oboes, etc., with
      flute solo or clarinet.*]

    DAYSAIR: (*re-enters*)
Well, my dears,
while that outsider is inside
chatting with the little victims of bow and spear
    before he pushes off,
let's figure out how we are to manage this cohabitation
        with
this virgin who isn't one any longer,
    'cause she's been yoked.
Too much cargo, contraband,
    but keep my mind afloat somehow.
"Double yoke
Under one cloak",
and I said he was so kind and dependable.
What I get for keeping house
               all this time.
But I can't stay mad at him long,
    I know what's got into him,
And yet . . .
    the two of us,
My husband, her man, the new girl's man.
    and she's young.
And:
    "E'en from fond eyes, olde flowers are cast away."

And
        it's not nice for a woman to be too crotchety,
the ones with nice minds are not peevish.
And
        may be there's a way out.
Nessus, that old ruffian with hair on his chest,
long ago, I was a green girl then,
and he gave me a little present
which I've kept stored away in a brass pot
        all this time.
He was dying from loss of blood
        there at the ferry over Evenus
where it's too deep to ford.
And he had me up on his shoulders
in mid passage
        and got too fresh with his hands.
I let out a shriek, and: WHIZZ!!
as he turned
Zeuson had an arrow into his lung up to the feathers.
Before he passed out he said:
        "As you're old Oineus' daughter,
I'll give you what I've earned by all this ferrying.
Scrape the drying blood from my wound
where the Hydra's blood tipped that arrow,
        Lernaean Hydra,
and you'll have a love charm so strong
that Herakles will never look at another woman
        or want her more than you."

Well, my dears, I been thinking 'bout that,
I've kept the stuff since his death
        carefully in a cool dark place,
and I've swobbed this jacket with it,
just as the Centaur told me,
        not like a philtre,
I don't believe it's too great a risk.

Deal with that young woman somehow,
        unless you think I am foolish.

KHOROS:
Don't seem a bad idea, if
    you think it will work.

DAYSAIR:
No absolute guarantee, of course,
    but you'll never tell till you try.

KHOROS:
Nope, no proof without data,
    no proof without experiment.

DAYSAIR:
There he is. Be gone soon,
keep quiet about this for a bit,
    what they don't know won't hurt us.
You can get away with a good deal in the dark.

LIKHAS:
I have considerably overstayed my leave, Madame d'Oineus.
Tell me, please, just what I've to do.

DAYSAIR:
While you've been in there talking to the girls,
I've wrapped up this present for Herakles,
a jacket I made him myself,
nobody else is to put it on first,
he's not to leave it in the sun
or near the fire inside the holy hedge
until he stand before the gods at the altar
for killing the bulls.
I vowed that if I should ever see him
safe home, or hear he had come,
I would make him a proper chiton
to wear when he sacrificed in the god's presence.
The packet is sealed with my signet
which he will recognize.
    Now you may go, and
remember a messenger's first job is

to do what he's told, not more, not less,
but just what he is told.
      Do that, and we'll both be grateful.

LIKHAS:
Properly trained in Hermes' messenger-service, Ma'am,
say I'm not, if I slip up on this
or don't take him the box, as is,
and your message exactly.

DAYSAIR:
Then go. You know how things are going inside.

LIKHAS:
Yes. I'll say: everything under control.

DAYSAIR:
And that I'm being nice to the visitor,
      you've seen that.

LIKHAS:
And I was most awfully surprised
      and cheered by it.

DAYSAIR: (*rêveuse*)
Anything more? No.

Mustn't say how much I want him
      until I know he's going to want me.

KHOROS: *Str. 1*
SAFE the port, rocky the narrows,
Streams warm to a glaze on Oeta's hill,
Malis' pool and Dian's beach
Neath her golden-shafted arrows
      Ye who live here and disdeign
      All greek towns less than the Pelean,

Ant. 1 (*fifes, flute & grosse caisse*)
SOON shall hear the skirl and din
Of flutes' loud cackle shrill return,
Dear to Holy Muses as
Phoebus' lyre ever was.
                    From the valours of his wars
Comes now the God, Alkmene's son
Bearing battle booty home.

Str. 2 (*clarinette, bassoon*)
TWELVE moons passing,
        night long, and day.
Exile, exile
Knowing never, to come? to stay?
Tears, tears, till grief
Hath wrecked her heart away,
Ere mad Mars should end him
        his working day.

Ant. 1 (*cello, low register*)
TO PORT, to port.
Boat is still now;
The many oars move not.
        By island shrine ere he come to the town
Day long, day long
If the charm of the gown prove not?
'Tis dipped, aye in the unguent
drenched through it, in every fold.
Told, told,
in all as she had been told.

[DAYSAIR *enters now in the tragic mask.*]

DAYSAIR:
Something's gone wrong, my dears, awfully,
terribly wrong, and I'm scared.

KHOROS:
Why, Daysair Oineus, what do you mean?

DAYSAIR:

I don't know, I dunno, I hoped
    and I don't hope.
Something awful will come of it.

KHOROS:

You don't mean your present to Herakles?

DAYSAIR:

Exactly. People oughtn't to rush into
what they don't understand.

KHOROS:

Tell us what you're afraid of.

DAYSAIR:

Something too creepy's just happened.
That thick wad of white sheep's wool
that I used to daub the jacket, just disappeared.
Nobody touched it.
                    Seemed to corrode of itself.
Ate itself up, there on the floor-stones.
When that brute of a Centaur
was in agony from the arrow in his lung,
he told me—and I can remember it
as if it were engraved on a brass plate—
and I did just what he told me: kept it cool,
away from the fire and sunlight, in a cupboard
until time to use it, which I did inside,
and nobody saw me take it out of the kettle
with wool I'd pulled out of a fleece from our own sheep
and put it inside the box that you saw.

But just now, something you wouldn't believe,
perfectly inexplicable, I found it all flaming
there in the sunlight. It had got warm
and just crumbled away, like sawdust
where somebody had been sawing a board,
but mixed up with bubbles

like the fat scum that slops over from the wine-press.
I'm out of my mind with worry and misery.
I've done something awful.
Why should that dying brute want to do me a favour?
He was dying on my account.
Wanted to hit back at his killer.
And I've found out what he was up to,
and it's too late.
I'm to murder him, damn it, fate.
I know that arrow hurt even Chiron
    and he was a demigod—
black blood from the death arrow,
    would kill any wild animal.
If he dies, if he's caught,
    I'll die too.
No decent woman would live after that horror.

    KHOROS:
Don't give up yet.
There's danger. But it mayn't necessarily happen.

    DAYSAIR:
There's no hope for those who have done wrong.

    KHOROS:
But if you didn't mean it, they won't
blame you as much as all that.

    DAYSAIR:
Talk that way if you're not involved,
not if you've got the weight of it on you.

    KHOROS:
Better wait to hear what your son's got to say.
There he is to tell you, himself;
he went to look for his father.

    HYLLOS:
Damn you, I wish you were dead,
or no mother, anyhow, or at any rate not mine.

DAYSAIR:
What's got into you, son,
     why do . . .

HYLLOS:
You've murdered your man, my father,
     and you did it today.

DAYSAIR:
What a thing to say. Oh, oh.

HYLLOS:
Well you've done it, and finished it,
and what's done can't be undone.

DAYSAIR:
How can you say this! Me! The most loathsome crime
     known?

HYLLOS:
I saw it myself, the way he suffered.
     This is no idle rumour.

DAYSAIR:
Where did you find him? You were with him?

HYLLOS:
You'll hear it. You've got to hear all of it.
He sacked Eurytus' city,
     you've heard of that place,
and was coming home with the spoils,
at the top headland of Euboea
where the sea swashes in on both sides,
at Kenaion, facing the North.
He orientated the altars, to the gods,
     our own.
Fixed the lay-out, cutting the leaves.
And I was glad to get the first sight of him

starting to kill all those bulls.
Then along comes Likhas the family herald
with that present, that marvellous peplon.
And he put it on, like as you'd said,
and started on the first dozen bulls,
going on to kill the whole hundred, hecatomb.
And the poor devil, at the start,
    was so cheerful about it,
seemed pleased with his vestments.
Made the prayer, but
    as the flame went up from the Holy Orgy,
bloody and from the fat oak logs,
sweat broke from his skin,
the shirt stuck to him, like it was glued,
shrinking in on all of his joints
as if made by someone who knew how to do it.
Gnawing into his bones, it seemed to be,
dirty snake poison gave him convulsions,
seemed like it was biting with hate.
And he howled for the miserable Likhas
    who wasn't guilty. You were.
To know who'd hatched the shirt trick.
And Likhas said he had brought it as it was
    fixed up and given him.

Then the stuff got another worse grip on him
and he grabbed Likhas by the foot,
    twisting his ankle,
and threw him out off onto a boulder
    that stuck up out of the breakers.
Hair! Brains came out of the skull
    mixed with blood.
The whole crowd groaned:
one dead, another stark raving.
Nobody dared to come near him. There he was
on the ground roaring, or groaning when
he reared part way up, and the rocks echoing
from Locris to Euboea,
    between the crags and the sea-cliffs.
Till he was clean worn out, writhing on the ground,

moaning, and cursing his marriage bed,
cursing you, and that he'd been fool enough
    to get you from Oineus
to ruin his life. The one woman.

Then with his eyes screwed up from the smoke
    that came out of him
and tears running down, he caught sight of me
and called for me:
    "Don't try to keep out of this,
even if you have to die with me.
    Get me out of here
to somewhere, anywhere, where no one can see me.
Get me out of here, quick.
                I don't want to die here."
    That's what he told me.

So we put him into the hollow of the boat
and brought him to the mainland,
hardly any more noise coming out of him
    but still in convulsions.
You'll see him pretty soon,
    living or dead.
That, my dear mother, is what you have thought up
    to do to my father,
Hell take you, and the Furies, and do you right.
Justice, eh, Justice, if . . .
    lot of justice you had for me!
You spewed it out when you killed
    the best man on earth,
what you see henceforth will be of a different kind.

    (DAYSAIR *exit*.)

    KHOROS:
Why does she go so quietly?
    Has she no answer?

HYLLOS:

Let her go. And a nice wind take her far enough
          . . . out of sight,
and another label to keep up her maternal swank,
fine mother she is, let her de-part
                              in peace . . .
and get some of the pleasure she has given my father.

KHOROS (*low cello merely sustaining the voice*): *Str. 1*
OYEZ:

Things foretold and forecast:
Toil and moil.
God's Son from turmoil shall
—when twelve seed-crops be past—
be loosed with the last,
                    his own.
Twining together, godword found good,
Spoken of old,
          as the wind blew, truth's in the flood.
We and his brood see in swift combine,
          here and at last that:
Amid the dead is no servitude
          nor do they labour.

(*contrabassi & drums muffled*) *Ant. 1*
LO, beneath deadly cloud
Fate and the Centaur's curse, black venom spread.
Dank Hydra's blood
Boils now through every vein, goad after goad
from spotted snake to pierce the holy side,
nor shall he last to see a new day's light,
Black shaggy night descends
                    as Nessus bade.

Str. 2
WHAT MOURNFUL case
          who feared great ills to come,
New haste in mating threatening her home,
Who hark'd to reason in a foreign voice
Entangling her in ravage out of choice.

Tears green the cheek with bright dews
                              pouring down;
Who mourns apart, alone
Oncoming swiftness in o'erlowering fate
To show what wreck is nested in deceit.

  Ant. 2
LET the tears flow.
  Ne'er had bright Herakles in his shining
Need of pity till now
  whom fell disease burns out.
How swift on Oechal's height
  to take a bride.
Black pointed shaft that shielded her in flight,
Attest
That
Kupris stood by and never said a word,
Who now flares here the contriver
manifest . . .
and indifferent.

  [*The dea ex machina, hidden behind a grey gauze in her
  niche, is lit up strongly so that the gauze is transparent.
  The apparition is fairly sudden, the fade-out slightly
  slower: the audience is almost in doubt that she has
  appeared.*]

  HALF KHOROS:
Am I cracked, or did I hear someone weeping?
In the hall?
  Did you hear it?

  2ND HALF KHOROS:
Not a muttering, but someone in trouble,
  wailing,
started again inside there.

  [*Enter* NURSE.]

HALF KHOROS:
Look,
look at the old woman's face.
                              Something awful,
it's all twisted up.

NURSE:
Children, children,
no end to the troubles from sending
    that present to Herakles.

KHOROS:
More, you mean more?

NURSE:
She's gone. . . . . .Daysair,
The last road of all roads
                        . . . without walking.

KHOROS:
What! Dead?

NURSE:
That's all. You heard me.

KHOROS:
You mean the poor girl is dead?

NURSE:
Yes, for the second time. Yes.

KHOROS:
Poor thing. How awful. But how . . .
How is she dead?

NURSE:
In the most violent . . .

KHOROS:
But how, say how, woman.
How did it happen?

NURSE:
Did it herself,
ripped herself open.

KHOROS:
But she crazy? What did she do it with?
How did she do it all by herself?
Dying one after another.

NURSE:
Got hold of a sword, a roaring big sword.
And a sharp one.

KHOROS:
But did you see it, you fool,
see this outrage?

NURSE:
Saw it. I wasn't far off.

KHOROS:
What? How? Go on and tell us.

NURSE:
Did it herself. With her hands.

KHOROS:
But what do you mean?

NURSE:
Plain fact. What you can see for yourself.

KHOROS:
That new girl's doin' it.
I'll say she's effective.
Bride is she, and a fury. Holy Erinyes!

NURSE:
And then some. You'd feel it more
if you'd seen it near to.

KHOROS:
But has a woman got the strength in her hands?
And to stand it?

NURSE:
Terrible, you can believe me. She came in alone
and saw the boy in the hall preparing the hearse-litter
to fetch back his father.
She hid herself down back of the altar,
sank down there groaning because her brood had deserted
    her.
Then pitifully stroking* the things she had used before,
went wandering through the best rooms—
didn't know I could see her, from a sort of kink in the
    wall—
drawing her hands over the things she was used to.

Then came on one of the maids whom she liked,
and with the look of doom on her
cried to her daemon, that she was more childless
than any woman. Then stopped. And of a sudden
ran into Herakles' bedroom, and threw her cloak
on to Herakles' bed, spread it out like a cover-pane,
then threw herself on to it and lay there quiet
for a moment as if asleep.
Choking with tears, then: "Bride's-bed,
good-bye my bride's-bed, never again
folded together!"

And she ripped the dress all off her left side
and the gold clasp with it.

* 2000 years later the Minoru had developed a technique which permitted the direct presentation of such shades by symbolic gesture. In Sophokles' time it had to be left to narration.

I ran for Hyllos, but she was too quick,
she had jammed a sword side-ways
through her liver into the heart, when we got there,
two-edged.

The boy screamed
and blamed himself for having driven her to it.
Father, mother, all in one day.
He'd found out that she'd only done what
that animal told her,
        hadn't meant any harm.
Too pitiful he was. Sobbing and holding her in his arms.

You can't count on anything for tomorrow,
got to wait till today is over.

   KHOROS (*declaimed*): *Str. 1*
TORN between griefs, which grief shall I lament,
which first? Which last, in heavy argument?
One wretchedness to me in double load.

   Ant. 1
DEATH'S in the house,
        and death comes by the road.

   (*sung*) *Str. 2*
THAT WIND might bear away my grief and me,
Sprung from the hearth-stone, let it bear me away.
God's Son is dead,
        that was so brave and strong,
And I am craven to behold such death
        Swift on the eye,
Pain hard to uproot,
        and this so vast
A splendour of ruin.

   Ant. 2
THAT NOW is here.
As Progne shrill upon the weeping air,

'tis no great sound.
    These strangers lift him home,
with shuffling feet, and love that keeps them still.
The great weight silent
    for no man can say
If sleep but feign
    or Death reign instantly.

    HERAKLES (*in the mask of divine agony*):
Holy Kanea, where they build holy altars,
done yourself proud, you have,
nice return for a sacrifice:
    messing me up.
I could have done without these advantages
And the spectacle of madness in flower,
    incurable, oh yes.
Get someone to make a song for it,
Or some chiropractor to cure it.
A dirty pest,
    take God a'mighty to cure it and
I'd be surprised to see Him
    coming this far . . .

    (*to the others*)
Ahj!
Get away,
let me lie quiet, for the last time
aaah. What you doin' trying to turn me over,
let me alone. Blast it.
Bloody crime to start it again,
    sticks to me.
It's coming back.
You greeks are the dirtiest,
    damn you, if you are greeks at all,
where do you come from?
What I've done on sea, and clearing out
    thickets,
killing wild animals.
And now I'm in torture, no one to finish it off

with fire, or with a knife,
 or do ANYthing useful,
or even let me alone.

If only someone would lop my head off
and get me out of this loathsome existence,
Aaahj.

> OLD MAN:

Here, you're his son, and I ain't strong enough
to lift him.
 Give a hand,
You could do more for him than I can.

> HYLLOS:

Right, but he's passed out from pain.
Inside or out here,
 he's dying on me.
God's will.

> HERAKLES:

Boy, where are you? Hoist me up
 and hang on. What rotten luck!
It keeps jumping. This beastly pain,
taken all the fight out of me.
 I can't get at it.

Pallas Athene! there goes that ache again.
Oooh boy, have some pity on the father that made you,
pull out something with an edge on it,
and get it in here

> (*with gesture; the exact spot*)

> (*low cellos, contrabassi, muffled drum in gaps between the
> phrases*)

and get it in here
 under my collar bone.
Your mother's to blame for this.

Damn'd atheist, that's what she is.
And I wish her the same.

(*pause, then sotto voce*)

Brother of God, Sweet Hell, be decent.
Let me lie down and rest.
Swift-feathered Death, that art the end of shame.

KHOROS:
Scares me to hear him.
    And when you think what he was.

HERAKLES:
Many and hot, and that's not just talking,
my own hands, and my own back doing the dirty work.
But God's bitch never put one like this over on me,
nor that grump Rustheus either.
And now Miss Oineus
with her pretty little shifty eyes
    m'la calata,
has done me to beat all the furies,
got me into a snarl, clamped this net on to me
    and she wove it.
It sticks to my sides and
    has gnawed through to my furtherest in'nards.
And now it's stopped the green blood,
got into the lungs and dries up the tubes along with them,
tears up all the rest of me.
Holds me down, like in fetters. I can't explain it.
No gang of plainsman with spears,
    no army of giants come up out of the earth,
no wild beast was strong enough. Nor Greeks,
nor foreigners whose countries I had cleaned up,
but a piddling female did it,
    not even a man with balls.
Alone and without a sword.

Boy, you start showing whose son you are. I.e. mine,
and as for the highly revered title to motherhood,

you get that producer out of her house
and hand her over to me. We'll see whether
you feel worse watching me rot or
seeing her cut up and brought to justice.

Go, pick up your courage. Get going and
      have mercy on me
or pity, that's it: pity. Me blubbering like a flapper,
no man ever saw me taken like this before
or said I groaned over my troubles,
now I find out I'm a sissy. Come here. Nearer,
see what your father is brought to.

      (*he throws off the sheet covering him*)

      Without the wrappings,
look at it, all of you,
      ever see a body in this condition?
Gosh!
      That's a death-rattle again. Disgraceful.
Got me here on the side again, eating through me.
Can't seem to get rid of it.
Lord of Hell, take me.
Thundering Lord God, if you've got a crash-rattle,
throw it.

God our father of Thunder.
      There it is gnawing again.
budding, blossoming.
      OH my hand, my hands,
back, chest, my lovely arms,
what you used to be. That lion that was killing off
the Nemean cattle-men, the Hydra in Lerna
and those unsociable bardots, half man and half horse,
the whole gang of them all together
arrogant, lawless, surpassing strong,
and the Eurymanthian animal, and that three-headed pup
from Hell down under, the Echidna's nursling
brought up by an out-size viper,
and the dragon-guard of the golden apples

at the end of the world.
And a great lot of other work,
and nobody took any prizes away from me.
No joints, no strength in 'em,
    all torn to pieces.
This blind calamity,
    and my mother was a notable woman
and my father in heaven, Zeus, mid the stars.
That's what they say.

But I tell you this much. I can't even crawl,
but bring her here and I'll learn her,
I'll make her a lesson: Alive or dead how I
    pay people for dirty work.

KHOROS:
Poor Greece, you can see troubles coming
    if you let such a man down.

HYLLOS:
You seem to expect me to answer.
You're quiet, as if expecting an answer.
Now if I may ask you for justice,
and tell you how useless it is to want to break her.

HERAKLES:
Say what you've got to say, and get it over with.
I'm too sick to be pestered with double-talk and nuances.

HYLLOS:
It's about mother's mistake.
    What's happened. She didn't mean it.

HERAKLES:
Well of all the dirtiest . . .
Your bloody murdering mother
and you dare to mention her
    in my earshot!

HYLLOS:
It's about mother's mistake.

HERAKLES:
No, I dare say past crimes ought to be—

HYLLOS:
And you'll mention what's happened today.

HERAKLES:
Speak up. But be careful,
    it won't show your breeding.

HYLLOS:
Well, she's dead. Just been killed.

HERAKLES:
By whom?
    That's a bad sign.

HYLLOS:
She did it.

HERAKLES:
And cheated me out of the chance.

HYLLOS:
If you knew all the facts, you'd quit being angry.

HERAKLES:
Thazza good tough start. Give.

HYLLOS:
She just didn't mean any harm. She meant well.

HERAKLES:
You louse! Meant well by killing your father?

HYLLOS:
An aphrodisiac. Thought it would
get you back, and went wrong, when she
saw the new wife in the house.

HERAKLES:
The Trachinians got witch-doctors that good?

HYLLOS:
Nessus told her a long time ago
that the philtre would start that sort of letch.

HERAKLES:
Misery. I'm going out
and my light's gone.
        The black out!
I understand perfectly well
where things have got to . . . Go, son,
call all my seed and their kindred,
and Alkmene, ill-starred for the empty name
of the Godhead, my mother,
so they can get my last report
of the oracles, as I know them.

HYLLOS:
Your mother is at Tiryns out of reach
and took some of the children with her.
Others are in Thebes-burg, I'll round up
the near ones, if that's O.K.,
and they'll do what you tell them.

HERAKLES:
Listen first, and show what you're made of,
my stock. My father told me long ago
that no living man should kill me,
but that someone from hell would, and
that brute of a Centaur has done it.
The dead beast kills the living me
and that fits another odd forecast

breathed out at the Selloi's oak—
Those fellows rough it,
    sleep on the ground, up in the hills there.
I heard it and wrote it down
    under my Father's tree.
Time lives, and it's going on now.
I am released from trouble.
I thought it meant life in comfort.
It doesn't. It means that I die.
For amid the dead there is no work in service.
Come at it that way, my boy, what

SPLENDOUR,
        IT ALL COHERES.*

[*He turns his face from the audience, then sits erect,
facing them without the mask of agony; the revealed make-
up is that of solar serenity. The hair golden and as
electrified as possible.*]

But you must help me
and don't make me lose my temper,
don't dither, and don't ask me why.
This is the great rule: Filial Obedience.

HYLLOS:
I will obey.

HERAKLES (*extending his hand*):
Put her there.

HYLLOS:
I'll do it. I don't need to swear.

* This is the key phrase, for which the play exists, as in the *Elektra:* "Need
we add cowardice to all the rest of these ills?" Or the "T'as inventé la jus-
tice" in Cocteau's *Antigone*. And, later: "Tutto quello che è accaduto,
doveva accadere." At least one sensitive hellenist who has shown great care
for Sophokles' words, has failed to grasp the main form of the play, either
here or in the first chorus, and how snugly each segment of the work fits
into its box.

HERAKLES:
Put it there.

HYLLOS (*complying*):
What am I swearing to?

HERAKLES:
Repeat: "By the head of Zeus,"
you will do what I tell you to.

HYLLOS:
I swear, so help me God.

HERAKLES:
"And God damn all perjurers."

HYLLOS:
I'll keep it anyhow.

(*adds after almost imperceptible pause*)

And God DAMN all perjurers.

HERAKLES:
You know the highest peak of Zeus' hill in Oeta?

HYLLOS:
Sacrificed there quite often.

HERAKLES:
You must get this carcass up there,
by hand, with as many friends as you like.
And cut a lot of wood from deep-rooted oaks
and from wild olive (male trees)
lopped off the same way.
Get it going with the bright flame of a pine torch.
And put me onto the pyre.
Don't blubber. Show that you are my son
or you'll have my ghost heavy on you
from below there,
        forever.

HYLLOS:
But father . . .
         have I got all this straight?

HERAKLES:
Got your orders. Do 'em,
         or change your name.

HYLLOS:
Good lord, you want me to be a murderer
         and a parricide?

HERAKLES:
No, a physician,
         the only one who can heal.

HYLLOS:
But how come, if I burn it?

HERAKLES:
If you are afraid of that,
         do the rest.

HYLLOS:
I don't mind carrying you up there.

HERAKLES:
And build the pyre? As I tell you to do?

HYLLOS:
So long as I don't have to light it
         with my own hands,
                  I'll do my bit.

HERAKLES:
And another little job
         that won't take long
after the big one.

HYLLOS:
I don't care what size it is. It'll get done.

HERAKLES:
You know that kid of Eurytus's?

HYLLOS:
Iole? I guess you mean Iole.

HERAKLES:
Ezakly.
When I am dead, if you revere your agreement,
remember it and marry the girl.
Don't disobey me.
She has lain beside me. No other man
but you is to have her.
You agree to the greater, don't jib at the less.

HYLLOS:
But I'd have to be possessed of a devil to do it.
Better die with you. She caused mother's death
and your torture. She's our worst enemy.

HERAKLES:
The fellow doesn't seem to want to carry out
his dad's last request.
God's worst curse falls on a disobedient son.

HYLLOS:
The delirium's coming back.

HERAKLES:
Yes, because you're stirring it up.

HYLLOS:
What *am* I to do, in this mess?

HERAKLES:
Start by hearing straight.
What I'm telling you,
the dad that made you.

HYLLOS:
Have you got to teach me crime?

HERAKLES:
It is no crime to gladden a father's heart.

HYLLOS:
If you order me to, is that legal?
Perfectly all right?

HERAKLES:
I call the gods to witness.

HYLLOS:
Then I'll go ahead. If it's set before the gods
that way, I can't be blamed for obeying you.

HERAKLES:
Fine. At last, and get going.
Get me onto that fire, before this pain
starts again. Hey, you there, hoist me up
for the last trouble.
        The last rest.

HYLLOS:
Nothing to stop us now. You're the driver.

HERAKLES:
Come ere the pain awake,
        O stubborn mind.

(*catches sight of* HYLLOS' *face and breaks off with*)

And put some cement in your face,
reinforced concrete, make a cheerful finish
even if you don't want to.

HYLLOS:
Hoist him up, fellows.
        And for me a great tolerance,
matching the gods' great unreason.
They see the things being done,
calamities looked at,
sons to honour their fathers,
and of what is to come, nothing is seen. Gods!
Our present miseries, their shame. And of all men
none has so borne, nor ever shall again.

And now ladies, let you go home.
Today we have seen strange deaths,
wrecks many, such as have not been suffered before.
And all of this is from Zeus.

        (*Exeunt: The girls left,* HYLLOS *and bearers right*).

PAVANNES AND DIVAGATIONS

Words for Roundel in Double Canon
(*Maestoso e triste*)

O bury 'em down
              in Blooms –
                       buree
Where the gravy tastes like the soup,
O bury 'em down in Blooms –
                    buree
Where the soup tastes like
                last night's
                    gra –
                         vee

O bury 'em down in Bloomsburee
Where the damp dank rot
Is never forgot
O bury 'em down
In Bloomsburee
Where the soup tastes like
                    last night's gravee

O bury
'em down
In Bloos –
buree
Where the gra –

vy tastes

Like the

Soup.

Guides to the Montanari Poems

AUTUNNO

Autumn, so many leaves
pass with the wind, I see
the worn-out rain
gather aloft again.

Aimless or vagabond,
a walking sadness, beyond
the deep-cut road:
horses weary of load.

A whirring noise, new night there
empty in monotone:
the Ave Maria
no prayer.

STAGIONE DI FIORI

Time of almonds in flower
and songs half spoken;
walnut's bough now
keeps sun off threshed oats.

Time comes again
from the shepherd's pens:
shy flowers in wind
each year, thus, with no pain;

Renews the rillets, and dews.
White thorn, darkens in pine
with new spikes, a heaven of birds
sing to line.

Comes joy's season, that does no ill
for our brother the sun, aloft,
keeps it too languid and still
for any evil.

NOTTE DIETRO LE PERSIANE

When the light
goes, men shut behind blinds
their life, to die for a night.

And yet
through glass and bars
some dream a wild sunset,
waiting the stars.

Call these few, at least
the singers, in whom
hope's voice is yeast.

POMERIGGIO DI LUGLIO

Road in the open there,
all sun and grain-dust
     and sour air
from the canal bank,

Ditch-water higher now
with the tide,
     turns violet and red.

A swallow for shuttle, back,
forth, forth, back
     from shack to
marsh track;
     to the far
sky-line that's fading now.
A thin song of a girl plucking grain,
a child cries from the threshing floor.

Werewolf in selvage I saw
   In day's dawn changing his shape,

Amid leaves he lay
    and in his face, sleeping, such pain
       I fled agape.

Chansson Doil

From the Provençal of Arnaut Daniel
(12th Century)

I

I'll make a song   with exquisite
Clear words, for buds are blowing sweet
Where the sprays meet,
And flowers don
Their bold blazon
Where leafage springeth greenly
O'ershadowing
The birds that sing
And cry in coppice seemly.

II

The bosques among   they're singing fleet.
In shame's avoid my staves compete,
Fine-filed and neat,
With love's glaives on
His ways they run;
From him no whim can turn me,
Although he bring
Great sorrowing,
Although he proudly spurn me.

III

For lovers strong   pride is ill won,
And throweth him who mounts thereon.
His lots are spun
So that they fling

Him staggering,
His gaudy joys move leanly,
He hath grief's meat
And tears to eat
Who useth Love unseemly.

IV

Though tongues speak wrong   of wrangles none
Can turn me from thee. For but one
Fear I have gone
Dissembling;
Traitors can sting,
From their lies I would screen thee,
And as they'd treat
Us, with deceit,
Let fate use them uncleanly.

V

Though my swath long   's run wavering
My thoughts go forth to thee and cling,
Wherefore I sing
Of joys replete
Once, where our feet
Parted, and mine eyes plainly
Show mists begun
And sweetly undone,
For joy's the pain doth burn me.

VI

Save 'neath Love's thong I move no thing,
And my way brooks no measuring,
For right hath spring
In that Love's heat
Was ne'er complete
As mine, since Adam. 'Tween me
And sly treason
No net is spun,
Wherefore my joy grows greenly.

CODA

Lady, whoe'er demean thee
My benison
Is set upon
Thy grace where it moves queenly.

For Right of Audience

From Arnaut Daniel

I

In a new cause my song again
Moves in my throat, with altered mien,
No, don't think any hope springs green
Of making fair song of my pain;
  But 'till she who hath blamed me wrongly 'll cry
"Mercy!" I'll sing it out before the crowd,
For she'll not let me speak with her alone.

II

'Tis grace and pardon I would gain
Did not her action come between
Me and my right of asking e'en,
Though mercy could the thief sustain,
  When all of his own deeds had passed him by,
Unto my life no respite is allowed
Unless, where my rights fail, mercy be shown.

III

Hath a man rights at love? No grain,
Yet fools think they've some legal lien;
And she'll blame you, with heart serene,
That ships for Bar* sink in mid-main
  Or 'cause the French don't come from Gascony.

---

* Literally: "That ships wreck ere they get to Bar (*i.e.*, the port of Bari),
and 'cause the French are not Gascons."

And for such faults I am nigh in my shroud,
Since, by my God! I've shown such faults or none.

IV

That place where his desire hath lain
A man leaves loath, this I well ween,
Yet there be some with breasts so mean
That they to take back gifts are fain.
    As for myself, my love can not run dry,
Not though she robs my all, where she's most proud.
My love, in lack of joy, is stronger grown.

ENVOI

Please ye, Lords fellows, now maintain
Me, whom she would in all demean.
Pray to her thus (until she lean
Toward me and make her mercy plain):
    "Fair for our sake let Arnaut's song draw nigh!"
I may not name her, cry ye all aloud
That Arnaut came to court, his heart is known.

Canzon: Of the Trades and Love

From Arnaut Daniel

I

Though this measure quaint confine me,
And I chip out words and plane them,
    They shall yet be true and clear
When I finally have filed them.
Love glosses and gilds them knowing
    That my song has for its start
One who is worth's hold and warrant.

II

Each day finer I refine me
And my cult and service strain them

Toward the world's best, as ye hear,
"Hers" my root and tip have styled them.
And though bitter winds come blowing,
The love that rains down in my heart
Warmeth me when frost's abhorrent.

III

To long masses I resign me,
Give wax-lights and lamps, maintain them
That God win me issue here.
Tricks of fence? Her charm's beguiled them.
Rather see her, brown hair glowing;
And her body fine, frail art,
Than to gain Lucerna for rent!

IV

Round her my desires twine me
'Till I fear lest she disdain them.
Nay, need firm love ever fear?
Craft and wine, I have exiled them.
Yet her high heart's overflowing
Leaves my heart no parched part;
Lo, new verse sprouts in the current.

V

If they'd th' empire assign me
Or the Pope's chair, I'd not deign them
If I could not have her near.
My heart's flames have so high piled them,
If she'll not, ere th' old year's going
Kiss away their deadly smart,
Dead am I and damned, I warrant.

VI

Though these great pains so malign me
I'd not have love's powers restrain them
—Though she turn my whole life drear—
See, my songs have beamed and tiled them.

Yes, love's work is worse than mowing,
    And ne'er pains like mine did dart
Through Moncli for Audierent.

VII

I, Arnaut, love the wind, doing
    My hare-hunts on an ox-cart,
And I swim against the torrent.

NOTE

Manning, in his "Scenes and Portraits," compares Dante's similes—similes like those of the arsenal at Venice, or of the hoar frost—to the illuminated capital letters in mediaeval manuscript. Daniel in this canzon has produced the same effect, and solely by suggestion, by metaphor that is scarce metaphor, by suggestive verbs; thus in stanza I he makes his vignette in the shop of the joiner and finisher, in II the metal-worker's shop with a glimpse through the open window; in III the church, and in the last lines of it: "I love her more than one who should give me Lucerne," he puts in perhaps a woman, with the light of the altar candles about her, paying dues to the ecclesiastical suzerain; in IV the low-lying fields, where the grain is fostered by the river-flush; in V Rome, of the church and empire; in VI the suggestion is fainter, though it may be of a farm hand working in a grey, barren stretch of field. I have translated it badly even if my idiom does mean about the same as the Provençal.

The last line of stanza VI on "Moncli n'Audierna" has given rise to a good deal of fruitless conjecture. Obviously Arnaut cites them as a pair of famous lovers, just as he cites Paris and Helen in his third canzon, but no such lovers are to be found either in classical myth or in romance tradition.

Turning, however, to Virgil's ninth eclogue I find the following in lines 10–11 and 44:

Omnia carminibus vestrum servasse Menalcan.
M. Audieras, et fama fuit; sed carmina tantum, etc.

. . .

Quid, quae te pura solum sub nocte canentem Audieram?

Given these lines in modern print, one would advance scarce further; Arnaut had been, however, to a monastic school: he knew some Latin; he knew not only of Paris and Helen but of Atalanta and Meleager, though only one of their names is given in Ovid's account of the hunting through Caledon. His Latin was, let us say, no better than mine—learning for learning's sake had not appealed to him. His Latin text was not only in miniscule manuscript but

Rica Conquesta

The Song "Of High All-attaining"

From Arnaut Daniel

I

Did Lord Love lay upon me his wide largess
As I bear mine to her, with open heart,
He'd set no bar between me and the great,
For I'm borne up and fall as this love surges;
Yet, reckoning how she is the peak of worth,
I mount in mine own eyes by daring her
'Till heart and mind cry out that I'll attain
This rich conquest that's set for my attaining.

---

it was full of all manner of abbreviations, and in the matter of unusual proper names—like Menalcas—the scribe would have been more than usually prone to go wrong.

This eclogue is not over easy to read. "Menalcas" appears in three different case forms—"-an," "-as," "-a." The content of the eclogue is very like that of a Provençal canzon; parts of it are almost pure Provençal in the matter of vocabulary. It would have charmed by being not too unfamiliar. One more detail: the "M" in line ii, which stands for the speaker, Moeris, is not unlike the "N" which is Provençal for "donna," or "lady." The parts of the verb *audio*, in lines ii and 45, both begin with capital letters; in both places the final consonant, "s" or "m," would or might have been written above the "a," with nothing to indicate whether it fell before or after. Translating on this hypothesis without too much regard to the Latin syntax, with which Arnaut would have been much less familiar than he was with the Latin vocabulary, we get, in the first case, something like this: "Monalca, or Menacla (or some such person), served with songs (all, yours, his, in all things), the lady Audierna or Audieras"; and in the second: "What, thou alone 'neath the clear night singing, Audierna." "Audiart" is, of course, perfectly good Provençal; de Born and others mention a lady of that name, so that if Arnaut had seen the first part of the name he might easily have mistaken it for a Latin form or variation; in any case, even supposing he had read it correctly and forgotten the spelling in the book, the transition was not beyond the bounds of the possible. At least, it is no worse a mistake than that by which "Sir Sagramore the unbridled" becomes "Sir Sagramour the desirous." I make the suggestion for what it is worth.

II

I care not though delay delay enlarges,
For I sweep toward, and pool me in such part
That the mere words she speaks hold me elate.
I'd follow her until they sing my dirges.
Sure as I can tell gold from brassy earth
She is without alloy; without demur
My faith and I are steadfast in her train
Until her lips invest me, past all feigning.

III

The good respite recalls me and then discharges
A sweet desire wherewith my flanks so smart,
Yet quietly I bear my beggared state
For o'er all other peaks her grace emerges;
Whoe'er is noblest seemeth of base birth
Compared to her; let him play justicer
Who 'th seen how charm, worth, wit and sense all reign,
Increase and dwell and stay where she dwells reigning.

IV

Don't think my will will waste it o'er its marges
(She is so fair!), divide it or depart;
Nay, by the dove, God's ghost, the consecrate,
My mind's not mine, nor hers if it diverges!
No man desires, in all the wide world's girth,
Fortune, with such desires as are astir
In me herward, and they reap my disdain
Who deem love's pain a thing for light sustaining.

V

Ah "All-Supreme," leave me no room for charges
That you are miserly. My love's sans art,
Candid, my heart cannot shake off its weight;
It's not the sort that bottle-madness urges,
But, as night endeth day, doth day my mirth.

I bow me toward you where my vows concur,
Nor think my heart will ever be less fain,
The flame is in my head and burns unwaning.

VI

A cursed flame eat through your tongues and targes,
Sick slanderers until your sick eyes start
And go blind; 'till your vile jests abate
We loose our steeds and mancs. And loss submerges
Almost love's self. God damn you that your dearth
Of sense brings down the shame that we incur.
Sad fools! What blighting-star grows you this bane
To kill in you th' effect of all our training?

VII

Lady, I've borne delay and will again
Bear long delay in trust of high attaining.

Lo Ferm Voler

From Arnaut Daniel

Firm desire that doth enter
My heart will not be hid by bolts nor nailing
Nor slanderers who loose their arms by lying
And dare not fight with even twigs and switches.
Yea, by some jest, there where no uncle enters
I'll have my joy in garden or in chamber.

I remember oft that chamber
Where, to my loss, I know that no man enters
But leaves me free as would a brother or uncle.
I shake in ev'ry part except my nails
As doth a child, for fear, before the switch
For fear I shall not come unto her arms.

"*Quant L'Herba Fresq el Fuell Apar*"

From the Provençal of Bernart de Ventadorn
(1145–1195)

When grass starts green and flowers rise
Aleaf in garden and in close
And philomel in dulcet cries
And lifted notes his heart bestows.

Joy I've in him and in the flowers joy,
E'en joy in me have I yet more employ,
Hath joy in her in whom my joy is cast,
She is such joy as hath all joys o'erpast.

I love her so and so her prize,
I fear her and such thoughts oppose
That my poor words dare not arise,
Nor speech nor deeds my heart disclose.

And yet she knows the depth of my annoy
And, when she will, she will her grace employ;
For God's love, Love, put now our love to test
For time goes by and we here waste his best.

Las Grans Beautatz

From the Provençal of Folquet de Romans

Her beauty and the fineness of her thought,
And her true heart and all the food of praise,
And her high speech and the newfangled ways
That color hath when to her cheek 'tis brought
Give me the will for song and knowledge of it.
Such were my song but such fears crowd above it
I dare not say 'tis you of whom I'm fain,
And know not what shall count me loss or gain.

My love of her so secretly is wrought
That none save I and Love know love's assay,
And on my heart the flame in secret preys;

Yet knowing this, you are not much distraught.
And yet I have such fear lest you reprove it,
That my heart scarce dares show you that you move it.
Yet if, when we're alone I daren't speak out,
At least my songs shall say what I'm about.

Certain Poems of Kabir

(Hindi: 1440–1518)

From the English versions of Kali Mohan Ghose

I

The spring season is approaching,
Who will help me meeting with my dearest?
How shall I describe the beauty of the dearest,
Who is immersed in all beauties?
That color colors all the pictures of this universe,
Body and mind alike
Forget all things else in that beauty.
He who has these ideas,
The play of the spring is his.
This is the word which is unutterable.
Saith Kabir: There are very few who know this mystery.

II

My beloved is awakened, how can I sleep?
Day and night he is calling me,
And instead of responding to his call
I am like an unchaste girl, living with another.
Saith Kabir: O clever confidant,
The meeting with the dearest is not possible without love.

III

The scar aches day and night.
Sleep is not come.
Anxious for meeting with the dearest,
The father's house is not attractive at all.
The sky-gate opens,

The temple is manifested,
There now is the meeting with the husband.
I make oblation of my mind and body:
To the dearest the cup of the dearest!
Let flow the quick shower of rain from your eyes.
Cover your heart
With the intense deep blue
Assembling of the cloud.
Come near to the ear of the dearest,
Whisper to him your pain.
Saith Kabir: Here bring the meditation of the dearest,
Today's treasure of the heart.

IV

It is true, I am mad with love. And what to me
Is carefulness or uncarefulness?
Who, dying, wandering in the wilderness,
Who is separated from the dearest?
My dearest is within me, what do I care?
The beloved is not asundered from me,
No, not for the veriest moment.
And I also am not asundered from him.
My love clings to him only,
Where is restlessness in me?
Oh my mind dances with joy,
Dances like a mad fool.
The rāginis of love are being played day and night,
All are listening to that measure.
Rāhu, the eclipse, Ketu, the Head of the Dragon,
And the nine planets are dancing,
And Birth and Death are dancing, mad with Ananda.
The mountain, the sea and the earth are dancing,
The Great Adornment is dancing with laughter and tears
    and smiles.
Why are you leaving "the world,"
You, with the *tilak*-mark on your forehead?
While my mind is a-dancing through the thousand stages of
    its moon,
And the Lord of all his creation has found it acceptable dancing.

V

O deserted bride,
How will you live in the absence of your beloved,
Without hunger in the day,
Sleepless in the night-watches,
And every watch felt as if
It were the aeon of Kaliyuga?
The beautiful has deserted you in the full passion of his April.
Alas the fair is departed!
O thou deserted,
Now begin to give up your house and your having.
Go forth to the lodge of the forest,
Begin to consider his name.
And if there he shall come upon you,
Then alone will you be come to your joy.
Eager as the caught fish for its water,
Be thou so eager to return!
Shapeless, formless and without line,
Who will be come to meet you,
O beautiful lady?
Take recognisance of your own wed Lord,
Behold him out of the center of your meditations,
Strip off the last of your errors,
And know that Love is your lord.
Saith Kabir: There is no second. Aeon
After aeon
Thou and I are the same.

VI

Very difficult is the meeting with him,
How shall I be made one with my beloved?
After long consideration and after caution
I put my feet on the way, but every time
They have trembled and slipped aside.
The slippery path leads upward and the feet can not hold
      to it.
The mind is taken in shyness,
For fear of the crowd
And out of respect to the family.

Oh where is my far beloved?
And I in the family dwelling!
And I can not escape my shyness!

VII

How shall it be severed,
This love between thee and me?
Thou art lord, and I servant,
As the lotus is servant of water.
Thou art lord, and I servant,
As the Chakora is servant of moonlight
And watches it all the night long.
The love between thee and me is from beginning to ending,
How can it end in time?
Saith Kabir: As the river is immersed in the ocean,
My mind is immersed in thee.

VIII

Rishi Nārad, that hast walked upon the winding path of the
        air,
That hast walked there playing the Vinā and singing thy
        song to Hari,
Rishi Nārad, the beloved is not afar off,
I wake not, save in his waking,
I sleep not, save in his slumber.

IX

O receiver of my heart,
Do thou come into my house.
My mind and body
Are but a pain, in thy absence.
When they say that I am your mistress
The shame of it is upon me.
If heart lie not upon heart,
How is the heart of love there?
The rice has no savor, the night is passed and is sleepless.
In the house and in the way of the forest my mind and
        thought have no rest.

Love-cup to the maid: water-cup to famished of thirst.
Is there one, bearer of fortune, to make clear my heart to
    my beloved?
Kabir is at the end of his patience
And dies without sight of his beloved.

X

O bearer of love, give voice to the well-omened song.
The great lord is come to my house,
After employing my body in his love
I shall employ my mind.
The five mysteries will be enlightened with love
The receiver of my heart, today is the guest in my house,
I am grown mad with my youth.
The pool of my body will be the place of pilgrimage.
Near by will Brahmā chant Vedas,
The mind will be fused with my lover.

O opportune, and well-omened,
The three and thirty tunes of curious sound here with the
    sound of Ananda.
The paired lovers of the universe are assembled.
Saith Kabir: This day I set out for my marriage
With a bridegroom who is deathless.
In the quarter of my body there is music in process,
Thirty and six rāginis are bound up into the burthen.
The bridegroom hath April play with me.
As Krishna with Rādhā, playing at the spring festival of
    Harililā,
I play at the spraying of colors, I and my beloved.
The whole universe is curious today.
Love and the rain of love are come hither with their showers.

Strophes

*From the French ("Symphonie de Novembre")
of Oscar Wenceslas de Lubicz-Milosz
(1877–1939)*

It will be as it is in this life, the same room,
Yes, the same! and at daybreak, the bird of time in the
    leafage,
Pale as a dead woman's face; and the servants
Moving; and the icy, hollow noise of the fountain-taps,

Terrible, terrible youth; and the heart empty.
Oh! it will be as it is in this life; the poor voices,
The winter voices in the worn-out suburbs;
And the window-mender's cracked street-cry;

The dirty bonnet, with an old woman under it
Howling a catalogue of stale fish, and the blue-apron'd fellow
Spitting on his chapped hands
And bellowing like an angel of judgement,

It will be exactly as here and in this life, and the table,
The bible, Goethe, the ink with the same temporal odor,
Paper, pale; woman, white thought-reader!
Pen, the portrait,
               It will be the same,
My child, as in this life, the same garden,
Long, long, tufted, darkish, and, at lunch-time,
Pleasure of being together; that is—
People unacquainted, having only in common
A knowledge of their unacquaintance—
And that one must put on one's best clothes
To go into the night—at the end of things,
Loveless and lampless;
It will be the same as in this life,
The same lane in the forest; and at mid-day, in mid-autumn
When the clean road turns like a weeping woman
To gather the valley flowers,
We will cross in our walks,
  As in the yesterday you have forgotten,
  In the gown whose color you have forgotten.

Sonnet to Guido Cavalcanti

From Guido Orlandi
(13th Century)

Say what is Love, whence doth he start,
Through what be his courses bent,
Memory, substance, accident?
A chance of eye or will of heart?

Whence he state or madness leadeth?
Burns he with consuming pain?
Tell me, friend, on what he feedeth,
How, where, and o'er whom doth he reign?

Say what is Love, hath he a face?
True form or vain similitude?
Is the Love life, or is he death?

Thou shouldst know for rumor saith:
Servant should know his master's mood—
Oft art thou ta'en in his dwelling-place.

Cabaret Vert

From the French of Jean Arthur Rimbaud
(1854–1891)

Wearing out my shoes, 8th day
On the bad roads, I got into Charleroi.
Bread, butter, at the Green Cabaret
And the ham half cold.

Got my legs stretched out
And was looking at the simple tapestries,
Very nice when the gal with the big bubs
And lively eyes,

Not one to be scared of a kiss and more,
Brought the butter and bread with a grin
And the luke-warm ham on a colored plate,

Pink ham, white fat and a sprig
Of garlic, and a great chope of foamy beer
Gilt by the sun in that atmosphere.

Comedy in Three Caresses

From Rimbaud

She hadn't much left on, and the big trees,
With no discretion, swished
Their leaves over the window-pane
Teasingly, so near, so near.

Half naked in my big chair,
She put her hands together
And her little toes tickled the floor,
Quivering comfortably, and so small.

I watched a little sprouting flush,
The color of wax, flutter
Like a smile over her neat breasts:
Fly on a rose bush.

I kissed her traced ankles
And she smiled a longish smile, bad sign
That shattered out into clear trills,
Crystalline.

Her little feet scampered under her shift:
"Will you *stop* now!!"
After the first permitted boldness,
The smile pretending coldness?

Her poor eyelids fluttered under my lips
As I kissed her eyes
And she threw back her weakling head:
"That's better now," she said.

"But I have something still to . . ."
I chucked the rest between her breasts

In a caress that brought a kindly smile,
Benevolence, all of it.

She hadn't much left on, and the big trees
Swished their leaves over the window-pane
At ease, teasingly, and so near.

Anadyomene

From Rimbaud

As it might have been from under a green tin coffin-lid,
A woman's head with brown over-oiled hair
Rises out of a theatre box, slow and stupid
With ravages in rather poor repair.

Then ups the fat grey neck and bulgy shoulder-blades,
The shortish back going out and in
And the fat, in clumsy slabs under the skin,
Seems ready to emerge without further aids.

Lice-Hunters

From Rimbaud

When the kid's forehead is full of red torments
Imploring swarms of dreams with vague contents,
Two large and charming sisters come
With wafty fingers and silvery nails, to his bedroom.

They set the kid by a wide-open window where
A tangle of flowers bathes in the blue air
And run fine, alluring, terrible
Fingers through his thick dew-matted hair.

He hears the rustling of their timid breath
Flowered with the long pinkish vegetable honies underneath
Or broken anon, sibilant, the saliva's hiss
Drawn from a lip, or a desire to kiss.

He hears their black eyelashes beat in that quietude
And "Crack!" to break his inebriated indolences
Neath their electric and so soft fingers death assails
The little lice beneath their regal nails.

And Lo! there mounts within him Wine of Laziness—a
    squiffer's sigh
Might bring delirium—and the kid feels
Neath the slowness of their caresses, constantly
Wane and fade a desire to cry.

Rus

From the French of Laurent Tailhade
(1854–1919)

What lures the antient truss-maker from his shoppe whose
    luxury
Sucked in the passers-by,
Is his garden at Auteuil where zinnias void of all odor or stink
Look like varnished zinc.

That's where he, of an evening, comes to taste the aromatic
    air
In his flannel coat and rocking-chair
As factories of suet and animal
Black spread out the whiff and flavor from Grenelle.

Although free-thinking and a quite free mason,
He thinks a favoring god in propitious hour
Gave him such refuge—a goldfish dying in the fountain
    basin—

While, with Chinese lanterns in a moorish tower
His "young lady" hums to and fro
Spicing his raspberry syrup with a couplet by Nadaud.

Catullus: XXVI

This villa is raked of winds from fore and aft,
All Boreas' sons in bluster and yet more
Against it is this TWO HUNDRED THOUSAND sesterces,
All out against it, oh my God:
                                   some draft.

Conversations in Courtship

*From Boris de Rachewiltz's Italian versions of
Egyptian hieroglyphic texts*

HE SAYS:
Darling, you only, there is no duplicate,
More lovely than all other womanhood,
        luminous, perfect,
A star coming over the sky-line at new year,
        a good year,
Splendid in colors,
        with allure in the eye's turn.
Her lips are enchantment,
        her neck the right length
                and her breasts a marvel;
Her hair lapislazuli in its glitter,
        her arms more splendid than gold.
Her fingers make me see petals,
        the lotus' are like that.
Her flancs are modeled as should be,
        her legs beyond all other beauty.
Noble her walking
                (vera incessu)
My heart would be a slave should she enfold me.
Every neck turns—that is her fault—
        to look at her.
Fortune's who can utterly embrace her;
        he would stand first among all young lovers.
Deo mi par esse
        Every eye keeps following her

even after she has stepped out of range,
A single goddess,
       uniquely.

SHE SAYS:
His voice unquiets my heart,
       It's the voice's fault if I suffer.
My mother's neighbor!
                       But I can't go see him,
       Ought she to enrage me?

MOTHER:
Oh, stop talking about that fellow,
       the mere thought of him is revolting.

SHE:
I am made prisoner 'cause I love him.

MOTHER:
But he's a mere kid with no brains.

SHE:
So am I, I am just like him
and he don't know I want to put my arms round him.
       THAT would make mama talk . . .
May the golden goddess make fate,
       and make him my destiny.

Come to where I can see you.
       My father and mother will then be happy
       Because everyone likes to throw parties for you
              And they would get to doing it too.

SHE SAYS:
I wanted to come out here where it's lovely
       and get some rest,
Now I meet Mehy in his carriage
       with a gang of other young fellows,
              How can I turn back?

Can I walk in front of him
    as if it did not matter?
Oh, the river is the only way to get by
    and I can't walk on the water.

    My soul you are all in a muddle.
If I walk in front of him my secret will show,
    I'll blurt out my secrets; say:
                  Yours!

And he will mention my name and
    hand me over to just any one of them
        who merely wants a good time.

SHE SAYS:
My heart runs out if I think how I love him,
    I can't just act like anyone else.
It, my heart, is all out of place
    It won't let me choose a dress
        or hide back of my fan.
I can't put on my eye make-up
                or pick a perfume.

"Don't stop, come into the house."
    That's what my heart said, one time,
And does, every time I think of my beloved.
    Don't play the fool with me, oh heart.
        Why *are* you such an idiot?
Sit quiet! keep calm
        and he'll come to you.
And my alertness won't let people say:
    This girl is unhinged with love.
When you remember him
    stand firm and solid,
        don't escape me.

HE SAYS:
I adore the gold-gleaming Goddess,
        Hathor the dominant,
           and I praise her.

I exalt the Lady of Heaven,
    I give thanks to the Patron.
She hears my invocation
    and has fated me to my lady,
Who has come here, herself, to find me.
    What felicity came in with her!
I rise exultant
    in hilarity
            and triumph when I have said:
                Now,
And behold her.
        Look at it!
            The young fellows fall at her feet.
Love is breathed into them.

I make vows to my Goddess,
    because she has given me this girl for my own.
I have been praying three days,
    calling her name.
For five days she has abandoned me.

SHE SAYS:
I went to his house, and the door was open.
    My beloved was at his ma's side
        with brothers and sisters about him.
Everybody who passes has sympathy for him,
    an excellent boy, none like him,
        a friend of rare quality.
He looked at me when I passed
    and my heart was in jubilee.
If my mother knew what I am thinking
    she would go to him at once.

O Goddess of Golden Light,
            put that thought into her,
                Then I could visit him
And put my arms round him while people were looking
And not weep because of the crowd,
            But would be glad that they knew it
                and that you know me.

What a feast I would make to my Goddess,
　　　　My heart revolts at the thought of exit,
If I could see my darling tonight,
　　　　　　Dreaming is loveliness.

HE SAYS:
Yesterday. Seven days and I have not seen her.
　　　　My malady increases;
　　　　　　limbs heavy!
　　　　　　　　I know not myself any more.
High priest is no medicine, exorcism is useless:
　　　　a disease beyond recognition.

I said: She will make me live,
　　　　her name will rouse me,
Her messages are the life of my heart
　　　　coming and going.
My beloved is the best of medicine,
　　　　more than all pharmacopoeia.
My health is in her coming,
　　　　I shall be cured at the sight of her.
Let her open my eyes
　　　　and my limbs are alive again;
Let her speak and my strength returns.
Embracing her will drive out my malady.
　　　　Seven days and
　　　　　　　　she has abandoned me.

Air: Sentir Avec Ardeur

La Marquise de Boufflers
(1711–1786)

Say what you will in two
Words and get thru.
Long, frilly
Palaver is silly.

Know how to read? you MUST
Before you can write. An idiot
Will always
Talk a lot.

You need not always narrate;
    cite; date,
But listen a while and not say: "I! I!"
Want to know why?

The ME is tyrannical;
    academical.
Early, late
Boredom's cognate mate
      in step at his side
And I with a ME, I fear,
            yet again!

Say what you will in two
Words and get thru!
Long, frilly
Palaver is silly.

Catullus: LXXXV

I hate and love. Why? You may ask but
It beats me. I feel it done to me, and ache.

Roma

Rutilius Claudius Namantianus
(flourished 416 A.D.)

Again and again I kiss thy gates at departing
And against our will leave thy holy door-stone,
Praying in tears and with praises
      such words as can pierce our tears.

Hear us, Queen, fairest in all the earth, ROMA,
Taking post twixt the sky's poles,
Nurse of men! Mother of gods,
                    do thou hear us.
Ever we hymn thee and will, while the Fates can have power.
No guest can forget thee.
             It were worse crime than forgetting the sun
If we ceased holding thy honor in heart,
Thou impartial as sunlight to the splash of all outer sea-boards.
All that Apollo over-rides in his quadriga
Hast thou combined into equity:
Many strange folk in one fatherland,
To their good, not seeking to dominate;
Gavest law to the conquered as consorts;
Made city what had been world.

They say that Venus was thy mother, that is by Aeneas,
Mars for father hadst'ou through Romulus,
Making mild armed strength, she in conquest:
One god in two natures;
                    Joy out of strife by sparing
O'ercamest the sources of terror
    In love with all that remains.

L'Ultima Ora

From Montanari

When the will to singing fails
and there be left him no choice
but to rest without singing voice,
forever, unending, arms crossed,

Let it be by the roadside
where the ditch is wide and deep
and the smell of his fields, in sleep
can come to him, and the note of the robin,

And the elms can be there companionable
to him, as evening draws to its close
in the savor of spring time,
melancholy a little, ending together.

"Ask not ungainly"

from Horace

Ask not ungainly askings of the end
Gods send us, me and thee, Leucothoë;
Nor juggle with the risks of Babylon,
   Better to take whatever,
Several, or last, Jove sends us. Winter is winter,
Gnawing the Tyrrhene cliffs with the sea's tooth.

Take note of flavors, and clarity's in the wine's manifest.
Cut loose long hope for a time.
We talk. Time runs in envy of us,
Holding our day more firm in unbelief.

(*Odes*, Book I, 11)

"By the flat cup"

from Horace

By the flat cup and the splash of new vintage
What, specifically, does the diviner ask of Apollo? Not
Thick Sardinian corn-yield nor pleasant
Ox-herds under the summer sun in Calabria, nor
Ivory nor gold out of India, nor
Land where Liris crumbles her bank in silence
Though the water seems not to move.

Let him to whom Fortune's book
Gives vines in Oporto, ply pruning hook, to the
Profit of some seller that he, the seller,

May drain Syra from gold out-size basins, a
Drink even the Gods must pay for, since he found
It is merchandise, looking back three times,
Four times a year, unwrecked from Atlantic trade-routes.

Olives feed me, and endives and mallow roots.
Delight had I healthily in what lay handy provided.
Grant me now, Latoe:
                     Full wit in my cleanly age,
Nor lyre lack me, to tune the page.

(*Odes*, Book I, 31)

"This monument will outlast"

from Horace

This monument will outlast metal and I made it
More durable than the king's seat, higher than pyramids.
Gnaw of the wind and rain?
                       Impotent
The flow of the years to break it, however many.

Bits of me, many bits, will dodge all funeral,
O Libitina-Persephone and, after that,
Sprout new praise. As long as
Pontifex and the quiet girl pace the Capitol
I shall be spoken where the wild flood Aufidus
Lashes, and Daunus ruled the parched farmland:

Power from lowliness: "First brought Aeolic song to Italian
       fashion"—
Wear pride, work's gain! O Muse Melpomene,
By your will bind the laurel.
                     My hair, Delphic laurel.

(*Odes*, Book III, 30)

UNCOLLECTED POEMS
AND TRANSLATIONS

Ezra on the Strike

Wal, Thanksgivin' do be comin' round.
With the price of turkeys on the bound,
And coal, by gum! Thet were just found,
    Is surely gettin' cheaper.

The winds will soon begin to howl,
And winter, in its yearly growl,
Across the medders begin to prowl,
    And Jack Frost gettin' deeper.

By shucks! It seems to me,
That you and I orter be
Thankful, that our Ted could see
    A way to operate it.

I sez to Mandy, sure, sez I,
I'll bet thet air patch o' rye
Thet he'll squash 'em by-and-by,
    And he did, by cricket!

No use talkin', he's the man—
One of the best thet ever ran,
Fer didn't I turn Republican
    One o' the fust?

I 'lowed as how he'd beat the rest,
But old Si Perkins, he hemmed and guessed,
And sed as how it wuzn't best
    To meddle with the trust.

Now Pattison, he's gone up the flue,
And Coler, he kinder got there, tew,
So Si, put thet in your cud to chew,
    And give us all a rest.

Now thet I've had my little say
I wish you all a big Thanksgivin' day,
While I plod on to town with hay,
    And enjoy it best.

1902

1149

Amor de Lonh

When the days be long in May
I love the song of bird afar.
When my lady is far away
I remember my love afar.
I love with such sad courtesy.
Nor song nor white thorn tree
Pleaseth me more than the winter's cold.

Of no love may I take my joy
Saving joy of my love afar.
I know no gentler fair nor coy
In no country near or far.
So is her worth full true and leal
For her caitif's shame I'd feel
In far Sarazin's kingly hold.

It seemeth me joy to seek thee,
For thy sweet love in land afar
It liketh me that my home should be
Near to her tho I be now far,
That with word of courtesy
When my far love is near me
With fair speaking pleasure hold.

Dole and joy is there to me
When I see my love afar!
I know not when the time shall be,
For our lands be parted far.
Many a path and weary way,
These shall not my coming stay,
For all shall be when God shall will.

Truly I trust the Lord on high
That I may see my love afar.
But for one good I get thereby
Have I two griefs, it is so far.
Aie! I'd take me the pilgrim's way
If my staff and my coat of grey
Might have her eyes to mirror them.

God why ye delay so long
Groweth my love for one afar
And my weak heart it maketh strong
That soon I see my love afar.
That sooth in fitting place
In bower or in garden space
Me seemeth paradise shall be.

Whoso me doth desirous call
Saith truth. I crave my love afar.
I have joy in nought else at all
When I rejoice in my love afar.
If to my love she bringeth hate,
Then hath my spirit given me fate
That I love with no return.

But if to my love she bringeth scorn
Then may my spirit be forsworn
That maketh me love with no return.

after Jaufré Rudel, ca. 1905

A Dawn Song

God hath put me here
In earth's goodly sphere
   To sing the joy of the day,
A strong glad song,
If the road be long,
   To my fellows in the way.

So I make my song of the good glad light
   That falls from the gate of the sun,
And the clear cool wind that bloweth good
   To my brother Everyone.

1906

To the Raphaelite Latinists

By Weston Llewmys

Ye fellowship that sing the woods and spring,
  Poets of joy that sing the day's delight,
  Poets of youth that 'neath the aisles of night
Your flowers and sighs against the lintels fling;

Who rose and myrtle in your garlands bring
  To marble altars, though their gods took flight
  Long ere your dream-shot eyes drank summer light
And wine of old time myth and vintaging,

Take of our praise one cup, though thin the wine
  That Bacchus may not bless nor Pan outpour:
Though reed pipe and the lyre be names upon
The wind, and moon-lit dreams be quite out-gone
  From ways we tread, one cup to names ye bore,
One wreath from ashes of your songs we twine!

1908

In Epitaphium

Write me when this geste, our life is done:
"He tired of fame before the fame was won."

1909

Clair de Lune

Your soul is a country chosen,
  Befit for maskings, and folk galliard-clad
    To touch the luth and dance in,
  Yet be beneath their masks a little sad.

  Where all shall sing in minor melody
That love is vanquisher, and life-chance's spoils among
    Yet seem mistrustful of their fortune there,
  Where moonlight tangles in the web of song.

The calm clear of the moon so sad, so fair,
Doth snare the birds within its net of dreams
    And mid the marbles where the water-jets
Sob for rapture in their pale, tall streams.

after Verlaine, 1910

Lied Maritime

Fadeth the sun on the sea afar,
The calm, unrippled sea;
Jasper wave falls silently
To touch the o'ershadowed shore.
Thine eyes, thy traitorous eyes, are closed;
Tranquil my heart so, as the sea is still.
Riseth the storm on the sea afar,
With moving rage of the sea;
Rise waves towards heaven mightily,
And wail to their deep troughs clamorous.
Thine eyes, thy traitorous eyes, look down
Into the wave-troughs of my soul,
Till my heart, tortured, doth exalt himself,
And break as gainst the rocks some mighty sea.

after d'Indy, 1910

Thersites: On the Surviving Zeus

(*With apologies to all the rhetorical odists*)

I

Immortal Ennui, that hath driven men
To mightier deeds and actions than e'er Love
With all his comfit kisses brought to be,
Thee only of the gods out-tiring Time,
That weariest man to glory ere the grave,
Thee do we laud within thy greyest courts!
O thou unpraisèd one, attend our praise!

II

Great Love hath turned him back but never thou,
O steely champion, hast let slip the rein.
Great deeds were thine in Rome and Macedon
When small gods gleaned the stubble of man's praise,
And silent thou alone didst know their birth.
Revealèd wast to none but thine elect
Who trod the chaff of earth's death-dusty crowns.

III

Immortal Ennui that hath saved the world
From dry contagion of man's great dull books,
O Wisdom's self that stillest wisdom's voice,
The frank Apollo never stole thy sheep,
No song hath lured thee from thy granite throne.
There is no bourne to thine insistency,
No power to turn the sword of thy disdain.

IV

All deeds are dust and song is less than deed
Thou dost beget such hunger in the soul.
To mightier conquests and to wars more vain
The sands of men are driven by thy breath;
Thine is the high emprise of lordly lays.
O thou inspiring Might, drink deep this praise,
Ere our great boredom pass its several ways!

1910

The Fault of It

"Some may have blamed you—"

Some may have blamed us that we cease to speak
Of things we spoke of in our verses early,
Saying: a lovely voice is such and such;
Saying: that lady's eyes were sad last week,
Wherein the world's whole joy is born and dies;

Saying: she hath this way or that, this much
Of grace, this little misericorde;
Ask us no further word;
If we were proud, then proud to be so wise
Ask us no more of all the things ye heard;
We may not speak of them, they touch us nearly.

1911

L'Invitation

Go from me. I am one of those who spoil
And leave fair souls less fair for knowing them;
Go from me, I bring light that blindeth men
So that they stagger.
              It doth ill become me.
Go from me. I am life the tawdry one,
I am the spring and autumn.
                  Ah the drear
Hail that hath bent the corn!
                    The ruined gold!

1912

Selection from Collection Yvette Guilbert

1. "Pursue ye beauty"
(*Villon*)

Pursue ye beauty, run to feasting,
Love light, desire all that ye will,
If 'tis naught save your heads you're wasting,
Ask naught beyond this get your fill;
'Tis love that men run most mad when a-tasting;
Solomon idolized a bit,
And Samson lost his specs through hasting;
Happy is he who'th naught of it.

2. *"When I behold"*
(Berthaud)

When I behold that which I loved so much,
Almost my flame doth spring up at the touch,
Till the lost love were thereby re-alighted,
Almost my heart, that did her captive live
Grows once more like some slavish fugitive
Who sees his lord and stops his flight affrighted.

Ah the discourse that had my soul waylaid!
Ah thought on thought and thereby thought gainsaid!
Doth then the heart mount up where thinking ceaseth?
How if my soul from her networks unloosed
Repents to find himself so disabused!
How am I sad where wisdom me increaseth.

3. *"The King's had flunkeys"*
(1599)

The King's had flunkeys beat the drum,
The king's had flunkeys beat the drum
To call all ladies proper;
But when the first fair dame was come,
The King's soul come a cropper.

Rataplan, rataplan, rataplan plan plan plan.
Rataplan, rataplan, rataplan plan plan plan.

"Now tell me Marquis* do you know (*bis*)
Who is this handsome lady?"
And then the Marquis replied so:
"Sire King, my wife, Miladi."

"You're luckier than I, Marquis, (*bis*)
"To have a wife so tender;
"Now just turn her over to me
"And I will well attend her."

---

* pronounce Marquis — Markee's

"Ah, my Lord, were you not the King (*bis*)
"I'd have my vengeance on you
"But since you are my Lord the King
"Obedience is done you."

"Marquis, now do not fuss yourself (*bis*)
"My justice is impartial
"And you shall have your pay and pelf,
"I'll make you first Field-marshal."

"So now put on your best, best clothes (*bis*)
"And deck your hair with laces.
"Yes, now put on your best, best clothes
"And show your girlish paces."

"Adieu, my dearest loveliest thing! (*bis*)
"Adieu, my hope, forever,
"For since I now must serve my King
"It seems that we must sever."

The queen hath plucked her flowers white (*bis*)
And made her garland ready.
The odour of these flowers, one night,
Hath slain the Marquis' lady.

4. *"In the rue Chiffonnier"*
(*XVIIième siècle*)

In the rue Chiffonnier,
En plin plan ran tan plan plan plan;
In the rue Chiffonier,
There dwells a nice young lady
There dwells a nice young lady,
Ran tan plan tire lire.

And there's a crook-back boy,
En plin plan ran tan plan plan plan,
And there's a crook-back boy
Who goes to see this lady;
Who goes to see this lady.
Ran tan plan tire lire.

Oh! he has kissed her thrice.
En plin plan ran tan plan plan plan;
Oh! he has kissed her thrice!
Ere she hath dared to say aught;
Ere she hath dared to say aught.
Ran tan plan tire lire.

When he'd kissed her four times,
En plin plan ran tan plan plan plan,
When he'd kissed her four times
Then she began her talking,
Then she began her talking:
Ran tan plan tire lire.

Oh the neighbours have seen,
En plin plan ran tan plan plan plan,
Oh the neighbours have seen,
And they'll tell all about it.
And they'll tell all about it.
Ran tan plan tire lire.

Dear let's begin again,
En plin plan ran tan plan plan plan,
Dear let's begin again
And laugh at all their talking,
And laugh at all their talking.
Ran tan plan tire lire.

For when they've told it all,
En plin plan ran tan plan plan plan,
For when they've told it all,
Then it will be talked over,
Then it will be talked over.
Ran tan plan tire lire.

In the rue Chiffonier
There dwells a nice young lady.

5. *"In Nant in prison there"*
(XVIIième siècle)

In Nant in prison there
Lies a poor prisoner
Lies a poor prisoner
Whom no one goes a-near
Except the jailor's lass
Ah! ah! ah! ah!,

Whom no one goes a-near
Except the jailor's lass,
Except the jailor's lass
And 't is she who supplies
His trencher and his glass.
Ah! ah! ah! ah!

And 't is she who supplies,
His trencher and his glass,
His trencher and his glass.
"They say through all the town
That you will die at morn.
Ah! ah! ah! ah!

They say through all the town
That you will die at morn,
That you will die at morn."
"Ah! If I die at dawn
Untie my feet for me.
Ah! ah! ah! ah!

Ah! If I die at dawn
Untie my feet for me,
Untie my feet for me!"
Then all the bells of Nant'
Began to ring around,
Ah! ah! ah! ah!

Then all the bells of Nant'
Began to ring around,

Began to ring around.
The jailor's lass was young
Her tears ran copiously.
Ah! ah! ah! ah!

The jailor's lass was young,
Her tears ran copiously,
Her tears ran copiously.
The ready prisoner
Hath leapt him in the Loir'
Ah! ah! ah! ah!

The ready prisoner
Hath leapt him in the Loir',
Hath leapt him in the Loir'.
Vive! all the girls of Nantes
And all their prisoners,
Ah! ah! ah! ah! ah!

6. *"These mothers always"*
(*1761*)

These mothers always
In great and small ways
Forbid their daughters to meddle with love.
Forbid them vainly,
Since girls so plainly
Feel in themselves the first tickling thereof.
No, there's no aid,
Innocence may restrain ye,
Yet there's no aid, 'tis for this we are made.

If we arrange our hair a Fontanger,
'Tis not for ourselves we go so arrayed.
If one admire us,
To smile should inspire us,
She who can please will not long stay a maid:
And we behave just as our hearts inspire us,
No, there's no aid, for this thing we are made.

At hearing description
Of what our soul trips on,
One trembles confused,
Turns red or looks abused,
If modesty shows what we'd not disclose:
How can one blush so for what one don't yet know?
A girl grows tender,
How could she defend her?
No there's no aid, 'tis for this we are made.

One sees a young man,
But timidly then
One lowers one's eyes
To gauge better his size
Ah, whence this desire?
And these sighs like fire
One's courage gives way
And one's heart goes Egh! Eay!
The man stops jesting
His pain's interesting.
No, there's no aid 'tis for this we are made.

Our nicest girl friends
Now less fit our ends
Than this young man whom we've only just met;
He thinks he suits
And his force he recruits
Then one excuses the boldness he'll use;
And then is our trouble redoubled
And then comes Love and he will be obeyed;
No there's no aid
Innocence may restrain us,
Yet there's no aid 'tis for this we are made.

7. "Love for you have fifteen years"
(*1781*)

Love for you have fifteen years
And the glories which that age has,
Guard against Sir Time's arrears

Ere you reach his dullard stages.
What to do when day is gone?
Go ask this of your play-fellows,
They'll say there's no god but one;
Love is he who paints the mallows.

Innocently one starts in
'Tis an easy slope for sliding,
Listen how when you begin,
Love doth teach you graceful gliding.
Many shepherds at the game
Tell you that they are devoted,
Soon you note that one of them
Is the one to be best noted.

And the slightest care of his
Will straight set your fancy roaming,
Set at naught the distances,
From afar you feel him coming,
If the fields that shepherd quit
In the townland to abide him,
Without thinking aught of it
You find yourself there beside him.

All the words of all the rest
Can then neither mar nor mend you;
If he speak you grave, or jest,
It doth please you or offend you.
If he sing of am'rous flame
You're embarrassed by his glances,
Lacking them it is the same
As if none made you advances.

Meet a moment sans design
And strange trouble seems to move you.
If he say "The day is fine."
Still you think he says, "I love you."
"Sure," saith Rosine, "tis this place
"That Amour comes forth to gain us."
"Ah! Themire, 'tis just my case
"Since I first saw my Silvanus."

CODA

Love for you have fifteen years
And the glories which that age has;
Guard against Sir Time's arrears
Ere you reach his dullard stages,
Ere you reach his dullard stages.

8. *"O but it is time"*

O but it is time, it is time, mama,
O but it is time now to marry me.

My daughter you are not yet half grown.
　O rot! mama fifteen years are gone.
Why don't they get on, why ain't something done,
　　now to marry me?
O but it is time, it is time mama,
O but it is time now to marry me.

But that needs a lover and you've got none. (*bis*)
　O rot, mama, we've got big fat John. (*bis*)
Why don't they take him? Why don't they like him?
　For marrying me?
O but it is time.　　　*etc.*

My daughter we've got no money to show. (*bis*)
　O mama, we've got six francs or so. (*bis*)
Why don't they take them? Why don't they change them?
　For marrying me?
O but it is time.　　　*etc.*

My daughter we have not any bread. (*bis*)
　O mama, we've got the yeast instead (*bis*)
Why don't they take it? Why don't they bake it?
　For marrying me?
O but it is time.　　　*etc.*

My daughter we have not any wine (*bis*)
   Mama we have got grapes on the vine (*bis*)
Why don't they get them? Why don't they set them?
   For marrying me?
O but it is time.   *etc.*

My daughter you've got no clothes to wear (*bis*)
   O mama we have got sheep to shear (*bis*)
Why don't they skin them? Why don't they spin them?
   For marrying me?
O but it is time.   *etc.*

My daughter you've got no covering. (*bis*)
   Well then, we'll just use any old thing (*bis*)
Why don't they sew them? Why don't they grow them?
   For marrying me?
O but it is time.   *etc.*

Still my daughter there's the house to buy (*bis*)
   O rot! mama we'll use the pig-sty. (*bis*)
Why don't they kill them? Why don't they sell them?
   For marrying me?
O but it is time.   *etc.*

9. *"Going through a wood"*

Going through a wood
   that had no leaves upon it,
I heard the pleasant voice
   of a lovely shepherdess.

—Tell me, shepherdess
If you will be my true-love?
—Sir, I think you will do
As well as any body.

—Tell me, shepherdess
How can you earn a living?
—Sir I can sew and stitch
And draw any thread divinely.

—Then stitch me a shirt
But use no thread and needle.
—O sir, you ask a thing
Which no one could accomplish.

—But tell me good sir,
   How can you earn a living?
   —I can read and write,
   You enchanting shepherdess.

—Well then, my good sir,
   Begin and write a letter
      But do not touch a pen
   And put no letters in it.

—Tell me shepherdess,
   Who taught you how to answer?
   —Papa and my mama,
   I'd have you understand, sir.

—Who is your Papa?
   —He is the King of England
   —And who is your Mama?
   —The Princess Some-one-else, Sir.

   10. "Yes, it is a poor man's daughter"

Yes, it is a poor man's daughter
Who's my heart's beloved;
Who has married with success,
Ah she is my heart's distress,
Ah, she is my heart's distress.

When that lady goes to service,
She's my heart's beloved.
She hath three lackeys no less,
Ah, she is my heart's distress. (*bis*)

The first bears her prayers and hymnal,
She's *etc.*
One hath her gloves to caress,
Ah *etc.*

The third bears a staff of office,
She's *etc.*
To push back the passing press,
Ah *etc.*

"Now stand back you base intruders."
She's *etc.*
See how Madame goes to mass.
Ah *etc.*

When Madam entered her chamber,
She's *etc.*
She hath called Jean Valleriess,
Ah *etc.*

"Tell me boy if I am lovely?
She's *etc.*
"Doth my mirror play a jest?
Ah *etc.*

"You are but a wee bit swarthy,
She's *etc.*
"It becomes you none the less."
Ah *etc.*

Then she hath tossed down her mirror,
She's *etc.*
Listened to her haughtiness,
Ah *etc.*

"Oh, shut up you silly wee thing,
She's *etc.*
"Just you quit your boastfulness,
Ah *etc.*
"When I bought your wedding dresses,
She's *etc.*
You had but six sous or less,"
Ah *etc.*

1912

Epilogue

(*To my five books containing mediaeval studies,
experiments and translations*)

I bring you the spoils, my nation,
I, who went out in exile,
    Am returned to thee with gifts.

I, who have laboured long in the tombs,
    Am come back therefrom with riches.

Behold my spices and robes, my nation,
My gifts of Tyre.

Here are my rimes of the south;
Here are strange fashions of music;
Here is my knowledge.

Behold, I am come with patterns;
Behold, I return with devices,
Cunning the craft, cunning the work, the fashion.

1912

from
Hesternae Rosae

"So pleaseth me joy"
B. de Palazol.
[*milieu du XIIième siècle.*]

So pleaseth me joy and good love and song
And merriment, fine ways and gentle breeding.
Nor silver nor rich rent has earth for heeding
That I would prize above such gifts for long
There are the things whereon my hope is cast
But she hath them so in her beck and call
That without her I can get none at all.

So have I wished her good and her advance
And so loved her and so wished to be with her
That if she'd send me off, I know I'd neither
Have strength nor sense to go, by any chance.
If I speak her great praise and hold it fast
In what I've said, no man can prove me wrong
For by her fact, I can prove true my song.

"Maiden and Virgin loyal"

Willaume li Viniers.
[*milieu du XIIIième siècle.*]

Maiden and Virgin loyal
In whom here Christ's Godhead.
As child glorious royal
Was conceived, born, nourished
Sweet maid be thy heart full fed
May his love and his grace allay
Thee this day,
When the Holy Ghost
By God's son be honoured Thee most.

Lady imperious
O marvelous fleur-de-lys,
The holy fruit for us
Thou hast born specially
Ah, rose branch and sovran tree
Thou hast the flower, and fleet
Odour sweet
Whereby paradise
Shall be brought before our eyes.

"The great desire"

Li Cuens d'Angou.
[*milieu du XIIIième siècle.*]

The great desire sheds fragrance o'er my thinking.
My thought for you, Madame, who'rt worth so much
Hath in it pain 'gainst which there is no blinking,
You have me made and have long held me such

Still my tormented heart lies in your clutch
Which naught shall loose save Death come nigh to touch.
Except thy grace should prove my pain's unlinking.

The great desire and the keen pain behind it
Have wrought on the true heart such honest grief
That as thou gavest joy thou now dost blind it
Ah, thou wert made for pleasure past belief.
And if thou grant me never sweet relief
And if thou grant me never thy relief.
Then mercy's hid where I shall never find it.

"Many people here miscall me"

Pierol.
[*fin du XIIième siècle.*]

Many people here miscall me
That I sing so seldom now,
But that fair whose thoughts befall me
I know not how long, nor how,
Hath bound my thoughts so woefully
That the chains thereon appall me,
And I've lost all joy and glee
So doth ill fortune gall me.

She hath banished all my pleasure
And is honoured naught by this,
With some well turned lies and leisure
She might well have wrought my bliss,
Such long delay before the kiss
Overfloweth folly's measure
And for payment cries I wis,
Shame's all I get to treasure.

"When cometh the clear time in"

Chanson à danser de la fin du XIIième siècle.

When cometh the clear time in, eya!
That our joys we may begin, eya!
To stir up the jealous men, eya!

Is our queen to show again
What gifts she has for playing.

    Refrain.
Jealousy Ha-a-i-e begone
Go we now, go we now a dancing our own way, our own way.

Ha! ha! here doth come the king! eya!
What a temper he doth bring! eya!
Bids us dancers break our ring! eya!
Lest his lady have her fling;
His April go a May-ing.

    Refrain.

But our sweetest lady here, eya!
Hath of old men little care, eya!
And for light-foot bachelors, eya!
Keepeth she that heart of hers,
Heigh-ho! what merry straying!

    Refrain.

1913

Pax Saturni

Once . . . the round world brimmed with hate,
. . . . and the strong
Harried the weak. Long past, long past, praise God
In these fair, peaceful, happy days.

                          A Contemporary

O smooth flatterers, go over sea,
                go to my country;
Tell her she is "Mighty among the nations"—
                do it rhetorically!

Say there are no oppressions,
Say it is a time of peace,
Say that labor is pleasant,

Say there are no oppressions,
Speak of the American virtues:
                    And you will not lack your reward.

Say that the keepers of shops pay a fair wage to the women:
Say that all men are honest and desirous of good above all
    things:
                    You will not lack your reward.

Say that I am a traitor and a cynic,
Say that the art is well served by the ignorant pretenders:
                    You will not lack your reward.

Praise them that are praised by the many:
                    You will not lack your reward.

Call this a time of peace,
Speak well of amateur harlots,
Speak well of disguised procurers,
Speak well of shop-walkers,
Speak well of employers of women,
Speak well of exploiters,
Speak well of the men in control,
Speak well of popular preachers:
                    You will not lack your reward.

Speak of the profundity of reviewers,
Speak of the accuracy of reporters,
Speak of the unbiased press,
Speak of the square deal as if it always occurred.
Do all this and refrain from ironic touches:
                    You will not lack your reward.

Speak of the open-mindedness of scholars:
                    You will not lack your reward.

Say that you love your fellow men,
O most magnanimous liar!
                    You will not lack your reward.

                                        1913

The Choice

It is true that you say the gods are more use to you than
    fairies,
But for all that I have seen you on a high, white, noble horse,
Like some strange queen in a story.
It is odd that you should be covered with long robes and
    trailing tendrils and flowers;
It is odd that you should be changing your face and
    resembling some other woman to plague me;
It is odd that you should be hiding yourself in the cloud of
    beautiful women, who do not concern me.

And I, who follow every seed-leaf upon the wind!
    They will say that I deserve this.

1913

Xenia

I

THE STREET IN SOHO

Out of the overhanging gray mist
There came an ugly little man
Carrying beautiful flowers.

II

The cool fingers of science delight me;
For they are cool with sympathy,
There is nothing of fever about them.

1913

Xenia

IV

Come let us play with our own toys,
Come my friends, and leave the world to its muttons,
You were never more than a few,
Death is already amongst you.

V

She had a pig-shaped face, with beautiful coloring,
She wore a bright, dark-blue cloak,
Her hair was a brilliant deep orange color
So the effect was charming
As long as her head was averted.

1913

Ikon

It is in art the highest business to create the beautiful image; to create order and profusion of images that we may furnish the life of our minds with a noble surrounding.

And if—as some say, the soul survives the body; if our consciousness is not an intermittent melody of strings that relapse between whiles into silence, then more than ever should we put forth the images of beauty, that going out into tenantless spaces we have with us all that is needful—an abundance of sounds and patterns to entertain us in that long dreaming; to strew our path to Valhalla; to give rich gifts by the way.

1913

Legend of the Chippewa Spring and Minnehaha, the Indian Maiden

If you press me for the legend,
For the story of this maiden,
Of this laughing Indian maiden,
Of this radiant Minnehaha
Who was won by Hiawatha,
I will answer, I will tell you
Briefly of her courtship,
And how Hiawatha won her.
She, of all Chippewa maidens,
Was the most fascinating,
And her charms were captivating;
Of the braves who sought this maiden,
And with passion almost frenzied
Led the chase and made hot battle,
Hiawatha was the bravest,
But his arrow was quite aimless,
And his game gave little heed to
Smiles of braves, or cupid's weapon.
Faint one day in early autumn,
Picking berries from the marshes,
And thirsting for a gourd of water,
She reclined upon the hillside,
Where a spring made merry laughter.
Hiawatha, from chase returning,
Saw the maiden thus reclining,
And, catching swift the inspiration,
Straightway brought the gourd of water,
Placed it to the lips so parching,
And bade her drink of 'Laughing Water,'
Scarcely had her lips been moistened,
By this fascinating nectar,
When she raised, with arms outstretching,
Bade her lover come and kiss her.
Thus it was that Hiawatha,
On the Chippewa's southern slope,
Where the fountain still is flowing,
And a city is fast growing,

Won and wed our Minnehaha,
Won and wed this beauteous maiden.

* * * * * *

Above, from happy hunting grounds,
Looking down, their watch they're keeping
On this rippling, laughing fountain,
Which gives health to all who drink it,
And with health, gives joy and gladness.

1913

Homage to Wilfrid Scawen Blunt

Because you have gone your individual gait,
Written fine verses, made mock of the world,
Swung the grand style, not made a trade of art,
Upheld Mazzini and detested institutions;

We, who are little given to respect,
Respect you, and having no better way to show it,
Bring you this stone to be some record of it.

1914

Pastoral

"The Greenest Growth of Maytime."
—A. C. S.

The young lady opposite
Has such beautiful hands
That I sit enchanted
    While she combs her hair in décolleté.
I have no shame whatever
In watching the performance,
The bareness of her delicate
    Hands and fingers does not
    In the least embarrass me,
BUT God forbid that I should gain further acquaintance,
For her laughter frightens even the street hawker
And the alley cat dies of a migraine.

1914

War Verse
(*1914*)

O two-penny poets, be still!—
For you have nine years out of every ten
To go gunning for glory—
                                   with pop-guns;
Be still, give the soldiers their turn,
And do not be trying to scrape your two-penny glory
From the ruins of Louvain,
And from the smouldering Liège,
From Leman and Brialmont.

1914

1915: February

The smeared, leather-coated, leather-greaved engineer
Walks in front of his traction-engine
Like some figure out of the sagas,
Like Grettir or like Skarpheddin,
With a sort of majestical swagger.
And his machine lumbers after him
Like some mythological beast,
Like Grendel bewitched and in chains,
But his ill luck will make me no sagas,
Nor will you crack the riddle of his skull,
O you over-educated, over-refined literati!
Nor yet you, store-bred realists,
You multipliers of novels!
He goes, and I go.
He stays and I stay.
He is mankind and I am the arts.
We are outlaws.
This war is not our war,
Neither side is on our side:
A vicious mediaevalism,
A belly-fat commerce,

Neither is on our side:
Whores, apes, rhetoricians,
Flagellants! in a year
Black as the *dies irae.*
We have about us only the unseen country road,
The unseen twigs, breaking their tips with blossom.

1915

Gnomic Verses

When the roast smoked in the oven, belching out blackness,
I was bewildered and knew not what to do,
But when I was plunged in the contemplation
        Of Li Po's beautiful verses,
This thought came upon me,—
When the roast smokes, pour water upon it.

1915

Our Respectful Homages to M. Laurent Tailhade

OM MANI PADME HUM
LET US ERECT A COLUMN, an epicene column,
                    To Monsieur Laurent Tailhade!
It is not fitting that we should praise him
In the modest forms of the Madrigale or the Aubade.
  Let us stamp with our feet and clap hands
  In praise of Monsieur Laurent Tailhade,
  Whose "Poemes Aristophanesques" are
  So-very-odd.
  Let us erect a column and stamp with our feet
  And dance a Zarabondilla and a Kordax,
  Let us leap with ungainly leaps before a stage scene
  By Leon Bakst.
  Let us do this for the splendour of Tailhade.
                Et Dominus tecum,
                    Tailhade.

1915

Et Faim Sallir les Loups des Boys

I cling to the spar,
Washed with the cold salt ice
I cling to the spar—
Insidious modern waves, civilization, civilized hidden snares.
Cowardly editors threaten: "If I dare"
Say this or that, or speak my open mind,
Say that I hate my hates,
      Say that I love my friends,
Say I believe in Lewis, spit out the later Rodin,
Say that Epstein can carve in stone,
That Brzeska can use the chisel,
Or Wadsworth paint;
          Then they will have my guts;
They will cut down my wage, force me to sing their cant,
Uphold the press, and be before all a model of literary
    decorum.
              Merde!
Cowardly editors threaten,
Friends fall off at the pinch, the loveliest die.
That is the path of life, this is my forest.

1915

Love-Song to Eunoë

Be wise:
Give me to the world,
Send me to seek adventure.

I have seen the married,
I have seen the respectably married
Sitting at their hearths:
It is very disgusting.

I have seen them stodged and swathed in contentments.
They purr with their thick stupidities.

O Love, Love,
Your eyes are too beautiful for such enactment!
Let us contrive a better fashion.

O Love, your face is too perfect,
Too capable of bearing inspection;
O Love,
Launch out your ships,
Give me once more to the tempest.

1915

Another Man's Wife

She was as pale as one
Who has just produced an abortion.

Her face was beautiful as a delicate stone
With the sculptor's dust still on it.

And yet I was glad that it was you and not I
Who had removed her from her first husband.

1915

Reflection

I know that what Nietzsche said is true,
And yet—
I saw the face of a little child in the street,
And it was beautiful.

1916

12 Occupations

by Jean de Bosschère

THE CHAIR AND TABLE MAKER

The chair-maker has democratized the throne.

The chair is the throne of all men. There now is something which even the bear who wisely sits himself down on the moss,—there now is something which even the bear has not invented.

Like the leech and the pig, man also eats. But decently the aforesaid maker presents him with a chair.

Ever since then he eats in state, higher than the beasts.

The maker of chairs and tables separates us from the earth.

"It is seemly," says he, "not to eat where the worms wait for us."

Then, by means of the table he brings the food half-way to our mouths. For the table is the first floor of the earth, as heaven is its garret.

Oh, admirable work of this man, which delivers the feather-less biped from the animality which lives on the earth.

The Greek has not done better for our sublimity.

THE ROPE-MAKER

If my arm be not long enough, I summon the rope-maker.

The rope asserts the will of the absent master.

The rope-maker also provides us with an amulet,—with the assistance of one who has been hanged.

SLEDGES AND SKATES

Pierrot, a sensitive person, tumbled down the hill.

From top to bottom, in the snow, it was a remarkable parabola.

His friends laugh long and loudly.

—"What are you laughing for?" cries Pierrot. "It's an experiment; you see I have invented the sledge. To-morrow you will be singing its praises."

—"The sledge," replies his lady-love, "I know, it's a double skate."

—"Skate?" asks Raton.

—"Yes, a long and narrow sole of iron. The skater plants himself on two of them; then on the ice he darts off like sheet lightning."

THE MOSAIC WORKER

A mason enamoured with painting, he paints in blows of many-coloured stones.

He has left his soul behind at Ravenna and Torcello.

THE JEWELLER

He endeavours to adorn our hides.

Humanity being long limbed, he devises how to knot it with rings, girdles, necklaces, bracelets and jewels. Such are the bands which fasten enamels, golden ornaments and diamonds to the person.

If the tailor has preceded him, it is with pins that he attaches his brooches, his clasps, and his cameos to the gown.

As the mosaic worker decorates the wall, so he decorates mankind with stones.

THE ELECTRICIAN

He weaves the nervous system into the flesh of houses.

He endows them with a sensitive epidermis. The house lives in all its corners, everywhere the wires creep along the crevices.

If one knocks on the wall, the nerves cry out, ring, crackle, blaze up: it is a loud hysteria.

The electrician with his long wires adds to our will. We are all at once in the cellar, in the garret, in the garden, at the front door. Prospero had no swifter messenger. Everywhere the winged sprite flies on our service taking the narrow road of the wires.

THE MIRROR-MAKER

The mischievous joker sticks something behind a pane of glass, and, if you look at what he is doing, you will see your own miserable visage only too clearly.

The mischievous joker looks at you sideways, and laughs like the black magician that he is.

THE GLOVER

He considers that the skin of human paws is too rosy and delicate.

He covers with gloves the hands of the ladies, and these perfumed stamens badly felt the need of them.

The glover deceives many people, but we are accomplices of his politeness which flatters our hands.

The glove is the mask of the hand. You know how precious this mask is,—you who understand the too expressive and too precise poetry of the hands!

The glove is also the weapon of a silent refusal.

THE GEOGRAPHER

He travels quicker than does a flash of lightning in the heavens.

His pilgrim's staff is a compass which moves over the painted maps.

His countries are of the colour of sugar-plums,—his rivers twist as the cracks in a wall,—his frontiers are chaplets of crosses,—his islands crumbs of biscuit.

But he lives happily in his unpopulated domains. His lands are without life, except now and then for a solitary lady-bird from the faded page of the atlas, which traverses a fishless ocean to alight on a desert continent.

THE ALCHEMIST

His wife each morning entreats him to remember that gold is the only god of the household. As regards himself, gold is not his care, nor the finding of it, nor the secret of life. The intoxication of research alone takes hold of him in its adorable cradle.

Death is his dreaded enemy, for undoubtedly it will come but a few hours before the moment in which he should have triumphed.

THE TOY-MAKER

He is the good magician of children.

He has only one eye, and smells of rotten gum and mouldy varnish, yet he knows how to hide the malicious spirit in a deluding puppet.

In his creations he excels even Phidias, for his toys are burlesques with the truth proper to them.

THE GILDER

He it is who alters the appearance of things by a veneer of gold.

Gold being a god which makes people crazy, the youngsters stick it and hang it up everywhere.

The gilder is a deceiver, who delights the simple peasantry, the children in the cradle, and kings seated on their golden stools.

1917

To a City Sending Him Advertisements

But will you do all these things?
 You, with your promises,
 You, with your claims to life,
Will you see fine things perish?
Will you always take sides with the heavy;
Will you, having got the songs you ask for,
 Choose only the worst, the coarsest?
Will you choose flattering tongues?

 Sforza . . . Baglione!
Tyrants, were flattered by one renaissance,
 And will your Demos,
Trying to match the rest, do as the rest,
The hurrying other cities,
Careless of all that's quiet,
Seeing the flare, the glitter only?

Will you let quiet men
        live and continue among you,
    Making, this one, a fane,
    This one, a building;
Or this bedevilled, casual, sluggish fellow
Do, once in a life, the single perfect poem,
    And let him go unstoned?
Are you alone? Others make talk
      and chatter about their promises,
Others have fooled me when I sought the soul.
And your white slender neighbor,
       a queen of cities,
A queen ignorant, can you outstrip her;
   Can you be you, say,
   As Pavia's Pavia
And not Milan swelling and being modern
      despite her enormous treasure?

If each Italian city is herself,
   Each with a form, light, character,
To love and hate one, and be loved and hated,
      never a blank, a wall, a nullity;
Can you, Newark, be thus,
         setting a fashion
But little known in our land?
           The rhetoricians
Will tell you as much. Can you achieve it?
You ask for immortality, you offer a price for it,
    a price, a prize, an honour?

You ask a life, a life's skill,
        bent to the shackle,
        bent to implant a soul
     in your thick commerce?
      Or the God's foot
        struck on your shoulder
         effortless,

   being invoked, properly called,
    invited?
I throw down his ten words,
   and we are immortal?

In all your hundreds of thousands
    who will know this;
Who will see the God's foot,
    who catch the glitter,
The silvery heel of Apollo;
    who know the oblation
Accepted, heard in the lasting realm?

If your professors, mayors, judges . . . ?
    Reader, we think not . . .
Some more loud-mouthed fellow,
    slamming a bigger drum,
Some fellow rhyming and roaring,
  Some more obsequious hack,
Will receive their purple,
    be the town's bard,
Be ten days hailed as immortal,
  But you will die or live
  By the silvery heel of Apollo.

           1917

Chanson Arabe

I have shaken with love half the night.
The winter rain falls in the street.
She is but half my age;
  Whither, whither am I going?
I have shaken with love half the night.
She is but half my age.
  Whither, whither am I going?

           1918

Dawn on the Mountain

Peach flowers turn the dew crimson,
Green willows melt in the mist,
The servant will not sweep up the fallen petals,
    And the nightingales
Persist in their singing.

Omakitsu

1918

Wine

Dew, clear as gilt jewels, hangs under the garden grass-blades.
Swift is the year, swift is the coming cold season,
Life swift as the dart of a bird:

Wine, wine, wine for a hundred autumns,
And then no wine, no wine, and no wine.

Rihaku

1918

A Canticle

(*Special to H.T., of St. Louis.*)

LIGHT OF THE WORLD! my country 'tis of thee,
Where booze is banned and letters are not free;
The classics on thy shores are tolerated—
As, in his summing up, Judge Hand has stated—
Because there are but few who will peruse 'em.
LIGHT OF THE WORLD, O freedom's chest and bosom!

America mine own delectable,
Such is the joyous news you have to tell,
To martyred nations in thick darkness cowering,
While you in your effulgence burst out flowering.
Light of the World, my country, list this tune
"Because of age, the classics are immune;"
Immune they are, although their legal portion
Is one with that of tools whereby abortion
Or birth-prevention may be vilely encompass'd!

'Twas 1919 that brought down the Rum Trust—
LIGHT OF THE WORLD, our grand-dads took it neat.

And Hokusais are still burnt in California
Because the woodcuts are thought ornrier
Than sons of Pilgrim Fathers ought to see,
Light of the World, my country 'tis of thee.
Our post office will not permit the traffic
Of things bald Lamar takes for pornographic.

Light of the World, my country 'tis of thee!
Nor forget this in long-remembering time;

Voltaire was printed in Leyden in the prime
Of Louis Quatorze, then styled the Grand Monarque,
Our pink-head bucks have hit this plimsoll mark
And lick the altar stones of this tradition,
God in our garden walks on kitty-feet.

Light of the World, once ruled by Andy Jackson;
Senate, and ancient bar wherefrom Calhoun
Beheld three crescents of one lonely moon
Serene above the streets of Washington!
Light of the World in splendid triplication!

Light of the World, look down upon our nation;
Behold the era of great Woodrow's race,
In ancient Andy's candid dwelling place.

1920

Fever Chart

NICE

For sale
the pagodas and fortresses and Khedival villas 1866.
The Russian wolfhounds mourn their princesses
collarless
in the pound.
Those Hungarian magnates, stringers up of cats, are setting
    up housekeeping

Farewell, precinematographic Mexican chieftains
whom one sole diligence used to enrich sufficiently,
old, dear monkeys basted with filigree,
Polish counts whose beds, at dusk, have not been made.

Farewell elderly British children
              their shadows right up to lunch-time
under the stupid perturbation of the swallows.
Victory, victory!
beside waves of taffeta
the Sanitariums go bankrupt,
NOBODY DIES ANY MORE.
Those big necrophores of the war
have minced Napoleon put in their soup,

Salmis of woodcock on platinum.
Ten thousand chandeliers.
Lunch, Lynch.
Who could have believed there were so many sables
in the American stocks?

The Paris-Lyon-Mediterannée azure has a flavour of aloes.

SAMPLE

My fingers are full of riots,
My bowler hat full of ideas,
My handkerchief is full of groans.
The people who pour out their hearts are spoiling
              unhappiness for me.
One would hunt in vain for two hours' mad laughter
in the Collection of Famous Authors.
Optimism is an hygienic beverage
from Boston, invented by Emerson.
Moist and wilful crocodile
J. J. Rousseau muddies the Evian water.
A couple make the acquisition
of a tube paste for reproduction
but nothing quiets their torment.
On the pavement
where an ovoid moon is already established,

a Magenta sky lies counterdrawn
among the jointed stalks and celluloid flowers.

As for me
I pursue my charming little road to the cross.

after Morand, 1920

Troubadour Songs

"Sad song ye hear"

Sad song ye hear, I speak a common grief
Among ye all, for valor's crown and chief
Is ta'en from us, His prowess overthrown.
'Tis mine to tell this tale who speak perforce and weep,
For Death unpitying hath laid this day his hand
Upon our Lord Richard, King of England.
Ah death, ah me: He fell before Chalu,
A quarrel bolt did pierce his vizard through,
Valor is gone from light into his tomb.
I marvel now that valiant deeds have ill desert
And manhood's flowers win but an early grave
And singers have no theme but so rest sorrow.
Think ye how firm his step, how great his largesse.
Plantagenet, our Lord, Richard, farewell!
Ah death! ah me: Who will pay singers now
That death hath laid thee low. Thy court and crown
And all thy gear, to lackland John shall pass.
Ah me—

after Faidit, 1920

"When new buds thrust"

When new buds thrust the leaves aside
And all the air is clear serene
And mid the boughs the birds confide
Then sweetness comes back to my heart,
Tis then each bird sings to his mate
And I who've such joy in my heart

Should turn to song for all my sorrow tells,
Are joy and song, I think of nothing else.

after Ventadorn, ca. 1920

"When cometh in the flow'ry time"

When cometh in the flow'ry time
And we farewell from winter take,
I love the merry roundelays
And light some songs the small birds make,
And then my thought doth turn upon
That fair who thinketh naught of me.
Ah will her favour ne'er return.
Ah will her favour ne'er return.

after Ventadorn, ca. 1920

"Although thou leave me now"

Although thou leave me now, so vixen strange,
'Tis reason none why I should change from song
Or leave my joy and plunge myself in tears;
But through new joys I will so wanton range
That none shall know what pain I bear within
Nor what sad lesson I have learned from thee:
How swift to change, nor hold one object long,
Thus much have I, from her who doth me wrong.

after Ventadorn, ca. 1920

"Call that not life"

Call that not life, wherein love hath no part,
It is but death disguisèd,
He hath no worth, and doth but irk his friends
Who liveth so, lives but to be despisèd,
Not by God's power, would I one day live on,
Had I not hope to gain her unison.

To see her eyes, her face, and her fair hue
Doth shake me as a leaf in wind
Is shaken and in all my mind
Not even a child's wit can I find,

Such in her presence I become,
Surely some kindness should start up
In her at sight of such a plight.

after Ventadorn, ca. 1920

"Say that sweet my sorrow was"

Say that sweet my sorrow was
That is all turned to pain.
For she that was so sweet and fain
And who'd held me all the summer
Hath now bid me to turn from her,
     Yea tho I cannot leave
Yet since she keeps me not
And I dare not ask grace
I can get no peace at all
Since from her all my sorrows fall.

after Marvoil, ca. 1920

"In sorrow now I know well"

In sorrow now I know well
That never do you think of me,
Since neither greeting nor friendship
Nor message comes to me.
Too long a wait I will have made,
And it seems really
That I will never get what someone else takes,
Since luck never comes to me.

Such pleasant fruit for me will be
Her iron heart, hard and enraged,
Until softened from all iron
With fair speech and grace;
This have I well found light,
This drop of water that falls
So often in one place
That it wears away the hard stone.

after Ventadorn, 1922

Highbrow's Translation from Horace

(Persicos odi)

The Persian buggahs, Joe,
Strike me as = a = rotten show,
Stinking of nard and = musk
Over the whole of their rind and husk;
Wearing their soft = shell clothes
Whichever way the wind blows,
The Persian buggahs, Joe,
Strike me as = a = rotten show.

1931

Drafts for
Guido Cavalcanti Rime (1932)

"I think that thou has looked"

I think that thou has looked on every valour and all
Of playe and good that any man may feel,
Thou'st put to proof that overlord of such weal
As, by his honour, holdeth the world in thrall.

Where he dwelleth unease ceaseth amain
For he hath reasonableness in a piteous mind,
When folk lie in dream he goeth softly to find
And pluck their hearts out, yet giv'th no pain.

He carried thine heart, seeing that death
Made claim against thy mistress,
And fed her with thine heart in her fearfulnesse;

That he appeared to weep as he went
Is a fair omen, whereby the presage saith
That the contrary of what was shown, is meant.

after Cavalcanti

"*Amore and Lagia*"

Amore and Lagia, Guido Orlando and I
May offer thanks to Ser Anonymous
Who by a certain severance serveth us,
From whom? I say not, loving purged memory.

Nor would these other three stand saying it over,
Although with such obeisance served they him
They could not more, had they held it in whim
That he were paramount to Lord Jehoveh.

May Love be thanked who was this in advance,
And then the lady who withdrew her affection,
And then Orlando, outside the whole connection.
The lady was timely, but so thank them all
And then thank me who in her virtue fall:
Be this my pleasure, think not it falls perchance.

after Cavalcanti

"*Guido, Gianni that saw you*"

Guido, Gianni that saw you yesterday
Or the other day; if you like, you may laugh me down,
But there's a young girl in Pisa, where the town
Is split by the Arno, who's a frown
Against love, and carries a dagger.
She asked me if you were fit (him who hath slain her)
To serve, and how far, the ladies you kill.
If she came, let us say, in such a way with him
That he alone, and Mr. Gaultier were aware.
So that the family: bent on slaughter
Could at most do naught, or no more than
Call mate (check-mate, that is) from afar.
I said, on my own, that you, and no sham,
Had your pouch full of munition,
And would indubitably, free her from the embarrassing
     position.

after Alfani

"In your gentle salute"

In your gentle salute,
Sent in rhymed sonnet
To boot.
You say the young lady said: 'Please
Make of me
What to thee
Give in ease.
Well, here am I
Ready and spry,
Obedient and equipted,
And Andrea, with his arrows tipped,
Bow in hand.
But have a care where you stand;
God's church
Wills not
That justice be left in the lurch.'
(Meaning perhaps: this prize is mine.
You pay the fine.)

after Cavalcanti

"Guard thee well"

Guard thee well guard thee well I say
Lest seest too late that
'Gainst stone of bombard steel vaileth little.
For much raw flesh and red flame
See I set at the game,
Many a sharper,
Fool spender and miser,
Snares stretched to harm without number.
E'en bold turn cowards
Seeing good bands of men set in disunion
With shames, scorns and complaining.
The she lion shows up for sharing.
Ever from rapine
Is born every ruin and every sorrow.
Oft loseth all for all
Who would have all for himself.

Thou knowst what grieves me:
To lose time and talking where deeds were needed.
Make we clear contract
And see how many loons need the lash
(Something to grin for).
'Who snare stretcheth, in snare is taken'; if so
'Twere justice.
Harsh hand, hard spur, bitter whip,
Ne'er yet did a colt good.
Bell without clapper,
Flash without thunder, ne'er made a man deaf.
And you that would
Bite in the whole pie
Show greed in wolf pack and then feel injured.
Be then provident
Even though I now speak to a mute that heareth and speaketh.
To make others thine own
Pleaseth not heaven.
To most men I bellow in vain,
But with good intention and honest.
Who will believe me?
Who will put under proof whether
Truth be it?
White coat or black coat
Fra Romero will make neither perfect.
Amend fault
Is a good step.
Know who is sickly?
Who bolts all without salt.
Let the taste warn thee
To say salt is asked with ever duty.
We shall make it avail
If we spend justly,
For loss with loaners
Wasteth all Ghibbeline substance,
That who seeketh glory against the just
As holy reason.
But I find too many boobs with ill will.
Yet move for good
To give egg here, grass there.

What thou findest bitter
Leave; and take the sweet, if there is a point.
Oft anointed with perfume
Mouse cometh to bitter eating.

after Cavalcanti

"We are the sad, bewildered quills"

We are the sad, bewildered quills,
the creaking scissors and the penman's knife,
who through our grief make strife
of words, till the parchment sheet distills

sound to your ear, that saith, what wills
caused us to leave, to come: saying,
'The moving hand felt such dubious
apparitions in the heart, such powers that destroyed him

and brought him so near to death
that naught of him, that was man, remains,
save the shaking sound of his breath.

And we crave with that power of prayer we have
that you let us stay with you a little, for long enough
till such time, that pity cast a small glance, your way.'

after Cavalcanti

"Gentle Jheezus sleek and wild"

Gentle Jheezus sleek and wild
Found disciples tall an' hairy
Flirting with his red hot Mary,
　　Now hot momma Magdelene
　Is doing front page fer the screen
　　　Mit der yittischer Charleston Pband
　　Mit

deryiddischercharles
tonband.

ole king Bolo's big black queen
Whose bum was big as a soup tureen
 Has lef' the congo
                and is now seen
  Mit der *etc.*

Red hot Mary of Magdala
Had nine jews an a Roman fellow
Nah she'z gotta chob much swellah
  Mit der yiddisher Charleston Band.
    mit der YIDDISHER
              Charleston BAND

Calvin Coolidg dh' pvwezident
He vudn't go but dh' family vwent,
  Vuddunt giff notding but his name vass lent
   For deh yidtischer Charleston pband.

N.B. I shant persecute you if you print the Yittisher without the music.

The final strophe rather dates it: in fact if you use it you shd. state it is from antient files of yr. correspondence.

(*Variant*)
  Mister Goolidge dh' pbvesident
  He vuddunt kgo putt dh' fvamily vent
  Vuddunt giff notdhink butt his name vuss lendt
   fer dh yittischer charleston pbadt.

You can note it belongs to the best and most active period of jazz; before the new neo sentimentalism set in.

                                   E. P.

                                 1932

Drafts for
"Cavalcanti: A Sung Dramedy in 3 Acts" (1932)

"Ever shall I be toward Amor"

Ever shall I be toward Amor
True and firm with honest heart,
For the fairest and best
Causes me to love and do service.
As soon as she does not advance me,
So increases her worth and honorificabilitudinity
That I take the honouring as reward,
For nobly is any true lover paid
Who is honoured by such gift.

after Sordello

"Ailas, what use are my eyes"

Ailas, what use are my eyes,
Since they see not my desired!

Now when summer renews and gentles
With leaf and with flower
She who is lady of delight
I will sing at once, for love
I die, for I love her
And see very little of her.
Ailas, what use my eyes
That see not my desired!

after Sordello

"If the prelates would take some honest advice"

If the prelates would take some honest advice from me,
They'd tell the poor: "See here, that belongs to you":
They'd then confine themselves to singing mass
And keep their cotton-picking fingers off other people's
     property.

They should, furthermore, remember they used to live on
    alms.
It was King Constantine who first cut them in on a share of
    the state's revenue.
If he'd foreseen the evil that would come of it,
He'd certainly have prevented it, for the good of the nation.
But their behavior, in those days, was still civil, not arrogant.

after Walther von der Vogelweide, ca. 1939–43

"King Constantine, as I will relate"

King Constantine, as I will relate,
Bestowed a whole lot on the Holy See.
Arms, cross, and crown—
At which the angel cried aloud:
"Woe, woe, and a third time woe!
Christendom once lived according to the Golden Rule.
Now poison has entered the system,
Turning its honey to gall.
The world will live to rue it bitterly."
All the princes are held in high esteem,
While their overlord is humiliated,
And this due to the prelates' decision.
O God, what a mess.
The prelates want to twist secular law.
The angel was talking truth.

after Walther von der Vogelweide, ca. 1939–43

Envoi'*

(from correspondence)

Prince, in this circus of three rings,
Hell, heaven and earth wherein is nothing clear
Void, mix'd and loose up to the stratosphere,
Pity the young who have not known these things.

* to a ballade unwrit re a past age, i.e., Verlaine's.

1946

"Thais habet nigros . . ."
—*Martial*

Thais has black teeth, Laecania's are white   because
she bought 'em last night.

1950

Papillon

For a small book unread

Do we suppose this is the price
Of association with Mr. Mac Nice;
Or of breathing "The Ariel" air
In cahoots with Walt de la Mare;
Or that England prays someone will send her
Another slender Spender?

In any case, let us lament the psychosis
Of all those who abandon the Muses for Moses.

Anon.

1957

Old Zuk

This is the grave of old Zuk
who wasn't really a crook
but who died of persistence
in that non-existence
            which consists in refusing to LOOK.

1959

More

When Elmer died the undertaker wiped his feet
            on the Criterion floor.
He felt that there had been
            other Elmers before.

1959

By the River of Stars

("Baijo's poem in the Koshigen")

By the river of stars, its brightness
    the ox herd far from stargirl
her white hand on the shuttle
    and at day's end no pattern yet made

a rain of tears for their distance
    tho' the river is clear and shallow
    they cannot cross it;

nor their pulse beat, come into words.

1959

"Age of Gold"

Age of Gold, I bid thee come
To this Earth, was erst thy home!
Age of Gold, if e'er thou wast
And art not mere dream laid waste!

Thou art not fled; ne'er wast mere dreaming;
Art not now mere feignèd seeming.
Every simple heart knows this:
Candour still thy substance is.

after Metastasio, 1964

Pigeons

To the Father of his Country (bronze)
Riva degli Schiavoni:
aloft on his helmet, on the top, the very top
a pigeon, as ever, a pigeon
comes to rest, looks down
and eases himself.

On the King's head and shoulders
on the head and rump of the horse
guano accumulates.
On the great cornices of civilized Istrian stone,
on the pinnacles against heaven
and on the brackets of street lamps
there are pigeons, the sacred cows of Venice,
pure and cooing doves
freeing themselves of corrosive superfluities suddenly
on the head of pedestrians—
(On the Grand Canal and out over the Laguna, the gulls
moving seaward and landward
rest, white, on the green water;
hale and hearty, birds of a different feather).
He-pigeon and hen-pigeon cavort on the pavement,
urban, outnumbering the citizens;
People! too many; they also besmirching crowned heads,
defiling brows and memorials. . . .
We demythicize, we raise our trophies of excrement.
Let no one impede us or affront pigeons—winged shapely,
having no talons—
Let no one contest our liberty to be empty,
regimented into dirty grey, mocking the monuments
which overshadow us.

after Fasolo, 1970

Prayer for a Dead Brother

May his soul walk under the larches of Paradise
    May his soul walk in the wood there
and Adah Lee come to look after him.

Queen of Heaven receive him.
Mother of the Seven Griefs receive him
Mother of the seven wounds receive him
    May he have peace in heart.

By a stream like Castalia, limpid,
   that runs level with the green edge of its banks,
Mother of Heaven receive him,
Queen of Heaven receive him,
     Mother of the Seven Griefs give him Peace.

Out of the turmoil, Mother of Griefs receive him,
Queen of Heaven receive him.
     May the sound of the leaves give him peace,
May the hush of the forest receive him.

pub. 1971

Chronology

1885   Ezra Loomis Pound born on October 30 in Hailey, Idaho, to Homer Pound and Isabel Weston Pound. (His grandfather Thaddeus Coleman Pound, of Quaker descent, had prospered as a partner in the Union Lumbering Company of Wisconsin, was elected lieutenant governor of the state in 1870, and served three terms, 1877–83, as its Republican representative in Congress. He also established the Chippewa Falls Northern & Eastern Railway, printing his own scrip redeemable at the company store; driven out of business by the lumber baron Frederick Weyerhauser, his railway was absorbed by the Northern Pacific Railroad. Abandoning his wife, ex-congressman Pound lived openly with his mistress, spoiling his political prospects under the administration of President Garfield. Through Thaddeus's political connections, his son Homer was appointed in 1883 as Register of the Government Land Office in the Idaho Territory, where his duties involved adjudicating miners' land claims and assaying ore.) Ezra Pound's mother, Isabel, daughter of Harding Weston and Mary Parker (a distant descendant of the poet Henry Wadsworth Longfellow), was born in Manhattan and raised by her uncle Ezra Brown Weston and his wife Frances ("Frank") in Nyack, New York.

1887   Suffering from the altitude and the frontier hardships of Hailey, Isabel induces her husband to leave Idaho. With their infant son "Ra" (pronounced "Ray"), they move to New York City, where they live with Uncle Ezra and Aunt Frank Weston in their boardinghouse at 24 E. 47th St.

1889–97   Homer Pound takes a job as assistant assayer at the United States Mint in Philadelphia, where he will work until his retirement in 1928. The family initially settles in the northern suburb of Jenkintown, then moves into its long-term residence at 166 Fernbrook Avenue in the adjacent suburb of Wyncote in 1892. "Ra" attends local schools and in 1896 his first published poem, a limerick on the defeat of William Jennings Bryan in the presidential election, appears in the *Jenkintown Times-Chronicle*.

He enters the Cheltenham Military Academy in 1897, where he learns Latin, fencing, tennis, and chess. He makes a formal profession of faith at the Calvary Presbyterian Church, while his parents undertake mission work in the slums of Philadelphia.

1898   Embarks on his first grand tour of Europe with his mother and her Aunt Frank; they visit England, Germany, France, Switzerland, and Italy.

1901   Enters the University of Pennsylvania at age fifteen, on the strength of his Latin. His freshman courses include English composition, public speaking, mathematics, German grammar and literature, Livy and Horace, American colonial history, and the principles of United States government. Befriends an art student, William Brooke Smith, who suffers from tuberculosis. Meets Hilda Doolittle, the fifteen-year-old daughter of a Penn professor of astronomy, at a Halloween party; she is struck by his "bronze-gold hair" and the green Moroccan robe he is wearing.

1902   During the summer of his freshman year, again travels to Europe (including visits to Gibraltar and Morocco) with his parents and Aunt Frank. Meets William Carlos Williams, a medical student at Penn two years his senior; Williams is discovering the romantic poets, but Pound, displaying his more advanced knowledge of the moderns (Browning, Symons, Dowson, and Yeats), quickly assumes the role of mentor in matters of poetry. Williams judges Pound "the livest, most intelligent and unexplainable thing" he has ever come across, while observing that he is generally disliked by his fellow students "because he is so darned full of conceits and affectation."

1903   Because of his poor grades during sophomore year, Pound transfers to Hamilton College in Clinton, New York, where he studies Romance languages with William Pierce Shepard and Anglo-Saxon with Joseph D. Ibbotson.

1905   Receives his bachelor's degree. Publishes a translation from the Provençal in the *Hamilton Literary Magazine*. Reads Dante intensively and dreams of writing a modern epic modeled on the *Divine Comedy*. Briefly infatuated with an older woman, the pianist Katherine Ruth Heyman. Enrolls as a graduate student at Penn, and sees a great deal of Hilda Doolittle, for whom he composes the poems in the handmade anthology "Hilda's Book." Together they read Swedenborg, Blake, William Morris, Dante Gabriel Rossetti, as well as Greek pastorals and books on Yoga.

1906   Pursues his studies of Romance languages and literatures with Hugo Rennert and attends seminars on Catullus and Martial. Receives his master's degree in Romanics and is awarded a fellowship to undertake summer doctoral research on the plays of Lope de Vega in Spain. Sails to Gibraltar, works in the Royal Library in Madrid, visits Burgos, and travels to Paris and London. Returns to Penn in the fall to continue work in Provençal, Italian, Spanish, and French with Rennert, but fails literary criticism and, disappointed with his professors, loses interest in his other courses.

1907   Learns his fellowship will not be renewed and that he will not be appointed as a instructor. Falls in love with Mary Moore. Accepts a job as an instructor of Romance languages at Wabash College in Crawfordsville, Indiana, where he teaches Spanish and French language courses. Composes dramatic monologues in the manner of Browning and cuts a colorful figure on campus.

1908   Accused by his landladies of harboring an actress in his rooms overnight, is dismissed from the Wabash faculty in February. Marriage proposal to Mary Moore rejected. Asks Professor Doolittle for his daughter's hand, but is turned down on the grounds he is "nothing but a nomad." At the recommendation of poet Witter Bynner, Homer Pound agrees to financially underwrite his son's career as a poet. Sails to Gibraltar in March; after working briefly as a tour guide, travels on to Venice, where he spends the summer acting as impresario for pianist Katherine Heyman and publishes *A Lume Spento* in 150 copies at his own expense; the book is dedicated to William Brooke Smith, who had died earlier in the year. Moves to London in mid-August. Frequents the bookshop of the publisher Elkin Mathews, through whom he meets poets Selwyn Image, Victor Plarr, Laurence Binyon, and Ernest Rhys. Publishes *A Quinzaine for This Yule*.

1909   Delivers six lectures on "The Development of Literature in Southern Europe" at Regent Street Polytechnic. Meets

Olivia Shakespear, Yeats's former lover, and her daughter Dorothy, with whom he soon becomes romantically involved. Through May Sinclair, becomes friends with Ford Madox Hueffer and his mistress Violet Hunt; Hueffer prints Pound's "Sestina: Altaforte" in his recently founded *English Review. Personae* published in April by Mathews. Attends the gatherings of the Poets' Club; meets T. E. Hulme and F. S. Flint, founders of the rival Secession Club, and discusses with them poetic possibilities of "absolutely accurate presentation and no verbiage." Following the success of *Personae*, is offered the ultimate London accolade—satirical mention in *Punch* as "the new Montana (U.S.A) poet, Mr. Ezekiel Ton, the most remarkable thing in poetry since Robert Browning." Publishes "Ballad of the Goodly Fere" in *The English Review*. Moves to 10 Church Walk in Kensington. *Exultations* appears in October. Over the course of the year meets Wyndham Lewis, D. H. Lawrence, and W. B. Yeats.

1910   Completes a second "Course of Lectures on Medieval Literature," published later in the year as *The Spirit of Romance*. Is in love with Evelyn St. Bride Scratton and romantically linked to a number of other women. William Carlos Williams visits London; Pound takes him to one of Yeats's Monday evenings, but Williams is not impressed. In March, leaves London for Paris, where the pianist Walter Morse Rummel puts him in touch with Margaret Cravens, who becomes his patron, guaranteeing him $1,000 per year. Travels to Sirmione on Lake Garda, where he is joined by Olivia and Dorothy Shakespear. Works on translations of the poetry of Guido Cavalcanti. Returns to the United States in June, hoping to start a business venture with Williams or to find academic employment. Divides his time between the Philadelphia area and New York City, whose new skyscrapers he admires ("squares after squares of flame, set and cut into the ether"), but whose literary scene he finds provincial. An American edition of his poems, *Provença*, is published in November. Renews contact with Hilda Doolittle, who, unaware of Pound's involvement with Dorothy Shakespear, still considers herself his fiancée. Meets Yeats's father, the painter John Butler Yeats, who puts him in contact with New York lawyer John Quinn, patron and collector of modern art.

1911   Returns to London in February, and immediately sets off
        for Paris, where he works on translations of troubadour
        poet Arnaut Daniel at the Bibliothèque Nationale and
        collaborates with Rummel on musical settings of trouba-
        dour poetry. *Canzoni* brought out by Mathews. Spends
        July in Sirmione, where he translates "The Seafarer" from
        Anglo-Saxon; travels to Germany to meet Hueffer, who
        ridicules the archaic diction of his latest volume of verse
        and directs him to concentrate on "using the living
        tongue." Back in London in the fall, meets A. R. Orage,
        editor of the Guild Socialist journal *The New Age*, which
        will be his major journalistic outlet over the next decade.
        His first series of articles for Orage's weekly, "I Gather
        the Limbs of Osiris," outlines his "New Method in Schol-
        arship": "The artist seeks out the luminous detail and pre-
        sents it. He does not comment." Hilda Doolittle appears
        in London, only to discover that Pound is intending to
        marry Dorothy Shakespear. Attends T. E. Hulme's lec-
        tures on Bergson. Friendship with Yeats becomes closer.

1912   Introduced by Hueffer to Henry James. In February,
        signs a ten-year contract with the London firm Swift &
        Co.; after publishing Pound's *Sonnets and Ballate of Guido
        Cavalcanti* in May and *Ripostes* in October, the company
        goes bankrupt and his projected bilingual edition of
        Arnaut does not appear. Introduces Richard Aldington to
        Hilda Doolittle; soon a couple, the two (who will marry
        the following year) accompany Pound to Paris in the
        spring, where he works on Provençal manuscripts at the
        Bibliothèque Nationale and begins reading in modern
        French literature. Travels alone through the troubadour
        country of southern France during the summer; halfway
        through his walking tour, learns that his patron Margaret
        Cravens has committed suicide in Paris. Upon his return
        to London in August, attempts to recast the notes made
        during his walking tour into a more general book about
        the troubadours entitled "Gironde," which he envisages
        as complement to "Patria Mia," his series of essays on his
        trip to America. Soon abandoning this project, he turns
        his energies to promoting his new school of Imagisme,
        publicly announced for the first time in the appendix of
        Ripostes. In August, he is contacted by Harriet Monroe,
        who is launching *Poetry* magazine in Chicago. Pound
        agrees to become the magazine's "foreign correspon-

dent" and promises her "whatever is most dynamic in artistic thought, either here or in Paris." Over the next few months, he submits to her his own "ultra-modern" sequence "Contemporania," as well poems by Yeats, Tagore, and Aldington, and *vers libre* by Hilda Doolittle, whom he names "H.D., Imagiste."

1913   In "Status Rerum" (in *Poetry*), he defines the two poles between which his poetry is now vacillating, the post-symbolist aesthetic of Yeats and the "prose tradition" of Hueffer. Meets Robert Frost and sends a laudatory review of his first book, *A Boy's Will*, to *Poetry*; praise for D. H. Lawrence's *Love Poems* soon follows. Arranges the publication of Williams's *The Tempers* by Mathews. The March issue of *Poetry* features Pound's manifesto of Imagism. Its poetic program involves: "1. Direct treatment of the 'thing' whether subjective or objective. 2. To use absolutely no word that does not contribute to the presentation. 3. As regarding rhythm: to compose in the sequence of the musical phrase, not in sequence of a metronome." Pound's haiku-like "In a Station of the Metro" appears in *Poetry* in April. In "America: Chances and Remedies" (in *The New Age*), he expresses his belief in a coming renaissance of American arts and letters. Travels to Paris in the spring to meet with Jules Romains, Georges Duhamel, Charles Vildrac, and other emerging French poets; his survey of contemporary French poetry, "The Approach to Paris," runs in *The New Age* in the fall. Hueffer and Violet Hunt introduce him to Dora Marsden and Harriet Shaw Weaver, publishers of *The New Free-woman*, soon renamed *The Egoist*, of which Pound becomes literary editor. Contributes to the New York magazine *The Smart Set*, whose editor, H. L. Mencken, he admires. Amy Lowell comes to London, July–September, and seeks out Pound, H.D., John Gould Fletcher, and others associated with the Imagist group. Pound meets the young French-born sculptor Henri Gaudier-Brzeska and is immediately convinced of his genius. Puts finishing touches on *Lustra*, although its publication will be delayed until 1916. Spends the first of three winters as Yeats's secretary at Stone Cottage in Sussex. Meets Mary Fenollosa, widow of the American Orientalist Ernest Fenollosa, and is entrusted by her with her husband's unpublished notebooks containing materials related to Chinese poetry and Japanese Noh theater; adapts three Noh plays contained in the notebooks. Yeats shows him work by Joyce; Pound immediately requests the latter's permission to use his poem "I Hear an Army" in his forthcoming Imagist anthology.

1914   Arranges for the serialization of Joyce's *A Portrait of the Artist as a Young Man* in *The Egoist*. His anthology *Des Imagistes*, containing poems by Aldington, H.D., Flint, Williams, Lowell, Joyce, and Hueffer, appears in book form in New York in March. Associates with writer and post-Cubist painter Wyndham Lewis and artists of the Rebel Art Center. Gaudier-Breszka sculpts "Hieratic Head of Ezra Pound." Marries Dorothy Shakespear on April 20; they move to 5 Holland Place Chambers, Kensington, her £150 annuity assuring a measure of financial stability. Praises Yeats's new "gaunter" manner and the "prose" quality of Hueffer's verse in *Poetry*. BLAST No. *1*, edited by Pound and Lewis, issued in July, proclaiming the birth of the "GREAT ENGLISH VORTEX" and containing a Vorticist manifesto signed by Gaudier-Brzeska, Lewis, Pound, and others. Amy Lowell returns to London in the summer to recruit contributors to her anthology *Some Imagist Poets*; Pound derisively refers to her group (which H.D. and Aldington have joined) as "Amygisme." Gaudier-Brzeska leaves for the front shortly after the outbreak of World War I at the beginning of August. An important essay on "Vorticism" in the September *Fortnightly Review* argues for "non-representative" art and defines the "image" as a "radiant node or cluster . . . a VORTEX, from which, and through which, and into which, ideas are constantly rushing." Introduced by Conrad Aiken to T. S. Eliot, Pound enthusiastically recommends "The Love Song of J. Alfred Prufrock" for publication in *Poetry*, despite Harriet Monroe's initial objections. Spends winter at Stone Cottage, where he completes his reworkings of Chinese poems in Fenollosa's notebooks. Publishes "Modern Georgics," a favorable review of Frost's *North of Boston*, in *Poetry*.

1915   Publishes a series of "Affirmations" in *The New Age*, praising the "pattern music" of Bach, the abstract sculpture of Jacob Epstein and Gaudier-Brzeska, and the "hardness" of Joyce. Becomes adviser to New York art collector John Quinn. Raises funds for Joyce and persuades Mencken to print two of the *Dubliners* stories in *The Smart Set*. "Exile's Letter," the first of the poems drawn from Fenollosa's notes, appears in *Poetry* in March. Unsuccessfully attempts to publish Fenollosa's essay "The Chinese Written Character as a Medium for Poetry," which he calls "a whole basis of aesthetic." *Cathay* published by Mathews in April. Gaudier-Brzeska is killed in action in France in June. *BLAST No. 2* appears. Arranges Quinn's purchase of pieces by Gaudier-Brzeska and Lewis in preparation for Vorticist exhibition in New York. Edits *The Poetical Works of Lionel Johnson* (Dorothy's cousin). Pound's *Catholic Anthology*, which showcases the poetry of Eliot (notably "Prufrock"), while also featuring Yeats, Williams, Masters, and Sandburg, appears in November. Rereads Browning's *Sordello* and begins writing "cantos" for "a longish new poem."

1916   Serializes Lewis's novel *Tarr* in *The Egoist*. Publishes memorial tribute to Remy de Gourmont in *Poetry*. Pound's *Gaudier-Brzeska: A Memoir* published by John Lane. In September, Mathews, skittish about the suppression of D. H. Lawrence's *The Rainbow* the previous year, brings out what Pound calls a "castrato" version of *Lustra*, removing several poems from its contents. *Certain Noble Plays of Japan* ("from the manuscripts of Ernest Fenollosa, chosen and finished by Ezra Pound") is published by the Cuala Press. Pound protests American censorship of the work of Theodore Dreiser in *The Egoist*. Reviews Yeats's *Responsibilities and Other Poems* for *Poetry*.

1917   *'Noh' or Accomplishment*, an expanded version of *Certain Noble Plays of Japan* (with Fenollosa's essays on Japanese theater), published by Macmillan. After rejection by several publishers, Joyce's *Portrait* (published in New York the year before) is brought out in England by the Egoist Press at Pound's instigation; in his review of the novel for *The Egoist*, he compares Joyce to Flaubert, Lewis to Dostoevski, and Eliot to Laforgue. Subsidized by Quinn, he assumes the foreign editorship of the New York–based *Little Review*, edited by Margaret Anderson and Jane Heap. Eliot's *Prufrock and Other Observations* published by the Egoist Press, with funds raised by Pound. "Three Cantos" appears in *Poetry* in June. T. E. Hulme is killed at the front. Expanded American edition of *Lustra* published by Knopf. October issue of *The Little Review* suppressed because of Lewis's "Cantleman's Spring Mate." Eliot's *Ezra Pound: His Metric and Poetry* published by Knopf. "Irony, Laforgue, and Some Satire" appears in the November *Poetry*. Has affair with Iseult MacBride, daughter of Yeats's great love, Maud Gonne. Yeats marries Dorothy's friend Georgiana Hyde-Lees, with Pound as best man. Writes art criticism (as B. H. Dias) and music criticism (as William Atheling) for *The New Age*. Raises money from Quinn for Joyce's glaucoma operation; receives first episode of *Ulysses*. Completely revises his 1911 translations of Arnaut Daniel for a bilingual edition to be printed by Clerk's Press in Cleveland, but the typescript disappears in transit and the book is never published.

1918   Writes about French literature in *Poetry* and *The Little Review*: "A Study in French Poets," "The Hard and the Soft in French Poetry," "Unanimism," "De Goncourt," and translations of Laforgue and Voltaire. First installment of *Ulysses* appears in the March *Little Review*, which also includes Pound's complimentary notices on the poetry of Marianne Moore and Mina Loy. *Pavannes and Divisions*, a collection of prose pieces, translations, and the poem "L'Homme Moyen Sensuel," is published by Knopf. Contributes to the special August *Little Review* number in memory of Henry James. The November *Little Review* is "devoted chiefly to Ezra Pound." Meets economic theorist Major Clifford Hugh Douglas through Orage (who considers him "the Einstein of economics"). Douglas's analyses of the ills of laissez-faire capitalism will take on ever greater importance for Pound in the wake of World War I. In particular, he will become an adherent of Douglas's monetarist doctrine of Social Credit, a scheme by which the state (and not private banking interests) would subsidize industries by issuing a "National Dividend" in order to ensure an adequate money supply for both producers and consumers.

1919   Edits February–March number of *The Little Review* devoted to Gourmont, whose "dissociation of ideas" and dismantling of clichés he finds "a symbol of so much that is finest in France." A truncated version of "Homage to Sextus Propertius" appears in the March *Poetry*, and in the following issue the magazine prints a letter from Professor W. G. Hale of the University of Chicago severely criticizing the poem's mistranslations from Latin; Pound severs ties with *Poetry*. Drafts a fourth and fifth canto. After numerous passport problems, spends April through September in France with Dorothy: Paris, Toulouse (where he reads Joyce's "Sirens" episode in manuscript), the Cathar fortress of Montségur (one of his "sacred places"), and a walking tour with Eliot through the Dordogne. *Quia Pauper Amavi* is published by the Egoist Press in October, containing the original "Three Cantos" and the full "Homage to Sextus Propertius." Writes Cantos 5, 6, and 7, but admits "each more incomprehensible than the one preceding it."

1920   Hired (at Quinn's recommendation) as foreign correspondent for the New York–based *Dial*, edited by Scofield Thayer and Gilbert Seldes. In *The New Age*, praises "Major C. H. Douglas's profound attack on usury"—a new (and increasingly anti-Semitic) theme in Pound's work. *Instigations*, containing Fenollosa's "Chinese Written Character," is published by Boni and Liveright in April. Makes futile inquiries about receiving his Ph.D. from Penn on the basis of his published work. Elkin Mathews publishes *Umbra: The Early Poems of Ezra Pound* and the Ovid Press brings out *Hugh Selwyn Mauberley*, his "farewell to London." Meets Joyce for the first time at Sirmione in June; helps settle Joyce in Paris in July, where he meets Sylvia Beach (proprietor of the bookstore Shakespeare and Company) and Adrienne Monnier, another Left Bank bookseller. In London, learns he has been fired from his lucrative job as drama critic for *The Athenaeum*. Publishes the first of his letters from Paris in *The Dial*. Publicly announces his departure from England in December.

1921   In a review of Cocteau's poetry in *The Dial*, states that the "young aesthetic" is "partial to a beauty very rapid in kind" because "in a city the visual impressions succeed each other, overlap, overcross, they are cinematographic." After a stay on the French Riviera, settles in Paris with Dorothy in April; meets Picabia, Cocteau, and Brancusi, and finds Joyce's new Circe episode in *Ulysses* "megalo-scrumptious." Reviews Eliot's *The Sacred Wood* and Douglas's *Credit Power and Democracy*. Quinn visits Pound and

Joyce in Paris. Meets E. E. Cummings through Thayer. Breaks a chair accidentally at the home of Gertrude Stein, who will later describe him as "a village explainer, excellent if you were a village, but if not, not." Plays chess with Marcel Duchamp; takes part in the Dadaist mock trial of conservative writer Maurice Barrès. With the help of Agnes Bedford, begins composing *Le Testament*, an opera based on the works of François Villon, on the piano of wealthy expatriate Natalie Barney. Escorts Bride Scratton around Paris. Has brief affair with Nancy Cunard. Publishes Cantos 5, 6, and 7 in *The Dial*, together with translations of Paul Morand and a review of Marcel Proust. The Autumn Brancusi number of *The Little Review* contains Pound's essay on the sculptor, together with his Dada "Poems of Abel Sanders." Marianne Moore's *Poems* published by Egoist Press at his recommendation. In mid-November, Eliot passes through Paris on his way to a sanatorium in Lausanne, showing Pound the manuscript of a "long poem" originally entitled "He Do the Police in Different Voices" (soon retitled *The Waste Land*). Moves into his new apartment at 70*bis* Notre Dame des Champs, in Montparnasse. Hosts American publisher Horace Liveright, who has just published his *Poems 1918–21: Including Three Portraits and Four Cantos*. Meets Ernest Hemingway and his wife, Hadley, who have recently arrived in Paris.

1922   In early January, Eliot, on his way back to London, gives Pound a revised draft of *The Waste Land*; he returns the typescript three weeks later with extensive comments and suggested changes. Organizes Bel Esprit, a scheme to solicit annual contributions from a consortium of patrons so that Eliot might be freed from his bank job (to Eliot's considerable embarrassment). Canto 8 and a review of *Ulysses* appear in the May *Dial*. From April through June, travels in Italy: Siena, Venice, Rimini (where he becomes fascinated with Sigismundo Malatesta's Tempio), Verona (where he meets Eliot and Bride Scratton), Sirmione (with the Hemingways). Back in Paris, he translates two volumes of short stories by Paul Morand (not published during Pound's lifetime) and completes rough drafts of Cantos 9 to 13. His translation (with a "Postscript" on sexuality) of Remy de Gourmont's *Natural Philosophy of Love* is published by Boni and Liveright. Listens "with rapt attention" to eyewitness account by Lincoln Steffens of the Russian Revolution. *The Waste Land* is published in the November *Dial*. Blocks out three cantos devoted to the life of Sigismundo Malatesta. Meets American violinist Olga Rudge at a reception at the home of Natalie Barney.

1923   "Criticism in General," published in Eliot's new magazine *The Criterion*, distinguishes between three major modes of poetry: melopoeia ("wherein the words are charged, over and above their plain meaning, with some musical property"), phanopoeia ("a casting of images upon the visual imagination"), and logopoeia ("the dance of the intellect among words"). The Pounds spend January through April in Italy, joined by the Hemingways for a tour of the coast between Pisa and Rome; Pound travels on to Florence, Cesana, Milan, and Rimini for further archival research into the life and times of Malatesta. His "autobiography," *Indiscretions*, appears in March, the first volume in a series he edits for William Bird's Paris-based Three Mountains Press; it is followed by Williams's *The Great American Novel*, and, the following year, by Hemingway's *In Our Time*. Thayer fires him from *The Dial*. American composer George Antheil arrives in Paris; Pound asks him to write violin sonatas for Olga Rudge. Three Malatesta cantos published in *The Criterion* in July. Completely revises the opening sections of *The Cantos*. Quinn visits Paris in October, meets Ford Madox Ford (formerly Hueffer) and provides him with the funds to start *The Transatlantic Review*. Bride Scratton's husband sues for divorce on grounds of adultery; Pound is cited as the co-respondent. Works on his Villon opera, with Antheil's assistance.

1924   After an appendicitis attack, recuperates in Rapallo, where British poet Basil Bunting joins him. Moves on to Assisi and Perugia, and begins to consider "American Presidents" as material for future cantos. Upon his return to Paris in June, Pound introduces the visiting Williams to his circle of acquaintances. A Rudge-Antheil concert is held at the Salle Pleyel in July. John Quinn dies. Goes on walking tour in southern France with Olga. Travels with Dorothy to Rapallo in mid-October and they spend December and January in Sicily. Three Mountains Press publishes his *Antheil and the Treatise on Harmony*.

1925   The first issue of *This Quarter*, published in Paris by American expatriate Ernest Walsh, is dedicated to Pound "as meriting the gratitude of this generation," with homages by Hemingway and Joyce. Eliot rededicates *The Waste Land* to Pound, calling him (in a phrase from Dante) "il miglior fabbro"(the better maker). Much delayed, *A Draft of XVI Cantos for the Beginning of a Poem of Some Length* is published by Three Mountains Press in January. By March, he has typed out another seven cantos and moved into a seaside apartment with Dorothy on the Via Marsala in Rapallo, their home for the next two decades. In July, Olga bears his child, Mary Rudge, in Bressanone; the infant is given to the care of a Tyrolean family in the village of Gais. Begins preparing *Personæ*, his collected poems (excluding the cantos), for Boni and Liveright. Eliot visits Pound and Olga in Rapallo around Christmas, while Dorothy is traveling in Egypt.

1926   Dorothy returns from Egypt in March. In June, they travel to Paris for the performance of Pound's opera *Le Testament de Villon*. Energetically promotes Antheil's *Ballet Mécanique* (scored for eight grand pianos, a battery of percussion, and two large airplane propellers), which premieres in Paris on June 19. Pound's experimental opera, scored for medieval instruments, follows ten days later at the Salle Pleyel, featuring the tenor Yves Tinayre, the bass Robert Maitland, with Olga on the violin and Pound on drums. Lukewarmly received, it is nonetheless considered by Virgil Thomson "the best poet's music since Campion." In early September, Dorothy gives birth to a son at the American hospital in Neuilly; Omar Shakespear Pound will be raised by Dorothy's family in England, with his mother returning from Italy for visits each summer. Joyce sends him a portion of *Finnegans Wake*; Pound replies, "Nothing short of divine vision or a new cure for the clapp could possibly be worth all the circumambient peripherization" and their relations cool. *Personæ*, his selection of his early work, dedicated to Mary Moore, is published late in the year.

1927   For the first and only time, Pound exercises full editorial control over his own little magazine, *The Exile*. Initially published in Dijon and then by Pascal Covici in Chicago, four issues will appear over the next two years, featuring such contributions as John Rodker's novel *Adolphe 1920*, selections from Joe Gould's "Oral History," Yeats's "Sailing to Byzantium," and poems by Carl Rakosi, Louis Zukofsky, and William Carlos Williams, as well as Pound's observations on Lenin, Mussolini, arms merchants, censorship, the city of the future, and contemporary German and Russian cinema. In late February, Olga Rudge gives a private performance of Beethoven and Mozart at the residence of Mussolini; noting Mussolini's encouragement of such artists as d'Annunzio, Marinetti, and Pirandello, Pound hopes to interest him in the avant-garde music of Antheil. Submits the manuscript of essay collection "Machine Art" (with accompanying illustrations of factory machinery taken from industrial catalogs) to Covici, but the project founders.

1928   With Marianne Moore now literary editor of *The Dial*, he renews his relations with the magazine, publishing various cantos there, as well as his "traduction" of Cavalcanti's "Donna mi prega," an essay on Williams, and a translation of Boris de Schloezer's book on Stravinsky. Awarded the annual *Dial* prize for 1928, he banks the $2,000 and withdraws the interest to offer aid to Ford, now impoverished, and other friends. Approached by Glenn Hughes, a scholar of Imagism, to write his autobiography for the University of Washington Chapbooks series, he instead submits a translation of the Confucian *Ta Hsio* ("The Great Learning"), based on Pauthier's French version. Spends the late spring in Vienna. *A Draft of the Cantos 17–27* is published by John Rodker in London. Eliot introduces and edits Pound's *Selected Poems* for Faber and Gwyer. Yeats and his wife move to Rapallo in the fall.

1929   Homer and Isabel Pound retire to Rapallo. Publishes "How to Read" in the book section of the *New York Herald-Tribune*, castigating the teaching of literature in American universities and proposing his own counter-canon as a corrective. The London-based Aquila Press agrees to publish his critical bilingual edition of Cavalcanti's complete works, as well as a volume of his collected prose and translations of the Confucian Odes. After printing the first 56 pages of the Cavalcanti edition, the press goes bankrupt. Olga moves to Venice, settling in a small house on the Calle Querini-Dorsoduro.

1930   Bunting returns to Rapallo, where he assists Pound and Olga in the organization of a local concert series. In the spring, Pound travels to Paris to oversee the publication of a deluxe edition of *A Draft of XXX Cantos*, published by Nancy Cunard's Hours Press and of *Imaginary Letters* by Caresse Crosby's Black Sun Press. In Frankfurt, attends the premiere of Antheil's opera *Transatlantic* and meets the German anthropologist Leo Frobenius, whose work he has recently discovered. Begins contributing literary and cultural commentary (in Italian) to the Genovese newspaper *L'Indice* and publishes cantos in the Harvard undergraduate magazine *Hound and Horn*, edited by Lincoln Kirstein and R. P. Blackmur.

1931   Convinces Harriet Monroe to allow the young Brooklyn-based poet Louis Zukofsky, with whom he has been corresponding, to edit an "Objectivist" issue for *Poetry*. *How to Read* is brought out as a pamphlet in London. In his survey of the contemporary literary scene in Samuel Putnam's Paris-based magazine *The New Review*, singles out for praise Lewis's *The Apes of God*, Williams's *White Mule*, Cocteau, Picabia, Brancusi, and the French surrealists. Begins dating his letters according to the Italian Fascist calendar, which numbers the years from Mussolini's October 1922 March on Rome. In October, the BBC broadcasts a performance of his opera *Le Testament*. Its relative critical success encourages him to write another radio opera (never produced) entitled *Cavalcanti: A Sung Dramedy in 3 Acts*.

1932   Publishes, at his own expense, a scholarly edition of Cavalcanti's *Rime* which features photographs of manuscripts, diplomatic transcriptions, and an elaborate philological apparatus, as well as translations, commentaries, and notes. Inquiring of the University of Pennsylvania whether he might submit this edition in fulfillment of his doctoral requirements, he is informed that he must first re-enroll and take additional courses. The Milanese publisher Giovanni Scheiwiller issues Pound's anthology *Profile* ("a collection of poems which have stayed in my memory"; the poets range from Arthur Symons to Basil Bunting). Orage founds *The New English Weekly* as a forum for the discussion of Major Douglas's Social Credit theories; Pound contributes regularly to its pages over the next eight years. Supplies cultural commentary (in Italian) to the literary supplement of the Rapallo newspaper *Il Mare*, lectures at an international conference in Florence with Pirandello, and meets with Marinetti in Rome. Collaborates on a scenario for a film (never produced) on the origins of Fascism, 1918–1922.

1933   Has his only private audience with Mussolini on January 30 in the Palazzo Venezia in Rome to discuss economic and cultural matters. Upon being presented with the deluxe edition of *A Draft of XXX Cantos*, Mussolini says, "Ma questo é divertente" ("How amusing"), a comment taken by Pound to indicate a deep understanding of the work. Organizes the Stagione Musicale in Rapallo; over the next several years, this regular concert series will feature works by Jannequin, Purcell, Bach, Vivaldi, Bartók, and Stravinsky, performed by Olga Rudge, Gerhart Münch, and Tibor Serly. Louis Zukofsky visits Rapallo. Faber publishes Pound's *ABC of Economics* (copies of which he sends to Mussolini and Roosevelt) as well as his *Active Anthology*, which includes Cummings's translation of Louis Aragon's communist poem "Red Front."

1934   Contributes a note on Frobenius and excerpt from his correspondence with Langston Hughes to Nancy Cunard's anthology *Negro*. Writes preface for George Oppen's first book of poetry, *Discrete Series*. Routledge & Sons and Yale University Press publish *ABC of Reading*, "a text-book that can be read for pleasure as well as profit by those no longer in school; by those who have not been to school; or by those who in their college days suffered those things which most of my own generation suffered." *Make It New*, his collected literary criticism, is published by Faber & Faber and, the following year, by Yale University Press. Farrar & Rinehart issues the American edition of *Eleven New Cantos XXXI–XLI* (including the Jefferson and Van Buren cantos, Cavalcanti's "Donna mi prega," as well as attacks on Jewish bankers and arms merchants). Harvard undergraduate James Laughlin spends several months in Rapallo at what he calls the "Ezuversity." Orage dies.

1935   *Alfred Venison's Poems*, a gathering of satirical verse on "Social Credit themes" first published in *The New English Weekly*, is brought out by Stanley Nott in London. Nott also publishes *Jefferson and/or Mussolini*, originally written in February 1933 after Pound's audience with Mussolini. Attends the Salzburg festival, where he is outraged by Toscanini's performance of Beethoven's opera *Fidelio*. Visits the Austrian village of Wörgl to observe implementation of economist Sylvio Gesell's new form of currency, *Schwundgeld*, or "shrinking money," which decreases in value if not spent. Writes articles for the *British-Italian Bulletin* supporting the Italian invasion of Ethiopia.

1936   "Canto—'With Usura'" (Canto 45) published in the London journal *Prosperity*. Canto 46 (on the founding of the Bank of England in 1694) appears in the first number of *New Directions in Prose and Poetry*, the annual magazine of James Laughlin's newly founded New Directions publishing house. With Olga Rudge and Gerhart Münch, makes photographs of Vivaldi manuscripts in various libraries in Italy and Germany.

1937   Faber & Faber publishes *Polite Essays*, which includes his essay (in French) on Joyce's *Ulysses* and Flaubert's *Bouvard et Pécuchet* as well as various pieces from Eliot's *Criterion*. Through the help of Ford Madox Ford, is offered a visiting professorship at Olivet College in Michigan, but declines the offer because he is too busy "challenging universal ignorance in Italy." Publication of the British and American editions of *The Fifth Decad of Cantos, XLII–LI*. In a contribution to Nancy Cunard's *Authors Take Sides on the Spanish War*, Pound declares himself "neutral," adding "Spain is an emotional luxury to a gang of sap-headed dilettantes."

1938   Delayed because its publishers decided that a number of its passages were libelous and had to be deleted, *Guide to Kulchur* (dedicated to Louis Zukofsky and Basil Bunting, "strugglers in the desert") is brought out by Faber & Faber in July. Elected member of the National Institute of Arts and Letters, Pound encourages it to publish the writings of Thomas Jefferson, John Adams, and Martin Van Buren. A center for Vivaldi Studies is founded at the Accademia Musicale Chigiana in Siena, where Olga Rudge holds the post of administrative secretary. Travels to London for the funeral of Olivia Shakespear; has last meeting with Yeats and first encounter with son Omar.

1939   Yeats dies. Eliot's *Criterion* ceases publication. After a
            28-year absence from the U.S., Pound sails for New York
            in April, where he is received by journalists as a news-
            worthy figure. Stays at E. E. Cummings's Greenwich Vil-
            lage apartment, then travels to Washington, D.C., hoping
            "to move the nation's policies towards paths to peace."
            Unsuccessfully seeks a meeting with President Roosevelt;
            contacts various isolationist politicians with whom he has
            been corresponding—among them, Rep. George Tink-
            ham (Mass.), Sen. William Borah (Idaho), and Sen. John
            Bankhead (Ala.)—and attends a session of Congress. Re-
            turns to New York with William Carlos Williams, who re-
            ports to James Laughlin that "the man is sunk, unless he
            can shake the fog of fascism out of his brain." Zukofsky
            warns him about his enthusiasm for the radio commenta-
            tor Father Coughlin ("Whatever you don't know, Ezra,
            you ought to know *voices*"). While in New York, meets
            with Ford Madox Ford (who dies in June), H. L.
            Mencken, Marianne Moore, and poet and Sappho trans-
            lator Mary Barnard. In Cambridge, records a series of
            cantos (accompanying himself on kettledrums) for the
            Harvard Vocarium; at Yale, meets with James Angleton,
            editor of the undergraduate magazine *Furioso* (and future
            chief of counterintelligence at the CIA). In June, receives
            an honorary degree in letters from his alma mater, Hamil-
            ton College; during the ceremony, Pound gets into a
            heated dispute with fellow honoree, the political jour-
            nalist H. V. Kaltenborn, whose speech is critical of Mus-
            solini's dictatorship. Upon his return to Italy in late June,
            resumes publication of articles in the Fascist-dominated
            Meridiano di Roma and has "a lot of jaw" about philoso-
            phy with George Santayana in Venice.

1940   *Cantos LII–LXX* (the Chinese history and the John Adams
            cantos) published by Faber; the original edition has a num-
            ber of blacked-out lines in Canto 52 which include anti-Se-
            mitic attacks on the Rothschild family. The New Directions
            edition is accompanied by a pamphlet with the essays
            "Notes on the Versification of the Cantos" by Delmore
            Schwartz and "Notes on the Cantos" by James Laughlin.
            Italy declares war on France and Great Britain on June 10.
            In October, makes tentative arrangements to return to
            U.S., but plans fall through. Writes a number of scripts for
            Radio Rome, which are read in English by others.

1941   James Joyce dies. Through his contacts with officials in the Ministry of Popular Culture (Minculpop), is finally granted direct access to Radio Rome, although some in the Italian government doubt his political efficacy or, indeed, his sanity. Makes his initial short-wave broadcast for "The American Hour" on January 21 to warn against U.S. involvement in the war—the first of some 120 extremely vituperative and often incoherent speeches that will be broadcast on a bi-weekly basis until the fall of the Fascist government in July 1943. He generally writes the ten- to fifteen-minute speeches (for which he receives approximately $18 each) at his home in Rapallo, then travels to the studios of the EIAR (Ente Italiana Audizione Radio) in Rome to record them on discs in batches of ten to twenty speeches for subsequent broadcast. Imitating elements of the American radio oratory of Father Coughlin and Huey Long, Pound adopts an exaggerated cracker-barrel idiom laced with anti-Semitic slurs. Over the course of the year, continues to attempt to clarify his passport situation and that of his daughter Mary with the U.S. embassy in Rome. In October, the Federal Communications Commission begins monitoring his broadcasts. After the Japanese attack on Pearl Harbor on December 7, he stops broadcasting for a month and a half. Italy and Germany declare war on the U.S. on December 11, and the U.S. immediately responds with its own declarations.

1942   Resumes his broadcasts on January 29, insisting that every broadcast henceforth be introduced by the statement that "Dr. Ezra Pound . . . will not be asked to say anything whatsoever that goes against his conscience, or anything incompatible with his duties as a citizen of the United States of America." The broadcasts continue to be characterized by anti-Semitic invective, personal attacks on Allied leaders including Roosevelt and Churchill, and condemnations of the Allied war effort, interspersed with commentary on Confucius, John Adams, and other topics of interest to Pound. A Princeton University–sponsored study of Axis radio propaganda describes Pound as "a fanatical admirer of Mussolini and an all-out champion of Fascism, totalitarianism, and anti-Semitism," while adding that their incoherence made it "difficult to apply standards of judgment to his broadcasts, which, incidentally, were the despair of the Princeton transcribers." The April number of *Poetry* magazine runs an editorial that states: "The time has come to put a formal end to the countenancing of Ezra Pound." Homer Pound dies in Rapallo. Publishes *Carta da Visita*, a summation (in Italian) of his economic and political philosophy, and an Italian translation of the *Ta Hsio*; they are sent to Mussolini as "two testimonies to fascist faith."

1943 Italian army in Tunisia surrenders May 13. Allies invade Sicily on July 10 and bomb Rome on July 19. Mussolini is deposed by Field Marshal Pietro Badoglio on July 25 and secret peace negotiations with the Allies are opened. On July 26, the U.S. Department of Justice officially indicts Pound for treason (along with seven other American citizens, all journalists or broadcasters in Germany). In an August letter to Attorney General Francis Biddle, Pound defends his broadcasts as an exercise of his constitutionally guaranteed right to free speech. Allies begin landing in southern Italy on September 3. Italy surrenders on September 8, but Germans occupy much of the country, resulting in prolonged fighting. Returns to Rome in September, but given the chaotic political situation, decides to make his way (some of it on foot) to his daughter's home in the South Tyrol. Travels to Verona and Milan, probably stopping en route at Salò on Lake Garda, headquarters of Mussolini's newly formed puppet government, the Italian Social Republic (or Republic of Salò). Badoglio government declares war on Germany on October 13. During the fall, contacts officials of the Fascist Ministry of Popular Culture in Milan. Receives permission to speak on the air in early December, but thereafter sends in radio scripts and commentary to be read by others.

1944 Under the aegis of the Ministry of Popular Culture, six collections of his Italian writings are issued; they include two volumes of Confucian translations, which he considers essential to the renewal of Italian Fascism and of civilization in general. With the Germans strengthening the coastal defenses at Rapallo, Pound and his wife are forced to leave their seaside apartment on the Via Marsala in May and resettle in Olga Rudge's house in the hills above the town of Sant'Ambrogio. For the next year, the three will live together awkwardly. After reading of damage inflicted on the Tempio Malestiano in Rimini by Allied bombing, composes, in Italian, Cantos 72 and 73, strongly supportive of Italian war effort. (Published in a small Fascist newspaper the following January and February, these texts will be omitted from collected editions of *The Cantos* until 1985.)

1945   Continues to draft cantos in Italian, recording a number of visionary experiences in the hills above Rapallo that will be incorporated into the poetry composed that summer in Pisa. Mussolini and his mistress, Clara Petacci, are shot by partisans near Lake Como on April 28 and strung up by their heels in the Piazza Loreto in Milan. German forces in Italy surrender May 2. On May 3, Pound is arrested at his home in Sant'Ambrogio by local partisans and briefly detained; released, he turns himself over to the American Counter Intelligence Center in Genoa, where he remains for the next three weeks, undergoing interrogation by an FBI agent and pursuing his Confucian translations. On May 24, Pound is transferred to a U.S. army prison camp in Pisa, where he is placed in a maximum-security roofed cage specially reinforced with steel used in building temporary airstrips. After three weeks in solitary confinement, exposed to the elements, he suffers a mental breakdown and is transferred to an officer's tent in the medical compound area. Begins composing what will become known as *The Pisan Cantos* (Cantos 74–84) in late June or early July and continues working on them into November. Notified of Pound's whereabouts by the American military authorities, Dorothy visits him on October 3; Olga and daughter Mary visit two weeks later. The commander of the camp allows him to send out batches of his manuscript to the three in Rapallo for retyping. After the FBI locates five technicians (none who speak English) from Radio Rome who are prepared to testify against Pound in court, he is flown back to Washington, D.C., on November 17, put in jail, and charged with treason (for which the Constitution requires the prosecution to provide two witnesses to each "overt" act). At his preliminary arraignment, he asks to act as his own counsel, but is informed by Judge Bolitha Laws that the charge against him is too serious for him to defend himself. At the suggestion of James Laughlin, Julien Cornell, a lawyer with experience in representing conscientious objectors and pacifists, agrees to take on the case.

Cornell advises Pound to stand mute at his November 27 arraignment, enters a plea of not guilty on his behalf, and asks for bail, arguing that Pound is mentally unfit to stand trial. Judge Laws orders a psychiatric examination, and on December 21, Dr. Winfred Overholser, superintendent of St. Elizabeths Hospital, a federal mental hospital in Washington, and three other doctors submit a report describing Pound as "suffering from a paranoid state" and "mentally unfit for trial." He is transferred to St Elizabeths and placed in Howard Hall, the prison building. Overholser rejects finding by six state psychiatrists that Pound is not psychotic. *The Saturday Review of Literature* and *New Masses* feature articles extremely hostile to Pound.

1946   First visits from poet Charles Olson in January ("Olson saved my life," he writes). Makes final revisions of *The Pisan Cantos.* After hearing testimony on February 13 from Overholser and three other doctors, the jury returns the verdict that Pound is of "unsound mind," and he is committed to St. Elizabeths until he is found fit to stand trial. Dorothy moves to Washington in July; tending to his far-flung correspondence and daily personal needs, she assumes his legal guardianship as the "Committee for Ezra Pound." Over the next few years, he receives a steady stream of visitors at St. Elizabeths, ranging from old friends H. L. Mencken, Marianne Moore, and T. S. Eliot to younger poets Robert Lowell, Allen Tate, Randall Jarrell, Elizabeth Bishop, and Robert Duncan, as well as scholars Edith Hamilton, Kenneth Clark, Marshall McLuhan, and Hugh Kenner. Random House announces it will not include any of Pound's verse in its *Anthology of Famous English and American Poetry*, but bowing to the protests of Conrad Aiken and W. H. Auden, its president, Bennett Cerf, reverses the decision.

1947   After an unsuccessful bail hearing on January 31, Pound is transferred from Howard Hall to Cedar Ward and then to Chestnut Ward, where he is eventually given a private room and permission to receive visitors on the lawn. Confucian translations *The Unwobbling Pivot* and *The Great Digest* published in James Laughlin's *Pharos* magazine. Writes to a Japanese friend, poet Katue Kitasono, about an eventual bilingual edition of the Confucian Odes.

1948   Cornell files a petition for habeas corpus on February 11. After it is rejected by the District Court, Cornell appeals the decision, but on March 28 Dorothy asks him to withdrew the appeal. In Italy, Olga Rudge prints a sanitized selection of Pound's broadcasts under the title *If This Be Treason* and organizes a petition in his favor which she sends to the State Department. After many delays by Laughlin, New Directions issues *The Pisan Cantos* in July. In November, the Fellows in American Literature of the Library of Congress (which includes 1948 Nobel Prize winner T. S. Eliot, Conrad Aiken, W. H. Auden, Louise Bogan, Robert Lowell, Katherine Anne Porter, Karl Shapiro, Allen Tate, and Robert Penn Warren) vote to award the first annual $10,000 Bollingen Prize to *The Pisan Cantos* (Williams's *Paterson* is the other candidate).

1949   Award of the Bollingen Prize to Pound is publicly announced in late February, with this statement: "Pound's works represents the highest achievement of American poetry in the year for which the award is made. . . . The Fellows are aware that objections may be made. . . . To permit other considerations than that of poetic achievement to sway the decision would destroy the significance of the award and would in principle deny the validity of that objective perception on which any civilized society must rest." Considerable public outcry follows. *The New York Times* headline reads "Pound, In Mental Clinic, Wins Prize for Poetry Penned in Treason Cell" and Congress prevents the Library from giving any further awards or prizes. Pound prepares a statement for the press ("No comment from the Bug House") but decides not to release it. Aided by Huntington Cairns and Veronica Sun, a Chinese student at the Catholic University of Washington, he undertakes a full-scale translation of the Confucian Odes, noting their phonetic features in a number of "Sound Notebooks."

1950   *The Letters of Ezra Pound 1907–1941*, edited by D. D. Paige, is published by Harcourt, Brace. Young disciples begin gathering around "Grampaw" at St. Elizabeths; right-wing extremists John Kasper and David Horton are among the first of these acolytes and over the next several years, at Pound's instigation, they publish the "Square $" series of booklets, which include Fenollosa on the Chinese written character, the *Analects* of Confucius, and selections from the works of Alexander del Mar, Thomas Benton, and Louis Agassiz.

1951   Translates Sophocles's *Elektra* in collaboration with the Greek scholar Rudd Fleming. New Directions issues a bilingual edition of *The Great Digest & Unwobbling Pivot*, with rubbings of the Stone Classics texts provided by Willis Hawley and an introduction by Achilles Fang. Publication of Hugh Kenner's *The Poetry of Ezra Pound*.

1952   Olga Rudge visits Washington. Also visiting Pound at St. Elizabeths: Eustace Mullins (self-proclaimed Director of the Aryan League of America), Dallam Simpson, Michael Reck, David Gordon, William McNaughton, and Sheri Martinelli.

1953   Visited by his daughter Mary, now married with two children and living in the Schloss Brunnenburg above Merano, Italy. Kenner edits *The Translations of Ezra Pound*. While rereading his 1916 translations of Japanese Noh plays, Pound is inspired to attempt a Noh version of Sophocles's *Women of Trachis*, which is published in *The Hudson Review* and broadcast the following year on the BBC. Discusses the new "Paradiso" section of the cantos with Guy Davenport and troubadour poetry with Paul Blackburn.

1954   T. S. Eliot edits *The Literary Essays of Ezra Pound*. After considerable delay, Harvard University Press publishes *The Classic Anthology Defined by Confucius*, with an introduction by Achilles Fang; the second projected volume containing the Chinese text never appears. Hemingway, on being awarded the Nobel Prize, observes "this would be a good year to release poets."

1955   Publication of *Section: Rock-Drill: 85–95 de los cantares*. In Italy, a petition to free Pound signed by Salvatore Quasimodo, Eugenio Montale, and Alberto Moravia is submitted to U.S. Ambassador Clare Booth Luce. After visiting St. Elizabeths and speaking with Dr. Overholser, Archibald MacLeish proposes to enlist the support of T. S. Eliot, Robert Frost, and Ernest Hemingway in a personal appeal to the attorney general for Pound's release.

1956   *Life* magazine, noting that the wartime broadcaster "Tokyo Rose" has been freed from jail, calls for a reconsideration of Pound's case, describing his room at St. Elizabeths "a closet which contains a national skeleton." MacLeish continues his negotiations with highly placed government officials, but is hampered by Overholser's reluctance to release his patient and by the negative publicity generated by the segregationist and anti-Semitic activities of Pound disciple John Kasper, who, associated with the Ku Klux Klan and neo-Nazi George Lincoln Rockwell, is eventually jailed for the bombing of a desegregated school in Nashville.

1957   Harry Meacham and Marcella Spann join the St. Elizabeths circle around Pound. Pound's unsigned contributions to Noel Stock's Australian magazine *Edge* include translations of Rimbaud and Catullus. MacLeish and Frost discuss the case with Deputy Attorney General William P. Rogers. Wyndham Lewis dies.

1958   At the request of Sen. Richard Neuberger (Oregon) and Rep. Usher Burdick (North Dakota), a report on "The Medical, Legal, Literary and Political Status" of Pound is published in the *Congressional Record*. Robert Frost lobbies members of the Eisenhower administration on Pound's behalf. Attorney Thurman Arnold moves on April 18 to have treason indictment dismissed on the grounds that Pound will never be fit for trial. After the government supports the motion, Judge Laws dismisses the indictment. Released from St. Elizabeths, Pound visits his childhood home in Wyncote, Pennsylvania, and drops in on ailing William Carlos Williams in Rutherford, New Jersey. Sails for Italy on June 30 with Dorothy and young secretary Marcella Spann. Is photographed on arrival in Naples giving a Fascist salute and tells reporters, "All America is an insane asylum." The three settle at Schloss Brunnenburg in the South Tyrol, home of Pound's daughter Mary and her husband, the Egyptologist Boris de Rachewiltz. Pound's initial euphoria over his release is followed by exhaustion and depression.

1959   Suffering from the altitude and family tensions at Brunnenburg, moves to Rapallo with Dorothy and Marcella Spann in March. The BBC films him at Brunnenburg in April. Purportedly proposes marriage to Spann on Lake Garda in May; by the end of the summer, she is no longer on the scene. Disconsolate, writes MacLeish in September: "Been no use to myself or anyone. . . . One thing to have Europe fall on one's head. Another to be set in the ruins of same." *Thrones: 96–109 de los cantares*, the last "paradiso" section of *The Cantos* written at St. Elizabeths, issued in December. Back at Brunnenburg, composes some of the cantos later published as *Drafts and Fragments*.

1960   Publishes "Conversations in Courtship," based on Boris de Rachewiltz's Italian rendition of an ancient Egyptian text. Moves to Rome as the guest of old friend Ugo Dadone. In March, Donald Hall interviews him for the *Paris Review*: "It is difficult to write a paradiso," Pound tells him, "when all the superficial indications are that you ought to write an apocalypse." Joins Dorothy in Rapallo in mid-May; the two spend the summer in Brunnenburg, where visitors include his Italian publisher Giovanni Scheiwiller, his German translator Eva Hesse, his future biographer Noel Stock, and his future bibliographer Donald Gallup. His mental and physical health failing, he is briefly hospitalized in the Martinsbrunn Clinic near Merano in the fall.

1961   His condition is marked by silence, depression, irascibility, refusals to eat, suicide threats. Condition improves when he travels in the spring to Rome, where he is photographed at the head of a neo-Fascist May Day parade, before again falling into despondency. At Olga Rudge's request, is transferred from a rest home in Rome back to the Martinsbrunn Clinic, where it is discovered he is suffering from a serious prostate condition. Hemingway commits suicide. H.D. dies.

1962   In early spring, moves back into his former Sant'Ambrogio home above Rapallo with Olga Rudge. Hospitalized during the summer for uraemic poisoning. After his condition improves, resettles on the Calle Querini in Venice with Olga; for the next ten years, the two will divide their time between Sant'Ambrogio and Venice, while Dorothy eventually moves to London to be near Omar. Awarded the Harriet Monroe Memorial Prize by *Poetry* magazine, he replies that he is content to be remembered as a "minor satirist who contributed something to a refinement of language." E. E. Cummings dies.

1963   Receives a $5,000 fellowship from the Academy of American Poets. Informs an Italian journalist, "I have lost the

ability to reach the core of my thought with words."
William Carlos Williams dies.

1964   Olga takes him to Switzerland for treatment of depression. Publication of *Confucius to Cummings*, the anthology of world poetry he had edited with Marcella Spann.

1965   New Directions issues *A Lume Spento and Other Early Poems*. Pound attends memorial service for T. S. Eliot in Westminster Abbey. Later writes of Eliot: "His was the true Dantescan voice—not honoured enough, and deserving more than I ever gave him." While in London, chooses the texts for Faber & Faber's *Selected Cantos*. Goes to Dublin to visit Yeats's widow, George. As guest of Gian-Carlo Menotti, reads from the poems of Robert Lowell and Marianne Moore at the Spoleto Festival. In honor of his 80th birthday, the British poetry magazine *Agenda* publishes a special number. Travels to Paris for the publication of an issue of *Cahier l'Herne* devoted to his work. Visits Natalie Barney on the rue Jacob and attends a performance of Beckett's *Endgame*, where he remarks, "C'est moi dans la poubelle" ("That's me in the trash can."). First visit to Greece.

1966   Hospitalized for depression in the spring; doctors note "ideas of self-accusation and hypochondriacal delusions"; refers in conversation to his *Cantos* as a "botch," and similarly asks James Laughlin and Peter du Sautoy of Faber & Faber, "Why don't you *abolish* the Cantos?"

1967   Allen Ginsberg visits Sant'Ambrogio and Venice; Pound reportedly tells him: "The worst mistake I made was that stupid, suburban prejudice of anti-Semitism." Publication of the *Selected Cantos* and of the *Pound/Joyce* correspondence. Ed Sanders's Fuck You Press brings out a pirated edition of *Cantos 110–116* "at a secret location on the lower east side"; in response, James Laughlin decides to issue late cantos even though unedited by Pound.

1968   Television interview with Italian poet and film director Pier Paolo Pasolini; Pound reads his responses from cue cards prepared by Olga Rudge.

1969   Publication of *Drafts and Fragments of Cantos CX–CXVII*. Visits the U.S. in June for an exhibit of Eliot's *Waste Land* manuscript at the New York Public Library.

Travels to Hamilton College, where Laughlin is awarded an honorary degree.

1970   Noel Stock publishes the first full-scale biography of Pound. A special issue of *Agenda* marks his 85th birthday.

1971   His daughter Mary's memoir, *Discretions*, is published.

1972   *Paideuma*, a quarterly devoted to Ezra Pound scholarship, is founded; publication of Hugh Kenner's *The Pound Era*. The American Academy of Arts and Sciences nominates Pound for its annual Emerson-Thoreau Medal, but the recommendation is overturned by its executive council. Dies on November 1 in Venice and is buried in the San Michele cemetery.

Note on the Texts

This volume contains poems and translations from 26 books published by Ezra Pound, as well as from the hand-bound "Hilda's Book," the "San Trovaso" notebook, the translations of the Provençal poet Arnaut Daniel meant for an edition that was never published, and the version of Sophocles' *Elektra* prepared with Rudd Fleming. It also includes a selection of 76 poems not collected by Pound, 19 of which were not published during his lifetime.

In general, this volume prints the texts of the poems and translations as they first appeared in one of Pound's books. There is often substantial overlap between volumes because Pound included previously collected poems (sometimes in revised form) in many of his books; the present volume does not include a revised version of a poem unless it is revised enough to be regarded as a new work. For example, both "Vana" (40.1–20) and its enlarged version, "Praise of Ysolt" (83.1–84.28), are included here. Pound translated poems by Arnaut Daniel and Guido Cavalcanti at various points in his career, and this volume contains more than one translation of a poem only if the translations differ considerably from one another. Most of Pound's revisions are not of this order, however; some examples of the more usual kinds of revision are listed in the notes.

Because of the overlap among collections, in most instances this volume does not print the complete contents of Pound's books as they were first published. In all but two cases (*The Spirit of Romance* and *Pavannes and Divagations*) in which a selection has been made, the poems omitted are limited to those already collected by Pound and thus included elsewhere in the present volume. In *The Sonnets and Ballate of Guido Cavalcanti, Guido Cavalcanti Rime,* and *The Great Digest & Unwobbling Pivot*, texts in the original languages accompanied Pound's translations; with the exception of "The Canzone" from *Guido Cavalcanti Rime* (which is included here because Pound's arrangement of the original Italian text is a creative act in its own right), these foreign-language texts do not appear here. (Pound's poem "Dans un Omnibus de Londres" at 309.24–310.24 was written directly in French.) Supplementary material not written by Pound in *Confucius: The Great Digest & Unwobbling Pivot, The Classic Anthology Defined by Confucius*, and *Sophokles: Women of Trachis* is omitted here as well; however, Ernest Fenollosa's essay on the Noh theater of Japan in *'Noh' or*

Accomplishment appears on pp. 388–405 because it was edited by
Pound and contains his glosses on Fenollosa's observations. T. E.
Hulme's poems, which appear as an appendix to *Ripostes* (1912), *Um-
bra* (1920), and the enlarged version of *Personæ* (1949), are printed at
note 229.2.

In a few instances, the first book publication of Pound's poems
and translations is best regarded as a work in progress, and the
present volume prints a later version of these works. For example,
Pound's translations of Japanese Noh theater were first collected in
Certain Noble Plays of Japan in 1916, a book that was expanded into
'Noh' or Accomplishment, published the following year. Because *Cer-
tain Noble Plays of Japan* is an incomplete version of *'Noh' or Ac-
complishment*, the later work is printed here. In the case of *Lustra*,
four versions of the book were published in 1916 and 1917; in three
of these versions, poems were removed from the contents because
the publishers were concerned about legal action; the present vol-
ume prints the only complete edition of *Lustra* (see below).

Hilda's Book (1907). "Hilda's Book" is a hand-bound book of
poems written between 1905 and 1907. The book is now in the
Houghton Library at Harvard. An edition prepared by Michael King
was published in *End to Torment: A Memoir of Ezra Pound by H.D.*
(New York: New Directions, 1979). For several poems, King has in-
corporated Pound's holograph revisions of the typed poems in the
book; because damage to the book has obscured part of "I strove a
little book to make for her," the King edition has established the text
of this poem with the aid of a manuscript in the Pound Archive at
the Beinecke Library, Yale University. The present volume prints the
text of "Hilda's Book" in *End to Torment*.

A Lume Spento (1908). At Pound's expense, *A Lume Spento* was
published in an edition of 150 copies by the Venetian printer A.
Antonini in July 1908. The present volume prints the texts of the
poems from *A Lume Spento* as they appear in *Collected Early Poems*,
edited by Michael King (New York: New Directions, 1976), which
corrects errors by reference to manuscripts and proof sheets at the
Beinecke Library and the Humanities Research Center of the Uni-
versity of Texas. Excluded from this section are four poems that ap-
pear in "Hilda's Book": "La Donzealla Beata," "Li Bel Chasteus,"
"Comraderie" (entitled "Era Venuta" in "Hilda's Book"), and "The
Tree."

The San Trovaso Notebook (1908). Shortly after arranging for
the publication of *A Lume Spento*, Pound began writing poems into
a notebook he called "San Trovaso." Two of these poems were pub-
lished in the *Evening Standard and St. James's Gazette*: "Histrion"

(October 26, 1908) and "Nel Biancheggiar" (under the title "For Katherine Ruth Heyman," December 8, 1908). In the fall of 1908, he decided to publish at his own expense 15 of these poems in a volume entitled *A Quinzaine for This Yule* (see below); several more were not published until Pound's daughter Mary de Rachewiltz's selection of poems from the notebook appeared in *A Lume Spento and Other Early Poems* (1965), and the rest were included in the posthumous *Collected Early Poems*. In the present volume, the texts in the "San Trovaso Notebook" section are taken from the 1976 New Directions edition of *Collected Early Poems*.

A Quinzaine for This Yule (1908). In early December 1908, 100 copies of *A Quinzaine for This Yule* were printed by Pollock and Co. in London. Later that month, Elkin Mathews printed an additional 100 copies, correcting printer's errors in the Pollock and Co. edition. The present volume prints the text of *A Quinzaine for This Yule* from *Collected Early Poems*, which includes sections III and IV of "To La Contessa Bianzafior." Possibly because of space limitations, these sections were not included in the copies printed by Pollock and Co. and by Elkin Mathews.

Personae (1909). Pound's next collection, *Personae*, consisting of poems from *A Lume Spento* along with 17 new poems, was published by Elkin Mathews on April 16, 1909. The present volume prints the texts from *Personae* as they appear in *Collected Early Poems*. Omitted from this section are 16 poems from "Hilda's Book" and *A Lume Spento*: "Grace Before Song," "La Fraisne," "Cino," "Na Audiart," "Villonaud for This Yule," "A Villonaud: Ballad of the Gibbet," "Mesmerism," "Fifine Answers," "In Tempore Senectutis," "Famam Librosque Cano," "Scriptor Ignotus," "Comraderie" ("Era Venuta"), "Masks," "Ballad for Gloom," "For E. McC.," "Motif" (entitled "Search" in *Personae*).

Exultations (1909). *Exultations* was published by Elkin Mathews on October 25, 1909. The book contained 27 poems, including five from *A Lume Spento* ("Plotinus"; "On His Own Face in a Glass"; "The Cry of the Eyes," now called "The Eyes"; "To the Dawn: Defiance," now called "Defiance"; "Song") and six from *A Quinzaine for This Yule* ("Night Litany"; "Sandalaphon"; "Greek Epigram"; "Christophori Columbi Tumulus"; "Histrion"; "Nel Biancheggiar"). Four of the poems had appeared in the *English Review* in 1909: "Sestina: Altaforte" (June), "Ballad of the Goodly Fere" (October), "Nils Lykke" (October), and "Portrait" (October, under the title "Un Retrato"). In the present volume, the texts of the poems from *Exultations* are taken from *Collected Early Poems*. Poems published in *A Lume Spento* and *A Quinzaine for This Yule* are not included in this section.

The Spirit of Romance (1910). Pound's collection of essays, *The Spirit of Romance*, contains more than fifty translations of works or fragments of works in Latin, Provençal, Italian, Spanish, and Portuguese. The translations in this section are drawn from those that Pound collected in the enlarged edition of *Translations* (New York: New Directions, 1964) and, for "Sequaire," in *Confucius to Cummings*, an anthology Pound edited with Marcella Spann (New York: New Directions, 1964). These translations were not revised for these volumes, though they sometimes include titles and accompanying source information that do not appear in the 1910 edition of *The Spirit of Romance*. The present volume prints the texts of "Inscriptio Fontis," "A War Song," "The Lark," "'Vedut' Ho la Lucente Stella Diana,'" and "Cantico del Sole" from the 1964 New Directions edition of *Translations*; "Sequaire" is taken from the 1964 New Directions edition of *Confucius to Cummings*.

Canzoni (1911). *Canzoni* began to take shape not long after Pound finished working on *The Spirit of Romance* and his translations of Guido Cavalcanti. Most of the poems were in the book composed in 1910 and 1911. After receiving proofs for *Canzoni* from Elkin Mathews in May 1911, Pound decided to withdraw three poems: "Leviora," "To Hulme (T. E.) and Fitzgerald (A Certain)," and "Redondillas, or Something of That Sort." *Canzoni* was published by Elkin Mathews in London in July 1911. Six of the poems had been published in periodicals: "Canzon: The Yearly Slain," "Canzon: The Spear," "Canzon" (published under the heading "Three Poems" in *English Review*, January 1910), "Canzon: Of Incense" (*English Review*, April 1910), "A Prologue" (entitled "Christmas Prologue," *Sunday School Times*, December 3, 1910), and "The Fault of It" (*Forum*, July 1911). In addition, 14 poems were included in *Provença* (Boston: Small, Maynard and Co., 1910), the first American edition of Pound's poetry, which was made up of selections from his four English collections as well as a section entitled "Canzoniere: Studies in Form." The following poems from *Canzoni* were published in this section: "Octave," "Sonnet in Tenzone," "Sonnet," "Canzon: The Yearly Slain," "Canzon: The Spear," "Canzon," "Canzon: Of Incense," "Canzone: Of Angels," "Sonnet: Chi È Questa?" "Ballata, Fragment" (entitled "Of Grace"), "Canzon," "To Our Lady of Vicarious Atonement," and "To Guido Cavalcanti" (as "Epilogue: To Guido Cavalcanti'). In the present volume, the texts of the poems from *Canzoni*, including those withdrawn from the 1911 Elkin Mathews edition, are taken from *Collected Early Poems*. Two poems are omitted from this section: "The Tree" appears in "Hilda's Book" and "Threnos" is included with the poems from *A Lume Spento*.

The Sonnets and Ballate of Guido Cavalcanti (1912). In 1929 Pound recalled that he had translated most of the poems in *The Sonnets and Ballate of Guido Cavalcanti* in the summer and autumn of 1910. Although the book's introduction is dated November 15, 1910, Pound claimed to have completed it in the spring of 1911. On April 27, 1912, the book was published in Boston by Small, Maynard and Company; an English edition was brought out by Stephen Swift and Company in May 1912. Although nearly identical, these editions vary in several passages. The texts of the translations in the present volume are taken from *Pound's Cavalcanti*, edited by David Anderson (Princeton: Princeton University Press, 1983). In preparing his edition, Anderson consulted the Small, Maynard and Stephen Swift editions as well as manuscripts and copies of both 1912 editions with corrections in Pound's hand. The Italian texts of Cavalcanti's poems, which accompanied the translations *en face* in the 1912 editions, are not included here.

Ripostes (1912). Pound submitted a typescript of *Ripostes* to the London publisher Stephen Swift and Co. in February 1912, and the book was published in October of that year. Using sheets from the Swift and Co. edition, the Boston firm of Small, Maynard and Co. published *Ripostes* in America in July 1913. Of its 25 poems, only "Salve Pontifex" (a version of "Salve O Pontifex" from *A Lume Spento*) had appeared in one of Pound's previous collections. Eight had been published in periodicals: "Silet" (*Smart Set*, May 1912), "Apparuit" (*English Review*, June 1912), "The Seafarer" (*New Age*, November 30, 1911), "Echoes" (*North American Review*, January 1912), "An Immorality" (*Poetry Review*, February 1912), "Dieu! Qu'Il La Fait" (*Poetry Review*, February 1912), "Δώρια" (*Poetry Review*, February 1912), "The Return" (*English Review*, June 1912). With the exception of "Salve Ponitfex," which is included (as "Salve O Pontifex") in *A Lume Spento*, the present volume prints the texts of the poems from *Ripostes* as they appear in *Collected Early Poems*.

Cathay (1915). In 1913 Pound was introduced to Mary Fenollosa, the widow of Ernest Fenollosa, a professor who had taught political economy and philosophy at Tokyo University before becoming Curator of Oriental Art at the Boston Museum. With the aid of Japanese assistants, Fenollosa had worked on translations from Chinese and Japanese literature, some of which were published posthumously in *Epochs of Chinese and Japanese Art* (1912). After Mary Fenollosa gave him her husband's notebooks and other manuscripts in the fall of 1913, Pound began to work on a series of translations based on Fenollosa's research. Pound's versions of Noh plays were published in *Certain Noble Plays of Japan* (1916) and then in an expanded edition as *'Noh' or Accomplishment* (1917); his adaptations of Chinese poetry were collected, with his Anglo-Saxon translation "The Sea-farer," in *Cathay*, published by Elkin Mathews in London on April 6, 1915. "Exile's Letter" had appeared in *Poetry* in March 1915. In the present volume, with the exception of "The Seafarer" (which appears with the poems from *Riposte*), the poems published in *Cathay* printed here are taken from the 1915 Elkin Mathews edition.

Lustra (1916–17). Pound gathered poems composed between 1913 and 1916 as well as numerous poems from his earlier books and submitted the manuscript of *Lustra* to Elkin Mathews in the spring of 1916. After the book was set, the printers and publishers asked that several poems be removed because they feared legal action, presumably on grounds of indecency. Elkin Mathews released a privately printed edition of 200 copies of *Lustra* in September 1916, with four poems from the original typescript omitted ("The Temperaments," "Ancient Music," "The Lake Isle," and "Pagani's, November 8"). The version published the following month by Mathews omitted not only these poems but nine others as well: "Salutation the Second," "Commission," "The New Cake of Soap," "Meditatio," "Phyllidula," "The Patterns," "The Seeing Eye," and "Ἱμέρρω." The title of the poem "Coitus" was changed to "Pervigilium."

When *Lustra* was published in the United States in October 1917 by Alfred A. Knopf, all but one of the poems suppressed in England, "The Temperaments," were restored. In addition, "Three Cantos of a Poem of Some Length" was included in the collection. A privately printed version of this edition, limited to 60 copies and with "The Temperaments" added, was made available in New York that same month. The present volume prints the complete text of *Lustra* as it appears in this privately printed version.

Lustra collected several poems from Pound's previous books. The complete contents of *Cathay* were included, as well as the following poems: "In Durance," "Piere Vidal Old," "Prayer for His Lady's Life" "'Blandula, Tenulla, Vagula,'" "Erat Hora," "The Sea of Glass," "Her Monument, the Image Cut Thereon," "Housman's Message to Mankind" ("Song in the Manner of Housman"), "Translations from Heine" ("Translations and Adaptations from Heine") "Und Drang," an untitled version of "Silet," "In Exitum Cuiusdam," "Apparuit," "The Tomb at Akr Çaar," "Portrait d'une Femme," "New York," "A Girl," "'Phasellus Ille,'" "An Object," "Quies," "The Cloak," "An Immorality," "Dieu! Qu'Il la Fait," "Salve Pontifex," "Δώρια," "The Needle," "Sub Mare," "Plunge," "A Virginal," "Pan Is Dead," "The Picture," "Of Jacopo del Sellaio," and "The Return." These poems do not appear in the *Lustra* section of the present volume but are included with the books in which they were first collected.

Of the poems first collected in *Lustra*, the following had been published in periodicals: "Tenzone" (*Poetry*, April 1913, and *New Freewoman*, August 15, 1913); "The Condolence" (*Poetry*, April 1913); "The Garret" (*Poetry*, April 1913, and *New Freewoman*, August 15, 1913); "The Garden" (*Poetry*, April 1913, and *New Freewoman*, August 15, 1913); "Ortus" (*Poetry*, April 1913); "Salutation" (*Poetry*, April 1913, and *New Freewoman*, August 15, 1913); "Salutation the Second" (*Poetry*, April 1913, and *New Freewoman*, August 15, 1913); "The Spring" (*Poetry*, March 1915); "Albâtre" (*Poetry and Drama*, March 1914, and *Smart Set*, August 1915); "Causa" (*Smart Set*, December 1913); "Commission" (*Poetry*, April 1913); "A Pact" (*Poetry*, April 1913); "Surgit Fama" (*Poetry*, November 1913, with the subtitle "Fragment from an Unwritable Play," and *New Freewoman*, December 1, 1913); "Dance Figure" (*Poetry*, April 1913, and *New Freewoman*, August 15, 1913); "April" (*Poetry*, November 1913, and *New Freewoman*, December 1, 1913); "Gentildonna" (*Poetry*, November 1913, and *New Freewoman*, December 1, 1913); "The Rest" (*Poetry*, November 1913, and *New Freewoman*, December 1, 1913); "Les Millwin" (*Poetry*, November 1913, and *New Freewoman*, December 1, 1913); "Further Instructions" (*Poetry*, November 1913, and *New Freewoman*, December 1, 1913); "A Song of the Degrees" (I–III in *Poetry*, November 1913 as "Xenia," III–V, and *New Freewoman*, December 1, 1913, as "Convictions"); "Ité" (*Poetry*, November 1913 as "Xenia," VI); "Dum Capitolium Scandet" (*Poetry*, November 1913, as "Xenia," VII); "Το Καλόν" (*Poetry*, August 1914); "The Study in Aesthetics" (*Poetry*, August 1914); "The Bellaires" (*Poetry*, August 1914); "The New Cake of Soap" (*BLAST*, June 20, 1914); "Salvationists" (*Poetry*, August 1914); "Epitaph" (*Smart Set*, December 1913); "Arides" (*Smart Set*, December 1913); "The Bath Tub" (*Smart Set*, December 1913); "Amitiés" (*Poetry*, August 1914); "Meditatio" (*BLAST*, June 20, 1914); "To Dives" (*Smart Set*, December 1913); "Ladies" (*Poetry*, August 1914); "Phyllidula" (*Others*, November 1915); "The Patterns" (*Others*, November 1915); "Coda" (*Others*, November 1915); "The Seeing Eye" (*Poetry*, August 1914); "Ancora" (*Poetry*, November 1913, and *New Freewoman*, December 1, 1913); "Dompna Pois de Me No'us Cal" (*Poetry and Drama*, March 1914); "The Coming of War: Actaeon" (*Poetry*, March 1915); "Fan-piece, for Her Imperial Lord" (*Poetry and Drama*, June 1914); "Ts'ai Chih" (*Poetry and Drama*, June 1914); "In a Station of the Metro" (*Poetry*, April 1913, and *New Freewoman*, August 15, 1913); "Alba" (*Smart Set*, December 1913); "Heather" (*Poetry and Drama*, March 1914); "The Faun" (*Poetry and Drama*, March 1914); "Coitus" (*Poetry and Drama*, March 1914); "The Encounter" (*Smart Set*, December 1913); "Tempora" (*Poetry and Drama*, March 1914); "Black Slippers: Bellotti" (*Smart

Set, October 1915, as "Her Little Black Slippers"); "Society" (*Poetry and Drama*, March 1914); "Image from d'Orleans" (*Poetry*, March 1915); "Ione, Dead the Long Year" (*Poetry and Drama*, December 1914, as "Dead Iönè"); "'Ιμέρρω" (*Poetry*, September 1916, as "O Atthis"); "Shop Girl" (*Others*, November 1915); "To Formianus' Young Lady Friend" (*Poetry and Drama*, March 1914); "Tame Cat" (*Smart Set*, December 1913); "L'Art, 1910" (*BLAST*, June 20, 1914, as "L'Art"); "Simulacra" (*Smart Set*, December 1913); "Women Before a Shop" (*BLAST*, June 20, 1914); "The Social Order" (*BLAST*, July 1915); "The Tea Shop" (*Others*, November 1915); "Ancient Music" (*BLAST*, July 1915); "The Lake Isle" (*Poetry*, September 1916); "Epitaphs" (*BLAST*, June 20, 1914); "Our Contemporaries" (*BLAST*, July 1915); "Ancient Wisdom, Rather Cosmic" (*BLAST*, July 1915); "The Three Poets" (*Poetry*, September 1916), "The Gipsy" (*Poetry*, March 1915); "The Game of Chess" (as "Dogmatic Statement Concerning the Game of Chess" in *Poetry*, March 1915, and *BLAST*, July 1915); "Provincia Deserta" (*Poetry*, March 1915); "Sennin Poem by Kakuhaku" (*New Age*, June 22, 1916); "A Ballad of the Mulberry Road" (*New Age*, June 22, 1916); "Old Idea of Choan by Rosoriu" (*New Age*, June 22, 1916); "To-Em-Mai's 'The Unmoving Cloud'" (*New Age*, June 22, 1916, and *Others*, July 1916); "Near Perigord" (*Poetry*, December 1915); "Villanelle: The Psychological Hour" (*Poetry*, December 1915); "Dans un Omnibus de Londres" (*Poetry*, September 1916); "Pagani's, November 8" (*Poetry*, September 1916); "Homage to Quintus Septimius Florentis Christianus" (*Poetry*, September 1916); "Fish and the Shadow" (*Poetry*, September 1916); "Impressions of François-Marie Arouet (de Voltaire)" (*Poetry*, September 1916); "Three Cantos of a Poem of Some Length" (*Poetry*, July 1917 and August 1917, as "Three Cantos").

'Noh' or Accomplishment (1917). Pound began publishing his Noh translations based on Fenollosa's notebooks in May 1914, when "Nishikigi" appeared in *Poetry*. "Kinuta" and "Hagoromo," along with quotations from other plays, were published in *Quarterly Review*, October 1914, and a shorter and somewhat different version of Parts I and II of *'Noh' or Accomplishment* appeared in *Drama*, May 1915. "Awoi No Uye" appeared in *Quarterly Notebook*, June 1916, and "Kakitsubata" was published (as "Kakitsuhata") in *Drama*, August 1916. Pound gathered the plays "Nishikigi," "Hagoromo," "Kumasaka," and "Kagekiyo" in *Certain Noble Plays of Japan* (Churchtown: The Cuala Press, 1916), which was then enlarged for publication in England (by Macmillan and Co.) and America (by Alfred A. Knopf) in 1917 as *'Noh' or Accomplishment*, these publications using the same sheets. The text printed here is from the 1917 Knopf publication of *'Noh' or Accomplishment*.

Arnaut Daniel (1917). As early as 1911, Pound had hoped to publish a book of translations of the Provençal troubadour Arnaut Daniel (see note 479.1). Late in 1917, the Clerk's Press in Cleveland agreed to print a book of Pound's Arnaut Daniel translations in a private edition of 80 copies. On December 14, 1917, Pound wrote to John Quinn that he had been "working ten and twelve hours a day on my Arnaut Daniel. . . . I have redone about half of it, and shall wholly rewrite the rest. Thank God it wasn't printed in its first form." He completed his revisions of the translations shortly thereafter. When Pound's typescript was sent to the Clerk's Press it disappeared in transit and the book was never published. Typescript copies of these translations with Pound's holograph corrections are part of the collection of Pound's papers in the Beinecke Library at Yale. Based on these typescripts, an edition of the Arnaut Daniel translations intended for the Clerk's Press volume was prepared by Charlotte Ward in *Pound's Translations of Arnaut Daniel* (New York: Garland Press, 1991). Ward's edition provides the texts for the Arnaut Daniel section of the present volume.

Many of Pound's earlier translations of Arnaut Daniel's verse, quite different from the "redone" versions completed in 1917, had appeared in *New Age* in 1911 or 1912 or in the musical score *Hesternae Rosae* (1912). Some of these were collected in *The Translations* (1953; enlarged version, 1964). As for the translations intended for the Clerk's Press edition, "Doutz Brais e Critz" was published under the title "Glamour and Indigo" in *Little Review* (November 1918), and complete or fragmentary versions of the following translations were included in Pound's essay "Arnaut Daniel," published in *Instigations* (1920): "Can Chai la Fueilla," "Lancan Son Passat li Guire," "Lanquan Vei Fueill' e Flors e Frug," "Autet e Bas Entrels Prims Fuoills," "L'Aura Amara," "En Breu Brisaral Temps Braus," "Doutz Brais e Critz," "Ans Quel Cim Reston de Branchas," "Sim Fos Amors de Joi Donar Tant Larga." One of Pound's translations meant for the Clerk's Press edition ("I only, and who elrische pain support") was incorporated into the sequence "Langue d'Oc" published in *Quia Pauper Amavi*, where it appears under the title "Canzon." For *Umbra: The Early Poems of Ezra Pound* (1920), Pound included "L'Aura Amara," "Autet e Bas Entrels Prims Fuoills," "Doutz Brais e Critz," "Lancan Son Passat li Guire," and "Ans Quel Cim Reston de Branchas," grouping them under the title "Five Canzoni of Arnaut Daniel."

Pavannes and Divisions (1918). In *Pavannes and Divisions*, a volume consisting mostly of essays, Pound collected "L'Homme Moyen Sensuel," which had appeared in *Little Review* (September 1917), and "Pierrots," a translation that had appeared in *Little*

Review (May 1917) under the pseudonym John Hall. *Pavannes and Divisions* was published by Alfred A. Knopf in New York in June 1918. There was no English edition of the book. The texts of "L'Homme Moyen Sensuel" and "Pierrots" printed here are taken from the 1918 Alfred A. Knopf edition of *Pavannes and Divisions*.

Quia Pauper Amavi (1919). The Egoist Press published *Quia Pauper Amavi* in London in October 1919. There was no subsequent edition of the book. "Langue d'Oc" had appeared (as "Homage à la langue d'Oc") in *Little Review* in May 1918 and in *New Age* on June 27, 1918. "Moeurs Contemporaines" also had appeared in *Little Review* in May 1918. Sections I, II, II, and VI of "Homage to Sextus Propertius" had been published (as "Poems from the Propertius Series') in *Poetry*, March 1919. *Quia Pauper Amavi* also contains "Three Cantos," which is not included in this section because it is a version of "Three Cantos of a Poem of Some Length" in *Lustra* (pp. 318–330). The present volume prints the texts of the 1919 Egoist Press edition of *Quia Pauper Amavi* for the poems contained in this section. At line 529.12, Pound changed "Wherefore" of the published text to "Wherefrom" by hand in numerous copies of the book; the corrected reading is printed here.

Hugh Selwyn Mauberley (1919). *Hugh Selwyn Mauberley* was first published in an edition of 200 copies by the Egoist Press in June 1919. This book was the first appearance of the poem in print and provides the text printed here. There was no American edition of *Hugh Selwyn Mauberley* as a separate publication, though the first six sections of Part I appeared in *The Dial* in September 1920, and a lightly revised version of the entire poem was included in *Poems 1918–1921* (New York: Boni & Liveright, 1921), as well as in subsequent collections such as *Personae* (1926) and *Diptych Rome–London* (1958).

Umbra (1920). *Umbra: The Early Poems of Ezra Pound* is a collection mostly of poems published before 1913, along with selections from his Guido Cavalcanti and Arnaut Daniel translations (and the "Complete Poetical Works of T. E. Hulme"). He also included five previously uncollected poems. "The Alchemist," dated 1912 in the table of contents of *Umbra*, was first published in this volume. "Oboes" had appeared in *Poetry Review* in February 1912 (where it contained a third section entitled "An Immorality," which had been collected as a separate poem in *Ripostes* and which was omitted from the *Umbra* version of "Oboes"). Two poems from *Little Review* (November 1918), "Cantus Planus" and "Phanopoeia," also appeared in *Umbra*. "Poem: Abbreviated from the Conversation of Mr. T. E. H.," written by Pound, was added to the "Complete Poetical Works of T. E. Hulme," which was printed as an appendix to the volume.

Umbra was published by Elkin Mathews in London in June 1920. There was no subsequent edition. The present volume takes the texts of the five uncollected poems from the 1920 Elkin Mathews edition of *Umbra*.

The previously collected poems in *Umbra* are "Grace Before Song"; "La Fraisne"; "Cino"; "Na Audiart"; "Villonaud for This Yule"; "A Villonaud: Ballad of the Gibbet"; "Mesmserism"; "Famam Librosque Cano"; "Praise of Ysolt"; "For E. McC."; "At the Heart o' Me"; "The White Stag"; "In Durance"; "Marvoil"; "And Thus in Nineveh"; "Guido Invites You Thus"; "Night Litany"; "Sestina: Altaforte"; "Piere Vidal Old"; "Ballad of the Goodly Fere"; "Laudentes Decem Pulchritudinis Johannae Templi"; "Aux Belles de Londres"; "Francesca"; "Prayer" ("Greek Epigram" in *Exultations*); "The Tree"; "On His Own Face in a Glass"; "The Eyes" ("The Cry of the Eyes" in *A Lume Spento*); "Nils Lykke"; "Planh for the Young English King"; "Alba" ("Alba Innominata" in *Exultations*); "Planh"; "Au Jardin"; "Silet"; "In Exitum Cuiusdam"; "The Tomb at Akr Çaar"; "Portrait d'Une Femme"; "N.Y."; "A Girl"; "'Phaseus Ille'"; "An Object"; "Quies"; "The Seafarer"; "The Cloak"; "Δώρια"; "Apparuit"; "The Needle"; "Sub Mare"; "Plunge"; "A Virginal"; "Pan Is Dead"; "An Immorality"; "Dieu! Qu'Il la Fait"; "The Picture"; "Of Jacopo del Sallaio"; "The Return"; "Effects of Music Upon a Company of People"; Sonnets I, II, III, V, VI, VII, VIII, XV, XXVI, XXXIII of Guido Cavalcanti, as well as "Madrigal" and Ballate I, II, III, V, VI, VII, XII, XIII, XIV; from Pound's Arnaut Daniel translations, "L'Aura Amara," "Autet e Bas Entrel Prims Fuoills," "Doutz Brais e Critz" (entitled "Glamour and Indigo"), "Lancan Son Passat li Guire," and "Ans Quel Cim Reston de Branchas."

Personæ (1926). Although a note in *Personæ: The Collected Poems of Ezra Pound* claimed that it was an "edition to date of all Ezra Pound's poems except the unfinished 'Cantos,'" the book was in fact a selection that omitted numerous poems. It contained seven poems that had not been included in Pound's previous poetry collections. Six of these had been published in the first issue of *BLAST*, June 20, 1914 (some of which were revised for *Personæ*): "Salutation the Third," "Monumentum Aere, Etc.," "Come My Cantilations," "Before Sleep," "Post Mortem Conspectu" (as "His Vision of a Certain Lady Post Mortem"), and "Fratres Minores." These were printed under the heading "Poems from BLAST (1914)." *Personæ* also collected "Cantico del Sole" as a separate poem; it had been published in *Little Review*, March 1918, and appeared as part of the essay "The Classics 'Escape,'" in *Instigations* (1920). The texts of the seven poems in this section are taken from the first edition of *Personæ*, published by Boni & Liveright on December 22, 1926. An enlarged version of *Personæ* was published in 1949 by New Directions (see below).

In addition to these seven poems, *Personæ* contains poems previously published in book form, many of which were revised for this collection: "The Tree," "Threnos," "La Fraisne," "Cino," "Na Audiart," "Villonaud for This Yule," "A Villonaud: Ballad of the Gibbet," "Mesmerism," "Famam Librosque Cano," "Praise of Ysolt," "De Aegypto," "For E. McC.," "In Durance," "Marvoil," "And Thus in Nineveh," "The White Stag," "Guido Invites You Thus," "Night Litany," "Sestina: Altaforte," "Piere Vidal Old," "Paracelsus in Excelsis," "Ballad of the Goodly Fere," "On His Own Face in a Glass," "The Eyes," "Francesca," "Planh for the Young English King," "Ballatetta," "Prayer for His Lady's Life," "Speech for Psyche in the Golden Book of Apuleius," "'Blandula, Tenulla, Vagula,'" "Erat Hora," "Rome," "Her Monument, the Image Cut Thereon," "Satiemus," "Mr Housman's Message" ("Song in the Manner of Housman"), "Translations and Adaptations from Heine" ("Translations from Heine" and "Oboes," II), "The House of Splendour" ("Und Drang," VII), "The Flame" ("Und Drang," VIII), "Horæ Beatæ Inscriptio" ("Und Drang," IX), "The Altar" ("Und Drang," X), "Au Salon" ("Und Drang," XI), "Au Jardin" ("Und Drang," XII), "Silet," "In Exitum Cuiusdam," "The Tomb at Akr Çaar," "Portrait d'une Femme," "N.Y.," "A Girl," "'Phasellus Ille,'" "An Object," "Quies," "The Cloak," "Δώρια," "Apparuit," "The Needle," "Sub Mare," "The Plunge," "A Virginal," "Pan Is Dead," "Dieu! Qu'Il la Fait," "The Picture," "Of Jacopo del Sellaio," "The Return," and "The Alchemist." It also included all the poems in the 1915 edition of *Cathay*, the poems (excepting "Preference" and "Three Cantos of a Poem of Some Length") first collected in *Lustra* (see above), "Langue d'Oc," "Moeurs Contemporaines," "Homage to Sextus Propertius," "Hugh Selwyn Mauberley," "The Alchemist," "Phanopoeia," and "Cantus Planus."

Guido Cavalcanti Rime (1932). The poems from this book printed here—translations from the 1920s as well as "The Canzone," Pound's Italian text of Cavalcanti's "Donna mi prega"—were first published in book form in *Guido Cavalcanti Rime* (Genoa: Edizioni Marsano, 1932). Pound's English versions of Cavalcanti sonnets in this section—Sonnets VII, XIII, XIV, XVI, and XVII—are new renderings of works first translated in *The Sonnets and Ballate of Guido Cavalcanti* (1912). A version of "Donna mi prega" and "The Canzone" had appeared in *The Dial* in July 1928. *Guido Cavalcanti Rime* was printed at Pound's expense after his edition of Cavalcanti's works scheduled to be published by the Aquila Press was canceled due to the firm's bankruptcy (see note 573.2). Pages set for the Aquila Press edition in 1929, including those containing the poems in this section, were used for printing *Guido Cavalcanti Rime*. There was no subsequent edition of the book. The texts printed in this section of the present volume are taken from the 1932 Edizioni Marsano edition of *Guido Cavalcanti Rime*.

Alfred Venison's Poems (1935). The poems in *Alfred Venison's Poems* were first published in the *New English Weekly* between February and November 1934. They were then collected as part of Stanley Nott's "Pamphlets on the New Economics" series in April 1935. Pound included them without revision in Appendix II of the enlarged edition of *Personæ*, published by New Directions in 1949. The 1935 Stanley Nott edition of *Alfred Venison's Poems* provides the text printed here.

Guide to Kulchur (1938). "The Lioness Warns Her Cubs" and "Praise Song of the Buck Hare," folk songs from Sudan and Siberia (respectively), were translated from German sources and published in *Guide to Kulchur* (London: Faber & Faber, 1938), which provides the text printed here. Under the title *Culture*, the book was published in America by New Directions in 1938 using sheets from the Faber edition.

Personæ (1949). An expanded edition of Pound's 1926 collection *Personæ* was published by New Directions in 1949. It included the full contents of the 1926 edition, as well as two appendices. The first contains "The Complete Poetical Works of T. E. Hulme"; "Pierrots" and "L'Homme Moyen Sensuel" from *Pavannes and Divisions*; a version of "Donna mi prega" (see *Guido Cavalcanti Rime*): and three previously uncollected poems: "To Whistler, American," "Middle-Aged" (both which were first published in *Poetry*, October, 1912), and "Abu Salammamm—A Song of Empire" (first published in *Poetry*, August 1914). A second appendix contains the complete contents of the 1935 Stanley Nott edition of *Alfred Venison's Poems*, along with "M. Pom-POM," first published in *Townsman*, January 1938. The present volume prints the texts of "To Whistler, American," "Middle-Aged," "Abu Salammamm—A Song of Empire," and "M. Pom-POM" from the 1949 New Directions edition of *Personæ*.

Confucius: The Great Digest & Unwobbling Pivot (1951). Pound's first version of "The Great Digest," one of the "Four Books" of the Confucian canon that he initially read in French translation (see note 615.1–2), was published by the University of Washington Bookstore in 1928 as *Ta Hio: The Great Learning*. Pound continued to study and translate Confucian works over the following decades, benefiting from increased familiarity with Chinese as well as existing translations. He published an Italian version of "The Great Digest" in two books in 1942 and 1944, as well as an Italian translation of *Chung Yung*, another canonical Confucian book, under the title *Ciung Iung: L'Asse che non vacilla* (1945). *Chung Yung* then appeared in English translation as "The Unwobbling Pivot," accompanying "The Great Digest" in an issue of James Laughlin's magazine *Pharos* (Winter 1947) devoted exclusively to these translations. These two works were then collected in *Confucius: The Great Digest & Unwobbling Pivot*, published by New Directions in 1951, which is the text printed here. Because the present volume does not reproduce the Chinese text on the pages opposite the English translation as in the New Directions edition, it does not reproduce the breaks in lineation and pagination that were meant solely to align the English with the Chinese text.

The Confucian Analects (1951). Pound first published excerpts from Confucius' *Analects* in English translation in the pamphlet *Confucius: Digest of the Analects*, published in an edition of 245 copies by Giovanni Scheiwiller in Milan in 1937. With very slight revisions, these excerpts became the first chapter of Pound's *Guide to Kulchur* (1938). Pound's translation of the complete work appeared in the *Hudson Review* (Spring–Summer 1950); it was lightly revised and published as *The Confucian Analects* in 1951 (New York: Square $ Series, 1951). A subsequent undated version of the Square $ Edition (published in Washington, D.C., with "Dollar" instead of "$" on the title page) added the two brief introductory sections, "Procedure" and "Brief Concordance" (most likely written in 1954), but made no other changes to the text of *The Confucian Analects*; these sections were also included in the book when it was published in England in 1956 by Peter Owen Limited. The text of *The Confucian Analects* was subsequently reprinted in *Confucius: The Great Digest; The Unwobbling Pivot; The Analects* (New York: New Directions, 1969). The undated Square Dollar edition of *The Confucian Analects* contains the text printed here.

The Classic Anthology Defined by Confucius (1954). Pound's first translation from the *Shih Ching* (*Book of Poems* or Confucian Odes), the anthology of 305 poems whose compilation is attributed to Confucius, was "Song of the Bowman of Shu" in *Cathay* (1915), based on a version in Fenellosa's notebooks. Around 1920, he acquired a Latin edition of some of the Confucian Odes; English versions of poems from the *Shih Ching* were intended for the aborted Aquila Press edition of translations and prose planned in the late 1920s (see note 573.2). A partial translation of Poem 108 (809.17–810.5), based on a French source, was included in *Guide to Kulchur* (1938). In the 1940s Pound studied the commentary and translations of the *Shih Ching* by James Legge and the Swedish scholar Bernhard Karlgren, and during the first years of his confinement at St. Elizabeths he began planning an ambitious "Scholar's Edition" of the Confucian Odes, much of which was never realized (see note 753.1–2). *The Classic Anthology Defined by Confucius* was published by Harvard University Press on September 10, 1954. Using unbound sheets of the Harvard University Press edition, Faber & Faber published the book in England the following year. New Directions, reproducing the Harvard University Press edition, brought the book out under the title *The Confucian Odes* in 1959. The present volume prints the text of the 1954 Harvard University Press edition of *The Classic Anthology Defined by Confucius*; it does not include the introduction by Achilles Fang, which is part of the Harvard edition as well as the subsequent Faber & Faber and New Directions volumes.

Elektra (translated *ca*. 1950). *Elektra*, Pound and Rudd Fleming's version of Sophocles' play translated while Pound was hospitalized at St. Elizabeths (1946–1958), was not published during Pound's lifetime. Based on the two existing typescripts of the play in the Princeton University Library, two editions of *Elektra* were prepared in the 1980s: Carey Perloff's acting edition, used for the first performance of *Elektra* in 1987 and published by New Directions in 1990 as *Elektra: A Version by Ezra Pound and Rudd Fleming*; and Richard Reid's edition, *Elektra: A Play by Ezra Pound and Rudd Fleming* (Princeton: Princeton University Press, 1989), an edition guided by what Reid calls "faithfulness to the historical documents" (some of Perloff's decisions, as befits an "acting edition," are designed for stage adaptation). The text of the 1989 Princeton University Press edition of *Elektra* is printed here.

Sophokles: Women of Trachis (1956). Pound's version of Sophocles' *Women of Trachis*, which like *Elektra* was translated while he was confined at St. Elizabeths Hospital in Washington, D.C., was first published in *Hudson Review*, Winter 1954. Nearly three years later, the London publisher Neville Spearman published *Sophokles: Women of Trachis: A Version by Ezra Pound*. Along with Pound's translation, this edition contained a foreword by Dennis Goacher, an "Editorial Declaration" by Goacher and Peter Whigham, and two essays: S. V. Jankowski's "Ezra Pound's Translation of Sophokles" and Ricardo M. degli Uberti's "Why Pound Liked Italy." The American publication of *Women of Trachis* (New York: New Directions, 1957) was created from reproduction proofs provided by Neville Spearman. The present volume prints the text of the 1956 Neville Spearman edition of Pound's *Women of Trachis* but does not include the ancillary material written by Goacher, Whigham, Jankowski, and Uberti.

Pavannes and Divagations (1958). *Pavannes and Divagations* (New York: New Directions, 1958) is an expanded version of

Pavannes and Divisions, published in 1918. Among the poems first collected in it are the following: "Words for Roundel in Double Canon," first published in *An "Objectivists" Anthology* (New York: To Press, 1932); "Guides to the Montanari Poems," first published anonymously in *Imagi* in 1951; and the translation (with accompanying drawing) of the French Jaime d'Angulo poem beginning "Werewolf in selvage I saw," which had appeared in the December 1950 issue of the Calcutta periodical *Kavita* as well as in *Imagi* in 1951. In a section called "Frivolities," *Pavannes and Divagations* also included the following poems: "The Sneeze," "Mr Housman's Message" ("Song in the Manner of Housman"), "The New Cake of Soap," "Ancient Music," "Our Contemporaries," "M. Pom-POM," "Abu Salammamm—A Song of Empire," "In 1914 There was Mertons," and "'Neath Ben Bulben's Buttocks Lies." The texts of "Words for Roundel in Double Canon," "Guides to the Montanari Poems," and "Werewolf in selvage I saw" in the present volume are taken from the 1958 New Directions edition of *Pavannes and Divagations.*

Translations (1964). Pound chose the contents of a selection of his translations while at St. Elizabeths in Washington, and the book was published under the title *The Translations of Ezra Pound* in July 1953 by Faber & Faber. The book was issued the following month in the United States by New Directions using sheets from the Faber & Faber edition. The collection included works appearing elsewhere in the present volume: the 1912 versions of his Guido Cavalcanti translations, selections from his Arnaut Daniel poems from 1917, translations after Chinese poems from *Cathay* and the "Cathay" section of *Lustra,* the Anglo-Saxon "The Seafarer," and (in a section called "Miscellaneous Poems") the following translations: "To Formianus' Young Lady Friend," "Her Monument, the Image Cut Thereon," "Rome," "Dieu! Qu'Il la Fait," and "Pierrots." It also contained the prose translation (not included in the present volume) of Remy de Gourmont's "Dust for Sparrows." An enlarged printing, entitled *Translations,* was published by New Directions on February 18, 1964. This printing reproduced *The Translations of Ezra Pound* and added poems to the "Miscellaneous Poems" section. Most of these translations had been published in periodicals and anthologies; they were not revised for inclusion in *Translations,* although they sometimes include titles and accompanying source information that do not appear in the earlier publications. The poems added to the enlarged *Translations* include five translations from *The Spirit of Romance* (see above), Cercalmon's "Descant on a Theme" (part III of "Langue d'Oc" from *Quia Pauper Amavi*), and the following poems printed in this section (with the sources of first publication): "Chansson Doil" (*New Age,* December 28, 1911); "For Right of Audience"

(*New Age*, December 28, 1911); "Canzon: Of the Trades and Love" (*New Age*, January 18, 1912); "Rica Conquesta" (*New Age*, February 22, 1912); "Certain Poems of Kabir" (*Modern Review*, June 1913); "Strophes" (*Dial*, November 1921); "Sonnet to Guido Cavalcanti" (*Dial*, July 1929, in the essay "Guido's Relations"); the five poems "Cabaret Vert," "Comedy in Three Caresses," "Anadyomene," "Lice-Hunters," and "Rus" (*Edge*, October 1956, reprinted in the pamphlet *Rimbaud*, published in 1957 by Vanni Scheiwiller in Milan); "Catullus: XXVI" (*Edge*, May 1957); "Conversations in Courtship" (*Wort und Wahrheit*, January 1960); the four poems "L'Ultima Ora," "Ask not ungainly," "By the flat cup," "This monument will outlast" (*Agenda*, September 1964). "Roma," "Catullus: LXXXV," and "Air: Sentir Avec Ardeur," all dated 1963 or 1964 in the table of contents of *Translations*, were published for the first time there. The texts of the 21 poems in this section are taken from the 1964 New Directions publication of *Translations*.

Uncollected Poems and Translations. The texts in the "Uncollected Poems and Translations" section are taken from their first publications, except for poems published in the following editions, abbreviated as follows:

CEP   *Collected Early Poems of Ezra Pound*, edited by Michael King (New York: New Directions, 1976).

FB   *Forked Branches*, edited by Charlotte Ward (Iowa City: Windhover Press, 1985)

P   *Personae*, edited by Lea Baechler and A. Walton Litz (New York: New Directions, 1990).

PC   *Pound's Cavalcanti*, edited by David Anderson (Princeton: Princeton University Press, 1983).

Note: the poems in FB and PC were not published during Pound's lifetime.

Ezra on the Strike. CEP. First published in *Jenkintown Times-Chronicle*, Jenkintown, Pa., November 8, 1902.

Amor de Lonh. FB.

A Dawn Song. CEP. First published in *Munsey's Magazine*, December 1906.

To the Raphaelite Latinists. CEP. First published in *Book News Monthly*, January 1908.

In Epitaphium. CEP. First published in *The Book of the Poets' Club* (London: The Poets' Club, 1909).

Clair de Lune; Lied Maritime. Transcribed from the program ("Book of Words") for a vocal and piano recital by Florence Schmidt and Elsie Hall at Bechstein Hall, London, Tuesday, March 1, 1910.

Thersites: On the Surviving Zeus. CEP. First published in *The English Review*, April 1910.

The Fault of It. CEP. First published in *Forum*, July 1911.

L'Invitation. CEP. First published in *Poetry Review*, February 1912.

Selection from Collection Yvette Guilbert. Transcriptions from the musical score *Selection from Collection Yvette Guilbert* (London: Augener Ltd., 1912).

Epilogue. CEP. First published in *Collected Shorter Poems* (London: Faber & Faber, 1968), which notes that it was "composed 1912."

from Hesternae Rosae. Transcriptions from the musical score *Hesternae Rosae* (London: Augener Ltd., 1913).

Pax Saturni. CEP. First published in *Poetry*, April 1913.

The Choice; Xenia ("The Street in Soho"). CEP. Both were first published in *Poetry*, November 1913.

Xenia ("Come let us play with our own toys"). CEP. First published in *Smart Set*, December 1913.

Ikon. P. First published in *Cerebralist*, December 1913.

Legend of the Chippewa Spring and Minnehaha, the Indian Maiden. CEP. Dated 1913 when first published in *Chippewa County: Wisconsin Past and Present*.

Homage to Wilfrid Scawen Blunt. CEP. First published in *The Times*, January 20, 1914.

Pastoral. CEP. First published in *BLAST*, June 20, 1914.

War Verse (1914); 1915: February. P. These two poems were not published during Pound's lifetime.

Gnomic Verses; Our Respectful Homages to M. Laurent Tailhade. CEP. First published in *BLAST*, July 1915.

Et Faim Sallir les Loups des Boys. CEP. First published in *BLAST*, July 1915.

Love-Song to Eunoë. CEP. First published in *Smart Set*, July 1915.

Another Man's Wife. CEP. First published in *Others*, November 1915.

Reflection. CEP. First published in *Smart Set*, July 1915.

12 Occupations. *12 Occupations by Jean de Bosschère* (London: Elkin Mathews, 1916).

To a City Sending Him Advertisements. CEP. First published in *The Newark Anniversary Poems* (New York: Laurence J. Gomme, 1917).

Chanson Arabe; Dawn on the Mountain; Wine. *Little Review*, November 1918.

A Canticle. *Much Ado*, January 1, 1920.

Fever Chart. *The Dial*, September 1920.

Troubadour Songs. "Sad song ye hear,": transcription from the musical score *Five Troubadour Songs: With the Original Provençal Words and English Words Adapted from Chaucer, Arranged by Agnes Bedford* (London, Boosey & Co., 1920).

"When new buds thrust the leaves aside"; "When cometh in the flow'ry time"; "Although thou leave me now, so vixen strange"; "Call that not life, wherein love hath no part"; "Say that sweet my sorrow was"; "In sorrow now I know well": FB.

Highbrow's Translation of Horace. *Readies for Bob Brown's Machine* (Cagnes-sur-mer, France: Roving Eye Press, 1931).

"I think thou has looked on every valour and all"; "Amore and Lagia, Guido Orlandi and I": PC.

"Guido, Gianni that saw you yesterday"; "In your gentle salute"; "Guard thee well guard thee well I say"; "We are the sad bewildered quills": FB.

"Gentle Jheezus sleek and wild": *An "Objectivists" Anthology* (New York: To Press, 1932).

Drafts for *Cavalcanti: A Sung Dramedy in 3 Acts*. FB.

"If the prelates would take"; "King Constantine, as I will relate": FB.

Envoi'. *Quarterly Review of Literature*, V, 2 (1949).

"Thais habet nigros. . ." *Imagi*, V, 2 (1950).

Papillon: *Edge*, May 1957.

Old Zuk; More: *European*, January 1959.

By the River of Stars: Mary de Rachilwiltz (ed.), *Catai* (Milan: Vanni Scheiwiller, 1987)

Age of Gold: *Confucius to Cummings* (New Directions, 1964).

Pigeons: *Sunday Times Weekly Review* (London), April 26, 1970.

Prayer for a Dead Brother: *Antigonish Review*, Winter 1971–1972.

Grateful acknowledgment is given to New Directions Publishing Corporation for permission to print from the following copyrighted works of Ezra Pound:

END TO TORMENT: A MEMOIR OF EZRA POUND, copyright © 1979 by New Directions Publishing Corporation. Copyright © 1979 by the Trustees of Ezra Pound Literary Property Trust/Copyright © 1979 by Michael King.

COLLECTED EARLY POEMS OF EZRA POUND, copyright © 1926, 1935, 1954, 1965, 1967, 1976 by The Ezra Pound Literary Property Trust.

PERSONAE, copyright © 1926 by Ezra Pound.

TRANSLATIONS, copyright © 1954, 1963 by Ezra Pound.

CONFUCIUS: The Great Digest, The Unwobbling Pivot, The Analects, copyright © 1947, 1950 by Ezra Pound.

WOMEN OF TRACHIS, copyright © 1957 by Ezra Pound.

PAVANNES AND DIVAGATIONS, copyright © 1958 by Ezra Pound.

CONFUCIUS TO CUMMINGS, copyright © 1964 by New Directions.

ELEKTRA, copyright © 1987, 1989, 1990 by the Trustees of the Ezra Pound Literary Property Trust and Rudd Fleming.

"Envoi," "Old Zuk," "More," "Pigeons (Fasolo)," "Prayer for a Dead Brother," "Thais habet negros (Martial)," "Papillon: For a Small Book Unread," copyright © 1991 by the Trustees of the Ezra Pound Literary Property Trust.

This volume presents the texts of the original printings chosen for inclusion here, but it does not attempt to reproduce nontextual features of their typographic design. The texts are presented without change, except for the correction of typographical errors. Spelling, punctuation, and capitalization are often expressive features and are not altered, even when inconsistent or irregular. The following is a list of typographical errors corrected, cited by page and line number: 24.7, "Bah; 24.28, here!; 31.28, "Sharing; 38.4, "When; 38.31, Beatrice.; 39.9, Beatrice,—; 50.24, So; 127.17, praised; 127.32, 36, Praised; 128.15, 18, Praisè; 187.23, Calvacanti; 224.16, servitor.; 303.23, Rochechouart; 305.15, fiction,; 305.37, Bertrand; 306.35–36, man,"/"I; 322.6, Panting; 344.6, going a; 468.4, roof.; 473.22, takadana*; 481.31, tho'; 484.16, fairest.; 487.10, but; 489.19, fearing; 491.35, hearing; 509.7, prized.; 510.34, hand; 522.27, Macchiavelli; 529.12, Wherefore; 535.1, it's; 535.28–29, [stanza space]; 536.26, gored is; 537.2, happpy; 537.15, Diana,; 542.22, ears; 542.30, kingdom.; 543.11, seabord; 543.19, pomegranite; 545.11, wreathes; 551.17, decor"; 558.26, NUKTIS; 559.5, seive; 560.17, neo-Neitzschean; 562.20, hedonist"; 596.17, doeting; 600.20, would; 659.9, milennium; 673.17, em'; 694.11, *french*; 710.9, peoples'; 731.18, XL; 731.21, XLI; 781.24, your's; 797.4, tother; 802.27, it."; 870.28, Hiang-ward; 882.11, then; 910.2, that; 958.28, state.; 994.10, *Agamnenon's*; 1025.22–25, 1037.20–33, 1038.9–19, [corrected line breaks]; 1080.4, here; 1082.30, compliment.; 1103.31, it.; 1107.33, me.; 1137.2, and; 1143.12, Boredome; 1144.9, sea-bords; 1156.25, lady?; 1157.13, lovliest; 1157.16, sever.; 1159.23, morn.; 1159.24, Ah!; 1159.29, me.; 1161.13, guage; 1162.27, embarassed; 1162.34, "tis; 1162.34, pace; 1165.30, hearts; 1166.31, less,; 1170.15, her's; 1185.17, back; 1186.14, then on; 1200.20, persistance.; 1203.9, him

Notes

In the notes below, the reference numbers denote page and line of this volume (the line count includes titles and headings). No note is made for material included in standard desk-reference books such as *Webster's Collegiate* and *Webster's Biographical* dictionaries. Biblical quotations are keyed to the King James Version. Quotations from Shakespeare are keyed to *The Riverside Shakespeare*, ed. G. Blakemore Evans (Boston: Houghton Mifflin, 1974). Classical references are keyed to the Loeb edition. Chinese romanizations, if not keyed to Pound's spelling, follow the Wade-Giles system. The following is a partial list of works consulted in the preparation of the Notes, Note on the Texts, and Chronology: Peter Brooker, *A Student's Guide to the Selected Poems of Ezra Pound* (London: Faber & Faber, 1979); Humphrey Carpenter, *A Serious Character: The Life of Ezra Pound* (Boston: Houghton Mifflin, 1988); Mary Paterson Cheadle, *Ezra Pound's Confucian Translations* (Ann Arbor: The University of Michigan Press, 1997); Christine Froula, *A Guide to Ezra Pound's Selected Poems* (New York: New Directions, 1982); Donald Gallup, *Ezra Pound: A Bibliography* (Charlottesville: University of Virginia Press, 1983); Simon Leys (ed. and trans.), *The Analects of Confucius* (New York: Norton, 1997); Akiko Miyake, Sanehide Kodama, and Nicholas Teele (eds.), *A Guide to Ezra Pound and Ernest Fenollosa's Classic Noh Theatre of Japan* (Orono, ME: The National Poetry Foundation, 1994); K. K. Ruthven, *A Guide to Ezra Pound's Personæ (1926)* (Berkeley: University of California Press, 1969); Carroll F. Terrell (ed.), *Paideuma: A Journal Devoted to Ezra Pound Scholarship, 1970–2003*; Carroll F. Terrell, *A Companion to the Cantos of Ezra Pound* (Berkeley: University of California Press, 1980); J. J. Wilhelm, *The American Roots of Ezra Pound* (New York: Garland, 1985); and *Ezra Pound: The Tragic Years 1925–1972* (University Park, PA: Penn State University Press, 1994). The editor would like to thank Mary de Rachewiltz, John Hamilton, and Eliot Weinberger.

1.1   HILDA'S BOOK]   In 1907 Pound gave these poems in a handmade book to Hilda Doolittle (1886–1961), his girlfriend at the time and later the poet writing under the pseudonym H.D.

3.15   light]   Michael King, the editor of "Hilda's Book," in *End to Torment: A Memoir of Ezra Pound by H.D.* (New York: New Directions, 1979) indicates that this is a probable reading. In the following line, words between "As" and "a cloak" (here represented by blank space) are illegible; "air" is a probable reading.

3.32   *Ecco il libro:*]   Here is the book.

4.3–8   *"Era mea . . . veniam"*]   For Pound's translation see 146.10–14.

4.12   *La Donzella Beata*]   The Blessed Damozel.

5.11   *Ver Novum*]   New Spring.

6.10   raed]   sound.

6.28   "Naethless, . . . go"]   Cf. Ruth 1:16.

8.22   *Per Saecula*]   Through Centuries.

12.5   *Li Bel Chasteus*]   The Handsome Chasteus.

12.32   Tintagoel]   According to legend Tintagel, a castle on the northern Cornish coast, was the site of King Arthur's conception.

13.20   *Era Venuta*]   She Had Come.

14.4   Daphne . . . bow]   See Ovid, *Metamorphoses*, I, where Daphne is transformed into a tree. Pound's term of endearment for Hilda was Dryad (a tree-nymph).

14.5   that god-feasting couple old]   Baucis and Philemon. See Ovid, *Metamorphoses*, VIII.

15.19   chançonnette]   Small song.

19.2   A LUME SPENTO]   When this book was reprinted in 1965 as part of *A Lume Spento and Other Early Poems*, Pound wrote the following "Foreword (1964)," signed "E.P." ("Bill W." is William Carlos Williams):

> A collection of stale creampuffs. "Chocolate creams, who hath forgotten you?"
>
> At a time when Bill W. was perceiving the "Coroner's Children."
>
> As to why a reprint? No lessons to be learned save the depth of ignorance, or rather the superficiality of non-perception—neither eye nor ear. Ignorance that didn't know the meaning of "Wardour Street."

20.12   in memoriam . . . primus]   In memory of him who to me was the first in dearness.

20.13   William Brooke Smith]   Painter friend of Pound's at the University of Pennsylvania; died of consumption (1884–1908).

22.6–9   The Legend . . . Vidal]   The "Legend" is Pound's invention. The story of the fictitious Miraut de Garzelas is a pastiche of the biographical *vidas* or *razos* of the troubadours. For Peire Vidal's story, see 107.10–16.

22.16   Malvern]   Forest in Worcestershire.

24.5   *Cino*]   An early pseudonym of Pound's (see also 302.27). One of the poem's typescripts reads: "C. Polnesi not to be confounded with the better known 'Cino da Pistoia'"—mentioned by Dante as one of his poet friends.

25.16   'Pollo Phoibee]   Phoebus Apollo.

26.1   *In Epitaphium Eius*]   Regarding His Epitaph.

26.5–6   "whereby . . . stars."]   Dante, *Paradiso,* XXXIII, 145.

26.13   *Na*]   Lady.

26.14   (*Que . . . mal*)]   Though thou wish me ill (see 26.28). Adapted from "Dompna Pois de Me No'us Cal" by the Provençal poet Bertrand de Born (*ca.* 1140–*ca.* 1214; alternately spelled "Bertran" or "Bertrans"). See 283.9–285.10 for Pound's translation.

27.25   Aultaforte]   Hautefort, Bertrand de Born's castle.

28.16–19   Towards the Noel . . . winds]   Lines adapted from Villon's *Le Lais*: "Sur le Noel, morte saison, / Que les loups se vivent de vent."

29.11   *A Villonaud. . . . Gibbet*]   In imitation of the catalogues of names in Villon's prison poem, *Le Testament,* Pound includes proper names drawn from Villon's poem (Caldou, François, Jehan, Margot, Marienne Ydole) as well as others of his own coinage.

29.13   "*En cest bourdel . . . estat*"]   The refrain from Villon's "Ballade de la Grosse Margot" (in *Le Testament*), translated by John Payne as "Within this brothel where we keep our state."

29.17   "*Frères humains . . . vivez.*"]   The opening line of "L'Epitaphe de Villon," translated by Swinburne as "Men, brother men, that after us yet live."

30.16   St. Hubert]   Patron saint of hunters.

30.27   "Haulte Citee."]   High city.

31.25   *Fifine*]   Central character of Browning's dramatic monologue *Fifine at the Fair* (1872), a latter-day Don Juan's defense of infidelity.

32.4   "I thirst." . . . sponge of gall.]   Cf. John 19:28–29.

33.1   *Anima Sola*]   Solitary Soul.

34.22   *In Tempore Senectutis*]   In the Time of Old Age.

35.26   *Famam Librosque Cano*]   Of Fame and Books I Sing. Cf. the opening of Virgil's *Aeneid,* "Arma virumque cano" ("Of arms and the man I sing").

36.29   Loquitur]   He speaks.

38.1   *Scriptor Ignotus*]   Unknown Writer.

38.2   K. R. H.]   Katherine Ruth Heyman (1887–1944), concert pianist for whom Pound briefly acted as an impresario in Venice in 1908.

39.20   "Youth's Dear Book"]   Dante's *Vita nuova.*

40.1   *Vana*]   Evokes Giovanna, the name of Guido Cavalcanti's first great love, according to Dante's *Vita nuova*. "Praise of Ysolt" (83.1–84.28) is an expanded version of "Vana."

41.1   *In Morte De*]   I.e. In Morte Di, "on the death of."

41.14   *Threnos*]   Dirge.

42.4   Tintagoel]   See note 12.32.

43.19   *Malrin*]   A typescript of this poem contains the note: "To give concrete for a symbol, to explain a parable, is for me always a limiting, a restricting; yet, because some to whom this has already come have not seen into it, I will say this: that it arises from a perception how the all-soul of mankind is one and joineth itself wholly at some time and returneth to God as a bride. And he the great hero of the new things spiritual is whoso waiteth for all the rest aiding as he may, yet daring to be last. / Ezra Pound, Milligan Place, Crawfordsville, Ind."

46.1   *Invern*]   Evokes "inverno," the Italian word for winter.

46.20   vortex of the cone]   "The 'cone' is I presume the 'Vritta' whirlpool, vortex-ring of the Yogi's cosmogony." [Pound's note in the poem's typescript.]

46.30   crescent . . . *me.*]   "Plotinus teaching 'that one could not dwell alone but must ever bring forth souls from himself.' The sonnet tho an accurate record of sensation and no mere (not) theorizing is in closer accord with a certain Hindoo teacher whose name I have not yet found." [Pound's note in the poem's typescript.]

47.15   *Aegupton*]   Aeguptus is the legendary conqueror of Egypt.

47.24   *Manus animam pinxit—*]   My hand painted my soul.

48.11–14   I . . . body.]   Lines omitted when the poem was collected in *Personæ* (1926).

49.15   *E. McC.*]   Eugene McCartney, a fencing partner of Pound's at the University of Pennsylvania.

50.16   *Salve O Pontifex!*]   Hail O High Priest!

50.19   Iacchus]   Cult name of Dionysus.

52.38   Vicisti, Nazerenus!]   You have conquered, Nazarene.

54.14–16   "No tongue . . . strong."]   From J. A. Symonds' translation of Michelangelo's poem "On Dante Alighieri" (included in *The Spirit of Romance*).

54.20   *Fistulae*]   Reed pipes.

55.10   *La Regina Avrillouse*]   The April-like Queen, name of a Provençal dance song which, as Pound notes in *The Spirit of Romance*, "may have been used in connection with such fragments of the worship of Flora and Venus as survived in the spring merrymakings: the dance itself is clearly discernible in its verbal rhythm."

57.9 "jolif bachillier"] Handsome youth.

59.15 *Oltre La Torre: Rolando*] Beyond the Tower: Roland.

61.3 *San Vio*] The Campo San Vio runs into the Grand Canal of Venice.

62.2 After Joachim du Bellay] A pastiche of *L'Olive* (1549), sonnet cycle by Joachim du Bellay (1522–1560).

64.1 *For a Play*] Entitled "Plot for Play" in Pound's table of contents for the "San Trovaso Notebook." Maurice Maeterlinck (1862–1949), Belgian author of symbolist dramas.

68.10 WESTON ST. LLEWMYS] Pseudonym of Pound.

69.1 *Ognisanti*] Canal in Venice near Pound's lodgings in San Trovaso.

69.17 O Dieu . . . coeurs!] O God, purify our hearts!

72.8 Malrin] See note 43.19.

74.26 "queren lo jorn"] "Goes crying the day." From Giraut de Bornelh's "Reis glorios," translated by Pound as "for I hear that bird a-singing / Who goes crying the day through the wood."

74.27 *Partenza di Venezia*] Departure from Venice.

75.15 *Caditurus*] Likely to Fall.

76.30 *forsitan*] Perhaps.

78.6 "*E paion . . . leggieri.*"] And seem to be so light upon the wind. *Inferno*, V, 72.

78.7 "*Ombre . . . briga.*"] Shades borne by that strife. *Inferno*, V, 49.

78.8 *Beddoesque*] In the manner of the poet Thomas Lovell Beddoes (1803–1849), author of *Death's Jest Book* (pub. 1850).

79.2 From the Latin . . . Capilupus] Pound discovered Capilupus' poem "Epitaph. Christophori Columbi" in a 1608 anthology edited by Ranutius Gherus.

79.25 *T. H.*] The English poet Thomas Hood (1799–1845).

80.15 the Florentine] Dante.

80.20 *Nel Biancheggiar*] In the Gloaming.

82.3 MARY MOORE] Pound's girlfriend in 1907.

86.1 *Xenia*] A gift of friendship; a title used by Martial for certain of his epigrams.

86.10   *Occidit*]   Sets. Entitled "Golden Sunset" in manuscript.

86.27–29   *Nel . . . dei.*]   Gazing upon her [Beatrice] I became within me such as Glaucus became on tasting of the grass that made him sea-fellow of the other gods.

90.4–5   "Quasi . . . soul."]   See Coleridge, "On the Principles of Genial Criticism": "the Greeks called a beautiful object καλόν quasi καλοῦν, i.e., *calling on* the soul, which receives it instantly, and welcomes it as something connatural."

90.24   "Veltro"]   Greyhound.

91.1   *Guillaume de Lorris*]   Author of the first portion of the 13th-century allegorical poem *Le Roman de la Rose*.

91.33   "Che lo glorifico."]   "In the Piazza dei Signori, you will find an in-scription which translates thus:
> 'It is here Can Grande della Scala gave welcome to Dante Alighieri, the *same which glorified him*, dedicating to him that third his song eternal.'
>> C.G. vi accolse D.A. che lo
>> glorifico dedicandogli la terza,
>> delle eterne sue cantiche.' " [Pound's note, in *Personae* (1909)]

92.13   *Cioè*]   Namely.

92.26   all things,]   "Ref. Richard of St. Victor. 'On the preparation of the soul for contemplation,' where he distinguishes between cogitation, meditation, and contemplation.

In cogitation the thought or attention flits aimlessly about the subject.

In meditation it circles round it, that is, it views it systematically, from all sides, gaining perspective.

In contemplation it radiates from a center, that is, as light from the sun it reaches out in an infinite number of ways to things that are related to or dependent on it.

The words above are my own, as I have not the Benjamin Minor by me.

Following St. Victor's figure of radiation: Poetry in its acme is expression from contemplation." [Pound's note in *Personae* (1909).]

92.33   Fenicè]   Phoenix; also the name of the opera house in Venice.

93.26   San Pietro by Adige]   "San Pietro Incarnato. There are several rows of houses intervening between it and the river." [Pound's note in *Personae* (1909).]

94.19   *Alba Belingalis*]   "MS in Latin, with refrain,
> 'L alba par umet mar atras el poy
> Pas abrigil miraclar Tenebris.'
It was and may still be the oldest fragment of Provençal known" [Pound's note in *Personae* (1909)]

The poem was first published in *Hamilton Literary Magazine* in 1905 as "Belangal Alba," i.e. "Bilingual Dawnsong."

97.1   *From the Saddle*]   An adaptation of one of the sonnets to Diane Salviati by Agrippa d'Aubigné (1552–1630), composed in the late 16th century but first published in 1874 under the title *Le Printemps*.

97.17   *Marvoil*]   The Provençal poet Arnaut de Mareuil (*fl.* 1170–1200). He was said to have fallen in love with Azalais de Toulouse, the wife of the Vicomte de Beziers, and was sent away when Alfonso II became jealous of their relationship. At the end of *Personae* (1909), Pound included the note:
> "The Personae are:
> Arnaut of Marvoil, a troubadour, date 1170–1200.
> The Countess (in her own right) of Burlatz, and of Beziers, being
>   the wife of
> The Vicomte of Beziers.
> Alfonso IV of Aragon
> Tibors of Mont Ausier. For fuller mention of her see the 'razos' on
>   Bertran of Born. She is contemporary with the other persons, but
>   I have no strict warrant for dragging her name into this particular
>   affair."

99.5   *Mihi pergamena deest*]   I do not have the parchment.

100.9   *Nineveh*]   Alludes to the funeral rites for poets in Nineveh, site of the royal residence of Assyria.

100.29   Raama]   Later publications of the poem read "Raana." Rana is a Norse sea goddess; Raamah is named as one of the sons of Cush in Genesis 10:7.

104.2   Carlos Tracy Chester]   Philadelphia clergyman who encouraged the adolescent Pound's literary aspirations.

104.3   *"amicitiae longaevitate"*]   In long-lasting friendship.

105.1   *Guido*]   Guido Cavalcanti (*ca.* 1255–1300), poet, mentor of Dante and addressee of the latter's Sonnet XXXII ("Guido vorrei"). Pound's poem is Cavalcanti's imaginary reply to Dante's suggestion that he, Guido, and Lapo Gianni together embark with their three ladies on an idyllic voyage of love.

105.14   *Sestina: Altaforte*]   Also known as "The Bloody Sestina" to Pound's circle in London. The voice of the 12th-century troubadour Bertrand de Born resonates through a number of Pound's early works ("Na Audiart," "Planh for the Young English King," "Dompna Pois de Me No'us Cal," "Near Perigord"). In *Inferno*, XXVIII, 118–123, Dante placed the poet (holding his own severed head) in Malebolge among the sowers of discord for setting Prince Henry against his brother Richard and their father Henry II.

105.15   LOQUITUR]   He speaks. *En*: Sir

105.18   Eccovi!]   Here you are!

106.10   destriers]   War-horses.

109.23   Simon Zelotes]   One of Jesus' apostles.

111.16   Flaminius]   Pound discusses the neo-Latin verse of the 16-century poet Marcus Antonius Flaminius in a chapter entitled "Poeti Latini" in *The Spirit of Romance*, which also includes the Latin original of this hymn.

113.2   "La Mère Inconnue"]   The Unknown Mother. Unidentified painting.

113.12   chere]   fondness.

113.17   *Rackham*]   Arthur Rackham (1867–1939), English illustrator and watercolorist.

114.1   *Laudantes . . . Templi*]   Corrupt Latin: Ten [Stanzas] Praising the Temple of Giovanna's Beauty. May allude to Cavalcanti's Giovanna; see notes 40.1 and 204.1.

115.17   Yrma]   An invented place-name, as are "Ahva," "Asedon," and "Ahthor" in the lines following.

117.9   *Aux Belles de Londres*]   To the Beautiful Women of London.

118.1   *Nils Lykke*]   A character in Ibsen's play *Lady Inger of Ostrat* (1855), dealing with the liberation of medieval Norway.

118.12–14   *A Song . . .* Vega]   Pound considered writing a doctoral dissertation at the University of Pennsylvania on the Spanish playwright Lope de Vega (1562–1635). "Los Pastores de Belen" ("The Bethlehem Shepherds") is discussed in *The Spirit of Romance*.

119.12   *Planh*]   Lament.

120.25   *Alba Innominata*]   Based on the anonymous ("innominata") Provençal "En un vergier sotz fue." The "alba" is a song form lamenting the arrival of dawn and the separation of lovers.

124.1   *A War Song*]   From Bertrand de Born's "Be.m plai lo gais temps de pascor."

124.21   *The Lark*]   From Bernart de Ventadorn's "Con vei la lauzeta mover."

125.25   *Sequaire*]   Or "sequence," a form of rhythmic Latin prose developed by the monk Notker Balbulus, also known as Godeshalk (805–869). Pound's interest in this form was sparked by Remy de Gourmont's *Latin mystique* (1892).

129.3–4   "*Quos . . .* PROPERTIUS]   "That I may bear them [i.e. "my three books"] to Persephone as my most precious offering." Propertius, *Elegies* II, xiiA, 26.

131.2   Manning's "Korè"]   Note by Pound on the poem's typescript: "'Korè or Maiden is especially used of Persephone with regard to her being stolen by Lord of Dis—and thereby causing death of summer." Frederic Manning (1882–1935) was an Australian-born poet, critic, and novelist.

131.3–4   "*Et huiusmodi . . . secuti semus.*"]   "This kind of stanza is used by Arnaut Daniel in almost all his canzoni, and we have followed him in ours." Dante is here referring to his canzone 'Al poco giorno ed al grand cerchio d'ombra,' which also provides the model for "Canzon: The Yearly Slain."

133.1   *Canzon: The Spear*]   In *Provença* (1910), Pound included the note: "This fashion of stanza is used by Jaufré Rudel in the song *'D'un amor de lonh.'* The measure is to be sung rather than spoken." For Pound's 1905 translation of Jaufré Rudel's poem, see 1150.1–1151.18.

135.1   *Canzon*]   "The form and measure are those of Piere Vidal's *'Ab l'alen tir vas me l'aire.'* The song is fit only to be sung, and is not to be spoken." [Pound's note in *Provença.*]

136.1   *Canzon: Of Incense*]   "To this form sings Arnaut Daniel, with seven stanzas instead of five." [Pound's note in *Provença.*]

138.1   *Canzone: Of Angels*]   "This form is not Provençal, but that of Dante's matchless *'Voi che intendendo il terzo ciel movete.'* Il Convito, II, bar the decasyllabic lines which one can scarcely escape in English but which do not, despite all statements to the contrary, correspond to the hendecasyllabic lines in the Italian." [Pound's note in *Provença.*]

140.27   *To Guido Cavalcanti*]   "This poem foreruns a translation of 'The Sonnets and Ballate of Guido' now in preparation." [Pound's note in *Provença.*] See pp. 183–227.

141.8   and hers of San Michele]   Pound considered the thaumaturgic image of the Madonna of San Michele in Orto a direct link to the pagan "cult of Amor" developed in Provence; see note 214.7–8.

141.10   *Tenzone*]   A Provençal poetic form consisting of an exchange largely in the form of invective.

141.11   LA MENTE]   The mind.

141.20   IL CUORE]   The heart.

141.22   '*Ronsard me celebroit!*']   "Ronsard celebrated me [when I was beautiful]," from Ronsard's sonnet "Quand vous serez bien vieille." Yeats had freely translated the poem as "When you are old and grey and full of sleep."

141.27   *Sonnet . . . Questa?*]   A free imitation of Cavalcanti's sonnet, "Chi è questa che vien, ch'ogni uom la mira." Cf. later versions, 199.31–200.10 and 575.1–14.

142.22 assoneth!] From "assonare," to rhyme in assonance.

142.23 *Canzon: The Vision*] "The form is that of Arnaut Daniel's 'Sols sui que sai lo sobrafan quem sortz.' " [Pound's note in *Provença*.]

146.2–8 Era mea . . .Veniam?] See also 4.2–10.

146.9 ANGLICÈ REDDITA] Rendered into English.

146.15 *Paracelsus*] Name of Swiss alchemist Bombast von Hohenheim (1493–1541). The poem is an epilogue to Browning's "Paracelsus."

147.5 Avernus] In Roman mythology, a crater giving entrance to the underworld; also a name for the underworld itself.

147.7 Iope] Cassiope, wife of Ethiopian King Cepheas and mother of Andromeda. *Tyro*: Poseidon assumed the shape of a river god and seduced Tyro, who then gave birth to the twins Neleus and Pelias.

147.8 Europa] Taking the form of a bull, Zeus carried off Europa and raped her. *Pasiphae*: Wife of Cretan King Minos, Pasiphae was made by Poseidon to fall in love with a bull; the result of their union was the Minotaur.

147.17–18 *Speech . . . Apuleius*] See the *Golden Ass* of Lucius Apuleius, Books IV and V. Pound wrote admiringly of Apuleius in *The Spirit of Romance*.

148.1 "*Blandula, Tenulla, Vagula*"] Cf. the emperor's Hadrian's dying address to his soul: "Animula, vagula, blandula, / hospes, comesque, corporis / quæ nunc abibis in loca, / pallidula, rigida, nudula? / nec ut soles dabis iocos!" ("Little soul, wandering, gentle guest and companion of the body, into what places will you now go, pale, stiff, and naked, no longer sporting as you did!") The adjective "tenulla" ("tender") is an interpolation from Flaminius (see note 111.16).

148.6 at Sirmio] Catullus' father owned a villa at Sirmio (now Sirmione), a town on the south shore of Lake Garda in northern Italy. Catullus XXXI praises Sirmio, "bright eye of peninsulas and islands," as a happy place of rest following arduous travels. Pound spent the spring of 1910 in Sirmione working on his Cavalcanti translations.

148.16 peaks of Riva?] The lower Italian Alps rise up behind Riva, a town on the northernmost part of the Lago di Garda.

148.17 *Erat Hora*] It Was the Hour.

149.9 *La Nuvoletta*] The Little Cloud.

149.27 *Rosa Sempiterna*] Everlasting Rose.

150.9 Pico della Mirandola] Italian humanist (1463–1494) and chief exponent of Neoplatonism at the court of Lorenzo de' Medici.

151.17 From . . . du Bellay] From his *Antiquetez de Rome* (1558).

151.18　"*Troica Roma resurges.*"] Trojan Rome shall arise. Propertius, *Elegies*, IV, i, 87.

152.1　*Her Monument . . . Thereon*] From "Sopra il Ritratto di Una Bella Donna" by Giacomo Leopardi (1798–1837).

154.34　*Sic . . . deest.*] Thus the end is always missing.

155.2　SATIEMUS] Cf. Propertius, *Elegies*, II, xv, 23: "Dum nos fata sinunt, oculos satiemus amore" ("while the Fates grant it, let us glut our eyes with love"), which was also used as the title of a poem by Ernest Dowson.

155.24　"*Pere . . . Denis*"] "Father Abelard at Saint Denis," from the *ubi sunt* of Villon's "Ballade des Dames du Temps Jadis."

157.26　"*Exultasti:*"] Exsultavisiti: You have rejoiced.

158.12　*Pax . . . natast.*"] Peace on earth is now born.

158.30　*dolentibus*] In pain.

158.35　*Explicit.*] The End.

159.1　*Maestro di Tocar*] The Master of Touch.

159.2　*(W.R.)*] Walter Morse Rummel (1887–1953), German-born pianist and composer; see note 1167.18.

161.1　*Translations from Heine*] Retitled "Translations and Adaptations from Heine" in *Personæ* (1926), which also includes as number VIII of the sequence a version entitled "Night Song" (in the present volume "After Heine" in "Oboes," 564.20–28). These are among Pound's first experiments in the kind of modern irony he would later define as "logopoeia." The sources in Heine's works are as follows: I: *Die Heimkehr* (1826), LXXVI ("Bist du wirklich mir so feindlich"); II: *Lyrisches Intermezzo* (1827), XXI ("So hast du ganz und gar vergessen"); III: *Die Heimkehr*, LXXXVIII ("Sag', wo ist dein schönes Liebchen"); IV: *Die Heimkehr*, LXVI ("Mir traümt: ich bin der liebe Gott"); V: *Die Heimkehr*, LXXIX ("Doch die Kastraten klagten"); VI: *Die Heimkehr*, LXV ("Diesen liebenwürd'gen Jüngling"); VII: *Die Harzreise* (1826), "Die Ilse."

163.13　*Philistia's*] The modern sense of "Philistine" derives from Heine, via Matthew Arnold.

164.17　*Und Drang*] After *Sturm und Drang* (Storm and Stress), movement of early German romanticism. In *Personæ* (1926), sections VII through XII of this sequence appeared as separate poems.

164.19　Binyon] Laurence Binyon (1869–1943), English poet, translator of Dante, and Keeper of the Prints and Drawings at the British Museum. He was a close friend when Pound lived in London.

165.10　"gray above the green"] See Swinburne, "A Ballad of Burdens" (1886): "Thou shalt see / Gold tarnished, and the grey above the green; /

And as the thing thou seest thy face shall be, / And no more as the thing before time seen."

165.30   And I . . . years,]   Cf. the closing lines of Yeats, "The Old Age of Queen Maeve" (1903).

166.3   "*Far . . . trionphare*"]   To have fine weather and triumph.

166.4   "I have . . . mind"]   Swinburne, "The Triumph of Time" (1866), line 49.

168.4   house not made with hands,]   II Corinthians 5:1.

169.3   Oisin]   Ossian.

169.15   "of days and nights"]   Cf. Arthur Symons's *Days and Nights* (1889), where he observes that since art's true subject is "man with trouble born to death," the poet's "song is less of Days than Nights."

169.23   Benacus]   Lake Garda (see note 148.6).

170.8   HORAE BEATAE INSCRIPTIO]   Inscription for an Hour of Happiness.

171.8   Roger de Coverley's]   Imaginary country gentleman created by Joseph Addison.

171.10   sic . . . mundi]   "Thus the glory of the world increases," ironic adaptation of Latin motto "Sic transit gloria mundis" ("So the glory of the world passes away").

171.14   aegrum vulgus]   Diseased rabble.

171.18   cari laresques, penates]   Dear family and household gods.

171.28   "The jester . . . garden."]   See the opening line of Yeats, "The Cap and the Bells" (1899).

173.3   *Leviora*]   These three sonnets and "L'Art" were grouped under the title "Leviora" in the proof-sheets of *Canzoni*. Only "L'Art" was included in the published volume. "Leviora" means "lighter matters."

173.15   "directoire"]   Alludes to the revealing gowns of the French "Directoire" period (1795–1799).

173.16   *sa chevelure*]   Her hair.

173.21   HIC JACET]   Here lies.

174.7   dericus]   Mockery.

174.7   ingides]   Greek nominative plural ending in the third declension.

174.21   *Hulme (T. E.) and Fitzgerald*]   T. E. Hulme and Desmond Fitzgerald, two members of the proto-Imagist group of poets (sometimes known as the Secession Club) with whom Pound associated in 1909 in London. For the "Complete Works of T. E. Hulme," see note 229.2.

174.28   guinea stamp] In his early typescripts, Pound often used the pound-sign (£) to signify an erasure.

175.4   breeks] Breaches, trousers (Scots).

175.6   birkie] Jocular term for a boastful man (Scots).

175.16   siller] Silver (Scots).

175.17   maun] Must, or manage to do (Scots).

175.28   wame] With diseased belly (Scots).

175.29   *Redondillas . . . Sort*] In *Canzoni*'s proofs the poem was entitled "Locksley hall, forty years further." Tennyson's "Locksley Hall Sixty Years After, Etc.," whose meter and matter Pound imitates (with bows to Byron and Whitman), was published in 1886. A *redondilla* is a Spanish form, an octosyllabic quatrain with an abba rhyme scheme.

176.10   Desenzano] Town on Lake Garda.

176.25   But Yeats . . . essay,] Pound's note in the *Canzoni* proofs: "*Yeats (W.B.),* specialist in renaissances."

176.29   *"Mi Platz"*] "It pleases me." Allusion to one of Bertrand de Born's war songs, translated by Pound as "Well pleaseth me the sweet time of Easter" (see 124.4).

176.35   T. Roosevelt.] Pound's note in the proofs: "President of one of the American republics early in the twentieth century. Not to be confused with Theodoric, Gothorum imperator."

177.4   Plarr] "*Plarr, V.G.,* of the Rhymers' Club." [Pound's note.] See note 553.15.

177.4   Fred Vance] "An American painter, chief works: 'Christ appearing on the Waters' (Salon, Paris '03) and the new bar-room in San Diego." [Pound's note.]

177.4   Whiteside] "An American landscape painter." [Pound's note.]

179.10   sound stave of Spinoza] "The particular passages I had in mind run as follows: 'The more perfection a thing possesses the more it acts, and the less it suffers, and conversely the more it acts, the more perfect it is.' *On the power of the intellect or human liberty. Proposition xl.* 'When the mind contemplates itself and its power of acting, it rejoices, and it rejoices in proportion to the distinctness with which it imagines itself and its power of action.' *Origin and nature of the Affects, xiii.* And another passage for which I cannot at the moment give the exact references, where he defines 'The intellectual love' of anything as 'The understanding of its perfections.' " [Pound's note.]

179.14   *rôti de dindon*] Roast turkey.

179.21   Tamlin] *Tam Lin*, a Scottish fairy ballad.

180.5   Arma . . . ab oris,]   Cf. the opening line of Virgil's *Aeneid*.

180.29   "Nascitur ordo"]   Order is born.

180.31   Ehrlich]   Paul Ehrlich (1854–1915), German bacteriologist, winner of the 1908 Nobel Prize for Physiology or Medicine for his work in immunology.

180.33–34   Fracastori . . . "De Morbo.")]   Perhaps "De Morbo Gallico" (1534), a study of syphilis.

181.2   Klimt . . . Zwintscher.]   Pound's note: "Klimt of Vienna, and Zwintscher of Leipzig. Two too modern painters."

181.3   *Admiror, sum ergo?*]   I admire, therefore I am?

181.39   *dégagé*]   Disengaged.

181.40   saeculum in parvo]   Century in miniature.

182.1   Bergson's]   "French postpragmatical philosopher." [Pound's note.]

182.8   Steibelt]   Daniel Steibelt (1765–1823), German composer and pianist.

184.3   VIOLET . . . HUEFFER]   The English novelist Violet Hunt (1862–1942) lived out of wedlock with the married novelist Ford Madox Hueffer (later Ford; 1873–1939) in South Lodge, Kensington.

186.1–24   *Oh dissi lui . . . perchè muta lato.*]   Dante, *Purgatorio*, XI, 79–102: " Oh," I said to him, "are you not Oderisi, the honor of Gubbio and the honor of that art which in Paris is called 'illumination'?" "Brother," he said, "more smiling are the pages that Franco Bolognese paints: the honor is now all his—and mine in part. Truly I should not have been so courteous while I lived, because of the great desire for excellence whereon my heart was set. For such pride the fee is paid here; nor should I yet be here, were it not that, having power to sin, I turned to God. O empty glory of human powers! how briefly lasts the green upon the top, if it is not followed by barbarous times! Cimabue thought to hold the field in painting, and now Giotto has the cry, so that the other's fame is dim; so has the one Guido taken from the other the glory of our tongue—and he perchance is born that shall chase the one and the other from the nest. Earthly fame is naught but a breath of wind, which now comes hence and now comes thence, changing its name because it changes quarter" (translated by Charles S. Singleton, 1970).

188.23   "*Vedrai . . . salita*"]   Then shalt thou see her virtue risen in heaven. From Ballata V (see 217.26).

189.21   "F.Z."]   Francesco Zanzotto, editor of the *Parnaso Italiano* anthology (1846), whose second volume contained the Cavalcanti base-text from which Pound worked.

189.27   Rossetti]   D. G. Rossetti's *Early Italian Poets* (1861) was revised and rearranged as *Dante and His Circle* (1874).

190.35   sonnet to Neronne.]   Sonnet XIX (206.1–18).

191.19   Brunelleschi]   In 1929 Pound added here: "Sacchetti's anecdote shows him so absorbed in a chess game that a small boy is able to nail down his coat-tails, first scrunching up several folds of the cloth, so that the nail might get a good hold." This scene figures in Pound's unpublished radio opera, "Cavalcanti: A Sung Dramedy in 3 Acts" (1932).

191.22   "*robustezza e splendore*"]   Robustness and splendor.

191.23   *sobrio e dotto*]   Sober and learned.

192.13   matchless . . . ballad]   Ballata XI (223.13–224.26).

192.15   before Dante saw the vision,]   I.e., of Beatrice.

192.24–25   sonnet . . . *vorrei*]   "Guido Invites You Thus" (105.1–13).

192.26–28   One modern writer . . . Paradise.]   See note 204.1.

192.34–36   "*Tu mi . . . primavera.*"]   Dante, *Purgatorio*, XXVIII, 49–51: "You make me recall where and what Proserpine was at the time her mother lost her, and she the spring." [Singleton's translation.]

193.12   otherwise]   The English edition of *The Sonnets and Ballate of Guido Cavalcanti* adds: "Such explanations might give us one more reason, which were superfluous, for the respect paid to Farinata (*Inferno*, X)."

194.7–8   *Sequitur. . . inest:*]   It follows, or rather belongs to this.

194.14–18   I consider Carducci . . . *tremare*.]   Nicola Arnone's *Rime di Guido Cavalcanti* (Firenze: Sansoni) was published in 1881; the poet Giosuè Carducci's anthology, *Antica lirica italiana: canzonette, canzoni, sonnetti dei secoli XIII–XV*, was brought out by the same publisher in 1907. Pound printed the original Italian of this line (from Sonnet VII) as "Che fa di clarità l'aer tremare," adding the following note in *The Translations* (1953): "This is by far the better reading if the sonnet is spoken, but the other reading: *tremare l'are*, can be sung, and that perhaps explains the persistent divergence between the best manuscripts at this point." Modern editors such as Contini print the line as: "Che far tremar di chiaritate l'âre."

194.24   Mithra]   Principle Persian deity, god of light and wisdom, closely associated with the sun; his cult, Mithraism, was one of the great religions of the Roman Empire.

194.37   *voi altri pochi*]   The few of you.

198.4   When . . . start]   The version in *Umbra* reads, "When dry words rattle in my throat and start."

198.7   from far]   "Cioè, io credo, da Venere—E.P." ["That is, I think, from Venus": Pound's note keyed to Cavalcanti's Italian.]

199.5   harsh place]   The version in *Umbra* reads "proud keep."

199.31   *VII*]   Cf. Pound's other translations of this sonnet at 141.27–142.9 and 575.1–14.

200.20   Amor]   The version in *Umbra* reads "Love's self."

201.20   haut]   High.

201.26   *XI*]   Above Cavalcanti's Italian there appears the note, "cf. 'Se fosse amico il re del universo' ('if the King of the universe were friendly to us')." *Inferno*, V, 91.

201.27–202.3   If Mercy . . . audience.]   "Of Guido's relentless irony, in this case directed against himself, the artistic temperament, and 'service' generally, this sestet may serve as example." [Pound's note, keyed to Cavalcanti's Italian.]

202.27   *XIII*]   Cf. later translation at 575.16–29.

203.20   *XIV*]   Cf. later translation at 576.1–25.

204.1   *XV*]   Beneath Cavalcanti's Italian, Pound includes the following quotation and note: "*E lo nome di questa donna era Giovanna, salvo che per la sua beltate, secondo ch' altre crede, imposto l'era nome Primavera: e così era chiamata.* Dante, Vita Nuova, XXIV. Cf. Purgatorio, XXVIII, 49 et circa; ref 'Matelda,' by Adolpo Borgognoni: pub. S. Lapi, Citta da Castello." Rossetti translates the passage from the *Vita nuova* as "This lady's right name was Joan; but because of her comeliness (or at least it was so imagined) she was called of many *Primavera* (Spring)." In a note, Rossetti explains that "there is a play in the original upon the words *Primavera* (Spring) and *prima verrà* (she shall come first) [i.e. before Beatrice]."

204.16   *XVI*]   Cf. later translation at 576.27–577.6.

204.17   Guido Orlando]   The Italian poet Guido Orlandi Rustichelli (1265?–1338), who addressed a number of poems to Cavalcanti, including one translated by Pound at 1134.1–17.

205.1   *XVII*]   Cf. later translation at 577.8–24.

205.3   Bernardo da Bologna]   This may refer to the Bernardo addressed in Cino da Pistoia's sonnet "Bernardo, io veggio ch'una donna vene."

205.19   *XXII*]   Cf. "I think that thou has looked" at 1192.14–29. Keyed to Cavalcanti's Italian, Pound's note reads: "In Vita Nuova III, Dante writes: 'Many replied to this sonnet (*A ciasun' alma presa, e gentil core*) with varying interpretations; among those who replied was he whom I call first of my friends; he wrote at that time a sonnet which began:
         "*Vedesti al mio parere ogni valore.*"
And this was, as it were, the inception of the friendship between us, when he learned that I was the one who had sent him this (sonnet).'"

208.2–3   Dante . . . Beatrice.]   Pound borrows the subtitle from Rossetti, who notes: "this interesting sonnet must refer to the same Period of Dante's life regarding which he has made Beatrice address him in words of noble reproach when he meets her in Eden (*Purgatorio,* C, 30)."

208.21   Lappo Gianni]   A mutual friend of Dante and Cavalcanti.

209.1   *XXV*]   "He is in part parodying Guido Guinicelli's technically questionable sonnet, "*Chi vedesse a Lucia un var capuzzo.*" [Pound's note, keyed to Cavalcanti's Italian.]

209.18   *Of . . . Vision*]   The subtitle is omitted from the version that appears in *Umbra,* which also prints the sonnet as a single strophe.

209.24   He will not . . . enured]   *Umbra* version reads: "He is, he will not have his spirit so inured."

210.18   *XXVIII*]   "To him who understands it this is the most derrible of all the sonnets." [Pound's note, keyed to Cavalcanti's Italian.]

211.7   Monna Lagia]   Lappo Gianni's lady. See Sonnet XXIV, p. 208.

211.16   *XXX*]   "A.C.S. Triumph of Time. Cf. stanza 30, ll. 7–8." [Pound's note, keyed to Cavalcanti's Italian.] The Swinburne lines read: "For the worst is this after all; if they knew me, / Not a soul upon earth would pity me."

212.20   Cecco]   In his translation of this sonnet, Rossetti notes that the poem is "very obscure . . . the person addressed may be Cecco Angiolieri after he inherited his father's property."

213.20   *XXXIV*]   Cf. "Amore and Lagia" at 1193.1–16.

214.7–8   the Madonna of Or San Michele]   The Florentine chronicler Giovanni Villani recorded that on July 3, 1292, a "painted figure of St. Mary in the loggia of Orto San Michele" began to work miracles, which the Franciscans (the "brothers minor" of Pound's translation) sought to discredit. In the unpublished notes to *Guido Cavalcanti Rime,* Pound observed: "For what it may be worth in general interpretation, the Mendicant orders were anti-Averroist." Cf. "To Guido Cavalcanti," 140.27–141.9.

214.29   over-gleams]   This reading is taken from 1910 manuscript version of the poem; all published versions read "over-gleans."

215.1   *I*]   *Umbra* version includes subtitle "Fragment of a Canzone, miscalled a Ballata."

215.3   saffron]   *Umbra* version reads "lapping."

215.17   D.V.E.]   De Vulgari Eloquio.

215.19–21   Ladies . . . were]   *Umbra* version reads "Fair women I saw passing where she passed; / And none among them woman, to my vision; / But were."

216.13–14   So . . . surely!"]   *Umbra* version reads: "With such benignity /
That I am forced to cry: / 'Thou hast me utterly!' "

217.4–5   "A vileness . . . your estate!"]   In the 1912 American edition and
in *The Translations*, these lines read: "Beauty within, Oyez! Within, is dying.
/ On guard lest Beauty see your present state!" (The text printed here from
Pound's Cavalcanti, edited by David Anderson, is based on the 1912 Stephen
Swift edition published in London.)

217.14   Forth . . . lips,]   *Umbra* version reads "Spring forth between her
lips,".

217.16   Another . . . marvelous,]   *Umbra* version reads "Another, in
beauty, springeth marvellous,".

219.4–5   Who . . . us."]   *Umbra* version reads "Who sang, 'The rains /
Of love are falling, falling within us.' "

219.13   Tolouse lately."]   According to Rossetti, Cavalcanti undertook a
pilgrimage in 1292, "apparently with the intention of reaching Compostella,
but he was stopped in Toulouse (Musicia Salimbeni says Nîmes) either by ill-
ness or by his affair with Mandetta." The "golden roof" (220.14) is usually
identified as that of La Daurade, a church in Toulouse.

225.28   For Death . . . bent]   *Umbra* version reads, "For Grief drags to
my heart a heart so sore."

225.31   O mistress . . . intent.]   *Umbra* version reads, "O mistress,
spoiler of my valour's store!"

226.4   Lo . . . me]   *Umbra* version reads "Death's cometh on me."

226.24   my self-slaying mournful soul]   *Umbra* version reads "my self-
torturing soul."

229.2   RIPOSTES]   *Riposes* bore as its subtitle "Whereto Are Appended
The Complete Poetical Works of T. E. Hulme With Prefatory Note." In the
spring of 1909, Pound was briefly associated with the group of poets (F. S.
Flint, F. W. Tancred, Edward Storer) gathered around Thomas Ernest Hulme
(1883–1917) and sometimes referred to as the "Secession Club." By including
Hulme's "Complete Poetical Works" (described by Flint as "little Japanese
pictures") at end of *Riposes*, Pound engaged in a playful publicity stunt in-
tended to provide a genealogy for the as yet virtually nonexistent "*Imagistes*,"
here said to descend from Hulme's "forgotten school" of 1909. Not included
in *Personæ* (1926), Hulme's "Complete Poetical Works" were added to the ex-
panded version of the book published in 1949. Pound's "Prefatory Note" and
Hulme's poems in *Riposes* read as follows:

In publishing his *Complete Poetical Works* at thirty,* Mr Hulme has
set an enviable example to many of his contemporaries who have had less
to say.

They are reprinted here for good fellowship; for good custom, a cus-
tom out of Tuscany and of Provence; and thirdly, for convenience, seeing

their smallness of bulk; and for good memory, seeing that they recall certain evenings and meetings of two years gone, dull enough at the time, but rather pleasant to look back upon.

As for the "School of Images," which may or may not have existed, its principles were not so interesting as those of the "inherent dynamists" or of *Les Unanimistes*, yet they were probably sounder than those of a certain French school which attempted to dispense with verbs altogether; or of the Impressionists who brought forth:

> *"Pink pigs blossoming upon the hillside"*;

or of the Post-Impressionists who beseech their ladies to let down slate-blue hair over their raspberry-coloured flanks.

Ardoise rimed richly—ah, richly and rarely rimed!—with *framboise*.

As for the future, *Les Imagistes,* the descendants of the forgotten school of 1909, have that in their keeping.

I refrain from publishing my proposed *Historical Memoir* of their forerunner, because Mr Hulme has threatened to print the original propaganda.

E.P.

* Mr Pound has grossly exaggerated my age. —T.E.H.

AUTUMN

A touch of cold in the Autumn night—
I walked abroad,
And saw the ruddy moon lean over a hedge
Like a red-faced farmer.
I did not stop to speak, but nodded,
And round about were the wistful stars
With white faces like town children.

MANA ABODA

Beauty is the marking-time, the stationary vibration, the feigned ecstasy
    of an arrested impulse unable to reach its natural end.

Mana Aboda, whose bent form
The sky in archèd circle is,
Seems ever for an unknown grief to mourn.
Yet on a day I heard her cry:
"I weary of the roses and the singing poets—
Josephs all, not tall enough to try."

ABOVE THE DOCK

Above the quiet dock in mid night,
Tangled in the tall mast's corded height,
Hangs the moon. What seemed so far away
Is but a child's balloon, forgotten after play.

THE EMBANKMENT
(The fantasia of a fallen gentleman on a cold, bitter night.)

Once, in finesse of fiddles found I ecstasy,
In the flash of gold heels on the hard pavement.
Now see I
That warmth's the very stuff of poesy.
Oh, God, make small
The old star-eaten blanket of the sky,
That I may fold it round me and in comfort lie.

CONVERSION
Lighthearted I walked into the valley wood
In the time of hyacinths,
Till beauty like a scented cloth
Cast over, stifled me. I was bound
Motionless and faint of breath
By loveliness that is her own eunuch.

Now pass I to the final river
Ignominiously, in a sack, without sound,
As any peeping Turk to the Bosphorous.

In *Umbra* (1920), Pound added to the "Complete Poetical Works" of Hulme his own "Poem: Abbreviated from the Conversation of Mr. T. E. H." (see 568.9–24).

231.1   *Silet*]   He is silent.

231.18   "Time's bitter flood"!]   Yeats, "The Lover Pleads with His Friend for Old Friends" (1899).

231.25   *Apparuit*]   Cf. Dante's *Vita nuova*, when he first sees Beatrice: "At that moment the animate spirit, which dwelleth in the lofty chamber whither all the senses carry their perceptions, was filled with wonder, and speaking more especially unto the spirits of the eyes, said these words: *Apparuit iam beatitudo vestra*. ['Your beatitude hath now been made manifest unto you.']" (trans. D. G. Rossetti)

232.22   Nikoptis.]   Pound's invention.

234.25   *N.Y.*]   The version in *Umbra* includes the note: "Madison Ave. 1910."

235.18   "*Phasellus Ille*"]   Cf. Catullus, IV, passage beginning "Phasellus ille": "The pinnace you see, my friends, says that she was once the fleetest of ships."

235.31   St. Anthony]   Saint renowned for resisting temptation.

236.6   *Quies*]   Rest.

236.11   *The Seafarer*]   When "The Seafarer" was first published in *New Age* on November 30, 1911, Pound included the note: "The text of this poem is rather confused. I have rejected half of line 76, read 'Angles' for angels in line 78, and stopped translating before the passage about the soul and the longer lines beginning, "Mickle is the fear of the Almighty [*Micel biþ se Meotudes egsa*] and ending in a dignified but platitudinous address to the Deity: 'World's elder, eminent creator, in all ages, amen' [*wuldres Ealdor, / ece Dryhten, in ealle tid./ Amen*] There are many conjectures as to how the text came into its present form. It seems most likely that a fragment of the original poem, clear through about the first thirty lines, and thereafter increasingly illegible, fell into the hands of a monk with literary ambitions, who filled in the gaps with his own guesses and 'improvements.' The groundwork may have been a longer narrative poem, but the 'lyric,' as I have accepted it, divides fairly well into 'The Trials of the Sea,' its Lure and the Lament for the Age." In 1912, when challenged about the liberties he had taken in the translation, Pound defended "The Seafarer," as "nearly literal, I think, as any translation can be," thus opening himself up to attacks by academic specialists. In a note to *Umbra* (1920), Pound described "The Seafarer," along with "Exile's Letter (and Cathay in general)" and "Homage to Sextus Propertius," as "major personae."

239.3   GUIDO ORLANDO,]   See note 204.17.

239.30   Asclepiades, Julianus Ægyptus]   The two Greek poets whose epigrams are adapted here: Asclepiades of Samos (*ca.* 230 B.C.E.) and Julianus (4th century B.C.E.).

240.16   For music]   Debussy had set to music this poem by the French poet Charles d'Orléans (1394–1465) in 1909; Pound later wrote admiringly of Debussy's settings.

241.1   Δώρια]   Echoes the Greek word for gift (δωρεά) while also evoking Victor Plarr's book of poems, *In the Dorian Mood* (1896). Biographers have also heard the name of his wife-to-be, Dorothy.

244.10   Cyprian]   Venus, who was worshipped on Cyprus in antiquity.

245.9–11   DEUX . . . *d'or*]   Two Movements / 1. Temple that once was. / 2. Fish of gold.

245.18   Vavicel]   Probably a misprint for "navicel[la]," a vessel-shaped ornamental object, often holding incense.

247.2–8   CATHAY . . . ARIGA]   Pound met Mary Fenollosa, widow of the American scholar of Far Eastern literature Ernest Fenollosa (1853–1908), in London in 1912. Impressed by the "Oriental" quality of Pound's poems, she presented Pound with 17 notebooks and other manuscripts belonging to her late husband in 1913. From these Pound would quarry *Cathay* (1915), *'Noh' or Accomplishment* (1917), and *The Chinese Written Character as a Medium for Poetry* (1919). Fenollosa's notebook texts (compiled in Tokyo in 1896–1899 with the help of the Japanese scholars Hirai, Shida, Mori and Ariga) contained the Chinese characters for the original poems, followed interlinearly by their Japanese pronunciations and rough translations. Pound's choice of Japanese names for Chinese poets (e.g. "Rihaku" for Li Po) signals the cultural mediations at work in his versions. The 1915 edition of *Cathay* (in whose heavy tan wrappers some have seen an allusion to the military apparel of World War I) contained 11 poems, with Pound's earlier translation of the 8th-century "The Seafarer" inserted between "Exile's Letter" and "Four Poems of Departure" to emphasize the contemporaneity of T'ang Dynasty and Anglo-Saxon visions of exile (see note 236.11). When published as a section of *Lustra*, five additional poems from the Fenollosa notebooks (see 299.12–302.22) were added to the section entitled "Cathay" (minus "The Seafarer," which appeared elsewhere in the collection). Other classical Chinese poems Pound translated from the Fenollosa notebooks include Po Chü-i's "Song of the Lute" (see 323.1–14 and note) and Mei Sheng's "By the River of Stars" (see 1201.1–11 and note).

249.28   *By Kutsugen.*]   Footnote corrected in all editions from *Lustra* onward: "By Bunno / Reputedly 1100 B.C." Bunno is Japanese for Chinese ruler Wen Wang (see note 621.6). For a later translation by Pound, see 846.6–847.5.

250.5   *Mei Sheng.*]   No longer attributed to Mei Sheng; one of the "Nineteen Old Poems," probably composed in the first century. Cf. "By the River of Stars," p. 1201.

250.7   *The River Song*]   A translation of two separate poems by Li Po; apparently confused by the pagination of Fenollosa's notebook, Pound conflated these poems into a single work.

250.14   Sennin]   Pound observed in a letter: "Sennin [hsien-jien] are the Chinese spirits of nature or of the air. I don't see that they are any worse than Celtic Sidhe."

251.22   *Rihaku.*]   Japanese form of Li Po (701–762).

254.26   Rihoku's]   Japanese form of Li Mu (d. 223 B.C.E.), general who defended China against the Tartars.

254.29   *Exile's Letter*]   When first published in *Poetry* (March 1915), Pound included the note: "From the Chinese of Rihaku (Li Po), usually considered the greatest poet of China: written by him while in exile about 760 a.d., to the Hereditary War-Councillor of Sho, 'recollecting former companionship.' "

259.1   *South-Folk in Cold Country*]   From a poem by Li Po. In his article "Chinese Poetry" (*To-Day*, April 1918), Pound cited this poem as an example of "directness and realism such as we find only in early Saxon verse and in the Poema del Cid, and in Homer, or rather in what Homer would be if he wrote without epithet. . . . There you have no mellifluous circumlocution, no sentimentalizing of men who have never seen a battlefield and who wouldn't fight if they had to. You have war, campaigning as it has always been, tragedy, hardships, no illusions."

259.13   Rishogu]   Li Kuan (d. 125 B.C.E.), known as "the Winged General."

261.2   LUSTRA]   Preceding the section entitled "Lustra" collected in *Personæ* (1926), Pound included the following note: "DEFINITION: LUS-TRUM: an offering for the sins of the whole people, made by the censors at the expiration of their five years of office, etc. Elementary Latin Dictionary of Charlton T. Lewis." On the page following the dedication he printed the lines:

> And the days are not full enough
> And the nights are not full enough
> And life slips by like a field mouse
>   Not shaking the grass.

261.3   *Vail de Lencour*]   Pseudonym for Brigit Patmore (1882–1965), English writer and literary hostess.

261.4   *Cui . . . libellum.*]   "To whom I am to present my pretty new book," the opening line of the dedication to Catullus's poems.

263.17–20   *A mis . . . pensamientos.*]   The opening lines of Lope de Vega's "La Doreata," which Pound had translated in *The Spirit of Romance*: "To my solitudes I go, / From my solitudes return I, / Sith for companions on the journey, / Mine own thoughts (do well) suffice me."

263.31   "*fantastikon*"]   In a letter to Harriet Monroe dated March 1913 Pound explained that this word signified "what Imagination really meant before the term was debased—presumably by the Miltonists, tho' probably before them. It has to do with the seeing of visions." In "Psychology and Troubadours" (1912), Pound distinguished between the *phantastikon* defined by the "Greek psychologists" (in which men's "minds are circumvolved about them like soap-bubbles reflecting sundry patches of the macro-cosmos") and what he calls "germinal" consciousness ("their thoughts are in them as the thought of the tree is in the seed, or in the grass, or the grain, or the blossom").

264.20–21   *En robe . . . Samain*]   From the prefatory poem to *Au Jardin de l'Infante* (1893) by the French poet Albert-Victor Samain (1858–1900), which reads: "Mon âme est une infante en robe de parade" ("My soul is an Infanta in fancy dress").

265.4   *Ortus*]   Origin, birth.

266.10–12   Watch . . . them:]   Replaced by the line "Observe the irritation in general:" in *Personæ* (1926).

266.28   "The Spectator."]   English periodical lampooned by Pound for its mediocrity and prudery; from 1898 to 1925 its editor was John St. Loe Strachey (mentioned at 266.34).

266.32   Cybele!]   Fertility goddess of Asia Minor, whose cult spread to Greece in the 5th century B.C.E. She was praised with music and ecstatic dancing.

267.7 *The Spring*] An adaptation of a poem by the Greek poet Ibycus (6th century B.C.E.); when the poem was collected in *Personæ* (1926), Pound added the Greek poem's first line as an epigraph: Ἦρι μὲν αἵ τε κυδώνιαι ("In Spring the Cydonian quinces"). Cydonia was a town in Crete.

267.9 Meliads] Spelled "Maelids" in subsequent editions; Pound's coinage for a fruit-tree nymph.

267.26–27 Gautier . . . whiteness] Cf. Gautier's poem "Symphonie en Blanc Majeur" (1849).

269.19 *Surgit Fama*] There is a rumor.

270.23 *Dance Figure*] Originally subtitled "A Thoroughly Sensuous Image."

270.24 For . . . Galilee] See John 2:1.

271.22 *Nympharum . . . disjecta*] The scattered limbs of the nymphs. Cf. Ovid, *Metamorphoses*, the closing lines of Book III describing the dismemberment of Pentheus.

273.7 "Slade"] London's Slade School of Art.

273.11 *Cleopatra*] Diaghilev's one-act ballet *Cléopâtre*, first performed in Paris in 1909.

274.6 Santa Maria Novella] A Dominican convent in Florence.

274.9 *A Song of the Degrees*] Psalms 120–134 in the King James Bible are each subtitled "A Song of Degrees."

275.1 *Ité*] Go.

275.7 *Dum . . . Scandet*] Cf. Horace, *Odes*, III, lines 8–9: "usque ego postera crescam laude recens, dum Capitolium scandet cum tacita virgine pontifex" ("I shall arise with fresh praise in the future, as long as the high priest climbs the Capitoline Hill with silent virgins").

275.16 To Καλόν] The beautiful.

275.24 *Guarda! . . . be'a!*] Look! She's beautiful!

276.1 Sirmione,] See note 148.6.

276.9 *sta fermo!*] Keep quiet!

276.18–19 *Aus meinen . . . Lieder*] Heine, *Lyrisches Intermezzo* (1827), XXXVI, in E. B. Browning's translation: "Out of my own great woe / I make my little songs."

277.5 Charles the Fourth] King of France from 1322 to 1328.

277.7 Henry the Fourth] King of France from 1589 to 1610.

277.12 espavin] Pound's coinage.

277.20   Agde and Biaucaire.]   Pound visited Agde, Beaucaire, and all the towns in the lines following (except Marseilles) during his 1912 walking tour through southern France.

277.31   Chesterton.]   In August 1917, Pound wrote to John Quinn concerning this poem: "If it were a question of cruelty to a weak man I shouldn't, of course, have printed it. But Chesterton *is* so much the mob, so much the multitude. It is not as if he weren't a symbol for all the mob's hatred of all art that aspires above mediocrity. . . . Chesterton has always taken the stand that the real thing isn't worth doing. . . . I should probably like G.K.C. personally if I ever met him. Still, I believe he creates a milieu in which art is impossible. He and his kind."

279.16   *Old . . . most.*]   Yeats, "The Lover Pleads with His Friend for Old Friends" (1899).

279.25   *Te . . . Bourrienne,*]   "So here you are, my Bourienne." L.A.F. Bourrienne (1769–1834), private secretary to Napoleon, and later his biographer.

280.5   *bos amic*]   Good friend.

280.10–16   *Iste . . . femina.*]   Translated by Peter Brooker as: "That chap was vulgar, / Thank god he's buried, / Let the worms feed on his face / A-a-a-a-A-men / Meanwhile, like Jove I / Shall move in / With his woman."

280.23   *Dives*]   The haughty rich man who suffers in hell in Jesus' parable (Luke 16:19–31).

281.8   lar]   Household god.

281.12   *Lesbia Illa*]   That Lesbia. Catullus, LVIII. Lesbia was Catullus' mistress.

281.18   *Lugete . . . Cupidinesque!*]   Cf. the opening of Catullus, III: "Lugete, o Veneres Cupidinesque" ("Mourn, you Graces and Loves").

282.22   *Ancora*]   Again.

282.23–24   They say . . . canzonetti!]   Harriet Monroe, editor of *Poetry*, had voiced reservations about some of Pound's poems published in the magazine in 1913.

283.7   Castilian]   Of Castalia, a sacred spring on Mount Parnassus.

283.9   *"Dompna . . . Cal"*]   For the story of this poem, see 26.15–27.

283.12   Lady]   Maent de Montagnac, who spurned Bertrand, thus inspiring this poem.

283.32   Bels Cembelins]   Pseudonym of an unknown lady of Limousin.

284.5   Midons Aelis]   Maent's sister.

284.8   Viscountess,]   Tibors of Montausier, Viscountess of Chalais, said to have reconciled Maent with Bertrand.

284.13   Anhes]   Viscountess of Rochechouart.

284.17   Audiart]   Audiart de Malemort; see "Na Audiart," 26.13–28.14.

284.24   Miels-de-bcn]   "Bcttcr than good," pseudonym of Guischarda de Beaujeu, whom Bertrand briefly courted, which caused his dismissal by the jealous Maent.

284.28   Faidita]   Probably the relative of an important baron named Peire Faidit.

285.1   Bels Senher]   "Fair Sir," i.e. Maent (the Lady often being addressed in the masculine in troubadour poetry).

285.11   *Actaeon*]   In Greek mythology, Actaeon inadvertently wanders into a grove where Artemis and her nymphs are bathing. The enraged goddess splashes him with water, transforming him into a stag, and his own hounds pursue him and tear him to pieces. See Ovid, *Metamorphoses*, Book III.

286.1   *Ch'u Yuan*]   Chinese poet (340–278 B.C.E.). This poem and "Liu Ch'e" are based on English versions in H. A. Giles' *A History of Chinese Literature* (1901).

286.12   *Liu Ch'e*]   Emperor Wu of the Han, patron of the arts (156–87 B.C.E.).

286.19   *Fan-Piece . . . Lord*]   Based on Giles's account of an incident in the life of Pan Chieh-yü, a favorite concubine of the Han emperor Ch'eng Ti.

287.1   *In a Station of the Metro*]   When first published as part of Pound's "Contemporania" sequence in *Poetry* in April 1913, the spacing of the poem heightened its "ideogrammic" quality:

> The apparition   of these faces   in the crowd   :
> Petals   on a wet, black   bough   .

287.21   Auster . . . Apeliota]   The South Wind and the East Wind, respectively.

288.1   *Coitus*]   In the English edition of *Lustra*, the poem was entitled "Pervigilium," a reference to the anonymous Latin poem *Pervigilium Veneris* (The Vigil of Venus), which Pound in *The Spirit of Romance* linked to the pagan May Day fertility rites of medieval Provence and Italy.

288.8   Dione]   The mother of Venus.

288.17   *Tempora*]   The times.

288.18   Tamuz!]   Adonis.

288.26   *Bellotti*]   An Italian restaurant at 12 Compton Street in London.

289.3   *Connaissez-vous Ostende?*]   Do you know Ostende?

289.14   *d'Orleans*]   Translation of eight lines of a song by Charles d'Orléans (see note 240.16).

289.23   *Papyrus*]   Based on a papyrus scrap of Sappho first published in Berlin in 1902.

289.26   Gongula]   Disciple and perhaps lover of Sappho.

290.1   *Ione*]   Perhaps the French dancer Jeanne Heyse, who used the stage name "Ione de Forest." She committed suicide in August 1912 at the age of 19 (this poem was first published in 1913). "Ione" was also the name of a muse of the English poet Walter Savage Landor (1775–1864).

290.11   'Ιμέρρω]   To long for. From Sappho, LXXXVI.

290.23   shepherdess . . . Guido.]   See Cavalcanti's Ballata IX, 221.23–222.18.

290.26   After Valerius Catullus]   Cf. Catullus, LXI.

291.24   woman]   "Prostitute," in the poem's first publication (*Smart Set*, December 1913).

292.8   Chicago]   *Poetry* magazine was published in Chicago.

292.23   (Pompes Funèbres)]   Funeral rites.

293.4   Avernus]   See note 147.5.

293.23–24   Winter . . . Goddamm,]   Cf. the Middle English lyric (*ca.* 1260) beginning "Sumer is icumen in."

294.5   Dr. Ker]   The scholar and essayist William Paton Ker (1855–1923). Pound wrote, "Dr. Ker has put an end to much babble about folk song by showing us *Summer is ycummen in* written beneath the Latin words of the first known example of a canon" (*Poetry*, January 1914).

294.24   *Epitaphs*]   The deaths of these two Chinese poets, Fu Hi (554–639) and Li Po (701–762), are recounted in Giles's *History of Chinese Literature*.

295.6   he . . . island]   Rupert Brooke (1887–1915) published a sequence of poems about his three months in the South Seas in *1914 and Other Poems* (1915).

295.8–13   Il s'agit . . . Anthology."]   We refer to a young poet who followed the Gauguin cult all the way to Tahiti (and who is still alive). Given that he was a very dashing fellow, when the tawny princess heard that he was eager to offer her his favors she displayed her alacrity in the manner evoked above. Unfortunately, his poems are merely filled with his own subjectivities, in the Victorian style of the "Georgian Anthology."

296.4–5   A.D. 1912 . . . the walk,]   The poem records an encounter toward the end of Pound's walking tour in southern France in mid-July 1912 near Clemont-Ferrand. Previous stops on this journey had included Arles, Beaucaire, Rodez, and Gourdon, where he had witnessed the festivities of St. John's Eve (June 23).

297.5   *Provincia Deserta*]   Title alludes to C. M. Doughty's *Travels in Arabia Deserta* (1888). The place names in the poems are sites visited by Pound during his walking tour through southern France in the early summer of 1912. Rochecouart, Chalais, Montagnac, and Hautefort are all associated with Bertrand de Born (see "Dompna Pois de Me No'us Cal," 283.9–285.10). Mareuil and Ribeyrac were the homes of, respectively, the troubadours Arnaut de Mareuil and Arnaut Daniel; Chalus is where Richard Coeur de Lion was killed; Excideuil is the birthplace of the troubadour Giraut de Borneil.

298.31   "Dorata."]   Church of La Daurade in Toulouse (see also note 219.13).

298.33   "Riquier! Guido."]   Troubadour Guiraut de Riquier and Italian poet Guido Cavalcanti; Pound speculated that the two might have met in Toulouse.

298.36–38   Two men . . . woman.]   After their coin toss, Austors de Maensac received the castle and Pieire de Maensac the poetry—with which he then seduced the wife of Bernart de Tierci and abducted her. Pound returns to this "second Troy" in the Auvergne in Canto 5.

300.1   *A Ballad . . . Road*]   Translation of the first 14 lines of a 53-line anonymous Chinese poem.

300.4   Shin]   Ch'in in Chinese, name of a state.

300.5   Rafu]   Lo-fu in Chinese.

300.20   *Rosoriu*]   Chinese poet Lu Chao-lin (634–*ca.* 684)

301.17   Butei of Kan]   The Emperor Han.

301.22   *To-Em-Mei's*]   T'ao Ch'ien (365–427).

302.24–25   *A Perigord . . . ab malh.*]   In *The Spirit of Romance*, Pound translated these lines of Bertrand de Born: "At Perigord near to the wall, / Aye, within a mace throw of it." "Perigord" is the Provençal town of Périgueux. The composition of this poem in 1915 is contemporary with that of the original "Three Cantos" (see note 318.1).

302.27   Cino]   See "Cino," 24.5–25.32.

302.28   Uc St. Circ]   Attributed author of commentary to some of Bertrand de Born's poems.

302.29   Solve me the riddle,]   In 1912, Pound closely inspected the topography around Bertrand de Born's castle of Altafort (Hautefort), attempting to determine whether the poet's "fine canzone" (302.30), "Dompna Pois de Me No'us Cal," was merely a lover's attempt to regain Lady Maent's favor or a warrior's ploy to infiltrate neighboring castles and thus consolidate power over rival barons. For Pound's translation of the poem, see 283.9–285.10.

303.17   "that . . . lamp."]   Cf. *Inferno*, XXVIII, 121–22.

303.21   "counterpass"]   Laws of divine justice. Cf. *Inferno*, XXVIII, 142.

304.25   Papiol]   Bertrand's jongleur.

305.6–7   (St. Leider . . . hidden.)]   As Pound explained in "Trouba-dours: Their Sorts and Conditions" (1913): "If you wish to make love to women in public, and out loud, you must resort to subterfuge; and Guil-laume St. Leider even went so far as to get the husband of his lady [the Viscount of Polhanac] to do the seductive singing."

305.10   *"Et albirar . . . bordon—"*]   In "Troubadours: Their Sorts and Conditions," Pound translated this line by Gaston Phoebus, Count of Foix (1331–91): "And sing not all they have in mind."

305.21   *al* and *ochaisos.*]   Rhyming words used in "Dompna Pois de Me No'us Cal."

305.25   "magnet" singer]   See "Dompna Pois de Me No'us Cal," the final stanza (not included in Pound's translation): "Papiols, mon Aziman" (Papiols, my magnet).

306.24   *trobar clus*]   A hermetic style practiced by some Provençal poets, notably by Arnaut Daniel.

306.25   "best craftsman"]   In *Purgatorio*, XXVI, 117, Dante calls Arnaut Daniel the "better craftsman" ("miglior fabbro")—a compliment T. S. Eliot would later pay to Pound in the dedication of *The Waste Land*.

307.10–15   *Surely I saw . . . counterpart.*]   Cf. *Inferno*, XXVIII, 118–23, 139–42.

307.18   *Ed eran . . . due*]   And they were two in one and one in two.

309.5   *"Between . . . morning?"*]   See Yeats, "The People": "The daily spite of this unmannerly town, / Where who has served the most is most de-famed, / The reputation of his lifetime lost / Between the night and the morning."

309.24   *Dans un Omnibus de Londres*]   In a London Bus. Translation: The eyes of a dead lady / Greeted me, / Set in a stupid face / Whose other features were commonplace, / They greeted me / And within my memory / I then saw many things / Stir / Awake. // I saw ducks at the edge of a pond, / Near a small cheerful hunchbacked child. / I saw the old fake columns / Of the Parc Monceau, / And two slender little girls, / Aristocratic, / with linen-colored shocks of hair, / And pigeons / Plump / as pullets. / I saw the park / And all the lawns / Where we rented chairs / for a few pennies. // I saw the black swans, / Japanese, / Their wings / The tint of dragon's blood, / And all the flowers / Of Armenonville. // The eyes of a dead lady / Greeted me.

310.25   *Pagani's*]   London restaurant, in Great Portland Place.

311.1   *a Friend*]   The poet Hermann Hagedorn (1882–1964), whose name is "anglicized" in line 1. The epigraph is from Hagedorn's 1915 sonnet "The Cabaret Dancer." *Vir Quidem*: A Certain Man.

311.27–29   CARMEN . . . la flamme]   Two excerpts from Théophile Gautier's poem "Carmen" ("Carmen is thin, a line of bistre / Encircles her gypsy eye . . . [and the hot gleam of her eyes] renders back the flame [to satieties]").

312.27   "Pauvre femme maigre!"]   Poor thin woman!

313.4   *"mica salis,"*]   A grain of salt.

313.6   Nell Gwynn's]   The actress Eleanor Gwyn (1650–1687) was Charles II's mistress.

313.21   Quintus . . . Christianus]   The Latinized name of the French scholar and translator Florent Chrétien (1540–1596), who published *Epigrammata ex Libris Gracae Anthologiae* (Epigrams from the Greek Anthology) in 1608.

313.24–26   Theodorus . . . death,]   Translated from an epigram of Simonides (*ca.* 556–468 B.C.E.).

313.28   Cyprian's]   Venus'.

314.3   *Anyte*]   Female poet (*fl. ca.* 300 B.C.E.) believed to have been from Tegea, a town in southwest Arcadia.

314.9   *Palladas*]   Palladas of Alexandria (*fl.* 400).

314.20   *Agathias Scholasticus*]   Poet and compiler of epigrams (536–582).

314.27   *Nicharcus*]   Chrétien attributes the epigram to the first-century poet Nicarchus of Alexandria, though modern scholars reject this attribution.

315.17–18   *Qu'ieu . . . sai.*]   That I am handsome, I know.

315.20   Arnaut de Mareuil]   See note 97.17.

315.23   *Impressions . . . Voltaire*]   Pound's adaptations omit many lines from Voltaire's poems. I: based on "Epître Connue Sous le Nom des *Vous* et des *Tu*." II: based on *Stances*. III: based on *Stances*, "A Madame Lullin de Genève."

316.12   *Mme du Châtelet*]   Voltaire's mistress during the 1730s and 1740s.

317.8   "Delia, . . . dying."]   Tibullus, *Elegies*, I, i, 59–60.

318.1   *Three Cantos . . . Length*]   Originally composed in late 1915. Almost as soon as "Three Cantos" had appeared in *Poetry* in 1917, Pound began to revise it, turning to T. S. Eliot for editorial advice. At Eliot's suggestion, he eliminated redundant or explanatory passages from the *Poetry* versions, removed some 21 personal pronouns in order to "impersonalize" the text, and in general rendered its transitions far more elliptical. Excerpts from the *Lustra* "Cantos," which further abbreviated and denarrativized these "Ur-Cantos," were printed in the London magazine *The Future* in February–April 1918 under the titles "Passages from the Opening Address in a Long Poem," "Images from the Second Canto of a Long Poem," and "An Interpolation taken from the Third Canto of a Long Poem." When Pound revised the beginning of the *Cantos* in 1923, he made his translation of the *nekuia* passage from the *Odyssey* (Book IX), originally part of Canto III (328.19–330.33), the opening of his epic poem and redistributed passages from the original "Three Cantos" into the newly revised Cantos II and III. Much delayed, the final version of *A Draft of XVI. Cantos of Ezra Pound for the Beginning of a Poem of Some Length* was published in January 1925 (Paris: Three Mountains Press).

318.3   "Sordello,"] Long narrative poem (1840) by Robert Browning based on events in the life of Mantua-born Provençal troubadour Sordello (died *ca.* 1270) and the struggles between Guelph and Ghibbeline factions in Florence.

318.17   Beaucaire's] See note 296.4–5.

318.18   Altaforte—] Bertrand de Born's castle. See note 302.29.

318.19   Alcazar] Moorish stronghold conquered by El Cid. See note 324.33.

318.27–28   Peire . . . Dante.] Pound noted of the troubadour Peire Cardinal (*fl.* 1210–1230) in *The Spirit of Romance* that "in so far as Dante is a critic of morals, Cardinal must be held as his forerunner."

318.31–32   font . . . passage] At the end of Book the Second of Browning's *Sordello*, the troubadour, despairing of his poetic vocation, throws his crown of laurel into a fount at Mantua: ". . . into the fount he threw / His crown / Next day, no poet!"

318.34   And no matter.] The 1917 *Poetry* version reads: "Does it matter? / Not in the least."

318.37   "Sordello."] The 1917 *Poetry* version continues:
    And you'll say, "No, not your life,
    He never showed himself."
    Is't worth the evasion, what were the use
    Of setting figures up and breathing life upon them,
    Were 't not our life, your life, my life, extended?
    I walk Verona. (I am here in England.)
    I see Can Grande. (Can see whom you will.)
        You had one whole man?
    And I have many fragments, less worth? Less worth?
    Ah, had you quite my age, quite such a beastly and cantankerous age?
    You had some basis, had some set belief.
    Am I let preach? Has it a place in music?

319.2   "Appear Verona!"?] *Sordello*, I, 59–61, "Then appear, / Verona! Stay—thou, spirit, come not near / Now . . ."

319.5   your "Great . . . Domini] St John's Eve (June 23). Cf. *Sordello*, III, 764ff.

319.11   barn-like church] San Pietro in Mavino, constructed on the ruins of an ancient pagan temple.

319.14   "Home . . . laughter,"] Catullus, XXXI ("Paene insularum, Sirmio, insularumque").

319.21   *Lo Soleils plovil.*] The sun rains. From the final line of Arnaut Daniel's "Lancan son passat li giure" (485.37).

319.23   "Lydian" . . . *undae*] Catullus, XXXI ("Salve, o venusta Sirmio atque ero gaude, / gaudente vosque, o Lydiae lacus undae")—in which Catullus compares his own lake to the Lydian waters surrounding Sappho's island of Lesbos.

319.24   *lemures*] Spectres of the night.

319.30   GLAUKOPOS] Epithet for the goddess Athena, traditionally translated as "blue-eyed," "grey-eyed," or "glare-eyed," but, according to Allen Upward's *The New Word* (1910), best understood as evoking the blinking, glinting light of an owl's eye or olive leaf.

319.33   *apricus*] Drenched with sunlight.

319.35   Asolo] Setting for Browning's "Pippa Passes" and later the writer's own residence.

319.36   palace step?] Cf. "I muse this on a palace-step / At Venice," *Sordello*, III, 675.

319.37   Dogana's] Chief Venetian customhouse on the Grand Canal.

319.38   "those girls"] Cf. "Let stay those girls," *Sordello*, III, 698.

320.8   Morosini.] Square and palace in Venice.

320.15   Pre-Daun-Chaucer] *Book of Daun Burnel the Ass* (*Speculum Stultorum*) by Nigellus Wireker (*ca.* 1130–*ca.* 1200): The following passage appears in the 1917 *Poetry* version in place of lines 320.14–17:

And we will say: What's left for me to do?
Whom shall I conjure up; who's my Sordello,
My pre-Daun Chaucer, pre-Boccacio,
        As you have done pre-Dante?
Whom shall I hang my shimmering garment on;
Who wear my feathery mantle, *hagoromo*;
Whom set to dazzle the serious future ages?
Not Arnaut, not De Born, not Uc St. Circ who has writ out the stories.
Or shall I do your trick, the showman's booth, Bob Browning,

Turned at my will into the Agora,
Or into the old theatre at Arles,

And set the lot, my visions, to confounding
The wits that have survived your damn'd *Sordello*?
(Or sulk and leave the word to novelists?)
What a hodge-podge you have made there!—
Zanze and *swanzig*, of all opprobrious rhymes!
And you turn off whenever it suits your fancy,
Now at Verona, now with the early Christians,
Or now a-gabbling of the "Tyrrhene whelk."
"The lyre should animate but not mislead the pen"—
That's Wordsworth, Mr. Browning. (What a phrase!—
That lyre, that pen, that bleating sheep, Will Wordsworth!)
That should have taught you avoid speech figurative
    And set out your matter
As I do, in straight simple phrases:
        Gods float in the azure air
Bright gods, and Tuscan, back before dew was shed, [. . .]

320.16   Uc St. Circ]   See note 302.28.

320.21   Panisks]   Small woodland Pans, half human, half goat.

320.22   Maelids]   See note 267.9.

320.27–28   Metastasio . . . us.]   See Pound's translation of Metastasio's
poem "Age of Gold" at 1201.12–21.

320.36   Ficino]   Under the patronage of Cosimo de' Medici, Marsilio
Ficino (1433–1499) translated many of the Greek classics into Latin, among
them Plato's dialogues and the writings of Plotinus. In *Gaudier-Brzeska: A
Memoir* (1916), Pound wrote: "Ficino was seized in his youth by Cosimo dei
Medici and set to work translating a Greek that was in spirit anything but 'clas-
sic.' That is to say, you had, ultimately, a 'Platonic' academy messing up Chris-
tian and Pagan mysticism, allegory, occultism, demonology, Trismegistus,
Psellus, Porphyry, into a most eloquent and exhilarating hotch-potch, which
'did for' the mediæval fear of the *dies iræ* and for human abasement generally."

321.1   Exult . . . squatness?]   Cf. Gaudier-Brzeska's "Vortex," published
in *BLAST* in June 1914 and reprinted in Pound's *Gaudier-Brzeska: A Mem-
oir*, in which the sculptor traces a universal history of art, moving from the
"Paleolithic Vortex," through the "Hamite Vortex of Egypt" and into the
"convex bronze vases" of China's Shang and Chou dynasties.

321.2   bronzes.]   Followed in the 1917 *Poetry* version by: "(Confucius later
taught the world good manners, / Started with himself, built out perfection.)"

321.11   Kuanon]   Japanese goddess of mercy who can also appear as the
armed goddess of war (spelled "Kwannon" in the 1917 *Poetry* version). Her

avatar is a lotus petal. The passage from 321.7 to 321.18 is adapted from the Noh play *Tamura* (see pp. 379–83).

321.21   *Or San Michaele*]   See Cavalcanti's Sonnet XXXV (p. 214) and note 214.7–8.

321.22   tomb he leapt]   See Boccaccio, *Decameron,* Sixth day, Ninth tale, which recounts how Cavalcanti eluded an attack by Betto and his company by leaping over one of the high marble tombs in the cemetery of the Church of Santa Reparata. The scene is featured in Act I of Pound's unproduced radio opera "Cavalcanti: A Sung Dramedy in 3 Acts" (1932).

321.23–24   street-charge.]   Followed in the 1917 *Poetry* version by:
Sweet lie, "I lived!" Sweet lie, "I lived beside him."
And now it's all but truth and memory,
Dimmed only by the attritions of long time.

"But we forget not."
No, take it all for lies.

321.28   phantastikon]   See note 263.31.

321.37   (Simonetta?)]   Giuliano de' Medici's wife, reputed model for Botticelli's "Birth of Venus."

321.38   Aufidus]   Stream identified with the male zephyr in Botticelli's painting.

322.1–2   "Apparelled . . . ("Pericles")]   Cf. Shakespeare, *Pericles, Prince of Tyre,* I.i.12.

322.7   Mantegna . . . us:]   The Italian painter Andrea Mantegna (1431–1506) created frescoes for the Gonzaga family of Mantua. After "us" these lines appear in the 1917 *Poetry* version:
Barred lights, great flares, new form, Picasso or Lewis.
If for a year man write to paint, and not to music—
O Casella!

322.9   Casella.]   Musician who set Dante's poems to music; in *Purgatorio,* II, 2, Cato rebukes Dante for loitering with Casella, reminding him that he must climb the mount.

322.12   Mantuan palace,]   Of the Gonzaga family.

322.20   Joios, Tolosan]   A minor itinerant troubadour whose poetry Pound discovered in the "Chansonnier du Roi" (Ms. Fr. 844) in the Bibliothèque Nationale in spring 1912—the "blue and gilded manuscript" at 322.27.

322.24–25   "Y a la premera flor," . . . plor."]   "And at the first flower I found, I burst into tears." Pound translated these lines for "Troubadours—Their Sorts and Conditions" (1913), collected in *Literary Essays* (1954).

322.32   When . . . Chalus;] See note 297.5.

322.33   Arnaut's a score of songs] In 1911, Pound traveled to Milan to consult Ms. R71 superiore at the Ambrosian Library—the sole manuscript containing the musical notation for two of Arnaut Daniel's poems ("Chansson doil mot" and "Lo ferm voler," translated by Pound at 481.1–482.24 and 502.25–503.31, respectively).

322.35   Dolmetsch] Arnold Dolmetsch (1858–1940), French musician and instrument maker (of early stringed and keyboard instruments in particular).

323.–14   Yin-yo . . . We heard her weeping] Pound's arrangement, based on the Fenollosa notebooks, of "Song of the Lute" by the T'ang poet Po Chü-i (772–846). For a full translation see Burton Watson (ed. and trans.), *The Columbia Book of Chinese Poetry* (NY: Columbia University Press, 1984), pp. 249–252.

323.15   her . . . sparrows.] Lesbia plays teasingly with her sparrow in Catullus, II; Venus' chariot is often pictured drawn by sparrows.

323.17   "Rêveuse . . . plonge."] "Dreamer, so that I plunge." The first line of Mallarmé's "Autre Eventail."

323.19–22 God's peer . . . me.] Catullus, LI. A four-line condensation of the complete eleven-line poem appears in the 1917 *Poetry* version.

323.23   *flamma demanat*] "A flame steals down through my limbs." From Catullus, LI.

323.24   "I love her as a father"] From Catullus, LXXII.

323.25   "Your words are written in water"] From Catullus, LXXX.

323.26–30 "O Caelius . . . Roman"] From Catullus, LVIII.

324.3   "D'amor . . . cossir"] "Of love my every thought." From "Tug miei cossir son d'amor e de chan" ("All my thoughts were of love and song") by Peirol (1188–1222).

324.4   The Lady of Pena] The Viscountess of Pena's further adventures with Elis of Montfort are recounted in one of the *razos* of Uc de Saint Circ (see note 302.28) summarized by Pound in "Troubadours—Their Sorts and Conditions." The 1917 *Poetry* version of this episode is considerably condensed here.

324.6   *bos trobaire*] A good finder of song.

324.24   Gordon] Pound visited the town of Gourdon toward the end of the festivities of St. John's Eve, June 23, 1912.

324.33   My Cid] "Commander" or "Lord" Cid, title given by the Moors to Ruy Díaz (1040?–1099), hero of the Spanish epic *Cantar de mío Cid* (*ca.* 1140). Part I of the epic ("The Exile") tells of the banishment of Díaz by Alfonso VI for bearing false witness against him.

324.33   Burgos] Díaz lived and was buried in Burgos, capital of Burgos Province in Old Castile.

325.4   (*Afe Minaya!*)] Alférez (or Commander) Alvar Fáñez, Christian warrior in *Cantar de mío Cid*.

325.6   *Muy velida!*] Most beautiful!

325.13   Y dar . . . hierros"—] And the arms and weapon gave new light.

325.19–20   Kumasaka's . . . him.] See the Noh play "Kumasaka" at p. 370.

325.22   *las almenas*] Cf. Lope de Vega's play *Las Almenas de Toro*, summarized by Pound in "The Quality of Lope de Vega" in *The Spirit of Romance*. King Sancho and his advisers the Cid (Ruy Díaz) and Conde Ancures beseige the gates of the city of Toro, which has been bequeathed to Elvira by her father King Ferdinand. Seeing Elvira appear on the battlements, King Sancho falls in love with her, unaware that she is his sister.

325.29   "Mal fuego s'enciende!"] An ill flame be kindled in her! (King Sancho speaking of his love for Elvira.)

325.33   Pedro] Son and heir of Alfonso IV of Portugal, who secretly married Inés de Castro. Alfonso IV joined in a conspiracy that succeeded in murdering her in 1355. Pound explains in the "Camoens" chapter of *The Spirit of Romance*: "When Pedro succeeded to the throne, he had her body exhumed, and the court did homage, the grandees of Portugal passing before the double throne of the dead queen and her king, and kissing that hand which had been hers."

326.2   "Que . . . Rainha."] Who, after she was dead was crownèd queen. From Camoens's *Os Lusiadas*, III, 132.

326.4–7   "That once as Proserpine . . . in Mondego."] Based on *Os Lusiadas*, III, 134–35.

326.9–13   Houtmans in jail . . . Renaissance.] In "Camoens" in *The Spirit of Romance*, Pound provides a prose gloss: "If one were seeking to prove that all that part of art which is not the inevitable expression of genius is a by-product of trade or a secretion of commercial prosperity, the following facts would seem significant. Shortly before the decline of Portuguese prestige, Houtman, lying in jail for debt at Lisbon, planned the Dutch East India company. When Portugal fell, Holland seized the Oriental trade, and soon after Roemer Visscher was holding a salon, with which are connected the names of Rembrandt, Grotius, Spinoza, Vondel (born 1587), 'the one articulate voice of Holland,'. . ."

326.15–16   Gaby wears Braganza . . . gullet.] The Braganza house ruled Portugal from 1640 to 1910 and Brazil from 1822 to 1889. "Gaby" refers to Gaby Deslys, the stage name of Marie-Elsie-Gabrielle Caire (1881–1920),

French dancer and actress famous for her risqué performances and her jew-
elry. She was mistress of King Manuel II of Portugal. In the 1917 *Poetry*
version these lines were followed by:

> Ah, *mon rêve*
> It happened; and now go think—
> Another crown, thrown to another dancer, brings you to modern times?

326.17   a man]   Fred Vance; see note 177.4.

327.2   John Heydon]   English astrologer and alchemist (1629–1667).

327.3   levitation,]   Followed in the 1917 *Poetry* version by:

> In thoughts upon pure form, in alchemy
> Seer of pretty visions ("a servant of God and secretary of nature");
> Full of a plaintive charm, like Botticelli's,
> With half-transparent forms, lacking the vigor of gods.
> Thus Heydon, in a trance, at Bulverton,
> Had such a sight:

327.6   "Decked all in green"]   From John Heydon's vision of the spirit
Euterpe who gave him the "Key and Signet" to the "mysteries of the Rosie
Cross," as recounted in Book VI of his *Holy Guide* (1662).

327.11   wisdom.]   Followed in the 1917 *Poetry* version by:

> "Pretty green bank," began the half-lost poem.
> Take the old way, say I met John Heydon,
> Sought out the place,
> Lay on the bank, was "plungèd deep in swevyn;"
> And saw the company—Layamon, Chaucer—
> Pass each in his appropriate robes;
> Conversed with each, observed the varying fashion.
> And then comes Heydon.
>   "I have seen John Heydon."
> Let us hear John Heydon!

327.12–15   "Omniformis . . . chapter,]   The quote, "Every intellect is ca-
pable of assuming every shape," is taken from *De Occasionibus*, chapter 13, of
Porphyry (*ca.* 232–*ca.* 304), Greek scholar and Neoplatonic philosopher.

327.14   Psellus]   Michael Constantine Psellus (1018–1105), Byzantine
philosopher, politician, writer, and Neoplatonist.

327.16   omniform.]   Followed in the 1917 *Poetry* version by:

> Magnifico Lorenzo used the dodge,
> Says that he met Ficino
> In some Wordsworthian, false-pastoral manner,
> And that they walked along, stopped at a well-head,
> And heard deep platitudes about contentment
> From some old codger with an endless beard.
> "A daemon is not a particular intellect,

> But is a substance differed from intellect,"
> Breaks in Ficino,
> "Placed in the latitude or locus of souls"—
> That's out of Proclus, take your pick of them.

327.18   Ficino's]   See note 320.36.

327.19   Valla]   Lorenzo Valla (*ca.* 1407–1457), Italian humanist and Greek scholar. Author of the *Elegantiae linguae latinae* (1444), a philological defense of classical Latin in which he contrasted the elegance of ancient Roman works with the clumsiness of medieval and Church Latin. This is the source of the line quoted at 329.24.

327.20   his Pope, Nicholas:]   Nicholas V, pope (1447–1455) renowned for his learning and piety, and founder of the Vatican Library. Patron of Lorenzo Valla.

327.27   Sir Blancatz]   I.e. Blacatz (*fl.* 1194–1236), "magnet" poet whose death was lamented in a *planh* by Sordello.

327.31–32   "nec bonus . . . Tullianus."]   Neither a good Christian nor a good Ciceronian.

327.33   Du Bellay . . . building;]   See Pound's translation of "Rome," p. 151.

327.36   Laniato corpore.]   His body torn to pieces.

328.1   Villari]   Italian historian Pasquale Villari (1827–1917).

328.8   Doughty's]   Charles Montagu Doughty (1843–1926), English author of *Travels in Arabia Deserta* (1888) and the epic *The Dawn in Britain* (1906). See note 297.5.

328.10   Andreas Divus]   In "Early Translators of Homer" (1918), Pound wrote: "In the year of grace 1906, 1908, or 1910 I picked from the Paris quais a Latin version of the *Odyssey* by Andreas Divus Justinopolitanus (Parisiis, In officina Christiani Wecheli, MDXXXVIII), the volume containing also the Batrachomyomachia by Aldus Manutius, and the Hymni Deorum rendered by Georgius Dartona Cretensis."

328.13–15   "Down to the ships . . . went."]   Pound's version of Andreus Divus's 1538 Latin translation of Book IX (the "Nekuia") of the *Odyssey*, which is continued from 328.19 to 330.17.

328.16   I've strained . . . –ensa,]   The terminal rhyme scheme of Peire Vidal's "Ab l'alen tir vas me l'aire," translated by Pound in *The Spirit of Romance*.

329.1   ell-square pitkin]   Pound's invention: a little pit.

329.14   dreary]   From the Anglo-Saxon "dreory" ("blood-dripping").

329.33   ingle]   Inglenook, from the Scots "chimney corner" (via Gavin Douglas).

330.27–29   Veneradum . . . est,]   Worthy of veneration, golden-crowned and beautiful, whose dominion is the walled cities of all sea-set Cyprus (Loeb). From Georgius Dartona's Latin version of the second hymn to Aphrodite, bound into Pound's copy of Andreas Divus.

330.32   orichalci]   Of copper, used by Dartona with reference to Aphrodite's earrings.

330.34   Argicida]   Slayer of the Greeks, a reference to Aphrodite's favoring the Trojans (and especially Aeneas) over the Greeks.

331.1–3   'NOH' OR ACCOMPLISHMENT]   In Japanese, Noh (or Nō, as Fenollosa preferred to spell it) means "ability," highlighting the emphasis placed on a meticulously rehearsed and finished performance. As he prepared these English versions in 1914–1916, Pound recast the literal translations that Fenollosa had made in his notebooks with the help of Kiichi Hirata (see note 360.15 below) during their study of Noh in Tokyo in 1898–1901. In addition to Fenollosa's notebooks, Pound used the following sources for his edition: Ernest Fenollosa, *Epochs of Chinese & Chinese Art*, 2 vols. (1913); F. V. Dickins, *Primitive & Mediaeval Japanese Texts* (1906); F. Brinkley, *Japan: Its History, Arts, and Literature*, vol. 3 of *Oriental Series*, 8 vols. (1902); W. G. Aston, *A History of Japanese Literature* (1899). He also was helped by Marie C. Stopes, author and co-translator of *Plays of Old Japan, The No* (1913).
   Inspired by Yeats's adaptations of the Noh for the Irish stage, Pound in 1916 attempted several of his own; *Plays Modelled on the Noh* remained unpublished until 1987.

332.7   Arthur Waley]   British Orientalist (1889–1966). Prolific translator from the Chinese and Japanese who published *A Hundred Seventy Chinese Poems* (1918) and *The No Plays of Japan* (1921).

335.13–14   warship . . . Miidera.]   "Miidera" is the popular name of Onjōji, a temple near Lake Biwa in Otsu City. In accordance with his wishes, Fenollosa's ashes were removed from London's Highgate Cemetery and interred at Onjōji in 1909. The Japanese warship was hearsay.

336.32–33   It is a theatre . . . approve.]   Yeats outlined his theories of ritual or symbolic drama in his 1900 essay "Theatre." Edward Gordon Craig (1872–1966), English scene designer, producer, and actor, published *On the Art of the Theatre* in 1911, in which he argued for a poetic rather than a realist theater.

337.1   Umewaka Minoru]   Famous Noh master (1828–1909) who preserved its theatrical traditions during the Meiji Era. He was Fenollosa's teacher in Japan in 1883 and again in the years after 1896.

337.2–3   the revolution . . . Tokugawa.]   I.e. the Meiji Restoration, which overthrew the Tokugawa, the ruling family of the Edo Era (1603–1867). The boy emperor Meiji was "restored" to power and the imperial capital was transferred from Kyoto to Edo (Tokyo).

337.5 Perry's arrival] In 1854, American naval officer Matthew C. Perry (1794–1858) forced the opening of Japan's trade with the West.

337.9 'kaiyu'] Kayu, rice gruel.

337.18 Ninwa] Ninna, name of an era (885–888).

337.25 Gotsuchi Mikado] Japanese emperor (1464–1500).

337.26 Bunmei] Name of an era (1469–1486).

337.28 (Monsuki)] Montsuki, clothes bearing a family crest.

337.30–31 "waka" . . . Umewaka.] "Waka" means youth or young nobleman; "ume" means "plum tree."

337.35 Bunka] Name of an era (1804–1817).

337.36 Kioroku] Name of an era (1528–1531).

337.39 koku] A unit of volume of about 180 liters, used to indicate the total amount of rice crop annually produced in a territory.

337.39 Nobunaga's battle] The warlord Oda Nobunaga (1534–1582) was betrayed and attacked by Akechi Mitsuhide, one of his own generals.

338.1–2 Tokugawa Iyeyasu] Founder of the Tokuygawa Shogunate (1543–1616).

338.2 Keicho] Name of an era (1596–1614).

338.3 Kambun] Name of an era (1661–1673).

338.11 Umewaka Rokoro] Fenollosa's teacher Umewaka Minoru. See note 337.1

338.33 Taketi Owada] Professor of English, poet, and scholar of Japanese literature (1857–1910).

338.37 Utai-zome] New Year's celebration marked by performance of the Noh.

338.38 daimyos] Land-holding military lords.

339.2 the five . . . companies] The schools of Kanze, Komparu, Kongō, Hōshō, and Kita.

339.3 Omaya] Architectural structure with two gables.

339.4 time of Toyotomi] The rule of Toyotomi Hideyoshiu (1587–1598).

339.8 large hall in Hon-Maru] The Tokugawa Shogun's castle in Edo (Tokyo).

339.9 the San-ke] The three main branch families of the Tokugawa Shoguns.

339.15 hayashikata ("cats")] Because they made sounds that reminded him of "back-yard fence cats," Fenollosa, so his widow Mary informed

Pound, coined this term for the Noh musicians playing bamboo flutes or various drums on stage.

339.32   IN and YO]   Yin and Yang in Chinese.

339.35   Empress Jingō]   Empress Jingū (d. 269), mother of Emperor Ojin (270–310), later deified as a god of war.

339.36   Ciyo-shun]   The mythical Chinese emperors and sages, Yao and Shun.

339.37   Hachiman Daibosatsu]   Name of the chief Shinto god of the Hachiman Shrine in which Emperor Ojin is deified. "Dai" means great, and "Bosatsu" is "Bodhisattva."

339.38   Iwashimidzu]   Iwashimizu Hachimangū, shrine located at Yahata in Kyoto Prefecture.

340.2   "Takigi-No"]   Literally "Noh by firelight," originally held annually on seven consecutive nights at the end of March outside the Kasuga Shrine in Nara.

340.8   Taiyu of Kanze]   Tayū, or lead actor, of the Kanze school.

340.22   gates . . . Kikyo]   Gates through which people entered the Tokugawa Shogun's castle.

341.16   Noh of the Gods]   I.e. Waki Noh.

341.37   "Bodai-shin")]   Literally, the heart of the bodhi (perfect wisdom in Sanskrit).

342.7   Jin, . . . Shin]   From the Chinese Jên (love), I (justice), Li (propriety), Chih (knowledge), Hsin (sincerity).

343.24   Chansons de Geste]   Medieval French epic poems.

344.11   Kiyotsugu,]   Kan'ami Kiyotsugu (1333–1384) originated Noh drama at the Ashikaga Shogun's court by introducing stories into local songs and dances. His son, Zeami Motokiyo (1363–1443), elevated Noh to its classical form. Nine plays in this volume (*Suma Genji, Shojo, Tamura, Tsunemasa, Nishikigi, Kinuta, Hagoromo, Kagekiyo, Kakitsubata*) were traditionally attributed to Zeami.

344.13   Ono no Komachi;]   Poetess at the court of Emperor Nimmyo (833–850) and archetypical embodiment of beauty in Japanese tradition, associated by Pound in his Cantos with the moon-goddess Isis.

349.20   tachibana]   Mandarin oranges.

354.13–14   libretto . . . meaning.]   Pound added the following note in *The Translations* (1953): "Several Noh, including the Awoi-na-Uye, had, by 1939, been recorded on sound-film, which is the only medium capable of conveying any true idea of the whole art, unless one can see it properly done in Japan." Pound saw several Noh films (including *Awoi No Uye*) on a visit to the Library of Congress in May 1939.

358.36   Buckle . . . unanimism.] Henry Thomas Buckle (1821–1862), English historian who emphasized the formative influence of climate and geography on the collective consciousness of nations. Jules Romains (1885–1972), major theoretician of the French "unanimiste" school of poetry, whose poetics of place and of the crowd Pound praised in several articles in 1913.

359.16–17   I watched . . . Gregory] Pound spent the winters of 1913 through 1915 serving as Yeats's secretary at the Irish poet's country home, Stone Cottage, in Coleman's Hatch, Sussex. The Irish playwright Lady Augusta Gregory (1852–1932), founder, manager, and director of the Abbey Theatre, pioneered the collection of Gaelic folklore for stage adaptation.

360.17   Mr. Hirata] Kiichi Harata (1873–1943), scholar of English literature and Fenollosa's translator and adviser while Fenollosa served as part-time lecturer at The Higher Normal School in Tokyo (1898–1900).

360.20   the mistake of years ago] In 1883 Fenollosa suddenly dropped his lessons with Minoru Umewaka, leaving part of his tuition unpaid.

360.26   Takeyo] Takeyo Umewaka (1878–1959), Fenollosa's principal teacher of Noh singing during his second period of Noh study (1896–1901).

360.29   Mosse] Edward Sylvester Morse (1838–1925), American biologist who taught evolution at Tokyo University from 1877 to 1879; he returned to Tokyo in 1882 and studied Noh under Minoru Umewaka, to whom he introduced Fenollosa.

361.8   present Danjuro's] Danjūrō is a title given to the leading Kabuki actor of the Ichikawa family.

361.21   Kobori Enshu] Koboria Enshu (1579–1647), tea master, architect and garden designer.

366.5   hinoten] Planks of Japanese cypress.

366.9   Awoyama . . . Roju] The ex-daimyo Awoyama Tadanaga (1807–1864).

366.18–19   the time . . . Iyeyasu] The general Toyotomi Hideyoshi subordinated all the war lords in Japan in 1590; Tokugawa Ieyasu founded Tokugawa Shogunate in 1603.

366.20   Tadasu ga wara,] The riverbed near the Shimogamo shrine in Kyoto.

366.27   Ise] Location of a major Shinto shrine on the Pacific coast.

367.11   "daiko"] Master carpenter.

367.19   Kano artists] Painters who belonged to the school of artists founded by Kanō Masanobu (1434–1530); Fenollosa joined the school and was given the name Kanō Eitan Masanobu in 1884.

367.26   three ken square]   One ken is about six feet.

367.34   "shaken"]   Shaku, the equivalent of one foot.

370.2   *Ujinobu*]   Better known as Komparu Zenchiku (1405–1470), he married the daughter of Noh master Zeami Motokiyo (see note 344.11).

379.15   Kioto]   Kyoto, capital of Japan from 794 to 1868.

379.16   Sakura]   Cherry trees.

380.5   Kwannon]   See note 321.11.

384.20   "Era già . . . disio."]   *Purgatorio*, VIII, 1: "It was now the hour that turns back the longing [of seafaring folk and melts their heart the day they have bidden sweet friends farewell, and that pierces the new pilgrim with love]."

388.2   FENOLLOSA . . . NOH]   Pound's edited version of one of seven lectures (two which were delivered at the White House at the invitation of Theodore Roosevelt) given by Fenollosa in Washington, D.C., in March 1903. The essay does not appear in the source listed at 388.35–36.

389.4   Bishop Percy]   Thomas Percy (1729–1811). In 1761 he edited *Hau kiou choaan, or The Pleasing History: A Translation from the Chinese Language* [by James Wilkinson] *to which are added the argument or history of a Chinese poetry with notes.*

389.8   Bishop Hood]   I.e. Richard Hurd (1720–1808), whose essay "On the Provinces of Dramatic Poetry" (1811) examines Chinese theater.

389.9–10   Voltaire . . . translation]   Voltaire's *L'Orphelin de la Chine*, first staged in Paris in 1755, was based on Le Père Joseph Henri Prémaire's translation *Tcao-chi-cou-eulh, ou l'Orphelin de la Maison de Tchao* (1731).

391.7   Danjuro's.]   Danjūrō was a renowned Kabuki actor.

391.10   the fifth period]   In his 1903 Washington lectures Fenollosa divided the national life of Japan into five periods or "acts": 1) the 7th and 8th centuries; 2) the 9th through 11th centuries; 3) the 12th through 14th centuries; 4) the 15th and 16th centuries; 5) the 17th through 19th centuries.

391.14   Ukiyo-ye]   School of popular painting and color woodblock printmaking that emerged in the early 17th century, notable for its representations of contemporary Japanese life.

395.5   Saibara]   Derived from folk songs often dealing with the subject of love and composed in alternating lines of five and seven syllables, saibara were sung to the accompaniment of reed pipes at the imperial court in the 12th century. The Saibara quoted was recast by Pound from Fenollosa's manuscript notes, where it is titled "Takasago."

395.38–39   the Provençal . . . clar."]   First line of the Provençal May Day dance, "La Regine Avrillouse."

397.24   Heike epic]   *The Tale of the Heike*, a prose chronicle which sings of the fall of the Heike family in the battles of 1180 to 1185.

397.24   Soga cycle]   Stories about the Soga brothers who avenged their father's death in 1193.

397.33   Dengaku]   Fourteenth-century music and dance performances at Shinto shrines and Buddhist temples that were prayers for abundance in the rice harvest.

398.28   Kwan]   Kan'ami. See note 344.11.

398.32   Zei and On]   Kan'ami Kiyotsugu's son, Zeami Motokiyo (see note 344.11), and the latter's nephew On-ami (1398–1467).

398.39   Kamo river]   A river which flows through Kyoto.

401.19   the epic cycle of the Yoritomo]   Told in *The Tale of Heike*.

406.2   *Motokiyo*]   Zeami Motokiyo. See note 344.11.

411.14   Butsu.]   Buddha.

412.16   Suzuki]   Pampas grass.

418.7   ("The Silk-board")]   "Kinuta" is usually translated as "Fulling Block"—a block of wood upon which cloth was spread and beaten with wooden mallets to render it supple and shiny.

422.21   Aoi!]   A cry of pain invented by Pound in his version of the Noh play *Awoi no Uye*, whose heroine is wracked by jealousy.

423.37   adzusa!]   Catalpa.

428.29–30   South Kensington Museum]   Now the Victoria & Albert Museum.

430.35–36   "Quale . . . eterne."]   "As in the clear skies at the full moon Trivia [the goddess of the three ways, i.e. Diana] smiles among the eternal nymphs."

431.30   sho]   Mouth organ of Japanese court music.

433.34   City-on-the-cloud]   The capital, Kyoto.

440.3   Bushido]   The way of the warrior. Pound singled out *Kagekiyo*, his favorite among the Noh plays, for its "Homeric robustness."

442.20   yamabushi exorcists]   Yamabushi was a Buddhist monk living in the mountains and exorcising spirits with incantations of Buddhist scriptures.

444.13   DAIJIN]   Minister; Lady Awoi's father.

445.6–7   Adzumaya]   A square building with no walls.

449.19   Bosatsu]   Bodhisattva.

450.4 Narihira] Narihara (825–880), well known in his lifetime as a poet, lover, and courtier; a character in *Tales of Ise*, an anonymous anthology of brief stories written in alternating passages of prose and poetry compiled in the 10th century.

450.6 "Kohi"] Koi, love between the sexes.

450.6 "Gobusaki's"] Perhaps Pound's misreading of Fenollosa's "Gokuraku," a Buddhist paradise.

451.18 Ise Monogatari] *Tales of Ise* (see note 450.4).

453.23 Gosetsu] Gosechi, ceremonial dance and music offered to the Shinto gods on the day after the Harvest Festival in November.

455.20 Genbuku ceremony] Rite of passage, formally acknowledging the attainment of adulthood.

459.2 *Nobumitsu*] Also known as Kanze Kojirō (1435–1516).

463.2 *Kongo*] Surname of one of the leading families of Noh players.

463.3 *Utai Kimmō Zuye*] "Illustrated Guide of Noh Chanting" (1802), a popular collection of 50 texts for chanting.

463.4 Tō dynasty] T'ang dynasty (618–906).

463.5 biwa] In the 9th century, during the reign of Emperor Nimmyo, three legendary lutes or "biwas" were brought back to Japan from China by the courtier Fujiwara no Sadatoshi. They were named Genjo (Black Elephant), Seizan (Blue Mountain), and Shishimaru (Lion Child).

464.30 A. D. W.] Arthur Waley (see note 332.7), who had translated "Stories from *Utai Kimmo Zuye*."

468.28 Hi-no-Moto] Poetic name for Japan.

469.25 the sacred era of Gengi] I.e. the era of Engi or Yengi, during the reign of Emperor Daigo (897–930), the father of Murakami (946–967).

473.21–22 triple takadana] Triple shelves to place offerings for worship.

473.22 "gohei,"] Mitegura, paper attached to a wand.

477.4 tansos] Tansu, a chest of drawers.

479.2 ARNAUT DANIEL] Pound translated the entire corpus of Arnaut Daniel in 1911, traveling to the Ambrosian Library in Milan in the summer to examine one of the rare manuscripts containing musical notation of the troubadour's poems and later completing his translation in Sirmione. By December, some translations were appearing in *The New Age* and Pound was optimistic that his bilingual edition would soon be published by Stephen Swift and Company, which had brought out his *Sonnets and Ballate of Guido Cavalcanti* in May. The project foundered after Swift and Company went bankrupt in the fall of 1912. The following year, Pound sent "The Canzoni of Arnaut Daniel" to the Chicago publisher Ralph Fletcher Seymour, who kept it for three years before returning it in 1916. By December 1917, Pound had found another publisher, the Clerk's Press in Cleveland, but his manuscript disappeared in the mail. (Pound noted in *Umbra* that "the intended 'Arnaut Daniel' " was to be dedicated to William Pierce Shepard, professor of romance languages at Hamilton College with whom he studied.)

Having given up on this edition, Pound published "Glamour and Indigo," his new translation of "Doutz Brais e Critz" in *Little Review* (November 1918) and subsequently included 11 translations (whole or in part) in the long essay "Arnaut Daniel," collected in *Instigations* (1920). One translation not included in this section, "Sols Sui Qui Sai," was incorporated into his sequence "Langue d'Oc," published in *Quia Pauper Amavi* (see 520.24–522.4). He based his translations on Lavaud's revised and expanded version (1910) of Canello's 1883 edition of Arnaut Daniel's works.

While completely revising his earlier Arnaut translations in the fall of 1917, Pound came across a copy of Gavin Douglas's *The XIII Bukes of Eneados* (1553), a Chaucerian version of the *Aeneid* prized by Pound because it was "by no means Elizabethan." Most of the archaisms in "Arnaut Daniel" can be traced to Douglas's Middle Scots idiom. The following glossary is a guide to Pound's archaisms in these translations:

Ameises: Appeases, assuages
Amene: Pleasantly
Apertly: Openly
Auzel: Bird
Bedene: Immediately; anon
Belikes: Likely
Burnet: Dark brown
Cates: Choice viands or delicacies
Chirmes: Warbles
Chit-cracks: Young boasters
Culrouns: Rascals.
Culvertz: Villainous persons
Dasted: Stupified
Doncel: Damsel
Dree: Endure
Elrische: Variant of "elrich" or "elrage," suggestive of elves, hence weird, strange, uncanny
Escheating: Forfeiting
Esperance: Hope
Feod: Fee
Fere: Companion, in this case love
Flacked: Fluttered
Flinder'd: Broken into fragments
Fordel: Preeminence

Forletteth: Hinders
Frieks: Variant of "freke" or "freik," a bold or fighting man; any man in general
Galzeardy: Cheerfulness
Genet: Broom plant
Gentrice: Gentleness
Gesning: Hospitality
Gimp: Neat
Glastre: Brag
Hewis: Steep hills
Holts: Woods
Hows: Valleys
Inkirlie: Secretly
Kern: Cause to granulate? Churn?
Leal: Loyal
Lynd: Lime
Lyt: Little
Make: Mate, fere, companion
Mam: Variant of "mament," moment?
Mansuet: Mild
Mearing: Bounded by
Mewing: Whimpering, recriminating
Mirk: Murk

Murrain: Pestilence

Par fay: Verily

Paregale: Equal

Parsement: Variant of "partiment," a division or company

Peirs: Blue

Perk: Perch

Pleach: Intertwined boughs; hedge

Prevene: Occupy

Quihitter: Twitter

Raik: Haste precipitate

Rates: Scolds

Resset derne: Secret retreat

Saineth: Blesses

Sege's: Man's

Shaveling: Contemptuous epithet for a tonsured ecclesiastic

Son Dezirat: His (friend) The Desired One

Song-locks: Bundles of song

Spalliard: Espalier

Spalt: Stone used to promote the fusion of metals

Stot: Steer

Swenkin: Laborer

Swevyn: Dream

Swinger: Sluggard

Teen: Anger

Traist: Faithful

Venust: Grace

Voust: Boast

Waith: Wandering

Walwit: Bewailed

Welkin: Sky

Wriblis: Warblings

Yape: Ape

Yare!: Without delay

481.1   *Chansson . . . Prim*]   Cf. the version published in *New Age* in 1911 and collected in *Translations,* 1118.3–1120.5.

483.30   Pontrangle]   "Pontremble," in the original, an allusion to (Albert?) Malaspina of the Italian town of Pontremoli.

485.20   Puy-de-Dome]   Mountain in the Auvergne region of France.

485.34   Sir Bertran]   "Presumably Bertrand de Born" [note in *The Translations*].

486.31   Elwand and Plow]   The Belt of Orion and Ursa Major.

489.1   *L'Aura Amara*]   "In this poem 'we have the chatter of birds in autumn, the onomatopoeia obviously depends upon the '-*utz*, -*etz*, -*ences* and –*ortz*' of the rhyme scheme, 17 of the 68 syllables of each strophe therein included . . . I have not been able to make more than a map of the relative positions in this canzo' " [note in *The Translations*].

491.16   Dome]   "Our Lady of Poi [Puy] de Dome? No definite solution of this reference yet found. H. and B. say: 'town of Périgord'. The same?" [note in *The Translations*]. According to Canello, an allusion to the monks of the town of Domme in the Périgord.

492.8   mearing.]   "Dante cites this poem in the second book of De Vulgari Eloquio with poems of his own, De Born's, and Cino Pistoija's" [note in *The Translations*].

492.30   Lucerne's dower]   According to Canello, Lucena, town in the Spanish province of Valencia.

493.19   Sir Mnalcas]   "Cel de Moncli" (Sir Moncli) in the original.

493.23   *En Breu . . . Braus*] "Notable for the opening bass ono-matopoeia of the wind rowting in the autumn branches. Arnaut may have caught his alliteration from the joglar engles" [note in *The Translations*].

494.24   Atalant' and Meleagro.] Atalante and Meleager, whose chaste loves are recounted in Ovid's *Metamorphoses*, VIII, 260f.

495.6–7   "agre" . . . "haro."] In a manuscript note, Pound glosses Canello's suggestion that this might be the family name of the lady sung by Arnaut: "variously conjectured as *agregon*, *agrismonte*, but not yet explained."

495.21   Vivien] "Vivien, strophe 2, nebotz Sain Guillem, an allusion to the romance, 'Enfances Vivien'" [note in *The Translations*, taken from Canello].

496.2   Longus'] "Centurion in the crucifixion legend" [note in *The Translations*].

496.28   Galicia's king to villeiny—] "Ferdinand II, King of Galicia, 1157–88, son of Berangere, sister of Raimon Berenger IV ('*quattro figlie ebbe*,' etc.) of Aragon, Count of Barcelona. His second son, Lieutenant of Provence, 1168" [note in *The Translations*, taken from Canello].

496.35   true king . . . Estampa.] "King crowned at Estampe, Phillipe August, crowned May 29, 1180, at age of 16. This poem might date Arnaut's birth as early as 1150" [note in *The Translations*, taken from Canello].

497.8   ameises] Appeases, assuages, a translation of "d'enoi gandres," Levy's reading of the enigmatic "noigandres." See Canto 20.

497.29   Meander's] Winding river in Phrygia.

500.24   Lernian mazes] The marsh of Lerne, according to Canello; cor-rected by Lavaud into the marsh formed by the Rhône at Userna, the ancient name of Beaucaire.

500.32   Sences] "Sanchas" (i.e. Saintes) in the original.

502.9   Miels-de-Ben] Lady Better-than-Good. See note 284.24.

502.12   brittle] " 'Brighter than glass, and yet as glass is, brittle.' The comparisons to glass went out of poetry when glass ceased to be a rare, pre-cious substance. Cf. Passionate Pilgrim, III" [note in *The Translations*].

504.3   *L'Homme Moyen Sensuel*] The average sensual man: phrase coined by Matthew Arnold in "George Sand," collected in *Mixed Essays* (1879).

504.4   "I hate . . . woman"] *Don Juan*, I, lxi.

504.18–19   infant tick . . . *Atlantic*] Ellery Sedgwick (1872–1960), editor of *The Atlantic* from 1909 to 1938.

504.20   Comstock's] Anthony Comstock (1844–1915), founder of the Society for Supression of Vice.

504.22–505.2   his taste . . . a publisher]   In 1913 President Wilson appointed novelist Thomas Nelson Page and publisher Walter Hines Page as ambassadors to Italy and to Great Britain, respectively.

504.32   Anonymous Compatriot]   American poet Fitz-Greene Halleck (1790–1867).

505.5   Henry Van Dyke]   Presbyterian minister and popular author Henry Van Dyke (1852–1933) served as minister to the Netherlands and Luxembourg from 1913 to 1917.

505.12   Mabie . . . Woodberry]   The magazine editors and critics Hamilton Wright Mabie (1845–1916), Lyman Abbott (1835–1922), and George Edward Woodberry (1855–1930).

505.18   Hiram Maxim]   Pound may be conflating Sir Hiram Maxim (1840–1916), inventor of the Maxim machine gun, or his son (1869–1936), inventor of the Maxim silencer, with the critic Hudson Maxim (1853–1927), author of *The Science of Poetry and the Philosophy of Language* (1910).

505.23   pantosocracy,]   Literally "equal rule of all," the name for Southey and Coleridge's unrealized utopian community to be established on the Susquehanna River in Pennsylvania.

505.28   Parkhurst's]   The reformer and Presbyterian minister Charles Henry Parkhurst (1842–1933), president of the Society for the Prevention of Crime in New York and author of *Our Fight With Tammany* (1895).

505.34   "Prolific Noyes"]   By 1915 Alfred Noyes (1880–1958) had published more than 16 volumes of poetry.

506.6   Gilder]   Richard Watson Gilder (1844–1909), poet and editor of *The Century* from 1881 until his death.

506.7   *De mortuis verum*]   Cf. the Latin proverb "De mortuis nil nisi bonum" ("Of the dead speak kindly or not at all"). *Verum* = truthfully.

506.26   "Message to Garcia,"]   Elbert Hubbert's widely circulated inspirational essay (1899) recounting the heroism of an American lieutenant during the Spanish-American War.

506.24   Mosher's]   Thomas Bird Mosher (1852–1933), publisher and editor of the magazine *The Bibelot* who was known for printing pirated books. He refused to publish Pound's *A Lume Spento*.

507.36   calor]   Warmth.

509.7–8   De Gourmont says . . . language]   In *New Age*, July 26, 1917, Pound quoted Gourmont on the coarsening of contemporary language: "Fifty grunts and as many representative signs will serve all needful communication between all thoroughly socialized men."

509.17   "As free . . . kings"?]   Cf. Byron, *Don Juan*, IX, xxv: "I wish men to be free / As much from mobs as kings."

510.32   Rodyheaver's] Homer Rodeheaver (1880–1955), evangelist and song-leader at Billy Sunday's revival meetings. Beginning in 1913, he made several recordings of revival hymns and temperance songs.

511.12   *Pierrots*] In *Poetry,* November 1917, Pound published "Irony, Laforgue, and Some Satire," an essay that discusses Laforgue's "verbalism" (later defined as "logopoeia"; see note 526.24).

511.14   (Scene . . . typique)] "A Brief but Typical Scene," title of the Laforgue poem as it appears in his *L'Imitation de Notre Dame* (1885).

511.17   *Vae soli*] Cf. Ecclesiastes 4:10 in the Vulgate: "Vae soli, quia cum ceciderit, non habet sublevantem se" ("but woe to him that is alone when he falleth; for he hath not another to help him up").

513.2   QUIA PAUPER AMAVI] Cf. Ovid, *Ars Amatoria,* II, 165: "Pauperibus vates ergo sum, quia pauper amavi" ("I am the poet of the poor, because I was poor when I loved"). Pound translated "Quia Pauper Amavi" for James Laughlin as "Love on the Dole."

515.1   *Langue d'Oc*] Language of southern France, in which the word for "yes" is "oc" (rather than the northern "oïl"). As indicated in the text, this poem is a sequence of translations after poems by Provençal troubadours: "*When the nightingale . . .* ": anonymous; I: Giraut de Borneil (1175–1220); II: Guillaume de Poitiers (1071–1127); III: Cerclamon, pseudonym of an unknown poet; IV: anonymous; V: Arnaut Daniel, a translation of "Sols Sui Qui Sai," intended for the unpublished 1917 Clerk's Press edition (see note 479.2). For archaisms, see glossary at note 479.2.

515.2   *Alba*] See note 120.25.

515.18   Plasmatour] Creator.

516.17   *Avril*] April.

519.26   *Vergier*] Orchard. For Pound's earlier translation see see 120.25–121.17.

524.2   "*Nodier raconte . . .*"] Cf. the first line of Théophile Gautier's poem "Inès de las Sierras": "Nodier raconte qu'en Espagne . . ." ("Nodier recounts that in Spain . . .")

525.6   poluphloisboious] "Loud roaring," a Homeric epithet. The line in Greek following translates "To the shore of the loud-roaring sea" (*Iliad*, I, 34).

525.8   SISTE VIATOR.] Stay, traveler.

525.10   *I Vecchii*] The old men.

525.13   Il était . . . garçon] He was like a very little boy.

525.16   "Con . . . tardi,"] With slow eyes and grave. Cf. Dante, *Purgatorio,* VI, l. 63.

525.20   Great Mary,"]   The novelist Mrs. Humphry Ward (1851–1920).

525.23   my bust by Gaudier,]   Pound's friend, the sculptor Henri Gaudier-Brzerska, completed his white-marble "Hieratic Head of Ezra Pound" in 1915.

526.8   *Ritratto*]   Portrait.

526.10   Lowell]   James Russell Lowell was American ambassador to Italy from 1880 to 1885.

526.24   *Homage to Sextus Propertius*]   Described by Pound as a "major persona" (or mask), "Homage to Sextus Propertius" is at once a tribute, a translation, and, as T. S. Eliot observed, a "criticism" of the first-century Roman poet "which in a most interesting way insists upon an element of humour, of irony and mockery in Propertius, which Mackail and other interpreters have missed"—an element that Pound himself defined as *logopoeia*, "the dance of intellect among words," a technique that "employs words not only for their direct meaning, but takes count in a special way of habits of usage, of the context we *expect* to find with the word, its usual concomitants, of its known acceptances, and of ironical play." Pound's tonal strategy in this "Homage" is deliberately anachronistic, for while attempting to capture "the spirit of the young man of the Augustan Age, hating rhetoric and undeceived by imperial hog-wash," he also sought (as he wrote in 1931) to present "certain emotions as vital to me in 1917, faced with the infinite and ineffable imbecility of the British Empire, as they were to Propertius some centuries earlier, when faced with the infinite and ineffable imbecility of the Roman Empire." When a considerably truncated version of the poem ("the left foot, knee, thigh and right ear," according to Pound) was published in Harriet Monroe's *Poetry* in March 1919, it immediately aroused the ire of University of Chicago classicist William Gardner Hale, who attacked its numerous errors and "howlers" in the April issue of the magazine: "Mr. Pound is incredibly ignorant of Latin. . . . For sheer magnificence of blundering, this is unsurpassable. . . . If Mr. Pound were a professor of Latin, there would be nothing left for him but suicide." Pound retorted: "No, I have not done a translation of Propertius. That fool in Chicago took the *Homage* for a translation, despite the mention of Wordsworth and the parodied line from Yeats." His real purpose, he explained, was less to "translate" Propertius than "to bring a dead man to life."

Homage: Pound later explained that he was following Debussy's usage of the term in "Homage à Rameau," i.e. "a piece of music recalling Rameau's manner." Thomas Hardy in 1922 told Pound the entire poem would be clearer if entitled (in the fashion of Browning) "Propertius Soliloquizes." In later editions the title is followed by the date "1917."

Pound's sources in Propertius are as follows: 1: from III.i; 2: III.iii; 3: from III.xvi; 4: from III.vi; 5: from II.x; II.i; 6: II.xiiiA; III.v; III.iv; II.viiiA; 7: II.xv; 8: II.xxviii; 9: II.xxviii; II.xxviiiA; 10: II.xxix; I.ixxixA; 11: II.xxx; II.xxxii; II.xxx; II.xxxii; II.xxx; II.xxxii; II.xxiv; 12: II.xxxiv.

526.26   Callimachus] Greek poet and critic (280–245 B.C.E.) from Cyrene. *Philetas:* Poet and grammarian (*ca.* 300 B.C.E.) from Cos, an island in the Aegean Sea.

527.32   Oetian] Hercules died on Mt. Oeta.

528.7   devirginated young ladies] Propertius' Latin reads "Gaudeo in solita tacta puella sono" ("Let my girl be touched by the sound of a familiar music and rejoice in it"). Pound reads "tacta" as the opposite of "intacta" (untouched, virgin).

528.20   Taenarian columns] Columns made of black marble quarried at Taenarus, Sparta.

528.28   wine jars)] In *Personæ* (1926), Pound added the line "Nor is it equipped with a frigidaire patent."

529.7   Bellerophon's horse,] Pegasus, who according to legend made the waters of the Hippocrene (a spring on Mount Helicon) flow when he stamped on the mountain. The spring gave inspiration to those who drank from it. Pegasus sprang into being from the blood of Medusa.

529.14   Curian brothers,] Three Curian brothers fought against the Horatii, three Roman brothers, to decide the conflict between Alba and Rome.

529.16   Q. H. Flaccus'] Horace's.

529.17   Aemilia . . . raft,] Aemilius Paulus celebrated his defeat over the Macedonians in 168 B.C.E. with a spectacular processional in Rome.

529.18   victorious delay of Fabius,] Against Hannibal's forces as they advanced on Rome.

529.19   battle at Cannae] In which the Roman forces suffered heavy losses at the hands of Hannibal's army.

529.20   lares] Spirits guarding Rome.

529.23   Jove protected by geese,] See Livy, V, 47, which recounts how the noise of geese alerted the outnumbered Roman garrison guarding the Capitoline hill of imminent attack by the Gauls in 387 B.C.E.

529.24   Castalian] Castalia, a sacred spring on Mount Parnassus.

530.1   Silenus] A satyr.

530.3   small birds . . . mother] In conventional depictions small doves draw Aphrodite's chariot.

530.4   Gorgon's lake.] The Hippocrene (see note 529.7).

530.19   Suevi] The Suebi were defeated by the Romans in 29 B.C.E.

530.21   "Night dogs,] Another celebrated "howler." The original reads "Nocturnaeque canes ebria signa fugae" ("you will sing of the tokens of drunken flight through the dark").

531.21   Cypris]   Aphrodite.

532.2   *Lygdamus*]   Propertius' slave.

533.18   Emathian]   Macedonian.

534.1   Pierides!]   The Muses.

534.33–34   Ossa . . . Olympus]   Pelion and Ossa were the mountains which the Aloade, two giants, piled on Mount Olympus in an attempt to scale heaven and overthrow the gods.

535.14   *ore rotundos,*]   With round mouth. Horace, *Ars Poetica*, 323f.

535.31   Jugurtha]   King of Numidia, captured and slain by Gaius Marius.

536.18   Syrian onyx]   Syrian unguents used in embalming were kept in onyx boxes.

537.15   Endymion . . . Diana]   The Moon (Diana) descended to visit Endymion, a handsome shepherd of Mount Latmos, and fell in love with him while he slept.

538.30–31   Io . . . Nile water]   Io, a priestess of Hera, was beloved of Zeus, who changed her into a heifer to conceal her from his wife. She was restored to her original form in Egypt after long wandering, and was worshipped there as Isis.

538.32   Ino]   Fleeing her Theban husband, Ino was transformed into the goddess Leucothea when she entered the sea.

538.33–34   Andromeda . . . Perseus,]   Perseus rescued Andromeda from a sea monster sent by Poseidon.

539.1   Callisto,]   Transformed by Juno into a bear after she bore a child by Zeus.

539.7–8   danger . . . Semele's]   When Zeus appeared to Semele in his full majesty, she was burned to ashes.

540.8   Iope, and Tyro, and Pasiphae,]   See notes 147.7 and 147.8.

541.31   Vesta]   Goddess of the hearth.

543.24–25   that woman in Colchis]   Medea.

543.26   Lynceus]   A rival poet who seeks Cynthia's affections.

545.2   Hamadryads]   Tree nymphs.

545.3   Ascraeus']   Hesiod's.

545.23   Varro . . . expedition]   In his translation of *Argonautica*, by Apollonius of Rhodes.

545.24–25   his great passion . . . parchment]   Varro's love poems have not survived.

545.29–30   Calvus . . . Lycoris]   Neither the poems of Calvus (82–47 B.C.E.) on his wife Quintilla nor those of Gallus (b. 70 B.C.E.) to his mistress Lycoris have survived.

547.4   "*Vocat . . . umbram*"]   The heat calls us into the shade.

549.2   (LIFE AND CONTACTS)]   In *Diptych Rome-London* (1958), the subtitle reads "Contacts and Life." Pound informed his publisher, "Note inversion in subtitle of Mauberley, NOT Life and Contacts but the actual order of the subject matter." In *Personæ* (1926), he added this note: "The sequence is so distinctly a farewell to London that the reader who chooses to regard this as an exclusively American edition may as well omit it and turn at once to ["Homage to Sextus Propertius"].

549.4   *Ode . . . Sépulchre*]   "Ode for the Selection of His Tomb," an adaptation of the title of an ode by Pierre Ronsard.

549.12   Capaneus]   One of the seven warriors dispatched from Argos to attack Thebes. Boasting that not even Zeus's thunderbolt could prevent him from scaling the walls of the city, he was struck down by lightning. Appears in Dante's *Inferno*, XIV, as an embodiment of defiance and unabated rage.

549.13   ʹΊδμεν . . . Τροίη]   *Odyssey*, XII, 189, from the sirens' song: "For we know all the toils that are in wide Troy."

549.22–23   *l'an . . . eage*]   "In the thirtieth year of his life"; adapted from the opening of François Villon's *Le Testament*.

550.13   barbitos]   Seven-stringed instrument resembling the lyre.

550.21   Shall reign throughout our days.]   Later versions read "Shall outlast our days."

550.24–25   We see . . . market-place]   The Greek words for "the beautiful" were featured on the label of a popular brand of soap.

551.4–6   τίν . . . upon!]   Cf. Pindar, *Olympian Odes*, II, 2: "What god, what hero, aye, and what man shall we loudly praise?"

551.9   pro domo]   For the home.

551.17   pro patria . . . et decor]   "For the fatherland, neither sweetly nor gloriously": Adaptation of Horace, *Odes*, III.ii.13: "dulce et decorum est pro patria mori" ("It is sweet and glorious to die for one's fatherland").

552.14   *Yeux Glauques*]   Glaucous eyes, phrase used by Gautier to evoke the dull grayish green or grayish blue gaze common in Pre-Raphaelite portraits of women.

552.16–17   When John . . . Treasuries"]   "Of Kings' Treasuries" was the opening chapter in Ruskin's *Sesame and Lilies* (1865).

552.19   Fœtid Buchanan . . . voice]   Robert W. Buchanan castigated the Pre-Raphaelite poets in "The Fleshly School of Poetry" (1871). Dante Gabriel Rossetti's poem "Jenny" (see 553.6) was singled out for attack.

552.23–26   Burne-Jones . . . rhapsodize]   Edward Burne-Jones' painting *King Cophetua and the Beggar Maid* entered the Tate Gallery's collection in 1919.

553.1–2   English Rubaiyat . . . those days.]   Edward Fitzgerald's version (1859) of *The Rubáiyát of Omar Khayyám* was virtually unknown until its discovery by Rossetti and the Pre-Raphaelites.

553.11   "*Siena . . . Maremma*"]   "Siena made me; Maremma undid me": Dante, *Purgatorio*, V, 134.

553.15   Verog]   Victor Plarr (1863–1929), librarian of the Royal College of Surgeons in London and author of the poetry collection *In the Dorian Mood* (1896), mentioned at 553.27.

553.16   Gallifet]   French general (1830–1930) who led a cavalry charge at Sedan.

553.17   Rhymers' Club]   Group founded in the early 1890s by W. B. Yeats, Ernest Rhys, and T. W. Rolleston; its members included Ernest Dowson, Lionel Johnson, Victor Plarr, and Arthur Symons.

553.25   Headlam]   The Reverend Steward D. Headlam (1847–1924). *Image:* Selwyn Image (1849–1930), Rhymers' Club member and professor of Fine Arts at Oxford.

554.6   Horeb, Sinai]   The mountains, respectively, where Moses saw the burning bush and was given the Ten Commandments.

555.1   friend of Bloughram's]   Gigadibs, literary hack in Browning's poem "Bishop Bloughram's Apology" (1855).

555.19   "Conservatrix of Milésien"]   The lubricious *Milesian Tales* did not survive antiquity. The phrase, adapted from Remy de Gourmont's short story "Stratagèmes" (1894), was later glossed by Pound as "Woman, the conservator, the inheritor of past gestures" in a postscript to his translation of Gourmont's *Natural Philosophy of Love* (1922).

556.2–3   "Daphne . . . hands"]   Translation of lines from Théophile Gautier's "Le Château du Souvenir" (1852).

556.24   "Which . . . nourished"]   Translation of the first line of Jules Laforgue's "Complainte des Pianos" (1885).

556.30   Pierian roses]   Cf. Sappho, LXXI: "for you have no part in the roses that come from Pieria."

557.3   Lawes]   Henry Lawes (1596–1662) set to music "Goe lovely Rose" and other poems by Edmund Waller.

557.28   *1920*]   For *Personæ* (1926), Pound added an epitaph adapted from Ovid, *Metamorphosis*, VII, 786: "Vacuos exercet aera morsus" ("His empty mouth snaps at the air").

557.31–32   "eau-forte . . . Jaquemart"]   Jules Jacquemart (1837–1880) engraved the frontispiece for the 1881 edition of Gautier's *Emaux et Camées*.

558.14–19   "*Qu'est* . . . CAID ALI]   "What do they know of love, and what can they understand? If they cannot understand poetry, if they have no feeling for music, what can they understand of this passion, in comparison with which the rose is coarse and the perfume of violets a clap of thunder?" "Caid Ali" is a pseudonym for Pound.

558.20   diabolus in the scale]   Medieval music theorists called the augmented fourth the "devil in music."

558.22   ANANGKE]   Necessity.

558.26   NUKTOS 'ÁGALMA]   "Jewel of the Night." From the Greek pastoral poet Bion's address to the Evening Star. All the editions until the 1958 *Diptych Rome-London* read NUKTIS.

559.4   TO AGATHON]   The good.

559.7   his urge]   The version in *Personæ* (1926) reads "his 'fundamental passion.' "

559.30–31   red-beaked steeds . . . Cytheræan.]   See note 530.3.

561.3   *apathein*]   Impassivity, indifference.

562.22   Luini]   The Lombard painter Bernardino Luini (*ca*. 1480–1532).

562.28   Anadyomene]   Foam-born (epithet of Aphrodite).

562.29   Reinach]   Salomon Reinach (1858–1932), French art historian; his *Apollo* (1904) is a study of ancient sculpture.

564.2   UMBRA]   At the end of *Umbra* Pound appended a chart (to be read vertically) entitled "Personae and Portraits: Main outline of E.P.'s work to date":

Personae—	Sketches (in "Lustra")—	
La Fraisne	Millwins	
Cino	Bellaires	
Audiart	etc.	
Marvoil	(*Later*)	Etudes—
Altaforte	I Vecchii	Guido
Vidal	Nodier Raconte	Arnaut
	etc.	Langue d'Oc

Sketches (in "Ripostes")—	Major Personae—
Portrait d'une Femme	Seafarer
Phasellus Ille	Exile's Letter (and
Girl	Cathay in general)
An Object	Homage to Sextus Propertius
Quies	

564.4   From *Poetry and Drama*]   The poem was in fact published in *Poetry Review*, with "An Immorality," page 240, as its third section.

564.20   AFTER HEINE]   From Heine's *Buch der Lieder.* ("Hast du die Lippen mir wund geküsst.")

564.24   haste.]   Later versions read "waste"; "haste" is closer to Heine's German ("Eil").

565.1   *Phanopoeia*]   Defined by Pound in "How to Read" (1929) as "a casting of images upon the visual imagination."

565.13   SALTUS]   A leap.

565.24   CONCAVA VALLIS]   A hollow valley.

566.6   *The Alchemist*]   *Umbra*'s table of contents notes: "unpublished 1912."

566.8 ·   Sail of Claustra]   A 12th-century female troubadour. The other women named in the poem are literary references. Some belong to Greek mythology (Alcmena, Briseis, Alcyon); others occur in Provençal literature (Aelis, Tobors, Audiart); several are derived from French and Italian sources (e.g. Cavalcanti's Vanna and Mandetta).

568.1   *Cantus Planus*]   Plainsong.

568.4   Evoe]   The frenzied cry of the Bacchantes. See Catullus, LXIV, line 255.

568.5   ZAGREUS]   Bacchus.

568.7   Hesper adest.]   Cf. the opening of Catullus, LXII: "Vesper adest, iuuenes, consurgite" ("The evening is come, young men, so rise").

568.10   *T. E. H.*]   Thomas Ernest Hulme (1883–1917), English philosopher and poet killed in action in World War I. See note 229.2.

569.4   *Salutation the Third*]   The version in *Personæ* (1926) considerably tones down the poem first printed in the debut issue of *BLAST*, June 20, 1914, which reads as follows:
    Let us deride the smugness of "The Times": GUFFAW!
        So much the gagged reviewers,
    It will pay them when the worms are wriggling in their vitals;
    These were they who objected to newness,

HERE are their TOMB-STONES.
　　They supported the gag and the ring:
A little black BOX contains them.
　　SO shall you be also,
You slut-bellied obstructionist,
You sworn foe to free speech and good letters,
You fungus, you continuous gangrene.

Come, let us on with the new deal,
　　Let us be done with Jews and Jobbery,
Let us SPIT upon those who fawn on the JEWS for their money,
Let us out to the pastures.

PERHAPS I will die at thirty,
Perhaps you will have the pleasure of defiling my pauper's grave,
I wish you JOY, I proffer you ALL my assistance.
It has been your HABIT for long to do away with true poets,
You either drive them mad, or else you blink at their suicides,
Or else you condone their drugs, and talk of insanity and genius,
BUT I will not go mad to please you.
　　I will not FLATTER you with an early death.
OH, NO! I will stick it out,
　　I will feel your hates wriggling about my feet,
And I will laugh at you and mock you,
And will offer you consolations in irony,
　　O fools, detesters of Beauty.

I have seen many who go about with supplications,
　　Afraid to say how they hate you.
HERE is the taste of my BOOT.
　　CARESS it, lick off the BLACKING.

570.7　　*Monumentum . . . Etc.*]　Cf. Horace, *Odes*, III.xxx.1: "Exegi monumentum aere perennius" ("I have built a monument more lasting than bronze").

572.1　　*Fratres Minores*]　In *BLAST,* June 20, 1914, the first and final two lines were blacked out with printer's ink.

572.9　　*Instigations*]　This poem was published in "The Classics 'Escape,' " in the essay collection *Instigations* (1920).

572.10　　*Cantico del Sole*]　See Pound's version of St. Francis's "Cantico del Sole," 127.1–128.18.

572.20　　Nunc dimittis]　Luke 2:29, from the Vulgate: "Now lettest thou depart."

573.2　　GUIDO CAVALCANTI RIME]　In 1928, Pound proposed to his English publishers, Faber and Gwyer, a new, limited edition of his *Sonnets and Ballate of Guido Calvalcanti*, supplemented by Dante Gabriel Rossetti's translations and facsimiles of the principal Cavalcanti manuscripts, but daunted by the production cost, the firm backed out of the project in early 1929. Meanwhile, he had contacted the Cuala Press of Dublin for an edition of his translation of "Donna mi prega," to be accompanied by a commentary by W. B. Yeats, but this project was canceled because of Yeats's poor health. In the spring of 1929, the Aquila Press of London agreed to a deluxe edition of "The Complete Works of Guido Cavalcanti" (including the Rossetti translations, the photographic facsimiles of the Cavalcanti manuscripts, and "Donna mi prega"), but after printing 56 pages of the book, the press failed late that year. Trying to salvage the edition, Pound (at his own expense) had the Italian texts and scholarly apparatus printed in Genoa by the Edizioni Marsano and the manuscript reproductions printed in Germany, to which he added the 56 pages of the aborted Aquila Press edition. The resulting book—printed on four kinds of paper and in various typefaces, with notes and commentary in Italian and English—was finally issued in January 1932. Bitterly subtitled "Edizione Rappazzata Fra Le Rovine" ("Edition Pieced Together Among The Ruins"), it appeared anonymously. Only the preface, entitled "Ad lectorem E.P.," hinted at its authorship.

575.1–14   Who . . . embrace.]   Cf. Pound's previous translations, 141.27–142.9 and 199.31–200.

575.16–29   A breath . . . see.]   Cf. 202.27–203.19.

576.1–14   Surely thy wit . . . playne.]   Cf. 203.20–34.

576.19–22   Sesto . . . etc.]   Sesto the Empirical. . . . Every syllogism is for him a vicious circle because the major premise has to be assured by a complete induction: whereas, in order that it may be said to be complete, it is evident that the conclusion of the syllogism, which has still to be demonstrated, must also be found to be therein included, etc.

576.28–577.6   This fayre Mistress . . . for its own.]   Cf. 206.16–36.

577.8–24   Every fresh . . . gentlehood.]   Cf. 205.1–18. Translation of Pound's marginal gloss in Italian: "It seems to me that this sonnet accompanied a commentary on or translation of some Arabic philosopher, say, Avicenna, of whom it speaks allegorically."

577.9   Galicia]   In the 1966 Madersteig edition of *Ezra Pound's Cavalcanti Poems*, the headnote reads: "Galicia (the modern Lizzano)."

578.1   *Donna mi Prega*]   In *Guido Cavalcanti Rime*, Pound's "traduction" of this canzone was placed between the first part of "Medievalism" (an essay first published in *Dial*, March 1928) and the second part (*Dial*, July 1928), entitled "A Partial Explanation." Canto 36 (1934) contains another English version of "Donna mi prega."

578.2   *Campion*]   English poet, composer, and lutinist (1567–1620), author of *Five Books of Airs* (1601–1617) and *A New Way of Making Fowre Parts in Counterpoint* (1613).

578.3   *Lawes,*]   See note 557.3.

578.23–28   (marginal gloss)]   There where and that which creates it.

579.1–3   (marginal gloss)]   Virtue and power.

579.17–19   (marginal gloss)]   Essence and movement.

580.2   *piacimento*]   Liking.

581.1–3   *The Canzone* . . . corrected.]   "The Canzone" is Pound's typo-
graphically innovative arrangement of the Italian text of "Donna mi prega."
Guido Cavalcanti Rime contains 40 plates of Cavalcanti manuscripts photo-
graphically reproduced by Pound from copies held by various European li-
braries and archives. Looking at the reproduction of the manuscript at the
Laurenziano Library in Florence (plate 4), one can observe that Pound took
the small dots and virgules that punctuate this unlineated text as guides when
creating his new version. "The canzone," he explained in his notes, "was to
poets of this period what the fugue was to musicians in Bach's time. It is a
highly specialized form, having its own self-imposed limits. I trust I have
managed to print the *Donna mi prega* in such a way that its articulations
strike the eye without need of a rhyme table. The strophe is here seen to con-
sist of four parts, the second lobe equal to the first as required by the rules
of the canzone; and the fourth happening to equal the third, which is not
required by the rules as Dante explains them. Each strophe is articulated by
14 terminal and 12 inner rhyme sounds, which means that 52 out of every
154 syllables are bound into pattern."

        In *Guido Cavalcanti Rime,* "The Canzone," the Italian text of "Donna
mi prega" (with English title and headnote), was preceded by Pound's "Par-
tial Explanation" and then followed by a lengthy section of commentary (first
published in *Dial,* July 1928) entitled "The Further Dimension," "The
Vocabulary," "The Canzone: Further Notes."

581.4   Giuntine edition.]   I.e. Di Giunta's edition of 1527.

587.1   ALFRED . . . POEMS]   Alfred Venison is a pseudonym for
Pound. These poems were first published in the *New English Weekly* between
February and November 1934. The letters preceding each poem and signed
A.V. were written by the newspaper's editor-in-chief, A. O. Orage.

587.2   *Social Credit*]   Monetarist doctrine propounded by Major Clifford
Hugh Douglas (1879–1952), a scheme by which the state would subsidize in-
dustries by issuing a "National Dividend" to assure an adequate money supply.

588.3   S.C.N.]   Stanley Charles Nott (1887–1978), publisher of *Alfred
Venison's Poems* in the series "Pamphlets on the New Economics" and an as-
sociate of Orage.

589.1   *Bread Brigade*]   In the late 1920s and early 1930s large groups of
unemployed workers, the "Hunger Marchers" (see 590.2–3), marched
throughout England and Scotland, protesting in London and other cities.

589.29   Beaverbrook] Willliam Maxwell Aitken Beaverbrook, 1st Baron (1879–1964), British financier, statesman, and newspaper owner.

590.30   Sime] John Allsebrook Simon, 1st Viscount (1873–1954), British foreign secretary from 1931 to 1935. *Mac:* James Ramsay Macdonald (1866–1937), British statesman. Prime minister of the second Labour government beginning in 1929, he agreed to lead a coalition government with Conservative support in 1931, thus losing the confidence of the Labourites.

591.10   Clerkenwall] District of Finsbury metropolitan borough in London.

592.31   Norman's kin] Montague Collet Norman, 1st Baron Norman of St. Clere (1871–1950), British financier and governor of the Bank of England (1920–1944).

594.2   the Co-ops] Social Credit political organization.

594.15   Selfridge] Harry Gordon Selfridge (1858–1947), U.S.-born merchant, founder (in 1909) of the London department store that bears his name.

596.22   Basil] Sir Basil Zaharoff (1850–1938), European munitions magnate who also had interests in oil, international banks, and newspapers.

599.3–4   Montague's] I.e. Montague Norman (see note 592.31).

599.12   Sir Hen. Deterding] Sir Henri Deterding (1866–1939), Dutch-born oil magnate, first chairman of Royal Dutch Shell Company.

605.3   *The Lioness . . . Cubs*] A Hausa song from Sudan. Its source is given in *Guide to Kulchur* (1938) as Eckart von Sydow, *Dichtungen der Naturvölker.*

605.15   *Praise . . . Buck-Hare*] A Siberian folksong, also taken from von Sydow's anothology.

608.5   *On the loan . . . Gallery*] July–October 1912.

608.20   "symphonies"] Likening his paintings to musical compositions, Whistler used the words "symphonies," "nocturnes," and "arrangements" in the titles of several works.

610.5   *Bonga-Bonga*] Victor Plarr (see note 553.15) published poems under this pseudonym in 1913.

611.2   *Caf' Conc'*] I.e. Café Concert.

611.4–14   M. Pom-POM . . . canons] Mr. Pom-POM went to war / To sell cannons / My handsome big brother / Can no longer see / To sell cannons. // Mr. Pom-POM is in the senate / To sell cannons / To sell cannons / To sell cannons.

613.1–3   CONFUCIUS . . . PIVOT] *Ta Hsio* and *Chung Yung* (in Wade-Giles romanization), two of the "Four Books" in the Confucian canon; the remaining books are *Lun-yü* (*Analects*, see pp. 657–751) and *Meng-tzu*

(*Mencius*). These works include quotations of poems from *Shih Ching* (*Book of Odes*; here often spelled "Shi King"), a collection of 305 poems whose compilation is traditionally ascribed to Confucius (551–479 B.C.E.). Pound translated the entire *Shih Ching* as *The Classic Anthology Defined by Confucius* (see pp. 753–992).

613.4   *Walter de Rachewiltz*]   Son of Pound's daughter Mary and Boris de Rachewiltz.

615.1–2   *Ta . . . Digest*]   "I believe in the Ta Hio," Pound declared in 1934, responding to T. S. Eliot's question, "What does Mr Pound believe?" Pound's first translation of this Confucian classic was published in 1928 (and then in 1936 and 1939) as *Tao Hio: The Great Learning: Newly Rendered into the American Language*—a version based on a French translation published in Guillaume Pauthier's *Doctrine de Confucius ou Les quatre livres de philosophie morale et politique de la Chine* (1840). Over the course of the 1930s Pound studied Robert Morrison's *Dictionary of the Chinese Language* (1815–1822) and the annotated bilingual text in James Legge's *The Chinese Classics* (1862–1871). In 1942 he published an Italian translation featuring the original Chinese text and an Italian-Chinese-Japanese title: *Confucio: Ta S'eu: Dai Gaku: Studio integrale*; a new edition was published without the Chinese text as *Testamento di Confucio* (1944). Pound's English revision of his Italian translation (which, as he notes at 633.11–12, was completed at the Disciplinary Training Center at Pisa in the fall of 1945), was published with "The Unwobbling Pivot" (see note 634.1–2) in the Winter 1947 issue of James Laughlin's *Pharos* magazine devoted to these translations. In 1951, New Directions issued a bilingual *en face* edition, *Confucius: The Great Digest & Unwobbling Pivot*, which included rubbings from the 9th-century "Stone Text" supplied by Hollywood bookseller and Orientalist Willis Hawley and "A Note on the Stone Edition" by Harvard sinologist Achilles Fang (neither of which are included here). Because Pound was working from the version of *Ta Hsio* in Legge's *Four Books*—namely the 12-century neo-Confucian Chu Hsi's rearrangement of the work, in which the main section was separated from Tseng's commentary and reorganized to include Chu Hsi's remarks (see 619.25–34)—Hawley cut and pasted the photographic reproduction of the 9th-century Stone-Classics text to fit Chu Hsi's version, thus producing an "original" Chinese *en face* text that had never existed. Pound protested against this "doctoring" of the original as "highly unscholarly," but in the end was persuaded by his publisher to agree to its publication.

615.18   TERMINOLOGY]   Following Pound's usage in his edition of *The Classic Anthology Defined by Confucius*, Chinese characters are keyed to the numbering and romanization in R. H. Mathews' *Chinese-English Dictionary* (Cambridge: Harvard University Press, 1943). Pound's visual etymologies, however, are largely taken from Morrison's dictionary. *Page 615:* Shih² (5788), Ming² (4534), Ch'eng² (381). *Page 616:* Shên⁴ (5734), Tê² (6162), Ch'ih⁴ (1044), Chih⁴ (971), Tê² (6161), Hsin² (2747), Jen² (3099). *Page 617:*

Tao⁺ (6136), Pao³ (4946) + Yu⁺ (7542) + Ming⁺ (4537), Kuei³ (3634), Szu¹ (5568), Jên² (3098).

617.6–7   *Odyssey*, I, 34.]   "Huper moron" ("beyond what is destined").

618.2.   Philosopher Ch'eng]   The neo-Confucian philosopher Cheng Yi (1033–1108).

619.12   *aliter*]   Alternately.

619.26   *Tseng Tsze*]   Philosopher (505–*ca.* 436 B.C.E.), disciple of Confucius and the purported author of the *Ta Hsio*; he figures prominently in *The Confucian Analects* (see pp. 657–751).

620.3   K'ang Proclamation]   Part of the *Shu Ching* (*Book of Historic Documents*), a compilation of documents pertaining to early Chinese history, including edicts and sayings of kings and their ministers. The "Great Announcement" (620.5) and the "Canon of the Emperor (Yau)" (620.8) are also included in the *Shu Ching*.

620.15   (Chinese character)]   Ming² (4534) ("The sun and moon, the total light process"); followed by Jih⁺ + Jih⁺ (3124) + Hsin¹ (2737) ('Day by day make it new").

620.21   T'ang's]   T'ang, founder and first emperor (*fl. ca.* 1766–*ca.* 1754 B.C.E.) of the Shang dynasty.

621.6   *King Wen*]   Chou ruler and founding ancestor; his son Wu ousted the Shang and became the first ruler of the Chou dynasty (*ca.* 1122–221 B.C.E.). Also "Wan" (as at 622.2).

621.26   Kung]   Confucius.

623.12   (Chinese characters)]   Corresponds to 618.17–18: "it is rooted in coming to rest, being at ease in perfect equity."

623.14–19   *Whether the ideogram . . . it.*]   Refers to Legge's translation of the passage at 623.2–4 as "Ah, the former kings are not forgotten." Pound also used the commentaries in Bernhard Karlgren's translations of the *Book of Odes*.

623.27   *the remark*]   At 618.26. The characters to the left are Pen³ (5025) + Mo⁺ (4546).

624.4   (Chinese characters)]   Chih¹ (932) + Ch'ih¹ (9365) + Chih⁺ (982).

625.5   (Chinese character)]   Ch'eng² (381) + I⁺ (2960).

625.5   (Chinese character)]   Cheng⁺ (351) + Hsin¹ (2735) + Hsiu¹ (2795) + Shen¹ (5718).

626.17   (Chinese characters)]   Chi² (560) + Chia² (594).

627.8   Yau and Shun]   Legendary wise emperors of the Hsia dynasty (of uncertain historicity); Chieh and Chou (Chou-Hsin) in the following line refer to the wicked rulers who were, respectively, the last kings of the Hsia and Shang (Yin) Dynasties. *See also* note 742.12.

628.13   (Chinese characters)]   Ch'ih² (1021) + Kuo² (3738).

633.2–3   A state . . . states.]   Corresponds to the Chinese characters on the bottom half of the page.

633.15   *Tami Kume*]   Tamijuro Kume (1893–1961), Japanese artist..

634.1–2   *Chung . . . Pivot*]   In February 1945 Pound published a translation of *Chung Yung* in Italian: *Ciung iung: L'Asse che non vacilla*. Most of the copies were destroyed after the war because the "Asse" ("Axis") of the title led authorities to believe it was pro-Fascist propaganda. The English version was published with *The Great Learning* in *Pharos* in 1947 and in the 1951 bilingual New Directions edition (see note 615.1–2). Pound omitted the final seven chapters dealing with the sincere man as sage and ruler.

636.18   *Yang Shih*]   12th-century Neo-Confucian philosopher, student of Cheng Yi.

636.26   chung *and* yung]   Chung¹ (1504) + Yung¹ (7577).

637.14   Shun]   See note 627.8.

637.23   *136th radical*]   Ch'uan³ (1441).

638.2   Hui's]   Yan Hui, Confucius' favorite disciple.

638.12   TSZE LU'S]   Disciple of Confucius who features prominently in the *Analects*.

639.28–30   *The falcon . . . deep.*]   Cf. Poem 242 in the *Classic Anthology*, lines 8–10.

640.13–15   *Cutting axe-handle . . . off.*]   Cf. Poem 158 in the *Classic Anthology*.

644.13   King Wen]   See note 621.6.

644.25   Duke of Chou]   12th century B.C.E. Chou minister and regent, as well as a founding ancestor of Lu, Confucius' home state. Son of King Wen and younger brother of King Wu, he established a universal feudal order in China.

646.1   DUKE NGAI'S]   Duke Ai, ruler of Lu from 494 to 466 B.C.E. The power of three aristocratic families in Lu made his reign ineffectual.

647.5   *ideogram in dispute*]   Huo⁴ (2412).

654.11   Hoang Ho]   The Yellow River.

655.18   Guicciardini]   Franscesco Guicciardini (1483–1540), Italian historian and statesman, author of *Counsels and Reflections*.

657.1   THE CONFUCIAN ANALECTS]   A few excerpts in English from the *Analects*, with Pound's commentary, were published as *Confucius:*

Digest of the Analects in 1937; these became the first chapter of *Guide to Kulchur* (1938). A full English version, translated from the Chinese, was published in the spring and summer 1950 issues of the *Hudson Review* and, the following year, as a pamphlet in the "Square $ Series" edited by John Kasper and Thomas David Horton. An English edition followed in 1956, adding the sections "Procedure" and "Brief Concordance"; the text was reprinted in the 1969 New Directions edition *Confucius: The Great Digest; The Unwobbling Pivot; The Analects.*

Each of the *Analects'* 20 books is named after its first two words, which Pound translates beneath his romanization of the Chinese.

Many of the characters in *The Confucian Analects* appear under various names in the original Chinese text. Pound's romanization and spelling are often irregular as well. To clarify the sometimes confusing naming of characters, the following list provides a partial glossary of proper names in Pound's translation, keyed to names as they appear in the text.

Ai, Duke: ruler of Lu from 494 to 466 B.C.E.

Ao: Legendary hero and sailor.

Ch'ai: Kao Ch'ai, disciple of Confucius (b. 523 B.C.E.) from Chi and governor of Pi. *Also* Tze-Kao.

Chan *or* Ch'an: State located in present-day Henan and Anhwei provinces.

Ch'an Kang: *See* Tze-Ch'in.

Ch'an Tze-ch'in: *See* Tze-chin.

Ch'an Wan: minister of Chi.

Chao: Name of a clan or, at 687.36, the duke who ruled Lu, 541–510 B.C.E.

Chau Zan: An ancient wise man.

Cheng: State in present-day Henan province. Confucius admired one of its prime ministers but thought its music should be prohibited; as Pound writes at 794.20, Confucius "seems to have regarded the tunes to these verses as a species of crooning or boogie-woogie."

Chi *or* Ch'i: State located in the present-day provinces of Henan and Shantung. *Also* the name of a powerful clan. At 718.1, an ancestor of Chou dynasty kings.

Chi Hwan: Father of Chi K'ang.

Chi K'ang: Influential lord in the dukedom of Lu, whose invitation prompted Confucius to return from exile in 484 B.C.E. *Also* K'ang.

Chi Lu: *See* Tze-Lu.

Chi Tze-chang: Functionary from Wei.

Chi Wan: Great officer of Lu.

Chieh: *See* Tsang Hsi.

Ch'ih: *See* Kung-hsi Ch'ih.

Ching: Duke of Ch'i who ruled from 547 B.C.E. until his death in 490 B.C.E.

Ch'i-tiao: Disciple of Confucius (b. 540 B.C.E.) from Lu.

Chiu: At 770.2, the ruler killed by his brother Duke Hwan.

Ch'iu: *Usually* Zan Yu (*see below*) but also Confucius' family name.

Chou: Name of a people and of the dynasty (*ca.* 1122–221 B.C.E.) which succeeded the Shang.

Chou, Duke of: 12th century B.C.E. Chou minister and regent who established a universal feudal order in China.

Chu Po-yu: Great officer of Wei.

Ch'ui-tze *or* Ch'ui: Great officer of Chi who killed his ruling prince in 548 B.C.E.

Chung-kang *or* Chung-kung: *See* Yung.

Chung-ni: *See* Confucius.

Chung-yu: *See* Tze-Lu.

Chwang of Pien: Soldier of Lu known for bravery.

Chwan-yu: Territory in Lu.

Confucius: *Also* Ch'iu (in Book 7 only; his personal name reserved for parents and elders), Chung-ni, Hillock, Hummock, Kung, Kung fu-tze, Kung-tze, (Kung)²-tze, Man from Tsau.

Fan Ch'ih: Disciple of Confucius (b. 515 B.C.E.) from Chi.

Fang: Territory occupied by Tsang Wu-chang.

Hsia: Legendary pre-Shang dynasty.

Hsia-tze: *See* Shang.

Hsien: *See* Yuan Sze. *A different* Hsien (720.23): great officer of Wei.

Hui: *See* Yan Hui.

Hwan, Duke: Ch'i Ruler (7th century B.C.E.) who killed his brother Ch'iu to usurp his power.

Hwan Tui: Enemy of Confucius who attempted to have him killed.

I Yin: Sage whose admonitions are included in the *Book of Historic Documents*; chief minister to T'ang (*see below*).

Kao-tsung: Shang dynasty ruler.

Kao-Yao: Minister of Hsia dynasty ruler Yü; reputed to have introduced laws for criminal punishment.

Kung *or* Kung-tze: *See* Confucius.

Kung-cho: Great officer of Lu.

Kung-hsi Hwa: Disciple of Confucius (b. 509 B.C.E.) from Lu. *Also* Ch'ih, Tze Hwa.

Kung-shan Fu-zao: Rebellious steward of the Chi family.

Kung shu Wan: Great officer of Wei.

Kung-Wan: Great officer of Wei.

Kung-ye Ch'ang: Disciple and son-in-law of Confucius; from Chi.

Kwan Chung *or* Kwang Chung: Prime minister of Chi who served Duke Hwan (*see above*).

Kwang: Place in Wei where Confucius, mistaken for someone else, was threatened and nearly attacked by a mob in 495 B.C.E.

Lao: Disciple of Confucius from Wei.

Li: *See* Po-yu. At 749.26, name for T'ang, first Shang ruler.

Ling: Duke who ruled Wei, 534–493 B.C.E.; Confucius sought employment at his court.

Lu: Confucius' native state, located in present-day Shantung province.

Mang Chwang: Son of a great officer of Lu.

Mang-I-tze *or* Mang-Sun: Lord in the dukedom of Lu.

Mang-Wu: Son of Mang-I-tze.

Min Tze-ch'ien: Disciple of Confucius (b. 536 B.C.E.) from Lu.

Nan Yung: Husband of Confucius' niece. From Lu (b. 530 B.C.E.); perhaps a disciple.

Nan-kung Kuo: Son of Mang-I-Tze.

Nan-tze: Duke Ling's wife, with a reputation for extramarital affairs.

Ning Wu: Great officer of Wei.

P'ang: Shang dynasty sage.

Pi: Citadel of the Chi clan.

Pi Shan: Aide to prime minister Tzu-ch'an of Cheng.

Pi-Hsi: Governor of Chungmou (the "Chung-mau" of 737.27); his rebellion occurred in 494 B.C.E.

Po-i: One of a pair of legendary heroes; see note 678.31.

Po-niu: *See* Zan Pon-iu.

Po-yu: Only son of Confucius (532–481 B.C.E.). *Also* Li.

Shan: *See* Tseng-tse.

Shan Ch'ang: From Lu; perhaps a disciple of Confucius.

Shang: Pu Shang, disciple of Confucius (b. 507 B.C.E.) from Wei. *Also* Hsia, Hsia-tze, Tze-Hsia.

Shang Dynasty: *ca.* 1766–*ca.* 1122 B.C.E.

Shao Hu: Minister who died in the service of the Chi ruler Chiu, who was ousted from power by his brother, Duke Hwan.

Shih: Disciple of Confucius (b. 503 B.C.E.) from Chan. *Also* Tze-Chang.

Shih-shu: Aide to prime minister Tzu-ch'an of Cheng (*see* Tze-Chen, *below*).

Shu-ch'i: One of a pair of legendary heroes; see note 678.31.

Shun: Legendary early ruler of China.

Shu-san Wu-shu *or* Shu-sun Wu-shu: Great officer of Lu.

Sung Chao: Prince of the state of Song, something of a rake.

Sze-ma Niu: Disciple of Confucius.

T'ang: Founder and first emperor of Shang dynasty.

Ting, Duke of: Ruler of Lu from 509 to 495 B.C.E. Confucius was an official in his administration.

Tsai Wo: Disciple of Confucius from Lu. *Also* Tsai Yu.

Tsai Yu: *See* Tsai Wo.

Tsang: *See* Tseng-tse.

Tsang Wan-Chung: Great officer of Lu. *Also* Tsang Wan the Elder.

Tsang Wu-chung: Great officer of Lu.

Tsau, Man from: Confucius, addressed in a disparagingly casual manner. Tsau was Confucius' home town.

Tseng-tse: Disciple of Confucius (505–*ca.* 436 B.C.E.) from Lu, attributed author of the *Ta Hsio. Also* Master Tsang, Shan, Tsang, Tsang-tze, Tseng-tze.

Tsing Hsi: Disciple of Confucius (b. 546 B.C.E.) from Lu, father of Tseng-tse. *Also* Chieh.

Tso Ch'iu-ming: Probably a disciple of Confucius.

Tze-Ch'an: A prime minister of Cheng whom Confucius admired.

Tze-Chang: *See* Shih.

Tze-Chien: Disciple of Confucius (b. 521 B.C.E.) from Lu.

Tze-Chin: From Chan (b. 511 B.C.E.). *Also* Ch'an K'ang, Ch'an Tze-ch'in.

Tze-fu Ching Po: Great officer of Lu.

Ts'ze: *See* Tze-Kung.

Tze-Hsia: Disciple of Confucius. *Also* Hsia, Hsia-tze, Shang.

Tze Hwa: *See* Kung-hsi Chi.

Tze-Kao: *See* Ch'ai.

Tze-Kung: Disciple of Confucius (b. 520 B.C.E.) from Wei. *Also* Granty, Ts'ze, Tze-King.

Tze-Lu: Disciple of Confucius (542–478 B.C.E.). *Also* Chi Lu, Chung-yu, the "Sprout," Tse-Lu, Tsze-Lu, Yu.

Tze-Yu: Disciple of Confucius (b.506 B.C.E.) from Wu, who served as governor of Wu-ch'eng. *Also* Yen Tze-yu.

Wan: Wen Wang, grandson of founding ancestor of the Chou and father of Wu (*see below*). At 681.8, river separating states of Lu and Chi; Duke Wan (719.38) ruled the state of Tsin, 636–628 B.C.E.

Wang-sun Chia: Duke Ling's minister of war.

Wei: State located in present-day Henan province; Confucius' first stop after leaving Lu in 497 B.C.E.

Wei-shang Kao: Character famed for his probity.

Wei-shang Mau: Probably a hermit.

Wu: Wu Wang, Chou ruler who led a successful rebellion and overthrew the Shang, establishing the Chou dynasty. *Also* music celebrating Wu's victory. *Also* a state in the present-day provinces of Chiangsu and Chekiang.

Wu-ma Ch'i: Disciple of Confucius (b. 521 B.C.E.) from Chan.

Yao: Early ruler who abdicated so that the wise Shun could rule.

Yen Ch'iu: *See* Zan Yu.

Yen Hui: *See* Yen Yuan.

Yen P'ing: Renowned great officer of Chi.

Yen Tze-yu: *See* Tze-yu.

Yen Yu: *See* Zan Yu.

Yen Yuan: Disciple of Confucius (522–481 B.C.E.) from Lu, said to be his favorite. *Also* Hui, Yan Hui.

Yi: Legendary archer.

Yin Dynasty: Shang Dynasty.

Yu: *Usually* Tze-Lu (*see above*). At 691.28, 692.13, 718.1, and 749.25, purported founder of the Hsia dynasty; the "historian Yu" (726.37) is Shih Yu, great officer of Wei.

Yu Zo: *See* Yu-tze.

Yuan Sze: Disciple of Confucius (b. 515 B.C.E.) from Song. *Also* Hsien.

Yuan Zang: Friend of Confucius.

Yung: Disciple of Confucius (b. 522 B.C.E.) from Lu, a commoner. The Chi family employed him. *Also* Ching-kang, Ching-kung, Chung-kung.

Yu-tze: Disciple of Confucius (b. 510 B.C.E.) from Lu. *Also* Yu Zo.

Zan Ch'iu: *See* Zan Yu.

Zan Pon-iu: Disciple of Confucius (b. 545 B.C.E.) from Lu. *Also* Po-niu.

Zan Yu: Disciple of Confucius (b. 522 B.C.E.) from Lu, aide to Chi K'ang. *Also* Ch'iu, Hook, Mr. Zan, Yu Yan, Zan Ch'iu, Zan-tze.

659.36   *Historic Documents*]   See note 620.3.

660.5   *Times'* critique . . . anthology]   A reference to the largely nega-tive review of Pound's *Classic Anthology as Defined by Confucius* in the *Times Literary Supplement*, April 29, 1955.

661.1–3   (Chinese characters)]   Hsin⁺ (2748); Ching⁺ (1138).

662.19–27   *Pauthier's French . . . Legge's studies*)]   See note 615.1–2.

662.28   *Frobenius*]   Leo Frobenius (1873–1938), German archaeologist and anthropologist whose seven-volume *Erlebte Erdteile* was partially trans-lated as *African Genesis* (1938).

662.29   *Karlgren . . . inscriptions*)]   See Bernhard Karlgren, *The Chinese Language: An Essay on Its Nature and History* (1949).

665.8–9   in the Odes . . . polish."]   Condensed paraphrase of Poem 55; see 622.12–26 and 782.15–783.14.

666.37   Gilson's statement of Erigena:]   While researching the philosoph-ical backgrounds to Cavalcanti's "Donna mi prega," Pound read Etienne Gilson's *Philosophie du moyen âge* (1925) and was struck by his analysis of Duns Scotus Erigena.

667.32   *verso il populo*]   Toward the people.

668.5–7   Pourquoi . . . publiques]   Why only consider those in public employment as fulfilling public functions?

668.15–17   Yin . . . added]   I.e. the Shang (Yin) dynasty retained rites from the Hsia dynasty which preceded it, and added some of its own; the Chou rulers adapted the rites inherited from the Shang.

668.27–29   Corps de ballet . . . stand for?]   I.e. the Chi clan was appro-priating privileges above their station. The "Head of Chi" was a great officer, a rank that entitled him to only four rows of dancers. 668.31–34 similarly laments the improper use of the Yung Ode (Poem 282) by aristocratic families. Cf. the Head of Chi described as an "evil overlord" at 681.5.

669.26–27   "The dimpled . . . black,"]   Cf. Poem 57 (lines 784.8–10) in the *Classic Anthology*.

670.23   the two dynasties]   That preceded it: Shang and Hsia.

671.12–13   *the first . . . anthology*]   See 755.7–29.

677.26–29   to Tze Ch'an: . . . them.] He is speaking of Tze-Chan's achievements, not speaking to him. Tze-Ch'an died in 522 B.C.E., when Confucius was in his late twenties.

677.34   Tsang Wan . . . tortoise;]   Reserved for lords; Tsang Wan is acting above his station as a grand officer.

678.31   Po-i and Shu-ch'i] Exemplary martyrs who chose starvation while hiding in the mountains rather than betray their lord and serve the Chou dynasty.

684.23–24   ses manières . . . prévenant!] His manners were gentle and persuasive! how affable and considerate was his demeanor!

684.34   cultural arts.] The "Six Arts": rites, music, archery, charioteering, calligraphy, and arithmetic.

686.11   Book of the Changes] *I Ching* (*Book of Changes*), the oldest of the "Five Classics" in the Confucian canon.

688.1–2   The prince . . . Wu-elder.] Which violated the "proper procedure" (688.3), the rites.

689.26–27   cautious . . . ice.] Cf. the concluding section of poem 195, pp. 873.32–874.4.

694.11   "il sait vivre,"] He knows how to live.

694.36   From Wei . . . Lu] Confucius returned to Lu in 484 B.C.E. after 13 years abroad, much of his time having been spent in Wei. The "Elegantiae and the Lauds" at 694.37 refer to poems 191–267 and 266–305, respectively, of the *Classic Anthology*.

696.18   No hates, . . . means?] Cf. 770.22–23: "He neither hates nor covets, / what wrong shall he do?"

697.3   (*villeggiatura*)] Vacation.

701.15–16   "The White Sceptre"] Poem 256 in the *Classic Anthology*; see 941.3–944.3.

704.22–23   "considerés . . . ministres."] Considered as having augmented the number of ministers.

713.22–23   *comment . . . autres?*] How could he rectify the conduct of others?

713.34   *cf*/Great Learning] At 627.4–5.

714.37   *Alors . . . bien.*] Then you will not understand them well.

715.16   *E poi basta.*] And then that's enough.

715.23   *s'abstiennent . . . raison*] Will at least abstain from practicing that which outstrips their reason.

715.38   *Lorenzo Valla in his Elegentiae.*]   See note 327.19.

718.37   *les examinait . . . ancients.*]   Examined them attentively and placed therein the sayings of the ancients.

719.8–10   the Chao . . . Hsieh.]   Here, Chao and Wei refer to clans, Tang and Hsieh refer to states.

719.34–35   asked Lu . . . successor]   To demonstrate that the state of Lu recognized Fang as his hereditary fief. Fang was conquered around the time of Confucius' birth in the 6th century B.C.E.

719.40   un fourbe sans droiture.]   A wily fellow without rectitude.

721.2   Chan Ch'ang murdered the Duke of Ch'i.]   In 481 B.C.E.

721.6   the Three Great.]   Heads of the three aristocratic families who had substantially eroded the ducal house's power in Lu. Cf. 733.17–19: "The government was seized by the great officers, four generations ago, the three lines of the Hwan (Dukes) are mere epigones."

721.10–11   *non possumus*]   Inability to do something, from the Latin "we cannot."

722.26   Hummock]   In the Chinese, "Chiu," Confucius' personal name. Wei-shang Mau is being insulting: except for parents and elders, it is forbidden to use this form of address.

723.19   *cf/ Aristotle*:]   Cf. Canto 74: "because as says Aristotle / philosophy is not for young men / their *Katholou* can not be sufficiently derived from their *hekasta* / their generalities cannot be born from a sufficient phalanx of particulars."

724.27   In the History, Tze-Chang said:]   The syntax is misleading: Tze-Chang is quoting the *Shu Ching* (see note 620.3), not speaking within it.

725.29   provisions cut off]   In 489 B.C.E., because of fighting between the states of Chan and Wu.

727.33   Music . . . pantomimes.]   The Coronation Hymn of Shun and the Victory Hymn of Wu.

729.1   cf/ Dial *essay*]   See Pound's "Paris Letter" (*Dial*, February 1922): "The verbal cliché wears out, the cliché of life and of type wears out. In trying to synthesize the change of the last years of calamity we may find that the type "gentleman" is played out, that the term should take its place with *corteggiano, muscadine, courtier.*"

729.23   the three dynasties]   Hsia, Shang, and Chou.

729.38   *Ovvero*]   That is.

734.36–37   *ref/* Ta S'eu . . . 3, 4.]   See 618.26–619.8.

737.6   Chou in the East?] The Chou were originally from Western China; Confucius imagines a government in Lu, his native state in the East, like that of the first Chou rulers.

737.32   Cf. G. Guinicelli] See "Vedut' Ho la Lucente Stella Diana" at 125.7–24.

738.38   2556] Number of the character Hsiang[1] ("country," "village") in Mathews' dictionary.

739.1   Rousseauequers] A disparaging reference to followers of Rousseau, formed on the model of the French word "rastaquouère."

739.2   cherchent . . . villageois.] Seek the approbation of the villagers.

740.19   three years' mourning] Customary period of mourning in which all routine activities are suspended.

741.14   chess] Here the game most commonly known as go, its Japanese name.

742.12   The Viscount of Wei retired.] Because of the tyranny of his step-brother Chou Hsin, the last Shang ruler. The Viscount of Chi and Pi-kan were Chou-hsin's uncles. See note 627.8.

748.3   "Crupper's"] Chou-hsin, the last Shang ruler (see notes 627.8 and 742.12).

749.26   the Shu] The Shu Ching (see note 668.1).

750.37–38 Occhio per la mente.] Eye for the mind.

751.25–26 on appelle . . . d'impots.] One calls this behaving like a tax collector.

753.1–2   THE CLASSIC . . . CONFUCIUS] Pound read the Shih Ching (the Book of Odes, an anthology of 305 poems whose compilation is attributed to Confucius) in Alexandre de Lacharme's Confucii Chi-King Sive Liber Carminorum (1830), a Latin prose translation that he had acquired around 1920. In 1929, the Aquila Press in England agreed to publish Pound's Cavalcanti edition, his collected prose, and his translations of the Confucian Odes, but the latter project foundered after the press went bankrupt (see note 573.2). During his first years at Saint Elizabeths, Pound procured Bernhard Karlgren's annotated translation and James Legge's bilingual edition of the anthology. By May 1947, he wrote the Japanese poet Katue Kitasono about plans for his own bilingual edition of the Odes, with translations and notes to be printed below the original Chinese. In addition, Pound had become increasingly interested in the sounds of Chinese: in a 1936 addendum to Fenollosa's Chinese Written Character As a Medium for Poetry, he wrote that he had been "bestially ignorant" of the melopoeia of Chinese poetry (whose "art of verbal sonority" was found in its "sequence of vowels"). In the late 1940s, aided by the romanizations in Karlgren's edition and by

Veronica Sun, a student at Catholic University, Pound compiled a 588-page "singing key" to guide the oral chanting of the poems (which, together with his "Sound Notebooks," are at Yale's Beinecke Library). Around 1950, he began to plan a monumental "scholar's edition" of the *Shih Ching*, consisting of his English translation, the "singing key" with word-for-word romanization, a rubbing of the Stone-Classics text, and the text written in ancient seal script. When James Laughlin of New Directions and John Kasper of the Square Dollar Series respectively failed to advance the project, Pound turned to Achilles Fang, then a graduate student in comparative literature at Harvard who was writing a dissertation on Pound's *Cantos*. Fang approached Harvard University Press, which agreed to publish a "trade edition" of the English translations in 1953; if Pound forfeited royalties, the press would raise funds over the next few years to underwrite the full "scholar's edition." Pound agreed and *The Classic Anthology Defined by Confucius* was published by Harvard University Press in September 1954. After much acrimonious correspondence between Pound, Fang, and the press's director, Thomas Wilson, the second volume of the "scholar's edition" was canceled in November 1958.

755.1   PART ONE]   Achilles Fang explains the book's arrangement in his introduction to *The Classic Anthology Defined by Confucius*: "*The Classic Anthology* is divided into four parts: *Feng, Siao Ya, Ta Ya*, and *Sung*. The *Feng* or 'Winds' (Part I, Odes 1–160) are folk songs of fifteen states in North China, of which four (Chou, Shao, Wang, Pin) were within the royal domain of the house of Chou. It has never been satisfactorily explained why songs from other states are not included. Conspicuously absent from the *Feng* section are the two states of Lu and Sung; it is hardly conceivable that no folk songs existed there. The absence of songs from Wu and Ch'u, however, has been explained by the fact that these two southern kingdoms were not within the orbit of China Proper. . . .

"The difference between Parts II and III of the *Anthology* (together known as *Ya*) is far from obvious. The generally accepted view is that both are concerned with the political life of the day and that matters of lesser importance are in *Siao Ya* or 'Elegantiae Minores' (Part II, Odes 161–234), while more serious matters went into *Ta Ya* or 'Elegantiae Majores' (Part III, Odes 235–265). Be that as it may, some of the *Ta Ya* poems resemble those contained in Part IV, *Sung*.

"Most of the *Sung* or 'Lauds' (Odes 266–305) are hymns sung on formal occasions, such as offering sacrifices to the royal manes, or spirits, in ancestral temples. The inclusion of the Odes of Lu (297–300) and Shang (301–305) in this section needs some explanation. The Duchy of Lu was, of course, Confucius' home state; but this fact hardly justifies the exclusion of sacrificial hymns of other states from the *Sung* section. Obviously something is amiss here. The same applies to the Shang poems, which have nothing to do with the defunct dynasty known as Shang or Yin. 'Shang' here stands for the Duchy of Sung, which was ruled by the scions of the Shang Dynasty and from which an ancestor of Confucius, a royal prince, had migrated to the

State of Lu. Possibly Confucius could be responsible for the inclusion of the four Lu poems and the five 'Shang' poems in the *Sung* section instead of in the *Ta Ya* section of the *Anthology*."

755.7   (1)]   The Arabic numerals here printed in parentheses are displayed as running titles on the side of the page (without parentheses) in the 1954 Harvard University Press *The Classic Anthology Defined by Confucius* and all subsequent editions.

758.2   καλὴ κἀ γαθή]   Beautiful and good.

780.3   "Dentes habet"]   Catullus, XXXIX, "Egnatus, quod candidos habet dentes" ("Because Egnatus has white teeth, he smiles wherever he goes").

782.16   πολύμητις]   Many-wiled, epithet for Odysseus.

783.26   "Sidney's sister"]   Mary, Countess of Pembroke, dedicatee of Sir Philip Sidney's *Arcadia* (1590) and co-translator of his versions of the Psalms.

785.33   "Grow old with you,"]   Cf. the first line of Browning, "Rabbi Ben Ezra": "Grow old along with me!"

786.8   SEHNSUCHT]   Longing.

789.5   "O thou man."]   In Hardy, *Under the Greenwood Tree* (1872), chapter 3, a local choir is about to sing Thomas Ravenscroft's "ancient and time-worn" hymn "Remember, O Thou Man"—of which one of the characters remarks "the first line is well enough but when you come to 'O, thou man,' you make a mess o't."

789.27   "Tous je connais"]   From Villon, "Ballade de menus propos": "Je connais tout, fors que moi-mêmes" ("I know everything except myself").

794.20   "Banish . . . Cheng."]   From the *Analects*; see 727.34.

796.32   "D'un air . . . Vlaminck]   With a mild manner. Maurice Vlaminck (1876–1905), French painter and writer.

803.13   NONDUM ORTO JUBARE.]   Not yet with the radiant rising. "Alba Belingalis": see 94.20–95.11 and note 94.20.

804.2   TOUJOURS LA POLITESSE]   Politeness at all times.

807.22   LA MADONE DES WAGONS-LITS]   The Madonna of the Sleeping-Cars, a reference to the popular novel *La Madone des Sleepings* (1925) by Maurice Dekobra (1885–1973).

808.14   "An ater an albus"]   Cf. Catullus, XCIII, "Nil nimium studeo, Caesar, tibi ville placere, / nec scire utrum sis albus an ater homo" ('I have no desire to make myself agreeable to you, Caesar, nor to know whether your complexion is light or dark").

809.19   "Families . . . etc."]   Cf. 632.15–16.

810.7   JE BOIS DANS MON VERRE]   I drink in my glass.

815.2   "Evviva . . . Pisa!"]   "Hurray for the Tower of Pisa!," title of a popular Italian song from the late 1930s.

825.17   HILARE DIE]   Glad gods.

837.22   *Aude me!*]   Take a risk with me!

846.6–847.5   Pick a fern . . . know).]   Cf. "Song of the Bowmen of Shu," 249.1–29.

861.6   SCALE ALTRUI]   From *Paradiso*, XVII, 60: "Tu proverai sì come sa di sale/ lo pane altrui, e come è duro calle/ lo scendere e 'l salir per l'altrui scale" ("You shall come to know how salt is the taste of another's bread, and how hard the path to descend and mount another man's stairs").

866.28   TRAHISON DES CLERCS]   *The Treason of the Intellectuals*, title of French essayist and novelist Julian Benda's book (1927) which argued that because of political commitments intellectuals were no longer devoted to the disinterested pursuit of truth.

866.34   Quis clavum afferat?]   Who mans the rudder?

870.7   Cultura Popolare]   The Ministry of Popular Culture (or "Minculpop"), founded in 1937 by Mussolini as a propaganda organ.

871.3   cark]   Burden.

874.33   responsus est?]   What is the response?

877.31   "Il n'y . . . l'acajou."]   There's nothing more annoying than mahogany. Cf. Canto 7.

889.14   nunc dimittis]   Now lettest thou depart (Luke 2:29, from the Vulgate).

889.33   BONIFICA]   Agricultural land-reclamation initiated in 1928 by Mussolini's government.

891.36   Corpus Domini]   St. John's Eve. See notes 296.4–5 and 324.24. The phrase following translates as "The procession goes across the fields."

917.30   Hagoromo.]   See pp. 426–432.

921.24   carrochs]   Chariots.

925.3   HOU TSI, John Barleycorn,]   Respectively, ancient Chinese harvest god Hou Chi (the "Prince Millet" at 925.12) and English figure of agricultural fertility (who was the subject of a ballad by Robert Burns).

928.15   "Per plura diafana"]   "More things diaphanous," from Robert Grosseteste (d.1253), *Of Light*. Cf. Canto 83, line 81.

929.3–4   olim de Malatestis]   Formerly of the Malastesta family. Cf. Canto 76, line 311.

943.29   *quot . . . sententiae*]   As many men, as many opinions. Cicero, *De Oratore* 2, 140.

954·33   K'ung 4.]   See 618.30–619.8.

955.19   palio]   Annual horserace in Siena.

970.33   *Ta Hio* IX.3]   See 627.1–7. See also 713.31–35.

971.15–16   θεῶ . . . ἄλλων.]   From the fragments of Theocritus, III, "Unto this goddess of one of the noble fishes which being noblest of all they call Leucos."

977.7   δικαιοσύνη]   Righteousness, justice.

979.10   εὔιππος]   Delight in horses, or famous for horses.

992.27–29   (Chinese characters)]   Translated by Pound at 665.22 as "Have no twisty thoughts."

993.1   ELEKTRA]   Pound's versions of Sophocles' *Elektra* and *Women of Trachis* are anticipated by a 1919 essay on Aeschylus translations which, after dismissing Browning's "unreadable" version of *The Agamemnon*, concludes that "a reading version might omit various things which would be of true service only if the English were actually to be sung on a stage, or chanted to the movements of the choric dance or procession" (*Literary Essays*, p.273). Around this time he encouraged T. S. Eliot to translate *The Agammenon* but grew impatient with Eliot's procrastination and attempted his own contemporary demotic version. He abandoned it after a few false starts. He described this aborted effort in "Paris Letter" (*The Dial*, March 1923): "I tried every possible dodge, making the watchman a negro, and giving him a fihn Géoogiah voice, making the chorus talk cockney, etc. This is a usual form of evasion in modern drama." Some 25 years later at Saint Elizabeths, Pound returned to the matter of the House of Atreus, his interest spurred by the 1949 visits of University of Maryland classicist Rudd Fleming, author of an unpublished novel about Agamemnon. Apparently intended as part of a series of translations in cheap bilingual editions designed to bring about a Greek "revival" in the U.S., Pound's translation of *Elektra* with Rudd Fleming in 1951 was undertaken with the understanding that it would appear under Fleming's name (lest the U.S. Department of Justice adjudge its publication by Pound as evidence of recovered sanity). Pound worked from the following books in preparing his translation with Fleming: a 1939 edition of the Loeb Sophocles, vol. 2; an English translation of Ellendt's abridged *Lexicon to Sophocles* (1841); Jebb's *Tragedies of Sophocles: Translated into English Prose* (1905) and *Sophocles: The Plays and Fragments, Part 6* (1894). The two existing manuscripts of the translation are located at Princeton University Library: Pound's typescript (referred to below as TMS) and the fair copy typed by Rudd Fleming (FC). Translations of Pound's Greek transliterations are listed in "Appendix B" of Cary Perloff's 1990 New Directions edition of *Elektra*. *Elektra* was first performed in the United States in November 1987 at the

Classic Stage Company in New York City, under the direction of Carey Perloff. Mary de Rachewiltz's Italian version was premiered at the Teatro del Vittorale in Gardone Riviera in July 1992, under the direction of Sandro Sequi.

1007.23   Need we . . . filth?]   See 1108.28–29: "This is the key phrase, for which the play exists."

1011.28   plant gifts or carry lustrations]   A note in the TMS connects these ritual offerings to the dead with the "nishikigi" ("wands used as a love-charm") that fill the funeral cave of the ghost of the disappointed lover in the Noh play "Nishikigi" (pp. 406–17).

1013.5   old screw]   The TMS indicates that Pound strongly considered translating ἡ τεκοῦσα (the genetrix, or mother, from the Greek verb τίκτω) as the "usuress" (derived from τόκος, or interest). In the FC, Fleming commented "I don't think the idea of usury is in the Greek, but the epithet fits the notion that the house of Atreus has fallen on vulgar days." Pound replied: "τοκκος. τεκοῦσα I am very firm on this shade of meaning."

1018.13   *nomina . . . rerum*]   Words are the consequence of things, a Latin phrase Pound associated with the writings of Richard of St. Victor (d. 1173).

1020.2   Gruss Gott]   German greeting.

1020.19   na poo]   British slang indicating that something is finished, in-capacitated, or dead (from the French "il n'y en a plus").

1034.12   and . . . dead]   After this line in the TMS, Pound wrote: "STRONGLY object to Wangerism [sic] i.e. making so much and so many kinds of noise audience get excited and dont know what's going on hence op-posed to SINGING save in emotional passages where nature of emotion is comprehensible, i.e. quite simple, usually elegiac (not always, as in THARSAI MOI [cf. line 234], etc. but simple and not doing with intellectual complex)."

1034.18–19   I'll keep . . . useless]   In the TMS, Pound provided this gloss: "Stendhal/ or dans ce genre on n'émeut que par la clarté" ("In this genre [i.e. prose] one can only move people by clarity").

1041.25   ELEKTRA'S KEENING]   In the TMS Pound commented on how this lament might be performed: "(I think sung from start) possibly in an-tiphony, El/ solo in english and line by line, greek echo from chorus. El/ gradual crescendo/ chorus starting pianissimo/contrapunto. (Chorus proba-bly, yes, I think perforce solo at start, and more voices later.) Vocal orches-tration. for the emotional passages translate the total emotion of the whole speech. for mental conflicts: the meaning, exact meaning word by word. or dans ce genre on n'émeut que par la clarté (possible ameliorations WHEN the music is actually written)."

1049.5   *Carmagnole.*]   Carmagnole, popular song and dance of the French Revolution, each stanza of which ends with "Dansons la Carmagnole

/ Vive le son, vive le son / Dansons la Carmagnole / vive le son du canon."
In TMS Pound added: "probably keep the drums till the end/ mebbe with
intervals. and beat the gk/ scansion probably if it fits/ NO other MOVE-
MENT possible/"

1050.6   You came . . . hope]   Pound notes in TMS: "(it's the reply, pos-
sibly inversion of the To hell with all the hens. (Question of TIME duration.
If cho/ doubles by singing BOTH gk/ and eng/ this cd/ be spoken. The
EMOTION in this antistrophe is ANTI that of the strophe/ not necessary to
give both in same register of trans/ rhythmic speech with kettle-drums, pos-
sible, got to have MEANING clear, before deciding. of ALL words/ gamut
of emotion very great from 1232 [in Jebb's numbering]"

1050.17   you "deign" . . . here]   In the FC Pound admitted that he was
here "kidding the crib" (Jebb's translation runs: "O thou who, after many a
year, hast deigned thus to gladden mine eyes by thy return").

1051.6–19   Oh dearest friends . . . thee.]   In the TMS, Pound added:
"Yours/ v[ery] t[ruly] Thos/Moore," in homage to the Irish lyricist (1779–
1852).

1057.22–27   In the end . . . Mars]   Although in the Greek original the
chorus refers to Orestes and Pylades emerging from the house after the mur-
der, Pound reads the passage as also evoking the ghost of Agamemnon.
Hence his transformation of Orestes's Φοινία δὲ χεὶρ ("blood-red hand")
into Agamemnon's "dead hand." At the end of the TMS, Pound added the
note: "Perfectly easy to throw (magic-lantern) ghost of Agamemnon on
white surface (flat white marble beside door or opening behind Orestes). ITS
hands dripping RED blood. probably better on wall by door so as to be vis-
ible to all seats in audience."

1060.9   Get these doors open]   At the end of the TMS, Pound provided
the following "Note for finale/": "The big double doors are open so the
WHOLE auditorium can see Klut's bier, and the scene of lifting the cloth/
Aeg/ is driven thru another door into the inner room where Ag/ was mur-
dered./ Restraint of S/ in NOT including Aeg's death in actual play. One
murder enough in action. One implied, with no doubt about it, but not vis-
ibly demonstrated. one doesn't at first realize that it is not actually in the
text." Other notes appended to TMS include:
     "LEX/ 1. there must be real person speaking possible speech NOT god-
dam book-talk. 2. Must be the stage SEEN, the position of the person speak-
ing and their movements. 3. Modification of speech MINIMUM or NONE
for the sung parts. They shd/ be as straight as Drink to me only with thine
eyes. BUT cantabile. 4. When danced, the foot-beat must be indicated BY
the words, from them to the tune. 5. for the sung part the translation need
NOT adhere to literal sense (intellectual) of the orginal but must be singable
IN THE EMOTION of the original."
     "Poetry = see/ stage/ = & hear"

1065.2   WOMEN OF TRACHIS]   According to Pound, his translation of Sophocles' *Trachiniae* "came from reading the Fenollosa Noh plays for the new edition [i.e. *The Translations*, 1953], and from wanting to see what would happen to a Greek play, given that same medium and the hope of its being performed by the Minoru company. The sight of Cathay in Greek, looking like poetry, stimulated crosscurrents" ("Ezra Pound: An Interview," *Paris Review*, 28, [1962]). First published in the *Hudson Review* (Winter 1953–54), then in book form by Neville Spearman in London in 1956 and by New Directions in 1957, *Women of Trachis* was first performed on the BBC's Third Programme in April 1954, produced by D. B. Bridson and Christopher Sykes. In the same spring, the play received its first U.S. performance at the New School for Social Research, a one-night reading double-billed with Gilbert Murray's translation of *Electra*, featuring a cast of actors that included James Dean as Hyllus. In 1960, The Living Theatre produced the play at the Cherry Lane Theater in New York, featuring Julian Beck as Herakles, Judith Malina as Daysair, and Martin Sheen as Hyllus. That same year, a Noh-inspired version was performed in Berlin, in Eva Hesse's translation.

1066.3   *God-Dance.*]   See 393.1–40.

1066.4   *KITASONO KATUE*]   Japanese poet (1902–1978) whose translations of Pound's poems appeared in the Tokyo literary magazine VOU between 1936 and 1951.

1066.5   *Miscio Ito*]   Trained in Japan, Paris, and Germany, and subsequently a resident of England, the dancer Michio Itow (*ca.* 1893–1961) participated in the production of Yeats's *At the Hawk's Well* in 1916 and in 1921 performed Pound's translations of the Noh plays *Shojo, Kagekiyo,* and *Hagoromo* at the Greenwich Village Theatre in New York. *Minoru:* Celebrated Noh troupe, named after Umewaka Minoru (see note 337.1).

1088.19   *rêveuse*]   Dreamily.

1089.1   *grosse caisse*]   Bass drum.

1103.17   *m'la calata*]   Part of a phrase spoken by Sigismundo Malatesta in 1450 when the Sforza, in league with Frederigo d'Urbino, had tricked him into making a useless attack on Pesaro. Quoted in Canto 9: "And he said: 'This time Master Feddy has done it.'/ He said: 'Broglio, I'm the goat. This time/ Mr. Feddy has done it (*m'l'ha calata*)."

1108.28–34   This is the key . . . box.]   Cf. 1007.23. In Cocteau's *Antigone* (1922), Antigone says to Creon: "You have invented justice." The Italian phrase (translated by Pound in Canto 86 as "All, that has been, is as it should have been" and in Canto 87 as "What has been, should have") is taken from a 1944 memoir attributed to Mussolini in which he evokes his ouster as head of state (*Il tempo del bastone et della carota: Storia di un anno, ottobre 1942-settembre 1943*).

1114.4   *Maestoso e triste*]   Stately and sad.

1115.1   *Guides to the Montanari Poems*]   These translations of four poems
by the Italian poet Saturno Montanari (1918–1941) were first published in
1951. *Autonno*: Autumn. *Stagione di Fiori*: Season of flowers. *Pomeriggio de
Luglio*: July afternoon. *Notte dietra le persiane*: Night behind the blinds.

1117.1–5   Werewolf . . . agape.]   Translation of a poem written in French
by Jaime d'Angulo (1888–1950), a novelist and expert on Amerindian lan-
guages and folklore whom Pound called "the American Ovid." The drawing
is by Pound.

1118.3   *Chansson Doil*]   This translation and the one following were first
published in 1911; cf. Pound's later version of "Channson Doil" at 481.1–
482.24.

1120.6   *For Right of Audience*]   A translation of "D'Autra Guiza e d'Autra
Razon."

1121.19   *Canzon . . . Love*]   From "En Cest Sonet Coind' e Leri." This
translation and the one that follows were first published in 1912; cf. Pound's
later version at 492.9–493.22.

1124.1   *Rica Conquesta*]   From "Sims Fos Amors de Joi Donar Tant
Larga"; cf. Pound's later version at 501.7–502.24.

1126.16   *Lo Ferm Voler*]   This poem, as well as the two translations that
follow it, were first published as part of the musical score *Hesternae Rosae* in
1913 (for the other five poems from the score, see page 1167).

1128.6   *Kabir*]   Hindu-Muslim eclectic preacher (1440–1518), who sang in
the Bhojpuri language. This translation was first published in 1913.

1133.1   *Strophes*]   First published in 1921.

1134.1   *Sonnet to Guido Cavalcanti*]   From "Onde si move e donde nasce
Amore," described by Pound as "the sonnet by Guido Orlando which is sup-
posed to have invited Cavalcanti's *Donna mi prega*." This translation was first
published in 1929.

1134.18   *Cabaret Vert*]   The following four Rimbaud translations and
Pound's version of Tailhade "Rus" were published as a booklet by Vanni
Scheiwiller in 1957, *Rimbaud by Ezra Pound*, with the following note: "The
Study of French Poets appeared in the *Little Review* nearly 40 years ago. The
student hoped that the selection would stimulate thought and that possibly
one or two of the thousands of aspirants for literary glory would take up the
matter. As no adequate translations have yet appeared, he now takes pity on
those who haven't had time to learn French but might like to know what the
French authors were writing about, and herewith *starts to provide a guide* to
meaning of the poems then given in the original only."

1137.11   *Tailhade*]   See "Our Respectful Homages to M. Laurent Tail-
hade," 1177.15–31.

1137.29   Nadaud.] Gustave Nadaud (1820–1893), French singer, musician, and author of popular light verse.

1138.1   *Catullus: XXVI*] Published 1957. Another version of this translation was printed in *The European* (January 1959):

> THE DRAUGHTY HOUSE
> A draft blows through this house,
> Furus, a draft not of Favonus,
> Not of the East wind, or of the West wind,
> Nor of Boreas. Not from the North-East is this
> Draft,
> But a thousand, fifteen two hundred sesterces
> Take this place fore and aft,
> My God, some draft!

1138.8   *Boris de Rachewiltz's*] Italian Egyptologist (1926–1997), husband of Pound's daughter Mary. This translation was first published in 1960.

1138.28   vera incessu] Cf. *Aeneid*, I, 405, "vera incessu patuit dea" ("and in her step she was revealed a very goddess").

1138.34   Deo mi par esse] Cf. Catullus, LI: "Ille mi par esse deo videtur" ("He seems to me to be equal to a god").

1142.27   *de Boufflers*] Marie-Françoise-Catherine de Beauveau, Marquise de Boufflers (1711–1786).

1144.23   *L'Ultima Ora*] The Final Hour

1149.1   *the Strike*] In June 1902, more than 100,000 anthracite miners in northeastern Pennsylvania went on strike demanding shorter hours, increased wages and recognition of their union, the United Mine Workers. The mines were closed until President Roosevelt ("our Ted" at 1149.12) appointed a committee of arbitration to settle the dispute. The miners returned to work in late October; five months later the arbitration commission awarded them a ten percent raise and shorter working days, but the union's demand for formal recognition was not met.

1149.23   Si Perkins] Byword for a rube, based on a stock character in popular theater.

1150.1   *Amor de Lonh*] From Jaufré de Blaye's "Lanquan li jorn son lonc en may."

1152.22   *Clair de Lune*] English lyrics for Gabriel's Fauré's setting of Verlaine's poem.

1153.6   *Lied Maritime*] English lyrics for Vincent d'Indy's setting of his own poem.

1153.22   *Thersites*] A man of evil tongue, severely chastised by Odysseus for speaking ill of Agamemnon. See *Iliad*, Book II.

1154.27 "*Some may have blamed you—*"] First line of Yeats's "Reconciliation" (1910).

1155.20 *Selection . . . Guilbert*] Translations for a score of songs "harmonized and arranged" by the Italian singer Gustav Ferrari (1872–1948), published in 1912. The original French text and Pound's translations appear beneath the music on the page. The titles here are based on the first lines of the translations; in the score titles are given in French, along with attributions and dates (listed as follows): 1. "Suivez, beautez" (de Villon). 2. "Quand je revis ce que j'ay tant aimé" (de Berthaud). 3. "Le Roy fait battre tambour" (1599). 4. "La belle fille et le petit bossu" (XVIIième siècle). 4. "Les cloches de Nantes" (XVIIième siécle). 5. "L'inutile défense" (1761). 6. "Aimez, vous avez quinze ans" (1781). 7. Il est pourtant temps de me marier." 8. "Les conditions impossibles." 9. "C'est la fille d'un pauvre homme."

Yvette Guilbert: Celebrated French singer, actress and diseuse (1865–1944). Later in her career, she toured extensively presenting historical and genre cycles of French chansons, accompanied Ferrari. In the 1931 BBC broadcast of Pound's opera *Le Testament* (1926), Ferrari, a baritone, played the part of Villon.

1155.21 "*Pursue ye beauty.*"] Villon's original French poem, "Suivez, beautez" was sung in *Le Testament*, one of two songs in the opera not written by Pound.

1160.28 Fontanger] The 18th-century fashion of *fontanges*, knots of ribbons worn in the hair just above the forehead.

1167.19 *Hesternae Rosae*] "Roses of Yesterday." Pound's translations appear in the second book of a two-volume score produced in collaboration with the German pianist and composer Walter Morse Rummel (1887–1953) in Paris. The score was published in 1912; four poems ("Chansson Doil," "Lo Ferm Voler," "Qunat L'Herba Fresq El Fuell Apar," and "Las Grans Beautatz") were collected in *Translations*; see pages 1118–20 and 1126–28. The remaining five poems appear in this section.

In his preface, Rummel writes: "The first volume (Nine French Songs of the 17th Century) is here followed by a collection of Nine Troubadour Songs of the 12th and 13th Centuries. . . . The two Daniel melodies ["Chansson Doil" and "Lo ferm voler"] are here published for the first time to the writer's knowledge, and he is indebted to Mr. Ezra Pound, M.A., for communicating them from the Milan Library . . . The writer with the help of Mr. Ezra Pound, an ardent proclaimer of the artistic side of mediaeval poetry, has given these melodies the rhythm and the ligature, the character which, from an artistic point of view, seems the most descriptive of the mediaeval spirit."

In addition to the music, each song has the original text, a modern French translation by M. D. Calvocoressi, and Pound's English version. The titles here are based on the first lines of the poems; in the score these titles are given in French, along with attributions and dates (listed as follows as they appear in the score): "*So pleaseth me joy*": "Tant m'abelis" (B. de Palazol). "*Maiden and Virgin loyal*": "Mère au Sauveour" (Willaume li Viniers). "*The great desire*": "Le granz desirs" (Li Cuens d'Angou). "*Many people here miscall me*": "Mainta ien me mal razona" (Pierol). "*When cometh the clear time in*": "A l'entrade" (Chanson à danser).

1170.18 *Pax Saturni*] The poem was published under its original title, "Reflection and Advice," in *Collected Shorter Poems* (London: Faber and Faber, 1968).

1170.19–23 *Once . . . Contemporary*] Cf. John Reed, the opening lines of *Sangar* (1913).

1174.1 *Chippewa*] Pound's grandfather, Thaddeus Coleman Pound, settled in Chippewa Falls in 1856 and lived there intermittently until his death in November 1914. On his mother's side, Pound was a distant descendant of Henry Wadsworth Longfellow.

1175.10 *Wilfred Scawen Blunt*] On January 18, 1914, Pound traveled with William Butler Yeats, F. S. Flint, Richard Aldington, Victor Plarr, and Sturge Moore to the country home of poet and political essayist Wilfred Scawen Blunt (1840–1922). This poem was among the manuscripts presented to Blunt inside a small marble box with decorative carving by the sculptor Henri Gaudier-Brzeska.

1175.21 A.C.S.] Algernon Charles Swinburne.

1177.15 *Laurent Tailhade*] French satiric poet (1854–1919), author of *Poèmes Aristophanesques* (1904). For Pound's translation of his "Rus," see p. 1137.10–29.

1177.16 OM MANI PADME HUM] Tibetan Buddhist mantra.

1177.26 Zarabondilla] Saraband. *Kordax*: Erotic dance accompanying performances of Greek comedy.

1177.28 Leon Bakst] The costume and stage-set designer Léon Bakst (1866–1924).

1177.28 Et Dominus tecum] And the Lord be with you.

1178.1 *Et Faim . . . Boys*] From Villon's *Testament*, XXI: "And hunger makes the wolves spurt out of the woods."

1180.2 *Jean de Bosschère*] Also spelled Jean de Boschère (1878–1953), Belgian-born writer and illustrator. The original French text and the author's illustrations were included in the chapbook in which these selections from Boschère's *Les métiers divins* (1913) were published.

1183.17 *To a City*] A response to the city of Newark's invitation to celebrate its 250th anniversary in verse.

1183.27 Sforza . . . Baglione!] Probably the Italian condottiere Francesco Sforza (1401–66) and the Roman painter Giovanni Baglione (1566–1643).

1186.7   *Omakitsu*] I.e. Wang Wei (699–759), whom Pound described as "the real modern—even Parisian—of VIII cent. China" in a 1917 letter.

1186.14   Rihaku] Japanese form of Li Po.

1187.8   bald Lamar] Joseph Rucker Lamar (1857–1916), American jurist.

1187.25   *Fever Chart*] From "Feuilles de Température" by Paul Morand (1888–1976). In 1922, Pound translated two volumes of Morand's short stories. Rejected by a British publisher and subsequently forgotten, *Fancy Goods* and *Open All Night* were published in a single-volume edition in 1984, accompanied by a preface by Marcel Proust (also translated by Pound).

1189.7   *"Sad song you hear"*] From "Fort Chant oiaz" (Faidit). In his "Proem" to the score of *Five Troubadour Songs . . . Arranged by Agnes Bedford* (1920), Pound notes of this translation that he has "made a condensation of the original poem, and interpolated certain data which would have been known to Faidit's audience, but of which a modern auditor may require some gloss or reminder."

1189.27   *"When new buds thrust"*] From "Can par la flors josta.l vert folh" (Bernart de Ventadorn).

1190.4   *"When cometh in the flow'ry time"*] From "Can lo dous temps comensa" (Bernart de Ventadorn).

1190.14   *"Although thou leave me now"*] From "Lo gens tems de pascor," III (Bernart de Ventadorn).

1190.24   *"Call that not life"*] From "Non es meravelha s'eu chan," II, VI (Bernart de Ventadorn).

1191.5   *"Say that sweet my sorrow was"*] From "Molt era dolz mei cossir" (Arnaut de Marueill).

1191.17   *"In sorrow now I know well"*] From "Conort era sai ben," I, V (Bernart de Ventadorn).

1192.1   *Highbrow's Translation of Horace*] Cf. Horace, *Odes*, I, 38. The translation first appeared in *Readies for Bob Brown's Machine* (1931). Brown's "machine" was a wooden box loaded with a strip of paper that was viewed through a special binocular lens. Hilaire Hiler's "Preface" to the collection explains: "The text in this book, contributed by experimental modern writers, has been expressly written to be read on the reading machine. The use of hyphens, arrows, other connectives and punctuation is solely to suggest that the reading matter is to pass in a pleasant reading size at a pleasing speed before the reader's eye on a tape unrolled by a motor."

1192.14   *"I think that thou has looked"*] Cf. 207.18–35.

1193.1   *"Amore and Lagia"*] Cf. 213.20–214.4.

1193.17   "*Guido, Gianni that saw you*"]   From "Guido, quel Gianni ch'a te fu l'altrieri," a sonnet to Guido Cavalcanti by Gianni Alfani.

1194.1   "*In your gentle salute*"]   From "Gianni, quel Guido salute," Cavalcanti's *mottetto* reply to Gianni Alfani's sonnet.

1194.21   "*Guard thee well*"]   From "Guarda Ben Dico, Guarda, Ben Ti Guarda," attributed to Cavalcanti by his earliest editors, but excluded from his canon by all editions since Arnone's (1881). A comic aria sung by the Giovanni the Cobbler in Act 1 of Pound's opera, after Guido has fled from a boisterous fight with Corso Donati Buendelmonte and his band in Florence.

1196.6   "*We are the sad, bewildered quills*"]   From "Noi sian le triste penne isbigotite," thought to be the first mention of writing instruments in Western lyric poetry.

1196.22   "*Gentle . . . wild*"]   Pound referred to this poem as the "Yittischer Charleston"; it is addressed to Louis Zukofsky, editor of the 1932 "*Objectivist" Anthology*, where it was first published.

1197.3   ole king Bolo's big black queen]   On October 31, 1917, T. S. Eliot sent Pound the first of what would become an ongoing series of off-color "Bolo" poems: "King Bolo's big black kukquheen / Was fresh as ocean breezes. / She burst aboard Columbo's ship / With a cry of gentle Jesus." [*The Letters of T. S. Eliot*, vol. 1, ed. Valerie Eliot (NY: Harcourt Brace, 1988), p. 206.]

1198.2   "*Cavalcanti: A Sung Dramedy in 3 Acts*"]   Following the BBC radio production of his opera, *The Testament of François Villon*, in October 1931, Pound was commissioned by BBC producer E. A. F. Harding to write a radio opera on the life and works of Guido Cavalcanti. Pound worked on the score of *Cavalcanti: A Sung Dramedy in 3 Acts* over the course of 1931–1933, but the opera (with libretto in English and songs in Italian) was never produced. These translations were perhaps intended for a full English-language version of the opera.

1198.3   "*Ever shall I be toward Amor*"]   From Sordello's "Tos Temps Serai Ves Amor," sung in the second act of Pound's Cavalcanti opera by the old servant woman Vanna, who claims she heard the aged Madame Cunizza sing this very song while she was a guest in the house of the Cavalcanti family. Significantly enough, this brief aria interrupts Guido's singing of the canzone "Donna mi prega." Hearing the easy, mellifluous Provençal of Sordello's song, Guido breaks off his solo, exclaiming "Damn, damn, damn, I ought to simplify."

1198.14   "*Ailas, what use are my eyes*"]   From Sordello's "Ailas, e Quem Fau Miey Huelh." Sung by a detachment of French soldiers beyond the walls of Sarzana, where the exiled Guido lies on his deathbed in Act 3 of the opera. Upon hearing the Provençal strains of Sordello's song, he launches into the aria "Quando di morte mi convien trar vita" (see "Ballata XII," 225.1–35).

1198.27   *"If the prelates would take some advice"*]   From Walther von der
Vogelweide's "Sollt Ich den Pfaffan Râten an den Triuwen Mîn"; the follow-
ing poem translates his "Künc Constantin der Gap sö Vil." Among German
poets, Pound ranked Walther von der Vogelweide (*ca.* 1170–*ca.* 1230) and
Heinrich Heine the highest. He was first introduced to this minnesinger's
work around 1912 by the translations of Ford Madox Hueffer, one which he
included in his anthology *Confucius to Cummings* (1964).

1199.32   i.e. Verlaine's]   Verlaine's "Ballade de la vie en rouge."

1200.1   *"Thais habet nigros . . ."*]   Martial, V, 43.

1200.5–6   *Papillon . . . unread*]   Papillon is the French word for butterfly;
the "book unread" is T. S. Eliot's *The Cultivation of Christmas Trees* (1956).

1200.17   *Zuk*]   The American poet Louis Zukofsky (1904–1978).

1200.24   *More*]   Paul Elmer More (1864–1937), American critic and
educator.

1201.1   *By the River of Stars*]   Translated in 1959. Mary de Rachewiltz's
Italian version of the poem was first published in her *Catai* (Milano: All'In-
segna del Pesce d'Oro, 1959); a revised 1987 edition of this book by Schei-
willer in turn included Pound's English text, together with the following 1959
note by Pound:

> At a time when academic persons are being subsidized to write about
> Fenollosa's influence, it might be permitted, not to wail, but to note with
> perhaps a touch of asperity, that apart from the first $200 Mrs Fenollosa
> dug, I believe, out of someone in Canada, the editing of Fenollosa's pa-
> pers was at my own cost and charge and the returns would not have paid
> a typist to make copies.
>
> The "Written Character" was abbreviated to get it printed at all, and
> the late Dr Carus deserves no thanks from anyone. In fact I could a hell
> derive from various obstructors of learning.
>
> I emphasized the points least known to the English-reading public,
> but that did not in intention imply Fenollosa's ignorance of other items
> known even to the best paid and stupidest sinologues. *The Little Review*
> did not appreciate the text though I finally got it printed in the back
> pages, and, if memory serves me, part of it on the back cover, then in-
> serted at the end of "Instigations."
>
> My own ignorance of the simplest matters was gradually and partially
> diminished. On return from incarceration I had the strength to tackle a
> few more pages of our author's not over legible penciling, from which the
> following items may serve.

1201.2   *"Baijo's poem in the Koshingen"*]   "Koshingen" is Japanese for
"Collections of Ancient Sayings." This poem was traditionally included in the
Chinese gathering of "Nineteen Old Poems" and attributed to the poet Mei
Sheng ("Baijo" in Japanese). See note 250.5.

1201.4   ox herd far from stargirl]   The Ox-herding Boy and the Weaving Girl are traditional figures for the stars Bega and Altair, estranged lovers who once a year cross the Han River (the Milky Way) to meet.

1201.21   *Metastasio*]   Pietro Metastasio (1698–1782).

1201.22   *Pigeons*]   When the poem was published in the *Sunday Times Weekly Review*, London (April 26, 1970), Cyril Connolly noted: "When I reviewed 'The Fall of Venice' by Maurice Rowdon recently I quoted Mrs Thrale from his book: 'St Marks Place is all covered over in a morning with chicken coops which stink one to death' and added my own complaint: 'Those pigeons! Strutting banality, flying sewers, with the photographers and exhibitionists who surround them; the hordes of Nordic tourists, many lying bibulous on the stones.' This brought an immediate telegram from Ezra Pound's Venice household [i.e. from Olga Rudge]. 'Cheers for you. Ezra delighted. Italian papers please take note.'" Connolly's note concluded: "At eighty-five the poet Ezra Pound has found a subject worthy of his fire and has sent us this translation of a poem by his friend Ugo Fasolo [1905–1980] to assist the cause. The "Father of his Country" is the statue of Vittorio Emmaneule II in front of Alberga Londra, Riva degli Schiavoni. It was erected in 1887."

1202.26   *Prayer for a Dead Brother*]   Accompanied by the note: "Sheri Martinelli is a close friend of Ezra Pound. In 1954 her only brother died. Her grief was so great that the writer put it into verse to soothe her soul." Sheri Martinelli: American painter (1918–1996).

Index of Titles and First Lines

Library of Congress Cataloging-in-Publication Data

Pound, Ezra, 1885–1972.
  [Poems. Selections]
  Poems and translations / Ezra Pound.
       p. cm. — (The library of America; 144)
  Includes index.
ISBN 1–931082–41–3 (alk. paper)
  I. Title. II. Series.

PS3531.082A6   2003
811′.52—dc21   2003040142

THE LIBRARY OF AMERICA SERIES

The Library of America fosters appreciation and pride in America's literary heritage by publishing, and keeping permanently in print, authoritative editions of America's best and most significant writing. An independent nonprofit organization, it was founded in 1979 with seed money from the National Endowment for the Humanities and the Ford Foundation.

*This book is set in 10 point Linotron Galliard,
a face designed for photocomposition by Matthew Carter
and based on the sixteenth-century face Granjon. The paper
is acid-free Domtar Literary Opaque and meets the requirements
for permanence of the American National Standards Institute. The
binding material is Brillianta, a woven rayon cloth made by
Van Heek-Scholco Textielfabrieken, Holland. The compo-
sition is by The Clarinda Company. Printing and
binding by R.R.Donnelley & Sons Company.
Designed by Bruce Campbell.*